INSEPARABLE ELEMENTS

Aboriginal and Torres Strait Islander readers are advised that this book contains references to and images of people who have died.

First published 2021 by
FREMANTLE PRESS

Fremantle Press Inc. trading as Fremantle Press
PO Box 158, North Fremantle,
Western Australia, 6159
fremantlepress.com.au

Copyright © Patsy Millett, 2021

The moral rights of the author have been asserted.

This book is copyright. Apart from any fair dealing for the purpose of private study, research, criticism or review, as permitted under the *Copyright Act*, no part may be reproduced by any process without written permission. Enquiries should be made to the publisher.

The quotation on p. 430 is from the English translation of the novel *Les Noyers de l'Altenburg* by André Malraux © Éditions Gallimard, 1948, reproduced with permission.

Cover design by Carolyn Brown, tendeersigh.com.au

 A catalogue record for this book is available from the National Library of Australia

ISBN 9781760990855 (paperback)
ISBN 9781760990862 (ebook)

Fremantle Press is supported by the Western Australian State Government through the Department of Cultural Industries, Tourism and Sport.

INSEPARABLE ELEMENTS

Dame Mary Durack

A Daughter's Perspective

by Patsy Millett

CONTENTS

Selected Durack family tree	6
Abbreviations	8
Preface	9
1 – Mildew (1939–1945)	11
2 – The Wider Circle (1946–1951)	33
3 – Broome (1952)	63
4 – Diversions and Deviations (1953–1956)	88
5 – Back on Track (1957–1960)	119
6 – The Rock and the Sand (1961–1964)	147
7 – 'A Surfeit of the Fullness of Life' (1965–1967)	168
Photographs	195
8 – The Coming of the Crows (1968–1969)	221
9 – Cross Threads (1970–1971)	249
10 – 'Everything that We Belong' (1972–1974)	273
11 – 'Can These Be the Same Stars?' (1975)	306
12 – The Main Job (1976–1977)	327
13 – Grounded (1978–1979)	351
14 – Bent to Burden (1980–1989)	379
15 – Ruffian Forces (1990–1994)	405
Epilogue	430
Conversions	432
Endnotes	433
Index	

SELECTED DURACK FAMILY TREE

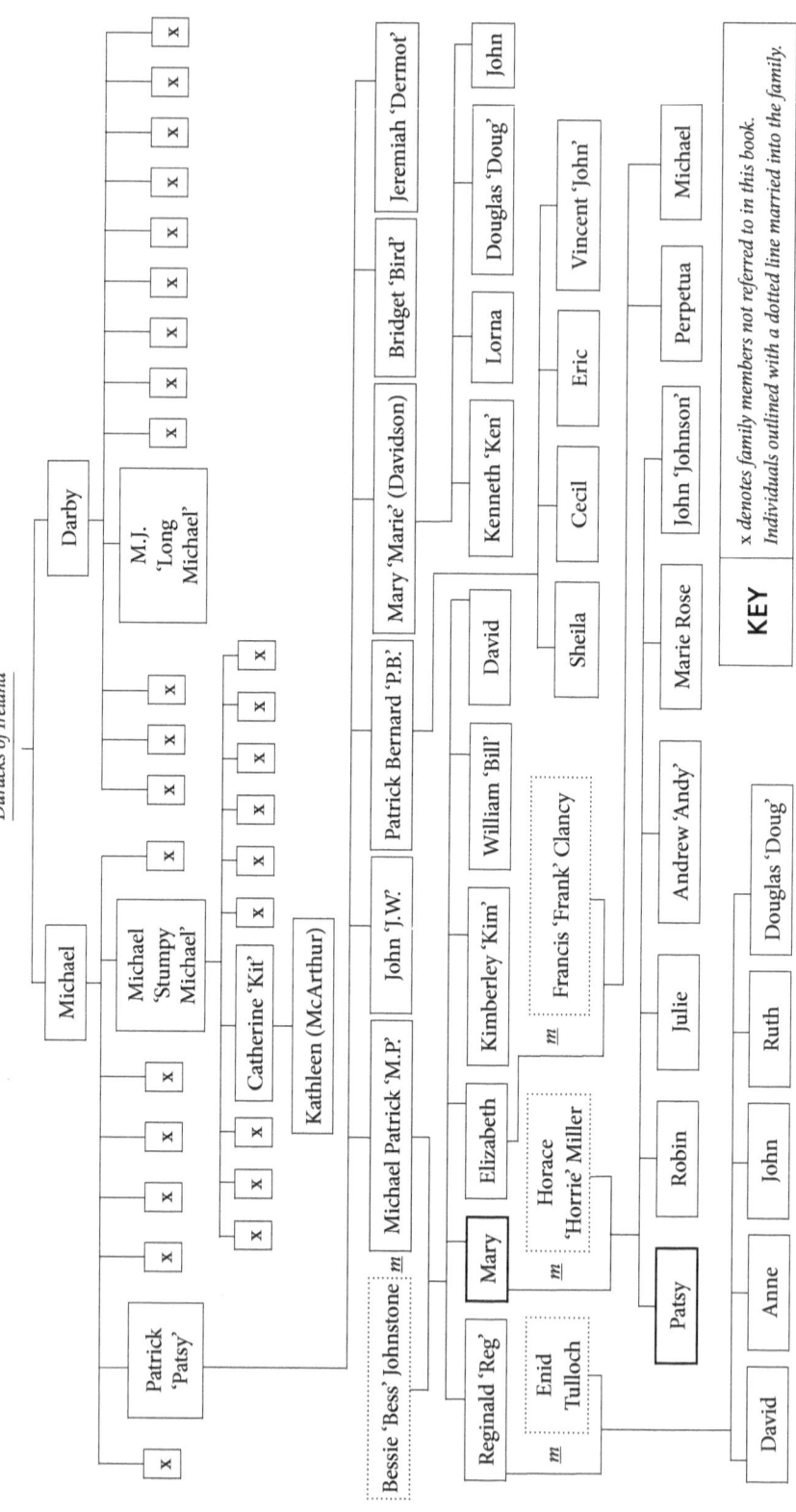

Mary Durack Miller with Patsy, 1940.

ABBREVIATIONS

ABC	Australian Broadcasting Commission (later Australian Broadcasting Corporation)
ACF	Aboriginal Cultural Foundation
AGM	Annual General Meeting
AC	Companion of the Order of Australia
ATF	Aboriginal Theatre Foundation
BBC	British Broadcasting Corporation
BHP	Broken Hill Proprietary Company
CD&D	Connor Doherty and Durack
CLF	Commonwealth Literary Fund
DBE	Dame Commander of the Most Excellent Order of the British Empire
DCA	Department of Civil Aviation
FAW	Fellowship of Australian Writers
PWD	Public Works Department
LISWA	Library and Information Services of Western Australia
MMA	MacRobertson Miller Aviation (later MacRobertson Miller Airlines)
NIDA	National Institute of Dramatic Art
OBE	Officer of the Most Excellent Order of the British Empire
RAAF	Royal Australian Air Force
RAF	Royal Air Force
RFDS	Royal Flying Doctor Service
RSL	Returned and Services League
SHOF	Stockman's Hall of Fame

PREFACE

'Spare me, dear,' my mother was wont to say in her old age, 'your analysis of me.' This plea usually countered one of my lectures on her weakness of will – principally, her inability to say 'no'. Did she also suspect, fixing me with an anxious eye, the posthumous biography: 'Mary Durack – A Put-Upon Life'?

'It's all in there somewhere,' she would say with a wave at the stack of journals containing the honest and reliable record of her days, bursting with photographs and other loose material by way of illustration. If not, it would likely be found in family correspondence files going back over seven decades or among those of exchanges with intimates and associates.

When contemplating how her story might be handled – as an episodic narrative, a soap opera, a vehicle for a dispassionate examination of her character and working methods, an intermingling of her many parts, principally the inseparable relationships with her sister Elizabeth and husband, Horrie Miller – consideration was given to whether it should be written at all.

Whereas she might not have been entirely averse to the notion of a biography, Mary Durack would have preferred 'a dear person' to tackle the task, particularly when it came to the selection of quoted material – someone perhaps like the author Brenda Niall, whom she had never met, but who would write a temperate and Christian summary of her life without offending living sensitivities.[1] Hopefully, such a book would also promote the work of her sister Elizabeth and complement their years of closely linked artistic and literary endeavour.

For the busy writer, regularly filling in the dated space in her diary was time-consuming discipline enough and, believing she had covered the contingency, she was not tempted to set about a formal autobiography.

What emerges here is as much a montage of the main players in her life as a biography of Mary Durack Miller, wherein while taking no more than the role of an extra, I stand at the end to take not a bow but rather the weight of the curtain fall.

CHAPTER 1

MILDEW (1939–1945)

We inherited opposite sides of the Irish coin, my mother and I. Hers belonged to a land of kith and kin, home and hearth, faerie folk and leprechauns. Mine lay with ancient clan wars, battles that rolled among the mountains by winter seas, grudges passed down the generations and the banshee wail. In keeping with a dark endowment, neither the timing nor the circumstances of my birth were auspicious, my mother's joy in her newborn tempered by the effects of a difficult delivery coinciding with the declaration of war and an ongoing rift with her father. Gran, making the best of it, visited the hospital and welcomed her first grandchild with agreeable noises. My grandfather, Michael Patrick Durack (generally referred to as 'M.P.'), still deeply pained that his beloved and amenable eldest daughter could have so disregarded his feelings and her own interests, was not to be consoled or won over by the new arrival. Inasmuch as barely nine months had passed since the letter informing him of her ill-advised choice of marriage partner, insult had been added to injury.

Having made up her mind, however unwisely, my mother was determinedly unrepentant. Sympathetic to underdogs, she had not been overly – or sufficiently – discouraged by the likelihood that in taking on Horace (Horrie) Clive Miller, she donned a hairshirt, and, given her steadfast disposition, a permanent one at that. Had she been in need of a companion for a desert island survival scenario, she would have been hard put to find a more ideal candidate for the position. As it was, for the daughter of a distinguished and manifold family to have connected herself to an individual who more or less existed in a vacuum without a single known relative was an act of folly scarcely mitigated by his claim to being 'a self-made man' and the founder of a Western Australian airline. She would spend a lifetime fortifying herself against the consequences.

Horrie had neither the courage nor the class to write to the parents of his prospective in the regular way, although she begged him to send a short note that she would help him compose. M.P. Durack cared not a jot that he was sober, hardworking, healthy, a 'provider' and, with the divorce, unencumbered. H.C. Miller was unsuitable in ways that in earlier times would have seen M.P. take preventative action, as he had done with his sister Bridget, ensuring her a miserable spinsterhood. Mary was not a daughter to be lightly given away under any circumstances, and here she was, stolen by a man without background or the education to appreciate her talent or share her literary inclination. Restrained from objecting to the non-Catholic aspect on account of his own marriage 'out of the church', in a letter to his son Reg he bemoaned her rash action as having sullied the family name.

While also disappointed at her daughter's decision, Bess Durack had applied feminine intuition to the situation. Her own spouse had initially been frowned on by members of both families: hers because 'Miguel' (as she always referred to the man who bore a resemblance to a Spanish don) had been more than twenty years her senior, and his because of her Presbyterian faith. But she knew that unexpected blessings were likely to emerge from the most unlikely unions, and, given time, men generally 'came round'.

In a desire to firmly claim my place within her family, my mother named me Patsy after her grandfather, the Durack patriarch whose migration from Ireland in 1852 had set the destiny of his lineage upon Australian shores. The artist Beatrice Darbyshire sketched me at eight weeks old, and there I am – pensive and wary. Katharine Susannah Prichard employed her author's licence to assure the new mother that 'your little person will be a fulfilment and source of consolation no matter what the Furies have in store'.[1]

~

Horrie had bought the double block situated at Bellevue Avenue in the suburb of Nedlands during the early thirties as a good investment. Ever his own man, he would reject his wife's subsequent hopeful appeals that he consider one of the many available riverfront blocks, his typical reasoning that such sites were 'too windy'. So it was that a decent distance from wind or water arose a one-storey version of the ubiquitous Californian bungalow designed, for a token fee, by Mary's architect brother, Bill Durack. There was then little regret felt for the upgrade from the rambling charm of the older style domiciles to modern guttering and plumbing, enduring Brisbane and Wunderlich tiling and narrow cement verandahs. As Gran put it: 'All very well, "Old World stylishness", but the upkeep, dear – the upkeep.' M.P. and Bess, in company with their old retainer, Nurse Stevens, lived in Goderich Street, a short walk from their former home at 263 Adelaide Terrace, where the Durack children had spent their childhood. The elegant city mansion lost to a downturn in the cattle industry, Gran never passed her former abode without memories and nostalgia but not real sorrow, as, from her practical viewpoint, it had served its term.

Beyond the Millers' ever-open green gate, paving slabs provided safe transit through a sandy wasteland to brick steps and the flywired, wrought-iron door with the letter 'M' at its centre, standing before the front door proper, sturdy and ripple-glassed. A number of features of the day were incorporated: porthole windows, Swiss-style shutters, brick window boxes, swing doors and a lounge-room ceiling sculptured like a wedding cake. 'Breakfast nooks' were a popular innovation and a section of the kitchen was allotted for this purpose. A passageway served as the spine of the house and, branching off, four modest bedrooms and one large, chilly bathroom tiled in hygienic green and cream. A three-seater couch and two chairs were installed in the lounge room, representing Horrie's idea of the maximum number who might at any one time be decently entertained. Notably absent from any display surface were wedding photos, since the nature of the Miller marriage had precluded conventional mementos or gifts. The back steps led down to a paved courtyard bounded on the far side by the laundry, outdoor toilet and Horrie's garage, which became in later years, as he drifted ever more into an outer zone, his room.

The house sat in the middle of an expanse, much of it never destined to emerge from a straggling wilderness into anything more sylvan or useful. A few grass trees and banksias had been salvaged, but the way was cleared for the planting of poplars, firs, lemon-scented gums and Rottnest pines, an ill-assorted mix of natives and imports, the roots within a few years putting paid to flowerbeds and the plumbing.

A rosebed, according to Gran de rigueur, was duly planted at the front, and Horrie saw to an elaborate reticulation system run by a capricious pump situated at the bottom of a deep well. As I watched him descend the vertical shaft, his feet clanging ever more faintly on the rungs, the courage required to venture into such an underworld seemed to me unimaginable. At the same time, I was seized with guilt at a small but recognisable hope that he would never resurface.

Atop the flat-roofed garage was an open balcony with an iron structure anchored in the centre for fixing and turning Horrie's giant telescope. Astronomy was one of his passing enthusiasms, although I have no memory of the instrument except as a mysterious elongated shape wrapped in green canvas. From this modest height, the river was then in clear view over the low roofs of an area as yet only semi-suburban. Among other long-vanished phenomena were the rising minor note of frogs at night, lions roaring across the river separating us from the Perth Zoo and the accelerating thrum of the pre-dawn DC3 take-off from the airport – sounds woven into our dreams.

Set for a long cycle of procreation, my mother decorated the nursery with a painted wall mural of themes copied from nursery rhymes and Ida Rentoul Outhwaite fairies and gnomes. Her five siblings at a distance, she particularly missed the confiding and sharing presence of her sister Elizabeth (known to her family as Bet), who was living in the Eastern States with her journalist husband, Frank Clancy, and out of reach except by mail which had gone beyond the moment by the time it arrived. Their lives during the war years largely confined to domesticity, the continued collaboration on children's books and an intense correspondence – a far cry from what could be described as regular exchange – represented a vital escape from the humdrum. So stimulating and cathartic became the frequent to and fro, they began to play around with the idea of a publication in the form of letters going back over a decade, under the title 'The Young Know'.

Incorporating their youth and formative years, they wrote of their time together on the family northern stations, relationship with parents and brothers, trip overseas during the mid-thirties, the war and general observations on the uncertainties and inevitabilities of life. Husbands and children were mentioned merely in passing before getting down to the next instalment of the retrospective journey towards some form of existential insight. As the concept took form and shape, to the disappointment of her sister who had worked hard on the project, Bet's initial over-enthusiasm cooled, with second thoughts about being too open with her inner turmoil and private life in a public domain. The manuscript, a unique journey into two extraordinary minds, was mothballed pending the demise of anyone who might be offended or pass judgement.[2]

Two girls with four brothers, the sisters were to remain bound to one another in a fashion that defied understandings of 'normal' sibling attachment – an inherency that could only have been maintained by women not destined to be intellectually or emotionally supported by men.

~

Missing the north and lonely during the long marital separations, in August 1941 Mary seized the opportunity to accompany Horrie on a Royal Flying Doctor Service (RFDS) aircraft delivery to Wyndham. Arranging for an onward journey to the family stations with her infant daughter, she gave her father and brother Reg advance reassurance: 'Patsy is quite tractable, with immense enthusiasm for life, movement and animals, full of cute ways and words.'

I seem to remember a friendly white cockatoo inviting my fingers through the bars of a cage, and the subsequent betrayal of trust. My inconsolability at this incident and overall performance during what my mother intended as an introduction to the Kimberley pastoral empire for the first of the new generation have been embedded in family annals, and my grandfather, no stranger to any number and variety of hair-raising occurrences, was reportedly reduced to a distressed and helpless 'Oh dearie, dearie dear'. Amusement was what was needed. Thinking it would be a fine entertainment, he carried me down to the yard where the beast selected to supply the station meat ration was about to be dispatched. My mother, hoping for a brief respite, heard the hysterical screams accelerating, until a panting Daisy delivered her stricken charge with the advice, 'She got'm chore heart b'longta bullock'. Three previous generations of Durack children had been introduced to bloody sights at an early age without suffering sore hearts. Such a to-do was not in the family tradition.

If carried, I became a dead weight or, with bruising force, struggled to be free. If put to ground, evading more wholesome company, I made a beeline for old Lucy, who was awaiting transfer to the leprosarium. On a diversionary walk down by the lagoon, we came upon the aged and near-blind former stockman Tommy.

'This your piccaninny, missus?'

When he reached a groping hand towards me, my mother, fearful of the endemic disease, instinctively drew me back.

'I can just see her, missus, like a little shadow.'[3]

And, considering the way of things, that was all I was ever fated to be upon that vast stretch of land believed then to be a dynastic heritage.

~

My mother retained few happy memories of my infancy. It was difficult not to feel aggrieved at the persistent grizzling that drew attention to her obvious inadequacy as a 'mummy', even the title denied her since I addressed her as 'Mrs Miller', which amused her enough to let it stand. My father, who was not a father's bootlace to me, was 'Horrie'.

My term as a solo prima donna, one perfectly satisfactory as far as I was concerned, was short-lived, and I did not then (or ever) take well to alteration of the status quo that left me, as I saw it, worse off.

Within the minimum possible gestation period, Robin and Julie arrived, presenting my mother with three infants under three. Consequently, a variety of young 'home helps' came and went in quick succession. None of them was a treasure, all to a degree inept, unobliging and encumbered with personal problems. But, in fairness to the girls, even for the sum of three pounds per week, it can't have been a job encouraging long-term commitment or enthusiasm, especially when the stifling conservatism of the small countrified city had been overtaken by the hot winds of wartime romance. With the realisation that the cost of female menials was greater than any service they could render, after six years my mother gave up on the whole idea, preferring instead to make use of relatives and friends willing to step into the breach when necessary. Live-in domestics, so taken for granted by the older generation, were a dying breed. With them went a primary component of conversation and source of complaint among those who considered household staff one of life's imperatives.

Visits from Gran and her live-in companion Nurse Stevens, or 'Snowy', as we were encouraged to call her since her role as midwife and child-carer had become superfluous, now included Grandpa. He had kept up the display of wounded chagrin until Robin's birth, refusing to listen to any news from 'Mildew', as the new domicile was drolly (and with the passing years ever more aptly) dubbed from a combination of the Miller and Durack names. Urged by Bet to apply his journalistic skills to the dilemma, Frank Clancy had written to his father-in-law in a bid to bring a little reason into the situation. Whether it was this or some behind-the-scenes no-nonsense talk from Gran, he came round, as everyone had always known he would. Nevertheless, I note in the few references to me in his journals my name is given inverted commas, as if in his mind I never quite attained legitimacy.

In his seventies, M.P. was still spending up to six months of every year in the north, his single-minded objective to pull station affairs back onto a footing that would pay off the accumulated debts of many decades. The success of these exertions would culminate in the sale of the seven million acre Connor Doherty and Durack (CD&D) estate, a prospect his children fought hard to prevent. He was a very old man, to me, tall and broad of girth, with tickling whiskers and amusing exclamations: 'Great living Scott, in all my born days …', the outrage ranging from the cost of a pair of his wife's shoes to the threat of wages for Aboriginal employees. Jovially instructing me to hold onto his walking stick, he would swing me up into the air, where I hung between his work-roughened, blue-veined hands in some nervous anticipation of release.

So he proceeded, when in Perth, down the yet unworn Mildew path, once more calling my mother 'Dearie', although he contrived his arrivals for Horrie's departures. While they would eventually come to an uneasy civility, the two were never able to look one another in the eye. Gran, who developed likings for people she considered 'different' or 'comical', got on well enough with her son-in-law, although she was inclined to address him with the cocked head and jocund tone of voice she adopted for 'characters'. Horrie, always respectful, called her 'Mrs Durack' and Gran never suggested he drop the formality.

~

When Robin was born, at the sight of her worried face and jaundiced colouring my mother thought her a somewhat unattractive baby. Horrie at once sprang to her defence: 'She looks like a Miller,' he said, 'and in my opinion, she's by far the prettier of the two.' So that was that. Horrie seldom deviated from first reactions. Robin, unlike his firstborn, seemed of gentler, more reasonable and possibly more solid stuff.

One name each had been considered by Bess Durack enough for her daughters, but my mother, perhaps to give us more substance, or in a bid for happy continuity, bestowed her eldest daughters with the second names Mary and Elizabeth.[4] Robin and Julie were apparently names derived from novels she had read prior to the births. Surprisingly, when naming her children, originality was not a priority for my mother.

My two great-aunts, M.P.'s sisters Mary Davidson and Bridget Durack, known respectively as Marie and Bird, left a lasting impression, although both were gone before my tenth birthday. Marie made stately descents on her niece for afternoon tea after protracted advance telephone communication and enquiries as to when Bird intended coming, thereby circumventing any possibility of a one-stone killing. Visiting regularly, they made the most of a time when, in the interests of establishing family acceptance of her dubious marriage, their niece was willing to indulge their foibles and the repetitious recall of bygone days.

Her tall, spare figure attired in a full sallying-forth rig of ankle-length dress, coat, hat and gloves, Aunt Marie's appearance was wont to provoke terror and inconsolable bellowing from minors. The principal purpose of her call seemed to be to off-load an inexhaustible inventory of trivial detail concerning other family members, friends and friends of friends. It was a matter of general speculation how these facts were ever conveyed to Marie in the first place, since she herself never stopped talking, her monotonous, palsied voice droning on into the afternoon until the rattling of cots and mutinous cacophony from the nursery became impossible to ignore and the narrative was put on pause while nappies were changed, shoes thrust over kicking feet and the menagerie confined to a rug within a playpen.

Bird, who was a 'maiden lady', did not avail herself of public transport. In defiance of the modest living allowance settled upon her by her brothers, she made reckless use of taxis and the toiletry products of Potter and Moore. My memory of this great-aunt is limited to her last days when she lay dying in a private hospital run by Matron Marjorie Marshall, a vivacious, somewhat haywire personality whose role as overseer of current and pending Durack deaths would earn her a place as an honorary family member. Our visits to Aunt Bird were in those days dependent upon Gran's stately paced and obliviously roadhog driving services. My father drove a roomy Chevrolet with running boards, hanging straps for passengers and cracked leather seats, available for Sunday jaunts to the Hills and to the beach in summer but not for errands, as might be helpful to his wife. Nor was there any question of her making use of it during his absences, when it was housed in an airport hangar, off limits to any but the mechanic who kept the battery charged; Horrie always exhibited an abhorrence of any two-timing with his belongings, particularly his vehicles.

The patient's mournful blue eyes brightening at the sight of Bess, Mary and the little ones, Aunt Bird would beckon me to the bedside and take three two-shilling pieces from beneath her pillow, one for each of us – an unheard-of sum to give children. There followed an excited conversation with Matron Marshall, whose sibilant whisper updated the room on the progress of death.

'Would you like to see?' she murmured, and even though no-one indicated much enthusiasm for it and the presence of those underage for such a viewing was overlooked, she swept back the bedcovers to reveal Bird's gangrenous leg. Since it had been her weakness for the bottle that had in the first place decided M.P. on removing his sister to a nursing home, it was to her credit that Marjorie Marshall quietly supplied the evening nip that brought a little comfort to Bird's tedious lingering.

Failing together, the two Durack sisters indulged in a competitive bid to reach the finishing line, the winner being the first to take up heavenly residence with J.W. Durack, their beloved bachelor brother Jack, who had departed in 1936. There had been a prearrangement that Bird should share his grave, one resented by Marie, despite her being a married woman with family to join her plot in the fullness of time. Matron Marshall, who took a lively interest in the oddities of her patients, had been amused by the ghoulish race, a diversion shared by my mother and Gran. An interesting postscript to the finale came to me only in half-heard undertones. The subject of disinterment at the behest of an infuriated Bird, who discovered her sister's victory and subsequent deception, was not really suitable for childish ears.

~

By all accounts a demanding child, clinging possessively to my mother's skirts in a bid to claw back the attention so rapidly usurped, I would torture myself with thoughts of being parted from or losing her – tears welling at the mere conjecture. But having decided from the outset that she would not give up her life to child raising, loving as she was, my mother maintained enough emotional distance to allow herself the occasional escape. Her children had come into being with little effort, neither planned nor unplanned, although she had supposed that one day she would have her own family. As for Horrie, he had managed to accumulate a sizable brood without giving it a thought either way, the effort involved far less than – for example – to produce an improved air filter. We were therefore born into an attitude that reflected the ease of our begetting rather than the coming into existence of small miracles.

As had been the case with the union of my grandparents, the combination of my parents produced unlike children. None of us bore much resemblance to the others in looks or temperament. Julie was a chubby, dimpled child possessed of an outgoing and sociable personality. She and Robin, both blonde babies, played contentedly together only so long as I, the dark interloper, was kept out of their games, and it had seemed something of a solution when a place was found for me during the mornings at a kindergarten run by a local church. Horrie, with the reluctance that marked his dealing with any domestic request, even one that put him out not a jot, was recruited to deliver me on his way into town.

These were the war years, during which he was faced with considerable problems to keep his airline running. MacRobertson Miller Aviation (MMA) aircraft were impressed at various times to assist Eastern States services, and by 1942 Japanese aerial attacks on ports from Darwin to Port Hedland saw regular schedules disrupted or cancelled. Obliged by now to shoulder managerial responsibilities rather than his preferred earlier role as pilot, mechanic and one-man-band, Horrie travelled daily to Yorkshire House, the city headquarters. After a dutiful appearance at the helm, he would slip away in the Chevrolet, now fuelled by a charcoal gas burner, to Maylands Aerodrome, where the roar of engines being tested, clang of tools echoing in the vast hangar and the heady smell of oil and dope soothed his nervy disposition. How familiar to the scene his diffident persona: the tall, wiry frame, thinning, windblown sandy hair, lean features – the face of an archetypal aviator. Chronically pessimistic, he daily awaited bad news. Dire warnings could not prevent his pilots making fool errors of judgement among the genuine accidents, and Horrie wasn't too particular about distinguishing between them. A hard man to please under the best circumstances, he was unforgiving of casualties, especially since it had been up to him on several occasions to tackle single-handed the gruelling salvage work. Jimmy Woods, the company's senior pilot and a close family friend, was finally sacked in 1947 after one crack-up too many. Horrie himself never made mistakes. If something untoward occurred, it was always either blind bad luck or someone else's fault.

~

The war years did not much disrupt the routine of our small lives. We went through practice runs to an air-raid shelter and registered the shortage of cakes and sweets being on account of the soldiers needing them more than we did. My mother's attempt to make up for meat rationing by serving slightly disguised offal met with such strong objection that brains, liver, kidneys and tripe disappeared from the menu. Gran, however, continued to relish these discards. If she felt some systemic craving for brains, there was absolutely no need for tripe!

Prior to the acquisition of a refrigerator, perishables were stored in a wooden icebox cooled by an enormous block of ice delivered by a man who hooked the dripping weight onto a sack draped across his shoulder. A horse-drawn cart trailing a delicious odour carried the bread from door to door, and a 'fisho' on a motorbike with a sidecar attached for the still-flapping produce arrived at the back gate on Thursday in time for the Catholic meatless Friday. But such old-world conveniences were coming to the end of their span. Grocery stores, a butcher, baker and pharmacy opened in Waratah Avenue, a walk of about fifteen minutes requiring, in the absence of a car, the services of the Miller children. It seemed to me a most extraordinary and interesting thing that the butcher was actually called Mr Butcher, and the baker Mr Baker. That the chemist was not called Mr Chemist, but Mr Coates, was a disappointment only made up for by the way his name handily rhymed with 'our throats', for the fixing of. A commercial traveller known as the Watkins man regularly called with an attaché case of toiletries. Before this relic faded away, my mother, groaning at the sight of him, would reach for her purse out of pity for the pathetic, jovial fellow.

I can also remember limbless itinerant men, hats raised politely at the door, asking if we needed any pots mended or knives sharpened. Thus were the maimed survivors of the First World War forced to make a living.

All round our house, others were springing up on the many spare blocks where once we had picked bunches of spider, donkey and enamel orchids, white honey flowers, cowslips and cat's paws, found bobtail lizards and set up cubbies. The arrival of newcomers within a wide radius saw Mary, who was indecently neighbourly, setting out to pay a welcoming visit, and hence, in addition to those carried over from previous locations, entered into family legend many friends for life. Proximity was the only qualification required. Some remained in the district for decades, but none so long as us. Had she known when her young feet first entered the Mildew gate that her corpse would ultimately be carried down the same path, it would probably have depressed my mother no end.

Directly across the road lived the McLeans, who had been the only people in Bellevue Avenue when we moved there. Shortly before the birth of Julie, their toddler son vanished, culminating in the discovery of the little body down a dry well on an empty block. In her vulnerable condition, Mary was deeply affected by this tragedy, and she felt some curious foreboding about the expected baby, not helped by a letter of similar portent from Bet. It came therefore as a joyous relief when in July 1942 Julie was born healthy and bonny. The only regret was that she was not the son Mary had seen in fond imagination as forming a bond with his father and perhaps sharing his aeronautic interests. For a while we were banned from playing on construction sites, but before long the momentary lull enjoyed in our absence would overrule all but a warning from our mother to 'be careful'.

So we three grew together, one no sooner out of the cot or pram than another occupant moving in, and en masse succumbing to chickenpox, mumps and anything else doing the rounds. My only claim to superiority was that I was the *eldest*, the reason given for all manner of asserted rights. Robin and Julie eventually came to counter this pushiness with the reminder that I would certainly die first.

Before I had reached the required age for formal schooling, my mother approached the nuns at Loreto Convent in the hope that her juvenile overload might persuade them to take me as a pupil. The rules were bent to accommodate her contingency, and my tiny form was inserted into a classroom where, for want of a spare chair, I was sat on the floor so that big people could trip over me. My mother's decision to have her children educated at the convent had been made with some reservations. Could she justify the religious aspects she had herself rejected? Seeking the wisdom of her brother Reg, who had married out of the Catholic Church, she went with his advice that it would probably be alright and that the kids would come to their own conclusions.

The kindly and in some cases academically well-qualified nuns were, by the nature of their calling, inclined towards eccentricity. Understood, excused and even loved by their pupils, the more bonkers among them could be regarded as existing in a zone of special sanity. For all they looked upon me with the interested goodwill born of my Durack association, their expectations were destined to be disappointed. At best, in terms of potential and character, I was poorly defined and I went to some lengths to keep it that way.

~

Her children expanded in short order to four under five, and feeling isolated from the wider and more erudite community, Mary sought the company of people she could relate to on a level above domestic matters. Re-establishing friendships made in pre-marriage days when she wrote articles and a folksy column for the *West Australian* newspaper, she soon had lines connected to most of those in the journalistic, arts and academic circles of Perth. No matter the inconvenience of the unexpected doorbell summons, at this stage she welcomed drop-ins and began to hold dinner parties, the edibles supplied from coupon rations that only required her imaginative adaptations to make them resemble the fancy recipes illustrated in the *Women's Weekly*.

Horrie always kept his wife poor. Paying for basic household expenses and, later, the school bills, he was convinced any personal allowance would only provoke her already excessive generosity towards indigent friends and kin, mainly her sister Bet, whom he judged as unstable and always 'on the take'. He also suspected she would hold more parties, since that was what she was already doing on a shoestring budget. There was an element of truth in his suspicions – Mary was incorrigibly convivial. It therefore became as much a necessity of life as an insistent urge for her to begin a serious writing career.

While her hands were full and concentration scattered, she churned out book reviews, radio talks, magazine articles and short stories. Constantly thinking up new ideas for children's books, she had at the same time begun working on a more ambitious project incorporating what she knew of Durack family history, tentatively titled 'They Reached a Land'. There was no thought other than this book, like the previous publications, would be illustrated by Bet. Another work in progress covering the history of the Swan River Settlement led me to the curious understanding that my mother owned the Swan River. My declarations at school to this effect were pronounced with such certitude that for a while the class was divided into the believers and the doubters. When hilarity met the confirmation sought at home, I was humiliated and resentful that I had been so carelessly allowed to harbour the wrong impression.

We fell asleep to the sound of the typewriter, clacking away far into the night. Children roused at any hour would be reassured by the sight of the mother on duty at the cluttered desk, stroking her upper lip with a bent right forefinger in a characteristic gesture of contemplation. We knew she was reaching into the back blocks of her mind where existed, so distinctly apart from 'Mum', that other person, the writer. Then a burst of typing would follow the clarified thought. We became used to her slightly abstracted state – one part of her mind, no matter the outward activity, inwardly working an assortment of themes that found her scribbling, and later trying to decipher, hasty notes. Even so, she always claimed her best thoughts evaporated into the ether.

Everything in short supply during the war years, we made do with second-hand clothing and a few homemade playthings. An odd assortment of 'presents', rare in straitened times, were valued and hoarded. Gran bestowed upon me a Japanese fan, a framed picture of the princesses Elizabeth and Margaret Rose and her empty perfume bottles for the pleasure of their lingering redolence. Other accumulated treasures lined the wall shelf in my room, where, like the bottles of Watkins merchandise in the bathroom cupboard, they became permanent accretions.

A Singer sewing machine acquired, there followed many years of dressmaking on the part of the conscientious mother. Sweating and harassed, her mouth full of pins, she treadled away into the night to make her 'bunnies' matching frocks, often embellished with an embroidery technique known as smocking, a tedious and stressful process usually accompanied by under-breath swearing. It was no surprise to me that it was an activity explicitly forbidden on aircraft. But somehow, we had a new dress every Christmas and were satisfactorily outfitted for Holy Communion, confirmations and special occasions. Otherwise, we wore shrunken woollies and faded cottons from sources connected to Gran and her frugal acquaintances. Fortunately, we were not fashion-conscious kids, and none of our friends looked any different. For many years, school uniforms and other unavoidable outlay were put on the Aherns store account, which became a fearsome thing – arrival of the bill causing cries of consternation followed by a period of serious application on the part of the writer.

For a few years we must have given the impression of a normal family. While she still strove for some semblance of a conventional situation, our mother had us lined up to greet Horrie of an evening as his vehicle insinuated itself down the drive. At the command 'give your daddy a kiss', each of us in turn gave the indifferently proffered cheek a dutiful peck. Always the last and most reluctant to comply, I would eventually dodge any further show of affection for one who growled in ceaseless complaint – whose shadow fell to darken my young existence. It seemed the best policy for dealing with my father was to keep him at arm's length.

In complete contrast to the man once declared by an associate as never *met* but just brushed up against like a wet tea-tree hedge, there emanated from his wife such warmth, intelligence and empathy that she was almost without exception loved at first sight. The combination of her cordiality, mobile features and charming smile transferred her to a special class of beauty. Undiscriminating and accepting of the varied foibles of her fellows, she simply liked some more than others, and sundry chaff drawn into the net of her appeal found a place at her table along with the valued harvest. Kindness ruled every aspect of her life, and it was to the great good fortune of anyone who came within the perimeter of her amazing grace. As time took its inevitable toll, she would be able to let dear friends go without inordinate sorrow, their passing made easier knowing that she could not have done more for them while they lived.

Everybody who crossed her path had a story, and she enquired with sincere interest into backgrounds and family histories and, encouraging of biographical effort, would gamely suffer the boomeranging results. Such magnanimity, however, would come at a price in terms of her own literary output, as would her uncritical approach to a broad diversity of humanity. But she was thus able to find affinity with many who did not share her acumen or interests, and therein lay a clue to her perplexing choice of husband. When pressed by the curious as to what – frankly – she had been thinking, she would resort to speaking in nebulous terms of her children and the felicitous link with an airline that allowed her travel north free of charge.

~

Horrie's romantic intentions had been announced during the 1930s by his performing aerobatics over Ivanhoe Station when Mary and Bet were in occupation. Unimpressed by such antics, Mary had nonetheless observed that Horrie was a rarity inasmuch as he had not been first attracted to her pretty and provocative sister.

The H.C. Miller bid for the tendered North West service in 1934 had come in at a marginally lower rate than that of the entrenched WA Airways operator, Major Norman Brearley, who knew he had been swindled but could never work out how it had been done.[5] M.P. Durack, a friend and supporter of Brearley, shared the general disapproval of the South Australian interloper whose aircraft carried the unfamiliar logo MMA. He little contemplated then the so much worse expropriation to come.

A trip abroad should have seen an end to any budding attachment, but Mary's letters to Horrie over this period reveal that she only half-heartedly put him off, and he was used to initial discouragement. Beneath the casual reserve of this singular and solitary airman, there ran a steely will and an ability to manipulate in a way that was at the same time transparent and deceptively subtle. If compassion rather than passion was needed, he could play heartstrings like a virtuoso, a performance to which Mary Durack was receptive. On her return, the friendship was resumed, but so informally that no-one suspected a romance. She herself could produce no real rationale for her decision to meet him in Melbourne on the strength of an uncertain arrangement and a roughly wrapped parcel containing a ring. There had been other, more fitting suitors, but none had captured her, and she was never to really lose her heart to any man.

Horrie's life experience had confirmed the achievability of many seemingly impossible goals, and in Mary Durack he had recognised a challenge worth a shot. She had a rare acuity capable, so he thought, of understanding his idiosyncratic personality. Realistically, this translated as a hunch that if she could be persuaded to take him on, she would probably put up with him.

His previous marriage in 1933 had been to Jean Knox, an Adelaide girl of his own working-class background. Jean and their daughter Auburn, born in 1934, joined him in Western Australia during the establishment of MMA – a demanding phase of Horrie's career that left him with scant time for the lonely wife and baby languishing in a city where they knew no-one. His then company accountant and later general manager Cyril Gare and his kindly wife Elsie had befriended them, but as the situation deteriorated, it had called for some discretion on the part of the Gares, who were also required to show unwavering loyalty to Horrie. Auburn always carried the dim memory of this unhappy period before they returned to South Australia, where her mother was persuaded by her indignant family to end the marriage. Following the uncontested divorce, Jean maintained herself and her daughter by working in a munitions factory until she died of polio in 1944. When letters to Horrie concerning his daughter went unanswered, Auburn was adopted by her grandparents, the understanding being that he had remarried into a 'society' family and any attempt on her part to make contact could only cause embarrassment.

Horrie's own childhood had been deprived in a Dickensian way. Born in 1893 and his mother lost to typhoid when he was an infant, he hardly knew his father, who had placed him and an elder sister in a foster home. It was as if from outer space that he had materialised on the scene in Western Australia. Orphaned as much in inclination as in actuality, his assumed status as flotsam of the storm gave him the licence to cut loose inconvenient or unappealing responsibilities. Fondly held recollections of neglect – freezing hands and shoeless feet, enforced work beyond the strength of a child, mentioned in tones of doleful self-pity – were dished up to us as children so that his shortcomings became somehow excused by his wretched beginnings.

Unfortunately, the misery of his early years did not render Horrie a more sensitive adult. The only trace of Auburn in our household being a photo in a broken frame hidden at the back of the linen closet, her father at this time did not acknowledge her existence. His daughter's welfare assessed by his having once driven past the place where she lived and seen her swinging on the gate,[6] Mary's suggestion that perhaps the child should be absorbed into the ever-growing Mildew menagerie was met with the flat statement that she was better off with her own relatives. Questioning matters considered by Horrie his business was inadvisable, as was pursuing any line contrary to his. The subject was dropped. In some ways, it was a relief to his wife that he came without attachments, so that she was spared being saddled with alien connections possibly affected by the same sad sack gene. The Durack family and its multiple branches were enough to cope with.

Accepting her karma, on 1 December 1938, at the age of twenty-six, Mary Durack went against her nearest and dearest, all sense of what was prudent and proper, and in a registry office, without family or friends present, she married a man who would soon downgrade her individuality (and perhaps define the intrinsic nature of the relationship) by calling her 'Mum'. The wedding day memorable only for the drama of her spouse in agony from a tooth abscess, there had been no discernible 'honeymoon period' before the new Mrs Miller was ensconced in the flat formerly occupied by the banished former wife and daughter, whose unhappy ghosts lingered. Aware of the general opinion that she had made her own bed, my mother kept to herself the discovery while expecting her fourth child that she was sharing the insubstantial affections of her husband with another woman. Her just deserts accepted as such, it was only through a few latter-day cryptic comments to me that I had an inkling of them. She also liked to maintain an image of sense and sensibility, the calm eye amid turmoil, and revelations of her own mess-ups would have affected the perception.

Whatever Mary's future justification for a match she would privately ascribe to some sort of astral casualty, Horrie certainly had no right to carry off the talented, much loved and valued eldest daughter of M.P. and Bess Durack simply because he could. What might be viewed as an unconventional but in some ways convenient union – one, as Bet predicted, 'doomed to last' – can also in hindsight be seen as a blighted mismatch that failed down the years to flourish in the way of the most commonplace.

~

My mother's bedroom contained a double bed, but I never saw my father in it. His room off the passageway outside, conjugal visits must have been carried out in furtive fashion. For that period in our young lives when he was in permanent residence, sporadic cheerful moods were indicated by the rendition of vintage music-hall numbers: *Nothing could be finer than to be in Carolina in the MOR-OR-OR-NING* ... or *Tell me pretty maiden are there any more at home like youuu* ... Profoundly melancholy, in a way reminiscent to his wife of Eeyore the donkey, his outlook was entirely pessimistic. Averse to commonplace civility, even 'Nice day, Horrie' was liable to be met by the sour rejoinder 'Not necessarily'. Queried on any subject outside his specific area of interest, with a shrug of his shoulders he 'couldn't say'. In later years, my mother would record in her diary the difficulty encountered in trying to fill out a census form with one incapable of a positive statement. Enquiries concerning his own health invariably bringing forth a preview of his imminent demise – a coming attraction, as far as I was concerned – the very sound of his light tenor voice on a dying fall had a dampening effect. It was embarrassing and boring that a great many ordinary things aroused him to shuddering antipathy: smokers, drunks, talkers, loud voices, shrill voices, whisperers, silence, funerals (avoided as if infectious), waste, too many kids, gas-guzzling vehicles, Yanks, Pommies, sneezers, wheezers and shoot-the-breezers – the list was fairly comprehensive. 'Clear orf' was a not-uncommon means of dismissal and he customarily prefaced pointless arguments with 'The point is ...'

While Horrie's durability could be attributed to an element of luck, even his apparently most hazardous ventures had been carefully calculated to optimise his chances of survival. As he grew older, with the knowledge that despite his every precaution, death would eventually prevail, the repeated declaration that he was on his last legs symbolised his method of knocking on wood.

There is no doubt, however, that Captain Miller was admired and respected by many of his contemporaries – those at any rate who had escaped his wrath. He personified the fading spirit of pioneering derring-do, the loner who negotiated confounding obstacles and defied odds to achieve an ambition. The very embodiment of the romance of flight and the flying ace – Lindbergh, Baron Von Richthofen, Charles Kingsford Smith – he had outlived his fellows to become a monument to an era when all eyes turned skyward at the drone of an airborne machine. Inventive and forward-looking, he took keen note of technological advances and he would later follow the space race with a close interest and conjecture on the future direction of humankind with the breaking of this barrier. Laconically recounting events from his colourful past, he could be amusing and entertaining. At times capriciously generous, since he was also neurotically parsimonious, this must be counted among his constitutional inconsistencies. His likes and dislikes established for fairly arbitrary reasons, Horrie stuck by them. The few who came up to his particular form of scratch (the qualifications for women: youth, good looks, of flirtatious disposition and pref. non-smoker) found him open and affable, while those who did not were cold-shouldered. His wife's friends fell into two categories: those who wouldn't have a bar of him, not even for her sake, and those who were prepared to tolerate him – for her sake. A few, like Gordon Colebatch, loved him.

Seemingly unhampered by a jobless and consequently penniless state, Gordon, the son of a former state premier, in the manner of a proper aristocrat, spent his days in rather disorganised but highly pleasurable pursuits. Introduced via a long association with the Duracks, Horrie was struck by and attracted to the charm and urbane sophistication of a man so unlike those of his usual acquaintance. People involved with the aviation industry tended to be rather conversely down to earth; Gordon, who never set foot in an aircraft, was mentally aloft, his interests covering great sweeps of subjects earthly and cosmological. While constructing a splendid Italianate villa at Gooseberry Hill on the crest of the Darling escarpment, where he planned to complete his 'History of the World', he drew Horrie like a magnet.

During the First World War, the RAF had attracted similar debonair blue bloods whose natural superiority had greatly impressed a fellow with no pretensions to background or breeding. For the most part devil-may-care, they had died young. Gordon himself had been wounded in the arm on a French battlefield, putting paid to a career (so it was bandied about) as a concert pianist. Horrie had always been what is referred to as 'a man's man', if only by dint of his being fairly clueless when it came to women. Now he found himself welcomed with glad cries in an Arcadia where he was taken seriously, and his theories on space, time and matter thoughtfully debated. In return, Gordon's vision of the ultimate failure of mankind found a receptive ear.[7]

As soon as an electricity connection permitted, the stone walls of the sunken drawing room reverberated to the sound of classical music and from their crates emerged books on every imaginable topic. The influence was recognisably behind the planting of a profusion of imported trees around Mildew and the acquisition of a large, very loud gramophone, along with albums of hifalutin records. We were all included in the transient summer of fun and games at Gooseberry Hill, but the core friendship was between the two men. When Gordon made a convenient arrangement that included marriage and moved Astrid into the villa, the food and beverage service made visits even more appealing, with the result that on several occasions emergencies in the airline had found the manager exasperatingly out of reach. That there might have been more to this rapport on Gordon's part than a deep, manly pal-ship would not have occurred to Horrie. He had somehow travelled through four decades without having knowingly encountered homosexuality, and when in some passing context it was finally explained, he chose not to believe it for a moment.

However attributed to his upbringing, when it came to relationships, there had somewhere been a short circuit in Horrie's wiring. Introverted, self-absorbed and emotionally damaged, his fondest feelings boiled down to a sort of mawkish sentimentality. At the age of forty-six, with a world war and twenty-eight years of pioneering aviation activities behind him, by the time he married Mary Durack the best part of his life was over and he would be gradually moved out of the way by the businessmen within the company who considered him an impediment to progress. As he became increasingly redundant to the scheme of things, there would be a marked division between those who remained grateful and loyal and those who looked upon him with dwindling benevolence and patience. Quite early in the piece, he became for his wife the most difficult of her children, to be indulged and placated for the sake of peace, and with the adoption of this approach, the shouting sessions were reduced to short, sharp spats culminating in his 'clearing orf', sometimes for lengthy periods.

Once at a remove, it was possible to correspond with Horrie on a surprisingly normal level. He wrote well, with a characteristic mixture of bathos and humour, keen-eyed accuracy and blind bias. In later years, living far from home, I looked forward to his wry observations on current affairs and family situations. But any impression of Horrie based on his letters alone would bear only a distant kinship to the man himself.

~

The Bellevue Avenue domicile was already proving too small, especially with the prospect of another baby before Julie had vacated the cot. Shortage of building material and manpower ruling out anything but a fairly rudimentary addition, the open verandah where we played in sunny weather was enclosed to become 'the new room' for the next twenty years. Following the birth in 1944 of Andrew, named after one of Horrie's vaguely mentioned Scottish ancestors, Mary succumbed to the strain, suffering the 'milk fever' prevalent prior to the advent of antibiotics and a temporary inability to face the hectic home scene. This was in no small part the result of her discovery of Horrie's indiscretion, albeit a passing affair with a woman who would make no claim for his alleged child. At the same time, she was troubled by frantic letters from her sister Bet and brother David, who had got themselves into predicaments hardly conducive to her recovery and certainly not to revealing her own problems.

An offer from an Italian friend to convalesce at her home was gladly accepted. A Madonna figure of extravagant gesture and voice, Maria Dent had come to Perth as a 'war bride' and set up house in Nedlands with her husband, who was a professional photographer. A decade or so before an influx of Italian migrants, Maria represented the Latin element in my mother's collection of diverse people. She would provide a welcome antidote to the very constant advice from Gran, in whose care Robin and I had been placed ('Well, I'm happy to take one or two, dear – but *three* …'), while Julie was accommodated elsewhere.

Staying with Gran and the entrenched Snowy, while lacking the cosy bedlam of home, had its advantages. The house in Goderich Street and her later abodes, always smelling so very distinctly of Gran – a flowery, lavendery, polishy *clean* aroma – were orderly in a way that stirred a dormant chord in my chronically untidy person. Gran lived under the dictate 'a place for everything and everything in its place', an old maxim that, while it meant nothing to me then, would one day come home to roost. There were graduating playthings for children, from the square wooden blocks in the green wheeled tray, to the daintily dressed porcelain dolls that had been hers as a child and the stereoscope with photographs springing to three-dimensional life and depth. Best of all, Gran owned a radio, a sculptured black bakelite item with a cloth-covered speaker box and a dial that glowed when in use. A two-minute warm-up was required as we sat in anticipation of entertainment that for Gran (adopting a fond and foolish look) didn't get much better than the strains of 'We'll Gather Lilacs in the Spring'. But she also enjoyed the serials that first emerged during the 1950s, especially *When a Girl Marries* and *Courtship and Marriage*, and before long I was listening in with equal thrall.

At this time, when in the care of Gran, it became necessary for me to deal with a nightmarish problem. From whence the malign fancy sprang I do not know, but my every exposure to passing strangers had gradually come to appear of mysterious significance. Surely there had to be a reason why invisible strings had pulled us, however fleetingly, together? Since we would likely be then forever parted, it seemed vital that I remember the face and form of everyone encountered, even in the merest glimpse from the window of a car. The man with the umbrella and raincoat crossing the road, the woman pushing twins in a pram, the old lady in a yellow felt hat, the grinning boy wobbling past on a bicycle – new lists to be memorised were added to previous lists, run over and over in my mind through sleepless nights. And daily, retaining the register grew more formidable.

'Pats, dear,' said my bemused grandmother, 'you won't enjoy the outing if you sit there with your eyes closed like that. It just doesn't do.'

Many things 'did not do', in Gran-speak, and if you persisted you might be declared as having 'taken leave of your senses' or 'gone mental'. We knew well the signposts culminating in a one-way trip to the lunatic asylum. Gran already had cause to wonder about me. Unlike normal children, I had not enjoyed recreational tours of the museum with its stiff and glassy-eyed collections of birds and reptiles, even though reassured as to all the exhibits having died of old age. Equally unnatural, my aversion to the zoo and the fun of viewing animals in restricted cages – desperate monkeys, noxious bear pits and endlessly pacing big cats with their worn pads and maddened eyes.

It did not occur to me to inform anyone of what I knew at the age of six to be a tiresome bug in my brain. It did not do, and something had to be done. Eventually, I worried my way towards an acceptable solution. The key lay in watching for the right person – just one – the stranger to be remembered all my life as a representative for the others who must be forgotten. For many days I looked, considering and rejecting. There was not the slightest doubt when I spotted the candidate. She was a large woman in a black dress and cream straw hat, sitting in a battered utility rounding the clock Gran called 'Edith' at the entrance to Kings Park.[8] There was something incongruous about the sight, and I have subsequently supposed she must have been a farmer's wife dressed up for a city visit. Carefully I filed her away and there she remains. The compulsion overcome, I was cured of that particular demon, but the syndrome remained.

~

Andy was a winsome golden-curled child, with a sweet turn of mouth, full of engaging antics from an early age. But with three before and two more to come, his childhood rapidly evaporated until he was a skinny, sandy-haired impressionable youth much, one must suppose, as his father had been. But for that affection-starved boy of a previous generation, the deprivation, while in some ways his emotional undoing, had made him self-reliant and motivated in a way that may not have surfaced had he been raised in a more advantaged environment. Andy's answer to the ordinary disciplines of life was to become more and more elusive until, amid the general melee, he somehow slipped away from us. There was a perception that the boys suffered for want of a father or an authoritative male in the family. Who knows? That we let it happen seems terrible now, but wild horses could not at the time have prevented it. It still gives me a sad pang to look at photos of the little brother destined to be spirited away by goblins and elves, mostly in the form of 'mates'.

~

After the war, Horrie became set on purchasing a house in Broome, an idea urged by his wife as one also advancing her hidden agenda of providing a possible solution to the immediate problem of Bet, who needed a refuge and somewhere to work. The purchase of a modest bungalow in the latticed and cyclone-shuttered local style, situated a few yards from Roebuck Bay, was to bring a new and joyous dimension to our lives – a period never surpassed and, once lost, never recovered. For himself, Horrie saw in the remote town a ready escape from everything he found unnerving about the city domicile, and thus would we be largely relieved of his presence. He was not missed by his children. He had never been a father along the lines of those kindly, jolly figures owned by other kids, attending school functions and sports days. When confronted by a hip-swinging little smart-arse threatening me with her father, who was a policeman easily persuaded to come and arrest me, I was momentarily floored for a comeback. Then, with a flash of invention, I sent her packing in wailing fear with the information that my dad was a pilot who was more than ready to fly over and bomb her house.

CHAPTER 2

THE WIDER CIRCLE (1946–1951)

At the end of 1945, Mary's sister Elizabeth arrived from Melbourne with her two children. She had fled, so the impassioned conversations between her and my mother revealed, an impossible marriage and privations way beyond those foreseen for one from a prestigious family. Determinedly 'glamorous', with her platinum blonde hair, dynamic personality and vigorous opinions, she made a tremendous impression on us. Although sharing certain family characteristics, the sisters were otherwise unlike and the disparity, which sometimes amounted to a polar opposition, was to us wonderfully diverting. Used as we were to a household of some scramble and disarray, there was about the Clancy ménage a heady sense of the wholly extempore, and with their effects soon taking up every spare space in the house, the walls would from this time become a permanent gallery. During her many homeless years, her life a turmoil of upheavals from one rented place to another, Bet had been obliged to hold in her head a mud map of belongings stored in storerooms and railway lockers and other people's houses, across the length and breadth of the continent.

We never doubted that she was a great artist, and with half our lives spent in sharing the lows of her setbacks and the highs of her too-infrequent triumphs we became deeply and loyally attached to her. Daring and funny 'Aunty Bumbles' was an aunt like no-one else's, and while she was in residence the tempo of our lives picked up; I cannot remember when, over many years, we were other than thrilled to see her and to incorporate the circus that came in her train. Our first cousins, Perpetua and Michael, pale refugees from the Eastern States, were beyond joy at being absorbed into a proper household and the bosom of numerous loving relatives. It must have been a cause of sad bewilderment that this mantle of apparent safety did not extend beyond Perth and their mother's next move.

~

Filled with the optimism that always marked her departure for fresh fields and the prospect of a clean canvas, Bet went north with the children to take up residence in the Broome house. But, as Mary noted, her sister had 'an extraordinary capacity to generate situations that cast her from one little hell to another'.[1] Heat fiercer than any lion or tiger prowled outside the bungalow, and no means of transport meant forays abroad for supplies in a place where white people did not walk. Without a telephone, they were isolated and lonely in a way not before experienced even in the furthermost outpost of the Durack properties. Established town silvertails, the wealthy pearlers and their wives, were wary and slow to make overtures to a femme as maverick and possibly fatale as Bet. She in turn could only shrink from the prospect of social contact with those she saw as a wrong element in the environment: 'All the whites', she observed, 'should be taken out of the north and put in a reserve. Not much we can do for them but we can make their passing easier.'[2] Predicting within decades an unstoppable influx from Asia, she declared the sooner the better.

Meanwhile, having set up quarters at the beach in an army vehicle salvaged from the war waste left to litter the town, Horrie had contrived this unsatisfactory arrangement for the purpose of public and private relations. His hope was that by making an apparently unselfish gesture, one that put him into a visibly pitiable hobo state, he might recover some ground if not his wife's unqualified forgiveness. Standing aloof for many months, it is a measure of Mary's feelings of betrayal that she kept it up so long. Whether or not she seriously considered ending the marriage, she was determined to let Horrie believe that she might.

He did little to assist the Clancys. Had he occasionally taken them to the local baths or given them a lift to the town stores, it would have made an appreciable difference to the neglected fugitive family. Only courageous pride and the lack of any viable alternative kept Bet there. Of all she had endured since her marriage, homelessness had been the worst – the agony of it outlined in a letter to her sister:

> *I have a terrible feeling all the time of being someone coming down on a long parachute descent, never seeing the ground, only cloud masses floating by and an occasional wave to a passing star…*[3]

Horrie knew that the worse it was, the sooner she would leave and no-one would hold him responsible.

In Perth, two children at school scarcely lightened the load for Mary, who had come to face the fact that however she might accommodate future relations with Horrie, the child raising was destined to be up to her. Finding space to resume her writing pursuits became a priority, not just in order to pay the bills but also to hold onto her sense of identity and purpose. The royalties from their books, which would have been a welcome supplement, going to a needy Bet, who also required art supplies and sundries sent to Broome, the budget was further stretched to assist brothers Kim and David. The reality that Horrie existed on the paltry self-imposed salary of five pounds per week from which he extracted her miserable allowance did nothing to alter the perception of her standing as the only family member attached to a wage-earner. M.P. had at various times been tapped as much as was thought possible by his impecunious children, but money from that quarter was taken with lashings of guilt and feelings of inadequacy not suffered when the loan came from 'dear old Mare'.

~

Because my mother stood for many things, but never certainty, as she earnestly sought to offend no-one and see all sides of a question, it was Gran who provided the element of assurance in our world. Always a beauty, with her soft brown eyes, high cheekbones and beguiling smile, Bess Durack exuded a practised sociability demanding of attention and deference. Formally elegant, her well-upholstered figure in a – perhaps – mauve frock, bouffant silver hair caught in a tortoiseshell comb, pince-nez spectacles, brooch and rings, neat, bunion-hugging shoes, hatted and gloved, she was a *presence.*

My mother could be dismissive of imagined, and sometimes real, childish trauma and I grew used to turning for comfort to my grandmother, who dealt efficiently with problems in terms of black and white rather than a penumbra. She was also the one to pass on vital survival tips: the dangers of eating unwashed fruit, not drying between the toes or putting in the mouth coins that might have been in a foreigner's pocket.

Amused as my mother was by Gran's fusspot axioms carried back to Mildew – especially by Robin, who trotted them out all her days – she was not without a few bugbears of her own. Witness in her youth to the forcible removal of afflicted Aboriginal people from the stations, she could not quite shake off the idea that leprosy lurked in their artefacts collected over the years, to gather dust in corners of the house. Decades after acquisition, she still warned us against any temptation to blow the didgeridoos or handle the corroboree clapping sticks – our multiple succumbing to prevalent diseases troublesome enough without having a leper among us.

Sitting in the playground under the ancient gum tree that had somehow survived the clear-fell of Christian enlightenment, I was aware that something was badly amiss. The bell rung and the other children dispersed to their classrooms, no matter how I tried to move them, my legs would not work. There they hung in drooping grey socks and scuffed black shoes, altogether disobedient to normal command. It was my worst fear come to pass: I had become *conspicuous* – an embarrassment that rendered inert limbs the lesser woe.

When carried up to the school by the gardener and placed in a passageway chair as an object of curiosity to groups of passing students, my embarrassment was as fierce as my thirst. Sweating and feverish, I was half-maddened by the sound of the nearby dripping cloakroom taps, and my tongue cleaved to the roof of my mouth. On a pedestal, beside a plaster statue of the Blessed Virgin Mary, stood a cutglass vase containing drooping flowers. The vase within reach, I swallowed its swampy brown water like nectar from heaven, but not without knowing I had committed at least a venial sin and I would not have been caught for the world. There must have been some problem locating Gran's transport service, for the school day ended, the nuns made their devotional way to evening benediction and I was forgotten. The age of litigation has forcibly raised the game of those in charge of children, but back then, had I died in that chair, it would not have entered the parental head to castigate the nuns, let alone sue them.

Medical opinion settled on rheumatic fever, and considering my silence on the mortifying symptoms of paralysis, I don't suppose there can be any blame for this. After a long period of convalescence I returned to school, but the illness had been a setback in my young life. Many months lost, I was no longer the cleverest in the class, and without a struggle I settled towards the bottom and – small for my age – the end of every line. My malady was never properly diagnosed. Looking back, I believe that I had suffered a relatively mild form of infantile paralysis, as the disease was known before it became polio. That terrible shark cruised the waters then, randomly snatching choice morsels.

'Patsy', wrote my mother to M.P., 'is very religious and is a great all-round believer but Robin is a harder nut to crack. She likes Father Christmas best; "He doesn't put you in hell".'[4]

I can remember this brief dalliance with the stagey aspects of church ceremony, a romance that did not survive experience of the real theatre. So starry-eyed did I become that my mother enrolled me, and an uncertain Robin, in the Linley Wilson School of Dance. Clad in white frills and weekly conveyed to a dingy hall in the city, our half-formed limbs were trained to accept turned out positions and extensions, and for me a few years later, the punishment of shoes designed for performing *en pointe*. Recognising an unprofitable pursuit, Robin soon dropped out. But for me, not renowned for sticking power, the next ten years saw the trek to and from ballet classes kept up with a dogged resolve.

~

Bet's fortunes had picked up with the advent of a number of attentive RAAF officers, one in particular with access to a jeep squiring her about the town. ('Ah ha!' Horrie had written triumphantly to his wife at the first sight of a vehicle parked in the early hours outside the house. 'The old, old story.')⁵ A telephone had been installed, the children absorbed into local facilities and the paintings regularly sent south for a coming exhibition. Ever-hopeful of Bet's achieving some financial independence, during the 1940s Mary would become a veteran of many time-sapping exercises on behalf of her sister. To allow herself the freedom to stay in the field, Bet needed helping hands in city centres, even if it meant temporarily mending fences with her otherwise abandoned husband.

Horrie, who was still camping in his army truck at Gantheaume Point, a place of best advantage for fishing, being seen by the townsfolk and making Bet feel 'just dandy', had not anticipated circumstances improving for the Clancys. When, somewhat spoiling his selfless facade, he made bold enquiries as to when they might intend returning to Melbourne, an indignant Bet had reported his tactlessness to her sister. Her brother-in-law had a devastating effect on her:

> *Dear God, for all Horrie's criticism of Frank, he knows nothing about spiritual support. He knows about work and the importance of it, but his presence kills something in me.*⁶

Horrie's judgement of Bet as the source of 'sudden, volcanic upheavals'⁷ had not in the end been disappointed. In a fix and not immune to scandalised small-town speculation, she left Broome in a hurry, and with her children once more happily ensconced at Mildew, she spent an interval recovering in a discreet Perth hospital while Mary prepared a booklet on the history of Roebuck Bay to accompany the *Time and Tide* exhibition. Frequently acknowledging she owed everything that came from her work to her sister, with her debts ever-mounting, Bet covered her 'sick feelings of obligation' with anguished wonderings how they might ever be repaid.⁸

~

On their sporadic visits to the city, my uncles Reg and Kim brought with them our connection to the northern properties associated with Grandpa and the pioneering days. Uncle Reg and his wife Enid, now with a firstborn son, managed a station in the Territory, while Uncle Kim was involved with an agricultural project that would do great things for northern development as a whole. Uncle Bill, having spent a few years in the north to escape the wartime draft, was also on the scene, before leaving for the Eastern States with his wife Noni and later taking up permanent residence in Queensland.

The strenuous and constant conversation with their sisters for the most part revolved around M.P.'s moves to sell the stations, a prospect that, after decades of half-hearted discussion and attempts to find a buyer, was suddenly likely. This, they agreed, would be the worst imaginable outcome – one that, if they stood united, might yet be averted.

The youngest brother, David, was to be only briefly glimpsed on home ground over the years. Graduating from a good-looking and high-spirited youth to a ruddy-faced Hogarthian figure of immoderately loud laughter, bearing bottles of expensive spirits and moving in a pall of cigar smoke, he seemed to me lacking the gravitas of my other uncles. As a school and university student perhaps the most promising of M.P.'s four clever sons, he had been the only Durack to 'join up'. Choosing to enlist with a parachute regiment in 1943, less from patriotism than from the possibility that it might be fun, he had subsequently broken out in a nervous rash that kept him clear of any action. The ailment appeared to have been brought on by a terrifying practice jump in a blackout, combined with the guilt of having let down his outspokenly anti-war and variously excused-from-duty siblings. It had, however, been something of a relief to M.P. and Bess that they were able to claim at least one in the services.

According to family legend, David had made a 'bad marriage' under wartime circumstances – one that effectively cut him off from his home in the west but for brief escapes, when he arrived like a schoolboy on holiday from unsparing discipline. His departure was marked by hangovers for family members unaccustomed to liquor and late nights, and he left in his wake a lingering smell of cigar smoke that provoked Horrie's dramatic throwing open of every window and door to get rid of it. An engineer of some esteem with prominent firms and latterly as an 'independent', the high-flying businessman was, over the course of a visit, apt to collapse into fits of remorse that everyone found hard to bear. External to the main action, once out of sight he was seldom called to consciousness except in sentimental terms and Gran's reproach that he never wrote.

~

Hovering in the wings, and emboldened by the absence of Mary's spoilsport consort, was a motley collection of writers, artists and people of varied talent, eccentricity and nuisance value. Formed in 1939, a West Australian branch of the nascent Fellowship of Australian Writers (FAW) had drawn together a group of previously isolated authors, largely unknown to one another. The fortuitous gift to them by Sam Furphy of a modest cottage in which his father Joseph Furphy had lived and been published under the pseudonym 'Tom Collins' provided a convenient headquarters. It was a gesture that ensured that the author of the novel *Such Is Life* was remembered in Western Australia, and that his old home in Swanbourne, known as 'Tom Collins House', remained a heritage-listed memorial to 'the father of the Australian novel'.

Mary Durack, the youngest and, in a no-contest line-up, certainly the best-looking of the newly formed organisation, enjoyed the patronage of senior members, who became intimates and regular callers. The most awesome of these was Henrietta Drake-Brockman, a woman of Junoesque stature, considered by my mother to be the epitome of social sophistication and style. A prolific writer on Australian themes, Henrietta was a game woman not averse to accompanying her engineer husband on surveys into the northern wilderness in quest of material, or at a senior age submerging herself to view a sunken ship. Enthralled by her accounts of diving on the wreck of the *Batavia*, my brother Andy called her Henrietta Great Frogman, an understandable confusion.

Katharine Susannah Prichard enjoyed a controversial aspect, less for her affiliation with the Communist Party than for her determinedly blinkered vision beyond eye-opening revelations of Stalinist Russia. Her politics always seemed to me to be at odds with almost every other perceptible facet of her personality. Perhaps it was to present an appearance contrary to what a biased society expected of a Red that she clad her angular form in fussy feminine frocks, restrained her wispy hair beneath flowery hats, covered her workmanlike hands in gloves and always preserved the soft voice so easily talked over by those of stronger opinion. During the Cold War, with McCarthyism on the rise in the United States, a small but vocal group within the FAW, led by the redoubtable Henrietta, had begun to give her a chill reception and there were calls to ban known communists. While Mary endeavoured to remain neutral, rifts formed and an element of witch-hunting emerged to persecute socialist dabblers like Irene Greenwood, who had helped in a campaign to send sheepskins to Russia, and Bert Vickers, who was a member of the suspect WA Peace Council. It spoke volumes for Henrietta's basic integrity that towards the end of her life, she would write an objective monograph of Prichard's work and form a genuine affection for the woman from whom she remained ever politically divided.[9]

Tolerance was the byword when dealing with Irene Greenwood, an intelligent and energetic force within a round, rather fluffy baker's wife exterior. Her unfortunate disability was garrulousness, especially when it came to the telephone. Bursting with interesting information, she was oblivious to the possibility that there might be more pressing demands at the other end. My mother suffered her share of champion telephone athletes over the years, but Irene continued to take the gold medal. Her very name became synonymous with a lengthy and inconvenient hold-up. Abiding lenity was because this magnanimous lady, whose authorship largely concerned women's causes, was possessed of an uncommon area of expertise. Writers could submit dog-eared manuscripts for her astute assessment and, if she approved of the work, her continued support and encouragement. She read the drafts of all Mary Durack's books prior to publication, her suggestions, notes and judgement trusted. When Mary visited her in hospital during her final days – and she had a miserable end at the dictate of iniquitous doctors – speechless at last, she could only take the hand of her beloved friend and, in frustrated anguish, bite it.

More able to indulge a creative pursuit, women predominated in the fellowship. Few men other than journalists were able to make a career from writing, and in the early days of the FAW only the renowned essayist Walter Murdoch could claim to live off his work. Peering over his glasses and puffing on his pipe in a wise and twinkling way, Sir Walter was a revered Australian icon much read and quoted by my grandfather, who kept between the pages of his journals cuttings from Murdoch's column in the 'Life and Letters' section of *The West Australian*, comprising sagacious and droll commentary on current events. During a latter-day encounter, Mary's perception of Rupert Murdoch would be cordially coloured by memories of his benevolent and high-minded great-uncle.

For the most part, male members of the fellowship were temperate and upright citizens whose published work remained confined to regional recognition. Back then, favoured mediums for literary expression were historical romances, travelogues – usually featuring a map inside the cover, with a dotted line indicating the route taken, and black and white photographs of vehicles crossing flooded creeks – and novels, many set in an outback no more than glimpsed through a windscreen. Dedicated authors had a go at them all. Despite a paucity of indexes, the travelogues survive as a useful reference on the country in a former era and a reminder of the gadabout nature of Aussie wordsmiths.

Prolific oddities, the bush balladeers were of a humble breed seldom aspiring to the elevation of FAW membership. Many of my mother's most dedicated correspondents fell into this genre, and to her embarrassment, a number were in possession of a treasured copy of *Little Poems of Sunshine*, a small vellum-covered volume of verse composed by the ten-year-old Mary Durack and published by her proud parents. William 'Billy Miller' Linklater, the best-known among the amateur bards, would bequeath to her a quantity of his scribblings, adding to what was to become a major legacy for her in the form of unpublished manuscripts from the living and the dead.

In the same vein, and a preliminary to what would in future years be unleashed by my mother's unfailing charity, was Jack Sorensen, erstwhile boxing champ and representative for R.S. Sampson's country newspapers. Bearing bags of oranges and mandarins from his orchard as a token of gratitude for an afternoon of uninhibited earbashing, 'Old Turnip', as he was privately known, began a rendition of his latest inspiration before he reached the door. As the writer Ernestine Hill described it, 'You could beat time to his verse with a dead fish on a marble slab.'[10] The habitual business suit, tie and smart city hat seemed somewhat orthodox attire for one so closely allied to a drover's life, being more in keeping with a man about to propose marriage. And always hopelessly in love with the one he regarded as his muse, he did make discreet enquiries as to his chances should, 'heaven forbid', anything happen to Horrie. In the way of many of her acquaintance, Mary made sure that Jack did not encounter the man of the house, whose occasional materialisation demanded full attention from his wife, and there was scarcely a moment when he was not competing with the telephone or a 'yoo-hoo' at the door. Nor was Horrie unaware of the relief and party atmosphere that went up when his wet-blanket presence was removed from the scene, and he darkly suspected 'boyfriends' lurking in wait for his departure.

As it happened, my mother's brand of 'just chums' discouragement kept at bay an odd assortment of suitors over the years, including the artist Beatrice Darbyshire, who had first been encountered during a Young Australia League tour in 1933. The friendship, one that after all survived the years, became strained after Bea made her passionate attachment pathetically evident. Devastated by the advent of Horrie and the marriage, for many months after the move to the Bellevue Avenue house she could not be persuaded beyond the gatepost, where she left piteous bunches of flowers. Finally accepting the hopeless nature of it, Bea ever after confined her devotion to a sad yearning behind her bifocal glasses.

Sorensen did away with himself in 1949 while on a ship travelling to Queensland. Prior to his departure, he had confided to Mary that he was on the run from 'a madman' intent on cutting his throat; not recognising the homicidal stranger in his cabin as himself, he died in the way he'd foretold. On hearing of his death, Ernestine Hill wrote of her surprise:

> *Given his buoyant nature, bouncing along to the rune of his rhymes, that he should find the grim resolution for such a final thing! You must have no regrets Mary. You were the light of his eyes – and I rather think he was content in having loved and lost – it suited his poetic vein.*[11]

To compensate for her victimisation by verse-mongers, Mary would develop a taste for the fruit of the genuinely 'innocent' among them. She kept a file of the best, happily shared with Barry Humphries, who was also a connoisseur, and his *Book of Innocent Austral Verse* acknowledges her generosity in allowing him to 'plunder her collection of rarities'.[12]

First among luminaries from further afield, Ernestine Hill sporadically surfaced to drift through our lives before vanishing again, a wraith-like figure who lamented her destiny as 'a shuttlecock to the battledore of chance'.[13] As if in recompense for the indulgence, the longer her stay in a civilised place, the further into the boondocks would she be eventually catapulted away. How vividly she comes to mind: her skeletal form, hands waving the cigarette in illustration, white face cracked like old china with a splash of rouge and a blaze of red lipstick and the thick, black hair streaked with grey. I hear her scratchy voice imparting to us as children some spooky bush tale: 'Ooooo, the min min light the old blackfellows call it, and if you see it, Ooooo, they say you are dooomed!'

Establishing her career as a journalist with Packer-associated papers, this deceptively frail pilgrim had first produced lively copy from outback places yet untouched by the writer's pen. Her charming, rather helpless manner proving an effective travel permit, she had turned up, on one of her early excursions, at Ivanhoe Station. Soon alerted to the family history and the famous marathon cattle drive, her florid, never-too-concerned-with-accuracy telling of it had in the nick of time been headed off by Mary Durack.

Ernestine's only son, Robert, known as Bob, travelled with her, sharing the sometimes tragic ups and downs of itinerant life and the ceaseless movement seemingly dictated by nothing more than an emotional pull of an almost tidal nature. While bound to a romantic fascination with history, 'Mrs Hill', as my grandfather deferentially addressed her, kept close-mouthed about her own. There had been a bitter and draining fight to prevent her son being called up to serve in the Second World War, one openly criticised by the wife of Brigadier Geoffrey Drake-Brockman. But becoming anxious about the need for some defined purpose and employment for Bob, Ernestine would gratefully accept Mary's offer to assist the engagingly dilettante young man in every way possible. It did seem that her friend, in whom she had every confidence, had accepted a charge of in loco parentis. In any case, Ernestine, exhorting her son to 'hitch your wagon to the stars', believed it so.

Other than those whose entire output was autobiographical, a good number of Western Australian writers managed to produce a creditable memoir before the funeral, such occasions well attended by FAW members and usually graced by a thoughtful tribute from Mary Durack. Perusing the local content of my mother's bookcase, with their fading personal dedications, one must suppose that few would find a publisher today. I am nonetheless struck by how prolific some of them were, most notably the line-up of volumes from Tom Ronan, Donald Stuart, G.M. Glaskin, Bert Vickers, Tom Hungerford and Dorothy Lucie Sanders. They and those of their ilk had their place in a more ingenuous era, before the emergence of a new galaxy of sophisticated national and international stars like Patrick White, Hal Porter, Tom Keneally and Peter Carey.

~

The Broome house now his primary place of residence, Horrie quietly re-established himself at intervals on the Perth front. By dint of much caulking up, the relationship with his wife settled onto the uneven keel that would see them somehow negotiate future rough water, and to the excitement of three girls old enough to appreciate a baby, a fifth child emerged in testament to the improved marital state. The nuns at St Anne's Hospital declared Marie Rose the prettiest newborn they had ever seen, and none of us doubted it for a moment.

~

When in 1950 the telegrams were dispatched to assemble members of his family, M.P. was almost beyond recognising them. Despite passionate appeals, he had sold the stations, accepting what Bet referred to as 'a mess of pottage in return for our great heritage'.[14] Deferring to her father's point of view, Mary's version would become the official reason for the decision:

> *Dad felt he was the only one left, his partners dead, his brothers gone before. He had survived the economic effects of two world wars and*

a depression and he was tired. He told us he would rather leave us a lump of money than a lump of land with all its problems. We tried to dissuade him from taking this step but he was quite resolved.[15]

Kim's final lone stand to stop the sale had done nothing but increase the distance between him and his father and exacerbate feelings of mutual betrayal. His son's 'impractical' ideas for company reform and criticism of CD&D's disregard for land management as evidenced in a legacy of erosion and devastated grasslands had only hardened the old man's resolve towards getting out. The offer to purchase on the table, and the majority of disinterested shareholders voting to take their long-awaited payout, in the end it had been a matter over which the managing director had no control.

With the weight of an immense but unprofitable estate lifted from him, instructing Bess to book their passage on a world voyage, M.P. set off on a farewell tour of his lost kingdom and to raise a plaque dedicated to his pioneering associates. After half a century of self-sacrifice, he looked forward to the rewards due a comfortably retired gentleman and his wife: travels abroad – perhaps a pocket-handkerchief property in the South West and a few stud stock? Something befitting his lifelong motto to 'travel hopefully and trust in God'.

But as he did the last round of the stations on tracks more familiar to him than the lines on his own hand, he saw a dreaming country that had never looked lovelier and, now just a visitor, felt the change in every face he saw and every wind that blew. He was heartbroken. The wearisome battle to pay off the debts and find a buyer at last achieved, he fell victim to a fatal spiritual debility beyond the diagnosis of doctors. As the end approached he seemed typically impatient, pushing life out as something over and done with. Once he called plaintively for Mary, and when assured she was there, he gazed sadly at her and said, 'No. I want the *other* Mary.' Perhaps he was looking for the beloved, obedient daughter who had written *Little Poems of Sunshine*.

Duly presented at the bedside, I gingerly brushed my lips against the sunken, bewhiskered cheek, and he gave my hand a feeble pump that might have been interpreted as his belated sanction, a charge to 'travel hopefully' or perhaps just goodbye. His own children only to some extent a known quantity, what mystery in the grandchildren? But beyond speculation, he sank back into the beckoning shades.

The tidings broadcast over the radio, relatives, family friends, associates and acquaintances hastened to send telegrams of condolence. Cards and letters came later. Whether personal or official, the format required attention and a degree of skill in condensing the heartfelt while retaining something of the character of the sender:

Saddest regrets Mary dear will write of him with love and honour tonight my thoughts with all – Ernestine

The citizens of Broome my Board and self extend heartfelt sympathy to you and your family in your sad bereavement STOP another great chapter in Australian pioneer history closed – D. Farrell Chairman Broome Road Board

Each one delivered by hand, more than three hundred such arrived via the loud and urgent doorbell ring: from the premier, members of parliament, clergy ('prayerful sympathies'), road boards, pastoralists associations, meatworks, station managers, hotel proprietors, distant cousins and former employees. From home phones, city offices and remote outposts per pedal radio, the immediate response was a wire. Horrie sent one from Broome: 'Deepest sympathy in your loss stop love and kind thoughts – Miller.' Some elderly and forgetful friends dispatched two or three. The significance of that yellow slip of paper from the Postmaster-General's Department, stamped by the telegraph office, printed in capital letters, its message components separated by peremptory STOPs, cannot be recaptured by modern means of communication. Opened with a thrill of excitement or trepidation, a telegram was something to keep down the years. And how many were destined to be conveyed to Mildew's door as the Miller family provided the general public with a multiplicity of occasions to be formally recognised, from triumph to tragedy.

At once on the lookout for a residence closer to Mary, Gran purchased a new car with a pop-out indicator – a very modern device in those days – to supplement her extended arm and imperiously gloved hand and got on with life. M.P.'s children also exhibited sorrow of a properly passing nature in the face of favourable prospects out of the paternal shadow and the rapid production of a new generation. Nevertheless, their father's demise at the age of eighty-five seems to have caught them by surprise, as it had done the old man himself. The unfortunate consequences of this lack of preparation would precipitate an imbroglio over the will that saw the bulk of funds from the sale lost to probate, and duty was exacted on gifts distributed to family in the interim. In the final reckoning, from the 250,000 pounds received for the stations, representing the sum total for a monumental pioneering endeavour and the lives given to and lost in the process, remained a mere

30,000 pounds – sufficient to keep the widowed Mrs M.P. Durack in modest security for the rest of her days.

~

The next phase of the writer's life came with a clearance of back rooms in the firm's city office. Mary had been astonished to discover among the CD&D records, the worm-eaten deeds, sealed parchments and stock books from Thylungra Station in Western Queensland pertaining to early Durack history and her grandfather, Patrick Durack. Resisting the 'clean sweep' urged by Bet and discouragement from Gran ('no room for the living, dear'), she had bundled up as many files as could be carried in her small car and brought them home with her for later perusal. In the haste of exodus, a good deal went out with the rubbish, the gaps in the record much regretted in later years.

Contemplating the go to woe of the Durack enterprise, Mary held no illusions about the reasons for the firm's ultimate failure to thrive. While she would spend many years of her life on the particulars, she believed the whole could be summed up in a paragraph written at the time to her cousin Kath McArthur, who would take up the task of assisting with information from the Queensland end for the coming opus:

> *They never had the Midas touch. Everything they touched turned not to gold but to dust and ashes. I feel somehow the heart was wrong. They were using the country without love or care – with the hope of selling out to the highest bidder as soon as possible – were in it on a speculative rather than a living basis – which is really the only way that land can flourish and prosper. It has to be loved.*[16]

Putting aside this simplified and perhaps arguable conclusion, Mary saw the enthralling family story begin to emerge from the brittle papers in far more detail than, and often in contradiction to, the version already written. At first supposing she could add to the original manuscript, it soon became evident that what was to hand meant scrapping the previous work. The scope of the research beyond the resources of the local library, assistance from the Queensland end would be vital.

The Durack saga began to take shape within a few weeks of M.P.'s death, its painful gestation later conveyed to Kath McArthur:

> *Oh the sorting out this maze of Michaels, Johns and Pats – not to mention Jeremiahs. I don't want to throw any libellous mud and a*

lot of pussyfooting has to go on. The work will be slow as everything has to be checked and verified as far as possible and I have my desk piled with references and cross-references, maps, old letters and documents. There are bits of clothing dotted around too – the socks I must mend tonight and the skirt whose hem must be put up before school in the morning. Days are swamped by the details of life and I am working at night mostly, which does not exactly bring the freshness of one's energy to the job.[17]

~

Expectation of continuing his agricultural experiments to benefit CD&D properties gone with the sale, Kim had agreed to form a partnership with a group of vested rice growers from the Murrumbidgee area. Impressed by his having successfully raised a variety of irrigated crops on the Ord River, this consortium had previously sounded him out for a scheme to grow rice at Camballin on the Fitzroy River. At the time committed to East Kimberley, Kim had rejected the offer. Now, in his dire need for employment in some ground-breaking proposition, the formation of Northern Developments presented as a solution of a sort. What the thirty-three-year-old visionary did not see behind the friendly handshakes and the involvement of known and trusted associates on the board of directors were the dangers and inequities lurking in contracts drawn up by the money-providers.

Setting out in a purpose-built caravan, Kim was to spend the next six years living under a boab tree while he coaxed rice from an alternatively drought-stricken and flooded land, invaded by hungry birds and plagues of land and airborne pests. His heroic perseverance in the face of visitations of almost biblical proportion became a drama we were to follow closely.

Prior to the disposal of the CD&D holdings, M.P. Durack had sliced off a remote Northern Territory section to accommodate his son Reg. Caught up for too long in the north and held by dynastic obligations, his dream of a medical career gone up in smoke, Reg had little choice but to use his experience to make a go of a station. His initial aspiration to manage a pastoral run on his own terms with a revisionary approach to the problems that had beset the firm was a long way from the actuality of establishing a foothold on Kildurk. All stock mustered off the property as a condition of purchase and his first task to build a homestead for his wife and children, he had been cast back to the privations of the first-comers. At this juncture, there was no member of the family – not even Kim – who blamed him for being the first to break the united stance against the sale.

There is an enduring propensity to lump the Durack name with those of other designated 'cattle barons' of their day, like the wealthy absentee operators Bovril and Vestey. Contemplating the hands-on management involving backbreaking labour and financial straits as endured by those of Patsy Durack's descendants who stayed in the Kimberley, there is little to connect them. In 1948 Kim had written to his sister: 'I cannot call myself penniless since I have two pence in my pocket, and posting this letter will needs await my coming by another four pence for a stamp.'[18]

~

The hugger-mugger of Miller family life had one downside in that we did not transplant easily to other households. None resembled our own in the slightest, and aside from the adjustment to periods of living with Gran, we felt sorely any separation from home. Travelling was a logistical headache for my mother: who to take, who to leave behind and who to look after them. More than one or two meant reduced creative output on her part and a strain on Horrie, so the excess was off-loaded onto a variety of makeshift and sometimes unsuitable proxies. Her activities and output would also have languished but for other than lightly held control in domestic areas. 'One can only do a whole lot of things', she concluded, 'by not doing a whole lot of other things.'[19] Involved as she was in many worthy causes, her compassion spread across a wide spectrum, her children grew used to being raised in a rain shadow of benign neglect.

In 1951, approaching forty, she went through an unsettled period, resulting in some poorly considered upheavals. The strain of raising five children without paternal support was the motive behind her going north to see if there might be an alternative, some possibly last-ditch means of putting the relationship with Horrie on a better footing. She took only Andy with her.

~

Feeling sidelined by MMA management, a situation instigated by himself but one he had not expected his associates to accept so readily, Horrie was considering the potential of a sheep station near Broome. Dampier Downs, a rocky wilderness of untamed beauty abandoned and for sale since the Depression, had become a haven for birds, donkeys and dingoes. While the lease could be had for a song, the catch lay in any mad ideas about turning the place into a going concern. Anyone could have seen at a glance that unless the plan was to create a sanctuary for wildlife, it was a potential money-sink way in excess of any potential pastoral profit. But for Horrie, it came to represent the next phase of his life, giving new meaning to his continued existence, and with something to occupy his mind, to his wife's relief, he decamped from a fairly settled post at death's door.

Braving many hair-raising trips in the army bus, he hacked a path through the bush and cleared an airstrip. On her arrival, Mary was able to fly out with him in the Wackett trainer aircraft he had acquired in 1947 as war surplus. A well-known sight around Broome, this two-seater aerial runabout was handy for detecting schools of fish, buzzing state ships and, if the pilot was lucky, startling a 'snappy line' sunbathing on Cable Beach.

Starved as she was for the Kimberley and open to avenues for change, Mary listened to Horrie's strongly argued case for selling the Perth house and establishing a permanent abode in Broome while he went to and from the property. When the kids grew too old for the local school, they could go south to board, like the children of other northern property owners. She could write to her heart's content without the pressures of city life. Of course, he added, it would be better if she could find a way to leave half 'the mob' in Perth. The thought of the entire family descending on his bolthole was not to his liking, but obviously there were going to be some penalties for the adjustment. After a week in the wilderness, Mary wrote to Bet of her first impressions:

> *Maybe the first sound that comes to mind in considering Dampier is the long drawn Ernestinian 'Oooooo'. I don't know that I have ever seen a place set down in such a weird or more seemingly remote locality. I've seen desolate places and arid places and heartbreaking looking places, but for sheer weird Dampier surely takes the bun.*

The food supply Horrie had assured her was enough to last six months consumed in three days, she found herself in the farcical position of 'following like an Aboriginal woman in the wake of my man who carries in grim pursuit of tucker, a loaded rifle.'[20]

While the rest of the north withered in the grip of drought, the oasis at the foot of the Edgar Ranges was replete with permanent water: brimming billabongs, spectacular waterfalls and meandering creeks running through lush vegetation. Rising from a forest of silky oaks, wattles, palms and flowering native shrubs, the towering walls of the range were pitted with caves, home to innumerable kangaroos:

> *[T]he place is teeming with them – beautiful creatures, the orange red of the rocks, some of them five to six feet tall – everywhere*

leaping, in silhouette or standing, stock-still against the cobalt sky. From the primitive homestead, Horrie keeps the dingoes at bay by firing the rifle at intervals through a hole in the mosquito wire, for all the world like grandpapa defending his family from marauding blacks.[21]

An upside of the new arrangement was conveyed to her Queensland cousin in a letter that drew rather a long bow in terms of Mary's actual involvement, given that she was only on a brief visit:

Imagine us though Kath, at this stage of our lives raising fences, reconstructing broken buildings, painting, planning and running boundaries! With the shared interest Horrie and I can now put up with one another for much longer at a stretch.[22]

Mary's ulterior motive was that while Horrie was otherwise occupied, she would have the house to herself and hopefully be able to get on with a new novel set in the town. The complicated murder mystery meant delving into the hidden history of the pearling port and many hours were later to be spent sitting in on local trials, the details preserved in notebooks along with the court procedure of the day. Another novel based on a northern station had been completed the previous year and submitted to several publishers under a male pseudonym, to avoid the possibility of prejudice against a woman in a man's preserve. Encouraging words had accompanied the rejections of 'Wandering River', and knowing it was good and only a casualty of the depressed market for novels, the writer resolved to send it to *The Bulletin* in the hope they might consider using it as a serial.

The Durack saga too daunting an undertaking without the definite prospect of seeing a book in print at the end of it, she extended a feeler beyond the dead-leg Australian publishing companies, posting off a precis and two sample chapters to her old friend Phyllis Kaberry in London. An eminent anthropologist, first met in the 1930s while she was undertaking fieldwork among Aboriginal women on the Durack properties, Phyll had contacts.

Dejected at her many projects in limbo and the production of nothing tangible, Mary felt she could scarcely count the small book *Child Artists of the Australian Bush*,[23] written at the behest of Florence Rutter, a philanthropic Englishwoman who had introduced the soroptimist movement to Australia. When shown some striking chalk drawings turned out by a group of disadvantaged Aboriginal schoolchildren in the south-west of Western Australia, the elderly lady had visited Carrolup Settlement and there met the students and their selfless and enlightened teachers, Noel White and his wife Lily. Taking the work on a tour of Australia and then to London and Holland, Rutter had been gratified by the interest and goodwill engendered. Mary Durack, recommended to her as the one to write about this phenomenon, had accepted the commission for 'Little Black Fingers' in the belief that, with a more appropriate title, the story could advance the Aboriginal cause. As it happened, it would have been hard to find a literary figure better qualified, and the book stands as an informed voice in an age of confusion and ignorance. Requesting no more than guaranteed publication for a work that encompassed the history of the dispossessed Bibbulmun tribe, Mary had also been happy to donate any profits from what Ernestine Hill described as 'a cameo of kindness' towards the Carrolup School. In a further altruistic gesture, she allowed Rutter's name to stand on the cover beside her own, on this occasion a modestly designated 'M.D. Miller'. Privately, she had informed Kath McArthur of a suspicion that her involvement would bring upon herself 'a whole packet of trouble'.[24] In answer to her cousin's queries about the family opus, she admitted to half dreading a positive response from London, at this point not caring which way it went.

Fully intending to fit Bet somewhere into the northern scene, she was spurred on by a letter from her sister bursting with enthusiasm for a move as impetuous and impractical as any she could have thought up herself:

> *You will work away from the petty fretting round of your Perth life and find happiness in spiritual survival, in the shunned, sun-inherited areas of our country. This swift new turn in your family plans seems wonderful, stimulating, a heroic thing. I love it. Once the house is sold, what's to stop a good size set of cubicles being erected broadside on my block if you need to come south?*[25]

~

Financed by the sale of the stations, after a decade of homelessness, by the end of 1950 Bet had at last moved into a house situated a short walk from Mildew. That M.P. had, prior to his death, insisted on holding the title deeds might have seemed unnecessary were it not that he suspected his daughter of a 'bohemian attitude' to material assets. Now, with the first winter and Mary's migration, Bet was becoming restless. To her sister she passionately expounded on how she could not live in a soulless prison away from the light of fresh new vision, and inspiration that started up within her like a glorious symphony of sound and excitement but was snapped off like broken string the minute she hit Perth. It was ages since she had felt a song coming on, as she did when in the grip of creative fever or the next mad idea. Why should she be chained to a suburban house, trying not to react in a violent way to the sight of her mother's impeccably polished little black car swinging into the clump of grass trees every day for the hour and a half of conversation?[26] Forgetting that her children – left over long periods in boarding schools and the care of strangers – had suffered badly for want of a home, she did not see why she should be denied the opportunity of a 'juggle'. Bet lived by juggles, and in future years often felt, in the absence of a song, another mortgage coming on. But here was this wonderful plan. A Broome transfer would require additions to the existing bungalow, an expansion that could also accommodate the Clancys, and she was 'rotten-ripe' to go north again.

Before her house was completed, Frank Clancy had got wind of it, and realising that a Perth base meant he would be cut loose, he arrived from Melbourne to make a last stand, 'protesting the removal of the children from beyond his jurisdiction and threatening all-sorts'.[27] Her sister expediently incommunicado, Mary bore the brunt of it, as she had done for many months while Frank used her in lieu for his long-distance phone calls, crazed letters and random subpoenas.

Whatever the rights and wrongs of it, Frank was unable to provide for his family. Sodden and enraged, he resembled a poor bull, outmanoeuvred at every turn by a more nimble opponent until, forced to concede the hopelessness of his position, he ceased to be a threat of any consequence. Personally, I liked him. On the few occasions we met he seemed kindly, humorous and, despite family consensus, reasonably sane.

Frank was considerably older than Bet, who had known him only briefly before their headlong marriage. Had she been better acquainted, or had it not been 'the next mad thing I could do', it would have been difficult to see him as other than a spent force – no sort of prospect at all – as, say, Horrie was. But his elder daughter having set the bar low, that he was a bachelor and a Catholic had for M.P. Durack been a mollifying factor. Also an author who had produced a creditable overview of Australian history from penal colony to nationhood,[28] Frank's Irish proclivity for rampage and living on the lam would put paid to his further aspirations in that direction. After a debilitating stroke he survived, after a fashion, until 1965, still officially married to Bet, who had not divorced him. It was always an option, but otherwise it was convenient to have a husband somewhere vaguely in the background, the discreet, respectable Clancy listing in the phone book and, later, the decorous umbrella of widowhood. Frank was shaken off without need for formal recourse to the law at a cost she could ill afford.

~

While my parents (not a term I often used) embarked upon a taste of frontier life at Dampier Downs, my only preoccupation was Marie Rose. Adorable but demanding, over the eighteen months since her birth, the toddler had with admirable endurance orchestrated sleepless nights for the household. Supposing a remedy lay in separation from her overindulgent sisters – and I had been the worst offender in this regard – for the duration, her mother had placed 'the demon bunny' with obliging friends – nice people but strangers to Marie. My angst can only be imagined. I knew my mother was not off her rocker, but that she could do such a thing was then – and is now – beyond my comprehension. Fortunately, Marie Rose was possessed of a strong will, and, despite the barricades, her frequent escapes caused her minders such consternation that, to my immense relief, there was nothing for it but to send her up to Broome. Robin and Julie meanwhile moved in with Gran, who had purchased an unpretentious Nedlands brick and tile dwelling in close proximity to her daughters, while I was sent to stay with the Korwill family.

Mary had met Marianne and Ferdinand (known as 'Ferry') Korwill at Maria Dent's place while recovering after Andy's birth. Fleeing Nazi Germany with daughter Kati and their parents, they had arrived in Western Australia in 1938. Ferry, who had managed a plumbing business in Vienna, was able to set himself up in a trade that fortuitously crossed all boundaries, but for his wife, a university girl with sophisticated tastes and political nous, Perth might as well have been Mars.

Proud of their Austrian background, here they were 'Germans' and, once war broke out, suspect persons. In company with a number of other ludicrously inoffensive refugees, Ferry was interned for a brief but humiliating term in Fremantle Prison. Marianne's elderly and distinguished father, Oska Taussig, who had been sponsored out by Rotary, settled in with remarkable aplomb, joined the local repertory and, although their lives could not have been more dissimilar, found an easy rapport with M.P. Durack. Somehow he adjusted to a narrow living space after the big town house and villa of his former top-brass post as head of the Austrian Railways. Marianne, less adaptable, fell into a Weltschmerz, seeing herself a castaway on a cultural desert island. Remembering that his wife had at least not expressed any active dislike of Mary Miller, Ferry in desperation suggested she pay her a visit.

And so it was that Marianne, dressed in her Austrian dirndl skirt and bolero with silver buttons, walked the half-mile from their home near the river to Mildew. An instant simpatico established between the two women, the Korwills were soon embraced into the Miller and wider family and included in revelries such as Gordon Colebatch's never-to-be-forgotten three-day house-warming fancy-dress party. That was more like it! Out of the doldrums, Marianne took up political activities, and for four decades she and Ferry became stalwarts of the Labor Party and champions of left-wing causes.

After the war, trips back to Europe were enjoyed but there was no doubt that, in returning to Perth, they came home. Perhaps as a counter to his pedestrian trade, Ferry became a dedicated amateur artist, holding exhibitions in his garden. Art not being Marianne's forte, she was able to stand by him in this outlet with a loyalty others found admirable. She understood the important thing was that it made him happy. Undaunted by a lack of success in terms of sales, Ferry would say, with a sweeping gesture at the paintings stacked in his studio, 'Vun day sey vill be vorz sousands.' An earnest, no-nonsense personality, he compensated for a lack of levity by telling jokes, but since he invariably mixed up the punchline, the joke became his telling of it, causing far more hilarity than had he got it right. Some were inclined to place the jokes and the artwork on about the same level, but among many glimpses of Perth, Fremantle and Rottnest Island, he captured with a poignant clarity the light and atmosphere of his relocated surrounds.

Kati Korwill, three years older than me, was a serious and scholastic girl. We became good friends and companions in rather staid activities: visiting the art gallery, attending Festival of Perth events, dressing up to entertain the old Taussigs who lived upstairs, picking lupin seeds for sixpence a bag from Ferry and being generally well-behaved. Before the attraction became more widely patronised, we had the almost exclusive enjoyment of the steaming thermal water bubbling out of the ground among the bamboos on the river foreshore. The Nedlands Road Board soon had it corralled into a concrete pool, and when this became the venue for some mild hooliganism, the 'Hot Pool' was cemented over and the water diverted to run away into the river. That showed us! Sure, members of Perth's road boards were not Nazis, but they typified the sort of Australian philistines that Marianne found so oppressive. And with a tolerance gauge pretty much stuck on zero, she would never accept some of the most sacred rites of her adopted country, starting with the ritual suburban lawn-mowing on a Sunday morning.

For my mother, the advent of the Korwills had the added advantage of lodgings for me in her absence. It was unquestionably better than being left with Mrs Bow, a deaf lady of Scottish extraction hired for twelve weeks in 1945 while M.P. took his daughter on a sentimental journey to Western Queensland. Or the woman someone had heard needed accommodation for a few months entrusted, without further investigation, to care for me and two-year-old Andy while my mother went north in 1946. A neighbour, getting wind of what was going on at the house, phoned Gran and a scandalised Bess gave the hussy, who had never cooked a meal or addressed a single word to her charges, the boot.

Regardless of the shortcomings, any home arrangement was preferable to the cold misery of a nun's cell at Loreto Convent, where in 1947 Robin and I were sequestered for what seemed a life sentence but was in reality only a few weeks. A day school, the Nedlands convent did not take boarders except in 'special circumstances' – in this case when the travel plans of our mother and grandmother coincided and no alternative offered. Unhappy children were simply absorbed into the nuns' austere regime: mass at dawn and benediction when the last bell had gone and long shadows fell across the empty playground. We ate flavourless food, were not permitted to share a bath and slept on narrow cots of holy hardness. It had been worse for Robin. Always a reserved and sensible girl, while I complained constantly to anyone who would listen, she stoically endured. Rising at six o'clock in the dark midwinter chill of a nun's cell to kneel through the deadly mass conducted by the monotonous Irish tones of Father Moss was a penance suitable only for adults under holy orders. Two years later, it was Bet's idea that Perpetua might feel happier about boarding at Loreto in the suburb of Swanbourne if Robin and Julie joined her. Despite her accommodating nature, Julie was frankly dubious, but for Robin, the helpful mainstay of the household, to be uprooted from the Nedlands convent and replanted in a bleak dormitory a bus ride from her home was unendurable. Her decline diagnosed as 'anaemia', she was taken to hospital and her appendix, as was the routine practice of the day, removed. From the north, where she was on another jaunt while her house was being built, Bet wrote with irritation:

> How extraordinary about Robin! I do hope you won't cave in on this one Mary – they really should be able to get used to the idea. Of course they will say they do not like it, but I am sure they will come round to it.[29]

While she believed in her inherent right to anything on offer from life – career, home, husband, children, pets – Bet also felt entitled to anything that might enable her to shunt the resultant responsibilities – childminders, boarding schools, obliging neighbours, the mixed-race couple housed out the back ... The difficulties involved in making such satisfactory accommodations were an eternal source of frustration.

The Durack sisters, who had never known other than a childhood within the bosom of an indulgent family, perhaps supposed that happiness was an in-built condition of juvenility. Mary never in the same league as Bet, both could be tough in defence of the freedom required to pursue creative lives. In truth, all the children placed in perfunctory care or boarding schools suffered for the experience, none more than Andy, who claimed he never got over it. And we were fortunate in comparison to the Clancy children, whose emergent spirits must have been dealt God knows what blows, especially the frequently abandoned Perpetua, observed by her mother as consequently 'in a thousand shreds'.[30]

~

When not quarrelling, Marianne and Ferry Korwill sang together in harmony as they went about the house. Musically educated, tuning in to classical music on ABC radio they would either know or be able to guess the composer. Never mind Mendelssohn or Schumann. *Ist Bartók?* asks Ferry. Marianne, finger raised, listens to the turgid discord for a minute: *Nein, Ferdie, ist Janáček.* Who then among our Australian acquaintances could have recognised either of them? Perth concertgoers still clapped between movements.

Music never a priority at Mildew, Horrie's souped-up gramophone blasting the neighbourhood with the early-morning entertainment of *Verdi's Requiem* was about as far as it went and he took care to dismantle the machine before he left for the north to make sure it stayed that way. The radio finally purchased was installed in my room, where it served to continue the unhealthy addiction to serials I had picked up from Gran. When we were small children, my mother, who had taken the piano lessons obligatory to nicely brought up girls of the day, played pieces from *The Nutcracker Suite* while we danced wildly about the lounge room with spring-busting leaps on the furniture. Before long, our out-of-tune piano became a permanent repository for an ever-growing stack of books, until the lid bowed under the weight. It is to the Korwills, and regular concerts at the Capitol Theatre, that I owe the introduction to a proper appreciation of music, destined for me to be a lifelong source of absorption and comfort.

Brought up the spoilt only daughter in a male household, Marianne indulged in tearful tantrums and long sulks. She generally behaved badly towards Ferry, who had always known what he was marrying and never got over his luck at having captured such a treasure. Once I was startled to come upon Mr Taussig weeping as he listened to Beethoven on the radio. Like the mere concept of parents who sang in accord, that was pretty outlandish too, as Gran would have been the first to agree. There was a sense of undercurrent and drama about the Korwill and Taussig households, running from pathos to farce. Indeed, Marianne's first cousin László Löwenstein, having found refuge in the United States, changed his name to Peter Lorre and became a film actor.

Happily, lodging with the Korwills provided me with a new source of reading material and anything in English was speedily consumed. It was an aggravation to me that the convent meanly doled out two books a week from the locked library cabinets – probably lest the demand exceed its meagre contents. The nuns' idea of literature suitable for their pupils was selective: British classics, a few American, nothing Australian except Ethel Turner, Mary Grant Bruce and Marcus Clarke's convict saga. When my mother supplied on request of the superior a list of Australian books appropriate for presentation to Loreto's mother general (supposedly a lover of fine literature) when she visited from Ireland, 'Mrs Miller' was reminded, in shocked tones, that most of the writers she had recommended were communists. Even Henry Handel Richardson featured among the banned, joining the local infidel, Katharine Susannah Prichard.

Mother General's visit was something of a highlight among the dull parade of forgettable convent visitors. On receiving advance notification that the head of the Institute of the Blessed Virgin Mary was both uncommonly lettered and a lover of music, we had prepared an entertainment including a bracket of colonial songs. Standing stiffly in our choral ranks, we watched, solemn and respectful, as a corpulent, near-blind elderly nun was guided to the row of chairs. A contrastingly skeletal religious companion, wearing round-rimmed dark glasses of the sort assumed by Daisy Bates, translated her Irish mutterings: 'Mother General thanks you for your welcome and your generous gift.' Frozen with anticipation, we could see that the old girl had been positioned by her apparently also blind attendant in a gap between the chairs. In slow motion, still clasping her plaster kookaburra, back she toppled, the dreadful legs never supposed to see the light of day exposed to rows of fascinated and unsympathetic eyes. What a charge of stricken nuns to the scene of disaster! You could see them wondering how the good Lord could have allowed such a thing to happen. But He was, after all, merciful. Mother G., no bones broken, was able to be propped up for a rendition of 'Where the Golden Wattles Rise' and 'Kookaburra Sits on the Old Gum Tree'. There was a 'mother provincial', too – the names they thought up for themselves!

In the way of one raised in a sophisticated milieu, Marianne spoke without embarrassment of subjects sidestepped by Australian society, and she expressed partiality in a very frank way. Not only did she loathe and venomously denigrate all but a chosen few politicians, she made no bones about her dislike of certain worthy citizens and literary figures embraced by my mother – some so beyond defence as to merit her derisive *Aber geh!* Geoffrey Drake-Brockman, the husband of the august Henrietta, fell into disfavour for having once slid his hand up her dress. It was not that he did it, as she explained, but that he did it because he thought that, being European, she would be broad-minded about it. And only from Marianne did I get a hint of why Gordon Colebatch's wife Astrid wore such a brave face.

The Korwills, however, drew a circle of peculiar acolytes of their own, and inevitably there was some mixing of oddities, like their compatriot, the artist Elise Blumann. The strength of our prevailing family bias meant that Elise was never regarded as anything but an amusing eccentric and her art, at best, inferior daubings. Clad in an assortment of defiantly bizarre garments, Elise sailed through the sedate Perth scene dropping memorable clangers that reduced all in her wake to a mixture of astonishment and hilarity. Arriving to view the newborn Miller son, she famously turned with indignation to the also-present Maria Dent: 'But Maria, he is not so hideous!' Blumann paintings, today respected by the art world, are sought by collectors and fetch high prices.

Nevertheless, perhaps as grist for some future literary mill, Mary indulged a variety of cranks and queer fish, many of them falling into the 'priceless' category, a word usually applied to someone of oddment value only. A posh-voiced devotee to the quasi-religious Great White Brotherhood comes to mind, and my eye is caught by an entry in Gran's diary that begs further investigation: 'Mary is still trying to help the poor dwarf woman with the brittle bones and the two big dogs who needs a life-saving operation in Switzerland.[31]

What made her almost fundamental Christian kindness more remarkable was that its practice had long been detached from religious belief. The outpourings contained in 'The Young Know' leave in no doubt an early breakaway from Catholicism on the part of the Durack sisters. In 1942 Mary wrote to Bet:

> *The church as she stands today cannot countenance the acceptance of progressive thought. The Catechism teaches us that we must pay*

the homage of our reason to God. Man pays to creation the homage of his reason because it is obvious that the cosmos and all creation are far beyond the limited scope of mortal mind. I do not feel that homage need consist of blindly accepting five highly improbable Articles of Faith and not eating meat on Fridays. There can be little progressive thought within the immutability of Catholic Dogma.[32]

As for Bet, her religious beliefs slipping before she left the convent, it was her opinion that in order to put up with the church one should keep away from it. So while their children trooped off to Sunday mass, the mothers were excused. We never questioned this. Going to church was included among the duties imposed upon children from which adults were exempt. Even so, both women were to hold a lifelong affinity with the clergy, nuns and priests making up a significant proportion of their acquaintances and, in Mary's case, correspondents. Given the adamant nature and intellectual scope of her long-held disbelief, Bet's latter-day devotional reversion can only be attributed to the miraculous. Perhaps a play of piety fell into the zone of just another of 'all my silly roles, from intellectual, housewife, pal, whore of Babylon to Winnie the Pooh.'[33] Mary would explain her own eventual return to regular mass attendance as a good way of catching up with members of the family and clerical friends, whom she did not like to offend by revealing her lapsed condition. From the 1960s, her growing involvement with clergy made a show of the faith unavoidable. Softened from atheist to a 'sincere agnostic', towards the end of her life she found spiritual comfort in the familiar rituals, so that they became for her more than just another expedient balancing act.

~

Horrie, galvanised by his wife's apparent acquiescence to the new order of things, began opening the faucet for what was to become a flood of drain-bound funds. That no-one thought to discourage him was an indication of what a trial he became when in the black depths of what he described as 'my constant companion'. To replace the tin shed at Dampier Downs, sheets of fireproof asbestos were shipped north.

Horrie had good reason to be nervous of fires. Hangars burned to the ground had marked his early flying career and he had seen aircraft with men inside consumed by flames. In 1947 the Broome house went up in a blaze that provided the town with a spectacular finale to race week and Mary with the fright of her life. Her later recounting of the episode always took in a subplot involving Dorothy Casey, who was a participant in the drama.

'Aunty' Dorothy was the aggrieved wife of the author Gavin Casey, a talented writer with a raw, vigorous style that potently captured hard times and mateship in Western Australia and on the goldfields. One of the more sprightly founding members of the FAW, during a wartime posting with the Australian News and Information Bureau in New York, Gavin had fallen for his secretary in a thoroughly clichéd way. Discovered in this what I understood to be (to my mother's mirth) 'candlestein' relationship, he opted to abandon his wife and young son in favour of his mistress. Dorothy's shock had been profound, the more so since Gavin's alcoholism had demanded of her such thankless forbearance that she had never imagined anyone else would take him on.[34]

Returning to Perth, she had sought solace from her dear friend Mary, who suggested a panacea might be found in a northern holiday and a spot of childminding. A recognisably good sport, Dorothy was easily absorbed into Broome society, the postwar frolics enlivened by an attenuated military presence. Left in her care while our parents visited the Kimberley stations, we were well entertained by spontaneous carousals at our house that frequently culminated in her performing routines from Broadway musicals. A sailor from a visiting ship gave her the curious gift of a captivating, huge-eyed sugar glider possum. Transferred to my pocket, 'Fluffy' became a major preoccupation for me – a sort of precursor to Marie Rose.

The carefree interlude at an end, and suitcases packed for an early-morning departure, the adults went off to a neighbour's race night party, leaving the four children asleep in the house. I do remember hearing a disturbing noise but knew nothing until I was pitched through the window into a puddle of water lit by the reflection of a lurid conflagration. As he threw me out, my father shouted an explanation, but the incomprehensible scene – milling people in evening dress, one drunkenly smashing into the freshwater tanks with an axe, the wind-whipped flames roaring through the openings, kids coughing and crying – bore no resemblance to the world when I had gone to sleep. One of the party guests, investigating a smell of burning, had discovered the already well-established cause: the kerosene refrigerator, languishing for an hour or more without Horrie's intensive care, had blown up. Mary never forgot the nightmarish sensation of struggling in her high heels towards the house and making no progress through the deep, vehicle-rutted sand. Taking up a heroic stance, the possum tucked safely inside his shirt, Horrie had managed to salvage the living room and sleep-out section, holding his post even as onlookers urged him to beat a retreat. Whooping from smoke-affected lungs, our belongings destroyed, we travelled to Perth in pyjamas.

When she married again, I sent Aunty Dorothy a card carefully inscribed: 'Hoping your new husband will be more sassfactory.' Apart from the spelling mistake, I still think it apt and never could understand the amused reaction. Sid Congdon *was* more satisfactory, although Dorothy was never able to properly free herself from the former connection, now lumbered with an equally intemperate American wife and the two children of the union.

When Gavin slipped quietly back to Western Australia in 1956, he was met by his staunch friend and former writing colleague Ted Mayman, whose continued fidelity cannot have been easily maintained. While there was minor reward in reporting the more comic aspects of the ongoing Casey shipwreck, only one as uncompromisingly decent as Ted would have stayed the distance. That my mother had not married a man such as he, intelligent, kind and humorous, seemed to me regretful – a sentiment shared by Ted.

At Ted's urging, the FAW threw a tardy welcome home for its former stalwart, who had felt sorely his unsung return. The second Mrs Casey did not entirely fulfil our expectations of a mantrap; in terms of a movie role, she was definitely better cast as a supporting actress – one in need of a Bex tablet and a good lie-down.

'Say, honey, where's the little ladies' room?' she enquired of a regally po-faced Henrietta.

'Common as muck', gleefully observed Irene Greenwood.

~

After the Broome fire, Horrie became super-vigilant. I had only to 'smell something burning' to witness his rearing up and charging through the rooms and surrounds of the rebuilt house with the belatedly introduced fire extinguisher in hand. Once on the way out to Cable Beach, I thought I saw a plume of smoke back in the direction of our block, and my father – instantly – swung the truck around in a narrow wheel-rut turn to head for home at engine-cooking speed. It was a pilot's reaction, the same that could immediately feather an engine or abort a take-off. Horrie never blamed me for these false alarms since, like all good pilots, he operated on the better-safe-than-sorry principle and he did not ascribe to the theory of one-off lightning strikes.

Now, in Perth to buy station equipment and sound out the sale prospects of Mildew, he found Bet had been using the house telephone, evidenced by a circle of matches and cigarette ash. Discovering a hole burned right through to the carpet underlay, he pronounced it a wonder that the place hadn't been reduced to a gutted ruin. What's more, the door had been left wide open for anyone to walk in. Divested of the key and telephone privileges, Bet was quick to turn the tables on Horrie, pronouncing his ideas for a move to Broome 'the biggest line of bull I've ever heard'. Notwithstanding the fact that she had always been counted in on the plan, Bet dispatched buckets of cold water northwards, her former enthusiasm turned to antipathy and scorn. Knowing well enough that Horrie would never have accepted her being 'fitted in', she suggested to her sister the better idea would be to rid themselves of all encumbrances, including redundant husbands, and take up sole occupation of the Broome house for collaborative purposes.[35]

Mary's first happy delusions were already suffering the onset of reality. Even so, she thought it only fair to Horrie that she should support him as best she could until the Dampier Downs venture proved itself one way or another. But her apprehension over such a drastic upheaval brought on a physical breakdown necessitating her removal to the rudimentary facilities of the Broome hospital. Although as a child a severe bout of measles had cost her the hearing in one ear, she again succumbed to the virus, along with an attack of what was diagnosed as hay fever. Susceptible to allergies when under stress, she had taken Gran's word for the trouble being pollen. But the trouble was constitutional rather than botanical or climatic.

She hoped that Horrie would himself eventually accept the obstacles involved, although he was still expounding on how the place 'could go ahead like wildfire' under the right manager. He was disappointed when, offering the job to Kim and then Bill Durack ('a lovely land here just wanting brains, youth and some cash'), they had been polite but definite in refusal. So it was that without warning or any clear understanding of why, we packed our belongings for an indefinite period of relocation. To save their feelings, my mother told the Loreto nuns that we would be going to the convent, but Horrie had booked us into the local state school.

CHAPTER 3

BROOME (1952)

To her cousin, Mary expressed her misgivings:

> *It is with mixed feelings I go Kath, and I think it is with mixed feelings that Horrie receives us. The truth is we are too many for him and he can never really understand why he should have us all. When I am up there he wants me to be off with him out to Dampier Downs and the kids make it impossible without imposing on people. However ... I do love the funny, little port with its cockeyed houses and cockeyed people and I hate a southern winter – haven't had to endure one for years in fact, and should probably die if I stayed.*[1]

There was a sense of almost irresponsible vagueness as people were bid farewell for an indefinite parting, although most were invited with foolhardy sincerity to visit us.

The emphasis placed on the consequences of interrupting my convent education, the main reason I had so often been left behind, seemed suddenly unimportant. Nor, I noted with some affront, did the suspension of my ballet lessons appear to be considered of any great moment. It was all to the winds, and in keeping with the whole capricious enterprise, we put away our schoolbooks and uniforms and took only our summer clothes and bikes.

The city having come to represent a winter purgatory and Broome a summer paradise, it seemed apposite that attaining this Shangri-la should be difficult and arduous. So that the 1,400 miles could be covered in an extended day, departures were always scheduled for ungodly hours, generally between midnight and five in the morning. Excitement having precluded sleep until, so we thought, the minute before the alarm went off, we hastened to dress and strap up the battered suitcases before the discreet doorbell ring announced the arrival of Cyril Kleinig.

Taken on by Horrie in 1930 as a fresh-faced boy looking for a career in aviation and offering to work for nothing, Cyril Kleinig had quickly made his way up the ladder of a regional airline company, his piloting days left behind with promotion to an administrative role. As assistant managing director in 1952, one of his duties was to collect and transport to Guildford Airport the family of the boss. Cyril and his wife Rhona were long-established personal friends, as were the Gare family. Cyril Gare, at the time MMA's general manager, was to the end Horrie's closest and most loyal associate. But Kleinig was cast in a different mould, and to uncomplainingly assume the role of chauffeur for the Millers at uncivilised hours during their frequent northern jaunts can only be supposed an exercise in playing his cards right.

Providing seats were still available a few hours before departure, we travelled free of charge, often in relays. En masse movement, as perhaps on this occasion, was unusual. I have forgotten individual flights, the whole having merged into a general recollection of many such.

At the airport an aircraft hangar served as a comfortless pre-departure lounge. Here luggage was checked, and if found to be over the allowance excess penalties were imposed, or the offending items left behind. Passenger weights were insensitively called across to the dispatcher, and my father, whose humour largely focused on the discomposure of others, would pleasurably recall the distress of one stout lady who insisted that the scales must be *dangerously* way out.

Shivering in the icy pre-dawn wind, we trailed across the wet tarmac to the dim bulk of a DC3, our means of conveyance for the next ten hours. Despite a smiling welcome from the air hostess suggestive of a treat in store, entering that claustrophobic tin can impacted powerfully on the senses, and seasoned travellers were liable to turn green at the door as the memory of past odysseys returned. Passengers were at once enveloped in a unique odour – a mixture of fuel, oil, metal polish, a hint of vomit lurking in the crevices and a permeation of the MMA brand flyspray used so liberally north of the twenty-sixth parallel.

A low tail-wheel meant an uphill haul to find one's seat and stow coats and hand baggage in the open overhead racks. Mary, who did not acquire a more compact portable model until 1957, sat throughout the journey with her bulky typewriter parked underfoot. Amenities for the comfort of the paying public consisted of an air vent, a dim reading light, a hostess call button and an ashtray. Designed to permanently digest any stowed articles, the subterranean seat pockets contained safety instructions and brown paper bags bearing the advice 'For Refuse and Air Sickness'. The door closed and barley sugars, pillows and blankets distributed, we sat captive, as are all air travellers, at the mercy of sundry elements.

I was well aware of other children who, not so long before, had been roused and transported through a stormy night, to similarly gaze blindly through a small, rain-dashed window when they should have been at home, tucked safely in their beds. From the terrible wreckage, someone had salvaged a few smouldering mailbags.[2]

The contract to carry Royal Mail was a sacred one, and once human life was extinguished, as with the regimental flag, no effort was spared in order to rescue the mail. Our family files carry two charred envelopes from separate disasters, returned with a note from the Postmaster-General. From the mire, Cyril Gare had plucked the inevitable teddy bear, the sad relic after his death passed to me for disposal. Prior to sophisticated methods of air-crash investigation, a molten hulk was generally beyond useful clues as to the cause. Apart from some basic deductions, it was not reassuring that the evidence in this case covered all bases, inconclusively citing the possibilities of engine failure, incorrect loading, misuse of the automatic pilot, a control lock left on an elevator or unspecified pilot error.

Being children of the founder, we took a proprietary interest in the airline. In Julie's case, this called for a tour of the cabin soon after take-off for the purpose of introducing herself to the passengers. A subdued lot, they made no objection to her affable overtures and queries if they were enjoying the flight 'so far'. The occasional Aboriginal person on board who had managed to survive the city hospital or police business, knowing her family connections, greeted her with genuine delight.

A series of explosive noises and puffs of smoke signalled the engines coughing to life. As we taxied at snail's pace there was seldom another aircraft to be seen; delays due to traffic, unimagined. Oh, that endless day! The monotonous sound of the engines, their fluctuating surge creating a slight swimming motion, droning on and on and on. Sunrise revealed the propeller's yellow-edged circle, the lines of silver rivets around the engine cowlings and over the wings that would, as the hours passed, be counted and re-counted, and the creeping dribble of oil watched until it blew off the trailing edge. Once the patchwork of rural allotments fell away, there was little to see through the haze below but the occasional glint of a river twisting through the flat green and grey landscape. Breakfast, served for the hardy, was laid out on a tin tray and the beverage cup only half-filled on account of turbulence. We had learned at a young age that empty air was not empty at all but filled with invisible violence and force. There must have been smooth flights, but my memory is of being lifted against the restraining belt and pushed into the depths of the seat, while objects fell from the overhead racks and trays crashed in the galley; poor little Andy gripping the sick bag throughout, Marie Rose reduced to a wrung-out waif.

Making use of the unproductive hours, Mary gamely waded into her ever-behind correspondence, and letters were subsequently dispatched bearing evidence of a pen barely under control. If rough conditions persisted it was almost impossible to avoid the nauseous effects, and with the unpressurised aircraft restricted to a maximum ten thousand feet, there was no climbing out of it. Prolonged exposure to a combination of reeking toilet and vomit made for exceptional unpleasantness, the application of air-freshener inadequate to the challenge.

But the trip to Broome on the West Kimberley border could not compare with a flight extending into East Kimberley. That was a trial intimate to my grandfather, who was a poor, if hopeful, traveller. Unwell from first to last, he yet endured gladly the marvel of a two-day stretch of discomfort as against a pre-airline wretched ten days at sea to cover the same distance. Gruelling peregrinations going back to the exodus from Ireland had put the Duracks in a unique class of travelling experience, one that left little room for complaint about the rigours of transportation by air.

Halfway to Carnarvon, a pink tinge crept into the coastal sand and then, by degrees, the red earth – for our family, always a sight to lift the spirits and stiffen the sinews. Halfway between Onslow and Roebourne, the first officer entered the cabin to formally confiscate cameras, a solemn assignment undertaken during 1952 on behalf of the Australian Government, to forestall any attempt to photograph the secret installations a smudgy distance out to sea on the tiny dots that were the pristine Montebello Islands. I can remember only an atmosphere of excited interest over preparations to explode atom bombs on our fragile and ecologically sensitive atolls. Led by the nose, Australians seemed flattered to have their outback areas chosen by Britain as a location to deploy this destructive power. But Mary, who had seen the splitting of the atom as the opening of Pandora's box, was moved to expound philosophically to Kath McArthur:

> *I think man puts too high a store on his ability to vitally disrupt the forces of nature, for nature hits back with weapons far more subtle and devastating than any within our power, for all our chemicals and atom bombs. We battle for survival along with the rest of the life on this planet and if our tampering with the ancient order of things has brought certain disasters to the earth and incidentally to man, the situation will be adjusted in time with all the ruthless cruelty of life itself, even if part of that adjustment entails the disappearance of homo sapiens as it has already numerous other species. It is my personal belief that man is relatively unimportant to the universe.*[3]

Regular ports of call provided spartan sheds containing a counter, set of scales, wall benches and toilets. All displayed the bed of purple vinca that denoted 'civilisation' throughout the north, some, for added decoration, lined with whitewashed vehicle tyres cut in half. Irregular stops, viewed through the aircraft window, revealed nothing other than a station vehicle waiting for mail or supplies, passengers compelled to sit and endure the heat and swarming flies until the transactions were completed.

Covering the same ground in the aircraft that bore his name, Horrie described the scene in vivid but sombre vein:

> *It was when coming in over Onslow that I felt the bitter sense of a harsh, forlorn country. A few blacks sitting under flapping hessian and torn canvas, looking up with no pretence of interest as our shining plane slipped through the shimmering haze a few feet above. On the ground, as the cabin door swung open, a wave of furnace heat almost seared the skin. Flies surged upon us – one could take no interest in anything, each port leaving a greater sense of dull despair. We flew into a towering mass of cumulus cloud and the plane was caught by the mighty currents and lost in a swirl of grey.*[4]

Port Hedland behind us, we set out over the Indian Ocean, the coast seen as a hazy line to starboard. Sitting with my nose glued to the vibrating window over the last dragging stretch, I looked hard ahead for the first glimpse of the narrow peninsula curving into the turquoise sea that was Broome.

Under the wing now, the pristine stretch of Cable Beach, kangaroos bounding away into the scrub, flocks of cockatoos rising, then the wheels squeaking down on the runway where white cones marked the boundary between bitumen and bush. There was the familiar terminal, the familiar figure of George Ockerby in his white shorts and long socks ready with the steps, and the all-too-familiar lean and loitering form of Horrie. Emerging wan, wobbly-legged and faint with fatigue, we stepped down onto a heat-baked tarmac, eyes dazzled by shafts from the setting sun. A rose and gold glow bathed the dusty scene, and blowing in on the evening wind, the clean, salt smell of the sea. Light-years behind us the house we had abandoned in the wintry dark, like rats a sinking ship. I did not just cease to think of any aspect of life in Perth, I forgot that it had ever existed.

In its ramshackle degeneration, its recession-driven exhaustion and acceptance of the substandard, Broome symbolised to us as children something beyond criticism. The pearling industry, dependent on Japanese operatives, had made only small recovery from the war, and hulks of luggers lay rotting in the tidal creeks and mud of Roebuck Bay. Of the boomtime hundreds, fewer than twenty vessels could be seen putting to sea during the season. Since every kind of prejudice can be upheld with no difficulty except that which might interfere with commerce, the pearlers had been prepared to put hostilities behind them as soon as possible. But tight restrictions on the importation of Asian labour continued to hamper the industry. In 1953, with no official announcement, thirty-five Japanese divers were admitted on three-year contracts, and the shell take for the season doubled. The Malays and Chinese, understandably, didn't want them back, and neither did the local branch of the RSL. But in the end, the general recognition that Broome was nothing for anyone without a profitable export saw a pragmatic acceptance of the inevitable.

Meanwhile, the once substantial and thriving centre had shrunk to three rows of rickety shops, and few of the fine homes built by the pearling masters were maintained. Broome had become a tropic backwater – one of history's has-been places, a happy hunting ground for visiting writers and journalists who kept its colourful history alive. Strewn with sorry souvenirs of the war and untouched by civic pride, it stank of decay, both physical and moral.

For the utterly captivated Miller children, that half-year from June to December embodied an unscheduled season of thrilling improvidence. It was the only time in my memory that we lived as a complete family in circumstances of happiness. While there remained a possibility of making a go of Dampier Downs, we were cast into a new life so much better than the old that it was probably as well it came to an end before we began to suspect that it might not be enough.

Loaded aboard Horrie's army van, we were borne past vacant blocks overgrown with weeds and wattle shrub, tumbledown houses, their junk-strewn yards shaded by mango trees and bottle-shaped boabs. In the grip of an unprecedented three-year drought, the place had never looked so dry and dusty. Such a failure of successive wet seasons along the marginal, desert-hugging coastal fringe had left a blighted land, the whitening bones of cattle and sheep scattered over thousands of square miles. It was a source of family anxiety that the disaster throughout the Kimberley was adversely affecting my uncles Reg and Kim in their struggling ventures.

A turn around Chinatown's jumble of white corrugated-iron shacks, the closed Japanese quarters with its graffiti-splashed walls, the stark community centre, the Catholic church and Bedford Park, where reminders of a buccaneering past lay rusting beneath tall spear grass – and the tour was complete. Swinging past the Continental Hotel, we joyfully returned the waved welcome from familiar figures seated on the verandah and at the bar, where they had remained, immobile, since our last visit – caught in the concentrated spotlight of the town as caricatures of themselves. And there was our house behind the pink oleanders, sprung out of the ashes to its former appearance.

Raised on cement piles topped with tin hats to thwart termites, the modest latticed abode stood with its wide cyclone-proof shutters propped open to the breeze. The sleep-out was shaded by an old mango tree, home to a squeaking myriad of the pungent-smelling flying foxes that plagued the town, their crisped corpses decorating the telegraph wires like funeral flags. Beyond the patch of hardy grass allowed two drops of water a day by Horrie, and halfway down the straggling double block, spread the feathery fronds of a gigantic poinciana, dangling dark brown pods full of rattling seeds. At the end of the year, its flaming head challenged any casual passing by. Displaying many such specimens in proximity to the dripping dazzle from golden shower trees – all rising out of the ox-blood earth against the clear jade sea – the town was splashed by primary colour as if from the brush of an overexcited artist.

At the end of the shell-grit path, under a riotous Mexican rose creeper, stood the outhouse, its noisome can emptied once a week by a 'night cart' manned during the day by a high turnover of quietly moving Aboriginal workers. Ancient civilisations of Egypt and Rome enjoyed more advanced sewerage systems than Australian country towns in the 1950s. While uninviting of any temptation to linger, at least the dunny's purpose was unambiguous in a way now lost to the first world. There was no question of paying a visit to wash one's hands, powder one's nose or freshen up. Bright green patches on the grass divulged not only our reluctance to make the nocturnal trek but the desperation of the grass.

A surprise awaited us on the top block. Horrie had begun, single-handed and without a discernible blueprint, to build a more modern house, incorporating walls of dependable asbestos. Worried about not having a ready escape from family, separate quarters seemed the answer, and as soon as the idea came to him he had begun work. Putting something through without delay was an ability he possessed envied by his wife. He had only been awaiting extra hands to help him with 'the principals', and subsequently a line of children raised the heavy wooden beams while the builder stood on the framework to guide them into place.

The old house was constructed with kitchen and bathroom off one side of a hallway leading to the main living room and, behind that, the single bedroom surrounded by a flywired verandah used by the children as a sleep-out. The word 'bathroom' may conjure up something more orthodox than Horrie's bush camp shower set up for purposes of ablution, a tool room having taken the space intended for the purpose. Rising costs, a constant theme, were responsible for the storage of tins containing Horrie's noxious and flammable mixtures of homemade substitute products that saved about sixpence on bottles of the real thing. (It had been the incendiary properties of a similar repository that had so effectively spread the blaze during the famous fire.) In the same cause, there were also glutinous concoctions of washing liquid and cakes of latherless soap.

'The frugality', wrote Mary to Bet, 'the reclusiveness and the possessiveness verge always on neurosis.'[5] For the most part happy to live in bachelor disorder, Horrie retained certain fusspot housekeeping habits. During her tenure, Bet had come up against them, although her situation allowed for only an inner seethe and a letter to her sister under the heading 'the dreadful house-proud misery that seems to grip hermits of both sexes'.[6] There was the mopping of wooden floors with a foul 'polish' of oil and grease, and the raking of shell-grit paths made untidy by careless walkers. Dim, twenty-five-watt light globes were covered with small pastel shades and tables hung with felt cloths. A Norman Lindsay etching of naked women chased by satyrs hung in pride of place, and on the sideboard was a Royal Doulton vase decorated with pictures of English village scenes. Unlike Mildew, so tastefully furnished by his wife, the Broome house was Horrie's domain and the worst could only be discreetly repositioned. Averse to insects, he stooged around pumping Flytox into breathing spaces and waited with a broom to sweep up the fallen corpses. There was no question of eating in the airy central room. Meals were conventionally confined to the hotbox of a kitchen, where a wood-fuelled stove had only recently replaced the primus, and a noisy electric fridge its disgraced predecessor. Horrie's phobia about the use of electricity forbade overhead fans, although prior to air conditioning there was no effective cooling device to be found throughout the Kimberley. In the old station days, a punkah, its operator out of sight, waved across the dining-room table when the cutlery was almost too hot to touch.

~

Our diet owed a good deal to tins, stews and fish. Situated as we were within one of the world's great cattle-raising areas, it was an eternal mystery why the town butcher could supply nothing but shoe-leather meat at an exorbitant price. A weekly box of fresh fruit arrived from Perth addressed in Gran's neat hand – sending provisions north a duty she had kept up for more than fifty years.

We ate from blackened cutlery rescued from the ruins of the fire. A coldwater tap served kitchen and bathroom needs, and fresh water, used to supplement the hard-as-nails scheme, was strictly rationed. Every morning, placing his ear to the tanks, Horrie rapped the corrugated sides and marked the level. Making no concession for the increase in numbers, he demanded explanations if the rappings revealed overindulgence. At night we fell asleep to the undersea distortions of the radio – a sound integral to remote locations – and the tap-tapping of typewriters. While Mary worked on the Broome novel (tentatively titled 'The Calm Eye'), Horrie wrote letters. He was an active correspondent, his missives going out across the continent to a diversity of recipients, from old flying mates to federal ministers. He had also begun to write his memoirs with an enthusiasm that was to wax and wane over the next sixteen years.

The feeler sent by Mary to Phyll Kaberry in London had finally turned up trumps in the form of Phyll's friend Florence James, a reader for Constable, who had been sufficiently enthused about the idea of the family saga to approach her firm for the requested guarantee of publication. A New Zealander raised and educated in Sydney, she came across to Mary, from first contact in 1952, as 'sounding like a splendid person'.[7] Consequently, although they did not actually meet until 1963, the formal 'Dear Mrs Miller' and 'Dear Mrs James' opening correspondence had within a blink evolved into a cosy personal association. 'Wandering River', retitled *Keep Him My Country*, was also packaged up and sent off to London.

Meanwhile, Mary worked on the completion of poetic translations of Aboriginal song cycles begun the previous year. The inspiration for this work had been her close association with Father Worms, a German anthropologist priest who, like Phyll Kaberry, had conducted fieldwork on the Durack stations in the 1930s. Renowned in the world of science and with many books to his credit, this gentle and erudite member of the Pallottine community, now re-encountered in Broome, had no difficulty in reconciling the two sides of his vocation. When queried as to why, as a priest, he was not appalled by the pagan rites he witnessed on his bush treks, he looked bewildered: 'Why do you ask? Is it not all in the heart of God?' The European Catholic, my mother noted, bore little resemblance to the Austro-Irish brand. She wrote to Kath McArthur:

> Father Worms' sort of religion suits me alright, but when it comes down to doctrine I am indeed a lost soul. I simply cannot follow the

line of reasoning and cannot even trot out the well-known cliché of 'envying their faith'. I do not envy it or want it.[8]

'Lament to Galalan – the Law-Giver', a translation from the songs of the Dampier tribes, traced the life cycle of a mythological figure in Aboriginal lore. Similarities to the Christ story led the author to muse that the martyred messiah in one form or another was a recurring theme emerging throughout ancient and modern cultures. Published first in a university journal, the combination of ethnography and literature created a considerable stir among academics and philosophers, and mixed reactions from anthropologists, including the purist Father Worms.[9] While skilfully wrought and faithfully translated within the perimeter of poetic licence, the work might be regarded today as an incursion and an experiment of its time. The 1950s saw a free-for-all in the appropriation of Aboriginal culture for Western adaptation: music, ballet, film and even opera, the latter being a future foray on the part of Mary Durack. The line between tribute and insult was indistinct and, aware of the pitfalls, it was one the Durack sisters had carefully negotiated for many years.

~

The usual concert of frogs silenced by the drought, night birds and crickets set up a shrill din, and in the distance could be heard the sound of the sea on an incoming or outgoing tide. When the swarm of insects battering their wings against the light and getting caught up in her typewriter became too distracting, Mary would draw them. Her many Broome sketchbooks are filled with creatures accurately captured from life – mainly those of the sea. Two self-illustrated children's books written in amusing verse would languish among projects put aside.[10]

Observing the southern pallor of his offspring, Horrie declared, as he always did, that he would soon have us as 'brown as berries' and 'fit as fiddles'. Encouraging nakedness in order to gain the beneficial effects of the ultraviolet rays, he enjoyed the fantasy of himself and family as a Neanderthal group. (It is comforting to remember my father's future battle with skin cancers. Not so comforting to remember mine.) Few townsfolk utilised the beaches, so we came to regard long stretches of coastline as our private resort, the army van a lone vehicle and no footprints but ours to mark the smooth sandhills.

Immediately on arrival, Robin and Julie set out to re-establish their network of friends. When circumstances had sometimes prevented Mary from leaving Perth during the school holidays, she had dispatched

Robin and Julie north, with instructions that they should look after their father and one another. Able to amuse themselves, they were also content to accompany him on his daily round of the town, the beaches and the aerodrome. Intelligent and engaging children, they were recognised and welcomed everywhere. It was a happy arrangement that in 1949 would be marred by an unfortunate incident.

One night Julie had been stricken with a severe stomach-ache, and it had become necessary, in the absence of the resident doctor, to call out a locum. Dr Mick Cook, a former chief protector of Aborigines, was reported by Horrie to have finally appeared at the hospital the worse for wear.[11] It is possible to speculate that his state was on account of his covert three-year romance with Bet, the difficulty being a wife and children he could not leave and the stratagems necessary to continue the affair. Examining the child of a family well known to him and demonstrating extra conscientiousness, Dr Cook had decided to remove the appendix rather than risk peritonitis. Had Robin been there, it is likely she would have sensibly put aside her loyalties and revealed that Julie, defying her father's warnings, had eaten portions of unripe mangoes. But sadly, no-one spoke out. Horrie later remembered an awful reluctance when filling out the requisite consent form, as if he were signing his daughter's death warrant.[12]

The operation had been a shocker. Unable to find the appendix but convinced of his diagnosis, the doctor kept cutting until, located at last, a normal and uninflamed appendix was removed. A long time recovering, Julie was left with a livid scar from the right side of her abdomen to the navel. Horrie had been seriously frightened at the prospect of losing a child in his care and having decisions forced upon him that he felt unqualified to make. But by 1952, the event was no more than a bad memory and Julie restored to good health and cheer. Not even Horrie, acquainted as he was with the concept of connective elements, foresaw the forging of the first awful link in a tragic chain.

~

Bet had managed to make a break from Perth earlier in the year, sailing up the coast on the state ship *Koolinda* to spend a few weeks in Broome. Not any longer in the running for a billet at the house, she and her two children had put up at the Governor Broome Hotel, with its rotting verandah boards and squalid, mosquito-infested rooms. They were informed that the better quarters in the far section were reserved for the expected arrival of the famous writer Ernestine Hill. The *Koolinda* had also carried what Bet described as 'wonderful Dampier Downs toys' for Horrie. She had been witness to him driving a tractor past the hotel, triumphantly waving his hat and grinning with the joy of acquisition, on his way to deposit the machine in his congested hangar beside his aircraft and a new truck, its seats still covered in plastic wrap and reserved for station runs.[13]

Hungry for the old springs of inspiration, Bet found 'the magic and melody of the north' had changed since M.P.'s death. The feeling of 'belonging' gone with the sale of the properties, she was no longer able to endure the low standards visible everywhere – those things that she had imagined would one day be amended by the personal effort of herself and other Duracks. 'We were too slow. Time played us false. Now I want to pick and criticise, condemn, blame, revile, hate and finally – leave.'[14]

Never really coming to terms with the new order but tied to the country beyond breaking the bonds, she would adjust her sights and for the remainder of her days continue by a variety of means to depict for better or worse an evolving situation. The question of what it had all been about would remain a perplexing issue for both sisters: the momentous groundbreaking enterprise, the placing of the Durack stamp upon the raw, red hide of the Kimberley, the long, profitless toil, the scattered bush graves. Had they after all cast upon the land no more than a shadow of a dream?

~

Word instantly out that the Miller family was in town, there began a constant jangle from the telephone that seldom rang with personal calls when Horrie was alone in residence. Reminders that it was a company installation to be used only for business purposes arose every time he saw his wife cranking the handle and requesting a number from the exchange. The open shutters that ordinarily admitted nothing more unwelcome than a flying insect now drew speculative eyes looking for a warm greeting from the lady of the house.

It was a matter of aggravation to Horrie that his wife would not join him in the avoidance and condemnation of every second person in town, especially Sam Male, who owned Broome's main store, and Derm Farrell, who ran the meatworks – both targets for his unrelenting hostility. On the contrary, she had speedily made and renewed friendships covering a broad spectrum of the white and multiracial community of a town that would over the years benefit greatly from her support and abiding interest. Yet he was proud of her popularity and had an inward sense that a good deal of the cordiality he enjoyed was on account of his admired better half. Reasonably, she would point out that Streeter & Male was also the agent for MMA, the Farrells were immediate neighbours, and to fall out with the town's bigwigs made things awkward. And reason was required, as Horrie could pitch any innocuous opener into a conversational battlefield via the 'Do you mean to tell me' route. To reassure herself that it was not she who was round the bend, Mary sometimes scribbled down his ludicrous interpretations of innocent remarks:

'Wasn't it nice of Jack Prior to give us those two lovely cauliflowers?'

'Do you mean to tell me you think Jack Prior's vegetables are better than mine? I might as well not bother. I'll pull them up and save on the water.'

'I hear the meatworks is contributing to the Christmas party for the kids this year.'

'Do you mean to tell me that I don't give all sorts of things to the kids of this town? The point is I'm paying out huge sums for the presents and sweets you give to the orphanage.'

'Do you mean to tell me that a man can't have his tools to hand? I might as well take them out and throw them on the dump …'

'Do you mean to tell me that you want the house to burn down again?'

'Do you mean to tell me that you didn't just walk right out of the store?'

When irritation got the better of her, my mother was not always able to resist the sarcastic or supercilious rejoinder:

'I'm sorry, dear, we'll just eat around the tools.'

'Oh, I didn't realise that removing the lock you've put on the tank tap would cause the place to burn down.'

'Oh, alright then, if you think it best, dear, I'll tell Sam Male that he has the town by the throat and that he is a racketeer and cancel our account with Streeter & Male.'[15]

Under protest, he went along for an evening with hospitable Phyll Male (affectionately retained by Mary among her 'priceless' collection) and the despised Sam. Over jugs of cold beer, the men yarned cordially as they sat on the verandah of a spacious residence, a classic of the early days built for a master pearler and befitting the chairman of the road board, owner of great slabs of pastoral country and a string of stores and agencies. It was more what Sam and his kind represented that my father abhorred than Sam per se. In a town like Broome, attracting a population bound on a treasure hunt, it was open slather until the few accumulated sufficient money and clout to sew it up. After that, the place could be run as a virtual fiefdom by the unchallenged heavyweights with their road board and shire council tie-ins and heirs lined up to carry on after them. In all matters to be decided, there was but one consideration: did it promote or hinder the welfare and profit-making activities of the power bloc? Businessmen, the movers and changers, cannot also be aesthetes or historians.

In later years, it would be hit-and-run outsiders who despoiled what remained of old Broome. Entering the town in the 1960s, the Reid family saw a more or less unexploited prospect for development. Down came the 'Bishop's Palace',[16] its legendary ghost sent packing, the historic Continental and Governor Broome hotels, Chinatown's timber-framed, corrugated-iron buildings and Horrie's unsightly hangar doors stitched with bullet holes from the wartime attack on the airport. Up went the Bali-Hai Caravan Park overlooking Cable Beach, brick flats and shopping centres. While no-one could really regret the passing of a slum like the Governor Broome Hotel, what replaced it, in the form of 'Tropicana Lodge', was worse. Sensing a possible small obstruction in the path of his bulldozers, the president of the Broome Shire Council confronted the president of the Broome Historical Society:

'The trouble with you, Mary, is that you, and people like you, live in the past.'

In a rare comeback, her answer was curt:

'The trouble with you, Peter, and people like you, is that you do not realise that Broome's future lies in its past.'[17]

The more enlightened vision of Alistair McAlpine towards the transformation of Broome into a balmy tourist resort making the most of its history was as yet decades away.

Horrie's antagonism towards various individuals extended to selective nations. His opinions openly aired, he detested 'Yanks' and everything they stood for; a trenchant critic of US Cold War activities, he rooted for Russia in the space race. And yet, while reclusive and unconvivial, he liked to be recognised. Disdaining most public events, he nevertheless expected to be asked and resented being passed over. Lacking the optimism required to reply positively to an RSVP, in the end he usually went, especially if the free aspects were attractive. He was as pleased when sought out or acknowledged by dignitaries at official functions as he was when black arms waved and cries of 'Hello, Captain Miller' came from the back of a passing ute.

~

Divided into junior and senior sections, there were only two classrooms at the local state school, where we were sent for the purpose of some semblance of a continued education. Our fellow students were the sons and daughters of Broome pearlers – Male, Morgan, Kennedy and De Castilla. Otherwise, apart from some white children of town employees, pupils were Chinese, Malay, Singhalese and of mixed heritage. So we had Fong, Ellies,

Dep, Rahmin, Ah Chee and Nasir. Aboriginal families were expected to send their offspring to the Catholic convent or the missions.

Three hundred air force and army people connected with the atom bomb tests had inundated the town for a season – a very prosperous one for the shopkeepers. During the war years, the former baths had fallen into disrepair and swimming outside an enclosure was risky on account of schools of predators attracted to the tons of offal pumped into the sea by the meatworks. In a gesture of gratitude for town hospitality and to give themselves something to do, the atom bomb boys rebuilt the baths. As far as I was concerned, such safe swimming was rather tame. Not content with being a walking fire alarm, I also had an uncommon ability to see and point out fins, missed by everyone else because they always looked too late. Somewhere along the line I had acquired a reputation for being a 'drama queen'. This label tended to put a damper on what I considered no more than a gift for ornamentation and a desire to brighten up a dull moment. Shark sightings always created a stir, as did the stonefish, stingray and deadly jellyfish I also managed to spot when things got a little slow.

~

Swirling over the mangroves, the high tide surged in, a vast, moon-pulled body of water reaching across the sand to suck and gurgle in the eroded hollows of the cliff. It was wonderful to plunge into the limpid coolness and swim out to the wire netting, where we hung with some care not to poke fingers and toes too far through the holes. The huge tidal drop also dragged the sea out until it was no more than a distant blue line, exposing the forest tangle of ash-grey mangrove trunks and ravaged roots, the oozing mud bristling with suckers. State ships stranded at the end of the mile-long jetty sat on their bottoms, to the diversion of passengers unfamiliar with such a phenomenon. This was the time for our reef expeditions. My mother's broad extramural talent included arranging shells and pretty things picked up from the beaches in bleached coral cups. These unique objets d'art were especially popular with Gran and her chums and, when all else failed, just the right gift. In truth, I was a little dubious about the merits of the kitsch articles, as I suspect was my mother, but they were fun to make, and collection of the raw material involved us in the fascinating pastime of reef-scouring.

While the commonplace loot could be gathered at any season, only the spring and king tides gave up the uncommon treasures. Mrs McDaniel, a town identity and keen shell collector, led us on these occasions, knowing as she did the tidal movements and the best places to explore. Setting shells arranged in graduated patterns under glass tabletops her speciality; one of these masterpieces was transported to the community centre during the never-to-be-forgotten excitement of a royal tour, where the Queen and Duke of Edinburgh were photographed gazing at it, quite clearly overcome with admiration.

In the early hours of the morning, as Mrs McDaniel drove us out to the selected beach, she was wont to complain en route about unscrupulous reef-robbers who were muscling in on a preserve once exclusively hers. A feisty, outspoken and sometimes belligerent lady, she made people nervous and it was considered wise to tread carefully in her company. Not only did I not tread carefully but in the half-light failing to see the weathered old biddy as she reached into the depths of her car for some piece of equipment, I firmly slammed the boot lid on her. It seemed to me very insensitive of Mrs Mac to spend the remaining months of our stay parading round in a neck brace, widely advertising my homicidal carelessness. Deprived of our guide, we had to make do with picked-over reefs and what we could find under the jetty.

Plunging into the shining grey expanse outside the baths was a perilous exercise, as the quaking, gelatinous mud sucked us down at every step. While occupied in what we called 'erk-perking', it was advisable to pull the sinking feet out quickly or extraction became too difficult, sandshoes lost in the boggy depths. Far out in the bay, the barnacle-encrusted wrecks of flying boats shot to pieces by the Japanese spilled their corroded innards among the rock outcrops.[18] Thirty unclaimed Dutch bodies still remained, small white rows of crosses overlooking the scene of their violent end. I often wondered how the returning Japanese felt about their handiwork so starkly displayed round the town. Perhaps they felt as I did when I caught sight of the encumbered form of Mrs McDaniel.

Clambering over the exposed reef on the other side of the peninsula, we splashed through tidal pools where small fish, bright as jewels, flashed among rainbow coral and undulating sea fern. We lifted the rocks to get at the live shells beneath, the prize discovery being the gorgeous sky-blue operculum hiding beneath the dullest of exteriors. But it was dangerous to become too absorbed, as the tide crept back with a swift stealth. A fossicking nun finding herself suddenly on an encroached island, and unable to swim, had drowned at Morgans Beach. Horrie was not able to understand why she hadn't taken off her enormous bloomers, tied the leg holes, blown them up and used them as water wings. We thought nothing of it at the time, but I don't feel proud of our ruthless garnering of sea spoils – witness now the stripped, dead reefs. It was limited only by how much we could carry, as Mary informed Gran:

> We need a packhorse to get up the cliff with the load – especially the big coral and many wonders we were not able to bring. I had to leave a magnificent teal one with a frilled mauve edge but the colours fade almost immediately you take them from the water.[19]

And after the coral cups were made and dispatched to sit on suburban mantle shelves, what to do with the shells, taken in glorious living sheen, their slugs cleaned out by ants under the poinciana tree? Since today they remain packed in cartons and wrapped in 1950s newspapers, we took them then with no other thought than that they were there for the taking.

~

In July a wire from Kim with the brief but poignant message 'Come Speediest' saw Mary on her way at once with Andy and Marie Rose. She found her brother haggard and hollow-eyed from waiting and obsessively scanning cloudless skies, his patience strained to the limit. The second anniversary of his arrival at Camballin had passed and he had not yet produced a crop. Drought had ravaged and reduced the country to the last shreds of life, the scraggy grey pindan and miniritchie scrub rising from the stony ground under a coppery sky. The campsite was basic but neat, with folding beds for visitors set up in tents alongside the caravan. On the evening breeze came the fierce stench of dead kangaroos. The waterholes dried to cracked mud, the poor, shy creatures had sought the shelter of the camp to die, crawling into extraordinary places in awkward attitudes, putting their heads under bags, pieces of tin, tank stands – anything to protect their eyes from the pitiless crows.

His itinerant labourers gone, in Kim's profound loneliness the ultimate atheist had found himself searching for God – and finding Him as he looked beyond the vast, cloudless firmament and starburst canopy of night to the boundless universe of cosmic mystery. Talking until dawn in exhausting marathons, explaining, justifying, rationalising, he tried to make sense of a situation where his scheme to grow rice seemed to be progressing fairly well until the awareness that there was nothing but work, and any vestige of 'living' or 'life' dried-up like the waterholes. Mary noted with trepidation that her brother was, like the country, down to the raw nerve of existence. Leaving Andy behind to keep him company for a spell, she hoped having a child about the place would keep the worst at bay.

A few weeks later, in the midst of the continuing drought, Broome was favoured with a relieving storm and soon green fields of new grass sprang up to offer a tiny corner of fertility in a desolate land. The scent of this bounty carried to bird communities more than a thousand miles away, and one day the sky was darkened and the air filled with the honking of hundreds – perhaps thousands – of magpie geese, refugees from their native feeding grounds in the Territory and along the Fitzroy River.[20] For more than fifty years, these birds had seldom been seen so far south, only two other such droughts recorded in the history of northern settlement.

Believing them to be legitimate wild game, many Broome residents took up their guns and shot them before it was realised they came under the provisions of the *Bird Protection Act*, introduced into the Western Australian Parliament by M.P. Durack. After that, they fed unmolested about the town, but not before Horrie had caught half a dozen in a net and caged them, with a view to fattening them up. It was a distressing sight to see the desperate geese battering their sleek-feathered bodies against the wire and becoming scrawnier by the day. Finally a bird was selected and slain, the carcass plucked and squeezed into the inadequate oven. But the flesh was bruised to a jelly and inedible. The others were released to join their fellows, whose long necks protruded like charred trees from the buffel grass around the town. They rose in a momentarily disturbed black and white commotion as Horrie's Wackett, with my nervous person aboard, vroomed overhead.

I was less keen on these aerial jaunts than my two fearless sisters, my natural sense of caution affronted by the insubstantial floorboards revealing the dwindling runway and earth below. As we flew above the azure sea, the pilot would turn a head encased in a leather flying helmet and point down at schools of circling sharks, causing me to concentrate fiercely on the back of his seat. Claustrophobic, I liked an unrestricted outlook, but not one with so little between it and me.

Trips beyond the town were always in the nature of a mystery tour, as Horrie never answered questions. We would head out through the low coastal scrub following the corrugated tyre ruts, until a turn-off signalled the destination: Cable, Riddell or Morgans beach, the old quarantine station, Gantheaume Point or Crab Creek – all stops greeted with equal joy. In the evening we took a run across the crusty salt marsh. Once the two spindly date palms marking the terminus of civilisation had dissolved in the heat haze, there was only the wreckage of a shot-down Japanese Zero to remind us of humankind's refining influence. Spinning along beside bounding kangaroos and racing emu, we turned back as the shafting rays filtered through our unsettled dust. A final stop for a beer at the Conti Hotel allowed us to go our own way, unsupervised.

Carefully negotiating the still unfilled wartime trenches where Andy once found a gold sovereign, we picked our way down the crumbling cliff and over the sand between the smashed bottles, rusted chains and anchors to the Roebuck Bay mangroves, the mud seething with the small motion of hermit crabs emerging to begin their night scavenge. Hauling one another aboard the tide-stranded luggers, we played pirate games and watched for a glimpse of the ghost in the Bishop's Palace on the hill, or a phantom flash from the broken warning light on Buccaneer Rock. We were drawn into gutted houses, relics of a past era seemingly of no further use or concern except to adventurous kids. What did we know then, as we tore about the glass-strewn concrete floors of Captain Ancel Gregory's derelict store, of how that intrepid character and his Japanese partner, Yasukichi Murakami, got their comeuppance from the town's established interests for daring to experiment with cultured pearls? That profitable gambit was a matter for the biggest snouts in the trough, not some maverick jumping the gun. Members of the Murakami family slipped back after the war, but Gregory and his partner were never to return.

Sighting the loping form of our West Indian friend Con Gill, escorted by his three goats, we joined him as far as our house, our high voices and his singsong lilt in a sort of harmonious exchange.

Once in a while we went to the Sun Picture Theatre in Chinatown. This creaky wood and iron structure, with its segregated seating for the Aboriginal and mixed-race communities, offered the locals a glimpse of the outside world and also provided a centre for informal pairings. The management was proud to assure customers that Sun Pictures would never show an R-rated movie. Considering the live show in their deckchairs, they didn't have to. Before a levee bank was built, the high tide brought the sea in over the steps to wash around the feet of patrons, who took off shoes and socks without taking their eyes from the screen or being deterred from any other activity. Otherwise, the town's main entertainment was provided by the Chinese gambling dens.

Chee fah was the most popular game, its intricacies designed for the Oriental mind. Twice a week a riddle was given out, with a ticket marked with printed symbols: fish, butterfly, turtle, spider, etc. The poser came in an enigmatic clue, such as 'quick thing now he go slow' or 'yellow leaf falling', and the answers, 'monkey on a string' or 'old man in his coffin', were equally puzzling. Con Gill kept us informed about the winners and losers. A roguish old remnant, full of sly observations and proud of his reputation among visiting journalists as Broome's most colourful character, Con had sufficiently schooled himself in the way of Chinese thinking to twice scoop the pool.

As he passed our house every evening, he would announce his approach by singing snatches of calypso songs, spiced with impromptu references to town gossip. The locals were somewhat wary of Con, believing him possessed of magical powers derived from his earrings, which had been put into his ears without any join in the circles of gold.[21] Hearing him, Mary would dart out with notebook and pen to jot down his rambling anecdotes of Broome's heydays and, recognising a writer of calibre, when talking to her he dropped the theatrical cackle, ragging and leg-pulls reserved for visitors. Recounting as many of the facts and ancient scandals as he could muster, he would struggle to get it right: 'Nooo, wait up, wait up a bit, I tell a lie', and that was surely an admittance from Con. His memories and character preserved, the old man also featured in a number of Mary Durack works and he is to be found as the central character of her unpublished novel 'The Calm Eye'. Other Broome identities were similarly fostered for their recollections of the past, the author crossing all borders without hesitation in her quest for material. She later maintained that by the 1950s, the epoch of marked economic disparity and clearly defined social strata topped by the pearling aristocracy had gone:

> *The present cosmopolitan population is a community in the true sense of the word, the permanent residents, however different their racial backgrounds being warmly united in the affection they bring to their town. Indeed as race relations become an increasingly important issue, the Broome community could well set an example to the world in mutual tolerance and understanding.*[22]

Had she been challenged to write a more discerning account of race relations in Broome, depending on the context, Mary could have risen to the task, but as it was, she preferred to take a positive line. While it is true that the 'colour bar' was less evident there than elsewhere, to deny its existence was just part of the utopian fantasy that she wrapped around a place she loved.

Apart from the racecourse, two tennis courts and a basketball court, the latter for which MMA had contributed the funds, there was little else in the way of local sporting facilities. It was Horrie's idea to mark out a golf course on Cable Beach, and he was to persist in this endeavour despite the tide daily claiming the 'greens'. His many golfing trophies testifying to his being something of a champion, my father was in fact an ace in many areas both acknowledged and unsung, with an ability to master almost anything he set his mind to. That he had survived the era of early flight confirmed his prowess as a pilot. Engines had always responded to his touch, 'knowing that all their problems were comprehensible to me',[23] and the revival of countless temperamental, wounded or pronounced-dead machines attested to his mechanical skill. Several of his inventions were patented and a lack of formal education did not deter him from trying his hand with some success, at short stories and personal memoirs. An affinity with animals, not including dogs, extended to an ability to tame wild creatures during long periods of lonely isolation in the bush – a theme he explored in the many fragmentary anecdotes intended for publication. Undeterred by his wife's not much enjoying the activity, he was a lively ballroom dancer, proficiency picked up as a young air force pilot in England during the First World War. With no patience for what he described as 'the shuffle shuffle ballsing around' of modern dancing, for him it was 'the long stride and whirl of legs and undies with the body sway of Bali-Hai. One dances with the mind, not the legs – they are only accessories to the dream.'[24]

And he was a great fisherman. Not only did he enjoy the exercise to the very roots of his being, but like our shell and coral collecting, it was the something-for-nothing rather than overpriced provisions from the shelves of Streeter & Male aspect of it that appealed. Every fish caught was one in the eye for the racketeer Sam Male and the meat mogul Derm Farrell.

Following the tide, he might cast a rod from the white sand of Cable Beach, or more dangerously from the Gothic rocks at Gantheaume Point, where the deep sea thundered angrily at its interrupted journey. He faced an open ocean that surged unbroken from the east coast of Africa. Naked escept for bathers rolled to his loins against the possibility of a snapping denizen of the deep rather than modesty or the fear of being observed, he was transformed into a primordial figure. Here, above the footprints of dinosaurs pressed into a molten Mesozoic slab, he hooked the big fish: barramundi, kingy, mackerel, and once a parrot fish, iridescently gorgeous but inedible.

'Deadly poisonous,' I told the others. 'You will die straight away if you touch it – if you even *smell* it you'll die.'

I will see my father forever standing in that fantastic setting, fearless against the surging sea, caught amid tremendous green and white curtains of spray. Could ordinary men with ordinary lives have conceived of such theatrically heady thrills as Horrie enjoyed on a daily basis?

When no breath of wind stirred and shreds of fog still lingered, dawn was the time to catch the silver and yellow skipjack and tailor running out with the tide. It was a fifteen-minute walk to the end of the jetty snaking out into the bay. Under our tread, the trembling boards made a hollow resonance, and between the cracks the grey mud and then the sea came and went. Occasional vibrations coming the other way heralded the appearance of someone to be greeted with a casual 'g'day'. Otherwise, Horrie seldom spoke except to tersely admonish or command – 'Look where you are going', 'Leave that where you found it', 'Don't touch that', 'Get a move on' … Then it was a climb down two flights of steps to the dim, dank platform left slippery and treacherous by the recently departed sea. From here the outgoing pull caused the massive pylons to creak and groan as if from some arthritic complaint. Standing on boards green with algae, Horrie expertly baited the hook and cast the line, before almost instantly pulling it in, a dancing silver fish slicing the smooth, oily surface.

This day, from the edge of the landing, I sat idly paddling my legs in the cool swell.

'Don't sit there,' said Horrie sternly over his shoulder. 'Get your legs out of the water at once.'

From above came an echoed pounding of feet as the others played on the jetty, their squeals and shouts strangely amplified below. They scared the fish, Horrie said, and were usually banished to a safe distance, my presence tolerated only for its paltry use in delving for items from the smelly sugar bag.

Now I lay at full length across the slimy boards, gazing down through a broad crack. The tide had dropped away to the tips of my dabbling fingers, and in the translucent water I could see magnified fish darting and flashing between the pylons. Dreamily I watched the hypnotic movement, until suddenly all the fish vanished – and at once the depth was blotted out by a great shadow, dark as death. I could see the width of it, the impossible length as it passed, never breaking the surface yet closer than breath or heartbeat. Soundless and relentless, it passed and passed beneath my small body, turned in that humid air to ice. A slight shiver of the boards, then the water was free of it and the clear downward view restored.

Fearfully I raised my head to scan the ocean beyond, but there was only the calm blue expanse and a white-sailed lugger hefting into view around the bay. Rearing up, I looked at my father who, in the act of re-baiting the hook, seemed to have noticed nothing. For a long time I sat, knees pulled up, occupying the smallest space, trembling in an atmosphere turned foul with menace from the nether region.

Six skippies in the bag, enough for breakfast, and we were making our way back down the jetty. Silently, I trudged behind. Several attempts to speak had failed, and now I would never speak of it, for the message of existent perils known already to Horrie had been for me – the drama queen.

~

With the flowering of the poinciana, the year was drawing to a close. As inky monsoonal clouds gathered and it seemed that at last the long dry might be broken, heavy-hearted we were packing for return to Perth. Our brief season of truancy was at an end, and although we would return over the years, the parting of ways from so much would be forever. For me, the pain of departure was eased only by the prospect of a renewed acquaintance with books, ballet lessons and radio serials.

While my mother was probably as happy then as she had ever been, the episode had confirmed the exchanging of the city for the outback to be an unrealistic proposition. The guarantee from Constable come through, she knew the weighty task to be confronted. Sadly, she put away the Broome material, the 'Calm Eye' manuscript tied up with string for another day. The shape of the marriage set and any chance of long-term togetherness dependent on maintaining a distance from Horrie, she wrote a gentle epitaph to the relationship:

> *Little left to ask of each other though much we will never know –*
> *of what lies between us as quietly as the shade between two trees –*
> *a tranquil covering of complicated roots*
> *seeking in the same soil their different nourishments.*
> *So much unspoken*
> *casual observations on our separate ways*
> *distilled for safe consumption –*
> *Comings and goings sudden and unimpassioned*
> *and long partings for time and reason now seldom specified*
> *but sufficient at least for two ways of life between which the bond fell*
> *too slackly for tension –*
> *for there is kindness between us beyond charity*
> *and that loose bond is too strong for breaking.*[25]

Horrie saw us off with the usual mixture of relief and maudlin regret. After countless treks and backbreaking lone toil, he had been forced to accept that any future for Dampier Downs was contingent upon finding a partner, preferably someone young and energetic who could live on the property. In light of the financial backing he was prepared to inject, locating the right man was proving unexpectedly difficult. Although he deemed himself the owner and no-one ever suggested otherwise, he still held only an option on the lease. Perhaps he mused some joining of forces with Kim's rice project. Or, in the interests of modern station management, would the purchase of a helicopter make a difference?

A few weeks alone and the old melancholy began to set in. He knew his wife would not reconsider settling permanently in the north, and contemplating the encumbrances that came with her, he was not certain that he wanted her to. Although few of 'the Duracks', as he was wont to lump the distaff relatives, found favour with him, there was an exception. His wife's attractive cousin Kathleen McArthur, who had once travelled with him on an overland trip from Perth to Broome and who he had heard was separated from her husband – now, there was a fine type of woman who might be open to a pioneering venture! And so the letter went off inviting Kath to visit him:

> *I would like you to come out and see the lovely country of which I am Lord and Master but which I feel regards me as an insect which time will soon resolve into some of its dust.*

Horrie was more than capable of underhand action if he thought he could get away with it, and expanding upon the reason for his lonely state he must have thought he was fairly safe, perhaps not aware of the close bond that had formed between the cousins over the writing of the family history:

> *Mary ... has a kind of retinue of people who are doing or about to do something in a big way for the natives, or the kindergarten or the school, or are writing a book or a play, a round of visitors who sit and mumble on for hours. Then with the continuous demands of the offspring, one becomes completely sunk in the ducking and dodging of domestic life ...*[26]

Clinging to his solitary and abandoned self-image, Horrie bypassed his extraordinary good fortune in having such a wife, such a family, such freedom and means of movement and adventure – none of that fitting the picture.

The unanswered letter, which would eventually come to my hands, was far from the last evidence of behind-the-scenes treachery that would home to the last person in the world who needed to see it.

Notwithstanding my jaundiced view of my father, I have always taken into account the fact that he was a product of his neglected upbringing, and what he achieved earned him a rightful place in the history of pioneering aviation. With this in mind when writing of him, I have throughout allowed him a cloth to cover himself, and the above letter quoted from has been censored.

~

Gran, meeting her skinny, berry-brown grandchildren at the airport, could see we had come back to civilisation none too soon. Back with us came little pieces of Paradise Lost: the branch of poinciana blooms incongruously drooping in Mildew's lounge room, pungent cartons of shells and coral cups, boxes of mangoes, rocks from Cable Beach. Taking one look at our clothes and shoes, Gran bundled them straight into the rubbish bin.

CHAPTER 4

DIVERSIONS AND DEVIATIONS (1953–1956)

Rested and restored by the Broome interlude, with the children back to school and heartened by the enthusiasm emanating from Constable, Mary began work on the family opus. Painstakingly assembling details of the 1867 trek from Goulburn to Western Queensland, she anticipated a journey taking many more months to cover by typewriter than by horse and buggy. For assistance from the Irish end, she would rely on her Uncle Dermot, the one remaining son of Patsy Durack, who had 'gone home' to Dublin after retiring from his post as a professor of mathematics at the Allahabad University. Sacrifices had been made by the older Durack brothers to rescue the youngest from a rough life in the saddle, but in the final analysis it could not be said that Dermot had enjoyed a better life. After meeting his nieces during a 1936 trip to Ireland, the lonely, fusty old scholar remained fondly close to them, especially Mary, for whom he formed unbounded admiration. In need of useful employment, he was delighted to be assigned the task of digging into old records in search of Durack origins for the book he would sadly not live to see. Dermot's capability and willingness had been a stroke of luck for the author, as had the participation of a generous relative in Queensland.

Kathleen McArthur, who lived in Caloundra, was a talented artist, writer and conservationist, activities in addition to her being a single mother to three children, and consequently the gift of her time to an external project was a noble one. In search of information and the last of old memories, Kath had from the start struck problems with the emergence of a longstanding family feud, the sort of rattling skeleton that Mary abhorred.

The dispute that had split the Queensland and Western Australian branches since 1895 had arisen over Kimberley land owned by Kath's grandfather, Michael ('Stumpy Michael') Durack, the brother of Patsy Durack. In the wash-up of debts following Michael's death, his northern station had been acquired for one pound over the mortgage by a cousin, M.J. ('Long Michael') Durack, who had shown himself adept at the fast footwork and flexible ethics required to make a quick profit. Among the ten children of the consequently impoverished widow, there was plenty of scope for bitterness and hostility towards the Western Australian Duracks for their continued congress with M.J. – enough to justify their refusal to cooperate with a history as might be written by one of that branch.

It was perplexing that the aggrieved parties would not have welcomed a chance to set the record straight, until the real difficulty emerged: the loss in the 1890s land crash of Durack assets worth half a million pounds had largely resulted from reckless speculation on the part of Stumpy Michael, and there was a fear that he would be shown in a bad light. This remained an obstacle for some years until Mary's diplomatic advice:

> *Your aunts need not be worried as your grandfather emerges as a wonderful character with extraordinary endurance and powers of leadership. Blow the business failures – they were in very good company – half of Qld went down.*[1]

She was more concerned about how she might tactfully disabuse the descendants of Jerry Brice Durack of their conviction that their father had accompanied the overland cattle drive. Or how to deal with the thorny subject of the casual 'picking up' of Aboriginal children to raise for station labour. 'I suppose we can't sit in judgment,' she wrote, 'no-one in the old days would have suggested blacks had human rights.'[2]

The Queensland quarrel had been only one of diverse pockets of resistance. A number of family members had been dismayed to learn, thanks to Uncle Dermot's investigations, that a cherished belief in their French origins (so much classier than bog-Irish) was discredited, along with their valued 'Du Rack' family crest supplied for a fee in 1908 by the Armorial General of the Paris Archives Royales.

~

In February 1953, to celebrate her fortieth birthday, Mary held a party at Mildew. Among family and the perennial guests, Ernestine Hill was there with her son Bob, who had brought the projector and screen to show colour slides in the courtyard. Pictures of the Miller family in Broome and Camballin and Ernestine's carpets of everlastings brought forth oohs and aahs from the company, for whom such entertainment represented having the time of their lives. Paying a first visit, the eminent ophthalmologist Professor Ida Mann, clad in a striking cheongsam, added her lively input and tales from a peripatetic life to the receptive assembly. Guided to a chair, and happy just to imagine the glories of the Kodachrome process, was our blind friend Nessie Kidson.

Mr and Mrs Kidson had been neighbours when M.P. Durack and his family were resident at 263 Adelaide Terrace, and their daughter, Nessie, a devotee of literature and things mystic, had formed a friendship with the adolescent Mary Durack. In 1931, at the invitation of M.P. and Bess, she had travelled by ship to Wyndham as a chaperone to their seventeen-year-old daughter before spending two weeks at Argyle Station, an event that would remain the highlight of her life. The only part she had not liked was every aspect of the brutal cattle industry. A few years later, in the process of an operation for a sinus problem, the bridge of her nose had collapsed and she woke from the anaesthetic to total blindness. She became my godmother, and once a week for as long as I could remember she paid us a visit to nostalgically recall the happy Adelaide Terrace days, the halcyon interlude in the north and her occult encounters. But she suffered greatly, and when word got around that a renowned London clinician was in Perth, Mary had consulted her on Nessie's behalf. In this instance, Professor Mann could do no more than alleviate the pain by replacing the dead eyes with artificial ones.

It was evident from their first meeting that the writer and the scientist were kindred spirits. Retaining for professional purposes her original surname, Ida Mann had come to Perth in 1949 with her ailing husband, the renowned cancer researcher Professor William Gye. When hopes that a change of climate might prolong his life came to an end three years later, Ida stayed on to purchase a house near ours and open a practice. In the intervals between her busy Australian and world travels she became absorbed into our lives.

With increasing demands upon her time, Mary had finally bowed to the necessity of employing a domestic. Katerina Boda and her husband John, refugees from Hungary, had carried with them the tragedy of a family wipe-out at the hands of the Nazis. Her light blue eyes clear as glass marbles, 'Bodie' had somehow retained a face of shining innocence and, herself childless, a motherly heart that embraced without reservation the offspring of any household to which she became attached. She was also a fast and efficient worker, and Mary was relieved of at least some of the more basic chores.

European migrants were beginning to arrive in numbers sufficient to make their presence felt around the city, although Perth was far behind the Eastern States in industrial expansion and the large-scale schemes employing unskilled labour. Initially, finding work for the predominantly southern Italian intake had fallen to municipal authorities, immigration centres and consulates. Reading the advertisements calling for volunteers to employ the newcomers, Kim had thought they might be the answer to one of his perennial difficulties. Uncivilised conditions and the harsh climate having defeated the hardiest Australian employees, perhaps a comradely group of this robust peasant stock might succeed where others had failed. He imagined their cheerful weather-beaten faces, the willing toil, evenings around the camp with a few bottles of vino and voices raised in the folk songs of their homeland. Soliciting Bet to approach the Italian Consulate on his behalf, he began to learn Italian.

The opéra bouffe that ensued with the arrival of Romeo, Romano, Luigi and Leo exceeded Kim's wildest suppositions of what could possibly go wrong. To say the men 'went troppo' is probably the kindest interpretation of the breakdown in relations between an incompatible mix of southern and northern Italians shipped to Camballin. Even had they not been engaged in trying to kill one another, they were unable to adapt to a life without the sustaining factor of a recognisable community.

Bet, who had meanwhile met Dr Mario Giachetti at the otherwise ineffectual Italian Consulate, was immersing herself in wonderful Italian culture. Her previous romantic encounters not having included a gentleman of Latin temperament, it was to be an introduction to a foreign variety of melodrama. Despite a more settled life, financial pressures (always on the edge of drastic) drove her to take on anything that paid the bills. In consequence, she had never enjoyed real artistic freedom, and the 1950s found her painting murals on suburban walls and in local cafes, illustrating books and looking for commissioned work. Of necessity she would become adept at the bold advance on the world of industry and commerce in order to charmingly promote the idea of a 'series'. Using drawings of Miller and Clancy children as her exemplars, she also sought a market for children's portraits. Mounting regular exhibitions, she could but suffer Perth's limited art-buying circle and all the slings, arrows and downright affronts aimed at a woman artist without a sponsor or protector, who did not paint flower studies and orderly landscapes. Not that she was herself entirely helpless, as a Sydney art critic who gave her 1947 exhibition a bad review had found to his cost.[3] Unsatisfied by Paul Haeflinger's response when she had fronted him to protest his attempt to 'annihilate' her, with admirable tenacity she went after his reputation and his job. Always caught between the reality of what she saw and what would sell, she toned down the neglect seen everywhere among Aboriginal children, 'perking up and rounding out' to make presentable for general consumption the dwarfed, emaciated and fearful-eyed:

> *If I did actually draw the limbs of poor little Djingyerri or Barbara, would [the public] not be repulsed? Would it not defeat our purpose in presenting them in attractive form?*[4]

There is no available record of the number of copies produced of *The Kid*, a 1947 watercolour of an appealing Aboriginal girl holding a goat, but the original, sold to Loreto Convent, paid Perpetua's school fees. Bet's underlying disdain for those who demanded this trade-off would belie latter-day critics who dismissed her 'romanticised images'. Weary of trying to convey the complexities of a situation beyond the grasp of her potential customers, asserting she was only interested in using Aboriginal subjects for her own aesthetic and philosophical purposes, she would distance herself from proscribed motivations and maintain that the dictates of commerce justified her employment of 'whatever little artifices and the like useful to me'.[5]

When unable to journey to the far north, Bet sought inspiration closer to Perth in the mid west and Murchison regions: Paynes Find, Wiluna, Wubin – godforsaken places with nothing to paint, so she painted the nothingness, coming back with red desert in her brain. 'Studio work for me', she said, 'can never compare with work done hot and fast in the field.'[6]

Emerging from the wilderness at the end of 1951, the children away on holiday, Bet had for the first time experienced the luxury of returning to her own home. While not by any means the place she had envisioned in innumerable sketched designs, the new abode served her need for a combined working and living space. Apart from the connected bathroom and children's quarters, the building comprised a single long room, with the bed at one end and at the other, hidden behind folding Chinese screens, the kitchen. The furniture was utilitarian: cupboards, drawers and trestle tables, a cane lounge suite and, as a talking piece, uncomfortable chairs standing as a reminder of her father's experiment in putting crocodile skin to commercial purpose. On the walls, a constantly changing panorama of the latest work, and on permanent display a large oil of an Aboriginal group in the river, one of a number painted at Ivanhoe in 1947 that Bet would find hard to part with.

Each exhibition demanded another train of thought, another style, and the artist moved fast and with new trends. For many years before the roneo process became a reality, she saw some means of reproduction beyond the formal 'print' as being vital to a more profitable turnover of work. Almost every artistic medium – pencil, ink, wash, chalk, charcoal, pastel, watercolour, oil, tempera, earth pigments, collage, pastiche, gouache, splatter, swirl, dribble, mixed media and the later watercolour and dyeline (under which euphemistic art jargon she churned out touched-up prints) – had at some juncture been applied to every available outlet: book illustrations and jackets, posters, cards, murals, big pictures, little pictures, comic strips, panels, friezes, diptych, triptych …

Rather than the direct handout, Mary sometimes bought a picture from Bet to mingle with the many others on loan at Bellevue Avenue. Over the years, the purchased and the loaned became somewhat confused, most of them taken back for exhibition purposes or retrospectives, to be sold or absorbed into Bet's studio storage. Bet believed that the gesture of buying her work had been merely to save her feelings. This was probably true. Their arrangements kept private, there was a tacit understanding that anything that might assist her was condoned.

During the early 1950s, the sisters were, in appearance, distinctive. With a preference for plain, rather bluestocking outfits, apart from a variety of cotton print summer frocks, Mary favoured tailored skirts and blouses, matching jackets and comfortable footwear, her fine hair, always defying restraint, usually kept in place by a headscarf. Bet, still an ample-figured woman, went in for more feminine attire, boleros and artistically knotted shirts adding a bohemian touch. Her image an extension of her creative self, Bet would go to lengths to preserve a glamorous front. She did this with some cynicism, asking herself why she felt compelled to continue with 'the shabby, outworn formula of attraction, the platinum blonde hair, plucked eyebrows and painted nails'.[7] Not infrequently declaring she could shed the whole facade, in the end she had lacked the self-assurance to renounce her strongly established persona.

~

By April things were going awry for the family saga. The currents turning Mary from the task were of the order that, with minor variations, would plague her writing career. As she had predicted, the child artists of the Australian bush, since matured to young men of the urban fringes, were becoming a cause for anxiety. Florence Rutter having gone her soroptimist way, her 'co-author' would be left to deal with the backwash.[8]

A call from the Fremantle Prison superintendent informed Mary that an Aboriginal inmate had been producing some outstanding crayon and pastel drawings, examples of which the impressed staff had put up in the main office. Enquiries into Revel Cooper's background raised the Carrolup story, and someone had thought the information might be of interest to Mrs Miller.

Behind bars for manslaughter, Revel was found to be one of four former Carrolup artists in the prison. The others, incarcerated for trivial 'receiving liquor' charges, were released at their former benefactor's behest and lodgings found for them by Cyril Gare through his involvement with the administration of Allawah Grove, a community which provided a transition for Aboriginal people from outskirt camps to urban living; Cyril's position with MMA was only the salaried part of a life of good citizenship. Jobs were also arranged, and to raise funds and further advance their artistic endeavours an exhibition was organised. Accustomed as Mary had become to single-handedly planning shows for Bet, in this case the Aboriginal element added an extra level of complication and stress. She was grateful for the assistance of Bob Hill, who was as yet unemployed and at a loose end. Having found a billet nearby, Ernestine was assiduous with entreaties on behalf of her son, sure her dear friend, with her many connections, should be able to find a position befitting a young man experiencing problems between his wagon and the stars' hitching mechanism. To keep him further occupied, Mary suggested he paint Mildew, in the process – ever open to innovation – allowing herself to be persuaded into a black lounge-room ceiling that had a very lowering effect.

'Different,' mused Gran, 'like a coffin lid.'[9]

Her finances parlous, Mary had been forced to undertake cash assignments, despite Constable's expectation of a book by the end of the year. For the ABC she gave a series of talks on the Swan River Settlement and began work on a play about Governor Stirling's wife, Ellen. Most of the story already covered in the as yet unpublished manuscript 'Black Swan River', she had, with her usual optimism, supposed the task would be comparatively easy. Articles for *The West Australian* and *Walkabout* brought in a few pounds here and there, and the books rolling in for review were hard to refuse, even if the job was seldom thrown off with the facility imagined by the publishers who sent them.

Allowing herself to be partly, then wholly, distracted from the family saga, the author turned the CD&D files over to a keen university history student to shuffle through in search of material for his thesis on the WA cattle industry. So frequently was Geoffrey Bolton on the scene that Mary let him answer the phone on her behalf, a task which for him would pay off. When the caller identified himself as from a radio quiz and the question was answered with alacrity, given his huge delight we could not begrudge him taking the prize. The mental picture of the future esteemed professor and Australian of the Year surveying his lifetime supply of Lucifer matches and ten tins of Dulux paint while lying under a candlewick bedspread to the pastel shade of his choice, made it worth the loss to ourselves.

To a large extent, inasmuch as she had become bogged down in historical puzzles and missing dates, it had been the lack of enthusiasm from her family that had stymied Mary at the two-hundred page mark.

Gran worried about all the other things that would slide during the process, Horrie questioned who on earth would wade through such a tome, Bet felt her sister could best exploit her talent through the medium of the novel, and her cousin Eric Durack, keen to get the family story straight, had begun his own version by way of scribbling hoary anecdotes and scraps of information on the backs of envelopes.

~

Accepted as a writer of note on the local scene, at this stage of her career Mary Durack had not yet achieved wider renown. In some quarters, she was only associated with Aboriginal causes, to the point where, not altogether happily, she had assumed the mantle of authority on anything broadly pertaining to Aboriginal people and, in particular, citizenship rights. A decade of regular talks had made her voice familiar to Perth ABC radio listeners, and later as a regular guest on *The Women's Session* with Catherine King, the daughter of Sir Walter Murdoch. At the time customary in the public domain to identify women by the surname and initial of their consorts, other than for literary purposes Mary Durack was Mrs H.C. Miller, and as 'Mrs Miller' was she conventionally addressed by the butcher, the baker, the nuns and the neighbours. Notwithstanding her writing activities, she had a house, husband and family, and first and foremost she was therefore a housewife.

Among old Perth lineages, the Durack name was still recognised and respected, but no longer supported by vast properties and the main players gone, their pioneering history was fading from public memory. The question has sometimes arisen since: 'What was it like to grow up in such an illustrious family?' In reality, the Duracks were not widely known until Mary made them so, and not until the 1960s, when her children were in their teens, did she receive national acclaim. Prior to that, there was more kudos attached to our link with the founder of MMA. While we never knew the stability and comfort of standard parenting, we were acquainted with many notable personalities of the day and raised within a creative milieu. In all other respects, we trod the same path as our contemporaries, and our roots were put down in the grey sand of the 1950s.

Not one to toil in the interests of recovering lost ground, I had found it hard to return to the narrow convent routine and regular curriculum after the spree at the ragtime Broome state school. Abandoning religious belief, I consoled myself for my disenchantment by paying narrow attention during Christian doctrine lessons for evidence of specious dogma. As a result of this application, to the wonder of my mother, I frequently carried off the annual prize. Meanwhile, overcoming Horrie's safety measure, I discovered the detached wire at the back of the gramophone and put it back in place. Now the records turned over so longingly in their heavy albums could be played, and played they were, until the needles were blunt and the tracks worn to a scratchy vestige of their former clarity.

~

From my hectically untidy room, I listen in a state of groaning ennui to my mother on the telephone in the hall outside. She is talking to the grocer, who for decades rang to take a personal order, delivered to the kitchen table through the ever-open back door, the bill, to be paid at her convenience, tucked into the wooden box.

'A pound of sugar,' my mother is saying, 'a pound of butter, a dozen eggs, half a pound of bacon, a pound of rice, a packet of Weeties' – the list goes on in customary tedious procession. That done, a second northern order is under way for Horrie.

'What's good in the fruit line at the moment, Walter? Oh, alright then, I'll have a pound of plums and a pound of apricots …'

As my mother prepares dinner, Gran's carrying voice is accompanied by that of her constant pal, 'Freddie' Piesse, a tiny, bowed cricket of a woman whose finely turned ankle once attracted the attention of a rajah, among others, during her career as a turn-of-the-century chorus girl.

'Well, Mary, I must say we only went because we had heard people talking about it and saying it was such a good film, but we were thoroughly disgusted.'

'I felt like asking for my three and ninepence back,' pipes Freddie.

'Such a disappointment to see Vivien Leigh looking so drab and faded,' says Gran, 'and I don't call that sort of sordid story entertainment, it just gave me a headache.'

'Quite lewd in parts,' says Freddie, whose risqué previous made her a fitting critic. 'I felt positively unclean watching it!'

'When it came to a scene of …' – Gran's hesitation indicates the presence of little listening ears – 'well, Mary dear, we walked out. I just don't know what has happened to entertainment these days. It was the same with *Medea* that we saw at the Sunken Garden.'

'Well, Mother dear, that's not a new play, you know …'

'Whatever it was, when you put on a show where two little children are … S-L-A-U-G-H-T-E-R-E-D by their own mother and expect people to pay to see it … well, I don't know! And,' (that bringing to mind another poor show), 'Mr Carcery tells me there's no good news on the Freney oil front. I just don't understand it!'[10]

~

It is after midnight and I am wakened by the sound of Horrie rattling round in the drawer of the kitchen cabinet. My mother also hears the noise and emerges from her room.

'What are you looking for at this time of night, dear?'

'Just looking for a pencil, Mum, any old kind of a pencil. You'd think, wouldn't you, that there would have to be just one working pencil in the house of a famous writer?'

'Well, I don't know, there's usually one in this drawer [rattle rattle], will a pen do? You can use my pen, if you like.'

'No, I don't want to use your good pen – just any old kind of a pencil will do.'

'Here's one ... you can sharpen it.'

'No, that's an indelible pencil, I don't like those.'

'Well, here's a crayon – use that and goodnight!'

In the morning, there is a note written in red crayon under an empty milk bottle: 'Mum. Gone back to Broome. H.'

~

The problem of the ageing founder's unwillingness to accept retirement had been finally solved when a Broome-based post was contrived for him within the MMA company structure. 'Regional manager', as far as anyone could ascertain, called for meeting the aircraft, chatting to the pilots, chatting up the hostesses and departing with a swag of booty: mail, newspaper, his regular supply of 'perishables' and leftovers from the in-flight meals. Travelling to Perth only to attend company functions or buy a new vehicle, with a hint of cold weather he was off again within days, going as he came: unannounced. We had no clue to his return other than our mother's intuition that he might be about to descend. Although we knew nothing of it, his city visits over this period also involved a restructuring of his financial affairs.

Cagey concerning money matters, other than to declare himself 'stony broke', on the advice of Cyril Gare he had only reluctantly assented to a review of his assets. Investigation revealed that he had 231,000 fully paid ten-shilling shares in MMA worth 80,926 pounds, Commonwealth bonds to the tune of 2,000 pounds, a Nedlands residence valued at 8,000 pounds, two houses in Broome at 4,000 pounds, and 7,000 pounds in cash. Not then an inconsiderable sum, such holdings were likely to attract significant tax and, eventually, probate duty.

With this in mind, Miller Investments Pty Ltd was established, to allow transfer of capital to family members, while Horrie, as governing director, retained full control for life. Articles of association were drawn up and a share portfolio recommended. Cyril nominated as principal trustee, from this time, for a trifling fee, he would take on the very real onus of acting for the Miller family as accountant and secretary. He was to become an institution, always there and always available, his wisdom sought and decisions trusted. From the records, however, it is plain that his charter was considered a very broad one by Horrie, and his Quaker patience must have been exercised to the limit to deal with the tangled affairs that presented themselves for his solution. As the years passed, it was to become increasingly difficult for a trustee to oversee the diversion of funds to the disadvantage of all but one shareholder, and to regulate the bottomless financial pit represented by Horrie's hobby – Debesa Station.

~

Meanwhile, Bob Hill had acquired a paint spray gun with the idea of making wooden trays decorated with wildflower and fish stencils. These handy artefacts in various stages of completion soon spilled into the courtyard. Negotiating our bikes through the obstacle course, we grew used to Bob's mess, and my mother was easygoing about it. While, for discretionary purposes, officially living in a rented boathouse on the river foreshore, he had by now moved into the garage, since converted by Horrie into his quarters.

This was the state of affairs until overnight, without reason or definable cause, I became addicted to order. Hitherto it had been a matter of rummaging through jumbled piles of clothes and other belongings in a perpetual search for lost items, at night the accumulation on my bed dumped on the floor and in the morning thrown back onto the bed. If cleanliness was next to godliness, then it held no attraction for an atheist like me. Now, as if come to pass a curse on some scatterbrained Sleeping Beauty, there grew within me a new demon in the form of Gran's old axiom 'A place for everything and everything in its place'. Half my life would be dissipated in the pursuit of systemisation and classification and, later, as every solid aspect of it proved transient, in keeping an index of the vanishing contents. What had seemed at first to my critical mother a miraculous cure became instead a more malign complaint, especially as the tables were to be so intolerantly turned upon her down the years.

'Call this clean?' I am saying.

'Clean enough,' says my mother, 'for anyone except someone as obsessive as you.'

I began to notice the chaos surrounding Bob Hill with some disquiet. Multi-talented as he was – what with the art, the cello, the woodwork and the photography – to be so disorganised was surely not conducive to success. Otherwise, as he was witty, amiable and good-looking, I did not object to his presence. A willing hand when it came to household chores, he picked up the tea towel unbidden, changed fuses and defrosted the fridge. ('Aha! This calls for steam work.')

Bet was having trouble shaking off Mario Giachetti, who was proving a more demanding subject than she could have imagined when she took up her Italian studies. Locking every door of her house, she installed a 'guard dog' from the local pound and 'went bush' with the children. To the diversion of the Korwills, Giachetti was observed running past their place and up the hill to Bet's carrying a long ladder – evidently for the purpose of scaling the roof and entering the premises via the chimney. After a decent interval, the fugitive group returned, and Bet having decided that the best deterrent was another man about the house, we began to see a lot of Canny Rose, a member of a West Kimberley pastoralist family, before her old flame Dr Mick Cook again entered the picture. Kim was disapproving of that side of his sister which cared nothing for the damage done in the process of her tempestuous affairs, a sentiment he knew was shared by Mary, to whom he wrote:

> Perhaps it is not a case of what people do, but how they do it. Elizabeth's relationships appear somehow disreputable mainly on account of how they are handled without regard for the destruction that can so easily follow. We must keep our actions within bounds.[11]

But Bet's actions outside her burning creative centre were of small concern to her. Few, including her siblings, were ever to fully understand her lack of respect for any other aspect of herself. She *was* her work – without it, as she confessed to her sister, 'I am superfluous, loathsome. I could crawl under a rock and die.'[12]

~

Word had come from Constable that they considered *Keep Him My Country* 'one of the best first novels ever to pass through our hands'. With an early publishing date anticipated, Mary was spurred into an immediate review of the manuscript and improvements that had occurred to her in the interim. The result was an almost complete rewrite of a romantic drama set in an outback so swiftly passing that its capture became a labour of nostalgia for the author. A year later she would still be working on the last of several 'final drafts'.

Queries for the Queensland end having dried up, Kath McArthur realised that her cousin was more than merely flagging on the family opus; there was a good chance that, having lost the impetus, she had laid it aside indefinitely. Strapped as she was, she sent Mary an advance payment for the estimated cost of three copies of the published book. Immensely touched but uncertain of her ability to fulfil the contract, Mary put the cheque away. After she thanked Kath for the perhaps unwarranted faith in her, nine months would pass before their correspondence was resumed, and then only to exchange passing pleasantries. In keeping with an errant period, there are few letters to be found for the next two years. Only the intrepid minutiae of Gran's diary continue the thread, and from her point of view things generally seemed on the rise if not quite, as she was fond of saying, 'going ahead with a swing'.

Mary's book would soon be published. Bet had received a boost with the sale to the University of Western Australia of her *Cord to Alcheringa* set.[13] One of her pictures had been selected for placement in the Government House bedroom to be occupied by the royal couple on a forthcoming Perth visit; she was also working on a jacket design for *Keep Him My Country*; and a new method for reproducing her paintings was achieving promising results. Against a full hand of odds, Kim had brought in and bagged his first rice harvest. Kildurk had seen relieving rain, and Reg's prospects seemed a little brighter. The best news had been the oil strike at Exmouth Gulf, and Gran was convinced, as she had been for the past thirty-five years, that her significant parcel of Freney and WA Petroleum shares would soon see her family rolling merrily on oiled wheels.

~

On a warm January evening in 1954, Bellevue Avenue was surrounded by cars and lit up for a party. The gathering was to welcome Ida Mann home from the north – where her travelling clinic had been treating trachoma – and Enid Durack, who was on a break from the station. The past three years had been arduous for Enid as she and Reg struggled with the adversities and tribulations of life on Kildurk. Now with four children to support, Reg, who could not himself afford to pay for labour, was contemplating the prospect of leaving the station and taking wages as a stockman for some other concern – or so he informed Gran in the hope she might find the wherewithal to avert such a pass.

Out came the projector to show Ida's latest coloured slides, and the guests, all well known to one another, mingled with Miller, Clancy and Durack teenagers and capering pyjama-clad children.

Gran and her spry companion Freddie sat beside Flora Bunning, a prominent patroness of Perth art and music and one of a family of wealthy timber merchants. When it later came to light that a quantity of the product was being acquired from Asian rainforests, Flora would deplore the falling into disrepute of her once-respected name and the sight of Bunnings stores splashed with 'greenie' graffiti.

Lang Hancock was there with his wife Hope, who was within a few weeks of producing her first and only child. Lang's industrial wealth was then based on asbestos mining at Wittenoom Gorge, but his new ambition involved the unexploited iron ore he had detected, from aerial surveys, literally falling out of the mountains. The Hancocks were not regular visitors, as Horrie had taken a set against Lang, but Gran, who was close to Hope and her mother Anne Nicholas, had invited them.

The architect Margaret Pitt Morison had walked over from Hobbs Avenue with the Korwills and John Wheeldon, later senator, who was being groomed for political stardom by Marianne Korwill – a situation stoically endured by her husband Ferry.

Bet, beautiful in a new green gown that complemented her hazel eyes, had arrived with her children and her latest gentleman friend. She did not wholeheartedly subscribe to her sister's party favourites just because they were always there, but she was much admired by them and, greeted effusively, was charming in return. Easily bored, she could take or leave social occasions ('my interest peaks with the arrival of the food and rapidly declines from that point'). She had little need for friends beyond the immediate family and the circle established by her sister, and outside acquaintances were for the most part actively cultivated only if she considered them useful. Her warning, 'Mary, you must keep people at arm's length or they will kill you', fell on ears, at best, hard of hearing. She could with a swift thumbnail sketch demolish anyone who crossed her path, including, without compunction, those held dear by her sister. Absorbed by her artist's eye, she disposed of Ernestine Hill as 'a little scorched-up leaf', and Henrietta Drake-Brockman as 'Nicely dressed, clear, fair skin, well done hair, hands that have done no hard work – a numbskull, not even likable like the average nitwit'.[14] Before the gathering broke up after midnight, there was some excitement among the children, not gone to bed as ordered, who had spotted the now near-suicidal Mario Giachetti darting along the lane outside.

~

In October, permission having been obtained from the bishop, who found some Catholic proviso allowing for the overlooking of recognised evils in the name of charity, Mildew became, at the request of the nuns, the venue for a 'gambling night' to raise funds for a leper colony on an island off Queensland. The guest list, with a few variations, was much as it had been for the January do and others in the interim. Mary's parties were unlike the run-of-the-mill, and invitations, for which prior engagements were cancelled, eagerly accepted. Although she believed that the most improbable people could find interests in common, she was nevertheless careful to avoid indigestible concoctions of the mundane – an assembly over which Gran reigned supreme – and the intelligentsia or the politically opposed. Literary friends required separate affairs.

The backyard casino raised a respectable sum for the lepers, a cause, while for most of the company happily remote, undeniably worthy. Nessie Kidson won a box of chocolates and the chook raffle. 'Blind luck,' chortled Bob Hill, whose infectious laugh and terrible quips jollied all proceedings. It was a typical Mildew turnout of the sort that had rendered Horrie a permanent refugee. The wonder of it to me, even now, is that my mother genuinely revelled in being sociable. The hard work and expense involved must have always been worth it, as for fifty years the lights went on, cars gathered and the neighbours said, 'The Millers are having another party.'

~

Worried by his many months of work on an unprofitable commodity, Mary made a concerted effort to find employment for Bob Hill, who had by his thirtieth year never held other than a few footling temporary jobs, and it was now or never. Ernestine had reservations about the position with the Perth Observatory, there being little opportunity for advancement without academic qualifications, but it was a start. Able to resume her wanderings, she departed happy in the knowledge that her son was earning a wage and within the safe haven of a family circle.

But there was an impediment to the arrangement. For reasons I could not fathom, Robin had taken exception to Bob's continued residence at the house. It was uncharacteristic of my generous sister and hard to believe her antagonism was on account of loyalty to her father, as Horrie did not particularly object to Bob. He had happily recruited him to draw up a plan for his rocket train monorail-across-the-Nullarbor idea and purchased several Hill trays for the Broome house. In hindsight, I realise that there were more than enough grounds for her objection, but as we were not then particularly confiding sisters she said nothing to me.

At the end of 1954, my mother told me, with contrived casualness, that she would be having another baby in five months. She asked me to tell the other girls. 'And Bob?' I asked. 'Yes, Bob too, if you would, dear.' Of course I knew. Entering her room one morning, I had seen the house guest going out the window, and my mind shied away from what seemed my mother's descent into some kind of French farce. And so, knowing as I did, I simply dismissed the possibility. In retrospect, what happened is plain enough.

Normal development stunted by a rootless, fatherless existence and an over-possessive mother, Bob's peculiar craving for a combination of the mother figure and the lover had converged on his benefactress, the only one, apart from Ernestine, convinced of his merit and potential. Perhaps Mary, at the age of forty-one, had succumbed as a consequence of the virtually celibate life circumstance had dictated for her. Or she had just been caught in a weak moment. Sympathetic to his plight, and ever vulnerable to manipulation, pity could move her in imprudent directions. And in this instance, once she had yielded, there was no going back.

Robin received the news in silent shock. From the window, I saw her confront the guilty party as she watered the garden. 'All I can say is ... why?' she exploded in a fury. It is a bad moment, and one difficult to recover from, when a parent is challenged by the censorious child. I knew that in this instance, it was not mine but Robin's reaction that my mother had feared. Nothing much disturbing her happy equilibrium, I have no memory of any particular response from Julie to the unexpected turn of events.

Over the washing-up that night, I offhandedly mentioned the coming event to Bob, who in his fright dropped and broke a plate.

Not then, or ever until the very last, was anything said that might discomfort her: no questions or insinuations. Not under circumstances of the worst imaginable row, and there were a few of those, could I have raised the subject of her indiscretion with my mother. What Bet thought about it remains a mystery. I have even supposed that she may not have known, but if she did (and how could she not have?) it must have given her quite a turn. She had always regarded Bob as a permanent adolescent who, for all his fooling about with paint and poetry, was no more than a likable ratbag. Predicaments of this sort not unfamiliar to her, it would have been utterly confounding that dear, sensible 'Mare' had fallen to such a folly, the worse for it not being in her sister's nature to avail herself of the practical means of extrication.

Apart from her natural revulsion for abortion, Mary felt she had to face up to the penalty dealt her, and while the too many children had hampered vital aspects of her life, she was possessed of a strong maternal instinct. If there was conjecture within the close circle, so solid was the wall of love and admiration surrounding her that no word of it got abroad. The very improbability of the thing was itself a protection. No-one, including Horrie, could have taken Bob Hill for other than one of the many to fall within the wide and often offbeat perimeter of her benevolence.

The next few months spent in a self-imposed retreat, my mother relied upon me for the politic fend-off and plausible excuse. Zealously taking up the role of sentinel, I advised relatives that as she was expecting a rather late-in-the-day addition, she needed peace and quiet.

Horrie's reaction just had to be toughed out. His own dereliction leaving him without a leg to stand on, he was placed in a tricky position. Discretion presented the wisest course and there were no accusations, no scenes – no more than a supposition that the matter would resolve itself. He also had a fairly shrewd idea of how the mischief was done and the ephemeral nature of the affair. That the child was accepted as another Miller was likely to have come about as the easiest course rather than something discussed between them.

Gran, informed when it became impossible to further delay, registered the news in her diary with the curt comment 'I don't feel happy about it.'[15]

~

The summer of 1955 brought an extended heatwave. 'Too hot to put my corsets on,' complained Gran, who moved her bedding arrangements to the front verandah, as did many Perth citizens in those carefree days. Accompanied by Robin, Julie and Perpetua, Horrie set out for Port Hedland to deliver a new company bus, while Bet flew up to camp with Kim at Camballin. With the novel completed and sent away and an unusual lull over the household, Mary began work on the *Kookanoo* children's series for ABC broadcast. Composing this story of an Aboriginal boy in witty verse was a pursuit she found relaxing, and there was the added bonus of an illustrating job for Bet if it went into book form.

Even though I possessed a natural aptitude for the task, a holiday spent turning away friends and neighbours did tend to pall, and since my mother was by this time moving towards re-establishing semblances of normalcy, I gladly accepted an invitation to spend a week at the Colebatch villa in Gooseberry Hill.

Despite the heat and the threat of bushfires, in Gordon's company I was in a seventh heaven of unaccustomed individual attention, my half-baked opinions on everything under the sun received with gratifying deference.

Gordon and I amused one another vastly and I can remember weeping with laughter as he rose to ever more extravagant heights of drollery.

'When people ask me if I have read such and such a book and I haven't,' he said, 'it puts me on a back foot rather. So now when they ask I say *certainly not* in tones of great outrage, and that puts *them* on the back foot.'

He may have been, as Bet labelled him, 'a slightly moth-eaten enfant terrible' but, perhaps as a consequence of my being so willing to appreciate him, he reciprocated in full measure, and that was all that was needed. While Astrid cooked and chored, he and I retreated with patrician indolence to the cool, stone-walled room, turned up the gramophone until the volume shook the glass droplets in the chandelier and submerged ourselves in a full repertoire of opera.

Nothing in my life before affected me as much as Gordon's death. At the end of that long, hot summer, he had gone out to fight a bushfire close to his house and was later found lying among the blackened and burning trees. His loss a devastating blow to his many devotees, no-one took it as badly as Horrie, who could never again bring himself to go near what he described as 'that stony bastion of memories'. For the first time, I came up hard against the unsalvagable nature of death. There was no way around this one, no backup plan, bargaining away or tackling the problem by another route. Where, if he was not at his home in the Hills, had he gone? Even as I grappled with the eternal dilemma, I knew he was nowhere but in my evocation, and still inhabiting his lofty Elysium, the reality, as he had predicted, long despoiled, he has continued to visit my dreams down the years.

~

The sixth Miller child was born after a slow journey to the hospital through almost impenetrable fog in the early hours of an autumn morning. Bob drove the car, crawling through the swirling haze while I urged him to hurry as the birth was imminent. We waited together until we heard that a boy had been safely delivered. No impolitic words were exchanged. If nothing was said, it was not so, but it was hard to ignore the awkward fact that the baby was of a different strain to the other Miller children. Whereas it was reasonable to suppose that Horrie had been responsible for the rest of us and that we were, although dissimilar, related, here was a cuckoo in the nest. Since she was determined to pursue a course of denial from first to last, my mother named the brown-eyed boy John, after Horrie's father, although she improved on the commonplace by calling him Johnson.

Thus, carefully cocooned in blandness from his name to his godparents, John was christened, with Cousin Eric and his wife Marjory Durack filling the requisite roles. On a permit from Robin to stay on the scene until the birth, Bob had now to prepare himself for exile. While another job, at a distance, was secured, for the next few weeks he hung about, fairly distraught and seemingly beyond making any rational decision.

~

Reading between the lines of letters from her son, Ernestine had detected something amiss in the west. A relative about to visit Perth was instructed to investigate.[16] The truth, as revealed by Bob, sent Ernestine into a state of near collapse. There was scarcely anyone she had admired and trusted more than 'dearest' Mary. Unable to write or by any means acknowledge what had occurred, she ceased all contact. One might have supposed that, given the circumstances and silence surrounding Bob's origin, she could have been broader minded.

As a journalist working for *Smith's Weekly*, the twenty-four-year-old Ernestine Hemmings had fallen under the spell of her powerful boss, Robert Clyde Packer, then a married man in his forties. The result of their liaison was her son Robert, who came to light after an expedient retreat to Tasmania, along with a story about a marriage to a man called Hill, a nevermore mentioned figment. Ernestine paid a heavy price for her, probably one and only, dalliance. She carried bravely the consequence of having allowed herself to be seduced by a philanderer and was consoled by her belief that fate had willed her someone of her own. And she was to loyally hold her tongue on the subject of R.C. Packer. There had been some support for the child and funds for his education at a private school until he was eleven and the death of the founder of the publishing dynasty. His widow had dealt with provision in the will for his 'secretary', and Ernestine and Bob, objects of speculation, were on their endless travels.[17] And so it was that the new Miller baby shared a grandfather with the future media mogul Kerry Packer.

Someone once called Ernestine's attention to a photograph in the *Women's Weekly* of the five-year-old John Miller, winningly outfitted in a cowboy hat, a lariat over his shoulder, posing with an Aboriginal stockman. 'The dear little chap,' she said sadly, before putting the magazine aside.[18] When in the 1960s she and Mary crossed paths a few times at the Adelaide Festival, she kept up an uncommunicative front. While not forcing a situation that Ernestine felt beyond forgiveness, Mary remained fond of her old friend, anxiously following news of her declining health and often recalling in her diary some aspect of the long, affectionate association.

~

By August, *Keep Him My Country* was in the bookshops and receiving laudatory reviews, with some comparisons made to *Coonardoo*, a similarly themed book by Katharine Susannah Prichard written some twenty-five years earlier. It was typical of Katharine's generosity that she herself would acknowledge in light of 'the inestimable value of authenticity' a vastly superior work.[19] An initial six thousand copies having sold out, a second edition was published within weeks and serialised by the *Sydney Morning Herald* and *The Countryman*. On receiving the first copy, Mary's feeling of accomplishment was overshadowed by her regret at the compromises that had been necessary to see it in print: decades of unique material, enough for three novels, condensed into one. She mourned characters that never made the distance and hoped they might yet be incorporated into short stories or a more factual account of the north as she had known it in the thirties. Similarly, she was loath to waste the laborious compilation of local history woven into the plot of the Broome novel, its resumption merely awaiting the completion of ABC commitments and the stack of books for review. She scarcely dared think further than that, as she informed Florence James, who wrote back kindly:

> For goodness sake if you don't feel like going back to the magnum opus and want to finish the novel, don't feel guilty about it. We are very anxious to have the first volume of the Durack story of course, but one can't always do these things to order ...[20]

There is little record of what Horrie thought of his wife's successful writing career, other than to privately wonder how much she was earning, but he conscientiously read and commented on her publications and passed on appreciative remarks from others. Taking for granted that her work was first-rate and compliments from him somewhat superfluous, he wrote to say he thought it a pity that the rights of such a fine book had gone to 'a Pommy publisher.'[21]

In return for favours extended to him by his sister, Reg offered to take a couple of unspecified Millers over the school holidays. A decision made to send me to Kildurk Station with my ten-year-old brother Andy, we travelled with boxes of perishables and a copy of the new book. As the central character had been based on her brother, Mary was not a little anxious about his reaction.

Our journey was a grim two-day marathon, Broome on this haul only halfway to the ultimate destination. Transported for the final leg in a chartered light aircraft, we set out from Wyndham at first light, flying low over the broad coils of the pink-tinged Ord, with its lush fringe of mirror-image trees. Clouds of white cockatoos rose in protest at our passing, slithering crocodiles submerged, a myriad of waterbirds briefly stirred their glassy reflections, and groups of dozy cattle broke and scattered beneath the wing.

My account of our visit has been preserved, two pages of neat Loreto handwriting covering the details that I knew would be of interest to my mother and grandmother. Moved from its original flood-prone location to higher ground, the homestead was no more than an open, crudely partitioned shed, with the furniture and Enid's piano sitting on a floor made from the flattened crust of an anthill. But thanks to some financial assistance from Gran, Reg's fortunes had improved. Chipper and fit, in his outback element, my rather homely uncle when got up in stockman's gear and well-worn hat assumed a gutsier guise as he niftily wheeled his horse around the cattle.

While we were made welcome, it was just unfortunate for me that the standard visitors' fare included those things to which I was most averse. Down at the site of the old station where we camped out for a night, an experience dear to my intrepid ancestors but new to me, no-one else seemed to notice the rivers of giant cockroaches crisscrossing the ground. Wrapped for protection in my swag, I sat up until dawn in the back of the truck. Reg was not too impressed. I could see him making critical judgements about his namby-pamby convent-schoolgirl niece.

In the Durack tradition of showing a tyro family member the ropes, he set about giving me a few lessons in the ways of the bush. When a half-dead horse was produced for me to ride, not only did it prove to be a safe mount but one that refused to take a single step. 'Get down, get down,' roared Reg. 'You have to show a horse who's boss right off!' And to demonstrate the point, he drove the baulking creature straight into a thorny shrub so that spikes tore at its cheeks and flanks. 'You see?' he said, turning it around to drive it back the other way. Yes, I saw alright!

But the worst torment for me was the business of the scrub bulls. A jaunt in any direction sooner or later brought us up against one of these alleged inferior breeders, and Reg had his rifle out at the double while I cowered on the floor of the jeep with my fingers in my ears. The scarred warriors never seemed more than mildly curious, turning their heads to watch the jeep being manoeuvred into a good position for the kill. Then the explosive percussion and the great brute down on its knees, blood pouring from its nose. With what awful apprehension did I await the sighting of each new victim, and with what sly amusement did Reg observe my shrinking reaction before deliberately taking aim and firing. He was reminded of foolish Nessie Kidson, years before, causing much hilarity by weeping at the spectacle of a bronco muster.

And with every passing day, what aspect of the pastoral industry made fitting holiday fun? Mustering? Earmarking? Crush branding? Spaying? It was hard for me to separate the allure of the outback from the reason for anyone being there: to produce dead meat from living flesh, in the process eliminating anything, however trifling, that stood in the way of the yearly 'turn off'. I did not, and do not, speak from the standpoint of a vegetarian but from a less defensible wish that my family had nothing to do with the production of the steak on my plate. In any case, it was clear that I was not cut from the right cloth. The irony was that if my Kildurk cousins were, then it was an inherency destined to be applied to city careers.

The nicely inscribed copy of the novel was not well received, Reg writing to his sister that the book had revived memories of incidents and characters that carried painful echoes and overtones. But he was glad that it had been favourably reviewed, as it made him feel better about his own 'possibly warped' reactions.[22]

Kim, an unhappy exile from the East Kimberley region, had also been deeply affected by the memories evoked: 'It made me wretchedly sad and depressed. Your book shocked me back into seeing. To no purpose I'm afraid for me. Having seen, I have no eyes to see again.'[23]

~

The lease on his riverside retreat terminated, Bob Hill pathetically pronounced himself 'homeless'. While he waited for confirmation of employment in Kalgoorlie, Mary made arrangements to depart for Broome with Marie Rose and the baby. Taking pity on the forlorn outcast, Gran, who had always been fond of both Ernestine and Bob, saw to his meals and gave him her spare bed. Determinedly clueless, she wondered how on earth he would get on without the support of the Miller family. Mary felt sorry for him, too, but she had also had enough. A poem she titled 'Dilettante' put the stamp of finis on the affair:

> *Here was an instrument for great playing*
> *And none dared scorn the pledge of its untried wood*
> *There was respect for doubt for he would know*
> *The day of decision, the time to turn*
> *And tighten the toyed strings*
> *But the years cast a pall of dust and a drift of dreaming*

You were the instrument for the wind's strumming
And that was all.

The same day she flew north, Bob left Perth. Back to a nomadic life, he married, had children, divorced and found someone else. Once in Adelaide he saw Mary in the street with other writers attending the festival. She had been kind enough, but he felt the distance between them – she now the famous author, he still the same ne'er-do-well.[24] He wrote to her often over the years, and at intervals received a sensible arm's-length reply. Although she filed all correspondence, Mary destroyed these letters from Bob, except for two that slipped through. One made perplexing reference to lasting remorse over bad behaviour towards Robin. Was it possible, I wondered, that an anxious mother had deflected an inappropriate fixation on her daughter? The other was a 'very terrible and upsetting' letter sent by Rene Foster, an Adelaide friend and erstwhile Ernestine Hill biographer, containing Bob's moving account of his mother's death: 'In the end they had to give her a needle to stop her strong heart.'[25]

I am saddened to imagine my mother diligently removing any reminders, but she must have believed it for the best. Why complicate life more than necessary when she was fairly confident she had got away with it? And to all intents and purposes, she had. Robin and I held our silence on the subject, with her and with each other. Horrie never to my knowledge raised a hair of it, and the other children were oblivious. Bob chose to believe that the relationship had nearly worked out and that Mary had seriously considered going away with him, as he had often begged her to do, just taking baby John and leaving the rest of us to fend for ourselves.[26]

We were old enough now, in the absence of parents, to no longer require outside accommodation or supervision, other than Gran's daily visit. Through the winter months of 1956 we saw ourselves to school, forwarded mail and looked after Andy and the pets. Left with a few blank cheques to cover expenses for the duration, we conscientiously spun them out while Robin carefully accounted for every penny. Other than in an emergency, we would not have thought of making a long-distance call, and all communication was by post. The distance between Perth and Broome, just as in earlier days between the city and the Kimberley stations, represented a psychological separation more remote than the actual mileage involved.

From Broome, Mary wrote to Kath McArthur, who had belatedly heard of the addition:

I am feeling tired to the bone of the eternal baby on the hip, the weight on the arm, the broken nights and the unavailing struggle for a moment to work and think. But I should be thankful that the little one is strong and beautiful. Thanks dear for your kind card and enthusiasm about the novel. It was merely a summary picture, deliberately curtailed and much blue-pencilling went on of what might be described as 'sensitivities.'[27]

It had been the advent of John, she explained, to blame for the unfinished family epic. Longing to get on with the Broome novel, she found 'six kids, no help and – as I now realise – not unfailing strength' had stalled that plan. Leaving open the question of what she intended to do next, the letter ended on a vaguely descriptive note:

The sound of the tide lapping through the mangroves, the sound of naked feet and soft voices passing outside. I love this place and see it as the world in miniature – all the races, the ideals, greed, intolerance and snobbery, all the kindness and love and warmth of mankind.

Taking a trip out to Camballin, she found Kim busy finding local markets for his rice, but, as he waited on various political concerns to be resolved, still cautious about expanding the project in any major way. Even so, the promise of eventual success having justified looking beyond the caravan to something more permanent, he had begun construction on an ambitious stone building surrounded by grand columns inspired by the Greek Parthenon. The battle, as Mary saw it, was that of the new agriculturalist versus established pastoralists. No-one was prepared for the looming collision between the idealist and big business.

The spell in Broome would produce no more than another in the series of Dampier song cycles, an article on citizenship rights and a catch-up on the mail. Physically and emotionally drained, Mary was content to occupy herself idling about the beaches, being mildly social, having philosophic discussions with Father Worms and enjoying a much lightened domestic role. An evening drive across Streeters Plain, a few beers at the Continental, a roast dinner, children put to bed, and the healing days drifted by in a pleasant dream.

She missed the passing songs of her friend Con Gill, who was the latest old-timer to be buried in the pioneer cemetery overlooking the bay. But one friend out and another in, there appeared on the doorstep a dashing young man in the form of Gerry Glaskin, an aspiring writer who received Horrie's standard brush-off with amiable aplomb.

~

For the purpose of buying a new car, Horrie accompanied his wife when she returned to Perth. The old Chevrolet long abandoned for more modern vehicles, his fancy had been taken by the rear-engine design and economical fuel consumption of a Volkswagen 'Beetle' sedan. Driving back to Broome with Robin and Andy squeezed in beside tractor parts, his journey came to an abrupt end when the vehicle rolled on a sand shoulder south of Port Hedland. It later emerged that Robin, who did not yet have a driver's licence, had actually been at the wheel, but nothing was said about this. During the three-hour wait for rescue, Robin had administered first aid and wisely kept her father immobile. She and Andy escaped with a few bruises, but Horrie's neck was broken and he spent weeks in a plaster brace, miserably moping about the house, looking, as Gran told him with sympathetic concern, 'like a walking corpse'.

His condition was not improved by news of a missing MMA Anson and, two weeks later, of the crashed aircraft located with no survivors.[28] Dolefully he informed Gran that dingoes had got to the bodies.

'Oh, you don't say! What a terrible thing,' said Gran, and on further contemplation of the horror: 'Why, it makes me feel quite fortunate.'

Knitting needles and other implements pushed under the heavy, itching plaster proving ineffective, a hacksaw finally solved Horrie's problem. The replacement a cardboard beer carton secured with an old necktie, consequently Horrie was never again able to turn his head, instead forced to swing his whole body around in a rather menacing manner. But he enjoyed the attention and the opportunity to buttonhole his wife's visitors with an account of the mishap that had been entirely due to the instability of the vehicle. He was also pleasantly surprised by the sudden metamorphosis of his three eldest daughters from scrappy kids to young women. We were off to drive-in theatres, listening to rock-and-roll, tying our hair in ponytails, flashing shapely legs in high-heeled shoes – and, less happily in the case of Julie and me, smoking.

Dull old Perth was brightening up. The more enterprising Italian migrants had opened coffee houses in the city, with espresso machines and gelato ice-cream. Bet painted a mural for the Della Marta cafe and began building a studio addition to her house to save on gallery costs. Her next exhibition would feature bright glimpses of Cottesloe Beach and yachts on the Swan River. Modest success had enabled her to buy a second-hand car, an acquisition opening up a previously undreamed-of freedom to move. Five years later, a station wagon would extend her ability to reach and capture the most godforsaken places on the map.

~

Held back by the pressing claims of an infant, during the next twelve months Mary could only complete the Ellen Stirling play, review books for *The Women's Session* and head appeals for community support towards Indigenous causes. The number of first-draft short stories and verses in the files over this period indicates scattered concentration and forestalled attempts. Her usual speaking engagements scaled down, there had been no escape from the yearly obligation to the Karrakatta Club. Largely wasted on well-upholstered, well-heeled Perth society ladies, 'The Aborigine in Australian Literature' was a first-rate dissertation that cost the author many hours of work and research and, as she dryly recorded, a new pair of shoes.

Ever-welcoming of overseas visitors, she held a party for James T. Farrell, the American author of *Studs Lonigan*, whose drunken Irish humour made him altogether more agreeable than his Pulitzer Prize–winning compatriot James Michener, the latter a big celebrity since the success of the musical composed from his *Tales of the South Pacific*. Bored with Perth, and abstemious throughout his visit, Michener had read magazines when seated in the rear of Horrie's Chevrolet for a local tour, while in the front his sophisticated New York Japanese wife was archly regaled by the driver: 'Is cherry-blossom time in Japan as good as they say?'

Although his sisters doted on the youngest family member, we noticed that our mother was indulging him in a way that she had not done with the rest of us. Remembering the firm stance taken with Marie Rose, I did not know what to think of her letting the child into her bed until he would not stay in his own. But he was a quaint little boy, quick to learn and amazing us with what we believed was his developing genius. Sociable, very aware of his disarming cuteness and ever-present, John was a different proposition to his elusive older brother Andy, who had become what his mother whimsically described as a member of the 'Cnaw' tribe. Initiated members, so went her premise, communicated their movements more by telepathy than telephone, but the occasional call and request 'Cnaw speak to …' – in this case, Andy – gave a hint to their tribal identity. She held that in their ability to move soundlessly and merge with the landscape, her son and his fellow nomads had taken on some of the characteristics of the original inhabitants of the area.

Bet's exhibition was opened on a humid March afternoon, with more than a hundred guests milling round her stylish home studio. Via a native garden, they entered through a black door emblazoned with the artist's dramatic white-painted signature. Innovative for the 1950s, the gallery walls were of red-brown vertical jarrah and white-painted exposed brick, lit by natural light from windows below the ceiling. Bet's daughter Perpetua, now an auburn-haired beauty, and her studious and reliable son Michael served the drinks and savouries. Gran, installed early with cronies Freddie and Mrs Shapcott, known as 'Shappy', tinkled the ice in her glass while proclaiming for the benefit of the assembly that she was sure the unusual weather was due to the latest atom bomb test. Her diary account of the day would end on a hopeful note: 'Bet does deserve success. The girl certainly is a trier.'[29] It was ever a disappointment to her that none of her hardworking and creative children could be declared 'in the money'. Considering that most of her Establishment friends and their families were comfortably off without having ever visibly exerted themselves, it seemed unfair.

Mary was pleased to meet up with the popular Perth actress Nita Pannell, and the two women sized one another up with a view to possible future usefulness. Nita was nourishing the idea of a dramatic monologue, and Mary had always been drawn towards writing for the stage. Both were for the moment otherwise occupied, but it was inevitable that their individual talents would one day converge.

Also among the guests, tall and tanned in his tropic whites, was the recently published writer Gerry Glaskin. By this time a regular at our social events, he was that rarest of living species and party assets then – as now – a very handsome bachelor. That he might also have been heterosexual was then – as now – too much to expect. A former stockbroker, he brought to the more illustrious business of being a novelist all the skills of his former profession. His first novel, *A World of Our Own*, had been surreptitiously passed among my classmates who fell for the limpid beauty of his photograph on the jacket and accordingly pressed me for invitations to events where he might be viewed.

Looking today at the line-up of G.M. Glaskin books, one can only conclude he was a recidivist author. But otherwise kind-hearted, good to his mother and savvy when it came to the business of marketing books, he was to remain on the FAW scene, between periods abroad, and in regular touch with Mary. Today he has become celebrated for his innovative foray into overtly homosexual literature.

Bet introduced the American Consul, Mr Winship, who had been deemed a person of sufficient clout to make the opening speech. The pictures were accessible: crayon, brushline, aquarelle and watercolour depictions of local scenes and some outstanding studies of shearers at work. If there had been reticence about Bet's representations of Aboriginal people ('well, they are very good, but you wouldn't really want one hanging on your wall') among Perth art buyers, then it might have been supposed that this showing offered less challenging motifs. Nevertheless, disappointingly, only three pictures sold on the first day. The mystery of what people would buy was ever for Bet a maddeningly hard nut to crack. She was to remain starved, not so much for praise, although that never went amiss, but for any indication from outside the family that her work was understood on a deeper level. She would also come to realise the limitations of the home studio other than as a viewing venue for interested parties between exhibitions in major galleries.

~

The year rolled by with renewed oil hopes, the Olympic Games in Melbourne and the theatrical breakthrough of Ray Lawler's *Summer of the Seventeenth Doll*, a play Gran felt, while clever, could have been improved with a happy ending. Gran enjoyed 'clever' entertainment, a commendatory adjective embracing many forms of amusement: acrobatics, Franquin the Hypnotist, Agatha Christie plots, songs by Noël Coward, films starring Cary Grant, Danny Kaye, Clifton Webb or Katharine Hepburn, and the picture of a dog on its hind legs wearing a top hat, tails and a monocle.

Family travel was constant and compulsive, the Duracks as a group seemingly mindful of Bet's dictum that to lose the power of movement was a form of death. On account of her being the only fixed element, Gran was assigned the position of 'Gran Central'. At her window seat in her upstairs study, from where it was still possible to see the river, she attended to the telephone, wrote letters and made a record of each precious day in her neat, minuscule hand:

> *Dec. 13. Listened in to the radio. Things in Hungary worse if anything, makes one wonder how it will end!*

~

A few weeks short of Christmas, travelling overland to Broome with Horrie, the Durack sisters set out on another joint adventure. Her older girls by now able to take over the household and little ones, Mary had accepted a commission to cover the journey for *The Countryman* – the main incentive being an agreement that the two-part feature would include illustrations by Elizabeth Durack. Recording her impressions along the way, she set to verse a typical dissertation from Bet:

> *Elizabeth says as the wheels turn the red miles under:*
> *'Why should I paint it like a landscape, I wonder?*
> *'"Red Hill at Sunset" – "White Gums Against Sky"?*
> *'There must be symbols more real to the heart than the eye.*
> *'These struggling branches and brave, scanty shoots;*
> *'These twisted, thirsty roots;*
> *'This carrion that brings*
> *'A baleful cluster of dark hovering wings;*
> *'This home of spinifex, supple-jacks,*
> *'Needlewood, lizard-lean blacks.*
> *'I must find symbols other than such things*
> *'To show why it is that my heart*
> *'Turns over when these red lands start*
> *'And something within me sings.'*

The journey had been a welcome break, but with her book royalties sporadic and no increase in her allowance since the birth of Marie Rose, Mary could not step off the treadmill of piecemeal work that produced the immediate payment.

On her return, her eye had been caught by a newspaper advertisement for a novel commodity that she thought might ease the problem of an inadequate house overrun by teenagers and only three bedrooms between the six. 'Genuine log cabins' were surprisingly cheap. The first one went up for Andy, complete with a rudimentary ceiling, straw mats, curtains and electric light. For some years serving a purpose, for the most part housing temporarily homeless Cnaws, when it proved too small and far from weatherproof, a stouter model was constructed further along the block. This was followed by another one for Marie Rose, shared with her many cages of semi-confined white mice. Later, the ex-house accommodation would include a substantial room for Julie and a workroom for the ever-encroached-upon author herself.

The FAW had been given a lift when Vincent Serventy took on the presidency. Full of gusto and fun ideas for the yearly 'Corroboree', the personable naturalist was such a windfall that it was inevitable Western Australia would eventually lose him to the Eastern States. Mary loved him and his wife Carol dearly, the connection kept up over the years in her frequent visits to Sydney and the Serventys' back to the west. Only Vin could have persuaded her to take on the vice-president's role, the prospect of working in tandem painless to both.

The void left by Jack Sorensen was occupied by a number of transient time-wasters until the entrance of Donald R. Stuart, who was to leave little room for anyone else. Born in 1913, the same year as the woman who would become his long-time supporter and promoter, after a decade in the outback as a jack-of-all-trades Donald had enlisted and served as a gunner in the Middle East and Java. Taken prisoner by the Japanese, he attributed his surviving the infamous Burma–Siam railway to a life already inured to hardship. On repatriation, reverting to an itinerant life marked by spells of prolific writing and short-term wives, he found work at Yandeyarra Station in the Pilbara region, where in 1946 the controversial trade union activist Don McLeod had helped organise the first strike of Aboriginal employees. Retiring to Perth with his million-word documentary novel of the dispute, much of it taken from the Aboriginal viewpoint, Donald was seized with the compulsion to read every word of it to someone who would not only appreciate his style but also assist him towards publication – and Mary Durack was his first choice.

Draft in hand, his quiet, gravelly voice followed her around the house, raised so that she might not miss a syllable through the bathroom door, paused for telephone calls, up the garden path to the letterbox and from the passenger seat as she drove to the shops. Unwary visitors were obligingly included in the performance, the very sound of his voice enough to send Gran's legs into reverse with unusual speed. Despite the daily incursion, recognising the merit of his work Mary did her utmost to find him a publisher. Meanwhile, his leathery visage, deep-set eyes and nutcracker-hard mouth had become as much a Mildew fixture as the lichen-mould spreading over the limestone foundations. His romance with a schoolteacher named Kathleen Anderson was generously shared with us, right through to the marriage, details of the honeymoon and subsequent expectations.

Ever-helpful with advice and the pulling of strings, Mary channelled hopefuls like Donald Stuart through to Florence James, where he joined a stream including Nene Gare, Tom Ronan, Gerry Glaskin, Bill Harney and Ida Mann. While Florence, tireless in her promotion of Australian writers to Constable and later from her position as literary agent for Richmond, Towers and Benson, would make discerning and pertinent comment on submitted manuscripts from an overseas publisher's point of view, Mary would sometimes question her personal taste. Florence did not care for Randolph Stow and could not 'get into' Patrick White, defeated by his 'turgid, self-conscious style'[30] – it was perhaps an understandable difficulty for the co-author (with Dymphna Cusack) of the banal *Come In Spinner*, although that novel, in its day, enjoyed considerably more popular success than Patrick White ever did.

Donald would ultimately find an Australian publisher for *Yandy*[31], his abridged rendition of the Aboriginal workers' strike, this first title followed by an impressive output of thirteen books before his death. No-one more suitable ever occurring to him, Mary launched every one of them.

Five years later, while on a round-Australia trip, the Stuarts were to meet up with the anthropologist Theodore ('Ted') Strehlow, to whom Donald's wife would defect. When the Aranda people of Central Australia ceremonially entrusted their sacred objects to Professor Strehlow, they knew nothing of white-man inheritance laws or Kathleen Anderson Stuart Strehlow, the eventual widow. Donald made sure we never missed a beat of that drama, too, or his subsequent marriage to Dawn Crabb.

CHAPTER 5

BACK ON TRACK (1957–1960)

Clearing her desk with the idea of resuming work on 'The Calm Eye', Mary discovered tucked at the back of a drawer the cheque sent three years before by Kath McArthur. Conscience-stricken, she remembered the amount had been an advance subscription for copies of the Durack family story, an unfulfilled act of faith. Reviewing the intervening years and seeing nothing but transitory effort and her own fatal inability to ward off irrelevant entanglements, she felt that even the novel took on the aspect of an indulgence. It was in this state that I found her, head in hands and tearful with the shock of the sudden return from her long mental and physical walkabout, already having decided that she would put aside all else until the task complete. My mother's self-restraint seldom allowed for tears, so it was apparent she had undergone some profound inner confrontation.

After informing Kath of her resolve, she hauled out the cartons of old documents and got down to work. As always starting with a complete revision, four weeks later she had overcome the previous impasse and found a title for her book from an ironic remark made by her grandfather in reference to his being dubbed a 'Cattle King'. Once this was hit upon, the disparate parts of *Kings in Grass Castles* seemed to come together in a workable form. Lists of queries to be answered and puzzles to be solved again winged their way to Queensland. Delving deeper among the documents salvaged from the company office, she discovered her grandfather's original station cashbook, a stock book and a bundle of his cheque butts that would enable her to reconstruct an inventory of goods purchased for the cattle trek. And she needed photographs so characters could be described. There was always the tendency, she explained, to build up a likeness of someone from letters and diaries, only to find they looked nothing like the figure of her imagination.

Once again Kath found herself trying to extract documents from relatives who, in their old age, had become possessive about things that should be family property. She also assured her cousin:

Do not worry about the time I give to you – it interests me so much. I have always had a rather pathetic desire to be useful to people I admire and you are writing to the ultimate glory of us all. I would do it just for the joy of your letters.[1]

Some photos, she reported, had been stuck too firmly for removal, so that the album had to be taken away and the aunts had little to do but anxiously await its return. They seemed unpersuaded by Mary's assurance that the images would be preserved for posterity, unlike so many gone to dispersals of deceased estates and bonfires. Another request for access to papers and a journal belonging to Stumpy Michael, inherited by one of his grandchildren, met a familiar response. Possibly having been 'got at' by the aunts, Ambrosine Wyles was wary, and her assistance came with many difficulties. Though these records were not essential to the book, the mere knowledge of their existence was sufficient to make them seem so. The author was experiencing what she herself admitted was

the awful greed of the historian – one wants everything. But what a thrill as forgotten stories unfold. But, this game could go on forever. One must draw the threads in some time.[2]

The last years of the story to be found in her father's diaries, begun in 1886 and continued until his death sixty-four years later, meant long hours working with a magnifying glass to decipher names and places from the spidery script, often penned at some remote camp by kerosene lamp.

The first draft sent off in June, an advance of one hundred pounds approved by Constable on receipt barely acknowledged the costs already incurred or the loss of income from other sources.

'No-one but the typist has read it,' Mary wrote to Kath on the eve of leaving for a month in Broome with the two youngest children, 'and I have no idea if it is any good.'[3] The typist was her close friend Marjorie Rees, whom she would acknowledge in the coming book as 'that indefatigable and always encouraging midwife of so many shaggy manuscripts of West Australian writers'.

~

Having finally accepted the impracticability of Dampier Downs, Horrie was now investigating the possibility of taking up the lease on Debesa, a station in the Fitzroy area with some established infrastructure. After her extended absence, he was glad to see his wife again. Lengthy spells on his own drew him via maudlin avenue to the slough of despond.

Travelling on to Camballin, Mary expected to find Kim buoyed by the visit of a party of businessmen and politicians who had been impressed by the small-scale achievement and favourably disposed to a larger commercial scheme. But to his mind, the optimism was premature, and he had been particularly disturbed by a feature in the *Daily News* proclaiming him 'Man of the Day'.[4] While Gran had been sure it meant that things would now go ahead with a swing, her son grimly predicted that emphasis on his pivotal role would not go down well with the financiers behind the venture. Work was proceeding on the 'Parthenon', its stone walls and columns rising from the wilderness like a strange mirage. Frank Rodriguez, a local stonemason employed on the construction, was living at the site with his family, and Mary thought the evidence of untidy domesticity improved the place. She worried that, at forty years of age, her brother was becoming an austere and distant figure to the outside world, and there seemed little hope of his ever finding a wife. Despite having won the first freehold grant for agriculture in the north, Kim was more than ever uneasy about the widely differing perceptions as to the purpose of the project. Holding fast to the principle of not being there to 'cook up' results for his partners but to establish the viability of extensive irrigated development, he knew that it had reached the stage with his backers where failure was not an option.

School holidays brought the eight members of the Miller family together in Broome for the first time in four years and, as it was so ordained, for the last. We did not stay long. Invited to a party at Liveringa, Robin, Julie and I were driven to the station by Uncle Kim, whose crop was growing on what had been their best sheep-grazing land. Judging from the gratified faces of owner-managers Pat and Kim Rose during this evening of music, dancing and youthful frivolity on the homestead verandah, their arduous pastoral epoch had all been worthwhile, which was just as well, because it was all coming to an end. The pioneers were looking for a way out.

Hurt that his girls had moved on so soon after arrival, Horrie felt further abandoned when his wife joined Ida Mann on her travelling eye clinic. Setting up a 'going concern' at Debesa seemed the only prospect to keep him occupied in his solitary old age.

Back in Broome, a letter awaiting her from Florence was Mary's first real indication of a positive outcome for her years of labour on the family saga:

> *I am so excited ... you've made a wonderful job of it. Once started I couldn't tear myself away, the story carried one along on a flood*

tide. The whole thing rings with the authority of meticulous research ... it's forceful and sinewy and there's not a spare ounce of fat on it.[5]

Much heartened by her friend's plaudits, Mary still held some private reservations about the judgement of Constable's reader, as she informed her Queensland cousin:

> I hate to say it, but I am afraid Florence is inclined to let sentiment rule the intellect. That dreadful thought entered my head when I got from her a couple of books for review about which she was unstinting in her praise but that I found about sub-magazine standard. I can only hope she has not made a terrible mistake about mine.[6]

A list of requests from the publisher for more historical background in the early chapters, fuller quotes from letters, additional financial details, an epilogue and an index calling for her immediate return to Perth, Horrie saw his wife's departure as a further indication of his redundancy in her life.

Faced with several more months buried in the past, she made up for her anticipated withdrawal by turning a birthday party for Marie Rose into a general invitation that included neighbours, friends and sundry relatives. The occasion served to precipitate her back into mundane suburbia via kids' pandemonium and Gran holding forth among the elderly component on such current topics as the Russian satellite ('whatever next!') and another let-down with the closure of the latest Freney oil bore. Attempting to abstract herself, Mary found sustained concentration impossible while beset by domestic affairs, visitors, the phone, FAW matters and an incontinent letterbox. Ricocheting mail would remain one of her constant irritations, and she protested the indecency of people who replied to more or less casual correspondence by return post.

Engagements on all levels and the conscientious patronising of both local and imported entertainment meant evenings at home were infrequent. Despite qualms about her gadabout nightlife and an apparently genuine desire for a less complicated social life, Mary was not to be entirely trusted on that score. Her outgoing disposition meant an equal and conflicting need for company, group activity or what Bet referred to as 'her insatiable appetite for more'. As much as she yearned for some remote hideout, when sanctuary was achieved, a good deal of its value would be squandered on this account.

Ida Mann, who was taking a weekly clinic at Busselton in the South West, had noticed an attractive bush block for sale at nearby Siesta Park. At sixty-six, Ida was a small, compact figure, with hair like the silver crest of a wise bird and boot-button dark eyes. Intolerant of muddlers, dunderheads and stick-in-the-muds, she was also down-to-earth, her realistic outlook emerging in provocative statements: 'All illness is either self-curing or terminal', 'Suffering ennobles neither the victim nor the onlookers', 'Sending food to the starving is both cruel and futile'. Ida was often to be seen wearing to effect saris, cheongsams and other exotic garb collected on her extensive travels, and her distinctive and distinguished presence raised the tone of any function. Running to a tight schedule of clinics, outback expeditions and world ophthalmologic conferences, between times she needed a holiday house in which to relax and unwind. Overlooking Geographe Bay, the wooded property had struck Mary as an ideal retreat for them both, since Ida seemed generously intent on a shared habitat. With admirable dispatch, the block was purchased and within a few months a dwelling constructed. The house stood in two sections divided by a covered walkway and incorporating modest facilities for guests, discouraging of too protracted a stay. Naming the property after some English connection, at the easy-to-miss road entrance Ida hung a sign indicating the turn-in for 'Adsett'. The electrical connection was erratic and water was hand-pumped from a tank by means of a constantly malfunctioning apparatus, so that 'the man' to fix it became an integral part of the rustic Adsett experience. There was no phone, no postal service or anything more intrusive than the sound of birdcall and gently breaking waves to disturb the peace. But as Mary arrived to set up her working area, in the back of the car along with the boxes of paraphernalia came the two-year-old Johnson, wheezing from his first asthma attack. A getaway a mere three hours from Perth achieved, escape from her last-born was a long way off.

Not yet confident about undertaking the overland trip on her own, in October Bet loaded her vehicle and herself aboard a state ship bound for Broome. Such caution short-lived, she would soon be setting out on marathon journeys across the continent, until that activity palled and she began to look beyond Australia. On this occasion, she had decided to try a northern exhibition to test the water there for buyers, an exercise, if Gran can be trusted, that was 'happy and successful'.[7] Longing to paint landscapes, her optimism that she would find ample subject matter at Camballin during a few weeks' stay with Kim was dashed when her brother's mounting crisis eliminated any chance of an artistic purpose. As the forces of perdition drew around him, she would be witness to the dramatic finale of the seven-year rice-growing venture.

In my Leaving year at the convent, I had in effect already left. Unlike my exemplary sister Robin, an obvious candidate for head girl, during the free periods that marked my thin academic portfolio I took full advantage of a newly acquired driver's licence and my mother's car parked in a street at the back of the school.

During the year, I had regularly attended a St Georges Terrace cottage in those days housing the local ABC radio station. Catherine King was pleased to include a less mature voice among her stable of broadcasters, and reviewing books aimed at the young adult market was an activity I continued after leaving school, the payment of five shillings per book a valued source of income. Bored with juvenile fare, I began selecting some of the latest publications sent to my mother, and she was glad enough to be relieved of them. Under pressure to take advantage of a university within walking distance, I embarked upon a part-time arts course, my studies including philosophy, a discipline I came to believe was some sort of academic practical joke. I never had a taste for anything not firmly grounded in date and fact, an apparent failing picked up with some anxiety by Uncle Kim, who wrote to my mother: 'Patsy has a good mind, but there is danger that she may lean too heavily on reason only to find it no haven of security and not as solid as she imagined.'[8] If he felt I lacked a flighty side, he need not have worried. Later in the year, Gran notes that I had apparently got myself engaged to a member of a visiting Spanish flamenco dance company.

~

A February 1958 headline in *The West Australian*, 'Durack ousted from key job at Liveringa', announced to the wider community what had been known to the family for some weeks. As a result of a cyclonic flood, the new Public Works Department (PWD) dam on the Fitzroy, essential to expanding the rice project, had collapsed within a month of its completion. Informing his associates in the Eastern States that increased planting was not feasible in the circumstances, Kim also advised that the team of contracted labourers sent up to do the work was no longer needed. In any case, the men had been foisted on him without any clear delineation of his own authority in regard to their management, so that he had been placed in an invidious position.

Alas for Kim's dogma of integrity: in the face of the dam disaster, reality and honesty were not the required policies. A glossy prospectus printed, investors had been brought in and Camballin pronounced through the press the new hope for the greening of the Kimberley. The drama captured in riveting letters from Bet, telegrams flew back and forth, until a solution was arrived at from the Sydney end. The stipulation had been not to actually plant five hundred acres before the end of January but merely to say that it could be done. Declining to go down this path, Kim was at once replaced by someone untroubled by such scruples, and thus would he unwittingly concede the field. To remove the man who had toiled those long years with the last of his youthful energy while living in a caravan – moreover a company director who had sunk every last penny of his salary into shares – some sleight-of-hand by his fellow directors was all that was needed. As from the start, in the end it was just business.

Gran was thrown into a terrific state of shock by the unexpected arrival of her son, who had called her from Guildford Airport with the incredible information that he and Northern Developments had terminated their association. Bringing nothing with him but a suitcase, he had thought at first, as did we all, that it was a difference of opinion that would soon be sorted out. Since his job description had never been clarified, the legalities of his dismissal would remain murky, and consequently the question of whether he had voluntarily resigned or been sacked would remain a moot point. He was not an employee of the company, nor officially the manager at Camballin, he *was* Camballin; it had just grown up around him, and his downfall had emerged from his making it a viable possibility. Countering public outcry on behalf of a widely perceived hero figure, his enemies soon found a suitably negative label for him. He was an 'obstructionist', and to make sure that he would be thwarted from ever again finding any door open, it was suggested by the sly word dropped in the right places that he was a possible security risk. There was no need to elaborate. In Menzies's Australia, the Red Menace lurked in the most unlikely places. Kim fought hard, but the struggle was to be a terrible one, for he fought blind.

Gran wrote:

> *The whole affair is knocking us all up. I don't think I've ever been so worried. It's a dreadful ordeal for Kim. How I do wish things would hurry in eventuating for him. The boy is broken-hearted.*[9]

For his own ratty reasons still resentful of Kim, Horrie distanced himself from the general outcry and hand-wringing over the affair – which is not to say that when it suited him he would pronounce upon those behind it – and in the way of ill winds, the now unemployed 'Parthenon' stonemason,

Frank Rodriguez, expressed interest in managing Debesa Station on a partnership basis.

~

Complications at home and on the part of the publisher having delayed the finalisation of *Kings in Grass Castles* until the end of 1959, the interim led the author down a familiar path. Re-reading the manuscript she could not but agonise at what she saw as the need for substantial editing, and she never really overcame the conviction that anything could be improved if scrapped and started again.

Now, with her three elder girls leaving school and boyfriends on the scene, the proceeds of her second advance payment went to refurbishing the 'new room' to make a place where they could entertain without taking over the entire house. And the door could be closed on the gramophone belting out an awful combination of Elvis and Wagner. She complained of the phone being constantly engaged, even though its relentless interruption was her primary bane. Fearing tidings of accident, illness or someone in dire need of her counsel, never taking my casual advice to 'just let it ring', more often than not she would find herself helplessly hooked on the line to Irene Greenwood or Donald Stuart, both quite impervious to our attacks on the doorbell and other false alarms. And then there was always the unforeseen.

In midwinter came a call from the prison official who had discovered the Carrolup artists among his inmates. He had another Aboriginal prisoner about to be released, with nowhere to go except back to the streets, and as he explained: 'This one is different. He reads books.' When Colin Johnson, bearing only a small parcel of clothes and a wary expression, was escorted to the door by a probation officer, Gran had a field day.

'But my dear girl,' she protested to her daughter, 'you can't think of having the boy stay – not with your girls in the house – and he looks such a … desperado.'

Physically bearing little evidence of Aboriginal heritage, indeed, he could have been a Mexican bandit or, had he chosen to go into the movies, one of those racially adaptable actors like Yul Brynner or Omar Sharif. Doubtfully inspecting the tall, thin nineteen-year-old clad in bodgie black, Gran was scarcely mollified when told that he would stay with us only until a better arrangement could be made, the concern being that he would otherwise drift back to the gangs and activities that had put him in jail.

Unlike the browbeaten (not always figuratively speaking) youths from Carrolup, Colin had an air of self-assurance. Remaining aloof and incommunicado, he accepted the hospitality of the house with lofty disdain.

No doubt tempted to abscond, he had stayed out of curiosity, and inevitably he was tamed. Hungrily scanning the bookcases, he unobtrusively drifted in the direction of the music from the renamed 'back room'. The Millers being articulate and opinionated, as argument erupted he was unable to resist entering the fray, and with liberal quotes from his wide reading he was soon expounding upon the world and life in general. We discovered our silent guest was, after all, voluble, and, as he scornfully revealed the flaws in our polemic, not a little arrogant.

Intrigued to find in this boy evidence of solidity and even ambition, so different from the others who had seemed to slip between her fingers like sand, Mary used her widespread influence to find him employment in Melbourne. 'I suppose,' she said as we saw his lonely figure away on the train, 'that's the last we'll ever hear of him.'

Within a week, she had received the first of his regular letters containing dutiful accounts of his circumstances. Gran was by now a firm fan:

> *Mary received a wonderful letter of appreciation from Colin Johnson. Not many young men could have written such a letter, he certainly is clever and deserves to get on well.*[10]

A few months later he informed us that he had a job while he studied for his Leaving exam and that by working in frenzied spells at night, he had managed to complete a novel, tentatively titled 'The Dispossessed'. Surprised enough to be reimbursed for the fare to Melbourne, Mary was delighted to have her judgement of Colin's intellect borne out. When the first chapters arrived in the post, after a quick edit she sent a draft to Florence, who assessed it as promising but still requiring a great deal of work. Despite the enormity of the task (the evidence of which is preserved in her archives) Mary would not begrudge the time spent in its production, as she wrote to Florence:

> *What a thrill if we could see this boy rise as a writer – the first articulate expression of the mixed-blood. No success that might ever come to me would give me as much satisfaction.*[11]

Colin Johnson's subsequent emergence upon the Australian literary scene and his rebirth as Mudrooroo is a well-known story. Mary did not live to see her discovery of an Aboriginal youth who had miraculously escaped the instability of the fringe dweller eventually 'outed' by an investigative journalist as being from an Irish and African-American background.[12] One of her positive stories, she would have been sorry to lose it as pieces of the puzzle fell so disappointingly into place. But she would have held his life no less worthy for the divulgence. To whatever extent Johnson genuinely believed himself to be of Noongar descent, or took advantage of Mary Durack's unquestioning acceptance that he was, he had during his youth suffered the common privations of Indigenous people in a racially marginalised country town and arguably merited their honorary adoption.

~

Constable must have wondered at times if they would ever see the Durack saga between covers; the original version begun in the early 1940s, the epic had been nearly twenty years in the pipeline. Seven years after the contract was signed, further months passed as additional material was unearthed, maps and photos assembled. But from her desk looking out through the peppermint trees to a serene and beautiful seascape, Mary was at last able to report to Florence that she was in sight of the end. Comfortably ensconced at Adsett, she and Ida were able to put in full working days before indulging in 'happy hour' libations, creative culinary concoctions and early nights. It seemed almost selfish to keep such a Shangri-la to themselves, and their resolve to hold the world at bay was already breaking down. Invitations to neighbours to join them for an evening meal soon extended to family, friends and other visitors, who came to stay for variable periods. Although for disciplined terms the two women did hold to productive solitude, it was inevitable that the intended concentrated writing environment would become enjoyably diluted. The twenty-year age difference of no moment, Mary and Ida were on the same page, wrote whimsical haikus to one another, shared their work and play, exchanged capricious Christmas presents – ever in harmony.

In the process of her research, going beyond the death of her grandfather in 1898, at which point she had decided to end the book, Mary had been troubled by the discovery of unedifying family financial dealings and the imprudence of the Durack partnership with Connor and Doherty, which she suspected had always weighted the pastoral enterprise towards failure. These would be difficult areas to cover frankly if she ever got round to a second volume. Firmly resisting the urge to enlarge upon the already comprehensive references, she fell instead for another enticement.

A request from James Penberthy that she provide a libretto for an opera meant putting aside the manuscript for a few weeks, but after two decades, the further delay seemed a minor diversion. Penberthy and his Russian-born dancer wife Kira Bousloff were the sort of exotics that Mary found irresistible. Instantly inspired by Mary's suggestion that she adapt for the purpose the Aboriginal love theme from her novel *Keep Him My Country*, James had written the music for *Dalgerie* in a few weeks. Having cleared the accumulated books from our out-of-tune piano, the composer gave us a taste of his genius. His long hair flying wildly, he pounded at the bass end to represent the sound of didgeridoos and bullroarers, and at the treble to illustrate the high-pitched wail of the Julunggul curse.

Gran, who had a propensity to get names wrong, especially if the person was disagreeable, did not really take to 'Mr Pickenson'. His composition was not music to her ears, and she complained that 'all conversation takes a depressing turn when he is there', which meant he was not interested in her memories of *Florodora* or how much she had enjoyed Gladys Moncrieff in *Rio Rita*.[13]

James had contacts with the Elizabethan Theatre Trust, and by mid-January 1959, arrangements were well advanced to stage the world premiere at the Somerville Auditorium, with *I Pagliacci* as a tried and true backup.

Dalgerie was a rare homegrown product that fell into the category for which the trust was formed and subsidised, and the motif suited an era when Aboriginal culture was being discovered and exploited by a diversity of artistic mediums. Certainly, there was nothing begun by John Antill that Penberthy did not feel he could improve upon.[14] Bet engaged to design the scenery, the project had soon developed into the kind of lunatic exercise that suited Mary down to the ground. Among his entourage, the director Stefan Haag had brought with him the mysterious person referred to by my grandmother as 'the dwarf woman with two big dogs and brittle bones who needed a lifesaving operation in Switzerland'. She seemed nebulously connected to the wardrobe and Haag's kindness.

With John Farnsworth Hall behind the baton, the West Australian Symphony Orchestra gamely tackled the difficult score, while the (all white) singers performed with mixed enthusiasm.

Described by one critic as 'an outback Madame Butterfly'[15], the show enjoyed a successful ten-day run, kind reviews and a complimentary leading article in *The West Australian*. It was wonderful how any enterprise gained credibility simply by the application of Mary Durack's name. Despite the predominant goodwill, certain relatives who had put in a loyal attendance were not uncritical. Eric Durack, speaking for the doubtfuls, announced tactfully that he thought it first-rate except for the music and the theme.

Dalgerie had been a detour for Mary but it was one she would remember. Thoroughly bitten by the theatrical bug, from now on if the ephemeral world of stage or film beckoned, she would answer the call. The season saw exhausting parties every night after the performance, not one of them missed by Gran, who was in her element among 'entertainers'. Even Kim emerged long enough from his terrible limbo to enjoy a brief dalliance with the soprano.

Ultimately, the troupe departed, enduring friendships made extending to the trust founder Nugget Coombs, but, alas for the hapless librettist, minus the little wardrobe lady. She was left behind, to become a colossal nuisance for Mary, who somehow found herself organising a public subscription to send the afflicted person to a Swiss clinic.

Believing the two men were made for each other, Mary introduced James Penberthy to Donald Stuart, and for some years they became bosom buddies, so that if she had one, she had both, often with wives. Then they quarrelled and never spoke to one another again.

~

The final draft of *Kings in Grass Castles* at last on its way to London, the author's uncertainty that she would ever get round to a second volume was covered by an epilogue summarising events up to the sale of the stations and her father's death. The book carried a dedication to the memory of her grandfather and, more poignantly, the success of her brother Kim's work towards the development of the Kimberley district. Meanwhile, with the helpful assistance of Gerry Glaskin, the boxes of source material taken from the office of CD&D were deposited with the State Archives for safekeeping and the interim use of other historians. There had been no formality about the arrangement. The Battye Library staff, most of them long-time associates, were well known to her.

Writing to Kath from Broome, Mary reported on Horrie's new preoccupation:

> Horrie looks fitter than he has for years. I put this down to his involvement in a pioneering sheep property outside Derby. He is the financial member of a partnership and drives up 200 miles every week from here. I don't expect he ever will get the money back of the thousands he has put into it, but it makes him happy and that is the main thing. Meanwhile I manage on the usual shoestring, very grateful for the odd royalties to pay off the bills. I don't resent the fact just as long as everybody is jogging along and not picking on me – nice and quiet with a party now and again.[16]

From the constraints of biography, Mary had often longed to get back to the world of her imagination, but attempts to continue with the Broome novel found it had gone cold. After the success of *Dalgerie*, she wondered if she should not concentrate more on radio drama and writing for the stage or, after years of turning out scripts on historical subjects, try more contemporary themes. On her return to Perth, she began devising a play inspired by news of the flight of the Dalai Lama, driven from Tibet by Chinese forces. While *The Dallying Lama* was a lighthearted approach to the quandaries faced by a fictional holy man, a good deal of research went into an accurate depiction of the Tibetan setting. The play, broadcast several times by the ABC, was picked up as far away as Kildurk, where her brother Reg managed to get a vague idea of the plot through the heavy static.

~

Reports from Kildurk during the year had been disappointing, the churlish bullocks not coming in well despite the price being the best for years.[17] Reading the latest letter from Reg, Gran informed us in a grieved voice that the mustered 'fats' had lost condition along the hard trek, and only 460 beasts had been delivered to the works. Her son was reporting on the dying days of the droving era. Within two years, he would be trucking his cattle to Wyndham.

From the frontline of the letters to the editor page in *The West Australian*, Kim was engaged in combat with the Minister for the North West in the newly elected Brand Government. Charles Court, hell-bent on gaining federal assistance for the Ord River Dam, was not interested in Kim's recommendation that there should be a comprehensive assessment of northern water resources before further wasteful spending on irrigation schemes.

Of more import to the Millers was whether or not we were going to join the hundreds of lucky people with aerials sprouting from their chimneys. Gran was still not sure whether television wasn't just a passing fad, although her idea of fine entertainment marked her for a certain devotee in the making. Not lacking discrimination, she had walked out on *Waiting for Godot* and given the thumbs down to the unamusing American crusader Billy Graham, whose show had attracted crowds that poured in 'like loquats'.[18]

Finally deciding to take a two-way bet, Mary consented to hire a set that could be returned if the novelty palled. Robin, who strongly disapproved of the time-wasting, rubbishy intrusion into a house of youngsters, already too idle in her opinion, did not alter her judgement when the set was purchased the following year. Horrie, equally scathing at first, was discovered one afternoon absorbed in black and white golf; for a sports fan, the potential was hard to deny. When in Perth, he did the rounds of cricket, football or whatever was in season and played golf at a variety of venues, catching up between times via a constantly blaring radio.

~

Mildew was its usual scrum. Reg, in Perth to buy a new truck, added two of his children to the Miller tribe while he stayed with Gran, who also had Kim. Grown apart after many years of disassociation, the brothers tried to find the common ground they had once shared, but there was tension over their competing claims on their mother's carefully managed savings. With his many dependants, Reg could not accept his case as less deserving of her consideration than his unemployed bachelor brother. Though the struggle to make a profitable concern of Kildurk would continue until the sale in 1973, not part of his reckoning were the compensations that came with the unstinting support of a good wife and five outstanding children, their education at private schools paying off with top places and prizes. Reg and Kim effectively occupied different planets, and this would be the last time they met.

Perhaps the strain of the situation became too much for Gran. Consternation spread outward in ever-widening ripples across the continent with the news she had suffered a 'nasty turn' that might have been a mild heart attack. Robin, now a trainee nurse at Royal Perth Hospital, was summoned to the bedside. From this time, there would never be a moment when Robin was not 'on call' for our family and relied upon for every medical matter. Horrie would have no treatment other than hers, and messages concerning his never-less-than-terminal ill health were relayed to her wherever she was and at whatever inconvenient moment. In this instance, she was reassuring as to Gran's chances of a rapid recovery. Family members, briefly gathered, were once again dispersed.

Losing interest in prescribed tertiary study, I went north to work as a governess on a Murchison sheep station. Kim packed up his meagre belongings and travelled to Canberra to put his case for the convening of a Northern Water Authority and plan to establish Kimberley water catchments to the prime minister. (Catching water was one thing, but catching Menzies between his leisurely world perambulations was going to prove another.)

Overlanding in a new Bedford truck, Reg and his children departed for Kildurk. Bet, with a three hundred pound commission from the lord mayor to paint fifty pictures of Perth and surrounds, was off to put a similar proposition to the Geraldton Road Board. The spectacular design of her *Black Swan Legend* murals, done the previous year for Sir Charles Gairdner

Hospital, had gained her considerable publicity. But with each assignment completed, there was always the taxing pursuit of the next and the anxious wait to hear if a contract had been approved.

Returning from the station, I brought with me a pair of piglets from a litter produced by a sow with poor maternal instincts. Over several nights standing guard to pull the slippery bodies out from under their rolling mother, I had taken such a personal interest in their survival that when I left, two 'at risk' weaklings also boarded the plane. Arthur and Martha, sporadically confined to an enclosure near the back fence, were welcomed into the hugger-mugger. On hot days I drove them to the beach for a swim, their trotters hanging out the open windows, eager snouts sniffing the breeze. We were quite a turn, me and the rapidly swelling pigs.

~

'Lord,' said Mary on receipt of the advance copy of *Kings in Grass Castles*, 'but it's a regular lump of a thing!' Surprised and delighted at the prominent bookshop window displays, she wondered if anyone would get through it or, at a cost of fifty-four shillings and sixpence, even buy it. Reviewed to high acclaim and serialised by the *Sydney Morning Herald*, the saga remained at the top of the bestseller list until the first edition sold out five weeks later. Prime Minister Menzies and the deputy leader, Shane Paltridge, sent copies for her autograph. 'You deserve full credit', wrote Horrie, who carried the book around with him and gave black marks to anyone who did not pass on heartfelt congratulations.

Kath McArthur expressed her joy:

> What a thrill to see how cleverly you have woven in and brought to life the dry bits of history scrounged up from this end. My involvement, so generously acknowledged with the lovely inscription, has never been anything but a privilege.[19]

In demand for press and radio interviews, the author, who had never imagined such attention, went into a mode of unaffected modesty, an irritating idiosyncrasy to me that went down a treat with the public. The Duracks were suddenly among the most famous pioneers in the country, and from this time, members of the family carried the lustre of association.

Already a twice-a-day exercise, the bulky mail blew out so that the post office had to make special deliveries. Rapturous readers sent telegrams of appreciation, and an avalanche of letters descended from strangers who had some firsthand memory of the Duracks or details of their own histories to add to the records; a number claimed to have been on the cattle trek. Overseas branches of the family also emerged and, in future years, came to visit. A press-cutting service was hired. Julie threw a party to celebrate family triumphs: the book, her Leaving exams over, Bet's son Michael achieving dux of St Louis School, and David, Reg's eldest, winning a bursary for his university studies. Sharing her mother's generous and outgoing personality, from this time Julie could be counted on to willingly participate in and contribute to the very considerable Mildew hospitality burden. Conversely, I am reported 'a reluctant hostess, prone to vanish at vital moments',[20] whatever they may have been.

A Christmas present of a 1960 diary inscribed in bold script 'to darling Mum with love from Julie' brought a regrettable omission to light. Having spent so many years documenting the lives of others, the author had neglected a formal record of her own, and in an affirmation of her return to a path that could be openly documented, she began the entries that would chart her every remaining day.

Keeping journals is a family condition, like the carpal tunnel syndrome affecting our hands. The first aide-mémoire, grown to an invidious habit, can extend over decades into dozens of books containing potentially explosive material. An intimate and detailed register also has the capacity to preserve, with dangerous immediacy, days that should have sunk into the bog of time with only the odd gaseous bubble to break the surface. The practice can interfere with the normal process of memory failure and its connective healing qualities, especially for those prone to harbouring grudges. Venturing into the time capsule of my own record, I can find myself fanning the embers or reminding myself never to speak to that particular person again. Over several decades, it is possible to examine the same event from the standpoint of Gran, my mother, Robin and myself. M.P. Durack kept a vigilant log, the front and back pages devoted to facts and figures: horse brands, cattle numbers, the speed of light and the time taken to walk from his Adelaide Terrace home to the city office. Circumspect when it came to painful or sensitive concerns, his anguish over news of his daughter Mary's marriage is reduced to a single sentence: 'Bess gives me a letter from Mary but I cannot bear to read it.'[21] Following a visit to the Kimberley station where an 'Air Beef' scheme was being established, his final entry of six decades is typically pedestrian:

> *Glenroy store pigs when killed about first week in August dressed 147 lbs and classed 100% for export. Caught 11.30am plane into Wyndham, flight 1 hour 20 minutes. Put up at Six Mile Hotel.*[22]

The first lines of what for Mary would become a daily discipline of thirty years also begin typically:

> Donald Stuart and John Joseph Jones here to discuss the Fellowship reading. Dinner with Paul and Alix Hasluck. Present Henrietta and Geoff Drake-Brockman, Gerry Glaskin, Mr and Mrs Sholl. Gerry, Eric Sholl (ABC) and self discussing the possibility of a radio forum – full of bright ideas. Alix and I autograph books for each other.[23]

The pages untidily bristling with press cuttings, photos, postcards, invitations, obituaries, letters and other material illustrating the text, her activities are played out against the backdrop of valiantly interpreted world and local affairs. It is evident that she wrote with an eye to history, since, supposing they would be transient, she reserves for letters franker comments on personalities or touchy subjects – airbrushed for the eternal record.

Robin emerges strongly from the fourteen years she kept a record of her crowded days as pilot and nurse for the RFDS. Pitting her wits and courage against a multiplicity of ground and aerial hazards, she is attending 'MVAs', packing a severed hand in ice, pumping a drowned child's chest, pulling stakes from eyes and loading aboard 'broken ribs, spine and a nut case'. Interspersed with momentous feats of courage and indicative of her having little time to eat properly, she never fails to list the full menu of a good meal. Entries jotted in transit evident in the undulating lines caused by midair turbulence, every page somehow carries an imprint of the moment, a smudge of dust or the faint smell of avgas. Her diaries make for enthralling and often awe-inspiring reading, and it is difficult to comprehend, unless one travels with her page by page, just what Robin did and the difference she made to so many. Two books compiled from her journals hardly touch the extent of her capable passage through a range of dramas on any tour of duty.[24]

My uncensored and uninhibited diaries, in a variety of hands according to the mood of the moment, fall into a different category altogether. Classified information and the sort of thing 'best forgotten' carefully noted, they supply the detail missing from my mother's more prudent summary.

~

From 1960, the demands of a now national profile further complicating the normal complexities of her life and defying more than a broad outline in her hastily scrawled daily record, Mary began to overtax her strength. During the hectic years while her children, aged from five to twenty, were still living at home, her disregard for ordinary human limits stood in some contrast to her sister's restraint and defence of her personal space. Over time, Bet reined in her youthful intemperance and, with Mary as an exemplar to be avoided, demonstrated a remarkable discipline, not only in terms of her work but also in other realms. While maintaining 'the look', she slimmed down to a svelte, elegant figure, gave up smoking and drank only moderately.

In recognition of a hard-achieved effect, Horrie was wont to remark: 'By Jove, Bet certainly knows how to make the most of herself.' Despite their crystal-clear vision of one another and past differences, the two had come to a mutual understanding. So long as she was safely independent, during her sojourns in Broome Horrie enjoyed the company of his sister-in-law and was complimentary about her work. Since Horrie's artistic tastes had evolved on an entirely untutored level, this is something to be remarked upon. He did gain some better idea with his Durack connection, but too late to be other than hit and miss. He had no instinctive feel for it as he had, for example, for the condition of an engine.

The introduction of two pigs into the conglomeration of children and teenagers, a fussy cat and a small irritable dog disposed to select the elderly, nuns and, rather off-puttingly, my boyfriends, for nether-region attack had become the last straw. Grown to large, barging creatures, they got into the rubbish bins, broke bottles, dug up the garden and free-ranged the neighbourhood. Reluctantly bowing to duress, I transported Arthur, the main offender, to the farm of a trusted friend, who assured me that my pet would not be put in with the common herd but treated like one of the family.

One hot night, while undressing in my room with the window open to the breeze, I saw a man's hand creep between and part my curtains. Maintaining a heart-pounding calm, I moved to the door and was in an instant up the passage to my mother's room. After some whispered discussion, we rang the police, who arrived with a dramatic screech of tyres and loudly signalled entrance. This was the start of a long relationship with the local constabulary over the intruder. They came to know us well, and the younger fellows turned up to a household of attractive girls, usually in night attire, with impressive alacrity and were in no hurry to leave. Urged to employ a more cunning approach, they succeeded in seizing the remaining pig, whose high-pitched squeals and heavy, odoriferous body seemed to momentarily conform to what might be expected of a swine of a prowler. We heard reports that other people in the district had also been bothered by a peeping Tom – or perhaps a number of them.

Two years later, the complacent population of Perth was to get a terrible comeuppance for having imagined itself immune to the sort of thing that only happened elsewhere. A girl was shot dead at a house just up the road from us and after a spate of other apparently random murders, it became evident that a psychopath was on the loose. Miraculously, that was one horror not written for our family, the long arm of fate striking from out a different darkness.

A neighbour's complaint that his children had been frightened by an over-friendly Martha saw her on a one-way trip to join Arthur. Unbeknown to me, my mother had made certain catering arrangements for an upcoming party to welcome Bill Harney – author, first ranger of what was at that time called Ayers Rock, and Australian legend.[25] Returning unexpectedly early from a trip to Rottnest Island, I was met by a portly minstrel warbling outback ballads from the front steps and fellowship members milling around the house and garden. The Catholic prohibition on the consumption of meat that had so compromised Friday functions mercifully revoked, the evening air was redolent with the smell of roasting pork. Bringing with him a pretty TAA air hostess from his flight to Perth, 'for a little bit show-off, like', the guest of honour's much-aired bush philosophy had the crowd in thrall and for a time diverted my attention from the anxious whispering offstage.

Did anyone really suppose that I would not recognise the face of my Arthur on a spit with an apple in his mouth or be fooled by the 'another pig' story? My reaction confined to Gran's diary with the brief line 'Pats left in an upset', I departed with Rollo, the elder son of Alix and Paul Hasluck, who seemed prepared to be sensitively sympathetic to my distress. He continued to be sympathetic for some time, collecting me from the alleyway after the night shift at Newspaper House, where I was newly employed in the research department, and transporting me to various places of healing among Perth's nightspots.

~

Unable any longer to avoid taking on an office that was dodged by those who were capable of doing it and much sought by those who were not, Mary became president of the FAW.

Burdened with the entertainment bill inevitably attached to the position, and the expense of constructing an outside room for Julie, Mary fell back on what she called 'fugitive stuff'. She contributed to ABC radio *Forum* programs produced by Kit Denton, returned to writing scripts for historical dramatisation and was regularly heard on 'Problem Pie', a segment of *The*

Women's Session debating posers of the day: Should doctors tell their patients the worst? Should school uniforms be abolished? Would you like your daughter to marry an Aborigine? Regarding the latter, my father would not have been too picky who his daughters married, as he remarked regretfully in a letter to Cyril Gare: 'Where the girls are concerned, plenty of nibbles, but no bites I'm afraid.' It is unlikely his callous desire to off-load us included Robin, who alone merited his holding on to. But while he had readily agreed to subsidise his favourite into Aero Club lessons to the level of her obtaining a private pilot's licence, he remained sceptical about flying being other than an expensive hobby that held no future for women, unlike a nursing career or commercial art course as embarked upon by Julie.

At this point, writing for stage and radio promised the most agreeable way for Mary to fulfil her lifelong desire to put herself on a firm economic basis. Taken to Reabold Hill with other interested parties, she discussed turning its old limestone quarry into an outdoor venue for community theatre. The idea shelved back then for want of sponsorship, she would continue to espouse any venture with the potential to promote local drama.

The only article to bear her name in many months was 'Postscript to History' for the *Sydney Morning Herald*, a two-part compilation of memoirs that had emerged from correspondents after publication of *Kings in Grass Castles*. The annual FAW 'Authors' Readings' commitment to the Adult Education Board seemed more than ever a dull chore, and she remarked on the all too representative audience: 'a coterie of oldish ladies, surely past being adultly educated?'[26] Constantly called upon, she wondered if she should take a harder line and broach the matter of a fee for talks. Perhaps she needed a secretary to avert over-bookings and mix-ups on varying levels of embarrassment. But the memory of past experiences with the home help and the knowledge that any help came at a disproportionate cost stayed a move in this direction. So she continued with the weekly assistance of Bodie 'making clean', a gardener, an ironing lady and her typist Marj Rees. The first person to even vaguely fill the post was fourteen years away. It was anyway an expense she could not justify, as was a detached working area for herself, as she informed Kath McArthur:

> We are at least three bedrooms short. Horrie refuses to do anything about it. He says the girls will be married in a few years and we will be left with a big, unsaleable place on our hands. Meanwhile we are really cramped up and my bedroom-cum-workroom is a sort of general passageway for everybody.[27]

Funds that might have been put to the purpose were at the time quietly going to Kim, who was virtually destitute in Canberra. Gran also sent as much as she could spare to her son. Kim had fallen into a black hole of waiting for action on his various submissions and finding employment vaguely commensurate with his area of expertise. Family assistance left him in an agony of obligation, but Horrie, who was highly critical of the long-term support, cared nothing for that.

In addition to Donald Stuart and James Penberthy, among her time plunderers Mary had now acquired John Joseph Jones. Of Welsh background and claiming kinship with Dylan Thomas, 'J.J.J.', as he was known, was an ambitious man. Officially a schoolteacher, he also described himself for publicity purposes as a civil engineer, journalist, anthropologist, playwright, poet and singer. Rotund, affable and gifted with a pleasing tenor voice suited to folk and ballad song, often of his own composition, once having secured the patronage of a well-known and respected lady of letters he would rise to some prominence on the local scene. While encouraging of his setting the poetry of her late friend Jack Sorensen to music, Mary was less sure about his belief in the stage potential of the Durack story. The Western Australian pastoral industry did not to her mind readily lend itself to a musical or even a rhapsody.

That there might be other claims upon her never seemed to occur to J.J.J. or his fellow offenders. Having persuaded her to write the story for an underwater ballet choreographed by Kira Bousloff, James Penberthy had next required verses for a choral piece to be submitted to a national competition. Within a week of Mary completing *Swan of the Bibbulmun*, he was begging for another opera idea for presentation at the 1962 Empire Games. A composer who needed a librettist, an actress who needed a playwright, a singer who needed a lyricist, would-be authors who needed an editor – the list went on, and Mary Durack fitted the bill in every case. Annoyed by his constant presence, Gran noted Mr Pickenson 'banging away at the piano looking terribly thin and emaciated'[28], which indeed it did since denuded of the toppling pile of books for the strange purpose of being played – to the extent that several keys shed their ivory in shock.

Raising his voice to accommodate the musical accompaniment, Donald inexorably continued reading his latest manuscript, which I suggested he call 'The Driven', since that was plainly applicable to what the grating recitative was doing to other callers, especially Gran – out the door. Waiting in the wings was Mick Kileen, a pensioner from Queensland, who, in common with many old bushmen, had fallen in love with the photo of the author in her book.

While Bet, riding high on the news of a contract for the Wool Board, took off for Leonora, Wiluna and desolate desert areas, Mary escaped Perth's winter cold by spending a few weeks in Broome with Marie Rose and Johnson.

Intending while in the north to visit her old friend Father Francis Huegel at Beagle Bay Mission, Mary first called on the Catholic bishop for his sanction. The story of how John Jobst had ended up at the Kimberley parish was a strange one, but no stranger than those of so many from far-flung European backgrounds whose graves stand in remote outposts beyond the wildest imagination of their holy calling.

As was the case with his predecessor Father Worms, who had won the Kaiser's Iron Cross in the First World War, his parishioners knew little of the bishop's military role in the Second World War. According to his unpublished memoirs, Jobst, who was born to a farming family in Bavaria, entered the Pallottine novitiate in 1939. A year later, the twenty-year-old was conscripted and attached as a medic to a heavy artillery platoon before being sent to the Russian front for the spring offensive of 1942. Promoted to sergeant for meritorious conduct in the ensuing battle, Jobst, while he condemned the senseless carnage, was to retain admiration for the leadership and discipline of the German army. It is not surprising that he emerged from the war with somewhat confused loyalties. Just who had been 'the enemy'? With no time for the Nazis, he reserved his greatest hatred for the Americans, 'killing thousands of innocent citizens and bombing our cities, reducing them to ruins'. Taken prisoner of war in May 1945, he was interned in what he audaciously declared was 'one of the four American extermination camps on German soil'. Here his wounded head was roughly shaved and his epaulets torn off before he was herded into an open field and exposed to the elements for three days. Since he was soon after released still alive, it would appear the Americans lacked German efficiency.

In 1950, while Catholic missionaries had adequately covered Africa, there were vacancies in Canada and Australia, and so it was that Jobst found himself looking through binoculars at the 'not very exciting sight' of Fremantle, Western Australia. Sent to Broome and out to Beagle Bay Mission, he clearly found not even the privations of the Russian front had prepared him for this infernal post. But Jobst, made of stern stuff, had faced the Kimberley as a test of his intractable Pallottine faith. He could not have foreseen that his ideas of church revivalism had arrived as the winds shifted in the direction of self-determination for Aboriginal people. Even had he some intuition of it, he lacked the flexibility to deviate from fixed precepts or accept more secular trends.

Now, seizing the moment, as was his way when divine providence intervened, he spoke winningly about his wish to publicise the fiftieth anniversary of the missions. Was this something that might attract Mary Durack? Or could she organise another writer to cover the occasion, expenses paid? 'Afterwards', Mary wrote in her diary, 'thought I might try to do it and perhaps Bet could do the illustrations.'[29]

How carelessly conceived, the monumental task.

Staying in Perth only long enough to line up a photographer from *The West Australian* to accompany her to the north, Mary hardly thought it worthwhile putting Johnson back into kindergarten, where he had in any case been only an erratic attendee owing to a variety of ailments and constant travels with her. Anticipating leaving the house for an unspecified period, our distracted mother could only quickly ascertain that her other children were in good health and usefully occupied. She had mild misgivings about evidence of teenage parties in her absence, for which only Julie could have been to blame, but Julie, with her boisterous spirits and gregarious nature, was a girl after Mary's own heart. Robin, she noted, though not overly keen on social affairs, had become 'a regular joiner', and it was a source of satisfaction that she belonged to the Australian American Association, the Aero Club, the Catholic Nurses Association and the Royal Commonwealth Society. As for me: set in separate orbits, my mother and I would come together for a stretch before going off on our individual tangents. For most of the 1960s, my withdrawal from Mildew conviviality, lofty disdain for membership of any recognised group and criticism of 'the sort of people you let in the door' were a cause of exasperation and offence to her. It was a relief to me when she left the premises and a semblance of calm and order could be re-established.

Flying to Broome on the new turboprop Fokker Friendship aircraft, Mary remarked upon the hitherto unimagined luxury of being able to sleep most of the way, although her son stayed awake, busily getting his full service out of the air hostess. The mission tour called for two arduous weeks travelling between Beagle Bay, Lombadina, La Grange and Balgo, with side visits to the Derby Leprosarium and Broome orphanage. She had been disappointed when the bishop rebuffed the idea of using Bet's illustrations instead of photographs, Jobst's vision of the Aboriginal people as might be presented to benefactors not extending to Bet's depiction of them. ('Vy must she give such a sombre impression and vy limbs like sticks?')

Travelling in a jeep provided from church funds and everywhere greeted with concerts from the well-primed children, Mary took notes and interviewed staff. Their traditional songs forgotten, a chorus of 'Heigh

Ho, Come to the Fair' welcomed her at Beagle Bay. But there was much of interest for the inveterate historian in observing how the missions worked and examining the chronicles of unsung clergy who had given their lives to a harsh land and its inhabitants. Taking down memories from the Njolnjol, Yaoro and Baard tribespeople, and along the way requisitioning documents and baptismal registers, on return to Broome Mary began correlating her scattered notes and references.

Alive to the bishop's unease as he registered the scope of her research and zeal for translating the correspondence of the early priests, Mary had supposed it was because of the sensitive nature of much of the material. From his memoirs, however, one can gather that the author and the cleric were always going to be poles apart when it came to any shared understanding of purpose. It is unlikely Jobst had an intimate knowledge of what lay in the dusty files, but he knew that all he wanted was a feature in the popular press and a nicely presented pamphlet aimed at attracting donations and suitable for placement with others of the kind in the reading racks of Catholic churches. Potential donors – wealthy widows, businessmen and the like – were not going to wade through a history of the propagation of the Catholic faith in the North West, and the last thing he wanted was an exposé on the innermost thoughts of anguished souls as much in conflict with one another as with God and His elements.

The mission project marked for Mary an ever-expanding involvement with the clergy. Submerging the youthful independence of thought that had enabled her to espouse the principles of agnosticism, it was almost as if she applied her intellectual gift to the church as a penance for her non-belief. While seeing those 'of the cloth' as individuals beset with human weaknesses, she was unable to separate them from the selfless observances of their vocation and, in so many cases, their shining goodness and enduring innocence. What a troupe of saintly characters had emerged from the stories unearthed or told in person, not least among them the valiant St John of God sisters and the Pallottine priests, particularly her dear friends Father Ernest Worms and Father Francis Huegel. The latter was an unassuming intellectual with whom she would share many years of affectionate comradeship and mutual admiration. Denounced by the bishop 'a zealous priest but a muddler',[30] Father Francis was one of the few missionaries who had accepted his vicar apostolic with good grace, not only because he was incapable of anything but God-given forbearance but also because, a fellow countryman, he recognised and understood the type.

Father Michael McMahon, the forceful and energetic Broome parish priest whom Mary would refer to as 'my priestly son', enters the picture from the mid-sixties, and is thenceforth frequently mentioned in her diaries. With his innovative community cooperative venture, he would personify for the bishop the dangerous drift towards left-wing policies conflicting with Pallottine canon law. For us, he would facilitate a continued connection with Broome after our old base there had gone.

Meanwhile, in the course of her trip to Geraldton to sketch shearing shed action for the Wool Board and views of the town for the road board commission, Bet had made a wonderful discovery – a new sign off the main road advertising a MOTEL:

> *In some ways ugly, but twentieth century. They call the rooms 'units' and you park your car right outside. Attractive rooms, each with shower and lav and it smells clean. Charge 30/- a night and breakfast or £2.10 a day full board. I am sure this is the trend for accommodation in Australia. What a wonderful set-up for Broome – I could even work in it.*[31]

Wasting no time, she moved in.

With the departure of his wife, Horrie allowed himself to freefall into the depths. He had spent some days out at Debesa, where the first shearing was in progress, but feeling rather unwanted since the instalment of the Rodriguez family, he had returned dejected. To his wife he gloomed:

> *I drug myself with work these days. To keep my mind absorbed I accomplish near impossible tasks, things that look beyond reason for one man. I have to take risks. This calls for concentration and thinking out ways to guard against major disasters. The sad part is that no-one appreciates. No-one cares about the other fellow. No mail. Letters are a thing of the past too I guess. One cannot expect such a thing from daughters and your time flows away like water from an artesian bore. Well, I suppose words are nothing, you will see them and they are gone … What else have we left though? How to express such things as love? I see all around human derelicts – I feel that I am one of them. One dare not place oneself on a higher plane.*[32]

~

The first problem for the FAW president on her return to Perth was what to do about the impending visit of the head of the Soviet Union of Writers,

Alexei Surkov, and his literary companion Oksana Krugerskaya. After a press report that Surkov had backed the official denunciation of Boris Pasternak as 'spiritually out of tune with Soviet literature', the fellowship executive had reneged on arrangements to receive them. Reminded by J.K. Ewers that, under pressure, Pasternak had been forced to refuse the Nobel Prize for *Doctor Zhivago*, Mary didn't much like the sound of them, either. Nevertheless, they were about to arrive and it was evident that someone had to show a hospitable face.

The immediate welcoming visage at Perth Airport, behind a large bunch of wildflowers and tasteful diamanté spectacle frames, was their fellow traveller Katharine Susannah Prichard. Other forces rallied had been Gerry Glaskin, Donald Stuart, James Penberthy and Kira Bousloff, the latter able to converse in the visitors' native tongue. To Mary's relief, there was a reasonable turnout at Tom Collins House, including George Howard, a local Aboriginal identity who greeted the winner of the Stalin Prize with a plea on behalf of his oppressed people.

A number of critical questions directed to Surkov dealt with by his compatriot Krugerskaya, whose circumlocutory and diplomatic interpretations took most of the impact from his rejection of Pasternak, in the end good old Australian politesse had prevailed. Prescribed excursions ensued: the Kwinana oil refinery, university, Kings Park, afternoon tea at Katharine's Hills home and a picnic in cold, drizzly rain at Mundaring Weir, where Vincent Serventy did the honours with the billy tea and J.J.J. sang colonial songs. Goodness knows the Reds' perception of Australia, but Krugerskaya, a petite, vivacious woman, gave every impression that the visit had been a tremendous event, which spoke more for her life in the USSR than for Perth's attractions. Accompanying and interpreting for other Russian writers at successive Adelaide Festivals, she would develop a reciprocal bond with Mary that led to several decades of correspondence.

~

My twenty-first birthday was celebrated with a surprise party attended by family and the few who could be rallied by Helen Cogan, my most long-suffering friend. Determined to mark the milestone, my dear mother knew that the only way to ensure the presence of the guest of honour was to catch her unawares. I am relieved that her diary gives no indication other than that I was mannerly about it.

For all that things seemed to be going normally, by the year's end a shadow had fallen over our house, made the darker by its improbable source. Posted as part of her training to a rehabilitation hospital for paraplegics, Robin had been depressed by the broken bodies and tragic stories of ruined lives. At the same time sitting for her aviation exams, she was tired and, her mother noticed, 'very subdued and unhappy'.[33] Julie and I, though we said nothing, had a good idea of the cause.

During the winter while walking in the city, Robin had been taken suddenly ill. With the help of a fellow nurse, she had found her way to a nearby medical centre and the rooms of Dr Harold Dicks. It was certainly providential for him: Robin later told me that at the very moment she appeared, Harold, unable to further endure marriage to a woman who did not understand him, had decided to end his life. In any case, the entrance of a lovely blonde girl in all her virginal freshness had set Harold's heart leaping hopefully, and he wasted no time in pressing his attentions on her. His connections with the RFDS and her interest in flying proved a winning combination. Before long his car was delivering her home late at night. When the penny did finally drop, our mother was dismayed: 'Oh no, Robin – not Harold Dicks! Why, he had a reputation as a womaniser in *my* day.'

It was evident that Robin, unpractised in duplicity, had fallen into a decline from the strain of concealing a relationship with a married man. Hoping that a holiday in Darwin and a stay with Horrie in Broome might bring an end to it, her mother made the arrangements. A subsequent letter from Horrie saying Robin had left for Perth several days before sent her into a panic, as there had been no sign of the traveller. Not knowing where to start looking for her 'missing little one', she had begun phoning and wiring up and down the coast. A frantic call to Horrie had met with a thoughtful pause. 'I think', he said cautiously, 'she will turn up tomorrow.' And so she had, horrified to find that she had been the cause of such anxiety. Horrie wrote to her, contrite:

> *Sorry I let the cat out of the bag – unintentionally. I am no moralist when it comes to behaviour dear, but I do not want to see you hurt. There will have to be some painful repercussions over your migrations. Men can get away with anything but H. Dicks is so well-known. You must see also that there is the Durack side to consider. My love for you goes for good and will be our comfort in our declining years.*[34]

For Horrie, the situation was one that he could hardly oppose on moral grounds. After all, Harold was seizing his most loved treasure in the manner of his own theft of the jewel in the Durack family crown. But Mary Durack had been in her mid-twenties and, bad as it was, the fallout and damage to others had been less severe. Robin was an inexperienced nineteen-year-old and Harold, at forty-six, was the same age as her mother and had daughters of Robin's age. On consideration, Horrie decided that Robin could do no wrong, and if that was what she wanted then he would not stand against her sad dignity. Like the rest of us, he just hoped it would blow over with not too much harm done.

The matter continued as a troubling undercurrent while Mary strove to complete a summary of the missions for the bishop; to improve *Tea Towels and Earrings*, J.J.J.'s bold essay into 'kitchen sink' drama; and to comfort Gerry Glaskin in his hour of humiliation following a charge of his having indecently exposed himself on the beach. Julie won the Jacksons art prize, Robin got top marks for nursing, and Mick Kileen turned up, described in her diary by Mary as 'a small, spry jockey-type – talks as he writes in short, staccato sentences, each stating a separate, concise fact'.[35] Sensing another bore moving in, Gran (never lost for a fitting simile) declared, 'The man looks like a peeled prawn'. But she had been very impressed on meeting Bishop Jobst, noting him as 'one of the most handsome men I've seen. He showed us a photo of himself taken with Pope John – he quite dwarfs the pope.'[36]

Mary had been amused when mention of a trip to Cape Leveque with Jobst had met with a stern warning from the visiting anthropologist Dr Helmut Petri: 'You cannot travel alone with such a man. He should not be a bishop when he looks like a film star.'

CHAPTER 6
THE ROCK AND THE SAND (1961–1964)

In later years, Mary would look back with nostalgia on that period during the 1960s 'when all the girls were at home': the constant traffic, the romances that developed and undid, the extra chairs around the table for dinner, the diversity of pursuits and contrasting personalities of her daughters:

> *Robin is so quietly confident about her flying activities – even a few near calamities. Julie thunders in and out and has the place in an uproar of activity – cooking, dressmaking, painting, entertaining arty friends. Patsy is more touchy than the others but she has held down her current job and is saving for a trip overseas. Marie Rose dreams along with her menagerie of beloved white mice.*[1]

The facilities for social events not up to the expanding requirement, a payment of one thousand pounds from the *Sydney Morning Herald* for the serialisation of *Kings* financed what Horrie would refer to as 'the bear pit': a sunken patio and general entertainment area surrounded by trees, suited to arty parties.

Despite his anxiety to see his daughters married off, when Horrie put in an appearance he did not always advance the cause by extending civility to their suitors. An innate old-stag mentality was apt to cause embarrassment, as when he rose for an early-morning departure to Broome and discovered me sitting in the garden 'spinning a line' to a boyfriend. Perhaps we gave him a fright, but wielding his lethal metal torch he took off after the fellow, who leapt the fence and made for the hills. 'Just "a little torch of Horrie in the night"', wisecracked my mother in answer to my affront. When told of the incident, Gran commented, 'Well, it makes one wonder!' Gran's wonderings covered a broad spectrum – news of the first man into space, pole-sitters, troubling reports of tension between Cuba and the United States and happy tidings that her wealthy friend Elsie Broad had won the lottery. 'To he that hath,' she murmured ruefully, 'so they say.'

For Mary, every new year was faced with a resolution purposefully penned on the last page of her old diary:

Main objectives for 1961: finish Yagan of the Bibbulmun *and article on Dad's 1906 journey to Canada and the USA for the* Texas Quarterly. *Also finish Broome novel and sundry plays and short stories.*

Still occupying the FAW chair, she was looking for a replacement other than J.J.J., who had been the only one to put his hand up for the position. A worry for the fellowship that so few young writers were joining, an approach to Randolph (Mick) Stow, the best of the emerging talents, had found a shy and retiring youth unsuited to such an antiquated group – or any group, for that matter. It was a sign of the times that several office-bearers were not legitimately published authors, once a stipulation of membership. Eleanor Page Smith's claim to literati was a biography in manuscript of the explorer and Canning Stock Route surveyor H.S. Trotman that had been rejected by every publishing house in Australia. When Olaf Ruhen reviewed *The Beckoning West* with the whimsical premise –

There must be an ichor in the air of WA carrying good nourishment for writers, promoting good literary health and a sovereign remedy against the cancers of non-accomplishment. How else can one account for the flow of excellent books?[2]

– the generosity of Mary Durack was another explanation.

Too lengthy and erudite for regular newspapers, the article for the bishop titled 'Missions in a Bypassed Land' was restricted to publication in *The Catholic Weekly*. The Lombadina section extracted and rewritten to suit the bishop's original purpose, the author's name did not appear on the brochure. Considering the effort she had put into it, a costly one since no fees were received for the commission, Mary began to contemplate writing a full history of the missionary endeavour while the research was still fresh in her mind. She also supposed that the labour of love involved would please Bishop Jobst. It was certainly a task for which she would need to brace herself, and to this end she stole two weeks of January at Adsett, where she happily painted a mural for the breezeway between the buildings:

Perfect holiday relaxation. Would like to do nothing ever again but paint the bright things of the sea. Feel quite light-headed and irresponsible with sudden release of pressure. Glorious freedom from the telephone.[3]

It was a blessed escape from the vandalism of her working hours by J.J.J., who convivially included his wife and growing tribe of children in his incessant visits. He would have followed her to Adsett had he not been, for good reason, afraid of Ida. And by the egocentric Donald Stuart, who before swallowing her day complained about the gall of people who interrupted his train of thought by calling in unannounced. The erstwhile swagman Mick Kileen, who prior to his arrival from Queensland was known to Mary only from his fan mail, had also become something of a millstone. Taking his welcome for granted, he arrived early before settling in for the day. Sitting the old fellow in the sun with a nice lunch, Mary gave him cheerful books to forestall the morbid discourse, usually a run-down on the sort of diseases he might expect to have, or get, at his age. After a while he merged with the landscape, like a garden gnome.

Shortly before embarking on the mission project, Mary had made a fortuitous acquaintance in Father John Senan Moynihan. An Irish scholar, for forty years editor of the iconic literary publication *The Capuchin Annual* and confidant to numerous political, lettered, artistic and musical luminaries, in 1959, at the age of fifty-one, he had accepted a position on the other side of the world for health reasons.

His diabetic condition brought under control, as chaplain for the Sisters of Mercy at St Anne's Hospital Father Moynihan jovially defined himself as being, along with an old maid's cat and a butcher's dog, among the three most spoilt creatures on earth. He was installed in the presbytery, overlooking a tranquil stretch of the Swan River, and in addition to his regular duties soon assumed the role of Perth diocesan archivist. A character priest and the very prototype of an Irishman, he would have been a gift to the movies. Over the next decade, Mary would come to consider him a loved relative, while she and hers represented a family to him. With his specific knowledge, feeling for language and ready wit, he was going to be invaluable to her proposed history. Unable, however, to decipher the mysteries of a bus timetable and without a car, he was in constant need of a chauffeur, services provided by the Miller family and a group of kindly Catholic volunteers.

~

With Mary again away to Broome and Bet in the Eastern States, Gran remarked on her denuded family: 'Not one of my own left in town. I feel quite bereft.'[4] After completing her first solo flight, Robin had gone to Brisbane for a student nurses conference, Harold Dicks in close attendance. I was on a cheering visit to Kim in his Canberra purgatory, and Julie was staying with the Forrest family on a Pilbara station.

Her latest work exhibited at the Athenaeum Gallery in Melbourne, Bet's depiction of the goldfields country and inland ghost towns was strange and intriguing. Haunting images of amorphous figures emerging from a desolate landscape confirmed a direction away from the graphic and into a more abstract form of imagery.

In Broome, Mary found that the poinciana trees had been infested with a plague of caterpillars, their cocoons dangling from the branches like Christmas baubles, ready to hatch and further ravage the former glory of a town, as she observed, 'still in decline and without much spirit'.[5] At the first opportunity she was off in the mission truck with Bishop Jobst and crates of cheeping day-old chickens, heading for Beagle Bay. Leaving behind the sound of Horrie's familiar protestations at being left in the lurch, the travellers disappeared northwards in a heat haze to share, in this instance, a somewhat adventurous but, notwithstanding the fears of Dr Petri, thoroughly above-board journey.

Persuaded by his companion into taking an unfamiliar side path, the bishop found himself with a 'lost in the wilderness' parable for his next sermon. The ensuing marathon, but for divine intervention, could have seen the end of both of them – and an interesting headline. But in terms of the project, while willing to assist in a limited and cautious way, Jobst was already trawling for someone else – a tractable lay nun, perhaps – to write the story of the missions in a way that suited his purpose. Meanwhile, Mary continued her own interpretation of his making things difficult for her:

> He had not looked at the files before and may have regretted my seeing some of the more private and personal letters. But too late now. He had to go out during the afternoon and did not like to leave the papers with me, so have to await his return. Working directly from the Beagle Bay records and trying to translate the French correspondence with the help of a school dictionary is slow and frustrating with many blanks to be filled in from documents I have not been allowed to see.

> Went to the presbytery and asked Bishop for other files – the ones he had tucked away. I know he is not comfortable about this, but if I am to write the story I must also know the seamy side. And there are plenty of seams all right.

> He would only let me read on the spot and I must try and keep information in my head – could take nothing home. So read the skeletons with a gimlet eye.[6]

Bit by bit, and grudgingly, Jobst did allow her access to documents bearing on the foundations of the Kimberley missions. When pressed, it must have seemed churlish to withhold them from a keen and, one hoped, charitable historian who was also a personal friend.

The bishop needed all the friends he could get. Things had not gone smoothly for him in terms of his relations with the entrenched clergy, who saw him as an insensitive new broom with no concept of long-established northern practices. Withdrawing from the waves of antagonism, he became more alien and hard to know. Financial matters, for which he found a natural predilection, occupying his mind greatly, between the fundraising drives he called his 'begging tours' he moved about the country, obsessively acquiring land on behalf of church expansion. In the course of checking on his isolated parishes, he covered thousands of road miles over his 280,000 square mile diocese every month, until in 1967 an aircraft came about after an appeal to Catholic sponsors. Quietly muddling-along outposts accustomed to no more than a (dreaded) biannual visit from on high were thenceforth exposed to more frequent descents, and resignations found their way to the Broome presbytery.

~

On return to Perth, as she had half anticipated, Mary was confronted by the FAW in disarray and dissent among its members. There had been trouble when Gerry Glaskin was assigned to judge a local short story competition, the winning entry held by the losers to be such a travesty that most of the submissions had, in her absence, found their way to the presidential desk for a re-judge. When she finally relinquished the chair to the eager John Joseph Jones, the executive quickly fell out with the pompous and overbearing newcomer. From the minute she landed back in Perth, all concerns were diverted to her, whether she held the chair or not. It came as an immense relief when Vincent Serventy agreed to take over the helm again, and, after him, Dorothy Hewett, who despite her somewhat confronting private life proved useful and competent.

J.J.J. continued to off-load his side of the story two or three times a day. When told she was not answering the phone, he descended in person to badger his patroness with his 'corker' of a play about the Berlin Wall or requests that she compere his singing engagements. 'Suppose I will have to,' records the diary, 'but crikey!' And here I parted ways with my mother. Whereas I tolerated Donald Stuart, who for all his less forgivable traits had a reliable streak that would see him serve as a useful president for both the

WA and federal fellowships, I drew the line at Mr Jones, and was scathing of her inability to free herself from classified 'leeches'.

~

During the summer months, the alluring aspects of Adsett were somewhat compromised by the plague of small bush flies that hovered in clouds, stuck in the corners of the eye and were swallowed by voluble guests. On the positive side, they acted as a deterrent to idling in the garden or on the beach before evening, when they disappeared. Establishing a quiet and uninterrupted routine, Mary and Ida made solid progress. As it was considered unethical in medical circles to write other than textbooks under a professional name, Ida, using the nom de plume Caroline Gye, worked on an informal account of her far-flung excursions in the cause of treating trachoma. As a consultant for the World Health Organisation, she also produced numerous reports and scientific papers. From her own muddle of half-finished projects, Mary was full of admiration:

> *Ida's approach to scientific experiment is that of the creative artists and like them she gets an idea which becomes an obsession till it is worked through. This ability to conceive a plan and bring it to fruition is outstanding and her work is both a passion and a delight.*[7]

For her own part, Mary's time was taken up completing *To Ride a Fine Horse*, a simplified version of *Kings* for schoolchildren, and working on her contribution to the Perth Summer School, held annually at the University of Western Australia. Since its inception, the FAW had taken part in the event, and Mary held it as an obligation. Hew Roberts, the director of the Adult Education Board from which the concept had sprung, was a good friend and 'a dear man' who had assisted the foundation of a combined fellowship and Adult Education branch at Albany in the South West. Other speaking engagements, some booked months in advance, fell like so many rods on her back, none more resented than the afternoon given to the Karrakatta Club: 'An ordeal for me this carry-on – Perth seen in every aspect that bored and bothered me as a kid – the dull "bright" chatter, the hats, the "belonging."'[8] If she declined to confirm a request, the more wily petitioners were not beyond publishing notice of her booking as a means of blackmailing her into it.

The Summer School educational dough was now being leavened by a newly established festival, incorporating some avant-garde drama and foreign films. With various daughters in tow, Mary attended the best of the season: *Hiroshima Mon Amour*, *The Sundowners*, Stefan Haag's production of *La Traviata* and a performance of *Under Milkwood* in the university's Sunken Garden. Television now offering such edifying programs as Bertrand Russell's *Sunday Night Discussions*, *The Critics* with Max Harris, *Four Corners* and Kenneth Clarke's series on art, friends who had held out against acquiring a TV set routinely came in to watch ours, including Marianne and Ferry Korwill, who sat through the grim Eichmann trial with fascinated horror.

I missed the excitement of astronaut John Glenn passing over Perth's illuminated city (Gran contributing her twenty-five-watt porch light), being by that time at sea, bound for England. As the aged P&O liner *Orontes*, flying its 192 foot paying-off pennant, disappears over the horizon on its final voyage, readers can wave goodbye to me until 1964. But, as Horrie glumly predicted, I will be back 'toot sweet'.

~

Properly convened for the first time, the 1962 Adelaide Festival Writers' Week provided Mary with so valuable an opportunity to meet and fraternise with new literary soulmates that the occasion became a subsequent calendar fixture. Over this period, her diary is crammed with the names of Australia's wordsmiths, the talks and themes explored and the airing of related and contrary views at impromptu gatherings. Some, like Nancy Cato, Kylie Tennant and Beatrice Davis, were destined to become intimates; others, principally Hal Porter, playmates.

Xavier Herbert, whom she had not before encountered, 'spoke splendidly – quite a surprise – and we liked him better than we expected but he is the supreme, uncertain egotist – bush way of speaking but an overlay of the outside world.'[9] Roland Robinson, Olaf Ruhen, Tom Shapcott, Flexmore Hudson, Frank Dalby Davison, Cyril Pearl, Stephen Murray-Smith, Tom Inglis Moore, Geoffrey Dutton, Colin Thiele and Douglas Stewart, the best of a growing number of celebrated Australian writers, all made a contribution and extended a warm welcome to the new celebrity from Western Australia.

Creating a stir among the ladies, guest speaker David Attenborough delivered his lecture on natural history with a charm and gift for communication described by Mary as 'completely un-Australian'. Poet Kenneth Slessor and his confrère Hal Porter were reported 'in fine fettle', the latter 'flattering, insulting and constantly dropping deliberate bricks'.[10] This would be Mary's initiation to the Porter phenomenon, and one whose nightly revels and tottery daytime emergence suggested light regard for other than the recreational aspects of the festival. While he was an undisputed personality boy, the Victorian writer had at that point produced only two minor novels, to mixed reviews, and some short stories. The following year, *The Watcher on the Cast-Iron Balcony* deservedly set his seal of fame, henceforth granting him the imprimatur to behave more or less as he chose. Miffed when Max Harris, 'with the speed of a serpent', trumped him with a summary of the festival for *The Bulletin*, he was heard ridiculing the famous creator of the *Angry Penguins* journal in a public place.[11]

Attending the festival had allowed Mary a short leave of absence from the tribulations of pioneer priests, the looming shadow of J.J.J. upon the doorstep, bearing his latest song ('I Am Your Satellite', dedicated to John Glenn), and the walking medical casebook that was Mick Kileen, whose admittance to the nearby Sunset Hospital for the elderly had made Mildew more accessible. At a loss to find another ear for his timeless narration, Donald Stuart had fallen back on old Mick, who was willing, though his tendency to be reminded of his own outback experiences was interruptive. Leaving them to the mercies of one another, Mary was soon heading north to pick up the mission book with renewed enthusiasm since (rejecting my suggestion of 'Faith and Fallibility') the title *The Rock and the Sand* had come to her.

Father Huegel offered to translate the German letters for her, but after meditation and prayer Bishop Jobst had received the divine message that he should not give his permission. With a hint of resentment, Mary decided that if he continued to obstruct her writing a history she would set it down as a novel, a prospect that might well have scared the cassock off his Lordship. As the emerging pages blew out through the open shutters in the strong easterly wind, she wondered whether anyone could possibly be as slow and write a first draft so impossibly badly:

> *There is seldom an original sentence I can leave as written and then what I correct I improve tomorrow. A very bad habit I fear that could only be cured by unbroken writing time given to this story of so many tangled webs.*[12]

That prospect was also blown out the window as the awful caravan of Donald and Kathy Stuart, with a child described by the startled hostess as 'a holy terror', disgorged itself upon the premises. What with Donald's gift of a huge turkey he had shot along the way – the cooking of which became a saga of strife in itself – and his habit of sticking his soggy butt ends on door posts and window ledges, Horrie, predictably, played up. Denying any responsibility for this visitation, Mary declared the problem was having two houses in Broome so that people were inclined to take seriously her foolish offers of accommodation.

Anxiously awaiting her return, James Penberthy was 'on the deadline' for the lyrics to his closing hymn for the coming Commonwealth Games. 'Wrote him a couple of punk verses but hated spending some rare, good, quiet time on this.'[13] When the hymn was eventually performed, she had a rueful laugh at a 'not entirely untrue' letter in *The West* criticising its 'drivelling sentimentality'.[14]

Retreating to Adsett for a brief respite, to her relief she suddenly found the opening line for the book:

The people of the dream watched the people of the clock come out of the sea and strike their flagstaff firmly in the sand ...

~

Up against the accustomed indifference and resistance, Bet's hopes of a favourable reaction to the *Mirage* series exhibition were fading. She was not really surprised: 'The public is the same anywhere and I will sell the same as anywhere – the "little girl" because of the "expression in the eyes."' What was the use of bouncing pictures back and forth across the Nullarbor when the only one to profit was the transport company? Reckoning that for the same cost she could have purchased a ticket to New York, she was now fixed on a trip abroad to see for herself what was going on in the wider art world. With this in mind, her letter took on the defeated tone she knew always distressed her sister. Why paint at all? What had ever possessed her to imagine that she was an artist? She was reduced to a pittance, with pressing demands from the bank obliging her to enter into 'a damn abomination of a thing called a "second mortgage" on the roof over the old head'.[15]

Mary's determined adherence to the collaboration era exasperated her. She knew that, regardless of how unnecessary the addition of artwork, anything that came her sister's way was considered in terms of 'what might be in it for Bet'. Without inspiration to illustrate *The Courteous Savage*, as the young person's adaptation of *Yagan of the Bibbulmun*[16] had been titled, or *To Ride a Fine Horse*, it was not easy to turn down the commissions while she still needed handouts. It had taken an arm-twist to produce 'decorations' for *Northern Gateway*, a book by the missionary doctor Father Frank Flynn, and she had only tentatively agreed to a similar chore on Colin Johnson's novel. As she saw it, her distinctive sketches incorporated into miscellaneous books had merely served to perpetuate her image as an illustrator and laid her open to the insulting specifications of publishers. She realised the foot-dragging over such minor assignments made her sister cross, but Bet could only work 'in a bubble'.[17] The 'thing' at an end, the publication of the children's book *Kookanoo and the Kangaroo* would be their last joint venture.[18]

Horrie came to Perth to accept an award from MMA in recognition of his thirty-five years with the airline and having held a pilot's licence for fifty years. The gold watch presented to mark the increasingly heavy hours of his retirement was received ungraciously and never worn because 'the band pinches the hairs on my arm'. The occasion was prominently written up by the *Daily News*, with a picture of the proud father going aloft as his daughter's first passenger.

Having obtained an advanced pilot's licence and completed her nursing training, Robin had decided to supplement her qualifications with a midwifery course at St Anne's Hospital. It was work towards a more cheerful end after six months on the cancer ward at Royal Perth Hospital, a term she had found more disheartening than the previous stint caring for paraplegics and spinal injury patients.

The tyranny of Christmas upon her, Mary gave herself up to it and a hospital round between Gran, recovering from an operation on her thigh, and Nessie Kidson, who was dying. A few book reviews and 'Afterthoughts on the Adelaide Festival' for *Overland* were written from bedsides. On the precipice of the greater void, Nessie held the loving hand and sadly confessed, 'Oh Mary, sometimes I almost despair.' Gran's practical decision at this time to give up driving would become a refrain of regret – one of which we were never to hear the end.

It was not until the new year that Mary made an escape. With Ida away at a conference, she wrapped herself in solitude at Adsett and wrote to Florence:

> *I have been here for three heavenly days speaking to no-one except myself. The complicated threads of the years and the strange psychological meanderings of all these characters begin to untwist or clarify themselves as I get down to the microscopic study of letters, deciphered dates, and with the help of Latin, French, Spanish, Italian and German dictionaries, make more careful translations. It is hard even to try to tell anyone what this book is 'about'. If I say it is the history of eighty years of missionary activity among the Aborigines of North Australia it sounds as if I've gone round the bend. I mean utterly un-me. However, over the past few years*

> *I realised that the whole history of the north was wrapped up in these crumbling letters and papers – the incredible story of a polyglot people, the elusive character and subtle psychology of the Aborigines shown up in relation to the problem they were to the missionaries and the problem these various missionaries were to them. The story of the Trappists from 1890 to 1900 is to me most extraordinary when examined in this way. They expected to find 'crosses' and to embrace them – even martyrdom, but the greatest crosses they had to bear were not from external discomforts or persecutions but from their own inner conflicts and each other.*[19]

Florence, in company with Bertrand Russell and fellow jailed ban-the-bombers, knew all about crosses and martyrdom. Unconvinced as to the efficacy of radical demonstrations, Mary's faith lay in the power of the written word, and though her name did sporadically appear on petitions for causes upheld by other literary figures, she was averse to giving public one-sided recommendation. Asked to sign an appeal banning horses from the Adsett beach, she solved the problem by means of a frequent resort:

> *I do not think the fairest course is*
> *To ban the beach to folks on horses*
> *In fact the threatened use of force is*
> *A thing no democrat endorses …*

~

On the first of his many sprees to Western Australia, Hal Porter's arrival at Adsett soon sent the ghostly monks fleeing. He was captivated by the unspoiled south-west corner, as was Florence, who had finally managed to meet up with her correspondent of so many years. Florence was, however, less impressed to find the author hard at work on the memoirs of a paraplegic ex-footballer. It seemed Father Moynihan's charity extended to offering the assistance of his friend the writer Mary Durack to tragic cases like Brian Collins, a good Catholic boy who had written of his travels to Lourdes for a cure. ('A sadly muddled account of a boy facing his disability with courage and faith – rambling, sincere, naïve.')[20] Alarmed to also discover Eleanor Page Smith's rebounding manuscript among a number of such projects littering the writing desk, Florence gave her a pep talk on the necessity to 'get tough'. Subsequently, Mary's letters to her are filled with lame excuses:

Cross my heart dear, I have not really broken any promise to you. I get up very early in the mornings and go on with my own work all through the day, conscientious as blazes. But I suggested [Eleanor] come in to run over what subbing I had done. (What E. can do to a sentence when she takes it to retype is nobody's business.) I think that with the verbiage slashed out, clichés deleted, uninteresting details summarised or left out it should read up quite lively and the next time might not be turfed back obviously echoing with some poor, exasperated reader's sighs.[21]

Not that Florence, a notoriously soft touch, could set herself up as an exemplar and Mary soon had her agreement to coedit Colin Johnson's novel in order to bring the newly titled *Wild Cat Falling* to publication standard.

A few more urgent jobs got out of the way, Mary lined up an article for *Walkabout* to justify the jaunt[22] and set off overland for Adelaide Writers' Week with Florence, Ida and the driver, Eleanor Page Smith.

Travelling via the goldfields, they visited outback towns and historic sites along the Eyre Highway, writing separate accounts of the journey and having the time of their lives. While crossing the desert, the women amused themselves devising elaborate plots to murder and dispose of one other. Ida, who loved thrillers and left a gypsy trail of them across the world, was the clear winner.

~

A commission from BHP to capture aspects of the iron-ore mine at Yampi Sound, and the added attraction of a vacant Bishop's Palace in Broome, sent Bet north. Driving overland, she came upon a sandstone hill near Port Hedland covered in Aboriginal rock carvings, almost lost in rubbish and broken bottles. A letter to her mother expressed her dismay at the discovery: 'I wonder if future generations will be as disrespectful of our present art as we are of this ancient survival of a past culture.'[23]

Settling into the remnants of the formerly fine house, she had at once felt its phantom presence. Receptive to the atmosphere of the many residences she had occupied over the years, Bet also picked up on bad portents. ('One day, given the certainty of accident and death, she is sure to be right,' commented Mary wryly.) In the evening she and Horrie would adjourn for a drink at the Continental Hotel, or take a drive to view the town's transformation for an anticipated royal visit. Calling on the bishop for permission to visit Beagle Bay, Bet wrote to her sister:

Jobst ... he really is a trick. The local priests talk openly about him. He is remote, hard to see, only stays [in Broome] a short time, hardly speaks. He does not fit in, which is a pity for him and the missions generally.[24]

Noting that he had formed a curious fellowship with Horrie, who stoutly defended him against his many detractors, for her own part she could not resist giving him a light lick with her forked tongue: 'I believe you speak several languages my Lord. Tell me, do you speak them all as *quietly* as you speak English?'

Oppressed by the 'cottonwool stuffiness' of Broome, Bet, putting aside her artwork, found release in 'a bit of fantasy', a story she called 'The House that Flew Away'. Thinking the lighthearted allegory possibly suitable, with her own illustrations, for television, she sent the manuscript to her sister for her appraisal. This proved a mistake. Instead of making a few supportive comments and suggestions, the incorrigible editor had started in on Bet's invention. Knowing the critique would not be appreciated, she added a succinct summary of a subeditor's role:

> *I realise that you will think I have edited out the brightness and spontaneity – but from all I have learned about the writing game, the old adage 'hard writing makes easy reading' rings more true every year. That is not to say your story is not good – a glorious idea – just needs a bit of tidying up. Subediting is for the most part thankless. I wonder how many books Beatrice Davis practically rewrote? Xavier Herbert's* Capricornia *was a sow's ear made into a silk purse by the hard work of Inky Stephensen, although Xavier denied that he had had any help. Writers nearly always conveniently forget. Ion Idriess and Frank Clune regarded the heavy rewriting and subbing of their stuff as a mere secretarial job. In a way it is. The editor may not have an original idea but can sort out others' ideas, tidy the sentences, rearrange the script so that it sounds competent and reads smoothly. Maybe I am a better editor than I am a writer? But I don't want to be.*[25]

Bet's reply indicates her deflation:

> *I feel in this instance our minds are moving as two parallel lines – never really meeting. The first impulse to rush it through has passed. I have gone off it.*[26]

Leaving Broome to its royal fever, Bet set out on the round trip to Darwin via Wyndham, Kununurra and Derby. Seeing Kildurk for the first time, she could properly appreciate the untold labour involved in making something of that great swathe of virgin country. Only a spirit of intrepid perseverance had kept Reg going through a decade marred by lack of capital and poor seasons. His sister noticed that he had 'shrunken into his shell somewhat', and the long grind taken its toll, the pliant elements of his character hardened to the pragmatism typical of most station managers. There seemed little future for the property, and she sensed a time coming when, in terms of a fixed place, the north would be lost to the Duracks. On account of Kim's plight and a country she saw as 'meandering aimlessly in its thought and activity without him', she gave the opening of the preliminary diversion dam a miss.[27]

All at once fired up with the idea of doing something to regain her brother's lost footing, without further ado she applied for a lease on a tract of Crown land for sale near Wyndham for pastoral and agricultural purposes. On hearing of it, far from being grateful, Kim berated her 'unruly emotions' and questioned how her apparent grasp of his redefined objective could suddenly evaporate to reveal only a tenuous understanding.[28] In fact, what did any of his family know as they urged him to contemplate the 'compromise' that had always been for him unthinkable. Why *not* go cap in hand to Northern Developments and beg to be allowed to salvage the ever-worsening situation for the Camballin rice project? In consideration of his debts and yet in hope of marrying the girl to whom he had become engaged, earlier in the year Kim had done just this. His futile meeting with the managing director Peter Farley, whom he described as 'the very Prince of Darkness', was possibly the lowest point in his life. Kimberley Holdings, as the company became, would sink into a murky zone of insolvency, its tangled affairs beyond accounting and its shares deemed worthless. His audience with Menzies also a farcical washout, Kim would at this point put behind him what he described as 'the phenomenon of hope'[29] and turn for spiritual comfort to philosophical and theosophical studies.

Bet's standard reaction to criticism from any quarter was outwardly cool, although she felt it sorely, especially when emanating from Kim or Mary. To whatever extent she then accepted censure and reined in her wild impulses, she confessed herself as basically despising 'moderation', never seeing the reason not to go the whole way. Meanwhile, she returned to Broome to write articles on the North West for the *Sydney Morning Herald*.[30] Examining a land that had 'cracked more hearts than jackpots', and using the mission at Beagle Bay as a 'symbol of futility', her treatise painted a stark picture of 'a whole country that somewhere along the line has become hideously, perhaps irredeemably, unstuck'. Mary, beavering away to put the best light on the Catholic objective, found Bet's pessimistic view 'lacked balance'.³¹ From her standpoint, taking in, as was her wont, all sides of the question, it probably did, but Bet's assessment of the situation at this time was devastatingly perceptive. There is a sense that she subtly dampened her sister's sally into the literary world, possibly believing Bet's road hard enough to hoe in the medium where her talents manifestly lay. With this in mind, she had kept her own love of sketching and painting low-key and strictly on a 'dabblers' level. As a professional beset by amateurs, she was in no mood to be less than frank with her sister.

Despite himself, Horrie had become quite caught up in the excitement over the Queen's visit in March 1963. With no let-up in his complaints about the incessant noise of road graders and the filthy newly laid tar besmirching the wheels and paintwork of every vehicle in town, the occasion acted on him as a tonic. A few months earlier, he had fallen into one of his declines, and his wife had received the brunt: 'Dust and spiders are taking over, the old house is falling into rack and ruin, dunny collapsed from white ants. My health and spirits are at low ebb.'³²

Writing a bracing reply, Mary suggested he try again to find a publisher for his biography, *Early Birds*.

A factor in Horrie's despondency had been the downside of a seemingly advantageous transaction when Ansett Airlines took over as the major shareholder in MMA, a move he belatedly realised would threaten his sinecure as regional manager. Another shock had arrived with a letter from the Department of Civil Aviation (DCA) informing him he must keep to proper radio procedure and wear headphones in the Wackett – his pre-take-off briefing 'Going for a bit of a spin, shouldn't be too long', deemed inadequate. This Early Bird was out of place in the modern world.

At first doubtful about Julie becoming an MMA air hostess, he soon got used to the idea and enjoyed the sight of his daughter opening the aircraft door and her cheerful, affectionate greeting.

Her mother thought 'inadvisable' Robin's decision to take a break from her midwifery course for the purpose of joining a group on a ferry flight to transport an aircraft from London to Perth. With the inclusion of Harold Dicks, she knew the venture would attract publicity and, possibly, 'talk'. When the Italian Piaggio aircraft was badly damaged landing in Athens and subsequently abandoned, she had been obliged to compose carefully worded reports for the press. For Robin and Harold, however, it was to be the first of many such overseas jaunts. Feeling that it was time she spoke frankly to Dr Dicks and urged by me from London to do so pronto, the troubled mother somehow always put it off:

> *It is not easy to broach the subject of this affair, especially as Harold has been so helpful coming in to treat Johnson's asthma and making himself indispensable in other household medical problems, of which there are always plenty.*[33]

Her room at Mildew maintained as a mere facade, Robin was by now unofficially living with Harold at his Hills property. Still contemplating her future, she had in the interim secured a position with the RFDS Air Ambulance, so they were also working together. While thrilled with Horrie's suggestion that he purchase an aircraft for her, Robin's acceptance would depend upon to what worthy end she might put such a costly acquisition. To defray some of the outlay involved in gaining a commercial licence, she applied for and was awarded a Dalgety Scholarship. Working on an idea for a 'Flying Nurse' scheme, she joined the Women Pilots' Association and was so seldom home that Johnson worried, 'How will I be able to tell when I'm sick and when I am only pretending? She always knows.'

With *Kings* into its third edition, Mary had finally managed to put together two thousand pounds towards a self-contained workroom to be built on top of the garage at Mildew. ('Oh no,' groaned Horrie. 'Don't tell me I'm going to have to put up with Mum tap-tapping over my head all night.') The extension finished and furnished with finesse, Mary moved into the first functional and private quarters she had ever had. The only drawback to the new arrangement was that no upstairs phone meant a run down to the house, so friends were asked not to call her before four in the afternoon, when she customarily descended. Only J.J.J. refused to accept this, saying he would hang on while she was fetched. She missed the presence of Mick Kileen at his post in the garden, greeting and often forestalling nuisances like J.J.J. The old bushman had decided not to wait around for his appointed disease. Taking himself down to the river, he had neatly folded his coat, placed it conspicuously with his last borrowed books and a note requesting Mrs H.C. Miller be informed of his demise, and drowned himself.

Only news as momentous as the assassination of President Kennedy could have knocked the Cooke murders out of the headlines, the panic over a madman on the rampage having ended with an arrest. Convinced our prowler was Cooke, her girls' narrow escape became one of our mother's 'urban legends' over the years (though who knows?).

With the dire diagnosis of breast cancer, Gran bravely faced her likely end with typical platitudes: 'Well, I have been very fortunate and can count my many blessings. When my time comes I can go thankfully.' Once, reflecting on a relative in the throes of senility, she had confided to me, 'Oh Patsy, dear, when I get like poor Aunty Nell, just hit me on the head with a stick.' At least she would be spared that. Unlike many of her contemporaries, she had retained her faculties remarkably well, as she noted in her diary: 'So many I know these days are very deaf for which I can be thankful.' We knew what she meant.

While she appeared to accept her sentence, the family did not. A second opinion having confirmed the need for an immediate breast removal, Robin called Harold in on the case. His advice against any treatment more drastic than a 'lumpectomy' proved right, the gratitude that came his way for allowing Gran to live out a further sixteen years in good health cannot be overestimated.

With Gran happily restored to her own home, the main difficulty was in finding a 'companion help' that met her somewhat exacting requirements. A number were hired, but after good beginnings she became peevish as they invariably fell into one of two categories: 'no worker' or 'always doing'. Melitza, a charming former opera singer, seemed for a while the answer to a prayer, but Gran, deciding 'their ways are not our ways', couldn't reconcile herself to a Ukrainian countess fallen on hard times who was not used to being told what to do. It would be Gran herself who decided she could cope well enough on her own. The only real opposition to this independence came from Reg, who thought his mother should be placed in an 'assisted living facility' and a family company established from the sale of her house. With Gran's reluctant agreement, after consultation with Bill and David but not his sisters or Kim, the businesslike plan was drawn up and presented to the others as a fait accompli. Kim's instant response explicit on the advantages to shareholders over the interests of his mother, the scheme died there, but the gap was to widen between the ideologically polarised brothers until contact became no more than a Christmas card.

~

During a Summer School discourse on the trend of the modern novel, Mary had become involved in a lively debate on censorship. Not in favour of busybody authorities taking measures to suppress books or ideas, she had been rather uncharacteristically unequivocal. When her stance raised some hackles among conservative and church bodies, she felt her phobia against public utterance on contentious issues borne out. Retreating to Adsett, she complained of further imposition:

> *This incubus of other people's manuscripts becomes a sort of torture I seem unable to escape. On account of frequent interruptions much of the heart I had for the job has been lost – just as the monks I am writing about lost heart in theirs. It would be much easier if I knew this story to be of general interest and that it was worth the time and neglect of other things.*[34]

The return from abroad of the censorious eye and caustic tongue of her eldest daughter only compounded her problems. There on her desk for me to see, amended pages of *Wild Cat Falling*, *The Beckoning West* and 'Miracles Are Everywhere' swamping the first draft of *The Rock and the Sand*. At least, I noticed, Eleanor Page Smith paid for the rewrite of her manuscript by giving her benefactress soothing facials, with applications of aromatic poultices: her skin had never looked better. And under the desk lurked something that looked suspiciously like a hot potato legacy to the FAW in the form of a tattered autobiography by the late Mollie Skinner. So deeply bogged had my mother become that there was nothing for it but to call off her expected appearance at the Adelaide Festival and accept J.J.J.'s offer to attend in her place. Her hopes of making good use of the time were optimistic.

Inspired by his Adelaide success, Xavier Herbert had decided to take up the offer of a Perth lecture tour sponsored by the Adult Education Board. His ulterior motive was to gauge reaction to his autobiographical *Disturbing Element*[35], wherein he had provocatively pronounced the capital city of Western Australia a poor place without character or interesting people, the population seemingly content to live within a system of self-imposed colonialism. But on discovering no-one had read his book and on that account no offence taken, according to the headline 'Author Lashes at Home City', he had contrived a row with the Adult Education director Hew Roberts and cancelled his tour. An allusion in *The West Australian*[36] to his having been cold-shouldered by local writers – Herbert apparently forgetting that he had received a good audience for a talk at Tom Collins House – saw Mary hastily organising a welcoming dinner for him 'before he leaves to spread terrible stories of inhospitable old Perth'.[37] Roaring in on his motorbike at lunchtime for an evening invitation, he denounced the Adult Education Board for having accepted his withdrawal from the talks for which he had been invited:

> *No ordinary logic in his arguments, but amusing. He insisted on taking me for a ride around the block on the back of his bike – sorry no press photographers present.*

> *Cooked food for an indefinite number. Among those who turned up – Vincent Serventy, David and June Hutchison, Mick Stow, Henrietta, Paul and Alix Hasluck, Ken Eades, David Haslehurst, Eleanor White, Ida and Bet. As the night went on, Xavier got loudly argumentative, an awkward moment being when Hew Roberts came in hoping to say a friendly goodbye. Xavier refused and called him 'a liar'. Henrietta suggested he was not above trifling with the truth himself and he took further umbrage, declining to shake hands with her before she left.*[38]

Henrietta's proffered handshake had been charitable considering the earlier insult when Xavier had rounded on her with drunken malice and the words: 'Get out of my way you ugly old bag, I want to talk to the beautiful Elizabeth.' Between the guest's mysterious disappearances, there were some droll moments. Leaving his meal half-eaten on the table, he had conducted a protracted long-distance telephone conversation of a private nature with a girlfriend, clearly overheard by the guests. After another lengthy absence, Mick Stow had found him outside, urinating against the house wall, and in the darkness 'he rubbished just about everyone at the party and in the country and in the world'.[39]

The hostess wrote:

> *I don't know if the night should be voted a terrible failure or a howling success, but it was certainly memorable. Xavier was discovered at one stage out the back trying to climb a tree. Patsy coaxed him into returning to the fray.*[40]

~

Persuaded by Julie and thinking that it might be a tolerable pursuit until something else occurred to me, I joined my sister as an MMA air hostess. There was also the draw of the cheap worldwide airfares attached to the job, a bonus of which we both took full advantage. My frequent passing through Broome brought new expectations from Horrie, ones that, if not met, produced a speedy letter of complaint to HQ. He was unforgiving of such sins as failing to leave the usual packets of biscuits with his newspaper or having 'only casually waved from the doorway of the plane'. There had been trouble following an occasion when I was stranded in Broome while he was absent. He would never have known I had borrowed his jeep from the hangar to get round town over a couple of days had I not made the mistake of filling the tank and cleaning the windscreen. The unfortunate individual entrusted with his keys was subsequently startled when confronted by a furious 'Who gave you the right to loan my vehicle to any old person?' There is no doubt that, for whatever reason, I brought out the worst in my father.

Sometimes, when flying between Broome and Derby, the plane passed over his loaded Land Rover beetling its way through the stark landscape below en route to Debesa. When he leapt out to wave in comradely fashion at the evidence of what he had personally wrought upon the skies, from my cool seat aloft, I looked down upon him with utter detachment.

~

Situated sixty miles from Derby, with a lease rental in 1964 of twenty-five pounds per annum, Debesa consisted of some 51,777 acres carrying about two thousand sheep. Always represented by Horrie as luxurious and modern, the 'homestead' was in actuality no more than a hot, primitive shack. Despite the best endeavours of Frank Rodriguez, the yearly gain on the station had never exceeded its losses. In the absence of any alternative, Horrie, very anxious to hold the status quo, paid Frank's store accounts, medical bills, airfares and school fees for his numerous children. Notwithstanding the entire wool cheque expended to pay his salary, Frank wrote his boss letters full of complaint. Poorly educated and, from the correspondence on file, unable to grasp the absurd inequities of the 'partnership', he became surly and, as Horrie put it (and he would know), 'went off the deep end'.[41]

Imagining himself vital to a going concern, Horrie continued to spend many hours in the hangar, repairing station vehicles and covering the distance several times a week for a variety of fatiguing purposes. Always insisting that he was working his fingers to the bone in the interests of his family, who were insufficiently grateful, he meanwhile steadily drained family company assets.

~

The extraneous manuscripts subbed or rewritten and sent off to publishers with generous forewords and endorsements, Mary could now apply herself to the short story entries from a newly established Albany branch of the

FAW. Apart from the Yagan book and a booklet about the pioneer Tom Kilfoyle[42], 1964 had gone to unpaid projects for other people. An article on Xavier Herbert for *The Critic*, 'The Friendly Highway' for *Walkabout* and a charming memory, 'Christmas at Ivanhoe Station, 1935', for *The Territorian* provided little more than the funding for the latest outlay. In anticipation of welcoming home a daughter not a whit more amenable for two years spent in London, the budget had been blown on refurbishing the entire house, the pièce de résistance being a handpainted frieze of roosters round the kitchen walls. My mother had more fun doing that than anything else in the entire year.

CHAPTER 7

'A SURFEIT OF THE FULLNESS OF LIFE' (1965–1967)

Receiving her new diary from Julie, Mary wondered how she could ever have managed without it: 'It is my memory and I hope I can continue.'[1] Only on firm ground when it came to relatively recent events, she preferred to look something up than hazard a guess from her own recollection.

An FAW reception for Eastern States visitors Stephen Murray-Smith, Max Harris and Richard Walsh was held in the new garden setting at Mildew. On the eve of leaving his home state for Sydney and the wider stage of environmental and conservationist issues, a jubilant Vin Serventy had also secured a television commission that would take him and his family on a 'Nature Walkabout' round Australia. Riding high on the success of his wobbleboard hit 'Tie Me Kangaroo Down, Sport', the entertainer and television personality Rolf Harris attended, as Mary noted:

> uncertain about his future direction but soon returning to the London scene via Darwin. He had a go at my two didgeridoos and decided he would like to get some for himself when in the NT.[2]

Also present was the now much-published Gerry Glaskin, who amused guests with an account of the joys of having me as his house guest in Amsterdam. I felt it unfair of him to make such hay from incidents beyond my control. I had not asked the American guy to follow me from Paris and I had not asked Gerry to throw him down the stairs, although it was a helpful gesture. Gerry, it seemed to me, had no scruples when it came to embellishing a story.

By now a catering service was hired for bigger Mildew functions, and the chef was often to be found in consultation with the lady of the house over the menu. Later in the year, an Australiana bash thrown for Barry Humphries featured ornamentally arranged and spicily sauced squid, grasshoppers, ants, snails and Bet's centrepiece comprising a giant lizard made from mince and cream cheese moulded on a wire frame in a setting of boiled potato boulders. The bill for the event came in at a steep 180 pounds, but the incorrigible hostess never baulked at the outlay for a party.

The arrival of writer Elspeth Huxley, at the invitation of the Simba Club for expatriate Kenyans, called for another fellowship gathering. Her visit had been preceded by that of Alan Paton, with his grimmer message of racial conflict and account of the anti-apartheid struggle.[3] The Mau Mau uprising had taken Huxley a long way from her popular novel *The Flame Trees of Thika*, one much enjoyed by Gran. As listed in her diary, Gran's reading did not in any way threaten her composure or demand any undue expansion of her well-corsetted mind. After Robin's gift to her of a television set in 1963, books, other than family productions, had become for her largely redundant.

Prior to these international luminaries, Perth had seldom been included on the list of Australian cities visited by famous writers. Disinclined to disembark from the liner *Arcadia*, Edith Sitwell had remained in her cabin to receive the greeting from the president of the FAW's local branch.[4] When Edith, clad in a black satin gown, graciously extended a heavily ringed hand that had never been put to any purpose more arduous than holding a pen, Mary, wishing she had worn gloves, quickly withdrew her own.

How isolated Perth was then, with its less than a million population stranded on the other side of the Nullarbor Plain, and what a splash a big-note name made upon our celebrity-starved city. Writers were of course less interesting to the general public than theatrical stars and pop singers, and the arrival in Western Australia of the Eastern States sensation Johnny O'Keefe had seen a scrum of screaming girls at Perth Airport.[5]

On board an MMA aircraft en route to a concert in Geraldton, the rock-and-roll legend would prove a difficult passenger, refusing to fasten his seatbelt and demanding liquor, which was not in those days provided. Spaced-out on 'purple hearts', the favoured recreational drug of the day freely circulating among the entourage, I noticed his face was scarred as a result of previous unbelted episodes, and his eyes were glazed. Overnight at Geraldton's Shepheard's Hotel, beloved of commercial travellers to whom it represented the acme of perfection, there was a further scene when his claimed sudden indisposition, to which I was summoned by his bodyguard, required the sort of ministration I was unwilling to give. In the morning, the stone-faced minder waited until I was seated at the breakfast table with other members of the crew before returning my wash bag containing aspirin, bandaids and other possibly lifesaving nostrums: 'You left this in Mr O'Keefe's room last night.' On hearing the story, one he enjoyed immensely, Father Moynihan had declared he knew someone back in County Kerry by the name of O'Keefe, the worst of scoundrels and a relative of this article, shure.

Exhausted by the continuous round of social and literary functions, Mary departed for Adsett, determined to get in a good burst of work before leaving a few weeks hence on a northern assignment to script three documentaries for television.

There had been previous undertakings at the behest of ABC producer Kay Kinane, a former Loreto schoolmate. Mary kept in touch with the friends of her youth, gathering them once a year for a 'catch-up' dinner, as she did with 'the girls' met on a 1933 Young Australia League tour to the Eastern States. Initially loath to be again sidetracked, she had given in to the combination of sentimental ties, the opportunity for a visit to Kildurk Station and the irresistible prospect of documentary films for television.

Several trammels had been cast off. The publication of *Wild Cat Falling* by Angus & Robertson had been a great coup, the book creating a stir and selling well, but as Mary afterwards confided to Florence:

> *One wonders how many reviewers would have paid serious attention to a slim volume by C. Johnson if he had not been introduced as a part-Aboriginal or his background made interesting.*[6]

Thanks to the esteem in which Mary was held by Angus & Robertson's editor, Beatrice Davis, the Eleanor Page Smith manuscript had also been accepted. When, on hearing the news, Mary had let out an unrestrained whoop of joy, Eleanor gave her a little lecture on the benefits of maintaining faith in one's talent and never losing hope.

Bet's grant from the Australian Institute of Aboriginal Studies to compile a thirty-year history of the Aboriginal people of the North West had also been cause for celebration. Twenty sketchbooks, redrafted into scrolls showing tribal customs and their gradual submergence in mission and station culture, formed the basis of this unique project. Enthusiastically publicised, the idea was too good for humdrum minds to allow it to proceed without obstruction, and the undertaking would not be smooth sailing for Bet.

Weeks of planning went into the groundwork for the television films. Matters such as procuring transport, accommodation, a helicopter and the cooperation of her brother Reg for an episode on Kildurk Station left up to the scriptwriter, it had come as a disappointment when Mary belatedly learned that Kay would not after all be part of the team, her place taken by another producer by the name of Moira Gambleton.

On arrival in Kununurra, she met the resident engineer Roy Hamilton, who arranged for a PWD vehicle to be made available, along with a driver. Thus did Jack Saville, an Aboriginal man from the Queensland Kalkadoon tribe, enter Mary's life, in his crisp white shirt and pressed shorts. Getting to know him well over the filming period, she feared he left something to be desired when it came to being an ambassador for his Indigenous brothers:

> *He has rather disconcerting views on the reasons for racial prejudice which he puts down to Aborigines not paying sufficient attention to personal cleanliness. He has three showers and changes of clothes a day and consequently does not suffer from any prejudice. In fact he is one of the most popular personalities in Kununurra.*
>
> *Asked does he think of helping his own people he says, 'No fear – they don't want another blackfellow to help them – they only want to clear him out of cash and drag him down.'*[7]

From first to last, the film venture reads as a chronicle of disunity. Since Mary generally got along with everyone, it had come as a troubling surprise to find no meeting point with the producer: 'Moira gives me a most peculiar feeling. It should be so pleasant but for some extraordinary reason, just isn't being.'[8] The ensuing debacle was summed up in a letter to Florence:

> *I have just returned from nearly nine weeks away on the ABC assignment, scripting three documentaries for TV – Kay's idea but she was unable to come so she sent a deputy, Moira Gambleton. I don't know where this association went wrong. Perhaps I tended to over-organise, or not keep in the background enough, or to talk shop at meal times or to behave in an unprofessional manner – (too enthusiastic? too interested? too eager?) No words – just an overpowering coldness and cold-shouldering, so I kept out of the picture from then on as far as possible. I thought much of the trouble lay in the fact that they were four more or less young people, two boys and two girls and a fifth old fuddy-duddy was superfluous, but on their return the girls and boys were not communicating with each other either except where absolutely necessary. The secretary was very grateful to Moira for letting her have the job and together they were in a constant state of exchanging upward glances of*

> *patient despair if I offered a suggestion. I at no time got a feeling of being anything but inadequate even when quite difficult hurdles were overcome by my negotiation. I don't want to say anything of this to Kay as it might cause real unpleasantness to no purpose. My livelihood is not dependent on any report of me that might get back to her.*[9]

Rostered on an overnight in Broome and informed of what was afoot, I sat in the garden of the Continental Hotel and covertly watched the film team in action. It was evident that insulting and belittling the famous author had become a kind of group bonding exercise, particularly between the two women. Blood boiling, I rose and stormed towards the party with a half-formed intention of mayhem but, catching my mother's beseeching eye, instead took her by the arm and led her away, with the advice she must pull out at once or at least threaten to do so. While their rudeness and discourtesy did the ABC team no credit, neither did her putting up with it in the hope of bringing things to a 'palsy-walsy' level.

For months afterwards, the lack of any civil communication from the producer continued to dog completion of the script. Many of her expenses going unclaimed, the writer eventually received a paltry one hundred pounds for each of the three episodes. One might have supposed that further solicitations from Kinane would be given a miss, but Mary never learned to be twice shy.

Alone at Adsett, as winter storms blew in she found the battering rain and raging sea an accompaniment helpful to picking up the threads of the tumultuous mission story. The ubiquitous wild cat with many kittens firmly discouraged by Ida was now being fed and let inside in bad weather: 'Crazy of course, having tried so hard to turn her away.'[10] When it went missing, she found herself worrying – venturing into the blustery night to call and rattle the plate.

> *I dare not look back to see how long I have been here. It is a luxury to have complete freedom to work but a sort of agony too for fear it is not worth such understanding on the part of the children and such fanatical concentration on my own.*[11]

Her return to Perth conveyed as if by telepathy, there immediately appeared her personal press-gang: James Penberthy with another opera in mind, J.J.J. with the script of his latest play and Donald Stuart urgently in need of a literary grant. Julie was in the midst of arranging a wedding reception at Mildew for a girlfriend, Robin preparing to fly in an air trial, and Johnson's musical career was reported suspended because he would not practise. Rather reliant on her nieces in the absence of her sister and daughter Perpetua, who was working in Zambia, Bet had achieved the happy state of widowhood.

The FAW was in bad shape, and with the formation of the Australian Society of Authors, Mary wondered if it had fulfilled its function; the few busiest writers were keeping it going mainly for the membership of non-writers who did not pay their subscriptions.

What lay waiting on the desk of her upstairs room was the cause of further consternation. Florence was given the gist of it:

> *At the moment I am surrounded not only with this year's Albany short story entries but no less than 180 [student] projects. The latter I got let into at Johnson's school. The teachers in sixth, seventh and eighth grade asked me to judge the kids' work, to which I agreed and also offered a prize. So far only three efforts with an Australian theme, the influence of American TV very marked.*[12]

Letters to Florence and Kath McArthur usually included another instalment of the running serial she made of her children's activities. Her inability to get a handle on me was largely because I never allowed my mother more than a keyhole view, so she was compelled to pad out and fabricate the invisible bits. She made well-defined characters of her family, and recipients of her correspondence found we seldom deviated from our given scripts:

> *Patsy has taken on book reviewing for the* Sunday Times *– four to six books a week. She does them well and enjoys it but wonder will she be able to keep it up at this rate with her other job? Robin is studying for her commercial licence and has a proposition to put to the Health Department for a flying nurse service if and when she gets through. Julie is in Melbourne interviewing union officials for better conditions for the hostesses. Andy is still working his way round Australia, last heard of in Mt Isa. Marie Rose who is in her sub-leaving year will be very artistic I think, like Julie. Johnson is – well Johnson!*[13]

With no hope of writing finis to *The Rock* while on the home front, Mary made a further call on the understanding of her children with another two-month sojourn at Adsett in order to complete and send away the second draft. Once that was done, she felt in better heart to front the neglected responsibilities awaiting her in Perth.

Amid the pile of mail was a gold-crested envelope with the advice that, via the governor-general, Her Majesty was graciously pleased to appoint Mary Durack Officer of the Civil Division of the Most Excellent Order of the British Empire:

> *This is an oddity. The chores I have done that might be called 'deserving' are usually so foolish and misguided I hardly dare admit them to myself. What else? Kings perhaps. Anyway, Julie sent my 'grateful acceptance' while I was still considering whether I would look more of a chump accepting or refusing. Mother will be impressed at all events.*[14]

Returning from a flight late on New Year's Eve and answering the phone ringing in the empty house, I was met by the mellifluous tones of Prime Minister Menzies. What with the seasonal good cheer, and perhaps in anticipation of his impending retirement to the Cinque Ports, he had evidently had a few. Sweeping aside my apologies for her unavailability, he decided he was speaking to the honouree in person – so I cordially accepted the felicitations and left a typically naughty note on the kitchen table:

> *Sticky mess on floor near fridge – I presume orange juice – cleaned up. Ants will get to the sugar bowl if lid left off. P.S. Prime Minister called re honour – thought I was you. I told him he was a political joke and only Labor voters here – said his call unwelcome!*

While the recipient of the OBE waded into the flood of congratulatory mail (and Gran graciously received compliments for having mothered her), Bet had been disappointed to hear that she had not won a Churchill Scholarship to subsidise her intended overseas travel. Under the circumstances, Mary had felt obliged to help out. Talking Gran into a loan of two thousand pounds, borrowed against Bet's expectations of a share in her house, she agreed to pay the interest herself. Purchasing some stylish clothes, Bet packed for a rapid getaway. There was no area of her life that she did not tackle with artistic flair: her face, her home, her garden, her handwriting (an artform in its own right) and her distinctive dress sense. Commenting later on his sister-in-law in her autumnal burst of energy, Horrie would shrewdly sum up her situation as he saw it:

Bet is the one who will come out on top really. Her groggy husband well under, her face lifted and the world at her feet – also the nerve to push herself to the top and a long pathway of interesting affairs still ahead.[15]

From now on, the diaries would be liberally adorned with postcards displaying Bet's distinctive penmanship from around the world: Mauritius, Africa, Paris, London, New York – a six-month globetrot.

Albeit on home ground, Mary was also on the move, running up a mind-blowing itinerary for the next three months, beginning with the Adelaide Festival. Her days packed with people and events, she attended seminars and gave lectures, caught up with federal FAW members and joined other celebrities for lavish parties held at the home of Lady Constance Bonython.

Travelling by road with Ida Mann to Melbourne and Sydney, all the Loreto convents visited en route, Mary then flew to Brisbane, where Kath McArthur eagerly awaited her arrival. Together they drove to Caloundra for family reunions, before a stopover at Mount Tamborine, the home of Kath's close friend and fellow environmentalist Judith Wright and her husband Jack McKinney. This was Mary's first meeting of many over the years with the poet for whom she would hold personal and professional esteem but whose approach to Aboriginal issues as influenced by her close cohort Kath Walker she found somewhat guileless and overemotional.

In 1945, Mary had made a pilgrimage across Western Queensland in company with her father. For M.P., it had been a last look at Thylungra Station, the home of his youthful memories left behind in 1886, and a farewell to remaining relatives and old associates. Now, with her brother Bill, she once again covered the two-thousand-mile trek over terrain that had emerged so vividly from the pages of *Kings in Grass Castles*. Standing on the ground pegged out and parcelled up by her grandfather and his Costello and Tully kith and kin, she captured the scene for her diary record in gripping and moving detail. Terachy, Ray, Pinkilla, Springfield, Bulgroo, Tobermory – familiar names that had fallen sentimentally from the lips of the older generation until their demise. Family connections still in residence, she had been warmly greeted by those who had hung onto their properties and withstood the droughts and floods until saved by underground bores.

Wending her way back via Goulburn, with its many Durack graves, and the Blue Mountains retreat taken up by Florence James, she made a final stop in Canberra, where Kim had rented a 'studio flat' in the suburb of Red Hill. There she found her brother engrossed in an essay on 'Man's Place in

Nature', his once unlimited outlook shrunk to a backyard of well-tended annuals. In terminology way beyond her, he had spoken of philosophical theories, intricate riddles of quantum and particle physics, maths and theology, the mystery of existence and the meaning of faith. But he looked tired and strained as he told her of the sixth-grade exam he had been required to sit before being hired as a lowly clerk with Canberra Parks and Gardens. Unable to believe that there had been no position suited to his unique intellect and expertise, when she suggested he may not have tried hard enough Kim sadly brought out the thick files of applications and rejections of many years. Evidence of something deliberate behind his exclusion from gainful employment had been deeply disturbing to Mary, and fearing her brother's endemic weariness being symptomatic of a more serious ailment, she had urged him to see a doctor.

~

On my mother's return, when I announced my intention to abandon Mildew for a quiet and orderly place of my own, the news had not gone down well. Dismayingly, with tears in her eyes, my mother admitted that she knew when she was in residence the house was chaos, but she could not bear to lose me. She had also been upset by the tone of Horrie's latest letter, intimating an increasing alienation from a changing Broome:

> *Hard to adjust with each return to the awful wreck of a joint. Dogs howl and bark at night, cars and trucks roar around through the small hours. Aborigines now confused by dollars and cents when buying their grog. Old age is showing by a tendency to hang on in bed until sunrise. Off to meet the plane now. Those planes know me and one day they will miss me bad.*[16]

Debesa rapidly losing its primary purpose, it was plain to Mary that Horrie needed a new interest. To this end her pen was soon at work on his memoirs of pioneering aviation, for which she sought advice from Florence:

> *I have finished doing a* Wild Cat Falling *on the ms and it's now pretty good. Horrie wrote it a few years ago in Broome and without any references except from his memory. It was a very human little story, but all over the place – you can imagine. He recently dug out the tatty old draft and left it with me. I thought it would take only a week or so to get it into shape, but as entirely unchecked and not a date in the whole thing it was a good month's work.*

It has a great deal of interest for South Australia in particular and would undoubtedly have wide sales there. All the big names come into it, most gone now. Norman Brearley, Huddy Fysh, P.G. Taylor and Horrie – the last of the old gang have survived to see an era of aviation beyond their wildest dreams.[17]

As his wife worried about his state of mind and embarked upon editing his book, Horrie was privately occupied in writing to Cyril Gare:

Mary, like the rest of us is dependent on what she is going to get from Miller Investments now and in the future. She may have a good income of her own, but she never mentions this. These days she has patrons, friends and others almost worldwide, all of who she generously entertains. Also she has a big circle of Catholic priests and nuns who have to be looked after. The Durack clan is clustered around her and some of them get lavish handouts, particularly Bet and Kim. My own friends have slipped away. Since our marriage I have also been separated by the typewriter, so I might need my own place for retirement. All this adds up to – how much will Mary need for future security?

Plenty of blokes zooming around the girls but only for fun I feel.[18]

Always believing her OBE should have been a shared award, Mary was glad to be able to wire her sister in New York that she too had now been honoured. The news following advice that she had received a Ford Foundation grant to enable her to travel within the United States, it had been a double triumph for Bet. ('Congratulate your sister on her decoration for me,' wrote Bishop Jobst. 'You will be next,' he predicted comfortingly.)[19]

~

Removed from the frontline at Mildew, I was able to make forays at my convenience and, with the entrance of guests, escape like a shadow out the back door. There was a distinct improvement in the relationship between my mother and me, and we were closely allied on most essentials.
But what was this?
Dr Edward Teller, the 'father of the H-bomb', was reported to be in Perth, residing at an anonymous city bed and breakfast, the visit's hush-hush nature likely to have been less from his modesty than from a desire to

avoid banner-waving protesters. The American Ambassador had arranged a reception for him to meet a selection of citizens and, worryingly, among them was Mary Durack. Apparently having modified her former view on the disruption of nature's forces by humankind, my mother wrote mildly of the encounter: 'Obviously one of the great brains of our time, but a simple, cordial man. Wish I could have tape-recorded his dissertation on nuclear power for peaceful purposes.'[20]

'And you wonder why I left this house? Have you no principles at all, Mum? *You shook the hand of evil!*'

'Well, I didn't know it was the hand of evil – all I know is that it was courteously extended.'

'It's a matter of having some code of ethics. I suppose if you had met Hitler, you would have said that he was a nice, unassuming man with a keen interest in history!'

'I don't know what I would have said. I don't see much purpose in ludicrous conjecture.'

'Oh, *don't* you?'

Increasingly muted by her literary prominence, public honours and the associations formed as a result, Mary's more radical views were always subject to no-one being offended by them.

No sooner had she written a new foreword and epilogue for the paperback version of *Kings*, arranged the celebration for Gran's birthday, attended a Perth Festival committee meeting, signed herself up for French and Spanish lessons and momentarily turned her attention back to the book, than an old onus returned. After the resignation of FAW president Bert Vickers following a row with the executive, it seemed there was no-one else available to take the chair.

The festival featuring a special 'Protest Seminar', the immediate concern was what stance the FAW would take on Vietnam. Adding her signature to the list of Australian writers opposing conscription, she held the opinion that to pull out of the conflict rather than diplomatically working a way out of it was a mistake. Consequently, in the 1966 election she had given her vote to the Liberal Party.

Officially a Labor supporter, she stepped but lightly in the chosen camp, and then only because participation was compulsory. Voting so often calling for a choice between equally uninspiring candidates, in 1959 she had endorsed the Labor Party in Western Australia, believing Kim's best interests lay in that political direction. The re-election of Brand in 1962 had been for her regretful, as had the advent of Charles Court as deputy premier. In later years, once again demonstrating her inability to hold a decent grudge, she would form a good neighbourly relationship with Sir Charles. With her cousin Peter Durack on the ticket, in the 1970 senate election she went with the Liberals, and in 1980, believing they represented the best option for some sort of 'impartiality', she gave the Democrats a go. Now, in 1966, it was Harold Holt and 'all the way with L.B.J.'

Horrie was very anti-Holt, and, in company with left-wing friends like Cyril Gare and the Korwills, he did not see any withdrawal from Vietnam under the Liberal Party. The wider Durack family, uniformly conservative, held contrary views. Bet could, over the decades, be found supporting some fairly obnoxious political figures, although Joh Bjelke-Petersen was not in the same ballpark as Hitler, for whom during the war years she had formed an ardent admiration. Perforce always chasing the money and power, had her stars been otherwise aligned she might easily have slipped into a role such as that occupied by Leni Riefenstahl.

~

These were the decades of continual comings and goings and path-crossings. Only Gran kept the full family movement chart up to date, and so many the returning travellers' tales that she was constrained to cut them short with 'Just give me the *highlights*, dear'. Julie set off for Hong Kong as I returned from another trip to London. Perpetua was in Africa, her brother Michael working on a remote northern oil bore. Andy was in Japan. Her commercial licence in hand, Robin was attending an International Aerospace Medical Conference in Sydney, while Bet, heady with the intoxicant of America, touched down once more on 'our bit of sawn-off lump of terrestrial dust'.[21]

Visiting Kim before returning to Perth, Bet had also been concerned. Tests had shown him to be suffering from aplastic anaemia, a condition temporarily corrected by blood transfusions. When Ida Mann heard the diagnosis, she made the connection with his exposure to pesticides at Camballin, but there was at this time no suggestion that the affliction was incurable or terminal. Sending him chapters of the mission book for approval or criticism, Mary had received his high commendation, one echoed by Geoffrey Bolton, who found it fascinating, and Father Moynihan, who was, in his Irish way, ecstatic. *The Rock and the Sand* had certainly been less challenging than Kim's eighteen-page dissertation sent for her comments: 'Teilhard de Chardin and where he conflicts with the doctrine of the fall. Gosh!'[22]

His health deteriorating, Father Moynihan was regularly losing fingers and toes. A natural bon vivant, when sternly warned by his dietician of the consequences of not sticking to his diet, he joked: 'She says that I am flirting with death and at my age, with my list of desirable ailments, I've got a suspicion she might respond favourably.' Although it should have been obvious that there was not going to be a strong rapport between the austere German and the Irish intellectual, when she invited them to dinner, Mary imagined their common calling sufficient to bring together her two clerical boyfriends. Manifestly incompatible, Father Moynihan behaved in a frisky and mischievous manner very perplexing to the bishop, who became stiff and correct in a somewhat military way.

The three-part television series on the Kimberley appearing to small notice, Mary did not receive a copy and it was subsequently lost and forgotten. After her death, the video retrieved from the ABC archives, it remains today as an oddity, a concoction of history and fiction. Nevertheless, some heart-stirring footage was captured just before it vanished, not least a glimpse of old Broome and station life little changed since the pioneering epoch.

~

With Tom Collins House in the process of being renovated, Mary felt obliged, as FAW president, to open her house for informal gatherings during the 1967 Writers Week and host parties for visitors to which she contributed welcoming words before her familiar invitation: 'Anyone else moved to speak?' Her car in dock, neighbours and university attendees had been amused at the sight of her squeezed into the back of Julie's toy-town red Messerschmitt, a vehicle not conducive to her making a dignified entrance or exit.

Iris Murdoch, the guest of honour, had proved a disappointment:

> *Her lectures ('The Writer in the Modern World' and 'Trends of contemporary English Literature') were highly academic and more for her peers in philosophy than such as the writers of WA. The acoustics were bad and she spoke as if to an intimate group – could not make more of it than the need to re-examine the basis of our opinions and redefine 'goodness' and 'evil'. Unsatisfactory to say the least especially as there was a packed and attentive hall including most of Perth's intelligentsia. Bet said it was all 'old hat' anyway.*[23]

My memory of Murdoch from her visits to Mildew is of a lady bravely individual in her choice of apparel: a floral-patterned dress from another era, dark blue cardigan and openwork pink stockings. Among the passing parade – *Meanjin* editor Clem Christesen, festival director John Birman, writers Tom Inglis Moore, Max Harris and Dorothy Hewett – appeared the Rumpolean form of Father Moynihan, eager to meet his celebrated literary compatriot and her academic husband John Bayley. There for the same purpose was Sister Ignatius Prendiville, an Irish Dominican nun described by Mary as:

> *a dear, puzzling person, as I suspect she is also to her community who don't seem to know where to fit her in. Her outlook is too broad for the confines of a convent.*[24]

It was a difficult transitional period for clergy in the wake of the Second Vatican Council and the Pope's stance on birth control. Nuns, unless they moved with the times, were in danger of becoming obsolete. Sister Ignatius, needing lay companionship and signposts in an uncertain topography, was to become a Mildew habitué.

Conversely, in a motley collection of questioners and doubters attending the lit-fest, a provocative attitude of certitude dogged the professional life of the Czechoslovakian Chief Town Planner Paul Ritter, who informed anyone who would listen that he was 'for truth, facts and common sense'. In so being, he had put himself at odds with his associates on the Perth City Council, regular Australians who had never stood for any of those 'foreign' principles. Seeking to curb the far-seeing and ebullient architect and inventor they had so imprudently employed, the councillors created a classic 'underdog' status for Ritter, who was strongly defended by the populace when he was controversially sacked. At one stage of his career, he had raised the hackles of local conservationists by proposing that areas of Kings Park's virgin bush, which he assessed as 'mediocre scrub', should be landscaped. The ensuing indignation via the letters page of *The West* had been put into whimsical perspective by Mary Durack, with the contribution of a verse she headed 'Really Mr Ritter!':

> *You can say that our intelligence is sub,*
> *You can rubbish everything we have to rub,*
> *But you shouldn't knock The Park …*[25]

Ritter had been delighted, as had the people of Perth. Local support, headed by Mary Durack, with whom he would remain buddies for life, saw him reinstalled on the council where, standing against the destructive 'economic rationalism' of the day, he fought to preserve heritage aspects of the city.

Within a few weeks, Bet had completed her impressions of New York in sketch and narrative form. In her diary, Mary was cautious in her praise:

> Bet's ms is fresh and original but too roughly written for publication. She is inclined to equate 'the writing game' with 'the painting game' – anything goes – bad grammar, dashes and dots in lieu of punctuation. Think she feels I am pedantic and that a book like this can surely be 'dashed off' or else lose its spontaneity. Hard to explain that sloppy writing does not sound spontaneous, only bad. But with a little more pulling together might be publishable.[26]

Intended as an artist's eye response to places visited rather than travel books, Bet's *Seeing Through* series was hampered by its impressions of the moment becoming rapidly outdated. But Bet, in a fever of travel-lust, scarcely paused to unpack her bags before once more taking wing for the Philippines.

~

Word of Mary's fruitful assistance with Eleanor Page Smith's book had got out:

> Another impossible ms in the post today for 'constructive comments.' This is one I begged off via the telephone, but it is sent to me regardless. Really, I don't know why people are so ruthless. What is more, every one of them expect me to be through to them within hours, thrilled or powerfully moved by the contents and not a little taken aback at the 'honest criticism' offered. Spoke to Hew Roberts about the need for someone to take over manuscripts on a professional basis. He says he knows – but no-one expects to pay for this service.[27]

She had also learned that if she helped by editing a chapter or two as an example, that was usually where it stalled. In light of what slid under the door, her defensive 'you should see what I knock back' didn't cut much ice. It was often just a case of who got through to apply the pressure in person. Considering what was to follow, the line to Florence 'One of a theme, an autobiography from a Mrs Drysdale turned down firmly' also rings hollow.

In an attempt to stave off an increasingly frequent imposition, she wrote to the Education Department, asking that teachers not encourage their pupils to ask busy authors for biographies, photos and hints on how to write. As a working environment, Perth had become impossible for her.

~

With Marie embarked upon a Technical College arts course, only Johnson remained at school – when he attended, which was as seldom as he could manage. Julie, tearing off on a trip to Peru, had left a room described by her mother as 'geological strata of rubbish'. Urged by us all to give it a try, Robin applied for a pilot's job with MMA. Her application was refused by managing director Cyril Kleinig on largely specious grounds, including a woman's inability to cope with asymmetrical flying in the event of engine failure. When Mary asked him to intervene, Horrie informed her:

> *I cannot influence the case. It is down to the operations manager and the present ban against employment of females as pilots is a ruling that can be only altered by a special meeting of executives.*[28]

One does not get the impression that he really approved of the idea himself. Prior to anti-discrimination laws, no airline would have a bar of it. Fortunately, by midyear Robin's scheme to distribute Sabin polio vaccine throughout the north had been approved by the Department of Health. Presented with a program planned for completion over three rounds in eighteen months, it was hardly an offer they could turn down. Prepared to work alone and for a modest wage, Robin also supplied her own plane. Granted no concessions, she was expected to find serviceable airstrips, make out flight plans from any available information, organise medical supplies, arrange accommodation and transport to the clinic, and see to fuelling requirements and aircraft maintenance. In comparison to the cost of the travelling clinic as previously proposed by the department, she had provided the government with a bargain price alternative. Now president of the WA branch of the Women Pilots' Association, she gave her Cessna 182 a test run across Australia for a Queensland branch meeting.

On her return, she took her thrilled grandmother for a spin over the city. For Gran, who hopefully enquired every day of her family if there was 'anything fresh' to report, her flight definitely constituted something fresh enough to keep her telephone line running hot for hours. As Mary wrote to Florence:

Mother has taken a new lease in life – it is quite miraculous and a great weight off my mind. She is very happy following the doings of her now twenty grandchildren.[29]

~

The final corrections on *The Rock and the Sand* proved hard going for Mary, 'so very stodgy and awful' did her writing seem to her after six years of construction.[30] She wondered what the bishop was making of the copy sent to him for comment. Having adhered to the rules of documenting history, she felt some pride in the fact that for the frustrated novelist in her, there had been 'absolutely no cheating on this book – at what cost no-one will ever know'.[31]

As much as she longed to ensconce herself at Adsett, Horrie's latest bout of depression and the necessity to deal with the page proofs of *Early Birds* drew her north. The greater distance also lessened the possibility of her getting caught red-handed in the act of blue-pencilling other people's manuscripts. When Ida was in residence at Adsett, or I threatened a visit, Mollie Skinner's biography had to be shuffled out of sight. After persuading Gerry Glaskin to take over the fellowship chair and wrenching herself from countless Perth traps, she set up house with Johnson in the old Broome quarters. Keeping a safe stretch of red sand between them, Horrie occupied the other place at the far end of the block. Constant intimations of physical decline and being 'passed over' did not inhibit his pursuing an active life.

An all-expenses-paid invitation to attend Hawker de Havilland's fortieth anniversary celebrations had lured him to Melbourne with little more than an overnight bag containing his moth-eaten dinner suit. As he flew over the familiar South Australian countryside, he had tried to remember the many different types of aircraft that had carried him across the Nullarbor, but the journey ended before he had finished the count. Most of the haunts and personalities from his youth now gone, for a few hours he wandered the Melbourne streets, feeling lost and forgotten, a perception hard to maintain when soon afterwards, among astonishingly distinguished company, he found himself accorded the VIP treatment befitting a living aviation legend:

There were the old blokes I thought were long ago dead and gone. How they had dug them up I don't know. Grey heads, bald heads, sagging jowls, one with no legs at all. Hereward de Havilland, the guest of honour, Sir Dicky Williams, Sir George Jones, Sir Lawrence Wackett, Guy Moore – none under 70 except Rollo Kingsford Smith, Smithy's nephew, now de Havilland's business manager and our host for the evening. The speeches were muttered sotto voice [sic], couldn't hear a word, long and boring. Called upon to respond on behalf of the old fellows, I refused to be so designated and made some attempts to liven things up with remarks about their youthful outlook on life, which drew wan smiles from shrunken faces. As we broke up and mingled, all were just old friends with one foot in the grave knowing we would not meet again ... soon we were drifting away to lonely places, each knowing that his day was past.[32]

The last-legs veteran was observed soon afterwards taking off the Ampol Open golfing trophy at the Kimberley Boab Festival. The purchase of another aircraft for Robin had also provided him with a new interest, compensating in some degree for the loss of the Wackett's certificate of airworthiness, as Mary wrote to Florence:

Robin has taken delivery at Bankstown, NSW of a second aircraft and should be flying back with it today. Horrie got the crazy idea that she should have two planes for the job she has undertaken for the Government. Robin feels one aircraft is about as much as she can look after at present but she thinks her dad really wants it for himself and it would be excellent therapy to say she needs it stationed in Broome where he can maintain it. I don't know what arrangement they will eventually come to but the thought of Robin juggling a couple of aircraft and talking about 'charter runs' is the breath of life to her old man and he is living every minute of her life as though it were his own youth over again.[33]

Continuing later with an account of Robin's arrival in the new aircraft, it seemed after all that Horrie had intended his daughter to have a 'spare machine'.

Robin swept in over the bay and down over the house, to let us know she had arrived. Her red and white Mooney is as light and bright as a dragonfly. She thought Horrie wanted it for himself but had to pretend it was for her. Now it appears he really means she should have two aircraft in order to keep up the continuity of flying both for the medical department and the charter work she is planning over the wet season. I don't know about the other business. It is still in the background – never anyone else apparently, although men trail after her, just longing to be of service. Julie is in South America, having a whale of a time. Oh goodness, they are a lot of fun (and a lot of anxiety of course).

Patsy has resigned from her air hostess position but has to carry on until Julie returns as they are short of training staff. She never tells me about her romance – or even whether it is still on, or if not why not.[34]

I was reticent about mentioning my personal life to my mother. Her response to my letting her know of private matters had not always been helpful, as when she had learned of my problem with Harold Dicks, one that had begun with Robin's frequent absences from Perth and my living in a flat allowing him to reckon me 'fair game'.

A stocky and rather swarthy-skinned man, Harold had an odd, abrupt manner, nervous mannerisms and a loud forced laugh. Well known to the MMA pilots, many of whom did their aviation medicals with him, he enjoyed what might be described as a 'mixed press'. Some complained he had nearly killed them, while others swore to his having saved their lives. There seemed little opinion in between. Firmly cast in Robin's world as a knight-errant, any evidence to the contrary was inadmissible. No raconteur, anecdotes from his history of pioneering work with the RFDS during the 1930s and the war years were tediously recounted. Politically opinionated, he trumpeted a far-right line regardless of the company, and in the way of many humour-challenged people, he told jokes and recounted risqué stories. The corny legend about the 'droit de seigneur' entitling the lord of the land to deflower maidens on the night before their weddings an oft-repeated favourite, I suspected it a personal fantasy.

Never more than barely civil to him, and then only for Robin's sake, I found it inexplicable that he seemed encouraged by my indifference. Exasperated as I was at his persistent pestering, I finally consented to go out to dinner with him, the pretext being that he wanted to talk to me about his future plans regarding Robin – not that I considered it any of my business. During the ensuing assault while he had me trapped in his car, the idea seemed to be that if I was 'kind' to him, significant rewards would follow. Despite my first instinct being vengeful, I had in this instance no choice but to hold my fire. Harold must have been confident that a desire to avoid upsetting Robin would prevail; even so, I was flabbergasted that he could pull such a stunt without any apparent safety net. His good sister Norah had on several occasions told me, in hurt tones, how unscrupulous women had accused her upright brother of sexual misconduct, and I had not disturbed her loyalty. Harold had been very lucky to capture Robin, and there is no doubt he worshipped her and that the set-up they established suited them both. Given the risk he took, it was less his morals in question than his sanity.

It is still painful to recall – and all too easily done via my graphic diary of the day – how I finally gave in to his pleading that I allow him to take me out again for the purpose of offering a proper apology for his 'impulsive' behaviour. The upshot of that cave-in was a late-night scene in my mother's room, where in consideration of my outrage I tearfully demanded some show of support from her. Pouring me a steadying brandy and saying that apart from a torn dress, she saw no serious harm done, she advised me to talk it over with Julie before doing anything rash.

Julie had been quite firm. Under no circumstances was Robin to be told. 'It would kill her,' she said, 'and anyway, you're not the only one – he's done it to me, as well.' Marie Rose was not to escape, either. Exploiting the safeguards we placed around Robin, it was apparent that Harold felt he could help himself with impunity to all the female kin of the beloved.

Harold was a ruinously flawed man, and his lack of rectitude in this respect alone must forever colour and affect the more commendable aspects of his character and life of public service. Always fiercely protective of our sister, Julie suggested that we should view him as suffering from a disability demanding of at least a degree of leniency.

~

Acting with the concern of a dutiful trustee, Cyril Gare had informed Horrie that in addition to the station debts, the large sums drained from Miller Investments to purchase two aircraft for Robin could be seen as inequitable to the other children, and he believed that something had to be done to put the remaining assets on a stable basis. Horrie's reaction to this letter indicates to what extent he had never properly understood company structure. He had thought the arrangement merely a formality that would not restrict him during his lifetime from using the funds as he chose. Moreover, he didn't give a damn what 'trustee' meant. Always reliant upon the faithful servant, he took umbrage at any apparent deviation from the required role:

> *The Mooney was purchased after the Cessna because it gives a better chance of survival in a tight spot and Robin may need both planes if one goes u/s. I am unable to understand why you are charging her interest from her shares on the money paid for her aircraft. I would like to see it discontinued. I do hope that you are with me and her.*[35]

~

Having sent him a draft of the book, Mary had been disappointed with the long-awaited response from Bishop Jobst. Wondering why he had not at least mentioned the donation placed between the pages, the reason then occurred to her:

> *The Bishop has not read any of the manuscript I gave him and does not seem very interested in doing so. He said he hoped he could find someone to continue the history to bring it from the 1930s to the present day. He had no idea apparently that I had brought it right up to the last census out only a few weeks ago. I asked him just to read the last chapter in case any important factor omitted. He is very taken up and thrilled with his new aircraft.*[36]

Kim's opinion sought on her concerns, he had replied:

> *Your book does somehow retain the character of an historical novel (and for such the more power to it) but I suppose the Bishop had thought of 'A History of the Missions' as something rather different; it is not often that the story of 'God's Work' makes compelling reading. Also it is possible that a woman could not understand the priestly life in any depth or even the layman if it comes to that.*[37]

With her writer's eye for the essence of those she met, had there been an opportunity to fictionalise Bishop Jobst (as, for example, was done by Jimmy Chi in his play *Bran Nue Dae*), Mary could probably have come up with an astute portrait. But unless put to the task, she preferred to take people at face value. An aspect of him she cannot have missed during their thirty-year affiliation was that for all his lofty bearing, the bishop was no intellectual and his powers of perception were prosaic, as borne out by his memoirs. At heart, he was a businessman and, given the reversal of church fortunes before his tenure was out, one might speculate better suited to a more temporal role. A banker, perhaps?

While Jobst's new aerial venture presented an opening for a variety of Luftwaffe jokes for the locals, it created a headache for Horrie. As word of the near misses and other mishaps circulated, he would spend hours at the airport waiting and fretting when 'Bish' was overdue or flying in bad weather. Nobly agreeing to share his hangar space, he also helped with maintenance on the aircraft, and the empathy was strengthened between the odd pair. But no camaraderie got in the way of the regular bulletins of broad-spectrum grievance to Cyril Gare:

> *Mary is a sitting shot for all comers. She has just thrown $100 at Bishop Jobst towards his plane when he has no need of this. Newspapers, books and magazines alone would be extremely high, some of them she never reads. Large consignments of sweets and other gifts for natives in Kimberley have been distributed. However, her generous nature is involved and I rather let her drift along than take any exception to it. I regard Robin's aircraft as an investment on her behalf, which she well deserves. Any allowance to Patsy and Julie is not justified as they spend on themselves and do nothing to pay the costs at home. I have heard – not from her – that Patsy is supposed to be involved with some pilot in Canada, but she has not mentioned anything of her plans.*[38]

Apparently, Horrie had not registered to my being self-sufficient since 1965 and he chose to ignore Julie's liberal contributions to the Mildew entertainment budget. Relegated to a compartment of maudlin fondness, Marie Rose was usually exempt from criticism, a neutrality for which her father would be rewarded in later years by her continued sufferance. We did not receive, or expect, any allowance and none of us had ever questioned Robin's having merited financial favouritism. Horrie also defined the characters of his children albeit in ways that suited his skewed narratives.

Meanwhile, putting the best face on it, Mary broached with Florence, among other sensitive matters, the adoption of the latest orphaned manuscript:

> *So far my time up here has been spent coping with the huge backlog of mail and correcting* Early Birds *proofs. I had no intention of starting on anything other but I did bring up with me poor old Mollie Skinner's* Fifth Sparrow, *which has languished for so long. I promised to read it over and see whether anything could be done*

> with it. There is a good deal of interesting stuff in it and early days atmosphere, as well as the D.H. Lawrence material which has since gained in interest. Of course, the usual sorting out, unscrambling and checking is required. Marj Rees typed it for Mollie when she was quite blind and near her end. I am doing this for Marj, who while she is meticulous in typing and checking, has not had this editing experience. I want to suggest that she should get any royalties that might accrue from the book, if it is published, as I'm fairly sure it will be when we have fixed it up between us.
>
> I won't go out to Kildurk this time as Reg and I seem to argue when we get together these days. He has to keep telling me how impossible the blacks are as though I was somehow responsible for their shortcomings. He says over and over again he'd like to sack them all and hire white men. I ask him why he doesn't and he says he can't get white men. I ask him why not pull out and leave it for someone else to solve? Then he gets wild and tells me I don't 'understand'.
>
> Good novel stuff of course, but I think I will finish the Broome story first.[39]

All her time spent on getting *Early Birds* away for publication before Christmas, once again the Broome novel would lose out – into eternity. Horrie would never have any idea what his memoirs had cost his wife, as she had revealed to Florence:

> It meant many weeks of work, delving back into early newspapers in Victoria and South Australia in order to establish the sequence of his various exploits and those of his contemporaries. He believes that it is just as he wrote it and I am thrilled about this as I was particularly careful not to give it an unnaturally 'polished' effect and I think it does sound exactly as he talks. Today, reading over the page proofs he is remembering other details I never heard before. 'I know I had them in my original version,' he says reprovingly, 'you must have cut them out during the re-typing.' (The editing job is tactfully referred to as 'the re-typing'.)[40]

Invited to a rehearsal of the Broome convent production of *The Merchant of Venice*, Mary had felt sorry for the all-Aboriginal cast:

*None of them had a clue what they were saying. A brave effort but totally unsuitable choice for these young people. Would love to write a play for them about Broome.*⁴¹

Ship of Dreams had begun its gestation.

~

Taking a two-week break from her role as the 'Sugarbird Lady' (by which term Aboriginal children described the woman pilot who dispensed medicine on sugar cubes), Robin was preparing for her first RFDS ferry flight across the Pacific with Harold.

During her polio vaccine tour and a side trachoma clinic with Ida Mann, she had been much missed at home. Without her, Gran's little day-to-day complaints had disappointingly cured themselves, and Mary was unable to sort her son's real ailments from the concocted:

*The symptoms are genuine enough but can't help wondering if he is getting adept at inducing them. Accused, he gives a heart-rending cough, looks unutterably tragic and says, 'Call that psychological.'*⁴²

It was at this point that Marie Rose innocently introduced to the house a pallid and spindly English youth in his twenties who had been travelling round Australia. Far from home and missing family, Iain Horner had been drawn to the warm Mildew atmosphere. Likely with some calculation, he made himself at first useful and then, by taking an interest in an increasingly difficult Johnson, indispensable, as far as the harassed mother was concerned. Personally, from no more than a passing encounter, I thought him probably harmless.

For me, the family and its associated problems were about to be left far behind. Noting my last-minute announcement that I was leaving for Canada to marry Robert Millett, an Australian pilot working for a float-plane company based in the far north of British Columbia, my mother declared me 'too like her father for words. Fear any attempt to give her an appropriate send-off will be thanklessly repulsed.'⁴³ Further to the discovery in her correspondence files of my doings over the years, I realise that, unhappy with the original draft, she rendered me more resolute, strengthened the plot and fixed up the general structure of my life. Filling in storyline gaps, her shameless blue pencil knew no bounds. She, in fact, subbed me!

Everyone came to see me off – a flashback to one hundred years earlier and the departure of my forebears for the New World. In photos taken of the occasion, even Horrie can be seen lurking in the background. But the question was there: who might I never see again? Looking from the window of the aircraft, I felt a pang at the last sight of Gran's dear familiar figure.

Full of dire prediction, Horrie prowled nervously within the vicinity of the Mildew phone while Robin and I crossed paths over the Pacific. When Julie moved out of the house, the daughters he had long complained still on his hands were now going to be hard to catch. Leaving him to it, Mary retreated to Adsett and unburdened herself to Florence:

> *My salvation is to get away occasionally when I manage to cover the ground and life becomes again supportable. I really have nothing to complain of except a surfeit of the fullness of life, and a sense of the swift passage of time when I never so much wanted to get down to consistent writing. Re Rock and the Sand – a pleasant surprise that Constables liked the book. In fact Mr Arnold says it held him 'spellbound' and that they are very excited about it. This is far more than I expected. Bishop Jobst said he found it 'dismal reading' from a missionary point of view but he supposed that as it was the truth it had to be told. He punctiliously 'corrected' or 'improved' the wording of quoted extracts which I had most carefully, under Father Moynihan's eagle eye, left scrupulously sic and he made a firm request that I delete the last section entirely – that is from his entrance on the scene. It is impossible of course.*
>
> *Robin is back from San Francisco with the Beechcraft Baron for the RFDS. She is looking blooming and appears to be leading a thoroughly fulfilled life. The old attachment persists, but does not dominate as her job keeps her in the north for weeks at a stretch and she has lots of other interests as president of the Lady Pilot's Association etc. Julie has taken over Patsy's flat. She feels she will get more rest there than at home. She won't of course as she is too gregarious and social. What she really wants is to have the flat and her room here as well for the overflow. But the dear girl is always a joy to me – as warm and extrovert as ever. I expect that now Patsy has gone off she will get married to one or another of her admirers.*[44]

Widely distributing Christmas cards with news of my marriage, meeting the in-laws and assuming her customary seasonal duties, Mary was already mentally preparing further episodes in the lives of her children, God-willing, including a new generation.

Complacently sunning herself in the reflected glory of her illustrious family, Gran busily snipped out the almost daily newspaper coverage of one or another, or with a blissful expression on her face took commendatory calls on their behalf – not least among them her grandson David Durack, awarded a Rhodes Scholarship.

The drowning of Harold Holt had provided an absorbing talking point, Mary observing that in his obituary appearances on television the late prime minister suddenly took on a sadness and dignity previously not noticeable. Horrie, visibly cheered by the tragedy, had remained sociably in residence for the festive season. He would find John Gorton, with his RAAF and crash-survival background, although unforgivably Liberal, more acceptable.

Christmas for Mary was 'noise, chaos and mess'. Somehow the dinner table managed to accommodate fourteen family, including her brother Bill and his wife plus four of his children. Larger gatherings, such as the annual FAW party for forty guests, had been spread around the 'bear pit'. Flying in from Port Hedland just in time to attend the festivities, Robin reported having felt so exhausted en route that she landed her aircraft at Learmonth and went to sleep under the wing – waking to find six pairs of hairy male legs standing around, the men looking at her as if she had arrived from outer space.

New Year's Eve was always spent with the Korwills, who generously catered for a fluctuating band of friends, mostly Labor stalwarts, European refugees and a few lame ducks thrown in. For a period before the socialist cause fell into disrepute, a rousing rendition of 'The Internationale' followed 'Auld Lang Syne'. The speciality of the house in those days of plenty, and a free-for-all upon it, was a delicious clam chowder, made from abalone taken from the rocks at Cottesloe Beach, to be consumed with Ferry's potent Haydn punch, a traditional beverage guaranteed to leave guests with a hangover on New Year's Day. I still see the familiar faces lurid under a string of green lights, looking, as John Wheeldon gleefully pointed out, like a meeting of the Irish Foresters, an impression enhanced by his rendition of 'The Wearing of the Green'. Wheeldon, possessed of a coruscating wit as well as an independent will, would eventually break from the long control of his patron Marianne Korwill and exit from politics in 1981. On this occasion, Mary also amused the company with an account of her recent sitting for an artist and his twelve pupils, who had produced paintings of thirteen different women – all plain.

~

From my snowbound exile on Shearwater Island in northern British Columbia, I looked out upon a vista of white-capped mountains, and islands crosshatched with fir forests rising from deep blue inlets – an unreal chocolate-box picture. Accounts in my letters home of marauding bears and wolves around the lonely trailer where I was holed up against a variety of novel hazards lost nothing in the recounting by Gran. It was certainly far from home – about as far as I could possibly have contrived.

'Mildew', 12 Bellevue Ave, Nedlands, 1940.

Mary with four under four at Mildew, 1946 (from left: Robin, Julie, Andrew, Mary, Patsy).

Above: Mary in Broome. Below: Mary at home at Mildew, 1946.

Above: Miller family in Broome, 1952 (from left: Robin, Mary, Patsy, Marie Rose, Julie and Horrie). Below: Argyle Homestead.

Elizabeth and Mary, 1946.

Elizabeth and Mary Durack with Ernestine Hill, about to attend a reception for the Queen in 1954.

The Durack sisters at Elizabeth's home, 1951.

Bob Hill, 1954.

Gran and the Millers, 1953 (from left: Robin, Bess, Marie Rose, Andrew, Mary, Patsy, Julie).

Loreto girls Robin, Patsy, Marie Rose and Julie Miller with cousin Perpetua Clancy (centre), Bellevue Ave, 1954.

Kim Durack (above and right) at the 'Parthenon', under construction, with Patsy Miller and other family members, 1957.

Mary Durack Miller and family (from left: Johnson, Robin, Mary, Julie and Marie Rose) with a first copy of Kings in Grass Castles, *1959.*

Horrie Miller with his Wackett aircraft, Broome 1961.

Above: Mary having just completed the first draft of The Rock and the Sand, *Adsett, Geographe Bay, November 1963.*
Below: Ida Mann and Florence James, Adsett, 1964.

Above: FAW gathering, January 1964. Back row from left: Irene Greenwood, Mary Lacy Selsmark, Eleanor Page Smith, Dr Donald Stuart, Coralie Congdon, David Foulkes Talyor, Julie Miller, Helen Wilson. Front row from left: Carol Serventy, Michael Page, MDM, Vincent Serventy, Elizabeth Durack, John Miller. Below: Horrie and Robin Miller, 1965.

Above: Lounge room at Mildew. Below: Millers with Gran, 1965.

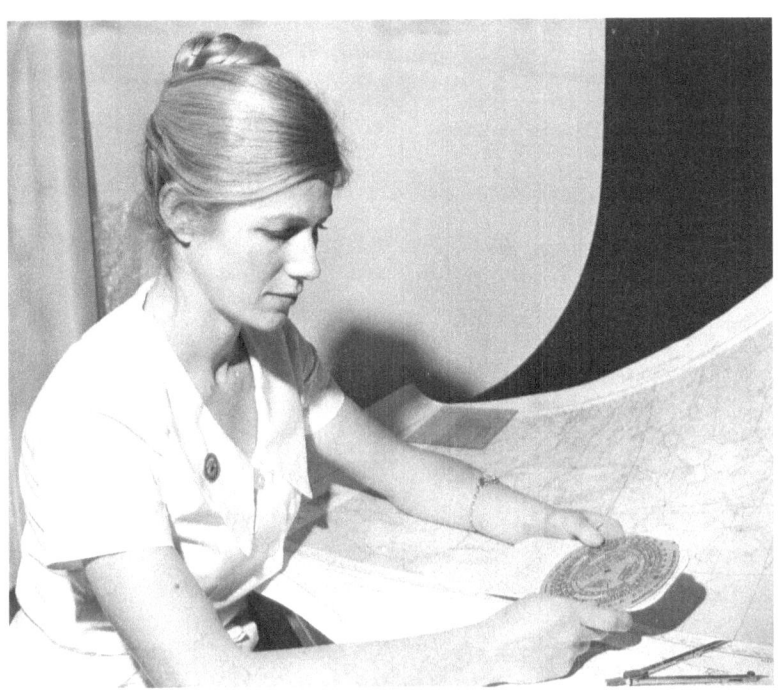

Above: Robin Miller, 1963.
Below: Robin with Dr Harold Dicks, 1967.

Bishop John Jobst, 1967.

The Ship of Dreams *opening night, 1968.*

Mary with Albert Barunga, Derby, 1969.

Julie Miller seated in an F27 MMA, 1968.

Diary entry December 1969.

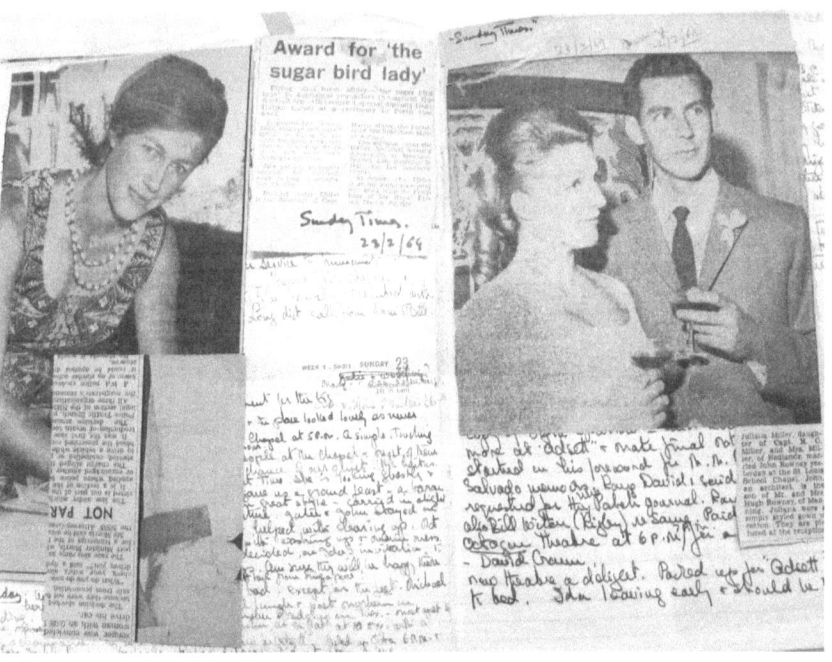

Bess Durack at her Nedlands home with son Reg and daughters Elizabeth and Mary, New Year's Day 1975.

Above: Mary with Hal Porter, 1975.
Below: Mary with Barry Humphries, 1979.

Mary with Horrie at the opening of Robin's Jandakot memorial, 1978.

The Durack sisters with honorary medals: Elizabeth's Order of St Michael and St George (CMG) and Mary's Order of the British Empire (DBE), 1983.

Nita Pannell and Mary backstage at Swan River Saga, February 1972.

*Mary with family and friends, Christmas 1988. Back row from left: Naomi Millett with Alex Megaw, Yagan Millett, Patsy Millett, Marcus Miller, Joseph Megaw, Marie Rose Megaw.
Front row: Jack Saville, Mary, John Miller, Penny Arrow.*

Mary with her 'sisters' (from left: Marie, Mary, Dot, Daisy and Peggy), Kununurra, 1987.

Newspaper clippings from 1994.

The author meeting with Bob Hill, 1995.

The last days of Mildew, 1996.
Marianne and Ferry Korwill, 1980.

Patsy working on the archives, 1996.

CHAPTER 8
THE COMING OF THE CROWS (1968–1969)

Within a well-defined social framework, we were yet in an era when fundamental components of our family remained in place. Thus would we confidently proceed with faith in a natural course until curtains slowly descended on epic lives, or closed with brutal suddenness upon those whose days were not destined to be played out. Mary would later remember as a malevolent portent the appearance of a crow in the Mildew garden, a bird hitherto never seen or heard in the suburbs. Turning her unease to verse, she wrote:

> *What has brought you to this ordered haven,*
> *This refuge of magpie and warbler,*
> *Wattler and wren, of pastel-feathered dove –*
> *And I – all come to terms*
> *Protesting your invasion?*
> *Importunate raven,*
> *Attendant of the dying, guest of the dead.*
> *When will you learn there is no carrion here*
> *And go your way*
> *Unwelcome crow!*

But en route to Geographe Bay, such forebodings seemed fanciful; with Iain Horner at the wheel and the boulder of the mission book about to roll away in the direction of her London publisher, she was able to relax and take in the passing coastal scenery and the towering karri and jarrah forests of the South West.

Brushing the dust from her work area, Mary got down to her mail, helped Ida with her trachoma survey report and (surreptitiously) continued editing Mollie Skinner's book. But the work was intermittent and put away by late afternoon to welcome visitors, the first being the celebrated English artist Lady Mary Rennell, to feasts of fresh seafood caught by Johnson and Iain. In essence, the pleasures of Adsett were simple and yet near enough to Paradise for the occupants that mild and transcendent summer.

In lighthearted mood, Mary began to shape in her mind the outline of a musical play for the children of Broome. Thinking up words for songs about buried treasure and ghostly galleons, she enjoyed the sense of doing something frivolous in complete contrast to the straitjacket of history.

Intuiting *Ship of Dreams* as not a vehicle suited to the musical acumen of James Penberthy, on her return Mary contacted an old friend who composed music, and she and June Fitzgerald set about combining their talents. Involvement with Kuljak, a new Perth theatre workshop formed to promote local playwrights, had also brought her in touch with a number of possible producers. The Broome nuns, hearing of the idea, had delightedly promised every cooperation.

It was a wrench to turn her attention to the somewhat tall order for the 1968 Adelaide Writers' Week theme: 'Biography and Comparative Values in Australian and World Literature'. She was grateful for the 'more cogent' input on the subject from Judith Wright, who, as guest speaker at the FAW Corroboree, was temporarily in residence at Mildew.

Arriving to make her contribution to the six-day panel session, which was usually held at a university venue, Mary found herself instead assigned with the group to a number of factories so that workers might be introduced to culture via lunch-hour literary recitals. This experiment, at the behest of the trade unions, was followed by a charter flight to Woomera and a talk on the history of the Kimberley for defence personnel and their wives. Moving on to Port Lincoln, she was gratified to find a packed town hall and a further crowd spilling outside the door for her address, until question time revealed that the majority had attended because they were fans of Horrie, who had long been a local hero. Many having taken a first unforgettable flight with him during his barnstorming and flying boat days in that area, treasured photos and personal memories were pressed upon her. Henceforth, the tour of the Eyre Peninsula became an unashamed plug for the soon to be released *Early Birds*.

It was at this time that Mary heard Henrietta Drake-Brockman had died suddenly in Perth. As with the deaths of many close to her, Mary would continue to commune in her dreams with her dear friend: 'As the baby crawled towards the fire I called out "Henrietta get that baby." "No, that's your baby now," said Henrietta.'[1]

After a brief break in the Blue Mountains with Florence James, she visited Kim, who had taken leave to write a theological thesis he hoped might evolve into a book. Now receiving regular blood transfusions, he assured her that he felt 'newborn'. Keen to catch up with his Miller and Clancy nieces and nephews, he asked, deceptively cheerful, that she 'shoot them through to me, Mary, fairly quickly'.

Robin was again the centre of press attention when she and Harold returned with two single-engine Sud Aviation Horizon aircraft ferried from Paris to Perth for a private company – an eighteen-day tandem flight involving ninety-three flying hours. It had been a dicey venture undertaken for nothing more than the fun of it, but the northern wet season had temporarily put the Flying Nurse on hold, and gambling with her life in foreign skies had somehow represented to Robin a respite from routine perils at home. Among other close calls, they had nearly been shot down after straying into restricted airspace over Beirut, and it had only been Robin's inspiration to tear the ribbon off her ponytail and let her long blonde hair blow in the air vents that had turned the hostile military jet away.

Despite the successful completion of a remarkable feat, the local front-page coverage boiled down to no more than a banal story about how Robin's Western dress ('Mini-skirt meant Maxi-trouble for Nedlands Pilot') had shocked the Arabs. Harold, however, had no objections to the 'Shapely Blonde in Historic Flight' aspect, and it suited him to have the ballyhoo directed her way. The following year, after an article about her activities appeared in an Italian periodical, she was taken aback to find herself awarded a 'Diploma of Merit for Services to Human Life' from the Mantova National Nursing Association. Mortified by the tabloid and television fanfare, she would have withdrawn her cooperation had not Harold persuaded her that such promotion was of benefit to the RFDS. Her entire working life, Robin sought for herself neither publicity nor praise, although she liked to receive a thank-you in recognition of some monumental rescue effort.

~

During his sister's stay in Canberra, Kim had produced a list of amendments he considered vital to *The Rock and the Sand*. With absolute confidence in his advice, Mary returned to the manuscript she had mentally left behind with Constable's approval of the final draft. A week at Adsett required for the complicated rewording of the parts designated 'disappointing', only one day had passed before she was awakened early by the sight of Julie's stricken face at the door.

> *While living all day with Kim's instructions I little knew that it was the last day of his life. Finally it was a sudden attack of pneumonia that caused his death as the drugs he was on for his blood complaint*

*rendered him immune to penicillin. He admitted himself to hospital and died a few hours later.*²

Flying that night to Canberra, Mary met Bill at the flat and, heavy-hearted, they began packing up Kim's modest belongings and copious papers. Disposing of them was a task complicated by his having left no will. When they faltered, Julie took over – 'a tower of strength and efficiency', as her mother noted. Bet, having received the news in Port Moresby where she was 'seeing through' Papua New Guinea, was spared the anguish of the funeral and having to deal with the practical details.

The last of the flowers and autumn leaves from his garden gathered to place on his coffin, Kim was buried in the Canberra cemetery, his grave marked by a plaque in the grass, far from home and the land to which he had given his life. Addressing to herself for transport to Perth the suitcases and cartons of documents – residue of an extraordinary life – Mary grieved in her diary: 'I cannot say what the loss of this wonderful brother means to me and to us all, though in a strange way he still seems close by.'³ Some day she hoped to find the space and spirit to write the Kim Durack biography, a story she believed should be told.

Nothing in her eighty-five years had prepared Gran for the sorrow of losing the son, of her four loved sons, closest to her heart. 'Why', she wondered, in the way of all bereaved mothers, 'was I not taken and my own dear Kim allowed to live and finish his work?'⁴

The press hailed him as a man whose burning faith in the future of the north had seen him pursue his vision without thought of personal gain or the sacrifices involved. A leading article in *The West*, speaking of the debt owed him, suggested that the new lake formed by the Ord River Dam be named in his honour.⁵ The political realities that had done for Kim while he was alive would see no such sentimentalities after his death. He had been mightily inconvenient to the course of ambitious men who perceived him as an impediment to progress, and within a few decades his achievements would be bypassed in rewrites of the history of northern development.

In through the doors of Mary's dreams he came, 'looking ghastly – saying something about the kind letters people had written. I asked how on earth they could have made a mistake about his death. He said, "They didn't," and vanished.'⁶

Kim's papers would join the archival boxes and files stored in the annex of her upstairs room. Opening one or two cartons, she found he had kept all the records from Camballin: copies of his letters, worksheets, growth charts, a daily journal and, penned in his neat Christian Brothers hand, the many exercise books containing his journey into elements of the higher mind. Dipping into a handwritten draft titled 'An Exercise in Refutation; Kant and the Ideal of Pure Reason' and finding the discourse out of her field of study, she had been too overcome with sadness to do other than put it all aside for another time.

With what was now a bounden duty to incorporate his suggestions into the opus, she left at once for Adsett and, putting all else aside, applied herself until the job was complete and the manuscript posted. It had been a cold and secluded interval of winter gales that threw up hundreds of venomous Portuguese man-of-war jellyfish to lie along the waterline like fragile blown glass. As she worked or ventured out to walk the flotsam-strewn beach, Kim's forceful presence never left her, so she did not feel alone.

On return to Perth, the too long deferred matter of dealing with her errant English agent was tackled by the roundabout means of writing to Florence James in the hope that she might deal with it for her. Like the former 'home helps', Mary's literary agents over the years had been barely better than having no-one, and hardly worth the percentage they extracted from earnings. Ursula Winant of Winant Towers, an associate of Florence in former and happier Richmond, Towers and Benson days, had proved under her own label a poor communicator, months passing without indication that she was handling even routine business. Word that the woman had suffered a mental breakdown won her not the sack from her neglected client but the sympathy vote. This unsatisfactory state of affairs continued until 1974, when Babette Johnson of NVG Agencies, another incompetent, was engaged.

The reluctance to get rid of hopeless hirelings extended to Mrs Haebich, the European 'ironing lady'. Invariably arriving with the fatalistic words 'Every day must be happening something bad', her loopy woes and the peddling of handmade dolls to disguise toilet rolls made Mary's Fridays fairly unbearable. To her mother's relief, Robin took it upon herself to dismiss Mrs Haebich, and but for my later sporadic attacks upon it, the ironing became an unattended mound in the laundry.

With tradesmen constantly needed to unblock drains, seal the leaky roof and fix wiring prone to deliver violent shocks to the unwary, the old house was showing its age. 'The day of reckoning must come and 12 Bellevue Ave will have to be sold up, nothing surer' was Horrie's prediction to his distant daughter.[7] But while less sure things came to pass, Mildew would hang together for another thirty years before the fall of the final hammer.

~

With the intention of involving Kuljak in the staging of *Ship of Dreams*, Mary soon found her association with this theatre group more than she had bargained for. Drafted to the steering committee and administrative side of a scheme to foster local drama, she had come up against the tiresome rivalries and divisions within Perth's theatrical factions. Over the next few years, while she would make use of a producer and director from among its members and retain the ties, she would otherwise exhaust herself with the mechanics and politics of a worthy venture that produced nothing of worth. *Ship of Dreams* was to set a standard far beyond the aspirations of Perth's budding dramatists.

With the help of local prisoners, John Joseph Jones had begun constructing an amphitheatre within a natural setting on land he had acquired at Parkerville in the Hills, the venue offered to Kuljak for their future productions. He was to persevere with this financially parlous undertaking in defiance of seemingly insurmountable obstacles that did nothing to dent his brash confidence or his belief that all he needed was the right backer.

Looking towards an opening date for the first week in October, Mary was already in a panic at the prospect of bringing an ambitious musical drama from scratch to stage in eight weeks. Before leaving for Broome, she had seen Horrie through the event arranged to launch *Early Birds*[8], hoping the expected media attention might defeat his determination to be a forgotten pioneer:

> *Thirty-six years since I surveyed the route to link with Qantas Empire Airmail Service. Only a few old-timers still recognise the fading old guy who was among the first to drive an aerial road over this isolated land.*[9]

Among the thinning ranks of air veterans, he was in fact well known and not unused to being approached by strangers wanting to shake his hand or mention some connection with his early flying career. The publication of his autobiography would merely bring him a new measure of fame. It also had the effect of unearthing a number of his former colleagues, including his First World War observer, not heard of for forty-five years, and praise from unexpected quarters. After reading the book, the Japanese Consul had sent an appreciative letter and an invitation to attend a celebration for the Emperor's birthday. Introduced as 'Captain Miller' among the many titled at the elaborate event, Horrie accepted with a laconic wave the Consul's bobbing obeisance. Mary suspected he was rather sorry now that when in the 1950s a group of former associates had put his name forward, he had flatly refused a knighthood. It was not so much his wife's accumulating honours he resented as the 1964 OBE (along with the Japanese Order of the Sacred Treasure) awarded to his old Broome adversary, the pearling master and merchant Sam Male, 'for service to the community, of all things', as he would bitterly remark.

With one hundred guests waiting at the new MMA passenger terminal in the city, the author was on his big occasion not an Early Bird. His flight from Broome delayed, he had arrived straight from the plane looking typically crushed and blown about. Nonetheless, he made an appropriate speech well seasoned with his best yarns.

Pleased as he was by the success of his book which in short order went through two editions and into a paperback issue, Horrie would cultivate characteristic umbrage. It was his bestseller, so he chose to believe, that set off lesser reminiscences from other aviation pioneers, and I was the recipient of the audacious information that he felt the story had lost a lot in 'the editing process'. Separated by the comfortable length of the world, my father and I were enjoying the best relationship of our lives. His letters, full of such nonsense, were always a source of amusement to me, as were Gran's daily diaries, sent monthly so I would not feel too homesick.

~

Under the auspices of Perth's Patch Theatre, of which company Mary Durack was a patron, David Crann and Jeff Carroll were lined up as producer and musical director for *Ship of Dreams*. Detached from his wife's doings, Horrie had been antagonistic to accommodating the theatre people in the old house; he was barely prepared to tolerate Johnson, who had come to Broome for his holidays. The problem was solved when Father McMahon offered the hospitality of the presbytery to the thespian cause. A cast selected and the community hall allocated for rehearsals, the town turned itself over to the excitement of a show shaping up as bigger than the royal visit. Frequently flying in to see how things were going, Robin took a keen interest in the proceedings, and with her enthusiasm Horrie began to warm to the idea.

Dealing with seventy-two multiracial children, the rivalries and infighting among the 'technical crew', the costumes, props, the live goat and the cockatoo, Mary had not envisaged having to be so personally involved. But as each new crisis arose and was overcome, it was plain that she was revelling in what might have taken years off the life of another. Keeping Gran up to date, she was under no illusion about the production being other than amateur:

I can't see it being in any way a polished show. Rehearsals don't seem to make much difference to the standard – the kids have just about reached the peak of their capability which is good in spots. Nothing on earth can induce them to speak their lines distinctly or remember from one rehearsal to another where they should be standing at different moments. However, the very look of them might be enough to make the show reasonably successful.

When they come on in full dress it makes up for much and the cockatoo is the star of the whole affair. Twelve Aboriginal boys are being tutored by their elders for the corroboree sequence. All turned up at the dress rehearsal most elaborately and correctly painted with white and yellow ochre that one of the grandfathers had travelled eighty miles to get. Can you just imagine the scene around the Shire Hall with these boys darting about armed with spears and boomerangs among a bevy of girls and boys in Malay, Chinese and Japanese costume and their proud parents crowding around the doors to get a look in?[10]

~

When the holidays came to an end and Johnson returned to Perth alone, Mary was faced with a situation that arose from her continued absence from the home front. Johnson's attendance at school evidently dependent upon Iain Horner being in residence at Mildew, Marie Rose, who was also living in the house, had been placed in an invidious position. She found his presence unbearable, and doubts may have also entered Robin's mind as to whether Iain's attachment to the teenage Johnson was entirely healthy. Intervening on her sister's behalf, Robin wrote to advise her mother that Iain would have to leave, especially as Johnson was anyway absconding. Mary's letter in return summed up the dilemma for her:

So sorry to hear you have copped this problem. We can't blame Iain. He has tried and in a few cases succeeded where I have failed in persuading Johnson to go to school, but he can't work the impossible. As far as I'm concerned he is the only one to run errands and do odd jobs around town and he is a real help to me – not that I would let that influence me if there weren't other factors to consider. You can't really wipe people off as being anything so simple as 'just revolting'. I realise Marie's hostility all too well and am not unsympathetic about it. I must write Iain firmly about this, but sadly as will also miss him.[11]

Another thorny problem to be dealt with from afar was the appeal from a deputation of fellowship members that she once again take the chair, as Dorothy Hewett was allegedly creating a bad impression by openly avowing herself a communist at a time when feelings were running high against the Soviet Union after the crushing of the patriotic resistance in Czechoslovakia. Aware that the writers group had long been considered politically suspect, a taint that had pained no-one more than Henrietta Drake-Brockman, Mary's response was a letter to Dorothy paying tribute to her valued contribution to the fellowship, one she sincerely hoped would be ongoing, with a postscript suggesting the exercise of a little more discretion in the light of political etceteras.[12]

~

A week from the opening, the musical still lacked cohesion, coming across more like a series of separate vaudeville turns. With hundreds of northerners planning to converge upon Broome and Bishop Jobst organising trucks for the mission communities, time was running out. Huge calico Japanese fish flapped from poles round the airport to greet a charter plane conveying invited guests, the press and an ABC film crew. Telegrams of good wishes arrived from across Australia and a high pitch of anticipation prevailed:

> *The whole town is caught up in it, the songs known by the entire population and walking through the streets you can hear snatches floating from foreshore shacks to pearlers' mansions. Dad, from being an uncooperative wet blanket, has ended up being more delighted about it than anyone – the only thing I've ever done, I think, that has really impressed him. It should work wonders towards giving the children a sense of pride in their own history and the richness of their different racial backgrounds.*[13]

Played to a capacity crowd, at the last minute the show miraculously took on a life of its own, and opening night was a triumph. Resplendent in a Thai silk evening dress loaned to her by Julie, Mary, taking her bow from the stage with June Fitzgerald, had been gratified to see Horrie lead the standing ovation from the front row. Attending all performances with the utmost enjoyment and as sorry as the rest of the town when the final curtain fell, he arranged a fitting tribute for his wife's departure:

Horrie had got permission for the cast to line up in a guard of honour to the aircraft and we were sung away on choruses from the play. It was really moving. Some of the children were crying and I felt like crying myself.[14]

This fleeting season of theatrical euphoria would become a local legend, never to be forgotten by any of the participants. A year later there was a Fremantle run with a new cast, but the predictable dramas of mounting a production involving children and animals were slight in comparison to the tour de force of the Broome performance. *Ship of Dreams* did not make much profit over expenses, but proceeds were returned to the community towards the establishment of a Broome Dramatic Society.

Over this period, I was disturbed to note that my mother encountered individuals implicated in the villainy that had seen Kim cast into the wilderness. With her brother so recently relegated to an early grave, her continued civility was a regular cause of discord between us that rather forced me to adopt counter attitudes more inimical than should have been necessary. But if your life's mandate is to get on with everyone, then there can be no room for animus and Mary had no capacity for the negative stuff of long memory.

~

In the final phase of her Sugarbird Lady round, when Robin deposited her thousands of record cards with the Health Department, she would have administered 37,000 doses of Sabin vaccine and flown 69,100 kilometres. Looking for another job that would combine flying and nursing, on return to Perth she began studying for a First Class Instrument Rating, funded by a Commonwealth Scholarship. Having disposed of the Cessna, she now put her Mooney (by chance bearing her initials R.E.M. in its registration) up for sale, not anticipating the albatross it would become over the next three years as 'tyre kickers', most of them angling to meet her, came and went. An application to the RFDS successful, Robin's first base was in Carnarvon, where her posting was met with antipathy from the two local doctors, who refused to fly with a woman pilot. When a more amenable medic from Meekatharra was seconded, Robin would report him as 'always diving for my legs and bosom – puts the pilot off'.[15]

Newspaper cuttings enclosed with Gran's journal conveyed to me the excitement of an earthquake that had destroyed the country town of Meckering and rattled Perth, cracks in walls around the city and suburbs attributed to the event. Further tremors promised by an equally excited press, Barry Humphries, who was in town with his show, became so nervous that he took to sleeping in the foyer of the Palace Hotel while his then wife Rosalind stayed awake to give early warning. Barry, whose characters Mary found more excruciating than amusing, would remain a good friend and she would take her place among a coterie of celebrated ladies to whom he would remain considerately faithful.

~

Checking the galley proofs of *The Rock and the Sand* and pronouncing the book 'incredibly dull', Mary handed the chore to Father Moynihan. The problems with Johnson were back on her plate, and from now on her diaries register these as an ever-increasing disruption to her life. There was no alternative but to fling into the fray a mixed bag of psychiatrists, counsellors, chaplains, the Child Guidance Bureau – all proving useless. Gradually, the formerly lenient and loving big-sister relationship we had with the baby of the family disintegrated into an exasperated battle.

While fully occupied with auditions and plans to stage *Ship of Dreams* at Fremantle for the Perth Festival, the lead-up to Christmas 1968 demanded of Mary no less a performance. She had made it for herself a tremendous yearly ordeal, the card list alone running into hundreds. There were parcels to be sent north for the Broome orphanage, the missions and Kununurra reserve residents, with special extras for the old Durack-era people. Rheumatic complaints (known as 'romantics') prevalent, they all received, in addition to sweets, tobacco, pannikins, dresses, shirts and scarves, a tube of Dencorub – or 'dingo rub', in the local parlance. Gifts were also dispatched to relatives, literary associates, Broome friends and people needing to be thanked, along with baby clothes sent to Canada, where I was not buying anything in the way of costumes in advance of the actual production.

Planning for the usual Christmas dinner at Mildew for her branch of the family and the inevitable ring-ins, with the expectation of Bet's imminent return, Mary also conscientiously observed the tradition of 'sweeping around' and putting the basics in the returnee's fridge. In the process, she could only contemplate the contrast between her sister's free-as-a-bird life and her own.

For two years more or less continuously on the move, home for Bet had become the place to assemble the output from her journeys. With the usual dispatch, having completed forty drawings, some mounted on copper sheets, for Conzinc Rio Tinto's Bougainville Copper, she already had her *Seeing Through* book in draft form.

Since her travelling money injection, Bet had corresponded liberally from abroad and caught up between times, but Mary picked up on a new caginess about her finances and supposed that this meant she was doing alright. As with Horrie and Ida, she envied her sister's ability to withdraw and single-mindedly apply herself.

For Mary's part, any hope of work had been subverted by the seasonal duties begun in November, and by mid-December she was 'nearly round the bend with this end-of-year tangle of which the merest minimum has been tackled. Getting out about fifty cards a day – each with a personal note.'[16] After being presented with a Kalgoorlie gold-smelting crucible as a token of FAW life membership (how many such had she bestowed upon other members?), she snatched a few days at Adsett to revise the play script. Actress Nita Pannell and her doctor husband Jim were now regular visitors, and from their mutual interest in the formation of Kuljak, the two women were discussing some form of cooperative venture. *Ship of Dreams*, which Nita had agreed to produce, would be their first collaboration.

~

In America with Harold prior to another Pacific ferry flight, Robin was absent for the Christmas Day gathering of twenty-two family members and friends, among them John Rowney, a presentable young architect brought along by Julie. On New Year's Eve, a tragic event would see the cancellation of the usual celebrations:

> News received about midday that the MMA Viscount aircraft had crashed with no survivors. It was a terrible shock, but human nature being what it is my original panic was relieved as soon as I ascertained that Julie was not on board. She would have been, but was grounded with a cold, so the sound of her voice was music to the ears as never before. Many calls from relatives and others inquiring about her. Heavy cloud of gloom. Good friends lost.[17]

Because of her connection to the airline's founder, and believing she should make a personal gesture, Mary wrote to relatives of the crew and sent telegrams on behalf of Horrie, who had succumbed to a stress illness over the disaster.

In her capacity as senior hostess, visiting the parents of the three air hostesses lost on the fatal flight, Julie had been shocked when one inconsolable mother, on seeing her out the door, had bitterly burst out,

'Why couldn't it have been you?' The poor woman immediately apologised for the remark, but Julie felt somehow guilty that it had not been her. At that moment, she decided to resign from MMA, and within days she had accepted a marriage proposal from John Rowney.

~

Committed to her yearly contribution, by now Mary had pronounced the Summer School a dead loss. Added to the penance were the numerous nuns and priests unable to attend festival venues without a lift to and fro, afternoon tea at Mildew usually part of the outing. A few members of the Moral Re-Armament movement, who had somehow become mixed up in the Catholic collective, also seemed to have a transport problem. As a group, Mary found them sincere but their morals, re-armed or not, confused and naive.

With family members urging she follow up on a suggestion that Argyle Station be salvaged from the Ord River Dam and re-erected as a permanent museum, Mary was soon discussing ways and means and the relocation of her father's monument to the pioneers and the headstones from Durack graves. But she could give no more than scattered attention to the ambitious plan while preoccupied with Julie's wedding, editing *The Fifth Sparrow* and being 'put upon with ridiculous tasks for other people'.[18] The booking office phone number somehow left off the newspaper advertisement for *Ship of Dreams*, calls were deflected to her and she was made personally responsible for fiddling jobs involving the wardrobe, props and finding the goat and cockatoo. After the last performance, in her own role as Lady Bountiful, she arranged a catered party for the children and distributed gifts to adult members of the cast and crew. But it had all been too much for her, and when she complained of 'feeling jittery with thumping noises in my head', Ida had advised her to take sedatives. She missed her daughter's healing hand, since Robin's employment as both pilot and nurse for the RFDS Air Ambulance required her to be based in Carnarvon.

Julie and John Rowney were married in February, the repainted house a bower of flowers for the eighty-five-guest reception, and to cap off a day of celebration came the joyful tidings from Canada of the arrival of a first grandchild. With assistance from Miller Investments, the newlyweds bought an old house in Claremont and, after a honeymoon at Adsett, set about renovating the place. Horrie, who had attended the wedding in sociable mode, was soon making a fuss over the cost. In a benevolent moment having agreed to pick up the tab, he warned his wife that when Cyril Gare retired, the family company would have to be administered by a stranger to her extravagance. Of those of his numerous children, Julie's wedding was the only one for which he ever saw a bill – the resented sum being five hundred dollars for a relatively simple home affair. But he had his justifications: 'Don't feel hurt dear if my poor childhood on the poverty brink makes it hard for me to accept such a lavish turnout. I feel the impression left is that the Millers are millionaires.'[19]

Mary never did lose sight of 'the motherless child' in her husband, and much is explained by this. The debts mounting on Debesa were partly responsible for Horrie's bad attitude to profligacy other than his own. When his partner Frank Rodriguez deserted him for a better offer in Derby, he had been forced to put the property on the market and keep it going for any potential buyers. He knew that it would have to be sold at a loss, most of the 100,000 dollars spent on 'developing' the place irrecoverable. To Mary's alarm, he was also talking about leaving Broome and coming south to work on a sequel to *Early Birds*, tentatively titled 'Out of the Blue'. The very thought of this, let alone the 'old man', as she increasingly came to refer to him, in permanent residence in Perth gave rise to foreboding.

For some peace from Mildew's ceaseless interruptions, she retreated to the 'awful pickle' of the newlyweds' house, a move that also briefly separated her from the daily conflict with Johnson. But for this off-the-rails element, everything seemed more or less satisfactorily on track. There were wedding photos on the mantelpiece, pleasant in-laws, a granddaughter in Canada and soon Julie's happy announcement of her expectant state. Her calendar full of unavoidable engagements, Mary's hopes of joining Ida on a trip to Vancouver to visit me were regretfully put aside, as had been other opportunities to travel overseas. While she would vicariously share Bet's latter-day gallivants, the trip to England and Ireland with her sister in 1936 would be her only experience of foreign soil.

With second thoughts about leaving Broome for the unquiet Perth house, Horrie was now considering relocating himself to Carnarvon to be with Robin, as his variations on a theme had informed Cyril Gare:

The situation at Bellevue Avenue is rather frightening to me. I saw a few of Mary's cheque butts and money flows out like water. She is on the 'up and up' these days. People are flocking onto the bandwagon of her popularity and success which means a constant stream of visitors, meetings of executives on this and that and mobs of relatives all seeing our spacious house and garden as an ideal place to gather. Then we have Iain Horner, the pommy salesman who is now regarded as indispensable to Mary and a downgrading of the old worn-out mechanic, myself. I am mentioning this to you Cyril, so that you will get an idea of my thinking, the need to have independence is really acute for me.[20]

~

A party on 6 July 1969 celebrated the combined birthdays of Julie and Bet, 'a very happy occasion', before Mary left for the yearly session with the South West branch of the FAW.

A few days earlier, Horrie had written to her of a strange and disturbing dream:

> *I have built a plane and am worried about testing it. There is a girl with glorious blonde hair running in the strong, dusty wind. She is crying, 'It's too heavy.'*
>
> *'How, why?' I ask her, 'Tail heavy or nose heavy?'*
>
> *'The centre of gravity must be wrong,' she says. Tears are streaming down her cheeks as she runs after a huge ball being blown away by the gale and dust flying; her lovely hair and beauty; it is Julie, darling Julie. Such sadness in her eyes. I hold her to me and run with her.*
>
> *She does not smile. No. Sadness is in her blue eyes.*[21]

After attending various functions held by the Albany writers, Mary returned to Adsett, where she was delivered an urgent message telling her to telephone Gran.

> *She told me that Julie had been taken suddenly ill with spasms of pain. They thought at first poisoning but yesterday traced the trouble to adhesions due to the clumsy appendix operation when she was a little girl in Broome – the pressure of the pregnancy causing intestinal obstruction. Harold called in a surgeon to operate last night. Mother said no real need to hurry back but I packed at once and got on the road quicker than ever before in my life. Picked up by John Rowney and down to Devonleigh Hospital. Julie not really with it but said a few words. Harold says so far so good, but not out of the woods.*[22]

Gran was meanwhile lamenting:

It is dreadful to think of the pain that the poor girl went through and what a very complicated operation. They pushed the womb to one side while operating but it will be a miracle to prevent a miscarriage. In her favour is that she is young and in splendid health. What a blessing Harold Dicks is so close to the family.[23]

The following morning, seeing it was a struggle for Julie to talk and that she was receiving good attention, her mother left her to sleep. Harold rang to report the patient was 'holding her own', but as the day went on Mary felt increasingly apprehensive. Unable to rest at home, having decided to stay the night at the hospital, she was caught on her way out the door by a call from Irene Greenwood, who settled into her usual voluble stride. When Mary disengaged herself at last, the phone rang again:

Harold said not to come – that Julie had just passed away. He came back at once with poor John and we just sat holding each other quite stunned. At last put through a call to Horrie in Broome. Everything suddenly a nightmare of desolation and grief.

With characteristic self-control, Mary would continue to make a brief daily summary, her familiar hand steadily recording the precipitous pitch from the routine confusion of her life into unchartered waters. Gran, in the midst of her prayerful platitudes, had been suddenly confronted by her granddaughters Perpetua and Marie Rose:

It seemed to make no sense what they were telling me. Our Julie has gone from us. I do not know full particulars but the ordeal was too much for her heart. I am writing this in a dream – but feel the urge to do it – perhaps to make the realisation come to me. Here I am at eighty-five with a full life of happy memories behind me and there is our lovely Julie who has been only a few months married with the hope and joy of motherhood before her – taken from her husband and all who loved her so dearly.[24]

Subsequently, several times and with some intensity, Robin assured me that Harold had done everything possible. Until then, it had not occurred to me that he may have been derelict, but over time his part emerged. Aside from some aggrieved talk, there would never be any question of sheeting the blame home to the original culprit. It would at any rate have been difficult, as Dr Cook was held in family favour for his unwavering loyalty to

Kim. As for Harold's role: only involved because he had been immediately available, it had been his decision to place Julie in a local hospital where he dealt with a few uncomplicated maternity cases.

There being no doctor on duty when she complained of feeling faint before losing consciousness, all the nursing aide 'specialling' her could do was run into the corridor to raise the alarm. By the time Harold arrived to attend an imminent birth, although he claimed to have made strenuous manual attempts to revive her, Julie was lifeless. In the B-class confines of Devonleigh, there had been nothing in the way of equipment to deal with a postoperative blood clot settling in the heart, and the patient died as a result of the operation rather than the actual disorder – the ship lost for a ha'pence worth of tar. The hospital was functioning on the level for which it was designed, so there would be no inquiry into her death.

After delivering twins, Harold arranged a relief pilot to take over for Robin and flew off to Carnarvon without a flight plan or runway lights, no doubt rehearsing his story en route. Robin was roused at dawn to the unexpected sight of his unshaven, hollow-eyed face, and knew at once there was something alarming to be imparted, but her mind running through the list of possibilities had stopped well short of the reality. Flying to Perth with two severe head injuries needing attention in the rear of the aircraft, she just managed to hold together until she got home, when she collapsed, to her mother's distress, 'utterly broken up'. Marie Rose understood that she had first gone to the morgue.

Mary woke to 'the cold, hard reality of having lost, for this life at least, our bright and beautiful darling – the sunshine of our lives – and the little one she had looked forward to with such joyous expectation'.[25] Maintaining a state of rigid calm and sparing herself nothing, she faced the morbid practicalities. By the following afternoon, most of the family had gathered at the house. Horrie arrived with Cyril Gare, 'shocked but not emotional', as Gran noted a little disapprovingly. He was later observed busily mowing the lawn in the rain, to the surprise of visitors coming up the path. In the interests of self-preservation, he must have felt he could not afford to take the loss too hard. 'Poor fellow probably needs to keep himself occupied,' said Gran with doubtful charity. 'Then the man from the funeral parlour came and it was too much for me and I asked to be taken home.'[26]

The black tidings went out across Australia and beyond to the other side of the world. By this time I had abandoned the northern wilderness for a more civilised Vancouver apartment, and it was there I received the brief phoned telegram: 'Sad news dear. Our Julie died yesterday after emergency operation.'

Dumbfounded, I walked out into the night and stood looking up into the firmament for some glimmer of an explanation. Her flow stopped in full force, was it possible my young and vital sister was now amid Durack shades like her grandfather and great-aunts Bird and Marie? Someone like Julie did not just 'die yesterday'. It had botch-up written all over it. But for two infants the previous century, through two world wars and hard lives in perilous locales, the family descended from Patrick Durack had been spared the anguish of premature death. I also had an intuition that our linchpin had been removed, and it was going to be a battle to restructure the family. A return wire – 'If Julie has gone then God help us all' – was the first expression of my sense that things may have turned permanently awry for the Miller family.

During the funeral, Mary looked away from the horror of the coffin to concentrate on the intricacies of a magnificent arrangement of white flowers. Noticing the air heavy with the sickly-sweet smell of massed blooms from wreaths, a thought crossed her mind that she should collect the cards they bore to show Julie. Nothing she was seeing or hearing seemed to concern her daughter or any aspect of her, and she found herself constantly turning for comfort to the one whose absence created the need for it. So far from comprehension that her golden girl was lost and silent, she had not wanted to view the body and Harold had taken care of the formalities.[27]

The same priest who had married Julie now conducted the bride's final rites. During the service, at the words 'For whatever reason our dear Julie has been taken, we must accept it as God's will', a devastated friend was heard (to some scandal) exclaiming from the back of the church, 'Well, fuck God then!' I could only endorse the sentiment.

Horrie, while grieved – one must, I suppose, take that much as read – remained behind defensive walls, his stoicism interpreted by Robin as 'taking a philosophical outlook'. He was, after all, not too far from the end himself, an eventuality he had been boringly anticipating for many decades. ('Julie certainly stole his thunder,' said Mary grimly.) Absenting himself from the funeral, only he had been there to answer the phone when from my limbo I had rung home. Assuring me that 'the weeping and wailing is more or less over here', he was unhelpful in supplying any details as to the cause of the catastrophe. From this time, there was no mention of Julie in his letters and he never again spoke of her in my presence. It was just a bad job. A crash!

To whatever extent she accepted Harold's version of events, Robin could not shake off the thought that the outcome might have been different had she been there. Bonded since birth, the sisters had never let one another down.

Andy had arrived in Perth for the dual purpose of attending the funeral and announcing his intention to marry Rosemary Birrell, a former 'Miss Kununurra'. A few weeks earlier he had sent a confidential letter to Cyril Gare – a classic of its kind – that more or less summed up his predicament:

> *I have landed my girlfriend in 'the family way'. I have been taking her out for some months now, presumably with the eventual intention of marrying her. She is a very beautiful girl – Miss Australia entrant for this area last year. I am at present faced with the decision whether to marry her or not – this being the most immediate problem as she is two months gone and the axe is due to fall shortly from her parents. Why I have run out of time with her is because I have been unable to decide but it seems I am left with no choice or else vamoose. So you see I am up that well-known creek. I can sort out my other problems on my own, the bull catching, the truck business etc, but not the woman department as there is now too much of a time limit on her. So what I need ASAP is finance or consolation urgent.*[28]

No prospective buyers for the property having emerged, it then occurred to Horrie that a more sober and domesticated Andy might be willing to manage Debesa.

An American syndicate acquiring properties in West Kimberley had so far not made him an offer, and he was anyway antagonistic to the idea of 'selling out to the Yanks'. Camballin and Liveringa had already been purchased by Australian Land and Cattle Co. Ltd[29]; over the next twelve months, the five remaining stations would also go the way of the 'big hat from Texas', Jack Fletcher.

The proposition was put to Andy and, in the absence of anything better, he agreed to give it a try. If he saw the offer as a prospect rather than a last-ditch stand against a sacrificial sellout, no-one else did.

~

When a blow can be shared between a close and loving clan, one gets through it. Robin, who understood this best, began to run a strong line for family unity, 'no matter how hard the effort', until I felt obliged to tell her to shut up. There was something about the good and gentle selflessness of Robin that reminded me uncomfortably of Beth in *Little Women*. She had also taken seriously the setback to the family investment company with Julie's intestate death, and the dangers in counting on likelihoods – such as that an elderly father will go before. In a letter urging me to make a responsible will, she underlined the words: 'We just can't afford to ever be casual again, Julie showed us that. We can never take it for granted that one of us might not die and muck up the company.'[30] A decision was made that the three remaining girls would leave their shares to one another. But, dwelling on the losses over Julie's probate, Harold Dicks began to feel Miller Investments needed the benefit of his business acumen to avoid further such careless mistakes. Convinced the shares were badly administered and anxious to review the portfolio, he had for some time been trying to obtain the articles of association and other pertinent papers. Persuaded to act upon his concern, Robin had requested a meeting with Cyril Gare, one Horrie endorsed on the understanding she wanted to know all about the functioning of Miller Investments.

Reluctant to pass documents, as he well knew would be the case, into the hands of Harold Dicks, Cyril received from Robin over the ensuing months increasingly curt demands for action. None of these letters sound like her, but they do sound like Harold Dicks. It spoke volumes for Cyril that, affronted by the suggestion that his careful husbanding of company affairs over the years had amounted to little more than conservative mismanagement, he did not resign forthwith. However, believing Robin to have been manipulated by a man who Cyril, but for Quaker principles, could not have viewed with charity, he did not hold it against her.

A sad family group had gone to the house in Claremont and packaged up Julie's belongings, among them wedding presents and still-unwrapped gifts from her twenty-seventh birthday, an event that seemed light-years away – the little cot in readiness too poignant for words.

As Neil Armstrong and the crew of Apollo 11 sped towards the moon, Mary could only acknowledge 'a breathtaking achievement and a pity our hearts find it hard to rise with them'.[31] Not knowing what to do with Julie's ashes, she had them temporarily placed in her father's grave.

A deluge of condolences ran the full gamut of the diverse means by which sympathy is conveyed in cases where words of comfort, particularly of the Catholic variety (and how many of these there were), seem inadequate. The apparent necessity to acknowledge them all personally became in itself a distraction and a consoling occupation for Mary. A fuller account needed for relatives and friends, each one became a separate heartbreak – the letter to Kath McArthur typical:

> It is the hardest blow I have ever been called on to face. Julie was not just a daughter to me but also a loving sister and a friend to me – always so helpful, understanding and full of commonsense. Since

her marriage to John we had all warmed our hearts in the glow of her happiness. It is some comfort I suppose to know that she packed more experience and love into her short life than many could do in a century.[32]

~

Within days the first copy of *The Rock and the Sand* appeared. In the circumstances, this momentous achievement gave her no pleasure. All was dust and ashes. Julie had designed an attractive jacket but, without consultation, Constable had gone with a weak montage, as they had done with *Kings in Grass Castles*, in lieu of an eye-catching drawing by Bet. Covers, it seemed, were an area publishers deemed theirs in which to wreak a sabotaging exercise, and Mary had never felt confident enough to stand up for her preferred option. Only Bet's pandanus palms on the jacket of *Keep Him My Country* had ever stood out.

While *The Rock and the Sand* would not receive the acclaim or sales of *Kings* and its sequel, in terms of it being an authoritative understanding of a complex history hitherto and henceforth so elusive to the best of minds, it is arguably Mary Durack's finest work. Arriving daily with more armloads to be signed before dispatch across the world, Father Moynihan practically bought out the first edition. At least his years as a literary editor gave him some idea of protocol. Requests from other clerical friends for gratis signed copies were so frequent that the author could only suppose they presumed she got them free.

Shortly before her death, Mary was perplexed to receive a book titled *From Patrons to Partners* by Margaret Zucker. She did not remember the woman, who had visited her for information about the missions without disclosing her commission from the bishop. Published through the Catholic University of Notre Dame in Fremantle, Jobst had finally got what he always wanted: a pedestrian history of the Catholic Church in the Kimberley that served to sum up at a stroke the gulf that had always existed between Mary and the man she thought she knew.

~

Three weeks after the funeral, Mary could be found speaking on 'assimilation' to the state council of the Country Women's Association and afterwards judging the cake, pickle and jam entries. Her good offices were also required to pacify warring parties within the FAW, brawling over the suitability of a stone bench memorial for Henrietta Drake-Brockman. A genuine attempt to disengage herself from the committee was thwarted when the new president Olive Pell, feeling out of her depth, begged her to stay. All the better-known literary figures having done their several stints, the position was increasingly falling to the lesser lights, and as a result the fellowship had begun to lose its former place as a force within the community and its relevance to writers themselves. The days of operating in a void had passed, and professional writers were developing a healthy self-interest in the disposition of their time. Without seasoned diplomats like J.K. Ewers, Vincent Serventy and Mary Durack in the chair, petty quarrels disrupted meetings, and it was difficult not to notice that functions were dominated by elderly women.

And so for the bereaved mother, life went on, the days too crowded with people and commitments to allow for the indulgence of drawn-out mourning. But holding herself together in public became subject to increasing strain: the sight of Ophelia in her coffin at a performance of *Hamlet* had been too much for her, and she had to be led from the theatre. Her family scattered far and wide, she would soon be looking for the old remedy of a return to her 'spirit country'.

Horrie and Robin, now sought-after celebrities, were in Adelaide for a memorial function to honour the aviators Ross and Keith Smith and another to commemorate Harry Butler's first airmail flight. After a season of gratifying media attention and recognition of his place among the flying trailblazers, Horrie would return to face the likely loss of his claim to legitimate employment.

In stark contrast to her previous trek into lush jungles of Bougainville, Bet was in Mount Tom Price on a new commission for Hamersley Iron. Observing that when it came to business ventures in the North West, taking something out was so much easier than putting something in, she was witness to bulldozers clearing the land for the iron-ore township, creating an instant desert with every Indigenous element removed. 'They would have carted away the red dirt if they could have,' she wrote to Mary, 'but will no doubt decently cover it with asphalt.'[33]

Marie Rose had gone to Kununurra to represent the Miller side of the family at the August wedding of Andy and Rosemary, who would spend their honeymoon in the comfortless abode at Debesa. To see how they were settling in and to meet her new daughter-in-law was all the excuse needed for Mary to board a flight north with Johnson. Her visit to the newlyweds found them yet 'in brave heart', and Rosemary a cheerful and good-natured girl.

The station now in the 'lost cause' bracket, Horrie's greatest fear was that his position in the airline was coming to an end. Since June 1969 a division of Ansett Transport Industries, MMA's cessation of activities as a limited liability company also meant no more directors. The restructuring had pitched him into a state of trepidation, awaiting from week to week some indication that he had been 'sacked'. By this stage, his salary (sent with a paper slip he was unable to decipher) was actually no more than a gratuity but one he felt he deserved in recognition of his status as founder.

On her return to Broome from Debesa, noticing Horrie's unusual level of despondency, Mary discovered that the blow had apparently fallen some three months earlier. Well aware that his sinecure had given him his reason for living in Broome, what he would do if not constantly running out to the airport she could not imagine. Feeling badly for him, she wrote to Cyril Gare:

> *Horrie is deeply hurt at what he has taken to be his dismissal from any part in the affairs of MMA. This may be so, in which case it is discourteous to say the least that he should not have been informed and simply left to deduce it from the fact his salary has not been paid for a few months. This may be an oversight, though H. himself is sure it is not. To me however, it seems incredible that the founder of a company and long-term director should be removed without so much as a formal letter of advice to this effect. For all he has gloomed about having 'had it' and his intentions of retiring, the figurehead role he has continued to play in company affairs has been extremely important to him and I think to the company as well. If what he suspects is correct I am afraid it will be a bad setback to his morale and ultimately to his health.*[34]

Whether it was an oversight or not, Cyril, bypassing MMA head office, soon dealt with the matter. Horrie was enormously relieved to receive a civil letter from Reg Ansett informing him that his salary would be paid for six months to mid-1970 and that he was extended free travel for life. With much in common, the cranky and idiosyncratic pioneers had always got on well, and Ansett was one of the few for whom Horrie never had a bad word. Privately, Mary and Robin thought the honorarium rather ordinary, but as far as Horrie was concerned the friendship had, by and large, paid off. Similarly, he kept up a genial lifetime association with Hudson Fysh, the founder of Qantas, to whom he sold that airline's first aircraft.

For a decade there continued some show of preserving the identity of a regional airline until a few months after Horrie's death, when the MMA logo and the aircraft named in his honour vanished beneath new Ansett livery.

~

Travelling to Kununurra, Mary consulted the PWD about the plan to dismantle Argyle Homestead and remove items of historic value before the anticipated flood. On a visit to see the station manager, she was met by 'Keep Out' signs and a padlocked gate. Mr Bell, she was informed, had been put out by the increase in tourist traffic since the publication of 'some book'. For the Aboriginal people who had accompanied her in the hope of seeing the site for the last time, locked gates and dams meant a much sadder separation. By 1968 most of them had already been evicted from their station homes by the badly implemented introduction of equal wages for Aboriginal pastoral workers, a long overdue policy which had devastating and demoralising consequence when they were replaced by white employees. The few whose services were retained, finding their dependents no longer cared for even on the previous rudimentary level, had soon drifted to the newly established township of Kununurra where they were swept up and relocated to outlying 'reserves'. And now their 'born country' was going under water for a project which they were being assured would be to their economic advantage.

Taking a tour of the diversion dam construction, Mary wondered for what specifically its vast supply of water would be used. Her musings were dismissed by Reg, who saw only the unlimited potential. Enid and Reg's frontier days were behind them, and after years under an iron roof and front open to wind and weather, they had more than earned their move into a modern air-conditioned homestead with a view over the surrounding plains and ranges. Further to their improved financial situation, their son John, a possible contender to carry on the enterprise, was flying around the station in a recently purchased aircraft – and what pride in the other children as they pursued paths of academic excellence. But even as he stoutly declared he would not sell at any price, Reg feared for the future of the pastoral industry, with Indigenous people, he believed 'stirred up by urban interferers', now demanding land rights. While Mary differed with her brother on many issues, she was not entirely sure herself, given entrenched attitudes throughout the north, that good racial relations would be served by the divisive issue.

Calling at Derby's Mowanjum Presbyterian Mission, she raised the question with the leading lawman, Albert Barunga, with whom she would over the next fifteen years share a close affinity. A member of the area's Worora tribe, he was less concerned about land rights than about uninitiated younger people losing interest in their tribal past and threatening to reject the disciplines and standards of both European and Aboriginal culture. Disturbed by evidence of dissension between claimants among his own people, he had attended land rights meetings while continuing to hold to the view that if their culture was to be rescued, his people were going to have to unite and cooperate with white sympathisers: 'I say two people got to be like brother, go arm in arm or we don't get anywhere – talk quiet and kind about each other.'[35]

With Albert's voice ringing in her ears, Mary returned to Perth to find a letter from the chairman of the Australian Council for Aboriginal Affairs, Dr H.C. (Nugget) Coombs, asking her for suggestions as to how Indigenous people might be encouraged to retain their pride of race.

It was in this way that the Aboriginal Theatre Foundation (ATF) came into being, with Mary as the Western Australian representative and Albert Barunga a principal member. Alert to an opportunity, and given only a few weeks by his creditors to demonstrate that his theatre could make a profit, J.J.J. was soon enquiring about the possibility of an Aboriginal dance group coming south to open his amphitheatre. Having managed to avoid becoming vitally involved in his project from its inception, it was with some misgivings that Mary consented to raise the matter with the relevant authorities:

> *This I did on the understanding that I could do no more than pull the necessary strings and, in the event of a positive answer, help on the sidelines. I made it clear that I had no experience of company organisation and no time to take on anything in the nature of the management of such a project. I was assured by J.J.J. that these minor aspects would be attended to efficiently so long as the money was forthcoming.*[36]

Under the auspices of the Australian Council for the Arts, the two-day inaugural ATF meeting in Darwin opened discussions on the means to establish a body to preserve, foster and develop Aboriginal theatre and related arts, along with the proposal that Indigenous representatives with voting powers be encouraged to sit on central and regional committees.[37] Heady possibilities were floated, such as an academy for performers and teachers, and tours and exhibitions of dance and related culture both at home and overseas. Allocated an initial ten thousand dollars, a budget was drawn up for the year's activities, including sending a group of dancers to Perth. Of an esteemed group of individuals invited to join the board, only Ted Strehlow refused on account of his fallout with Nugget Coombs. His presence would be missed.

~

At the end of her tether with Johnson, and using to good effect her ineffectual mother's brief absence, Robin removed him from Aquinas College and placed him at a local high school, where he could sink or swim. On the eve of her departure for the United States and another ferry flight marathon, she believed the problem, for the moment at least, solved. There was nothing much she could do about the pet cygnet picked up by Marie Rose, an incontinent duckling adopted by Johnson wandering the house, and the bees that had taken up residence in the wall of her mother's upstairs flat. Part of the wall and door frame would have to be pulled out to expose and remove the hives, but for some reason the bees had chosen Mary's working area and nothing over the years would discourage them. In the end, when honey was oozing from the electrical outlets, the place had to be demolished to see them dispersed.

Until Robin and Harold arrived in Vancouver en route to collect a new RFDS aircraft, other than a dutiful call at the behest of my mother from Randolph Stow, who had sat for a tedious hour in a scene of harassed domesticity, sans booze, there had been for me no visitors from home. Harold, whom I had not seen since the assault on my still-affronted person, entered bland and affable. But for my relentless chronicle of events, I might have doubted my own memory. On hearing the grim details of how a drunken man from the local Indian reserve had forcibly entered the Shearwater trailer and beaten me senseless, he displayed every proper sort of indignation and sympathy. With sincere concern he urged my return to the safety of my home state, taking it upon himself to assure my pilot husband of 'an open door' should he want a job with the Flying Doctor.

~

Among a large crowd of mourners, on 4 October 1969 Mary and Bet had attended the funeral of Katharine Susannah Prichard. The eighty-five-year-old author's coffin, covered in the red drape of her conviction, otherwise displayed only a bunch of local leschenaultia and smoke bush. Instead of a conventional service, a 'Song to a Dead Comrade' rang out before her communist associate Vic Williams read his tribute:

> *The future gathers in your words and deeds.*
> *The hands you joined, no bombs can break apart,*
> *Writer and fighter in one human heart.*[38]

Her ashes were later scattered from the top of Greenmount Hill within sight of her home, which would be preserved and in future years become a writers centre.

Having avoided discussing politics with Katharine, Mary would always defend her friend against her contemporary and latter-day critics, publicly arguing the case for a separation of the writer's political views from her literary works. Her grand cause mocked by the grinning skulls of martyred millions, one might deem Katharine as having failed a fundamental test of character; witness (among other writers) Dorothy Hewett's leaving the discredited party in 1968. Ultimately holding her place as a leading figure on the Australian literary scene, she will be remembered for having the courage to express a different view in a narrow-visioned, like-minded community.

~

With lyrical fatalism, Horrie wrote from Broome of packing up and disposing of his gear of the years stored in the hangar:

> *Just the right thing for the job – now to the tip. The wind moans through the old corrugated iron walls, rising and falling in the saddest cadences. I have a swag of tools. I wonder if it will be my destiny to wander off in the Land-Rover looking for work on engines? No spirit left for that anymore. I work in a kind of a dream talking to myself and mostly I say 'Oh no,' but go on with it. I am packing things up as if I'm going on a long, last journey. Every now and again my dear old Wackett standing beside me looks over and shouts, 'What about me?' As the sun lowers, the sound of a plane's engine that has become for me the world's saddest tune fades on a note. It speaks of distance and farewell, of loves, hopes and of youth when one had to run to catch time; now stumbling footsteps, limbs like old gum trees, gnarled and drooping – down the long trail we go.*[39]

Giving it away, he closed the huge doors and took off for Melbourne and the opening of a memorial at Moorabbin to his associate, the intrepid Sopwith test pilot Harry Hawker, who had dived into the ground in 1921.

~

As she surveyed the group gathered for the Christmas evening party, no brave attempt at normalcy or the trappings of seasonal cheer could dispel for Mary the spectre of a scene out of kilter and 'everything that seems unnatural':

Seeing John standing among the guests where he and Julie stood at their wedding reception less than a year ago was nearly the last straw for me. All I could do to hold myself together. I felt it was a sombre little gathering – an ordeal perhaps for everyone.[40]

Included in activities and travels, for a while John Rowney remained within the comfort of our family, but gradually, no longer with a fixed place there, he retreated into a life of his own. Still living in the Claremont house, he would retain cordial ties with us over the years.

Taking with her to Adsett Robin's 'astonishingly extravagant' present of a new typewriter, Mary found any thought of work forestalled by the arrival of Hal Porter, intent upon his version of recreation. Riding high on the production of his play *Eden House* and the success of his latest book *The Actors*, with its acerbic view of postwar Japan, 'he looked very fit – dried out and tanned and being his catalytic self – interesting, amusing and sometimes, with his moments of truth, shocking'.[41] A man composed of many parts, Hal could also play the courtly admirer. Observing the hostess moving graciously among the guests gathered to welcome him, he raised his glass in salute: 'Here we all are, dear lady, basking in your infinite beneficence and the sunshine of your smile.'

CHAPTER 9

CROSS THREADS (1970–1971)

From her desk at Adsett, not without a twinge of guilt, Mary put aside 'the job in hand' to sketch the distractingly beautiful view from the window. Her working time already at the mercy of the house guest, she excused the leisure moment as bolstering her spirits to face the coming year:

> A whale splashing around in the bay, a blue wren and its brown mate, gulls, terns, butcher birds, western warblers, cicadas and all the lovely sounds of the Australian summer.[1]

With Hal Porter in residence, the party began with his noon rising and ceremonial cooking of oriental eggs, his belated breakfast speciality. Resolutely on leave, Hal was happy to shake out pockets and suitcase to demonstrate that lest he be tempted towards anything more sober, he had not even brought a pen with him. Initially dubious about her overtly hedonistic guest, Ida had soon fallen for him. Who in the end did not succumb to his practised charm and play along with his expectations of bacchanalia? By sunset he was just getting into his stride, and at midnight goading the flagging assembly (including, to his snobbish delight, the aristocratic Lord and Lady Rennell of Rodd) into marathon talkfests until, vampire-like, he vanished with the dawn.

Using as a weapon his extravagant verbosity, Hal was wont to crush any opposition to an outlook curiously narrow for a writer: reactionary, monarchist, in favour of censorship. Seldom was there a better case for detaching the writer from his views. When Ida suggested as a good subject for the theatre a local case involving a doctor and matron who had been charged with manslaughter, Hal loftily declared that the principal function of any playwright was to entertain. Would such sordid matter entertain? He thought *not*! Among a group of dedicated conservationists, when the hot topic arose he reverted to a sphinx-like silence – indicating a theme that did not interest him. Whatever his private convictions, passionate exponents of right-mindedness bored him. But provocative displays contrary to popular convictions were forgiven as he launched into flights of zany wit and piercing commentary. It was, however, advisable to remember that, self-confessed, Hal was essentially un-innocent.

At this time much occupied with theatre groups, Mary would ultimately pronounce the medium, in terms of bitter infighting, on a par with anthropologists – who seemed to her a similar field of vitriolic competition – but for the moment, caught up with Kuljak, the ATF and a choreographed interpretation of *The Way of the Whirlwind*,[2] she was still enjoying the novelty. From her willingness to discuss with Kay Kinane adapting a series of plays and stories for Aboriginal schoolchildren, it was evident previous experience had not deterred her from giving the ABC another go.

Her first and most challenging duty of the year was to help organise the rescue of Aboriginal culture as proposed by Nugget Coombs. Accompanied from Derby by Albert Barunga, she flew to Darwin to clarify the aims of the ATF and her role in establishing regional branches. The old port, so familiar to her in the 1930s, was now unrecognisable – 'a splendid Woolworths in place of the old Chinese stores' – and the modern amenities made available by the funding authority luxurious beyond anything she had previously experienced in the north.[3] After a tour of Melville and Bathurst islands to examine local arts and crafts, she travelled south for the purpose of catching up with old friends in Kununurra.

Gazetted in 1963, the Native Reserve was a site of some ten acres, two miles from the town and discreetly out of sight behind the bulge of Kelly's Knob. It was here and in other such outlying camps that many 'Durack-time' people would end their days. For the predominantly Miriwoong-Gajerrong inhabitants, a good number affected by trachoma and other prevailing diseases, living conditions were basic and time fell heavy on their hands. Johnny Walker, head stockman on Ivanhoe in the 1930s, his sight gone, relived day after day in a rambling discourse the minutiae of his droving tracks – every stick, stone and passing bird of it.[4] So particular and unique were the memories of the Aboriginal people who had been witness, for better or worse, to pioneering history that Mary had begun to consider how she might best capture such a valuable resource. Already a familiar and much-loved visitor, she explained the objectives of the ATF to an interested audience, while Albert Barunga talked up the importance of retaining traditional artforms, as demonstrated by the dancers from Mowanjum who were preparing for a performance at the Parkerville venue. While he launched into his favourite homily about the need to go 'arm in arm', their stalwart chauffeur Jack Saville, in his pressed white shirt and shorts, kept his distance.

Preparing a report for Dr Coombs, Mary broached the prospect of developing industries and the manufacture of traditional objects, weaving, basket making and textiles. As nothing of this sort had ever been organised in Western Australia, she felt the ATF could break new and profitable ground. Though her participation was taken for granted, she spoke cautiously of retiring 'after the convening stage', as was her wont before committing herself to time-consuming projects.

Returning to Perth only to host a family gathering for visiting Canadian Duracks (come to light since publication of *Kings in Grass Castles*), she was away again almost immediately on another Northern Territory and island round before her Adelaide Festival lecture tour. But for a few brief breaks, she would be continuously on the move for the next six months. Aside from set itineraries, Mary seldom missed a chance to travel in another direction, no matter how short the notice, uncomfortable the means of transport or barren the destination. If there was a plane, truck or vehicle of any kind heading towards an Aboriginal community, she was along for the ride, and her yearly tracks across Australia were formidable.

There had been little time for more than a quick assessment of doings at Mildew. Marie Rose was absorbed in designing an anti–Vietnam War poster, and Robin, between RFDS duty, had begun work on her autobiography. Solicited by an agent for Rigby to put together an account of her flying adventures from her diaries, she had agreed because Horrie had seemed so keen on the idea.

With Bet's latest *Seeing Through* completed and an accompanying book of sketches depicting Papua New Guinean women already in print, she departed for England, via Iran. The plan was to meet up with Enid and Reg for the Oxford wedding of their eldest son before a tour of Ireland and, later in the year, Nigeria.

Mary's strenuous schedule temporarily relieved her of John Joseph Jones's daily bulletins on his fiscal morass, or finding words for the latest James Penberthy creation. She had lost patience with both Penberthy and Donald Stuart who, despite their falling out, had accepted a collaborative commission which meant communicating with one another through her. Pressing appeals for her participation in a Vietnam War moratorium were left behind, with the hasty addition of her signature to a letter from writers deploring President Nixon's bombing incursions into Cambodia.

While attending ABC meetings in Sydney to discuss the *English for Aborigines* radio series, Mary and Kay Kinane arranged to meet in Darwin midyear to record suitable material. Staying with the Serventys at their Pearl Beach holiday home, she prepared a report on the ATF for Dr Jean Battersby, who had recently been elected to the position of foundation executive officer for the Australian Council for the Arts. Then it was away to Queensland and a round of widespread friends and relatives, before a crowded Adelaide itinerary comprising the customary mix of official and private duties, with side trips to accommodate son Johnson and Iain Horner, who had on this occasion accompanied her.

Lying low to avoid ambush from her lurking pests, soon after her return she slipped away to Adsett with Robin to work on *Flying Nurse*.

Until informed by Gran, Mary had not heard that her daughter had been named Australia's most outstanding woman pilot and bestowed with the annual Nancy Bird Award. Robin was the ideal choice for any number of awards seeking a worthy recipient. Having accumulated 2,300 flying hours, she was one of only two female commercial pilots in the state, a situation indicative of the general prejudice against women in the airline industry. With five ferry flights across the world in her logbook, she was also the leading member of the thirty-five-strong Women Pilots' Association and WA president of Zonta, an organisation dedicated to empowering and finding opportunities for women. Doing what was perceived as a man's job, she took some trouble to project a feminine image, keeping her blonde hair long and customarily cladding her slim figure in light cotton frocks rather than trousers or the ubiquitous jeans. The press found her irresistible.

~

My homecoming with baby Naomi introduced Mary to the pleasure of being a grandmother, a role she would enjoy more than her own motherhood. But from an existence akin to solitary confinement, I was unnerved by the pitch back into a riotous flow of personalities and activities. Dymphna Cusack and her husband Norman Freehill were temporarily in residence at Mildew, sharing the house and Mary's attention with semi-permanent fixtures Iain Horner, Father Moynihan, Sister Ignatius and sundry others who had felt neglected during her long peregrinations. Aboriginal children, brought down from the Territory to perform in the *Whirlwind* ballet, sat wide-eyed in the back of her car. Gran, in hospital undergoing a gall bladder operation, needed visiting at hourly intervals. Doting in-laws appeared on the doorstep. I was also painfully aware that no amount of traffic could fill the void left by Julie. My misgivings were noted: 'Patsy seems to think it's a circus and perhaps regrets coming back.'[5] Re-establishing a respectable distance, I found other accommodation before the arrival of my spouse, who had accepted a job with a local airline company.

In my wake floated unresolved a number of hotly debated topics. Whereas I could appreciate the merits of my mother participating in an episode of *A Big Country* for the ABC, it was a mystery to me why she should contemplate repeating any exercise under the auspices of Kay Kinane. And what madness had moved her to endorse a project involving J.J.J.? Why did she feel obliged to be at the beck and call of the clergy, especially nuns – so many of them with a seemingly small aspiration or ambition: to take up growing orchids, cultivate bonsai trees, see the north, have a memoir published, get an autograph from Morris West on a precious copy of *The Shoes of the Fisherman* ... each one a saga of sapped time and energy.

Writing to Florence, Mary was reticent about admitting the extent of her involvement with the ATF:

> *I am trying to get the Aboriginal Theatre Foundation off the ground in this State. At the suggestion of Dr Coombs I agreed to being the organisation's WA representative at least in the convening stage. It is an exciting project but means a good deal of running round. It has its crazy side of course, but is not hopeless by any means. The Aborigines get the idea very quickly – all are natural actors and understand the medium, so we are hoping to develop a repertoire of simple plays using dialogue and mime to illustrate situations, stories and legends.*
>
> *I have decided that my next effort should be a sequel to* Kings. *It seems a shame to let Dad's diaries lie there unused while there are people around who can help me fill in the gaps ...*[6]

A mere mention in passing of what would become the ever-subverted 'main task' for the next thirteen years.

The novelist in her had died hard, as she revealed in a 1979 biographical piece:

> *That the greater part of my literary output has been of a documentary or historical nature was a matter of chance rather than of choice. I would have preferred to concentrate on fiction or drama but my inheritance of historical documents decided otherwise. I could, of course, have deposited this material in state or national archives to be dealt with by some better-qualified historian, present or future, but I realised that whereas others could produce better novels and plays than myself, no-one knew as much as I of the events and people with which these documents are concerned. Only I have had the opportunity, over many years of supplementing these records with the personal recollections of those involved who remembered the*

> *circumstances surrounding them. The majority of these, black and white, are no longer living and much of their story remains to be told. Bearing in mind Napoleon's definition of history as 'a fiction agreed upon', I try to ensure my interpretation is as factual as possible and to remember that my characters, enmeshed in their times should not be judged by standards imposed by different backgrounds and other generations. I look hopefully to the future while living, to a great extent, in the past.*[7]

By now, however, Mary was up to her neck in the ATF, visiting Aboriginal outposts, submitting reports and working towards the establishment of regional councils. From its inception, Mary would be for the foundation the much needed up-front diplomat and most constantly reassuring force for all the participants. Nor could the fund-strapped organisation have found a more providential arrangement than a representative whose airfares were covered and who did not claim for numerous small expenses.

By the time Mary joined Kay Kinane in Darwin, her old chum had already fallen out with the co-producer. The ABC women were scarcely speaking to one another, in a way reminiscent of the previous debacle.

> *An embarrassing situation ... Roberta demanding nothing less than sole charge of the production, Kay refusing. I told Kay I could not work on the program in an atmosphere of animosity and dissent. Thoughts of Julie very close today – the first anniversary of her death, although every day is an anniversary for me.*[8]

It was hard to miss the fact that Kay's emotional entanglement with her female colleague was at the back of the trouble, but Mary was fairly obtuse in some areas. As it was, having already run off several scripts, she still found the idea appealing, and with Kay's guarantee that all would now proceed smoothly, she continued to participate. Mucked about from Sydney in a way only one of excessive forbearance would have tolerated, she tried to accommodate contradictory communications and ever-changing requirements. The many hours spent taping Aboriginal legends were wasted when this concept was abruptly scrapped in favour of conventional dramatised stories. On the eve of another departure north in search of suitable material, a trip involving elaborate arrangements and juggled schedules, she received a wire from ABC head office: Kay Kinane (already demoted from television back to radio) had been transferred to another department and the series cancelled. But Mary's only protest was for the diary: 'Feel very fed up with them. My experience of jobs undertaken in good heart for the ABC has never been satisfactory.'[9] The subject of a cancellation fee was not raised. Kay's once stellar career with the ABC went into decline after this, as did her professional association with Mary.

Again paying the piper for an interlude at Adsett, Mary, during her absence, lost her dear comrade and indefatigable supporter Father Moynihan. It had not escaped her notice that despite the certainty of a blissful afterlife, many of those under holy orders found their mortality no easier to contemplate than non-believers. Having almost perversely avoided the practicalities, the priest had left his will unsigned and incomplete, thereby initiating a tussle between Irish relatives for his possessions. Acting as go-between in the matter became for Mary just another thankless task, culminating in ill-mannered complaints from rival family branches as if she had been a hired retainer. She more than paid for Father Moynihan's help on *The Rock and the Sand*. The unpleasant affair was to drag on for five years before all effects were put up for auction, including a valuable set of correspondence from the Irish Republican leader Patrick Pearse.

While working on the obituary, Mary was again 'visited'.

> *Last night most clearly saw Father Moynihan in his cassock standing in the doorway at the end of the passage. It was so real I exclaimed, 'They told me you had died!' His genial face remained quite impassive and the door closed slowly behind him.*[10]

The cancellation of the ABC series having created a momentary vacuum, the errant author turned her attention to Nita Pannell's request for 'a little solo character sketch'. Investigating the possibility of a drama languishing among early settler material held by the Battye Library, she came across some letters and a journal kept by a Swan River pioneer. From the yellowing pages, Eliza Shaw emerged as an intrepid woman whose triumphs and travails represented those of so many who came with high hopes to Governor Stirling's new colony. Before the day was out, Mary had drafted a short vignette. The piece first aired to encouraging applause at a fundraising soiree, Nita was soon pressing for a more substantial monologue, one she might perform for the visiting English producer Tyrone Guthrie.

~

Meanwhile, there was trouble brewing as relations, never too amicable, had begun to break down between Andy and Horrie:

> *Andy is difficult, non-committal and lacking in a sense of humour. He gets everything at the wrong angle and disparages people including all the family. He doesn't know a bee from a bull's foot about managing a station and he also smokes and drinks and wears pointed shoes. He pushed off after spending a few days here without leaving a note.*[11]

It had been a shock for Horrie to find himself at the receiving end of irrational talk and casual arrivals and departures. His son was very much a chip off the old block. But he liked Rosemary's 'carefree and sunny disposition' and he considered her to be of basically sound character.

After another trek out to see for herself how the couple and their infant son were faring, Mary found little cause for optimism:

> *The poor kids struggle on in the squalid house – furnace hot and flies bad – no fly-wire and the electric light feebler than our lamp at Ivanhoe in the old days. The country is drought-stricken, stark, arid – the only signs of life a few dejected cattle and birds feeding on dead stock. There is no hope for their future in this place but they do not want to walk out on Dad and leave him with the problem.*[12]

For Horrie, the former tranquillity of Broome had gone. Trucks roared past the house at all hours, Derm Farrell's new air conditioner across the road made an infernal racket and the dog menace was shocking. He noted only twenty-one dogs officially registered in a town where there seemed to be three per person. Observing the new hotels and motels pouring sewage straight into the lovely sea, he wrote letters of complaint. The rebuilt Continental Hotel up the road he considered an eyesore and a living obscenity: 'Evening swill at the pub. As I passed it, its arsehole at the side opened and hundreds of beer cartons were shat out.'[13]

His position as regional manager long redundant, Horrie still met every aircraft, if for no other reason than to greet the 'hosties', whose good welcome he sentimentally declared his 'last lovely spot in life'.[14] He would be cheered a few weeks later by the arrival in Perth of members of the Women Pilots' Association to compete in the Aviat 70 air race, an event he was invited to flag away. With Robin among the competitors, it had provided him with an opportunity to air his line about the pilots flying by the seat of their panties.

Soon after her return from Debesa, while making her usual call on the St John's nuns, Mary tripped over a convent step and broke two bones in her foot. Irritated and unsympathetic over her helpless state, Horrie asked if she meant to tell him that her minor injury could be compared to his crippling ailments. Before leaving Broome for treatment in Perth, Mary confronted him about his plans for the Broome houses, worried that he might be considering selling them, and, a matter of equal apprehension, about the consequences for her if he did. Her plea that he not make any move without letting her know met with a surly silence.

Acting upon his covert agenda of self-preservation at all costs, which meant being looked after in his old age, Horrie judged the time ripe to launch a series of advance raids for the purpose of removing Johnson from Mildew by fair means or foul. Suggestions the boy consider enrolment in the air force and other standard solutions that would get him among 'a crowd of decent blokes' meeting the response they deserved, he ramped up the aggression. One incident only semi-recorded in Mary's diary was typical of his offensive:

> *Horrie blowing up on Johnson who sleeps all day and when awake spends hours on the phone. Afraid the sudden nature of today's attack will do nothing but confirm J's idea of the impossible mentality of his parents.*
>
> *Very primitive scene.*[15]

~

Greatly encouraged by Tyrone Guthrie's complimentary reaction to her depiction of Eliza, Nita urged all stops be pulled out for a three-act monologue in time for the Perth Festival. Yielding to the strong-willed actress, Mary put aside the final editing of Mollie Skinner's *The Fifth Sparrow* and *Flying Nurse* and repaired to Adsett for the task of bringing back to life an Irish gentlewoman of the previous century. Still encased in uncomfortable plaster, she was relieved when Ida returned to take over the cooking and other chores. The indefatigable traveller had this time been on a trip to Canada and the Arctic Circle to visit her penfriend of long standing, the Flying Doctor to the Eskimos. While there she had learned of a danger to be avoided when in the northern hemisphere, prompting an amused response from Mary:

> *Today – Confucius Ida Mann say*
> *Human being get by on very little vitamin A.*
> *When visiting Arctic always beware*
> *Not consume liver of polar bear …*[16]

To safeguard the traditional pursuits of reading, writing and conversing, Ida had banned television from Adsett. Now, as her friend expressed regret that she was missing favourite programs enjoyed in Perth, Mary saw the writing on the wall for 'this intrusive fact of our age'.[17]

Briefly once more on home soil, Bet was in her disciplined way working on *Seeing Through Nigeria*. Having largely abandoned illustrating other people's books and collaborative jobs, now and again she made an exception, as with the striking poster advertising the Mowanjum dancers, which troubled enterprise had become by the end of 1970 Mary's almost total preoccupation. Nita's aspirations for a festival premiere of the Eliza play ruled out as unrealistic, she was far from certain that the Parkerville concept was any more feasible:

> *I really don't know how this January performance is to be brought off and with so many cross threads I would happily withdraw from the whole deal. It hardly seems possible, but I will take it as far as I can.*[18]

From among the frictional strands emerged Mary Selsmark, daughter of a Kimberley pastoralist and wife of an MMA pilot stationed in Derby, who was proclaiming herself promoter and artistic director of the Mowanjum group. Our family had known Mary for many years, and her involvement had raised some misgivings.

The hastily convened 'project committee' was already up against an increasingly despotic J.J.J. Once certain the wheels were in motion and Commonwealth money approved, he had begun to throw his weight around and make unreasonable demands. Registering the scale of what was shaping up as a total debacle, I introduced my censure motion to the house, where it was kitchen tabled, and washed my hands of the matter.

Away with Harold on a fourth Pacific ferry, Robin was again absent for Christmas, but family numbers were swelled by the inaugural presence of in-laws and two babies. After giving up on Debesa, Andy and Rosemary, now parents of a boy they named Drew, would find city life no less a struggle.

Jack Saville, a seasonal guest, had recently been enjoying his fifteen minutes of fame. Refused service at the bar of a city hotel, he had lodged a complaint with the Native Welfare Department, and when a journalist noticed the plaintiff's referee was Mary Durack, Jack found himself in the news. The proprietor, who routinely asked Aboriginal customers to leave the premises ('bad for business'), never knew what hit him. Since their meeting five years earlier, Mary had become used to the yearly telephoned request 'Can I come 'ome, Mum?' To the surprise of taxi drivers who delivered him, sometimes under the influence, he did indeed appear welcome at the Nedlands residence, embraced in a motherly way. Soon after this incident, Jack gave up drinking and instead spent his money taking overseas tours.

~

Mary's report on the performance of Mowanjum Aboriginal dancers at the Parkerville Amphitheatre, as subsequently submitted to the ATF and the Australian Council for the Arts, bore little resemblance to the more candid diary account of the three punishing weeks that would leave her 'shattered'. By the time Albert Barunga arrived with an advance party of dancers, J.J.J. had become almost impossible to deal with, as evidenced by the diary entry for 7 January 1971:

> *His attitude is intractable and aggressive. He reiterated demands for all the money advanced by the ACA, all power over the production and TV contracts for performers on or off the site over the period. I blew up on him over his sudden mention of the right to veto if the performance not up to his standard. Also his insistence that the $800 I had given him as an advance against arrival of the Arts Council cheque was a personal loan and that I had no right to mention it to the committee. Our solicitor told him his contract was unacceptable. He refused to listen. Insisted on his terms to the letter or the whole deal was off including the disclaiming of any responsibility for cost or work involved in filling in the large hole he calls his 'orchestra pit' in the main stage area. This meant frantic late night discussions about stopping all publicity – suspending everything until we investigate the possibility of another venue. I am utterly exhausted and terribly worried about disappointment to the Aborigines, not to mention my $800 and breakdown in relationship with J.J.J.*
>
> *Having known him and his crazy over-confidence for many years I should never have let the matter go so far...*

As Jones was aware, the money already expended on advertising the Parkerville site ensured no alternative but to stay with him.

After the abrasive exchanges with one she suspected truly 'off his rocker', Hal Porter on his annual recess had assumed a semblance of decorous sanity and his trespass on her time, light relief. Knowing Mary Durack never produced anything of substance in under half a decade, Hal could not see that the week spent on warm-up celebrations for his impending sixtieth birthday would make much difference. Travelling on this occasion with a female publicist friend, he suggested they move into Mildew while she attended a Darwin ATF conference and crisis discussion on Parkerville. With Hal breezily waving aside her concerns about his qualifications for looking after Johnson, puss, duck and garden, Mary could only hope for the best.

On the return journey, having sent the usual advance notification of her arrival in Broome, she was surprised to find no sign of Horrie at the airport and the further discovery of both houses left as if abandoned in haste. When Father McMahon broke the news that the original premises had been sold to the bishop, she realised that in order to avoid the immediate repercussions, Horrie had removed himself to Debesa. Her subsequent appeals that he consider why it meant so much to her to keep a last little foothold in the Kimberley had met a dour refusal to discuss the subject. There was no doubt in her mind that his quarters would remain off limits, and though both residences were legally his, in every other sense it had been her house he had sold. When confronted, the bishop claimed he would not have made an offer if he had known she was opposed to selling. But the church, on whose behalf he was buying property with the backing of a recent 500,000 dollar government grant, took priority, and having secured one Miller dwelling at bargain price, purchase of the other was on his agenda.

In reply to Robin's plea that he hold on to the house, Horrie had explained the difficulties for him in maintaining the place during her mother's absences, and the problems with tenants who had repaid him for a cheap rental by trashing it, and other such that he knew would sound better if it came from her.

Still reeling from the shock and the betrayal, Mary could hardly take in a request from the local festival committee for assistance with a re-creation of Dampier's 1699 Roebuck Bay landing and the hope that she might also facilitate the participation of local Aboriginal dancers.

Aware that an Aboriginal component could be expensive, the Broome Shire had detected in the federally funded ATF a gravy train just waiting to be boarded. With an eye to a tourist drawcard, it had persuaded the various racial groups within the town's population to combine their separate annual celebrations, and the Shinju Matsuri Festival had been launched the previous year. Kim Male, the son of her friends Sam and Phyll, was committee president, and Mary, never able to resist a Broome event combined with old association, would patronise the festival for the next twenty years. As was ever the case, in the light of her many commitments, she agreed to cooperate only to the extent of helping with the ATF element, writing the script and acting as an 'adviser' on the staging of the project.

In Perth, she was relieved to find that Hal had conscientiously looked after both the house and Johnson: all was in order and the garden thriving. When it suited him, she concluded, Hal could be dependable, especially if there had been an intimation of mistrust. Won over by his special brand of soft soap, Gran had found his company 'as good as a tonic', and he had earned her full endorsement.

Marie Rose had another story to tell of Hal shenanigans, not the least her mortification at finding him in the bath with a person of uncertain gender, whom he affably introduced as 'my taxi-driver'. Whatever he got up to – and those waiting impatiently at the door heard stentorian gargling, hawking, snipping and, possibly, chest-slapping – he had been guilty of unforgivably 'hogging the bathroom'.

While in no doubt of his literary talent, on hearing of his less commendable stunts I had thus far avoided the groggy, late-night frivolity of Hal's visits. Supposed in some quarters a 'ladies' man', he was known to capriciously court unreconciled spinsters, for whom the sun briefly came out and then bewilderingly set, and there had also been reports of a cruel game wherein he singled out some vulnerable member of the company for 'psychoanalysis', in the process stripping the victim of self-esteem. He would defend this practice as the prerogative of a writer, in order to reveal a character in its sundry facets.

Sister Ignatius, who had a penchant for dipping her modestly stockinged toe in worldly waters, had been among the guests one evening. The titillation of her nunly presence in a secular alcohol-laced environment had provoked Hal into pulling from his seamiest depths the most ribald observations and reminiscences. Hal believed that holy women should maintain a divide and his performance was intended as a warning that she should not stray from the cloister. On being introduced to Bishop Jobst, he had, with every show of deference, enquired if it would be appropriate to ask if he might kiss his Lordship's ring.

Our one uncomfortable meeting occurred during my mother's absence. Forgetting he was in situ, I had entered via the back door, singing at the top of my voice as a warning to intruders and those who would prefer not to encounter me, before being suddenly cut off mid-note by his hungover presence lurking in the breakfast nook. Confronted by a female soprano in a state of advanced pregnancy, he had remained silent behind his bland, unreadable visage and a cloud of blasé cigarette smoke. We narrowly eyed one another off, not a shred of pulled wool between us; I spotted worn boozer, he born wowser and goodness knows what else contra to his idea of diverting company. Better value for him was the sought out and apparently enjoyed society of the younger set, in the form of my brother Johnson and his laid-back mates.

~

Five days before the scheduled opening, the Parkerville project committee received advice from the Native Welfare and Public Health departments that nine of the Aboriginal performers were under active treatment for leprosy and could not be allowed to travel:

> *The others were, according to the PHD doctor 'all old crocks' anyway. He couldn't see what use we could have for any of them. Mary Selsmark was contacted to search for 'clean' substitutes. Albert is very troubled. He says the Parkerville site is no good and that we should start looking for another one in 'open bush.' Above all there was a cement hole in the middle of the dancing area into which they would all probably fall and break their legs. In all a thoroughly volcanic situation and one such as I hope I never get involved with again as it is completely dominating my life to the exclusion of everything else.*[19]

Accommodated at the Parkerville site in unseasonable weather, the dancers were not on good terms, the remnants of the original group refusing to dance with the hastily convened 'myall mob'. With only a few days to rehearse, quarrels soon erupted between J.J.J. and Mary Selsmark, who had disliked one another on sight. Kira Bousloff, called in to bring some semblance of professional order to the performance, was able to reconcile the two Aboriginal groups, but not the whites. The cement hole representing the 'orchestra pit' remained a source of contention, J.J.J. adamant it should not be touched and constantly threatening to withdraw his venue if crossed on the matter. The impasse continued until he held a private conference with Albert Barunga, during which he explained that the pit was tantamount to his own 'spirit place' – a situation accepted with some sympathy by Albert. While Mary privately recorded 'an increasing nightmare, just counting the days until it is over'[20], her official rendering was an exemplar of her editing skill:

> The show opened to an overflowing house, although about five hundred tickets had been given to invited guests and helpers.[21] All things considered, the performance went off very well. The setting, despite the hole, was appealing and suitable for such an exhibition. The dancers made a good impression and Mr Barunga's address at the conclusion was a highlight of the evening. Afterwards they mingled with invited guests at a champagne supper organised by a social sub-committee. Mr Lance Bennett arrived in Perth just in time for the first performance.
>
> He did not know about the show and had actually come to Perth to interview me after his recent appointment as Coordinating Director of the ATF. It seemed advisable that he should remain throughout the season as an observer, meanwhile making such local contacts as might be helpful to his job in future. He undertook the role of compere and was generally of great assistance.
>
> The Aborigines remained throughout amazingly good-humoured and cooperative and gave of their best under difficult circumstances. All twelve performances including two matinees, were well attended. The weather remained fine and no show was cancelled. Publicity was very gratifying and included a daily coverage of some kind – either a press feature story, picture or TV review.[22]

Determinedly upbeat, she made no mention of the uneven standard of the performances, illness, drink problems, the shortcomings of the venue – and John Joseph Jones. Miraculously, the venture came out 2,500 dollars on the right side of the budget. Her renown as a veteran of this and other offbeat undertakings confirmed Mary's belief that any chance of success depended upon her involvement, and, like childbirth, the pain was forgotten as she fell into the next – usually unplanned – conception. But for once in her life she drew a line, and Parkerville spelled the end of J.J.J., as far as she was concerned. His subsequent attempts to re-establish good relations and use her as a referee were regretfully declined.

While never questioning the worth of the undertaking, Mary ruefully accepted that about a third of her year was going towards the ATF. But there was no turning back now. It was largely due to her promulgation and contacts that the project had been received with a wave of goodwill and promises of support from among the most influential in circles of the arts, entertainment, academia and religion. The appointment of Lance

Bennett to the role of director and coordinator had been a positive step towards getting the show on the road. Through the work of his mother, Dorothy Bennett, a well-respected collector of Aboriginal art, Lance was familiar with Top End communities, and with his NIDA training and theatre experience he had outclassed the many other applicants for the role. Another choice might have brought to the position someone with less temperamental and emotional baggage, but none likely to have shown such dedication for the twenty-five-year tenure of the enterprise.

Setting out again for Darwin, Mary attended the first ATF meeting with Lance in the chair, before the customary all-ports southward return. In Kununurra there had been some signs of progress, with the formation of the Mirima Council for the purpose of preserving the tribal languages of the area and visible improvements in health and social services. The Aboriginal population now included in the national census, Mary would note every small step forward had been against a tide of racially biased citizens and self-interested pastoralists lobbying weak and inadequate politicians.

Confirming the eagerness of the people on the reserve to relate their memories of the past, she told them she would return with a tape recorder later in the year. As always in parting, the women embraced her tearfully and waved the car out of sight. With their happy capacity to take adoptive relationships seriously, Dot, Ruby, Marie, Peggy, Daisy, Biddy Rockhole, Nida and Sheba had designated themselves her tribal sisters – or in their parlance, her 'chisters' – the affectionate kinship going back to the 1930s when she and Bet had taken on the cooking and homestead management at Ivanhoe. In that isolated setting there had developed between them a subtle interdependence and affinity born of mutual respect.

A similar fond attachment extended to the former station stockmen Johnny Walker, Ernie Chapman, Daylight, Watty, Jack O'Sullivan, Bulla, Bungledoon, Mundae and Jeff Chunuma. She visited them regularly in Kununurra and, when health problems brought them to hospital in Perth, they were invited to her home and on departure sent away with a supply of their valued 'mungoo' plug tobacco and parcels of gifts to be distributed. The installation of a telephone at the reserve enabled the community to keep in touch, and news of illness or death was relayed to her as to any relative. In such cases, she never failed to send formal wires of sympathy, and when tidings of some misfortune affecting her reached their ears, a meeting was called to discuss how best they might help.

Travelling to Kildurk, Mary found Reg more or less reconciled to selling the station. With his son John embarking on a law course, none of his children were left to carry on after him. Contact with her older brother, while in most respects that of a devoted sister, had begun since the mid-1960s to register some exasperation: 'Reg on his old theme – told him it had gone on and on over the years like a gramophone record.'²³ In his view, Mary had no understanding of realities that could only be grasped over a lifetime managing Aboriginal employees. She 'idealised' them and needed 'straightening out'. Discouraging of her visits to the reserve, he warned her that she was leaving herself open to all manner of cadging from 'that lazy sit-down mob'.²⁴

Mary's search while in Broome to find a replacement house had proved fruitless. Foreseeing a land boom, the town profiteers were buying up, and genuine contenders like her had little chance in such a climate. Returning to Perth feeling dispossessed, she attended Tyrone Guthrie's production of *Oedipus Rex* and was well able to empathise with the stricken outcasts of Thebes.

Sympathetic over the loss of the northern base, Ida suggested a combined purchase might allow more leeway to meet current Broome prices. Mary was cheered by this proposal and, still placing her faith in old chums, asked them for tip-offs on residents who might be thinking of selling. The coming Dampier re-enactment, for which she had agreed to write the script, would give her some leeway to look around. Meanwhile, going through the letters sent from her grandfather to his sons, she found a quote pertinent to the ongoing family saga:

> Got an idea for possible start to the sequel for *Kings* and scribbled it down at once. Must collect Dad's diaries from where I left off. Decided the title of the next volume might well be *Sons in the Saddle*. It will probably have to be a trilogy.²⁵

Retrieving the documents and files deposited with the Battye Library, she began the slow trawl through her father's journals, picking up the strands of the story from 1898 and the death of her grandfather Patsy Durack. Unlike the shortage of firsthand information available for the first volume, this time she would be dealing with an overabundance, some of it sensitive material involving still-living personalities. From 1930 the book would have to become largely, and possibly uncomfortably, autobiographical, but she was optimistic that all obstacles could be tactfully handled along the way. Julie's former room was cleared of the sad residue and set up with shelving to house the ever-expanding archival collection.

Once again leaving Iain Horner in charge of her son, whom she noted with some trepidation as having developed 'a desperate ambition to be a bass guitarist in a band and in urgent need of equipment'[26], and with Marie Rose acting as her assistant, she departed for Broome to work on the Dampier segment for the 1971 Shinju Festival.

The accommodation problem had been temporarily solved when the bishop agreed to let her use the old house for the duration. Horrie, still in occupation on his end of the block, aware that his wife was investigating every possibility of an alternative residence, was equally intent on thwarting her. He had been responsible in the first instance for opening the Broome sanctuary, and now he was set on closing it. With the disposal of Debesa, nothing stood in the way of his pulling out for good and retiring to his home in Perth.

The Texan entrepreneur Jack Fletcher had eventually made a walk-in, walk-out offer of 12,000 dollars for the property. It was the best Horrie would get, but he turned it down. For many West Kimberley station owners, Fletcher's buying spree allowed them to sell out at undreamed-of prices; some became overnight millionaires. Local scepticism about the long-term prospect of an outsider succeeding where Australians had failed dictated a policy of grab and run. Horrie chose instead to sell out on a handshake to an Australian couple, 'good sorts' according to him, for 11,000 dollars on a two hundred dollar deposit. Without a word of advice from anyone or inquiry into their bona fides, he had only himself to blame for the outcome.

Mourning the hard work come to nought and his unrelenting battle (as he saw it) to prove that 'the small holder' could retain a viable place in the pastoral industry, Horrie calculated he had travelled the long and lonely road to and from the station more than eight hundred times. In the wash-up, he wondered if he should have stuck to the game he knew. Reckoning another air service across Australia would need only about three million dollars, he pondered getting Lang Hancock interested. But even for the money, could he stand Hancock? The answer was no.

Dealing with Debesa's hapless financial story had never been other than a burden to the company secretary Cyril Gare. News of the sale must have come as a tremendous relief, but there would be another three years of infuriating muddle before the books could be closed on the luckless venture. In the end, the sum of seven thousand dollars was painfully extracted from the purchasers, the remaining debt just another to be written off. As he continued to gripe over his wife's reckless, spendthrift ways, no-one ever confronted Horrie with the plain facts concerning the ill-conceived, wanton waste of it all. But Debesa had provided him with an occupation for sixteen years and perhaps that was enough.

Broome's many factions and influences had complicated the formation of an ATF branch with a united cultural vision. What to do, for example, about the Aboriginal women from La Grange Mission, who modestly insisted on dancing in white bras and pink slips? Aside from her ability to sort out such vexed issues, Mary had undertaken with her usual aplomb the confronting task of coordinating diverse groups from outlying areas to perform in a vaguely blocked out tableau for the Shinju Festival.

With a crew comprising Marie Rose, John Rowney, director Ray Omodei and Lance Bennett, she moved into a dark house stripped of furniture and utensils in preparation for its being demolished. Neither Jobst nor Horrie, who was completely 'hands-off', had given a thought to reconnecting the power.

While she was still in a tangle of sorting costumes, sound and lighting and a yet untried script, two thousand Aboriginal participants converged on the town.

Catching sight of Butcher Joe among the crowd, Mary knew him to be

> the last dreamer of the Ngigina tribe of which Paddy Roe is the only other member here – most of them wiped out in police punitive raid following spearing of Panter, Harding and Goldwyer.[27]

A loosely coordinated beach briefing organised, she set up kitchen on a rock from where bread, tea and sugar were distributed.

> The tide very high and then very low – really a glorious sight – the Aboriginal people in family groups under bough shades with their cooking fires all over the red sand hills, silhouetted against Broome's incredible sea. A thrill to see the lines of jumping fish on the incoming tide in the beam of the big lights.[28]

Without the benefit of a formal rehearsal, the re-enactment, performed over two nights, somehow took a shape, if not the shape scripted. It did not really matter, as the Aboriginal people came good with a spectacular corroboree – one Mary supposed 'as may never more be witnessed'.[29] And once again, the whites came up to no standard at all. The Broome Shire Council insisted that the ATF be charged for every trivial expense, and only when pressed did it agree to send a letter of thanks and appreciation to the foundation. The ATF was a clearly a body to be exploited for all it was worth, and as long as Mary Durack was the acting agent, argument would be short-lived, as she caved in for the sake of continued goodwill.

In a sewn-up market, Mary could find nothing in the way of a suitable house for sale, and a derelict government building she had thought could be converted into something livable was declared by the shire 'out of the question'. When looked into, anything on offer turned out to be in the 'smell-zone' at the back of the meatworks or in desolate areas, far from the sea and the town centre. She found it hard to adjust to the children of old acquaintances having become hard-as-nails businessmen talking 'solid investment' and 'top dollar'. While happy enough to use her labours, no leniency was shown by the good burghers of Broome to a lady whose presence had graced the town as none other before (or since). Her cause was not helped by their resentment at missing out on the Miller house, which had been quietly sold for a song to the bishop, nor by Horrie's keeping to himself any information that came his way about a likely prospect. She could stay no longer. 'A heavy heart knowing this is the last time I will be cleaning up this dear place of so many happy memories.'[30] In an apparent desire to have his cake and eat it too, Horrie dogged her footsteps mournfully. 'I however refrained from any comments of regret and maintained brisk brightness throughout.'[31]

As she boarded the Fokker Fellowship jet aircraft for the swift three-hour flight to Perth, the front gave way. That there would be no home in the north for members of the Miller or Durack family was an irony too sad for contemplation. Entering a turbulent scene at Mildew set to a soundtrack of her son's electric guitar amplified to soul-penetrating level, she contracted a virus that left her in a state of inertia, where from beneath the weight of her neglected duties she feared things were getting on top of her.

Andy and Rosemary had split up in the unhappiest of circumstances, and the mother and babe needed support. Donald Stuart called to crave ten minutes of her valuable time, and stayed for five hours:

> [T]he pretext his forthcoming book Ilbarana *written on the $6,000 Fellowship for which I sponsored him. He now wants me to help publicise with a radio talk and review for* Westerly. *Donald always assuming and confirming that I miss nothing he writes but makes no apology or pretence of reading anything of mine and talks much of vulgar intrusions on his time!*[32]

The issue of public lending rights – allowing authors a modest fee for the loan of their books from public and other libraries – was also discussed at length with Donald and, as the phone rang nonstop, it seemed with every other writer in Western Australia.[33]

The house plunged into darkness by an electricity strike, Mary was near collapse when, in the dim light of candles, like an angel, Robin appeared. Administering medications and laying on soothing hands, she put her mother to bed. But with her full-time air ambulance work and another ferry flight from the United States in the offing, it was evident Robin could no longer be expected to attend every call on her services from her family. After painting a dark picture of 'Mum's very bad state of mind', brushing aside my assurances that it was 'all crap anyway' and for the most part self-imposed, she mobilised my reluctant person into the breach.

Within a week, somewhat rallied, Mary was back in Darwin to discuss with the ATF committee a show for the opening of the Ord River Dam. All suggestions for an impressive display prorogued by the newly elected Tonkin Government, the lack of response was optimistically presumed by members to be on account of the difficulty in selecting from the variety of performances on offer.

There had been disappointment for the Durack family concerning the relocation of Argyle Homestead, a project for which Mary had lobbied hard, lost to state budget cuts. A promise of the previous Brand Government, the idea had been promoted by Charles Court, who favoured anything that brought the Ord River scheme into public focus. Now it seemed only a nominal 'reconstruction' job was feasible, incorporating very little of the old station. Various individuals and historical societies would endeavour over the following months to keep the plan alive.

~

Working from Adsett on the play for Nita Pannell, Mary cast herself back to the era and pioneers of the Swan River settlement. Revelations from Eliza's diaries of her tragic latter days meant the story would have to be more sombre than originally intended, an adjustment that suited Nita, who welcomed the opportunity to portray enduring strength through adversity.

Ida arrived from her trip to Israel still looking very much the globetrotting professor, but Mary wondered how long her friend would be able to keep up the pace. She hated to see vital people slowed by age or illness. Hearing that Marj Rees had been diagnosed with emphysema, she hoped *The Fifth Sparrow*, now accepted for publication, would not be unduly held up.[34]

Gran, who had been feeling neglected, was included on this occasion, and evenings at Adsett usually followed a comfortable pattern:

> *After one of Ida's superb curries she entertained us with an excerpt from her autobiography while I sketched an arrangement of Strelitzias in the ikebana bowl and Mother dozed bolt upright with an interested expression.*[35]

Gran's complaints of a 'flat' social life could be interpreted as meaning a party only every *other* day; neither could she claim to be 'overlooked' in her old age. Did she need reminding that she had recently been presented with a painting of Argyle Homestead by artist Frank Pash, with an accompanying full-page coverage by the *Sunday Times*? Encouraged by public response to her lively recollection of early days in the north, Gran had begun to write her memoirs.[36] The Duracks featured so regularly in the press that it was a dull week when she wasn't adding a cutting to letters sent abroad.

Appearances of family on television were also frequent – unfortunately, before anyone had the means to record them. Horrie, looking the part, always performed well for the camera, as demonstrated by his scene-stealing contribution to a documentary history of Qantas during the year.[37] While she knew she was not in the glamour class like Bet, on viewing herself for the first time on television in 1966, Mary had been 'profoundly shocked at the sight of myself on this merciless medium'.[38]

Without her sister's fashion sense, she made do with inexpensive clothes from local shops. Blue a favoured colour, the utilitarian 'little cotton frock' emerged for most occasions, the ensemble including clip-on earrings and a set of unremarkable beads. It was in just such an outfit, with the addition of a perfunctory scarf to keep her hair in place, that she sat beside the Queen at the 1988 official opening of the Stockman's Hall of Fame in Longreach. Next to the costly ensembles and silly hats, she looked singularly unpretentious, if a little surprised, since prior warning of the prestigious seating had somehow escaped her. The loose perm given way to a neat French roll, she presented a respectable but homespun figure.

~

Shortly before setting out for the United States with Harold on her fifth ferry flight to pick up a pressurised twin-engine Beechcraft Duke for the RFDS, Robin left her itinerary with me 'in case Mum loses it'. Rather than her usual high spirits prior to another great adventure, she seemed a little subdued and, wondering if she might have reservations about the many risks involved, I pressed her for the reason. Having operated via her connection with the RFDS president in a zone of unquestioned impunity, Robin had only lately become aware that there were a number of hardworking RFDS pilots, some of long standing, who were indignant that they never got a look-in on the overseas junkets. Getting wind of the resentment, Robin had been upset. What should she do? Looking at the options, there seemed nothing but to tough it out. Harold, who made all such decisions, would not have given a moment's consideration to anyone other than her as his travelling companion, his argument being that she generated good publicity for the service and that they were the only ones with sufficient experience. And she was equally convinced that their safe passage depended upon her 'check and double-checking' him every step of the way. It was perhaps fitting that the 'patient' for whom Robin was showing such solicitude in the photograph on the cover of *Flying Nurse* was a disguised Harold Dicks.

~

On a deadline to finish *Swan River Saga* for a full-length festival performance, Mary, realising she had in the process accumulated enough material for a book, believed a modest publication could be completed while awaiting word on her Commonwealth grant application for *Sons in the Saddle*. The delay had been something of a blessing, since working with Nita called for a daily revision of Eliza's character, and the author relegated the subordinate partner, any mention of obligations drawing her elsewhere met with a show of annoyance from the temperamental actress.

Departing for the final ATF conference of 1971, Mary records Marie Rose driving her to the airport with a young friend – she was unable to gauge if an official boyfriend – by the name of Michael Megaw. Required in her mother's absences to run a message bank, Marie, who was a good cook, had also of late been relied upon to cater for guests. The situation was hard on her, and Mary felt bad about it in a helpless way.

The Darwin meeting was dominated by mundane problems of a budget dependent on federal funding and internal politics, but with the inclusion of the academic anthropologist John von Sturmer, the ATF executive had been brought to a more realistic view of what might be achievable. The sixteen present for the AGM included the requisite four Aboriginal members, two of whom, 'looking much the worse for wear', Lance Bennett had bailed out of the lock-up to make the quorum. The Ord River Dam opening celebrations having thus far received no government grant to incorporate an Aboriginal presence, it seemed hardly worth raising the proposal from one delegate that the Indigenous contribution should be in the form of a ceremony mourning the loss of country.

~

New Year found Mary at Adsett, regretfully surveying the inroads made upon the secluded bush block by bulldozers ruthlessly opening firebreaks and the beach invaded by workers constructing a seawall. But with blue wrens flashing in to pick insects from the rioting red geraniums, dolphins frolicking in the jade-blue sea and black swans paddling close to shore, it was an enchanting scene, and she wondered how she could have found the willpower to carry on without it.

CHAPTER 10

'EVERYTHING THAT WE BELONG'
(1972–1974)

At this stage of her career, radiating an unassuming self-confidence that masked any show of nerves or fear the balancing act might collapse, Mary had reached a level of competence encompassing diverse spheres, sometimes only peripherally connected to her literary talents. An accomplished public speaker, if called upon she was also able to talk knowledgeably off the cuff on a range of subjects. In boardrooms, she was comfortable with formal proceedings and in full command of all aspects under discussion. Expert at organising committees – steering, executive, ordinary and emergency – her standing and expertise almost invariably propelled her into the chair. She was familiar with stagecraft and the many modes of the theatre – not least the pitfalls. Absorbing the latest fields of scholastic enquiry and keeping up with current publications, she read prodigiously. A self-taught anthropologist, she was one of the foremost non-Indigenous authorities on Aboriginal mythology for the area between Dampier Peninsula and the East Kimberley, and among a mere handful of white Australians disposed to sit down with Aboriginal groups and, knowing their names, genealogy and individual characters, speak to them on affectionate, equal terms.

On a more private level, she was an accomplished hostess, able to organise parties at short notice and produce meals for a fluctuating crowd. She could do a loaves-and-fishes with the meanest of ingredients, and never was there such a dab hand at decorative floral contrivances from the thinnest garden pickings. Without secretarial assistance, she maintained a staggering professional and personal correspondence, rising early, usually after a late night, to once again gather and hold taut the multiple threads that made up her life, with no more than the occasional tangle. Universally loved and without an enemy in the world, she bore her ever-expanding pre-eminence with endearing modesty.

During the course of fact-finding for *Swan River Saga*, Mary had visited Belvoir, the original Shaw property, and met descendants of the family. Filling in the gaps over the century since Eliza's death had meant unearthing clues from obscure sources, and the detective work had made for a lively Summer School talk. Publicity generally had been good and the play was the first festival production to be sold out in advance, those who missed out on tickets fortunately having recourse via the phone book to the author in the hope she might have a few up her sleeve.

Opening night at the Hole in the Wall Theatre was a gala occasion attended by Perth's top society, and an enthusiastic Jack Saville, who had a complimentary front-row seat beside the vice-regal party. A tour de force for Nita, her adept handling of the intricate monologue brought her standing ovations and rave notices. The season was extended to accommodate public demand.

~

As always when Robin was at the mercy of the elements, Horrie paced anxiously within earshot of the phone. Their ferry flight returning via Newfoundland and Europe, the last news from the travellers to say they had departed Athens and were heading for the Persian Gulf meant they now faced the great stretch of Indian Ocean that had done for so many intrepid aviators. But for Robin, Horrie would have left behind with his youthful days the high anxiety of awaiting tidings of landfall from a tiny airship somewhere abroad.

'A very emotional moment for Horrie and I when the aircraft eventually touched down and Robin and Harold emerged before a barrage of cameras'[1], noted the proud mother as a large assembly of family, officials, politicians and press turned out to meet the flyers. But that accomplishment behind her, within days Robin was looking for a sponsor to fund her entry in the US Powder Puff Derby for the following year. Back at her base in Carnarvon after a temporary transfer to Port Hedland (from where she had reported the night flying 'bloody dangerous'[2]), and on call for the certainty of human casualty, she makes reference in her log to having flown to Meekatharra three Aboriginal people from the desert who were experiencing their first white contact – one boy with a tumour on his eye in a state beyond incredulity. By then a rare event, she speculated – perhaps the last? Regularly bending the rules and fudging duty hours to accommodate every contingency, while her good standing allowed for some latitude from the not entirely unaware DCA, Robin was on occasions called to account. Coping with emergencies and tragedy that transcended regulations, she confined the true overtime record to her diary. In that vigilantly maintained journal, amid graphic description of injury and illness can be found a unique insight into the behaviour of patients in circumstances of mortal stress: drunken abuse, terrified screaming, stoic endurance, frozen fear, and the children, heartbreakingly good even as they died. She noticed that the very elderly and the very young seemed to conduct themselves best in the face of suffering. Men were often fortified by the mere sight of her. One dying prospector, looking with wonder at the vision transporting him on his last journey, finally whispered in his cracked old voice, 'Your parents must be turrible turrible proud of you.'

~

The March Adelaide Festival brought out 'the usual crowd with addition of the new Premier Don Dunstan, Irish actress Siobhan McKenna and Les Murray – the latter a new one on me but a most impressive talent'. The influence of the Aboriginal poet Kath Walker evident in a new and militant voice among pockets of writers, Mary was concerned to hear Judith Wright pronouncing on the hot subject of mining leases in the Kimberley. Philosophically and intellectually opposed to the popular demand for complex issues to be defined in cut and dried terms, Mary noted: 'bad as it is, the situation is not as Kath has painted it. But I doubt if Judith accepted my interpretation – "goodies" and "baddies" not clearly defined.'[3] Uncharacteristically for one so generous to fellow writers, she never had much regard for the later Oodgeroo Noonuccal in terms of both her literary merit and her brand of political activism based on the American 'Black Power' movement. Advocating and working towards the same goals, they came from opposite directions.

When media attention became focused on the visit of a BBC TV team to Alice Springs and producer Bob Saunders's reference to 'drunken, stinking blacks' was backed up by Germaine Greer's comments on the town's 'disgusting conditions', Mary became the mouthpiece for a moderate viewpoint. Citing the impossibility of withholding drinking rights and mentioning the many 'remarkable and responsible people' of her acquaintance, she emphasised Aboriginal efforts to hold to their own culture through the ATF.[4]

At the ATF meeting, prior to discussions on the forthcoming Pacific Festival, it had been necessary to soothe injured feelings. The derogatory remarks from Saunders and Greer, which were likely intended to draw attention to Australia's neglect of their Indigenous people, taken personally by the Aboriginal delegates, redressing their indignation was a problem somewhat beyond the jurisdiction of the foundation. The same applied to Albert Barunga's complaint that a Chicago missionary group had taken control at Mowanjum: the Aboriginal communities, now so handily corralled, were sitting ducks for all sorts of cranks and quasi-religious sects. On the positive side, the white members believed the potential of the venture, verified by the emerging dance spectacles from the Indigenous people and some outstanding individual talent, predominantly David Gulpilil from Maningrida, who had already won acclaim as an actor in the film *Walkabout*.

Urban tom-toms announcing her return, Mary complained 'the net of life in Perth drawing tight about me once again'. Through the free-for-all entrance of the telephone came impositions in one form or another:

> *Ring from Father Russo wanting me to read his thesis on Bishop Salvado. But the 'quick read' intended got bogged down inevitably in badly constructed sentences and muddled thinking – though the content good. Slow going and he wants it back soon. No hope of his getting a degree without a lot more work on it. He is a gentle young man, but, gentle people can be so tough.*[5]

This regular caller fitted very well into her gang of importuning toughs. Mary's diaries for the remainder of the decade attest to persistent forays from one who would not even, as per Eleanor Smith, pay her with soothing facials. He would also leave the church, so the clerical imprimatur she found so hard to refuse had been bestowed under false pretences.

On hearing from the headmaster of Johnson's school that her son had been absent for ten days, Mary investigated.

> *Johnson says he was there, nominally, just not attending classes. Spoke to Iain and told him as much as I appreciated his efforts he did not appear to have done anything to help J. work himself out.*[6]

That my mother brought herself to close this association may have been partly down to me. Seating her firmly on the uncomfortable edge of Occam's razor, I had asked her to consider the most likely explanation for Iain's persevering patronage of her son. That is not to say, as in many cases where former friendships fell to the censure of her daughters, that she completely cut off one who had been genuinely helpful in the absence of any alternative, but she kept future contact to herself.

Anticipating an injection of funds from the successful *Swan River Saga* season, Mary presented Bet with five hundred dollars 'to help further her plans – only a lack of finance tying her down.'[7] It had always been so and, despite her sister's improved circumstances, would continue. With her son Michael now working in Papua New Guinea and daughter Perpetua in New York, there was nothing to hold the footloose Bet on the home front.

She would next surface in Rockhampton on a commission for the vast conglomerate in possession of the former CD&D properties, and later in the year, after attending Michael's wedding in PNG, embarking on a tour of Indonesia.

Alas for Mary's happy expectations, it would come as something of a shock to discover that her lack of business acumen and a poor contract had cost her dearly on the *Swan River Saga* front. From a season that ran into thirty-two performances and gross takings of 10,381 dollars, she and Nita received payment of 259 dollars each. As her brother Kim rightly observed: 'Mary always seems to conduct her business in a hurry with as little concern as she signs a grocery bill.'[8] Plainly, she now needed recourse to both legal and financial advice, as well as secretarial help. Meanwhile, she continued with the extraction of information from her father's journals and other firsthand sources, the data handwritten in long Spirex notebooks under alphabetical listings: northern identities, people general, stations, Aborigines, Durack family. It was concentrated work, especially as many months had passed since it was put aside, but not yet demanding the greater application of construction. News of her approved grant for the sequel meant that, for the time being, the Eliza book would have to wait.

Putting together the background story for the producer of a television program to coincide with the Ord River Dam opening was a commitment she gladly undertook. An added attraction was the inclusion of her friend the naturalist Harry Butler, on a mission to rescue wildlife from the inundation. Investigating the prospect of obtaining a PWD house in Kununurra for the duration, she hoped to be able to stay on afterwards to begin recording the memories of the Aboriginal elders.

As a result of the unusually early wet season, there were signs the dam was filling up apace. The scheme's astounding statistics were still hard to comprehend. Over four hundred miles of fertile pastoral country comprising the entire Ord Valley was to be submerged by the biggest artificial reservoir in Australia. So unexpectedly swift was the inundation that the working party at Argyle assigned to dismantle the homestead was caught on the hop, and in the rushed evacuation the station went under largely intact.[9] All that had been salvaged was a stack of verandah flagstones and M.P. Durack's memorial to the pioneers. The property's final manager, citing the proprietor, had discouraged and hindered earlier attempts to retrieve the historic saddles, branding irons and mule chains, the tin trunk brought to Argyle by Patsy Durack in 1890, and other equipment going back to the first-comers, still housed in the sheds. The surrounding caves and rock crevices disappearing within days, Daylight, the last official holder of the Miriwoong sacred objects, had rescued and buried some of them and burned the rest, explaining that these emblems belonged to the spirits of a place that no longer existed. The song cycles of the area as given by Boxer would recede into the eternal silence when their keepers, he and Johnny Walker, passed on. Bulla, keeper of the ancient stones and tjuringa boards, forfeited his entire cache to the waves. Why, he continued to ask, had 'the old boss' left his properties to strangers rather than to the Aboriginal workers he had trained and who belonged there? He was genuinely bewildered by this. 'We feel we lose everything that we belong,' he said, and his sorrowful summary of the situation for himself and his people became the title of the coming ABC *Big Country* episode. A bottle laid beneath the Argyle cornerstone with greetings from the first Duracks on the site to future generations had been dug up but, rather fittingly, the termites had got through the cork and consumed it.

The birth of my son provided a timely diversion. It was his grandmother's suggestion that we call him Yagan, after the Aboriginal warrior who had dominated the early years of the Swan River Colony in Western Australia and about whom she had written a number of articles and a book. An impressive if ultimately tragic figure, he would within a decade be picked up on as a folk hero, but in 1972 only a few scholars of history knew his name and acknowledged his part in the colonial story.

~

Without saying where he was going, Johnson packed a bag and decamped, leaving his mother frantic about what sort of bed and board her son would find for himself. Marie Rose having moved to a flat, the once crowded house was sadly vacant and quiet. Who to turn to? Driving to Jandakot Airport in the hope of catching Robin between flights, there she discovered her harassed daughter unloading stretcher patients while at the same time selling her qualifications to a possible sponsor for the Powder Puff Derby. But Robin's main source of distraction and apprehension was the menacing figure of Mr Todhunter from DCA, who stood by, awaiting explanations.

Still traumatised by the events of the previous day, that morning Robin had experienced a strong urge not to get back in an aircraft. Meticulous in planning every detail of a flight, she was castigating herself for an aberrant mistake that had led, in a chain of unforeseen circumstances, to near disaster. After a busy day picking up and delivering medical cases, in the absence of a relief pilot she had agreed to carry from Carnarvon to Perth a soldier injured in a parachute training mishap. Normally, she enjoyed weather and unexpected challenges adding up to what she described as 'a flight with character'. But not this time. Caught in a series of storm fronts and with the radio compass unserviceable, she had deviated over the ocean, and when turning back on track made a heading error that put her well off course and in fact still ninety miles out to sea. Unable to pick up any of the Perth navigation aids, she had been forced to call for radar assistance, and there had been consternation from the tower as they failed to locate her even as she landed, in her exhausted state, on the wrong end of the runway.[10] She had been by this time ten hours in the air and twenty on duty without a break. Rising early to face another full shift, she found herself under critical review for working out of hours and for the inconvenience to the off-duty radar man. Although Robin gave her mother no more than a summary of the less hair-raising details, Mary had a sinking sense of a close call and realised that it was not the moment to raise her problems with Johnson.

Robin was no longer able to operate with anonymity. She moved within a network of invisible concern, a lofty unseen guard ready to support or assist if required. When she had once relayed a radio message that, in her haste to depart, she had left a pot of soup boiling on the stove, the airwaves had instantly come alive with jocular comments from many listening ears. Backtracking after a long day to collect a late-presenting patient, her request for a cold drink on arrival was met with aerial propositions from Broome to Bundaberg. She had become famous. This had the effect of opening doors for her – but not always. She had on occasion been subject to resentment and even malice from those who saw her as an incorrigible 'do-gooder' for the cause of the despised Aborigines. Sometimes there was humour in it. Stepping out to post a letter one evening in the town of Derby, she had been suddenly confronted by an Aboriginal man looming out of the dusk with the suggestive enquiry 'How're ya goin', baby?' Then, recognising her: 'Oh, it's you, Sister. Well ... how're ya goin', anyway?'

Not cut out to live a fugitive life, within a few days Johnson was back. Picking up on the situation from Broome, Horrie suggested the solution:

> *The house at Bellevue Avenue must now be sold. You should find a small, suitable place that might accommodate me for a night or two, but not big enough to jam in a dozen others. Selling the house will unload a lot of worry – we can always go around and sit under the old trees.*[11]

Packing kitchen equipment and linen for the house in Kununurra, Mary contemplated 'a flat' without enthusiasm. She knew well enough that empty rooms had a way of finding occupants, and situations altered so that disposing of the family centre was not really a viable option in her lifetime.

~

It had been *Big Country* producer Ron Iddon's inspiration that the flooding of the former Durack properties would provide a unique opportunity to capture the memories and sentiments of those who had once lived there, Mary and Bess Durack ideally representing two generations involved. Initially declaring she could not possibly make the journey, Gran was persuaded that it would be a chance to see the old haunts once more and make a first visit to Kildurk. Assured that not only would she be speedily transported but commodiously accommodated, Gran found it strange to adjust to the concept of a north, always in her experience synonymous with a level of discomfort, since transformed. Every moment of the journey recorded, on her arrival at her son's Northern Territory station, she could hardly believe she was seeing the place 'after more than twenty years of writing to Reg and Enid here – it is like a dream come true'. Awakened by the familiar screech of cockatoos flying overhead, she had watched, in raptures, the golden dawn rise behind the ranges – sights, colours and sounds last experienced in 1936.

> *Mary has brought her father's 1910 diary to revive memories of our first arrival in Wyndham after our honeymoon. So wonderful to have such a detailed account of everything and my reaction to a first glimpse of the Kimberleys – all the residents curious to meet M.P's bride.*

On her arrival in Kununurra, Ron Iddon wasted no time in transporting her to the reserve and a meeting with those who had remembered her so fondly down the years:

> *An interesting but trying day in many ways. Of course impossible to recognise any of them but they seemed to recall so much of the past, some as far back as when Reg and Mary were babies. They were very demonstrative – arms around me, cheeks pressed to mine ...*[12]

In Gran's day, the relationship with the Aboriginal staff had been more arm's-length and she was ill at ease with the new informality. Not really able to appreciate how much her return had meant to the old people, her attention, rather, was focused on when she had ever stood so long in the sun without a hat.

Escorted by Harry Butler, she attended the evening function in the park, where enthroned and holding court she had regally received the sociable Prime Minister McMahon, whose insignificant stature had been compensated for by his wearing an all-white ensemble, including shoes. As the widow of a distinguished person, Bess Durack was well versed in dealing with VIPs, the practised cordiality now serving to disguise deafness and failure to identify the face or admirer from way back. Swept up by Harry for midnight champagne at the Kununurra Club, in a Cinderella whirl she quite forgot her eighty-nine years. But the next day, seated among the guests at the opening ceremony, she had mixed feelings about the festive scene as sad thoughts of Kim intruded. In 1941, with a vision of a north revitalised by irrigation schemes, her son had been among the first to explore the Ord Gorge for a dam site. Now his contribution had been virtually forgotten. It was a hard thing for a mother to bear, as she later told a sympathetic Sonia McMahon.

Horrie had been thinking of the family gathering:

Duracks will be well-represented and no doubt sumptuous food and booze flowing. Reg will feel a tilt in his tummy as the past comes rolling along, like a tired mustering horse. There will be the shadows of past acquaintances and adventures floating among the nooks way down.[13]

The round-up at the immense artificial watering hole was to be the last for many family members. Diehard old Durack cousins Reg, and Eric and Doug Davidson, whose careers had begun with CD&D, might well have pondered what the decades of bad blood between them had been about. They had all in the end become wealthy men, but the possibility of ending up as no more than footnotes to history was galling, particularly for Eric, who was still determined to place himself in a definitive role – one that set him well apart from relatives he had always considered 'ratbags'.

The time spent on consultation and planning for a memorable spectacle, more as a promotion for the ATF than a celebration of a grand engineering feat, came down to a handshake proffered by the prime minister to Mundae Moore, who presented him with a carved boab nut.

Boating out on the lake to see the last of Argyle Station, Gran looked with wonder at the vast expanse and the rapidly submerging mass of Mount Misery. 'We came to rest over the site of the homestead, about where the dining room must have been – hard to take in.'

As shown on the film, it is evident that, even in her old age, Gran had retained her charm. Bridling and chortling, her eyes lively with pleasure at the attention from the photographers, her panoply of feminine artifices and winning little gestures are well captured. But there is rueful irony for me as my mother gives her the verbal prods and activates the push-buttons: 'What about the time Charlie asked you to name his piccaninny? Do you remember when you and Nurse Tiddy made the butter?' Soon enough it would be my turn to prod her: 'What about the time the Aborigines sang you better, Mum? Do you remember what Bulla said about the stations being sold?'

Although at the age of fifty-eight Mary was still an attractive woman, the loss of Julie three years before is writ plain upon her, the cruel blow visible in her sad smile, the wistful and sometimes watery eye.

A lasting source of gratification for Gran would be the warm bond she had established with the prime minister and his wife. She would be among the few to mourn William McMahon's ousting a few months later, and the Whitlam Government was going to win no favour with her.

~

Before long, the small PWD house in Kununurra had become the town's social centre, the author's resolve to get down to work on *Sons in the Saddle* at variance with invitations to share her domicile with numerous others. Robin and I concluded that the addition of Johnson would not matter and, concerned about his lack of proper supervision, we shipped him north. It was a move after the boy's own heart: back with his mother, clear of any further threat of school or 'study', and fun times on the roll. The nightly gathering for feasts of Kildurk beef or baked river fish incorporated nuns, an unorthodox priest who had inaugurated an Aboriginal mass, an ornithologist employed to deal with the thousands of brolgas endangering aircraft, two film teams, Harry Butler, a helicopter pilot, Nita and Jim Pannell, Ida Mann – and, blowing a didgeridoo in the moonlight, Rolf Harris.

Using a little dramatic licence, Mary would later claim that her decision to write a sequel to the family saga had been made at this turning point in Kimberley history:

> *The precise moment when I knew that I must carry on was when watching the waters of the Ord River dam rising above the site of the old homestead, blotting out the course of the Behn River and its tributary creeks, drowning the yards and the cattle camps and sacred sites of the Miriwoong tribes-people. As the remaining old-timers, white and Aborigine, were so quickly passing away, I felt my most urgent task was to interview anyone left for first-hand information.*

> Fortunately the Aborigines are now even more at home with this modern device for interviewing than the average white. In fact if I started writing notes they became suspicious. As one of them put it: 'How do we know what you're writing down there? More better you turn on that recorder, then we all know where we are.' I have found them curiously objective about the past, recalling events with no hint of bitterness, meting out neither praise nor blame to their white associates.[14]

One veteran she interviewed brought out a tatty copy of *Kings* for her signature, showing her a flower pressed in the page with her photo. What a pin-up girl she had become for lonely outback men.

Every day packed with rigorous activity, in the course of recording the mythology of the region, she gamely tackled faint trails to find places no longer on any map and make an inventory of cave paintings. With varying success, she sought to extract historical records from the hands of new managers on the old stations, and to mark gravesites. Overgrown or gone mouldy in swampy ground, some of the family tombstones were located and moved with others rescued from the flood, to be later re-erected at the Argyle Homestead Museum. Spending many hours at the reserve, she compiled an up-to-date index of the area's tribal groups and their genealogy.[15] Disturbed by Bulla's perplexed and sorrowful questions, Mary also began preparing a submission to the state government requesting the relinquishment of Long Michael Plain, Carlton Hill Station and two irrigation blocks for those who claimed the area as their 'born country'. Her compliance with this appeal had some overtones. She was not unmindful of the possibly adverse reaction from local authorities and a consequential withdrawal of cooperation with the ATF. In frequent communication with those who would be most affected, while supportive of moves towards land rights, she saw the potential to cause rifts between black and white – and, worse, among the various Aboriginal claimants. The Mabo decision would come too late for her to grasp this significant step forward, which in terms of settling the matter was all it was. Advised that her submission was received and would be considered, she heard no more of it.

Over the four months spent in Kununurra, with side trips to Darwin and Broome, Mary would never be without house guests. And not just the living. In the dim light of dawn, she was awakened by three gentle taps on the neck from what appeared to be a slight figure bending over her, but on investigation she found the room was empty. Hearing that Marj Rees had died, she was convinced her dear friend and typist of the years had dropped in to say goodbye. Tidings also came at this time that, after a hard-fought struggle with her increasing infirmities, Ernestine Hill had finally surrendered.[16]

Enid and Reg came to stay for a few days. Holding to his promise to Enid that he would sell Kildurk and settle in the south, Reg half hoped that no buyer would emerge. Now sixty, he was torn by conflicting feelings for the north. In his youth, fired with a desire to improve the lives of and prospects for Aboriginal people, he had written a manifesto outlining 'native problems under capitalism' and the means of equitably adjusting the entitlements of a dispossessed race – a document of compassion and foresight. But hard years and the persistent sabotage of his best efforts by Indigenous people themselves had narrowed his perspective, and with the improvement in his fortunes, socialistic principles were jettisoned for the opinions of a dyed-in-the-wool conservative. In Mary's opinion, his original mistake had been in line with those of numerous well-meaning bodies and individuals who imagined Aboriginal problems could be 'solved' by this means or that. It was her belief that the enigma rendered by their disinheritance was appositely beyond the deciphering of whites.

Reg was remembered in later years by the people who had worked for him as a good man in all respects. It may have been just an attempt at a chiack, but I shall always see Ruby waiting for a chance to talk to him among the crowd at the Argyle Homestead Museum. Shyly she came forward: 'Remember me, Mr Durack?' And her fallen face when her old boss dourly returned: 'Oh yes, I remember you, Ruby. You used to steal all my towels.'

A letter from Marie Rose announced her intention to marry Michael Megaw. She wanted no fuss or formal invitation affair in the style of Julie's wedding, but it had been a strange turnabout that Horrie should be the parent representative for the occasion. His belongings and boxes of tools were, by degrees, being transferred from Broome to the Mildew garage, and with his peculiar bachelor arrangements creeping into the empty house, he had begun to mark out his territory.

Flying out of Kununurra after her four-month sojourn, Mary looked down at the place where her intrepid relatives had set pioneering footfall – all the familiar landmarks gone to a watery grave. 'Well, that's the end of that,' she thought. And then, 'Or is it?' Bulla had seemed to regard the dam as just another phase that would pass. When its future benefits were explained to him, shaking his white head, he had declared emphatically, 'We don't know what's going to happen *after* the future.'

There came to Mary's mind a vision of an old woman throwing a fish back into the lake with a message to the 'spirit fellows':

You go back – go back now – talk strong my country. You tell him that spirit can't leave 'em. You tell him – wait! Hang on! This not the finish! Might be close up, might be fifty t'ousand year. Some time you gonna see that sun again. You gonna find all that moon and star. You gonna feel that warm wind blowing. You gonna look-out that sky!

As she winged her way south, she began composing the long poem 'Lament for the Drowned Country'.

Horrie, who was showing no signs of mellowing with age, met her at the airport with his fait accompli. In a typical and unexplained U-turn, he was now dead against disposing of the Bellevue Avenue home, and with the promise of the other Broome house to the bishop, he was leaving the north for good. When Mary had suggested that she and Ida buy the place from him, he told her that he would rather give it away first, an assurance also conveyed to Jobst. The penny finally dropped. Her long-errant seventy-eight-year-old husband, while remaining to his mind independent, meant to be looked after in his dotage.

'I do believe,' she said incredulously to me, 'he wants a sort of Darby and Joan situation here.'

Producing a bottle of champagne and a cooked chicken to celebrate their thirty-third wedding anniversary, Horrie implied that they would henceforth live together in regular connubiality. He would, however, establish a brisk and separate social round: playing golf, following a variety of sports, attending honorary functions and air-club rallies, dining out with selected friends and fostering a new network of acquaintances in Carnarvon. Robin provided most of his needs, her RFDS base a destination to head for in his car and her accommodation providing him with temporary refuge from the Perth elements that did not suit him. In a symbolic antisocial gesture, he advertised his return to Mildew by raking up the leaves and burning them on the verge so that smoke pervaded the whole neighbourhood.

Mary's admirer of many years, the recently widowed writer Leslie Rees – a frequent caller – saw his hopes of getting a foot in the door vanquished and resigned himself to joining the legions of 'just pals'.

The move to Perth had called for other irritants to be sent packing. While he was officially resident in Broome, Horrie had put up with my frequently calling in from our nearby house, handily situated opposite Gran. Now he did not want the intrusion of a daughter diverting the attention of his wife or cleaning the place in her absence. To this date, he had resisted acknowledging his grandchildren in any normal way. Never calling them by name, he would address them as 'Hey, you …', usually followed by a reprimand. Another man might have been proud of such bright and well-behaved progeny and, had he known it, a grandson made of the right stuff, into whose capable hands an old mechanic could have happily passed his treasured tools. Suffice it to say, he made our visits unpleasant, and no-one was more pleased than he when my husband took up a position with Air Niugini that would remove us to a safe distance. While he had no complaints about his son-in-law, the downside was the attachment in the form of his wife, plus two. In truth, he would not have lost a night's sleep if we had disappeared for good.

News of the old stager's departure from the north after thirty-eight years of association soon had the attention of the press. 'You can stay in a place too long and I feel I've worn out my welcome,' he was quoted as saying in explanation.[17] His final act before leaving had been to donate his Wackett to the Broome Shire Council. Returning two years later for the ceremony to open the Horrie Miller Museum housing the aircraft, he felt he had made a decision in the interests of preserving a small piece of aviation history. His gift allowed to fall into disrepair by the shire, it would take twenty-eight years of increasingly irate correspondence from me to correct that mistake and find a good home for the wartime relic.[18]

When the *Big Country* feature was aired nationwide, Gran was doubtful about her wrinkles on show, but the program caused a commendatory stir and an increase in mail and phone calls for the leading ladies. The next occasion for a Durack get-together in the north would be the opening of the Argyle Homestead Museum, a project now given the go-ahead via Commonwealth and state grants. The boost from Canberra had been in no small part thanks to Gran's fan, William McMahon.

A year after the opening of the dam, Kildurk was purchased for 829,000 dollars by the Australian Government on behalf of the Aboriginal community of the area, a lucrative deal that Reg, for all his regret to see the station go, had been waiting on over an anxious period. This would allow not only the purchase of a suburban mansion for his retirement years but also full rein for his well-worn theme as he made nostalgic visits over the years and mourned the deterioration of the run.

Although it could no longer be said – or perhaps ever said – that the country belonged to them, for Reg, Mary and Bet, shaking off their sense of belonging to the country would be another matter.

~

Opening her 1973 diary, Mary wondered, 'What story to be unfolded on the clear pages of this new journal?'

Inevitably, the first story was someone else's. Ingrid Drysdale's reminiscences of a lifetime given by her and her husband to managerial and caring roles in remote Aboriginal communities had landed back on her desk.

> *Ingrid is another one of these gentle, good souls but her interesting material not well enough written for publishing. She feels she has now somehow relegated this whole problem to me and has no conception of the time involved, though her original request was that I 'run my eye over it' and give general advice. Oh dear! Hope Ida won't find out as she will be cross with me if she knew I had taken on another of these chores and I did promise her.*[19]

Eventually published under the title *The End of Dreaming*,[20] the book would steal many months from Mary's life, as would further raids from Father Russo, now aspiring to see his thesis on Bishop Salvado between covers. Another request too difficult to refuse had been Father Francis Huegel's determination to have the stories of Butcher Joe Nangan, the last of the Ngigina song men, edited for publication.

Following a second successful season of *Swan River Saga* at Fremantle, and with an Eastern States tour planned, Nita needed a rapid production of the Eliza Shaw book to promote her stage performance. This idea, something Mary had rather carelessly brought upon herself in the mistaken belief that it was already virtually written, would have to be again given priority while the sequel to *Kings* and other exigent commitments were put on hold. When, after several pressing letters from the publisher, she had got down to re-reading *Keep Him My Country* for new edition errata, Mary found it a better reporting of an era and an idiom than she remembered.

> *Only wish I had gone on developing as a novelist. Now I suppose I am lumbered with this great family chronicle which may prove after all to be less true than fiction. Trying to work with a finger swollen by bee sting from my besieged room. Feeling rather desperate.*[21]

On observing how much of her time was taken up with treks to the Battye Library in pursuit of small pieces of history, Geoffrey Bolton recommended a research assistant who had been helpful to him, a suggestion that came to a dead end: 'Nice girl but she wants $80 a week, can't type and is having a baby – so I don't really think …'[22]

James Penberthy's excited call raising the possibility of a Sydney Opera House production of *Dalgerie* during the 'warm-up period' prior to the official opening of the opera house later in the year was presumed by Mary to be 'just another of his castles in the air'. She had got wind of trouble in the Penberthy household. Jim, according to his wife Kira, had left her for another woman. 'Don't want to get mixed up in this, but sorry for Kira. She says he has treated her with abominable contempt, as he did his two former wives.' Mary was not altogether certain about his musical talent, either, his opening fanfare for the new Perth Concert Hall 'a discordant *noise* to me'.[23]

It was with mixed feelings that she recorded what should have been a happier event: 'Harold and Robin in with bottle of champagne – they are getting married. I suppose they have proved their devotion to one another and Robin seems never to have looked at anyone else.'[24] The civil ceremony held a few weeks later in Canberra was a private affair not mentioned in Robin's diary. In a subsequent attempt to explain the gap in her record, Harold inserts himself into *Sugarbird Lady* to suggest that her reluctance to take the formal step was because she did not want to lose 'her cherished independence'. Her hesitation was more likely on account of his being a grandfather, supposedly well past having more children and the possible sensitivities of his former family. In addition, as they had become a widely accepted couple there seemed little to be gained by it. Under pressure, she had agreed, and in anticipation of a legitimate union they had begun constructing a house by the river in Mount Pleasant.

Despite Horrie's own mysterious and often unannounced movements, he had no compunction about making his wife feel guilty for 'deserting' him. Resolved as she was not to curtail her activities, never again would she travel without an awareness of 'the old man' dejectedly awaiting her return, even if in fact he was quite happily otherwise occupied. She had not yet grasped the full implications of a reinstated spouse, or the major changes to her customary lifestyle and hospitality that would result from his antipathy to sharing the same living space with anyone except her. Having dealt with a period of proximity to Johnson, who had returned from Kununurra and embarked upon a fine arts course at tech, Horrie was as yet exercising some caution as he manoeuvred his way back into a position of control.

~

During the first ATF meeting of the year, the agenda became bogged down in the question of how to present the foundation's current position at the coming National Seminar on Aboriginal Arts in Australia, in Canberra. Foreseeing that the foundation would be under fire for its white-dominated image, a rapid restructure was vital to allow for an unambiguous presence and voice. With director Lance Bennett on the verge of a nervous collapse, and differing views at every turn among the white executive, it had seemed to Mary that an Aboriginal board could hardly do worse. She felt more comfortable on the familiar ground of an FAW workshop in Kununurra for five would-be writers, including one who intended to rewrite *Kings in Grass Castles* as a novel and bring it to life, as she found it very dull – 'cut me down to size properly!'[25]

With no more than an overnight in Perth, she was off again to attend the Canberra seminar organised by the redoubtable anthropologist Dr Robert Edwards, who would later become a founding director of the Aboriginal Arts Board of the newly created Australia Council.[26]

Opened by Prime Minister Whitlam, in company with Nugget Coombs and Jean Battersby, chair and CEO of the Australian Council for the Arts, the vastly ambitious occasion had brought together four hundred national and international delegates for a week of talks and presentations. Mary's diary provides a summary of the factious congress:

> *An Afro-American from New York read some black power poetry – not applicable to Australia – wildly applauded by a group of urban Aborigines. ATF speakers were then attacked with a barrage of questions and strident accusations. Main objections, white image and failure to bring the Aboriginal culture on a sort of perpetual tour of southern and urban areas so that city dwellers could learn about and regain their lost identity. Also a conspiracy to drive a wedge between full-blood and part-Aborigines.*

It was a disparate assembly, the locals interspersed throughout the audience in full cry while the northern Aboriginal visitors held a dignified silence. The following day, the confrontation became more heated:

> *The radical sector demanded that all whites leave the room to allow them to communicate with their people. The full-blood Aborigines objected, insisting all stayed together. The elders spoke strongly on issue of urban Aborigines fostering race-hatred and bitterness that was leading only to trouble. In reply, the part-Aborigines made a passionate plea that they be accepted as tribal brothers and sisters. After the conference a statement was read out to the effect that they are henceforward not to be referred to or regarded as part but as full tribal Aborigines. It is indeed the subject matter for satire in view of the previous struggle to be accepted as full European – the*

slogan is now 'Back to Black'; they have failed to get the elders' point that colour should not come into it. Everyone wrung out at the end of the day. Kath Walker in evidence on her various over-emotional themes. Too much talk on all sides.[27]

So raucous and unruly became the crowd that Mary had been obliged to take over during the question and answer open session. Aboriginal arts projects officer Anthony Wallis would later remember her as 'brilliant and brave, she could handle even the roughest and most partisan mob'.[28] Wallis would also note that this would be the start of a long-running battle between conservative and radical elements.

~

Stefan Haag from the Elizabethan Theatre Trust having confirmed approval for a Sydney Opera House production of *Dalgerie*, a budget was drawn up to allow the participation of twenty Aboriginal men and women dancers from Port Keats and Kununurra, and the Aboriginal tenor Harold Blair was engaged for a leading role.

After an eight-day roller-coaster of events and people, Mary attended Canberra's opening night of the touring *Swan River Saga* and took her bow with Nita to a standing ovation. She returned to Perth in time for Bet's latest exhibition of the Kimberley and goldfields areas, held at the Parmelia Hotel in the hope that a plush city venue with comfortable chairs and a handy bar might engender a buying atmosphere. Invitations targeting a cross-section of Perth society – vice-regal, titled, academic and nouveau riche – the guest list had included governor-general Sir Paul and Lady Hasluck, Sir Charles and Lady Court, Lady Colebatch, Sir Claude and Lady Hotchin, Captain and Mrs H.C. Miller, Professor and Mrs Fred Alexander and Mr and Mrs Alan Bond. With the sanction of the magnetic elite, Bet hoped to encourage the hoi polloi.

Robin and fellow pilot Rosemary de Pierres left for the US Women's Transcontinental Air Race wearing their Wool Board donated green tunics with paisley-patterned blouses. Three weeks later, a *Sunday Times* headline, 'Hats Off to the Powder Puff Pair', informed the people of Perth that their hometown lady pilots, flying a Beech Bonanza, had gained a creditable thirty-sixth place in a field of 104 aircraft, with a prize for the best foreign entry. Following close in their wake, Harold had organised a ferry flight home for himself and his new wife in a second pressurised Beechcraft Duke, this time via Iceland, London, Basel, Teheran, Bombay and Singapore – a leisurely month-long holiday.

The midyear Sydney Opera House production of *Dalgerie* was, as Mary would describe so many episodes in her life, 'a book in itself'. Many obstacles having emerged in the weeks since the plan was first mooted, the often inadequate 'solutions' tested the fortitude and nerves of the scriptwriter, composer, producer and music director, Rex Hobcroft. Accompanied by Marie Rose, Mary was met by a disillusioned Stefan Haag with advice that the magnificent new House of Culture was 'a shambles'. An advance group of Aboriginal dancers from Port Keats who had no clue what was expected of them were reported already 'on the grog'. The Kununurra participants were visibly relieved at the sight of her and game for anything she asked of them, as was she in return, since the grant covering airfares and modest lodgings had not taken into account extras such as the cost of warm clothes, food and outings. Private sponsors to provide additional funds had been hard to find – and even a performance fee for the dancers was still 'under consideration'. They were a few months too early for the Australia Council revamp, when money to promote Indigenous projects was suddenly no object. All sundry outlay fell to Mary.

The 'urban element' soon entered the picture to make demands on behalf of their 'tribal brothers'. Unwilling to recapture their lost culture to the extent of assisting with the construction of stage humpies from the tons of bark brought down by the Territory group (at considerable hassle to the carrier airline), the local representatives were more concerned with the drawing up of a proper 'itinerary' that would allow for smokos and three meals a day. The most vociferous of these was Mundae Moore's niece Shirley ('Mum Shirl') Smith, a large, irate woman who roundly abused the organisers for 'dumping' her uncle in a cold city hotel. Mundae was busy meanwhile buying up all the Asian-made boomerangs he could find in Kings Cross, with the intention of selling them to unsuspecting tourists in Kununurra. 'Save a lot of trouble,' he said.

An electricity strike sent Stefan into a zone of calm resignation and James Penberthy into hair-tearing despair; panic and confusion prevailed. With the assistance of an eclectic group including ATF member John von Sturmer, the Aboriginal activist Gary Foley (who had the previous year established the Aboriginal Tent Embassy in Canberra), Bob Hannon, lawyer for the Aboriginal Legal Service, several kindly nuns and John Durack, a hastily convened nephew, the participants were gathered and transported to and from rehearsals. With no stage manager available to cue the dancers on and off, Marie Rose was delegated this position, while sound engineers were called in to solve some acoustic fault that enabled the audience to hear conversation from the dressing-rooms. For the shambolic dress rehearsal, the theatre was packed with schoolchildren, who laughed heartily at the hammy lovemaking act and the tragic death scene.

On the day of the opening performance, the black activist Chicka Dixon surfaced. Speaking for his 'tribal brothers' and their treatment at the hands of white exploiters, he declared he would stop the show and expose the scandal on television. After interviewing the dancers, he emerged with the news that they had agreed to one matinee – then *finished*. Five minutes later, when Stefan spoke to them, they said they had no complaints and what he wanted was alright with them. Mum Shirl Smith, now come round to the thoroughly decent person she was, told the 'urban factor' to get on his bike. The wind somewhat taken from his sails, Dixon amiably attached himself to Mary for the remaining time. Recounting his life story, he could not be removed from the hotel room, even as she and Marie Rose hurriedly dressed for the big night. On arrival at the 'breathtakingly splendid and lit-up Opera House', called to sort out trouble in the dressing-room, Mary had somehow managed to separate two male performers fighting over discovered tribal differences and lock them out. At the prospect of missing the show, having shaken hands and found the front entrance, the men ran through the applauding audience to make a dramatic leap onto the stage as the curtain went up.

The two performances, with the companion offering, Larry Sitsky's *The Fall of the House of Usher*, were well received by a capacity audience, and *Sydney Morning Herald* critic Fred Blanks pronounced 'operatic virginity' at Bennelong a thing of the past. Dryly summing up the plot of *Dalgerie* in the parlance of his time – 'Young white boss loves lubra, her tribe intervenes with ancient rituals, lubra vanishes, catches leprosy, has deathbed reunion' – he went on to praise the authentic and thrilling sequence of native dancers.[29] The librettist would later defend herself in a letter to Florence: 'I made a serious attempt at some sort of poetic or literary style – but J. Penberthy got at it and reduced it to the utmost corn.'[30] There is no evidence she ever received 'the riches' promised by Jim Penberthy for her part, and it is unlikely he made anything, either.

No sooner had she unpacked her suitcase on home ground than Mary was surprised to be reminded that she would be required within two weeks to act as guide to a party of ladies on a joint *Sunday Times* and MMA adventure tour of the North West. Hadn't she turned that one down when Horrie expressed disapproval of her taking a demeaning part in a commercial venture? Her initial refusal and then forgotten half-hearted agreement was a familiar route to many of her peculiar involvements.

Sorting through the amassed mail, she had mixed feelings about notification from Rigby that publication of *The End of Dreaming* was contingent upon her supplying an introduction and allowing her name to stand on the cover with that of Ingrid Drysdale. Assured it would help sales, she assented with the hope Ingrid would not think she had pushed in on her act. An earnest appeal from a livestock magazine editor that she write a 'comprehensive, thoroughly researched but popular article on the history of bovine pneumonia in Australia'[31] was declined. Wondering what the return postage (never included) on unsolicited material cost her per year, she groaningly put aside two manuscripts sent for 'constructive comment'. A screed from Kathleen, the wife of anthropologist Ted Strehlow – 'impossible to comment on the sinister plots she believes surround her and Ted – even anticipating bombs in the mail! Dr Coombs apparently the arch villain'[32] – was added to a substantial file of Strehlow condemnations of everyone, bar themselves, involved with Aboriginal affairs. Gerry Glaskin ('like Donald Stuart a regular old woman on the phone, long on illnesses'[33]) rang to tell her of waking dreams about his former life in the Neolithic Age. Iain Horner called in

> with the quite preposterous suggestion that I appear on TV advertising Aherns' Summer Sale! He wants me to say, 'For as many years as I can remember I have looked forward to this fabulous sale …!' Can't imagine what can have happened to the boy's judgment![34]

Public notice of Mary being awarded a full-time writer's Commonwealth Literary Fund (CLF) grant, with a guaranteed income of six thousand dollars for three years, gave many an excuse to telephone with their congratulations:

> However the majority of calls from strangers just inquiring how one muzzled in on this Government dough paid to allow people to knock off work. Several had unpublished mss that they wanted me to give an opinion on and if approved sponsor them for the next handout. Can only maintain patience by remembering that each one thinks he is the only one to have thought of ringing …[35]

Word of her contribution to the Drysdale biography prompted dozens of calls, the line of logic simple: 'Mary Durack helps people write books. I have an interesting story. Mary Durack will write it for me.' Mary Durack was surely the last eminent writer willing to take on the scribblings of amateurs. So errant in this respect had my mother become that I felt obliged to point out the responsibilities that came with a publicly funded subsidy.

In spite of her misgivings, Mary enjoyed the northern adventure tour as guide for a group of appreciative ladies. Many places visited had been new to her, and on a trip to White Peak Station in the Geraldton area, she had been deeply moved to discover the neglected ruin of Eliza Shaw's grave. She toured a prawn factory, wore a hard hat to walk among mountainous dumps of iron ore, conjured up spirits in the historic ghost town of Cossack and in the evenings entertained the party by reading palms. Everyone got their money's worth. As a special bonus, her arrival in Port Hedland had coincided with Robin and Harold's Australian landing after their long ferry flight across the world.

~

It was as she once more surveyed the untidy accumulation on her Perth desk that Mary received a call from Connie Hooker offering her secretarial services. For Mary, wary of hiring strangers, Connie was not only comfortingly familiar but, in terms of her qualifications, a known quantity. She had been first met in the 1930s, working in the research department at Newspaper House, when Mary had done a brief stint writing a folksy column for country readers of *The Western Mail* in the guise of 'Virgilia'. Hired at the rate of twenty-five dollars a week courtesy of the CLF grant, Connie soon established a semblance of order, and she was reported as doing wonders of organisation on drawers and filing cabinets. She was also a speedy and efficient typist, a position vacant since the death of the sorely missed Marj Rees.

To an elderly lady at the end of a life of useful employment, the position – one that would last for nine years – had come as a godsend, and worked well when it worked and when Connie was well. An ardent Labor supporter whose political convictions were no less articles of faith than those of her Catholic religion, Connie began each morning with a run-down on the latest atrocity from Vietnam and violations of the ceasefire, through to the ensuing Watergate drama. A non-driver, she would also require Mary's transport services, and allowances for time off when, within a few months of her engagement, she developed a carcinoma on her nose.

For Mary, the mere presence of someone expecting her to produce the goods was a rallying charge. Desperate to concentrate on her own work, she resolved to resign from the ATF, a decision that demanded her presence in Darwin. Her intention was received with a negative reaction from those delegates opposed to any executive retirement until the actual handover to Aboriginal control. During the discussions (known to the Aboriginal participants as 'the disgustings') on the means to an interim fifty-fifty restructure, one of the main difficulties was to ascertain just who the black 'leaders' were. They were not necessarily the men pushed forward as suitable for liaison with the whites, and the power set-up envisaged was not properly in keeping with Aboriginal concepts. It was going to be a difficult but unique transition.

Gran's ninetieth birthday in October was a big catered affair at Mildew, a highlight being the entrance of the chef brandishing a sword over a saddle of beef. It had been especially pleasing for Mary that among a preponderance of geriatric guests, she had managed to gather for the occasion her five children, three sons-in-law and two of her grandchildren. The function was also notable inasmuch as Reg made an unprecedented offer to share the expense. The long, hard years in the north apparently accepted as being behind him, he had recently purchased two rural properties in the South West. While they lasted, the farms were handy for family picnics and one memorable reunion. Gathering to enjoy the hospitality (BYO) of Reg Durack's seven-hundred-acre spread, Gran and all her surviving children would assemble for the first time in thirty-five years.[36]

Leaving Connie to the mail and the phone, Mary departed for Adsett, where she was greeted affectionately by the flies and the sight of the bright jewel spiders that strung their webs everywhere in summer. In the absence of Ida, she pottered in the bush surrounds, did some desultory weeding, sketched the peppermint trees framing the lovely seascape and took solitary sunset walks along the beach. At night she fell to the temptation of television for the latest news of President Nixon's threatened impeachment and the equally improbable melodrama *Certain Women* ... 'then I closed the curtains, cooked eggs and bacon and went to bed with one of Ida's thrillers.'[37] (Disappointingly, she was referring only to a book.)

After completing a summary of Argyle Homestead for the time-capsule buoy to be floated on the lake, and the foreword to the Drysdale manuscript, she began a preliminary draft of the Eliza history with a weak reproach: 'I know I allow main objectives to be fragmented and dissipated but I am somehow powerless to overcome the trend.'[38] The trend included her bearing in mind Nita's heavy hints that in addition to the book she was hungry for more and wider fields of conquest via another dramatic collaboration.

~

Other than for my censure over the subversion of her own literary output, during the 1970s my mother and I were in close accord. With the bleak acceptance of Julie's unavailability, mustering some good humour and sidestepping Horrie, I became more visible and obliging to circumstances that went against my usual practice of 'vanishing at vital moments'. Mindful of her overload, between 1974 and 1980 while travelling to and from Papua New Guinea, problems in my own life were carefully confined to the more transient, so that she was happily able to relegate her eldest daughter to an area of concern that caused her no loss of sleep.

Unable to renege on her obligation to Perth Writers Week, Mary bowed to Horrie's remonstrations and cancelled plans to attend the Adelaide Festival. Since she would spend seven months of the year away from home, it had been a gesture. The underemployed retiree had begun to devise subtle punishments for being left partnerless – chopping down garden trees and painting areas of the house in unusual colours from discounted hardware sales. And he was clearing the decks. Johnson had been removed to rented digs involving the good offices of a girlfriend. Andy was discouraged from so much as thinking of calling in, and terror tactics were applied to keep me and the children at bay.

To the best of her ability, Robin relieved her mother of his presence, inviting her father for meals at her new abode, taking him on flights and jaunts such as to see the much-vaunted Sarich orbital engine on public display. When up north, she encouraged him to join her and he would regularly set out on the long haul to Meekatharra, Carnarvon or Port Hedland. There was nothing he liked better than taking to the open road with a goal in mind. Robin would sometimes wryly remind me that she paid a fairly high price for being her father's favourite.

As a recipient of a literary endowment, the author suffered a certain backlash from unsuccessful applicants. Within the wide embrace of Whitlam's largesse, exclusions were relatively few, but someone had drawn the line at Gerry Glaskin. He was incandescent with rage and offended pride. His latest book, *Windows of the Mind*, espousing the 'Christos Experience' with parapsychology and expanded consciousness, had transported him from the realms of a modestly successful writer into the Twilight Zone. The publication had followed a series of personal revelations wherein he was taken back to Egypt, 4,000 BC. It was a matter of disquiet to Mary that he was now badgering his friends to redress the failure of the Australia Council's Literature Board to recognise his worth:

> *Gerry is literally demanding a grant under threat of exposure of the Board for conspiring against him and trying to force him to leave the country. He pours these charges into my ears.*[39]

This sad descent into paranoia on the part of an old friend had come at a time when so many others dear to her were physically failing. Visiting her dying cousin Doug Davidson, she mused on the ill stars that had taken so many family members in middle age. She had only recently attended the funeral of another relative, the well-respected lawyer Neal Durack, who had been killed in a car accident – at fifty, oddly enough the same age as his own father, grandfather and great-grandfather, all of whom had died either suddenly or violently. Most concerning to Mary had been that her ageless friend Ida was out of spirits and seeming 'not herself', talking of 'the downhill run' and quietly contemplating at what point she might exit before reaching the bottom.

Mary's 1974 diary was shaping up to be one marked by margin crosses denoting deaths and first mentions of dire events to come. Seeing me away to Port Moresby with the children left her bereft, and shortly after our departure she developed a curious pain in her right ankle that seemed impervious to the family cure-all – an aspirin and something known as 'a ten-minute flop'. The mystery affliction was to dominate Mary's every waking hour for the next three months. Distracted by the nagging ache, she began on a round of doctors and specialists. With nothing showing up on X-ray, a pinched nerve was suspected, but a neurologist found no evidence of it. Through a woolly haze from painkillers and compresses administered by Robin, she had only vaguely registered that her daughter herself appeared unwell and worried about some trouble with a lymphatic gland. But the matter was grave, as confirmed by Robin's own diary:

> Got Harold to remove the lump in my groin that I noticed two or three months ago. Prepared equipment in the surgery and assisted with a delicate and difficult operation. Later developed a huge haematoma over the wound so had to remove stitches and pack a dressing. Harold very kind and helpful and sympathetic.[40]

The decision for the two of them to go it alone was typical of Harold's reckless overconfidence and Robin's total trust. Two days later, on her return from an emergency flight, a red-eyed Harold was waiting with two whiskies poured. 'The pathology report had come back secondary malignant melanoma. I was heartbroken to see him so upset.' She chose to go into Royal Perth Hospital

> because I have friends there from training days and I am also curious to see just how things are there now and cast a critical eye as it

> were. I want the operation done as soon as possible as I couldn't wait
> many days reckoning the disease was ripping through my veins.[41]

Her first thought was to protect her ailing mother from the news, but its drastic nature would force the awful disclosure. Unable to bring herself to write in more detail of the diagnosis, Mary confined herself to the barest account and her daughter's courage:

> Robin brave and trying to be matter of fact but under no illusions
> though hopeful of being alright in three weeks time and still able to
> go with Harold to bring back a new Beechcraft for the RFDS.[42]

Horrie's dejection was awful to see. He had long harboured a dark instinct that something would snatch the darling of his life, and to the exclusion of so much else, this fear had made him cling ever faster.

In an arduous procedure, the lymph glands were removed from Robin's right leg and a mole, the suspected primary, from her back. After ten gruelling days she went home and for the first time beheld the damage:

> Looked at myself in the long mirror and saw a deformed body – only
> a week ago perfect and now with a hideous long scar and swollen
> upper leg. But was able to view with interest, as if it were not me.
> Told myself it would improve. Scar should fade, leg should go down,
> hollows fill in etc. The sort of thing I would have told a patient.[43]

Her schedule now including radiotherapy treatment, she went straight back to work and within six weeks declared herself fit enough for the ferry flight.

~

After painful exploratory surgery on her ankle, Mary soon realised the trouble was still there – if anything, more intense. Nothing had been found and the doctors were baffled.

The rising imperative to make a political choice rattled her. From her hospital bed, she again voted for Whitlam in the double dissolution election, with the explanation: 'While I still represent one of the swinging voters one can only conclude that Labor should be given a chance to carry out unfinished business.'[44]

She also felt Whitlam merited reciprocal support on account of her literary grant. (It was not an obligation that troubled a similarly granted

Hal Porter.) Observing that no politician seemed to have ever before stirred such vehement hatred among Liberal supporters, Mary further warmed to him as to all underdogs, and she was pleased when he was returned with a small majority. She and Bet had long parted ways politically, and the latter's new enthusiasm for the Westralian Secession Movement, a self-interested scheme devised by the mining magnate Lang Hancock, had not met with her approval.

After a week in hospital and uncomforted by Ida's theory that all ailments were either self-limiting or fatal, Mary came home to convalesce. Gran, always sympathetic to illness, forgetting she had already rung, phoned her two and sometimes three times a day with particulars regarding the ailments of those of her acquaintance who were worse off.

Depressing news was filtering through from the north. Albert Barunga had been assaulted by his own son, and Mowanjum Mission, beset by juvenile delinquency, was falling apart. The Drysdale West Kimberley welfare project, on the strength of which apparent success story Mary had donated her time to Ingrid Drysdale's book, was not prospering. Callers, in the guise of concern for her, passed on details of their own infirmities:

> *Irene Greenwood ringing to say her doctor had diagnosed her throat complaint due to talking too much and that she now had to remain silent. She talked about this non-stop for a solid hour until her voice gave out completely.*[45]

The grocer suggested she try an acupuncturist, 'a now much talked of ancient hocus-pocus. Practitioners have medical degrees. A Chinese doctor recommended.'[46] Ida advised hypnotism. Harold gave her his special quinine mixture. A blessed scapular was delivered from the Carmelite nuns, to be placed on the foot, and a Catholic friend sprinkled the area with 'Lourdes water'. But the affliction defied both Christian and pagan remedies brought to bear upon it.

~

Bet's exhibition on the theme of Aboriginal people and their interrelationship with the landscape featured her arresting *Rim* pictures depicting the forlorn remnant of an indigenous race on the margin of a brittle and disintegrating world, interestingly displayed along with her field sketchbooks dating back to the 1930s. Hobbling around the University of Western Australia's Undercroft Gallery, Mary felt herself an old crock in contrast to her vigorous and elegant sister.

Returning to Perth for a few weeks, as free airfares would enable me to do on a regular basis, I found my mother, still preoccupied with her disorder, about to head north. There had been several visits to an acupuncturist, of questionable benefit I thought, but possibly eventually ascribable to the sudden disappearance of the demon thing a few weeks later, vanishing as mysteriously as it had come. Or perhaps the magic atmosphere of Broome, whence it departed, had done the trick. The nuns at the convent where Mary was lodging claimed they had prayed it away, while her Kununurra friends later told her they had sung her better.

With our recently purchased Perth abode rented out, we took the risky step of moving into Mildew:

> *Patsy upset by her father's refusal to address a word to herself or the children since their arrival – not even 'good morning' and making his disapproval of their being here all too obvious. Horrie himself tells me he is merely being 'neutral'. Hard to know how to tackle him on the areas of personal dislikes and resentment he generates for no apparent reason. Finally lost my temper with him. Quite the wrong approach I suppose.*[47]

Finally there was nothing for it but to accept the offer from Harold that we move into the vacant house attached to his surgery in Crawley. In the hope of making it a formal arrangement rather than a favour, I insisted on paying him a rental fee, an offer he agreed to with some alacrity.

From this time, Mildew, with its now many empty rooms, was placed more or less out of bounds, and our visits home were conditional on the availability of temporary accommodation elsewhere. Horrie was not to be reasoned with. It had been hard enough for my mother to be parted from a daughter and grandchildren for long periods, but to be obliged to hold us at arm's length when we did come home was an added hardship, and embarrassing to explain to surprised friends and family members. I knew that she was concerned at what she discerned to be our somewhat cheerless existence ('Patsy never relaxes or enjoys life, though a great capacity for it'[48]), and she went to some lengths to think up recreational diversions, such as the zoo. I can still see her pained face when, to her mild enquiry, I informed her that deplorable conditions for the animals persisted, and a letter of complaint was on its way to the superintendent.

Anything in the way of leisure off the agenda, I found the task of sorting a number of muddled correspondence files from the Durack archives suited my fetish for order, the documents returned in plastic sleeves, numbered and dated with a summary of contents. Deciding to officially recognise my role in her life, my mother made a will around this time, naming me her literary executor, and those enquiring about the deposition of her papers were notified they should deal with me at some time in the future. Long into the night, with reciprocal foot-rubs, we discussed aspects of the sequel to *Kings* and the Eliza Shaw book and how she might clear the decks to finish anything at all.

Attending the midyear ATF meeting and confronted by the unwillingness of hotels in Darwin to accommodate delegates, Mary feared the growing alcohol problem could jeopardise the future of the project. When the subject was raised with the forty Aboriginal representatives from different cultural groups, 'Many of the leaders expressed anger about the drink – even some of the drinkers – one or two still drunk'.[49] The restructuring process was addressed, with numerous sidetracks and interruptions as the men dismissed the women for secret ceremony discussions or, following a power failure, refused to sit in a darkened room without being able to look one another in the eye. A number of them continued to argue against any plan for the exclusion of white participants, whom they felt they could trust more than members of their own groups. This did not go down well with Chicka Dixon, there to combine the urban faction with the tribal, a merger causing the director and the majority of executive members considerable misgiving. The meeting broke up, with delegates going away to obtain a consensus opinion of elders on methods of voting in a committee acceptable to all.

Returning via the usual stopover in Kununurra, Mary was accompanied by Rolf Harris, who had been making a film in the Territory. She found the 'Boy from Bassendean' quite unaffected by his fame and unfailingly good-humoured, to the extent of generously turning on an impromptu concert for waiting passengers when the aircraft broke down. Prior to his fall from grace, the multi-talented entertainer was proudly claimed by Western Australia as a homegrown success story and an exemplar of the Aussie personality as sold abroad.

Prospects for an irrigation utopia in Kununurra were fading, the cotton project defeated by bugs and bad economics. Confidence at an all-time low, desperate farmers chased elusive alternatives: sugar? Sorghum? Peanuts? The situation only confirmed Mary's conviction that the building of the dam had been premature, Kim's every prophecy uncannily fulfilled.

~

During a gathering at Mildew to welcome the travellers home from their ferry flight, for the first time in many months Robin and I managed a few quiet words together. Drawing me into the kitchen, my sister, after a brief, clinical run-down on her surgery, showed me the terrible scars. By this time, anything else being unthinkable, the family had decided that the prognosis was favourable and Robin was on the mend. She herself had not discouraged a general relaxation of anxiety, and Gran's diaries had the unhappy episode as something done with, like her daughter's painful ankle problem. Officially declared 'clear', she was not at all certain the primary cause had been discovered, and while keeping an optimistic face for others, Robin wanted me to have a precise understanding of the situation. Standing close and speaking quietly in the dim wintry light, without a trace of self-pity she said, 'If I am very lucky I will be alright. If I am not so lucky, I've got about two years.' A chill of foreboding fell between us, a glimpse of something so cruel and bleak as to defy and confound the supposed reality of cheerful family chatter from the next room. We will stand in my memory forever thus, frozen, eye to eye – a moment caught among deep shocks to the system that never move on.

Within a day of her return from the long flight across the world, the indefatigable Flying Nurse was back to a full round of medical casualties. Used as she was to every imaginable catastrophe, during the next two months Robin would be faced with some of the worst cases of her career. Through her hands passed a gruesome parade of burns, bashings, botched suicides and incomplete abortions; victims massively haemorrhaging within the confines of a small aircraft all over her and other patients aboard. And always for her the most heart-rending sight: the limp little hands of dead or dying children. Unmasked and vulnerable, she sat cheek by jowl with infectious diseases: tuberculosis, hepatitis, glandular fever … One unsuccessful bid to save a miner crushed by an ore truck was memorable for the all-stops-out battle involved.

Delivering up patients at the end of the intimate contact required to hold life, she seldom heard from them again. After resuscitating a station manager's wife who had been accidentally shot, she later received a card from her husband enclosing a donation of thirty dollars to cover the flight. 'It cost us $160 – but we were duly gratified.'[50]

So much did Harold consider their jaunts abroad a double act that he was astonished and hurt when she accepted an independent charter to fly a party of stranded Burma Oil employees to Timor. Despite the alarmed faces at the sight of their pilot, the passengers were delivered safely, although the trip was not without incident – at one stage, the geologists aboard attempting to locate Dili with their land contour maps, which were more up-to-date than those supplied by the charter company.[51] To mollify Harold, on their infrequent days off together she made time amid her busy household chores to spoil and cosset him – cutting his hair and nails, massaging his back with baby oil, laying him out like a Roman emperor on sheepskin rugs and feeding him peeled grapes.

~

With waning faith in the value of the task, Mary applied herself to completing the Eliza Shaw book, wearily going through fusty files of maps and early pastoral leases. Explaining yet another deviation from the main job to Florence, she would soon be lamenting:

> *Who was it who thought that this would be an easy project because so much research had already been done to write the play? It has become a dogged chore, like serving a sentence.*[52]

Relieved at having passed the parcel of editing the Butcher Joe legends to the Western Australian writer Hugh Edwards, she received a reality check when it was revealed that his services would require a five thousand dollar grant for doing the job: 'which rather took me aback in view of the months of work I have put into other people's manuscripts for less than nothing'.[53]

Looking back on her three-year involvement in the ATF, she wondered if their plan of action to rescue the rituals of Aboriginal ceremony, which had been supposed just in time, may have always been too late inasmuch as the foundation had come into being at the moment when urban groups were finding their voice and power. There would be no support from this quarter for federal funding to sustain in its purist form what they saw as a 'fossilised culture' from which they felt disconnected. In future years, their culture would be as they made it, an evolving means of expressing their Aboriginality with token gestures towards authenticity. Mary was not altogether unconvinced of Lance Bennett's conviction that government enterprises being set up for the purpose of assisting Aboriginal arts attracted 'every nut case in Australia'. But a Literature Board appeal for her help with an Indigenous writers workshop in Darwin was gladly accepted as being closer to her area of expertise, and her co-tutorial team, Nancy Keesing, Judah Waten, Don Crick and Anne Bower Ingram, were old associates. The experiment went well, with participants eager to preserve their legends and individual histories.

Travelling to Mowanjum Mission, Mary had been saddened to find the people no longer united as they used to be, noting 'the country full of "experts" and "prophets" as never before but nobody knows what to do for the best'.⁵⁴ The fine elders she had grown to know well seemed not to be communicating as formerly, or even particularly pleased to see her other than to eagerly accept a bag of much-prized hair swept up from the floor of her Nedlands hair salon for the making of hair belts. It amused her to think of the ultimate destination for the locks of genteel society matrons.

Land rights, given a vital boost by the recommendations of the federal government's Woodward Commission, still had the potential to become a divisive issue among competing claimants. Also signalling future trouble, the report's outlined basis for control of mining on Aboriginal land had not been accepted by the Court Government – unsurprisingly, given Western Australia had much more to lose than other states. During the subsequent Western Australian Royal Commission into Aboriginal Affairs, headed by Judge Furnell, the counsel of Mary Durack was regularly sought. In consideration of advice given, she was alarmed when Furnell took an even more conservative line on land rights.⁵⁵ Six years on, when Premier Court provided a police escort for a convoy of trucks carrying oil drilling equipment to sensitive Aboriginal sites on Noonkanbah Station, Whitlam's political career was over and Eddie Mabo an as yet unknown Torres Strait Islander.

~

As the Gerry Glaskin saga continued, with Mary Durack cited as his main advocate, Nancy Keesing (writing as a member of the Literature Board) had explained to her the difficulty:

> *There is no way the Board can help here. In the intense competition for first year Fellowships he simply was not in the race. This area worries the Board most. It is also the area that attracts our most vocal critics, some understandably equating quality with quantity. There is nothing petty about rejections. The ALB just can't be a charitable body.*⁵⁶

All the same, while Gerry was to remain unsuccessful, 136 grants totalling half a million dollars, including nine from Western Australia, were awarded in October 1974, among them a number of debatable merit. Earlier in the year, there had been a stormy Perth reception for the prime minister from farmers angry at the cessation of the bounty on superphosphate. Criticised for both reckless munificence and penny-pinching, one by one would the nails be driven into Whitlam's coffin.

Nita Pannell had meanwhile come up with an idea for a new solo show requiring four sketches about women under the title *Adam's Rib*, to be produced by Stefan Haag. With the Eliza Shaw book consuming her every moment, Mary unwillingly turned her mind to her contribution. The gloss attached to writing for the stage had begun to wear somewhat thin. An approach from an American corporation wanting to film *Kings in Grass Castles* had again opened the possibility of greater reward than had so far come her way from theatrical ventures.[57]

Hal Porter's arrival, bag and baggage, with the intention of taking up his usual role as Mildew's writer-in-residence saw Horrie vanish quick smart. He had not appreciated being 'dear boy-ed' or uprooted from his viewing of the TV sports programs. There was something about Hal that defied his rebuff and deflected the pointed barbs. Robin and Harold's house offered him a refuge and an alternative TV set. He had become quite hooked on 'the box', unlike Robin who, with not a moment to spare and despite her own frequent appearance in heroine mode, gave television barely a passing glance.

The guest of honour at an FAW party, Hal set about entertaining his fans with

> *fascinating dissertations on his absurd adventures and devastating opinions on his peer writers, White, Keneally etc. More kindly comments on the lesser fry and affectionate accounts of his wide range of 'mates' drinking, travelling and talking companions – his conversation becoming more and more extravagant and savage as the night advances and the contents of the Vat 69 retreats. He never wants to go to bed.*[58]

Cyclone Tracy and the destruction of Darwin put a damper on Christmas, and with all communications cut and the death toll rising, the New Year was ushered in for Mary with an anxious wait to hear news of many friends in the port, while her own refugees from New Guinea, held up by the airlines' shambolic involvement with the evacuation, did not arrive.

CHAPTER 11

'CAN THESE BE THE SAME STARS?' (1975)

After three decades of the balancing act required to raise six children and maintain a creative output, Mary should have been reassessing her priorities in terms of the remainder of her working life and a once longed-for freedom. But for the roughly stowed belongings of former occupants, the house was empty and the garden extensions ramshackle relics of a bygone era. When not warding off invaders or engaging in other antisocial acts, Horrie more or less kept himself entertained. While fate would intervene to deny her any clear run, it became evident as the years passed that somewhere along the way she had lost the capacity to take advantage of emancipation – or even to recognise it.

Ida liked to plan for the year ahead and stick tenaciously to an itinerary. Why, she asked, could Mary not also draw up a proper schedule for the completion of goals and firmly lock herself into it? 'Why not, indeed,' said my mother wearily when I endorsed the sensible advice. A listing of objectives with no set timetable seemed to be the best she could do. Having got the yearly gathering for the neighbours out of the way – an unprecedented success, thanks to the lively presence of Hal Porter – Mary turned to the next duty, a literary gathering for Tom Keneally's visit to Perth. At Hal's insistence, Gran had attended the event and, with coquettish delight, bent to his compliments and admiration of her splendid appearance in a pink chiffon gown purchased for Georgina Hancock's twenty-first birthday. Ignoring Keneally, Hal made it obvious that he preferred her conversation and views on current events: 'I won't vote for daylight saving,' she confided, to his entire sympathy, 'because it will be quite dark when I get up at six to water the garden.'

Robin and Harold had also attended the Gina Hancock coming of age. Mixing with the big-money men at the function, Harold had heard talk of the insidious effect on their fortunes from inflation and the falling value of the dollar. Consequently, he became set on removing from the bank his cash reserves to put them, as had been the word, in 'bricks and mortar', and Robin had accompanied him in looking at investment flats around the suburbs, the best of them beyond Harold's means. An attractive unit in

South Perth could only be purchased by pooling their resources. Entailing as it would further nuisance for her in dealing with Harold's business matters, Robin was unenthusiastic. There had been enough trouble finding tenants for his Crawley house and seeing to the maintenance and picking of orchard fruit at Camelot, the Roleystone property. She had also sunk funds into the building of *Inshallah*, his cruise yacht due to be launched during the year. But loath to oppose him when it came to something on which he had set his heart, she withdrew the necessary amount from her account. Robin's contribution to his investments not registered on any title deeds, it must at some point have occurred to him that her will, with its kindly distribution of her belongings, assignment to her mother of book rights and the shares in Miller Investments left to her sisters, was unsatisfactory.

In the throes of bagging up her old clothes for the Good Samaritans, Robin had a sudden grim premonition: 'Felt very depressed, just as I did when going through Julie's things after she died. Had a feeling I was clearing my life away for someone else's.'[1]

With a trepidation that later proved justified, Mary allowed Nita to talk her into appearing on stage to provide the linking passages between the *Adam's Rib* segments. It would be a Perth Festival offering, like *Swan River Saga*, entirely suited to a block booking by nuns, elderly people and her adopted Aboriginal relative, Jack Saville, who in Horrie's continued absence had taken the guest room on Hal's departure for Adsett with Ida. ('Dear boy ...', murmured Hal faintly and dubiously when introduced to Jack.)

The solo vignettes a critically acclaimed success, Nita was once again feted for her sensitive portrayals. Valiantly taking her position on stage between acts, the author also received heartwarming applause from the audience – a reception not lost on Nita. When the actress called at Mildew before taking a short break at her South West holiday home, it was plain something was amiss:

> *Nita looking fretted ... I think she is wondering why I have to be in the play at all, which indeed do I. Told [director] John Milson later that if any way of bowing out I will gladly do so. John says 'Oh dear, no' etc. But I suspect that Nita has mooted it with him that, although having pressed the idea in the first place, there is really no need for my feeble support. I think I will wriggle out of this and the further commitment to a Canberra run ... it isn't at all convenient if not attended by the warmest goodwill.*[2]

Sharing the limelight was not a part of the theatre Nita enjoyed, or had anticipated when suggesting Mary's minor role, and, possibly distracted on this account, she crashed and overturned the car along the road to Dunsborough. Her husband Jim escaped with cuts and bruises, but Nita's injuries were severe, and during the many weeks in traction with callipers plugged into her skull, it must have taken all her acting skills to remain bright and brave. The Canberra season cancelled, as a gesture of consolation Mary set about editing the *Swan River Saga* script for publication, illustrated with photos of Nita as Eliza Shaw.

~

In April, Mary attended her last meeting as an active participant in the Aboriginal Theatre Foundation, since renamed the Aboriginal Cultural Foundation (ACF) to reflect its broader ongoing aims. With no aircraft seats available to the cyclone-damaged port, she had been chauffeured by road from Kununurra, and when stopped by military security at Katherine and asked her business in Darwin, it had been no easy matter to persuade the authorities that the foundation meeting constituted anything vital. ('Who did they think I was? A camp follower?') Although the army had the town roughly cleaned up, Mary was unprepared for the scene that confronted her:

> *Running round the outer suburbs in the late afternoon, the destruction is incredible – street on street of houses laid waste, weird beyond description in the evening light – glass and debris piled into great heaps for disposal. I hear 29,000 of the previous population of 49,000 have already returned, making quick repairs to blasted houses, running up temporary shacks or living in caravans in a general atmosphere of cheerful activity.*[3]

A variety of makeshift lodgings found for them, an Aboriginal committee had been convened to discuss their participation at the forthcoming World Black and African Festival of Arts and Culture in Nigeria. There was a noticeable undercurrent among local members when they learned that of 140 delegates chosen to attend the event, only thirty were initiated tribal people.

From Darwin friends, Mary heard about a filmmaker in the area somehow connected to a Bishop Jobst project. It had sounded ominously like the kind of thing into which she would inevitably be drawn, and sure enough, when she stopped off at Broome on her way south, the bishop was waiting to discuss his plan for a television series, one that would require her to write the script. After firmly explaining the impossibility of it, Mary succumbed to the triple inducement of a clerical request, a film project and the offer of accommodation for the duration.

Since his previous venture into propaganda had not achieved the desired result, the bishop had come to the conclusion that publications of any sort were an outmoded means of disseminating the word on the good works of the church. To this end, Karl Stellmach, a cameraman and fellow countryman with impressive credentials (whom Jobst had chanced upon by the grace of God), had been engaged for a television series. A group of Catholic businessmen and Channel 9 were persuaded to finance the proposed 36,000 dollar budget, the reckoning not including paying the scriptwriter.

From his residence on the site of the former Miller house, the traditional bungalow since replaced by a modern two-storey structure, Jobst, in his almost inaudible voice and rather vague terminology, outlined his concept for something reflecting the missions' approach to changing times and a less paternal attitude to Aboriginal youth. His objective was to show the outside world the new schools and training centres providing education and technical skills aimed at reducing the high local unemployment rate. Mary suggested focusing on one teenager who could typify the dilemmas of his fellows and the mission's role in helping Indigenous people adjust to a white world, a storyline Jobst thought would do quite well. Touching wood, Mary hoped the project would not turn out to be 'another regrettable involvement'.

Karl Heinz Stellmach had come across just as described by the bishop: a bright, optimistic young European from a rich and successful filmmaking family dating back to *The Blue Angel* and including participation in no less than *Gone with the Wind* and *Born Free*. Speaking English fluently, from the start he had emphasised that his Pacific Islander wife Aborina, somewhat hampered by an infant, was to be part of 'the crew', which apart from the bishop and the scriptwriter consisted of the two of them.

Setting out on a seven-day tour of the missions, the party viewed the many advances being made in the way of housing, schools, workshops and amenities. In its desert setting, Balgo now had a power station, a hospital and tanks for limitless water to irrigate lawns and vegetable gardens. Guest quarters were comfortable, and after an excellent evening meal, colour slides (known by the children as 'stiffies' to distinguish them from 'movies') illustrating the transformation in progress were shown for the benefit of the famous filmmaker. With the recruitment of teaching sisters and brothers to staff new schools and hostels, and the community agog with excitement over the coming ordination of Pat Dodson, the first Aboriginal priest, prospects for the church holding and expanding its northern domain had never seemed so encouraging. Surrounded by inspiration, Mary soon mapped out 'a fairly comprehensive and attractive sequence' that was endorsed by Karl Stellmach.

She gladly accepted an invitation to visit the St John of God nuns at the Derby Leprosarium, and was greeted joyously and treated, as always, to what she had come to think of as 'the best hospitality in the Kimberley'. But on this occasion she sensed a cloud over the community. Patient numbers in decline since the development of antibiotics, there was growing speculation about the future of the spacious old hospital built in 1942 that had once housed more than three hundred victims. It would be hard for the saintly women who had dedicated their lives to caring for outcasts of the fearsome scourge to accept redundancy and of no further use their rare expertise and decades of research into treatment and rehabilitation. It was only empathy for their situation that prompted Mary to write the begged-for article supporting modern additions for the continuation of an institution that was manifestly and mercifully soon to be no longer needed.

~

A number of problems, predominantly medical, awaited Mary's return to Perth. Ida had suffered a 'bad turn' and, at eighty-two, been compelled to retire from her clinical practice. Recovering in hospital, both Ida and Nita had hardly been cheered by their hired hospital TV sets showing the fall of Cambodia and Saigon. Irene Greenwood rang daily to inform Mary at length of how conscientiously she was resting her bad throat. Connie's ailment required prolonged and complicated treatment that limited her usefulness. Planning for the possibility of not living a great deal longer, Gran was thinking of making a new will leaving her house jointly to her two daughters. She saw no reason why 'the girls' might not happily reside there together in their old age, and a family member was called upon for his legal advice. Cousin Ken Davidson, who was in his retirement caretaking one of Reg's South West properties, wasted no time in contacting Reg. Hearing of her mother's whimsy, Bet, on the eve of departing for another visit to Africa, was derisive of an idea she considered ridiculous and impractical. She would later regret not having properly thought it through.

Complaints of the elderly were par for the course, but it was with a deep sense of misgiving that her mother got wind of Robin's having received a doubtful result from her regular check-up. The advice had not come from

Robin who was talking confidently of another ferry flight with Harold midyear. I had also found out that in attending to her aviation medical, Harold made no mention of any previous health problem.

Deciding Ida was her foremost priority, Mary left Horrie to his incendiary and deforestation activities and drove her ailing friend to Adsett. With the Eliza Shaw biography, now titled *To Be Heirs Forever*, away to the publisher, she brought with her boxes of material relevant to the lapsed family sequel. Greatly missing her clinic, her lengthy autobiography[4] finished, and bored with reading, Ida needed an occupation. She picked up the CD&D business files and letter books, at first idly dipping, but soon became drawn into a story with as many twists and turns as any of her thrillers, and perceiving a task to keep her brain from atrophying she volunteered to summarise the contents. With a note that 'such good fortune seldom befalls me',[5] Mary took her up on the offer.

Travelling with her father through his diaries from 1886, Mary felt almost overcome with the enormity of covering the period from where she had left it in the first volume to the intended conclusion with the sale of the stations in 1950 – an ongoing pioneering story that would otherwise be lost to posterity:

> *Having thus far gone through to 1915 there are thirty-five more years to go. Any single year enough for a book in itself and this is only a fraction of the material stashed away in other boxes and trunks. I have the feeling that I could stay buried in the past, in fact it may be the only way to cover the enormous distance and keep the intricate details in mind.*[6]

Some of the letters were in a state requiring 'a Dead Sea Scrolls level' of pasting the jigsaw-puzzle pieces onto sheets of paper to make the gist of them legible. With a working schedule set down by Ida and visitors discouraged, the two old friends worked on by candlelight before a roaring fire when the lights failed. Outside the bush retreat, heavy winter seas brought up great banks of brown weed to be negotiated during the prescribed daily walk on the beach. Two weeks went in a flash. It was a wrench for both of them to pack away so much work in progress for the return to Perth.

Adding to Mildew elements hostile to concentration, Horrie had purchased a chainsaw, his hellish new tool sabotaging all coherent thought and drowning out conversation. Removing herself to Julie's old room, Mary left Connie to cope with the insistent interruptions: Colin Johnson, lured back from monastic life in India by an Australia Council grant; Broome nun Sister

('Iggy') Ignatius[7] needing help with her biography; FAW arrangements to welcome Nobel Prize–winning *Lord of the Flies* author William Golding; the talkers – Irene Greenwood, Gerry Glaskin and Donald Stuart. But Connie's secretarial skills did not extend to putting off callers any better than Mary did.

There would be months of pulling information from scattered sources and clarifying with her cousin Ken Davidson the many complicated legal aspects of the firm's business and endless court cases before Mary was at last able to record the triumphal moment when 'Chapter One' appeared at the top of the page.[8] At first the writing would be forced and stiff as she awaited 'the voices' coming through to her. The desultory correspondence of the intervening years with her cousin Kathleen McArthur was resumed, with regular calls for information and updates on her headway.

Family problems continued as background noise. To the overt disapproval of his father and sister Robin, Andy was temporarily on the scene. Seeking escape from the pub culture dominating his social life, he planned to travel abroad, an idea somewhat dampened by his mother's pronouncement: 'We change our stars but not our hearts who cross the sea.' Johnson's hippie lifestyle, lately influenced by Eastern mysticism, continued at a distance, with some input of funds from Miller Investments for the purpose of setting him up as a silver jewellery craftsman. We had all been impressed by his original designs and the latent talent emerging, but none more than his mother.

Ensconced in his fine home, playing stud farmer from his southern properties and in his spare time translating Greek poetry, Reg, rather than enjoying a reprieve from the many years of backbreaking work, was restless and unable to reconcile himself to exile from the north. He now had a fresh target for boring invective – the Whitlam Government. Like others of his ilk, he was disturbed and affronted by his taxpayer's dollar going towards a social agenda that spelled economic chaos. The fact that his prosperous retirement was due to the first acquisition of land for Aboriginal enterprises enacted by Labor, no other viable offers to purchase Kildurk having been received, did not now seem worth consideration.

In her own way, Bet was an exemplar to them all. Aware of her dwindling life span, she knew how essential it was to live it to the full and shake off shackles such as those that bound her sister. With no scaling back of her activities, and well practised in overcoming obstacles to her regular forays abroad, she had few scruples when it came to raising the finances to pay for them. The impressions collected from her trip to Africa applied to pictures for the next exhibition, as if to re-discipline a vision dazzled by exotic climes she would soon be heading for Western Australia's bleached and monochrome inland desert.

In mid-July Robin and Harold left for the United States to collect an aircraft from Wichita before a ferry flight home across the Pacific. Prior to departure, Robin gave into the temporary care of her mother her will, the document received by Mary with the unhappy awareness that the trust was now something more than just a formality. As his darling disappeared over the horizon, Horrie donned his ever-ready cloak of pessimism and took up his post within earshot of the phone in expectation of her distant voice, or word of disaster.

In the light of Mary's commitment to the salvage and promotion of Aboriginal culture, she was annoyed and embarrassed to discover that for a new edition of *Yagan of the Bibbulmun* the publisher, Thomas Nelson, had commissioned Clifton Pugh illustrations. 'Pugh has produced the pseudo, out of context "pinch" of the kind the Foundation is fighting and anyway Arnhem Land is totally un-Bibbulmun.'[9] Endeavouring to contact the scattered remnant of the Carrolup Aboriginal artists, she started with the most obvious place: Fremantle Prison. The search soon turned up Revel Cooper, who was pleased to be given the assignment, his neat and legible script in correspondence remaining a tribute to the dedicated teaching of Noel White. Unfortunately, Nelson had not budgeted for colour plates, and the sketches disappointingly rendered in sepia merely attest to Mary's determination to adhere to the principles of the ATF at any price. Seeking some biographical details for the jacket, she sent the artist a simple questionnaire. The result was a tragic document of confusion and alienation that could be applied to so many of his countrymen, and the subsequent jacket information a classic compromise. And all too poignantly predictable was the end of the story.

On his release, having blown his cheque from the publisher, Cooper began to turn up at Mildew to demand further payment from his patron. With a waiting taxi full of his extended family, if he found no-one home he would bail up neighbours. Sadly knowing that it was just a matter of time, Mary could only see him away with the contents of her purse. Periodically re-incarcerated, he would eventually be killed in a drunken brawl.

Decamping again to Adsett, Mary settled into a steady stride. With Ida's assistance, it seemed that if the pace could be maintained she might have the sequel written in five or six months. (Had she been told it would be another eight years, like blind Nessie Kidson on her deathbed, she might have almost despaired.)

~

After a six-week voyage, Robin and Harold returned with a Cessna Flying Ambulance, pressurised and air-conditioned. The last stop before Perth had been Warrnambool in Victoria for a reunion with fellow aviators from this farming community, met the previous year in Honolulu. Among photos taken there is one that caught Robin unprepared, and instead of the usual wide smile there is only strain and apprehension.

Met by a large contingent of press and family, as had become the routine over nine years nine and overseas flights to collect new RFDS aircraft, the travellers unpacked their usual stash of duty-free gifts and other items that had escaped a check from customs.

All seemed well with Robin. Since her operation the previous year, she had thrown herself into an unceasingly demanding schedule. Only in dire cases were auxiliary nurses or doctors requisitioned on her flights, and finding escorts to accompany the allegedly 'walking wounded' was one of her constant headaches. She would try anyone she considered even vaguely suitable and willing to drop everything at a moment's notice: family members, old school chums, neighbours, members of the Women Pilots' Association, Jandakot Airport office workers, visitors to Western Australia who had seemed interested ... The trouble was that no matter how enthusiastic the recruit, they were likely to be available only once. Flights over featureless country were long and, if the weather turned bad, sometimes frightening. At stark outposts, sufferers were loaded aboard in states requiring a variety of ministrations from those unused to giving it. Problems arose – and what was in a day's work for the Flying Nurse became an experience never forgotten by another. Having quickly grasped the principles of a modern twin-engine aircraft, Horrie was helpful inasmuch as he could take over the controls while Robin attended to the cabin, but the insurance implications had there been a mishap constrained her from using him too often. When no assistance was forthcoming, Robin heroically worked alone. On one occasion she flew the plane with a diabetic male in the rear and three babies – a critical bronchopneumonia, a chronic diarrhoea and a violently fitting case of meningitis – their small bodies chocked around her in the cockpit:

> *I managed four nappy changes, three vomits and much screaming, but it was difficult, especially as a night landing. I actually had two kids on my lap, they simply wouldn't let go and the seatbelt was useless as they just slid out. Big mess to clean up afterwards.*[10]

Usually professionally composed in the face of death, she had been horrified when a woman dying of cancer had passed away in the seat beside her. Given her own encounter with the loathsome disease, she had the impression the germs were leaping from the corpse onto her.

A happier outcome had been achieved when, with the help of nurse Audrey Jordan, an obstructed birth had proceeded and a midair baby was successfully delivered.[11] ('How did you boil the water?' came the enquiry from a plane in the vicinity.) Since both the midwives were already walking in the valley of the shadows, it was a blessing the infant lived.[12]

All too often the RFDS was belatedly called in and moribund patients handed over with little hope of surviving the journey. Robin liked to deliver her charges alive, and she went to lengths to revive and hold seemingly hopeless cases. She did not enquire about ultimate fates, although the information was often passed to her anyway. After a long struggle to fan a spark of life, it was disheartening to hear it had been in vain. The aircraft regularly bore witness to the exertion: seats and walls awash with blood, vomit and the detritus of medical equipment. It was the pilot's responsibility to restore the cabin to a sanitary state, and that for Robin included taking linen and seat covers home for washing and mending. If she discovered a careless clean-up, the offender was left a disapproving note, and she was openly critical of fellow pilots who were unwilling to exceed the flying time restrictions when a life, or lives, were at stake.

Not all those employed by the RFDS were as dedicated as Robin and Harold, who ran the service very proprietarily, and there is no doubt that they did between them double the work of others. Beyond their flying duties, they indoctrinated new staff, supervised hangar activities, accepted speaking engagements and gave their services to fundraising activities and community causes. In addition to his other duties, Harold ran a weekend outback clinic. Disrupted attempts at a social life were testament to their round-the-clock availability. It had therefore come as something of a shock to them both that total commitment to the job and acting always 'in the interests of the service' did not protect them from adverse forces, their more discretionary ventures increasingly subject to new rules and regulations. During his absences, there were moves to undermine Harold's entrenched position and initiate changes as upsetting to Robin as to him: 'Harold very worried. While we have been away he has more or less been ignored and disposed of in a "new concept" they have dreamed up.'[13]

It is evident that on her return from the ferry flight, as she continued the rigorous workload, Robin's normal realism deserted her. Surely knowing, but not admitting, the likely reason for her failing health, she ascribed oddly disparate symptoms to a number of lesser conditions. Contemplating the unthinkable, she wrote: 'I'd die if I couldn't continue in this job and at present I know that I am quite safe flying. The episodes don't incapacitate me in any way.'[14] Tests for Addison's disease proving negative, she attributed the pain in her right buttock and groin to 'sciatica'. Her nights sleepless, she lived on aspirin and shots of Fortral that made her violently sick.

With Robin safely on home ground and Horrie mollified, Mary went north to work on the bishop's film. On her arrival, it seemed little progress had been made with *Tjakamarra – Boy Between Two Worlds*, other than the bishop having approved a title that more or less summed up the theme. Unable to work on what was still an ephemeral notion, she travelled to Darwin to sit in on the convening of the first all-Aboriginal ACF committee.

Eighteen delegates representing 140 outback communities had turned up. The retiring Judge Foster welcomed the new chairman, Lazarus Lamilarmi from Croker Island, and Lance Bennett's careful explanation of how government money was dealt with and books audited seemed to be understood. No easy task to help the Aboriginal contingent organise without actually organising, the meeting was generally declared a success, though Mary was cautious about whether or not it had really achieved any more positive purpose than an appearance of the original plan being achievable. John von Sturmer, whom she noted as always seeing the situation with disconcerting clarity (albeit in terms sometimes too philosophically and technically profound for the other members), pronounced the restructure 'precarious'.[15]

From a house in Kununurra loaned by the North-West Department, Mary continued recording Aboriginal memories and consulting over the Argyle Homestead reconstruction process. Karl Stellmach, in town filming Catholic Church activity, was seemingly not yet ready for a script that might restrict his freedom to take random footage of anything he fancied. His requirement for aerial views of Wyndham gave Bishop Jobst a permit to dive-bomb the town in a manner not seen since 1942, an experience that Mary, in the rear seat, described as 'terrifying'.

On return to Perth, there had been no time before departing for Adsett to do any more than note: 'Robin suffering from a persistent pain in her thigh, a condition she hopes alleviated by next month when she has agreed to address the International Aeronautical Association in Canberra.'[16] Unable to put off the long-term arrangement made to tour the South West with her brother Bill and his wife Noni, for a week Mary was thus spared the terrible burden of knowledge that awaited:

> *Sensed at once from the manner of Marie Rose and Horrie that all not well with Robin. Soon the distressing news was revealed. The pain she has been having in thigh and leg has been shown by recent tests to be the result of an inoperable growth in the pelvic region. Lost no time in dumping luggage and getting over to her. She is brave and hopeful – the pain kept at bay by drugs of various kinds. She was worried mainly at the inconvenience caused by her 'possibly' she said, having to cancel her speech in Canberra. She said if she could not go she would dictate to me and Connie could type in case they could not find alternative speaker.*[17] *I will move in with the dear girl tomorrow. Poor Horrie, what to say to cheer him?*[18]

From the outset there was never any hope. Mary expressed none, apart from the pitiable line in a letter to Kath McArthur that 'some miracle may yet give her back to us'. Nor did she dwell on why she might have been thus twice visited. The insupportable is recorded factually and with affecting understatement. In tacit acknowledgement that earthly hands were powerless, an early alert to the clergy that brought about masses of special intention and fervent petitions to the Lord met a disappointing response. It was just matter of seeing it through.

Two days before her fatal diagnosis, disregarding her own acute discomfort, Robin had flown to Meekatharra and helped Harold with a busy clinic. No sooner had they returned home than there was an urgent call:

> *MVA at Lake Grace. Got back to the hangar and we were away within thirty minutes of the call. My leg bad and very tired. I flew down, Harold back. Injured my left hand in a door accident on the Cessna. At Albany found a woman a paraplegic and her six-year-old son with deep lacerations and internal injuries. It was freezing and the wind really stirred up my sciatic nerve – entire leg intensely painful – but others worse off.*[19]

It was her last living flight. The next day Harold called in a neurosurgeon, who made a house visit to examine her. ('A favour to Harold. Terribly embarrassed about this and on a Sunday too.')[20] He advised she be hospitalised for tests. After an excruciating run through the diagnostic mill, she flatly records the verdict: 'Surgeon and neurosurgeon told me that I have secondaries in the pelvis. I just feel sick and terribly lonely. Harold went off looking haggard.' During the fitful night, she woke frequently to wonder if it was only a dream.

No, true. I have inoperable cancer. How will I spend the time I have left? How will I tell Mum and Dad? Poor Harold! Will I have to live on drugs? How will Harold manage on his own? He needs me.

Treatments of last resort were organised – cytotoxic drugs, cobalt therapy and the already discredited Tronado machine: 'Depressed me no end to hear of it. Side effects include loss of hair, nausea, vomiting, gastric ulcer, dizziness, sterility.' With a supply of morphine, she went home, the death sentence from the medical laboratory stapled into her diary. There was no more the surgeons could do for her.

Between trips for the purpose of being blasted with lethal rays, she worked on her Canberra speech and discussed with her mother how she might occupy her idle hours; perhaps putting together a sequel to *Flying Nurse*? And until the last, with discipline and clinical objectivity, she logged the deadly details. At times her hand wanders in arcs across the page, but she writes over indecipherable words and corrects herself. Clinging to the refuge of her specialist knowledge and hard-won expertise, she continued to rally, organising escorts, phoning requests for emergency strip lighting and making out flight plans for Harold.

Although there had been no suggestion, including from Robin herself, of other than that she be put through the mill of last-ditch treatment, in retrospect it was a cruel road to have embarked upon. The ordeal lasted ten days.

'Feel poisoned off, like death,' she wrote after the first session. 'Terrible sweats and all night waking with the idea that someone was going to "check" me. Thought I was in some perilous situation in the air.' Her condition after one of these frightful tests of endurance, as recorded in her wavering hand, did not deter Harold from taking her to the bank, where she managed to withdraw the last seven hundred dollars from her savings account for upholstery on the boat.

As a result of an erroneous blood count from the hospital pathologist, she was given an overdose of radium therapy on her fourth visit. Developing a swinging temperature with splitting headaches and other grave symptoms, Robin documents what followed:

Mum and Harold working over me, sponging me down for hours on end. Meanwhile I was delirious and irrational. Doctor called in and took iv blood. The news was bad, I had septicaemia, my white cells very low and contradicting the blood scan we had last week. Seems I may have been handed the wrong report. Harold furious. Bowel

> now paralysed. At 3pm I went into the bathroom and felt myself going – cold, far away, desperate ... fell to the floor. Harold found me and for an hour we battled for life. I nearly died twice. No blood pressure. Pulse weak and thready. It's the way Julie died, I know – horrible, horrible! Felt the pain very great and my heart just couldn't take it. It actually stopped then came OK with every nerve, muscle and skin surface acutely sensitised. Harold shouting out couldn't raise Mum who was lying on her deaf ear. When she came down she was terribly upset but I'm glad she didn't see the worst part.[21]

'Just a bit off-colour,' she airily reassured the thunderstruck ambulance driver who regularly attended the RFDS at the airport and knew her well. Her final lines are from the South Perth Community Hospital:

> Having terrible rigours. In terrific fever. First of twenty 500 mls whole blood fresh. Restless night. Swinging temp, 104' [sic] to 37 (normal) shivering with cold then scalding with heat. Feel totally knocked. The sisters were marvellous – by me hour after hour.[22]

It is characteristic that her last written thought was an expression of gratitude for the good services of others ... and oh, the poignancy of the unmarked pages that follow.

Drugs now put her into a semi-coma, but not all the time, and the moments of lucidity were the hardest to bear. During 'long days at my darling's bedside', her mother continued with her own sorrowful account:

> She tells me it comforts her to come to and see me beside her – thanks me most touchingly. Today she said 'Mum, I can feel your spirit flowing into me.' I thank her for wanting me. But the days so slow for the poor darling – drifting off while trying to talk and her remarks a mixture of dreams and reality.[23]

Scarcely able to swallow food, Robin suddenly asked for a mango. The message conveyed to the Broome nuns, boxes of mangoes were speedily dispatched and delivered by MMA staff. Managing to eat a tiny slice, she appeared to enjoy a taste of the fruit that reminded her of her childhood days. Her hospital room began to fill with flowers and cards, the senders not able to grasp the remove of the dying.

On rambling flights of fancy, she fumbled at her tray, feeling the sides as if looking for the controls of an aircraft, and now and again issuing brief, exasperated instructions: 'We won't be long. Tell them we're starting off immediately.' In her brisk lost-Robin voice, she told her mother to 'go home and stop wasting your precious time', and impatient with attempts to spoon feed her: 'Put that away. There simply isn't any time for fooling – we've got to cope – this is an emergency.' All at once began the horror of a last burst of frantic energy:

> *No sleep or relaxation for her all day. She suddenly leapt out of bed and ran to the door of her room, fought me off quite strongly when I tried to deflect her – opened the door and ran out into the courtyard where she fell on the grass face down, crying distractedly. Once she clung to me weeping and said, 'Oh Mum, where am I going?' I brought out her rugs and a pillow and she lay there for about two hours.*

In her far-off way, Robin seemed to register the decision to remove her from the hospital. Knowing well enough the limitations to palliative care administered at home, it had been her earnest request that for as long as possible she should remain with her family in familiar surrounds.

But as the fiendish pain broke through the morphine barrier and the doctors discussed severing her spine to end the torment, we were faced with terrible decisions. With the need for a qualified attendant during his absences rejected by Harold as out of the question 'financially', the offer from Audrey Jordan that she take over as a relief nurse was gratefully accepted. During long and nerve-racking hours on watch, Harold had kept up a diatribe on the evils of Gough Whitlam and his pernicious Medibank and bulk-billing schemes. On 11 November, with the astounding news of the dismissal, Mary reported him 'in a state of jubilation'. In the kitchen, for all to see, he had pinned up a verse he seemed to consider the height of wit:

> *I'm glad that I'm Australian, glad that I am free.*
> *I wish I were a little dog, and Whitlam was a tree.*

Staunch Labor supporters, however, like the Korwills, were outraged, and Connie Hooker was rendered inconsolable:

> *The reactions from both sides over these past months have been more violent and bitter than anything I remember. Politics no longer a matter of reasonable debate. I feel personally torn in many directions and worried by the vituperative counter-utterances of those so close to me. And all the while, my beloved girl, struggling so bravely ...*[24]

Receiving the wire urging me to make all haste, within a day I was there. At first glance I knew that the battle was lost. My frantic calls from Port Moresby had been answered by Horrie, who had not informed me – other than 'she's out' – that my mother had moved to the Dicks house. 'No need for you to come down,' he had assured me. 'You're not wanted here.' The question remains: why did he do it? Civility had long ruled the day from my end. Apparently able to justify writing off his two sons, where was the pretext when it came to a reprehensibly well-behaved daughter? I suppose he did it because there was a need in him to lash out at anything he perceived as the least antagonistic or threatening to his will, and now because it was not me lying so gaunt and drawn in the last throes. Even so, I felt sorry for him, his focus narrowed to the single fading beam that, once extinguished, would leave him in stygian gloom. And how he did spare himself! During fleeting visits, he sat on the bed, shoulders bowed, his back turned to the ruin of his beautiful star. Sadly he reached down and picked up a swathe of her long blonde hair.

'Oh, Dad,' she sighed from her dream world, 'I've got so many things to tell you.'

'And I've got so much to tell you, sweetheart,' he choked before slinking away.

Never again would his spirits soar to the sight of 'our blondie, stepping down from the aircraft, looking so pretty and fresh in a pale green mini frock and with a smile like the sweetness of flowers in spring'.[25]

Marie Rose, attending the bedside and coping efficiently, had taken on some of Julie's 'tower of strength' qualities. In the circumstances, it was almost beyond belief that she too should have become subject to Harold's perfidious behaviour. Once, Robin had opened her eyes and seen her embarrassed sister fending off the vulgar embrace (not, she later revealed, a one-off occurrence.) 'Stop it, Harold,' she said. 'I know what you are doing.' And that for all time was the only hint we were ever to get that she might not have been entirely blind. In the final reckoning, it had been right that we had protected her from the worst of him.

On 5 December, Mary fell back on an old bushman's expression: 'Robin generally in low water.' It was only for our sakes that she tried to take a little nourishment and, nodding to encouraging words, allowed herself to be sat up as yet another well-meaning visitor came to her bedside. With every passing hour, she was clearly losing ground. When she no longer knew where she was, we had her taken back to hospital. How tenderly the faithful ambulance driver supported her poor little head as it fell back on her thin neck. What a light burden lifted onto the stretcher. As we followed her, in a strangely detached way my mother raised the subject of the funeral and other post-mortem arrangements. When she remarked matter-of-factly, 'Harold will of course remarry,' with all due respect to Robin's long infatuation, I thought her supposition fanciful.

Put on oxygen, blood transfusions and every possible intrusive thing, perhaps Robin would have expected this effort when all was lost, as she had done for countless patients. It seemed wrong to me, a sort of ultimate indignity, and when someone came in with a machine to polish the floor I left, wondering why we could not have been allowed to just hold her hand. She slipped away in the early hours of the morning.

> *Horrie and I looked our last on our beautiful girl. There was one tear caught in the corner of her eye and an expression on her face as if to say, 'well, that's that!'*[26]

~

When her preferences had narrowed to no more than a thought for the disposal of her mortal remains, Robin had 'expressed a wish', as it is said, that she be buried in Broome. Deciding it appropriate that the sisters should be laid to rest together, we gave instructions for the retrieval of Julie's ashes from where they had been temporarily placed in her grandfather's grave. The logistics of coordinating a coffin plus a large family party in two aircraft certainly acted as an immediate distraction, and one must admire her for having thought of it.

All the while, Gran had done her best to keep up with the inundation of sympathetic concern deflected her way in the absence of Mary on the home phone. The calamity really beyond the scope of her cliché-ridden diary, she had 'hoped and prayed' in apprehensive but generally optimistic terms until the end, when she went into a mode of disbelief. It had been almost beyond her bearing to sit at the bedside and hold the inert hand of the one she had counted on to see her out. The shock would lead to her final phase.

The sudden passing of the 'Flying Nurse', so well known for her life-saving exploits, made headlines across the continent and tributes poured in – from civic leaders to unsigned expressions of sympathy from 'just a member of the public'.

'Such a heart-warming demonstration from friends far and wide but goodness how can I deal with them this side of Christmas?'[27] As after the death of Julie, Mary was not going to lay down a single stone of her responsibilities, or what she saw as her ongoing duties to her daughter.

For the death notice, we chose a few lines from *Night Flight*, a novel by the French aviator Antoine de Saint-Exupéry. Robin, who had also experienced the relief of safe harbour on the other side of great danger, had marked the passage in her copy of the book. *Can these be the same stars? Is this the same sky? How bright, how clear, what safety I have reached.* These words were later placed on her gravestone.

Divided between commercial and private aircraft, the mourners gathered for transportation north. Horrie's fragile constitution not up to either the requiem mass at St Anne's Hospital chapel or the funeral, his withdrawal had been sympathetically accepted. Under a blanket of flowers and wreaths, Robin's coffin was loaded aboard the new aircraft she had only two months earlier ferried back from America. Flown by Harold, the Cessna also carried RFDS personnel and family members. Civil Aviation officials followed in another private aircraft, and an MMA flight, on which Mary chose to travel, was filled with mourners, among them Albert Barunga, who had been so suffused with grief for her that he could only hold her hand and weep.

In the white weatherboard church, an impressively solemn and noble Bishop Jobst conducted the requiem mass with fathers Michael McMahon and Francis Huegel. A group of local Aboriginal boys acting as pallbearers, the cortege afterwards wended a leave-taking path down the familiar streets and past the site of the old house, the poinciana ablaze with colour. Harold having absented himself immediately after the service, we tried not to make what Robin would have declared 'spectacles of ourselves' during the lengthy ritual of the traditional Broome burial, where all remained until the grave was filled. Amid the throng, the sorrowful mother stood, steadfast, but as she turned to walk away at last, the breaking point came as the Cessna appeared overhead and, in a gesture Mary thought perhaps his finest moment, Harold dipped the wing in a salute to the one who lay far removed from all that had once been so vital to her.

In later years I met a man who was among a paying backload of miners on board the aircraft. Unknowing of the tragedy, they had all been astounded when told by Harold as he came in low over the cemetery, the red earth of the grave-digging process clearly visible below: 'That's my dear little wife being buried today.'

~

Horrie's defence mechanisms had kicked in within hours of his daughter's death. Terribly anxious about him, Marie Rose had gone to the house and found him watching the women's golf on television. He appeared less affected than we had feared, and those who had predicted he would not survive, though it was a reasonable anticipation, did not know Horrie. He had spent a lifetime installing insulation against outrageous fortune, and even the things that meant most to him were placed, when lost, behind a wall of selfishness too fast to be broken by any death but his own. Over the weeks of his lone occupation, Mildew had become an old man's hovel and he was well entrenched in it. From his squalid garage lair, he had moved to a disordered den in Robin's former room, where he mournfully slept in her bed. Repelling invaders like a territorial animal, he awaited the return of his mate, who had decided to remain with the St John of God nuns for a few days to brace herself for the Christmas ordeal.

As I toiled to put a clean surface on the house, the resident raised a spirited resistance. 'The point is, you're not needed here. This is my house now. Clear off! Get back to where you *belong*.' Vacuuming away with a grim resolve, I wondered where he thought I belonged. I supposed he meant Harold's place, where we had once again been compelled to take up occupation. But it was obviously an unbearable provocation to him, his patch invaded by one his wife was wont to pronounce 'cleanlier than thou', and aware I had no expectation of his behaving other than in character, he would not disappoint me.

On the first night of Mary's dismal homecoming, there they were, Horrie and Harold, in furious disagreement over Gough Whitlam. 'Bloody mad old bastards' was the verdict of my diary.

Bet, who had been on an overland trip across Australia and absent for the last weeks of Robin's life, returned ten days after the funeral. A letter to her brother Bill with an account of 'a sad homecoming' was revealing of her remove from a situation that did not in any practical sense affect her. Critical of our handling of the case, she described how she had learned to her horror that 'poor darling little Robin', rather than being hospitalised for the duration, had for the most part been left to the ministrations of her loving but unskilled mother and sisters. To have allowed such a state of affairs was almost beyond her comprehension, 'and Enid agrees with me'. However, she believed that the Millers were 'over the crest' and that Gran, who was 'pretty knocked', would soon become buoyant again. Mary, she felt, needed to get away for a laze in the sun. Then, moving right along, she filled twelve pages with a description of her journey.[28]

The removal of Robin's gentle, considerate and civilising influence would be felt in many ways over the ensuing years. Already severely diminished by the loss of Julie, the Miller family was now further weakened and made more vulnerable to hostile forces. There may even have been a subliminal perception from her siblings that 'dear old Mare's' generosity had extended to allowing herself to be the family lightning rod, thus somehow sparing them.

In his own fashion grieved by the loss of Robin, Harold would nevertheless remain true to type.

'It is,' he said to me, 'the custom in Samoa for the dead wife's sister to step into the breach.' He had not been speaking in jest.

Each day he arrived early to sit for hours, unshaven and dishevelled, in his surgery, waiting for patients who were tactfully staying away. Did he suppose the suicide dodge that had hooked Robin might work again? He had an old aircraft out at Jandakot Airport, he told me, worth only the insurance money, tanked up and ready to take off on what he described as 'a Viking funeral'. 'It would be better than how things are now,' he said with utmost pathos. Encouraged by my hollow discouragement of such a conspicuous exit, he suggested I provide him with 'a ready-made family' by moving into his riverside house. My existing marital status apparently a mere peccadillo, he needed a replacement for Robin, pronto. Would I perhaps like a trip to the South of France? No? Well, then, how about a cruise to Fiji on the new yacht? Clearly, there was nothing that Harold was not prepared to do for the favoured one. Another ferry flight to the United States was in the offing. Would I come with him? In return for a negotiable salary, would I take over as a receptionist in his surgery? The vacancy, temporarily filled by his sister Norah, had come about as a result of Harold's having sacked his former assistant because, so he said, she had refused to help him answer his many sympathy cards. From the distressed girl I learned that he had insisted she work from his home. 'I'm engaged to be married,' she explained, 'and – well, you know Dr Dicks!' When I tackled Harold on the subject, he had looked at me with a menacing eye. 'She wasn't kind,' he said. 'Girls who are unkind get punished.'

Robin's clothes and belongings needed to be dealt with, but unwilling for what he described as 'a job lot' of relatives to undertake the task, Harold wanted me on my own, with hints of 'special little things' on offer. After receiving a negative response with every appearance of hurt bewilderment, he suddenly announced, 'You know Patsy, it's a funny thing but I can't find Robin's will.' 'Don't be absurd, Harold,' I said. 'It will turn up.' But the will that Robin had been so assiduous about putting into proper order had vanished. Mary was astonished.

> What a strange thing to happen for such a careful and meticulous girl. She had certainly made out her will, and before her overseas trips she always left it in the care of either Patsy or me.[29]

She also observed Harold to be 'in a better frame of mind, having found a girl to go with him to the United States for another RFDS ferry flight. He is a remarkably quick worker.'[30] It was three weeks since Robin's death, and within six weeks there would be another woman installed at the Mount Pleasant home among her belongings.

~

While most members of the Durack family celebrated the December landslide victory for the Liberal Party in the federal election, Mary remarked that she and Horrie were 'very much in the minority in our political eccentricity.'[31] On Christmas Eve, the coming event not having been mentioned in her diary, Mary received news of the arrival of another grandchild, born to her son Johnson and his partner Barbara Pedersen. Whatever misgivings she had about the irregular addition to the family, Marcus, an entrancing child, would provide a distraction from a grief that found its way into her nightly perambulations. Now she had two daughters to seek out from the shades:

> *Dreamed of my dear girls – asking Robin what she wanted for her next birthday knowing there would not be a birthday. Julie in the doorway, smiling. Found myself impelled to turn the other way, going from room to room in some sort of vain search – woke weeping and desolate.*[32]

CHAPTER 12

THE MAIN JOB (1976–1977)

Acting on public sentiment for a fitting memorial, Harold Dicks suggested Robin's Mooney be repurchased and put on display at Perth Airport, a proposal he hoped would be backed by a Miller family donation. Horrie's agreement came with the stipulation that unless the aircraft was placed beside his Wackett in Broome, it would be for Harold to raise the funds. My reaction to the idea was not enthusiastic:

> *There is still $10,000 on it owed Miller Investments by H. Dicks without the cost of getting it back. Robin only used the plane for eighteen months and it became a millstone to her before she finally managed to sell it, at Dad's insistence keeping the sale money. She spent six years with the RFDS so if the plan does go through it should be placed at Jandakot Airport where the service has its base and she was such a familiar figure.*[1]

We did our best with the grave in the Broome cemetery, planting trees and raising a slab of rock from Cable Beach onto which we attached her Flying Doctor wings. In another sentimental gesture, because she had been so strongly identified with the job, Julie's air-hostess wings were added to the shared tombstone.

Before she was halfway through answering the letters of condolence, Mary was again under siege:

> *Sister Alphonsus has sent me her anecdotes to accompany the other nun's biography I edited last year. I can't refuse the dear soul this little service in view of the great service she has rendered.*[2]

The ghoulish spectre of Mrs Haebich, the former ironing lady, materialised again: 'Listened for an hour to her recital of past and present ailments, mishaps and injustices before firmly dropping her on the bus stop.'[3] Mrs Haebich was only one of many to gain entry for the purpose of a personal unburdening or the pursuit of some other agenda in the guise of a sympathy call.

The political fallout from events of the previous year still a contentious issue, Irene Greenwood rang to hoarsely whisper her outrage at the iniquities of the new government, while from her hospital bed Connie Hooker continued the invective. During a gathering of Durack family for her brother David's visit, Mary notes: 'my wan defence of Labor no match for their vehement Liberal views and their solid conviction that Whitlam had all but wrecked the economy'.[4]

Her memory noticeably deteriorated since Robin's death, Gran required close monitoring, and Mary's attempt to absent herself for a few days at Adsett had been curtailed when her mother fell and was found hours later lying helpless on the floor. And what to do about Horrie, who had taken to sitting in darkened rooms with his head sunk in his hands, a pose designed to discourage her from leaving him alone for a moment. If she was to move in any useful direction, she supposed there was going to have to be some toughening up on this front.

Despite his recently having become a father, there was little change in Johnson's lifestyle. But the new generation was for Mary a source of consolation, and she was delighted when Marie Rose announced she was expecting.

An advertisement for a carer to look after an elderly lady had turned up only one suitable applicant. Given Gran's problems with live-in help, a South African lady of mature years had seemed reassuringly humble and compliant. For a start, she would have to put up with the noise factor, since sooner than wear her hearing aid Gran preferred to turn up the television and radio volume. Edith Joshua was installed, and although it would be no easy task to foster the novel idea of a 'companion' relationship rather than 'mistress and servant', to which her mother so easily reverted, the situation would endure.

With her mother in good hands, Mary made a sudden decision to attend the Adelaide Festival Writers' Week. For many months caught up in domestic binds and stalled by Horrie's despondency, she feared slipping from the mainstream or being sidelined on compassionate grounds. For all the taxing social aspects of it, attending the festival would confirm her ability to soldier on and allow her to meet her new Sydney-based literary agent, Tim Curnow of Curtis Brown. After a series of less than satisfactory intermediaries, she considered his willingness to take her on a lucky break.

Reconnecting with literary and festival associates, Mary felt herself back in her rightful milieu. She had been crossed off the list of attending writers, so the event called for nothing more arduous from her than a reading of 'Lament for the Drowned Country' ('to great applause') and a contribution to historian Hazel De Berg's recording of writers for the National Library.

In the course of what she dismissed as her 'babbling on', she made a revealing – if a shade coy – apologia that might stand as her epitaph:

> *I could never absolutely abandon mundane things and become abstracted, as one really needs to do to succeed in the writing game. I feel that I have never realised my potential as a writer. I could have written a very great deal more and better than I ever have, though in some ways, perhaps it is surprising that I wrote anything at all. Perhaps I enjoyed life too much, enjoyed just being a person with lots of people in my life. I could have been more disciplined, perhaps less outgoing and more ruthless. As it is, my life has been very much taken up with being a mother, a sister, an aunt, a daughter, a wife, a grandmother and I hope, a friend.*[5]

My latter-day dwelling on what might have been would tell her nothing for which she had not castigated herself.

In festival circles Mary had registered a general unease over Prime Minister Fraser's threatened budget cuts to ABC funds. Soon after her return to Perth, under duress from 'regrettably heavily-loaded political sources', she added her name to the list of prominent Australians calling, via an 'open letter', for the financial and political independence of the ABC. This signalled the onset of Liberal Party interference with an Australian sacred cow; by the end of the year there would be public outrage when *This Day Tonight*, *Four Corners* and *State of the Nation* were put on the list of programs to be excised. With no secretary between Mary and the phone, she would receive the brunt of calls from the press and concerned members of the community. The following year, when asked to endorse an anti-mining environmental cause[6], she declined, fearing her name would be used 'as a front for a more or less communist body of people – all other members signing as quoted to me are party members'.[7]

~

Flying out of Port Moresby with the intention of sorting out problems arising at home, I found I was too late. Horrie had left all matters of Robin's estate to my mother, and as ever when it came to business that required close scrutiny, she had perfunctorily signed off on demands from Harold Dicks that all Robin's company debts be forgiven and he be reimbursed for the not inconsiderable funeral expenses involving hire of an RFDS aircraft. This was done against the advice of Cyril Gare, who had never to my memory spoken a bad word about any living soul – but he had a struggle when it came to Dr Dicks. He had been particularly disturbed by the matter of Robin's shares, as outlined in a letter to Horrie:

> *I gave him the advice from Corsers law firm as to how he could transfer the shares to Patsy and Marie without incurring any penalty. However, he decided to stick by the distribution as laid down by law in such cases. I am unable to comment on this.*[8]

Cyril knew that the significance of what would likely go to Harold and the ensuing damage to the beleaguered family company was not fully apprehended by the Millers, who were amateurs when it came to their financial affairs.

~

Shortly before leaving for Broome to continue work on his film, Mary received a letter from Bishop Jobst: 'I wonder if you could leave out of the story anything controversial, without representing facts with a bias, which could be detrimental to the image of the church?'[9]

With this appeal to curb any wayward tendency to be discerning, from the outset there would be no call for other than the bland and literal. On Mary's arrival, it was evident that she was not the only one straying from the bishop's preferred script. She wrote indignantly:

> *Karl vociferous about racism towards his wife being shown by local citizens, including the nuns – of all people. His interpretation of inoffensive incidents most ill-considered and embarrassing. He thanks God there are no such tendencies in his own country.*[10]

Taking up residence in Horrie's former quarters, she had wasted no time in mustering her family to share what would be an increasingly rare opportunity. But there would be no respite from misfortune: 'Awakened by Patsy in early hours with disturbing news Marie Rose threatened with a miscarriage, the process of labour irreversible. A terrible day for us all.'[11] There followed a long ordeal for Marie and her husband Michael until a baby girl was born, too small for survival. The little one who had lived just two hours was buried beside her aunts Robin and Julie.

As arranged earlier in the year, a party of Warrnambool faithful arrived to lay a wreath on Robin's grave, the tribute reading: 'In memory of a happy Pacific meeting.' Once again the mother stood by the place marking the end of her daughters, and now the granddaughter she would never know:

'A simple ceremony. I unveiled the newly raised stone and plaque while Father Michael McMahon said a few well-chosen words.'[12] Subsequently the Warrnambool friends would continue the association by collectively and individually sending Christmas cards to perplex her as the years went by.

Kith and kin gone their various ways, Mary put together a draft script for the daily filming schedule. As evening fell, feeling bereft in the empty house, she gravitated towards the bishop's residence, and he was glad of her company for a convivial glass of beer while he cooked up fried rice in a thoroughly domesticated manner. Together they flew the round trip to Balgo mission over desert country the bishop found boring but that for her was entrancing:

> *crisscrossed with sand ridges from east to west, broken ranges, escarpments and dry creek beds, winding and looping north to the Fitzroy River – the whole country a patchwork of different shapes – some abstract and some curiously tracing the outlines of spirit heroes, fish, birds and prehistoric animals.*[13]

After a week of waiting for Stellmach to devise a coordinated plan of action, and unable to shake off the premonition that at any moment she might be summoned home by another family calamity, Mary could no longer justify staying on at the bishop's pleasure.

As it happened, nothing worse awaited her return than a (deceptively innocuous) letter from R.M. Williams asking her to accept a position on the board of the Stockman's Hall of Fame (SHOF). Not having met the man who had risen from outback itinerant to millionaire by creating an Australian style of bush-wear, she had replied with her standard response: 'Said I must forgo the Committee but would help where I could.'[14] She would soon learn that Williams was not a man to take no for an answer. Pressing most earnestly that she at least attend their inaugural meeting, he enclosed a bundle of *Hoofs and Horns*, a publication foremost among the reading matter of every station in Australia. 'I was at last able to place the celebrated entrepreneur, his name a by-word in pastoral circles.'[15] Since resigning from the executive of the ACF, Mary had missed the purposeful travel towards a worthy objective. Were it not for 'the main job', she might have been tempted.

Advice that she had been unanimously elected as patron of the Broome Historical Society, without having been notified of her nomination, was received with the line: 'All very nice, but I seem to do anything except the task in hand.' She wondered was there really no other volunteer. Or anyone else to judge short story and play competitions, give talks to so many groups, gatherings and clubs – or 'just cast an eye'.[16]

Would-be poets and playwrights she noted as the worst offenders, these challenging disciplines being particularly attractive to those of toughest hide and least inspired. Refusals or put-offs were not always met with understanding. Her obliging reputation having travelled far and wide, resistance seemed to play false with public expectations. Why, she was known as a literary St Jude, and arrival at Mildew the equivalent of a visit to Lourdes for any number of crippled and terminally afflicted manuscripts. While protesting these visitations, my mother was affronted by my assertion that she 'asked for it', not least by her willingness to personally snatch up the phone as if expecting (as I scathingly put it) a summons from the Central Committee for the Continuation of the Human Race. What a victim she would become to the 'you don't know me but …' variety of caller.

For many months, screeds of incomprehensible ramblings had been mailed to her from a person who signed himself, in his own blood, 'Little Jimmy MacLachlan'. Freakish enclosures for return post – a balloon to be inflated by her own breath, a recipe for damper to be made by her own hands – had earned for Jimmy pride of place among an unsavoury pack relegated to a special file labelled 'Letters Lunatic'. Mary Durack's staid literary output and unassuming public persona somehow managed to attract religious maniacs, conspiracy theorists, strangers declaring family relationship (and claims to its fabulous wealth) and obsessed fans. Scrutiny revealed that nearly all had been sent a courteous reply and, to my alarm, replies to their replies – including Jimmy MacLachlan.

In August, as Mary at last got back to work on *Sons*, the call came from Karl Stellmach to say his filming was complete. Ida, busily abstracting M.P.'s diaries, argued against breaking the Adsett routine, but it seemed to Mary prudent that she finish the job for the bishop while the going was good. Marie Rose had recovered her health, Connie had resumed her secretarial duties and Horrie, having picked up his golfing round, was reported in the press as having holed in one while playing with a group half his age. Gran, as she informed enquirers, was 'well in myself' – implying unspecified external factors less well – and frequently thanked the Lord for her faultless memory, even though that increasingly threadbare faculty now played odd tricks on her. She could have sworn she had not seen Mary for weeks, even when assured that her daughter had visited that very day.

It was not until she arrived in Broome that Mary found the bishop's offer of accommodation had evaporated. Too much reliance on divine providence and not enough on the regulations of the DCA had seen the cancellation of his licence to fly, and a substitute pilot now occupied Horrie's former residence. A billet with Phyll Male, a widow since the recent death of her pearling master husband Sam, came with penalties. As revealed in long sessions over the ubiquitous glass of gin and tonic, Phyll was fixed upon an ambition to sell her Broome house at full market value, while at the same time ensuring it would be preserved for posterity. Unwillingly drawn into the ensuing morass and Phyll's 'quite loopy' thought processes, Mary paid a high price for her free room. Nonetheless, in the light of the demolition of so many traditional features of the old town, she considered the salvation of a fine early Broome bungalow a worthwhile cause and she would continue to lobby towards this end.[17]

Thankful for the bishop's offer of his study during the day, Mary shared evening meals in his 'sedate company', usually followed by a viewing of Stellmach's latest footage – haphazard material disconnected to any cogent storyline. Keeping to her original idea, Mary drew together the broad concept of a thriving missionary venture, woven in with the reactions of an Aboriginal youth to the sometimes conflicting worlds of black and white. As the time was approaching when mission Crown grants would have to be relinquished, the main theme as constantly stressed by the bishop was to spread the message that a continued church presence was imperative to plans for autonomous Aboriginal settlements.

With the selection of Keith Boombi, a handsome Aboriginal boy from Kununurra, to play the part of Tjakamarra, over the next three weeks Mary cut and pasted, stitching the narrative to the images. But for the promised promotional booklet to accompany the film, she considered her part in the project at an end.

~

The posthumous honours somehow for us emphasised the magnitude of her loss, but Harold revelled in the continued attention to Robin. Royal Perth Hospital was planning a commemorative plaque, and from abroad she had been awarded the Paul Tissandier Diploma by Fédération Aéronautique Internationale and the Brabazon Cup by the Women Pilots' Association of Great Britain. The latter trophy to be presented by Prince Charles, it occurred to Harold that I might accompany him to London to collect the award. Undeterred by my mother's warning that he should not get his hopes up, he rang Port Moresby. When my husband took the call, while I made throat-cutting gestures, Harold explained with the practised affability of one pilot to another why he thought I should attend the royal event. The off-putting response giving him no pause, he sent a proposed itinerary, including a side jaunt to Paris. But perhaps there was some decency in him yet. He also wrote saying that 'in due course I intend to do the things I know Robin would have wanted'. Brusquely passing on London and Paris, I posted him a list of bequests as recalled from the missing will and a copy of a letter written six weeks before Robin's death concerning the distribution of her shares. After 'receiving advice', Harold soon let me know that the letter constituted only a non-binding 'statement of intent'. As for what Robin would have wanted, it seemed that he had been subsequently visited by the spirit of his dear wife, informing him of her wish that he should be the sole beneficiary, her assets his and any liabilities the responsibility of the Miller family. Cyril Gare was presented with the final bill. I was summoned home for a shareholders' meeting to discuss ways of raising the money.

The only alternative to decimating the company portfolio was to raise a mortgage on Mildew, a prospect Robin could not have imagined herself bringing about. Standing firmly against letting Harold get away with it ('as I'm sure all the neighbours will be pleased to hear', remarked my mother), I determined during my few weeks in Perth to search for the will. Horrie, who had additional cause for regret with the belated memory of his having gifted to Robin the proceeds from the Broome houses and a sizable parcel of Ansett shares bought at the time of the transfer, urged me to pursue every possible course of action.

~

Having, as she thought, made plain her resolve to play no more than a minor part in the establishment of the SHOF, Mary decided to kill two birds with one stone when the first meeting in Brisbane happened to coincide with Warana Writers Week. Apart from Joy Katter, the wife of chairman Bob Katter, MP, she found herself the only woman among a group of successful self-made men ('typical Queensland rough diamonds') personified by R.M. Williams and the artist Hugh Sawrey. Once the location of the main venue was chosen, the plan was to cultivate regional offshoots, and it was hoped that Mary Durack might agree to participate in that area. Consenting to a temporary place on the board, she explained that she would not be able to attend regular meetings or do more than promote the idea in the West. Her first piece of advice was that the project's title was too restrictive to encompass the extensive Australian pioneering story, and the suggested addition of 'Outback Heritage Centre' was in due time accepted.

Satisfied that she had, for once, managed to take a firm stance, she set out on another round of the Queensland stations, with the intention of gathering information for *Sons in the Saddle*. Visiting Kath McArthur in Caloundra, she rallied her cousin to the local research and further wheedling of photos from reluctant hands, a task made easier this time by the discovery of a coin-operated photostat machine in the public library that would allow documents to be shared without losing the originals, as had happened so often in the past.

The trip in this instance had been courtesy of Warana, but R.M. Williams assured her that on whatever level she chose to pitch in, the SHOF would meet all future travelling and accommodation expenses. The offer would prove a powerful enticement.

Anticipating a gloomy reception on her return, Mary was pleased to find Horrie occupied with his official part in a commemorative Perth to Sydney air race. In 1929, when he had flown a flimsy double-wing DH9 to carry off the coveted Centenary Cup, the 2,500 miles from east to west had represented the longest point-to-point race to be held anywhere in the world. (Among the crowd to cheer him across the line had been a group of schoolgirls from Loreto Convent, including a sixteen-year-old Mary Durack, blissfully untouched by any divination.) Always in character, he failed to find a rapport with his fellow celebrity starter Sir Douglas Bader, whose noxious pipe had seen Horrie retreat, with exaggerated coughing, to the back of the VIP aircraft accompanying the race. But he received a standing ovation for his speech at the reception dinner in Sydney, and in Adelaide he caught up with his old friend Bob Chamberlain, the tractor magnate, who was a nephew of his 'Early Bird' hero Harry Hawker.

~

To Be Heirs Forever[18] was launched in December 1976 from Baskerville Hall on the upper Swan, close to the place where Eliza Shaw and her family had set up their first home. It was a memorable day. After a stirring address from Geoffrey Bolton, Nita Pannell performed an excerpt from the *Saga* for the four hundred appreciative guests. Speculating on how Eliza might have felt about her precipitation into a world a century beyond her grave, the author commented that the pioneer lady would certainly have been familiar with many of the names present in the form of descendants of the early families.

While a new publication was always a boost and the first edition would be sold out before Christmas, Mary privately found cause for self-reproach. During the twelve months since she had completed the book, small progress had been made on *Sons*. She had yielded to Nita's desire to see the Shaw history in print, and then had allowed herself to be further led astray by the bishop's project, and 'the ridiculous booklet' to accompany the film was yet to be tackled. In addition, the deadline loomed for her to complete an epilogue for the paperback version of *Flying Nurse*. In the circumstances, she had gladly accepted an offer from Harold Dicks to edit Robin's diaries for the sequel, although she anticipated having to do some final polishing.

It had been a year of sidetracks and work at the behest of others, the latest being the sorting of Ernestine Hill's unidentified photos for the Queensland Fryer Library. When three large boxes had arrived on the doorstep, her heart sank, but going through them she had been filled with admiration for the old friend from whom fate had parted her:

> *What a record of her roaming life – and how she relished every remote corner of Australia from the Central Desert to Tasmania and Tropical Queensland – from the Dandenongs to the Carr Boyd and Leopold Ranges – from Thursday Island to Roebourne and Broome ...*[19]

Bet's equally roaming life had returned her from the Pilbara with landscape paintings Mary thought the best she had yet done. Subjected to an interview in the course of the successful exhibition, the artist must have wondered whether to laugh or cry – or just be grateful for any publicity:

> *Elizabeth Durack has a frail Dresden china look. It is hard to imagine this pastel lady sitting in the harsh red dust of the Pilbara ... Born to a gilded existence as a member of one of Australia's best-known pastoral families she could have led a life of leisure. Instead she has mounted thirty exhibitions and has written and illustrated many books. Her current exhibition is the result of four weeks in Hamersley National Park ... [She] has been accused of being a born draftsman and illustrator rather than a painter, a charge that irritates her; 'There is a strong illustrative streak in my work,' she says, 'but so there was in Michelangelo's.' She prefers to organise her own exhibitions. This, some say, has led to her work being undervalued and perhaps leads to the question whether she is an amateur or a professional artist. She only knows that she has spent a lot of time at it.*[20]

Christmas having lost for Mary all feeling of festivity, the tranquil atmosphere of Adsett provided a soothing antidote to the affliction of memories in every corner of Mildew. Unlike her widely heralded arrival in Broome, here she could make a more discreet entry and departure, and on Ida's insistence hold to the new discipline of not inviting guests. With two weeks of New Year peace before her, she set to work on the background to her father's account of the early days of the century:

> [The] politics, business problems and human issues of 1904–1905 is like creating an intricate mosaic. The actual writing of the chapters a minor task to that of chasing up the data and shaping many facets to read as smoothly as possible.[21]

Dealing with 'living sensitivities' remained for her as problematic as ever.

An encounter the previous year with the grandson of Francis Connor, one of the partners in CD&D, had led to a meeting with his surviving daughters, Kitty and Moira. Hoping to record their firsthand memories, Mary had found herself talking to two old ladies raised on misinformation and myth about their father and the reason for his resignation from the firm. Since they had never accepted the fact of his disgrace and suicide, when it eventually came to that point in *Sons*, Mary anguished over how least to offend them.[22] Fearful of unpleasant repercussions, the historian, while vigilant on accuracy, did sometimes choose what facts to omit.

As always during hours sitting at her desk, now and again the task at hand was put aside: 'As I pause to think, I start drawing just one cactus and suddenly find that the garden with the sea behind has evolved around it.' Many beautiful and intricate pencil sketches remain as a reminder of Mary's attachment to every corner of the bush sanctuary. She knew the day was approaching when the place would be lost to her, as Ida intended leaving the property to relatives of her late husband, who would likely sell it. The next-door block was tantalisingly for sale, but the fifteen thousand dollar purchase price put it out of the question.

Recently returned from a trip to Moora as an invited guest on a trachoma survey, Ida had unhappily accepted the fact that her ranking as a VIP indicated the end of her professional life. Received with speeches and accolades from shire councillors and the town's hospital and welfare staff, she was wryly amused to observe that only in her obsequious welcome had much changed. Beyond the talk of community effort and money spent, she found the Aboriginal camp in most respects the same as when, in 1953, she had first enraged the Public Health Department by announcing the presence of trachoma. A stranger to idleness, Ida, as in her clinic days, would continue to occupy herself at Adsett from nine to five, abstracting from the old documents.

On the rare occasions she was allowed a clear run, Mary covered the ground fast. Two chapters written within the week, it was only the job for someone else that forced her to break her train of thought. She supposed that Nita, who had been deservedly bestowed with a New Year's OBE, would be unhappy with the slow advance on her new monologue, but so much time had gone into providing material for the actress that Mary had decided to put this one, along with all theatre projects, on the backburner. 'Grandmother Costello' would remain in draft form among her unpublished works.

In contrast to the productive Adsett routine, Perth had for Mary become a writing wasteland. Her birthday now subject to a press notice providing an excuse for calls from the public at large, the onus of caring for a geriatric mother and husband rather prevented any relaxation into her own sixty-four years. Gran, she observed:

speaks with all her old precision and assurance declaring something happened today or yesterday that happened weeks or months ago – or not at all. 'Don't ask Edith anything,' she says in that lady's hearing, 'she gets everything muddled – doesn't know this week from the last.'

Occasionally she shows concern about the memory lapses and the continuing pain in her thigh ... 'Sometimes I begin to wonder ...' the sentence always remains unfinished.[23]

Andy remained a recurrent worry for Mary. Nearly a year gone by without a word or clue to his whereabouts, the sight of the birthday and Christmas presents for him gathering dust depressed her into stowing them away. Johnson, advanced funds for a van to travel north, was a more visible cause for concern, his impecunious state very much her problem. 'Sometimes I begin to wonder too ...' My lecture on her unruly generosity not dissimilar to those well aired by Horrie reminded her not to mention this or other such matters to me – in particular, her arrangements with Bet.

Blaming poor sales of her latest *Seeing Through* book on the changing political scene in Indonesia, Bet was once again in urgent need. Devising a 'juggle', on the security of her anticipated share in Gran's house, she appealed to her siblings for a loan of ten thousand dollars to construct a studio separate from her house on the far end of the block. Reg and Bill were willing to accept the proposition to the tune of two thousand dollars each and Mary made up the remainder. On this occasion, knowing Bet's expectations already encumbered, the cheque from Mary came with a rueful reminder to her sister of the disparity between the ease of asking for money and the difficulties involved in getting it repaid.[24] Her bank statement now descended into the red.

The revelation from Harold that after a full year he had managed only a rough draft of one chapter of Robin's book came as a bad let-down:

He now proposes getting the material 'sort of together' and passing the lot to me. I see six months solid work on this. Nothing closer to me – but how can I …[25]

Having divested himself of that task, Harold departed for the United States to arrange the purchase and shipment of a defunct Mooney for the Robin Miller memorial now to be situated at Jandakot Airport.[26] Maintaining a doleful front, he made no mention of his altered marital situation. Six months after the event, rumours that he had remarried were finally confirmed by his tearful sister Norah. Mary could make no sense of it:

I told Harold from the beginning that I would be pleased for him to marry again and can't imagine why, seeing us as he does so often he has kept it from us. It would seem the girl is the one he brought down to meet me soon after Robin's death. Norah is very upset.[27]

The registration of the missing will with the Law Society initiated a protracted and ultimately fruitless paper chase. Two witnesses to the document and a record of its location with her bank prior to her death were discovered, but, when at last tracked down, the solicitor involved was on his deathbed and removed from such earthly affairs. I knew all along it was probably hopeless, but an attempt seemed important for Robin's sake – and for Harold's, too, since his story of a 'mysterious disappearance' hardly deserved the benefit of the doubt.

Horrie had become increasingly disconsolate as he came to understand the extent to which Harold had betrayed both Robin and her family. While unveiling a commemorative plaque at Royal Perth Hospital, his normal aplomb deserting him, he had broken down while trying to say a few appropriate words. Harold, springing into the breach, had been given the cold shoulder on this occasion and forever after. Animosity was abroad, and Harold was not going to take lightly our resentment at having been rolled over and hung out to dry. Learning of my endeavours, he lost no time communicating his offence to Mary:

A letter from Harold who is most incensed to hear (from Norah) that Patsy has been trying to locate the will – under the impression she has employed a lawyer although this is not so. He seems to feel it is a personal affront of some kind. He told me (knowing the cat now out of the bag) about his marriage last October and birth of baby daughter. Rang Norah and read her the letter. She was amazed as she was sure Harold would be pleased as she had supposed him as upset as we were that he had been unable to fulfil Robin's wishes.[28]

From his letter, Harold's affecting point of view emerges:

Robin's departure left me with a sense of irreparable loss which I am sure I will never get over. After that horrible day 7/12/75 for months I was like a lonely shag on a rock. Although you phoned me from time to time, invited me to dinner and so on, no other member of the family ever sought to visit or phone me.

I was welcomed if I appeared but I was not sought in any way. The administration of the estate was left entirely to me without offers of assistance. At this late stage I have been amazed to hear that Patsy has employed a lawyer to search for a will. After all my efforts to allow the lowest possible valuation of family shares when State and Federal Governments valued them at 2–3 times as much.

I feel sickened and sad and insulted by Patsy's action. Not that she did it but that she appears to have done it without any advice to me, advice to which I was surely entitled as Administrator and in the line of our friendship. I am told she did this out of concern for the family company. The trouble with the family company is its built in headwind and not the deaths in the family. Inflation has affected it to an extent of over 100%. I am sorry I have to unburden myself in this way, but news of Patsy's stirring made me wonder what was the use of all that I have tried to do for everyone. Since my marriage last October and the birth of my daughter I now have people to love and care for me. All the same it is a lonely road.

Deeply troubled by the high feeling on all sides over the issue, Mary sought to reach behind the eternal curtain for some explanation:

Had a curious and vivid dream last night. Robin was back with us again, seemingly happy and normal. Told her it wasn't important now seeing she was back, but that we had been unable to locate her will. I tried to tell her of Patsy's efforts to find it and that Harold was upset about it … kept being interrupted and couldn't get the story over. She said, 'It doesn't matter Mum,' – didn't seem to want to hear. When I said how wonderful it was to have her back well again she looked at me doubtfully and I felt an awful sadness and apprehension.[29]

For all his claimed insult and offence, Harold soon began a new avenue of attack in the form of a proposed film of Robin's life, to be scripted and produced by a freelance filmmaker with whom the grieving widower had signed a one thousand dollar option. Needing Miller family sanction, he was disappointed at the cool reception to this plan, and taken aback by Mary's reaction to his announcement that he intended selling 'his rights' to *Flying Nurse* – as she conveyed in a letter to me, fuming helplessly in Papua New Guinea:

No suggestion that any such might belong to us. I regret that any discussion with Harold about rights, contracts or money sinks into an irrational zone. He repeats over and over how much the Robin memorial is costing him personally and his conviction, against all evidence that he is and has been generous to a fault. We have not thus far been privy to the amount he has raised for the Mooney aircraft per public donation. I said that he must at least split the proceeds from any contract or royalties on the book and our share would be the Miller family contribution to the memorial fund. Reminding him of the fact that Robin had made a point of assigning to me the rights to her book in her missing will, he replied, 'I doubt that.' When tackled on the matter, it seemed that the difficulty in mentioning for so long his remarriage was as a result of a problem with another woman in Carnarvon – one he felt 'honour bound' to first sort out.[30]

Harold's concession to allow us to repurchase Robin's shares at probate value in return for a signed indemnity against further claims on her estate did little to reduce the sum owed him. Horrie's last-minute refusal to mortgage the house had left Cyril Gare with no alternative but to sell parcels of the family portfolio, hasty transactions that denuded the company stock. We would lose everything Robin owned: her private savings, personal possessions, photo albums and many of her diaries. In 1987, with Harold's death, all fell into the hands of outsiders. Thus did Dr Dicks punish 'unkindness'.

~

Before Karl Stellmach returned – ostensibly to Germany – to do the final editing on *Tjakamarra*, no-one had thought to get his address or telephone number. As time passed and the film failed to appear, the bishop and the main sponsor could find no trace of him. Oddly, the Munich phone book failed to list a company by the name of Stellmach International, and wider enquiries met with a blank. Mary remembered how it had been something of a mystery, considering his credentials, that the filmmaker had been so guarded and uncooperative when a visiting *Times* journalist from London sought an interview.

On the eve of the Shinju Festival, at which event the 'world premiere' showing was an advertised highlight, the fugitive and restrictively copyrighted item arrived, along with a bill to the bishop for 490 dollars in postage.

Packing for Broome, Mary did her best to see the frail family components – principally Gran – set for her three-week absence. Fortunately, the latest carer continued unflappable and tolerant of certain annoying eccentricities:

> *Mother has developed a private art form – playing with the remote control, switching rapidly from channel to channel – a curious mixture of American cowboy film, Uniting Church service, the football and advertisements – all at a deafening volume.*[31]

Informed at last of Harold's new situation, the bereft grandmother made a note of it in her diary, along with the words 'something I find impossible to believe …', and did not mention him again.

My husband's training on the latest Air New Guinea aircraft having temporarily returned all the Milletts to Perth, we faced the familiar problem of nowhere to stay. Intending to accompany my mother to Broome for the festival, and interim shelter at Mildew as unappealing a prospect for me as Horrie would let us know it was for him, this time I decided to ignore the fallout and risk a few days under the same roof at either end. Despite my mother's exertions in anticipation of the arrival of 'dear fuss-pot old Pats', I found the house dusty and neglected, crockery showing traces of many a Christmas past, and when not snapping in situ, Horrie's teeth snarling at me from the washbasin.

My mother was pleased to have family travelling with her, but I knew she hoped there would be no incidents that might stir any over-the-top reaction from me. Absent on a clerical conference in Rome, the bishop, as a gesture of gratitude to the scriptwriter, had seen to the accommodation arrangements. On our pre-dawn arrival, the taxi-driver's torch had been needed to find the small caravan parked outside Jobst's closed residence. Our bags dumped in the dust and with no access to water or electricity, my mother's circumspect 'hopeless except under the most dire emergency' was in contrast to my own outraged response:

> *How could he have done this to Mum, after all she has done for him? His comfortable house on land sold to him at rock-bottom price by foolish Dad locked up, also his car. The matter is already quite a town scandal but no-one with any lodgings to offer. Father McMahon is trying to arrange a refuge for us with the Loreto nuns.*[32]

The party for the big night including her daughter Marie Rose and husband Michael, our mother's assurance that at a preview showing she had judged the film 'first rate' was at variance with the more savvy verdict of her family.

Over a muzak score, an English narrator spoke in plummy tones for the Aboriginal boy, who conveyed via solemn face and self-conscious smile, wide shot and close-up, that he was trapped between two worlds. The cameraman had also devised a (copyrighted) whirl-around technique wherein 'confusion' was indicated, while the sledgehammer symbolism (animal skull on sand – harsh land) owed a good deal to the zoom lens. Taking into account the low budget, *Tjakamarra* was the cinematic equivalent of innocent verse. Mary, who had so wanted a success for the bishop's sake, confined her diary account to 'crowded house, appreciative comments'.[33] Aware that it was not quite the 'world beater' Stellmach had led her to believe, she hoped that general goodwill might yet carry the day.

Her family dispersed, she set off for the far north accompanied by Geraldine Byrne, a young woman who was researching the history of her pastoralist relative Jack Kilfoyle. On meeting this member of a family closely associated with the Durack pioneers, Mary had taken to her at once, and she came to look upon her over many years and on a number of shared journeys as a much-needed surrogate daughter.

Showing the newcomer over the town of Wyndham, she observed, in place of the cattle ships of her memory, one fragile wooden craft tied to the wharf. Vietnamese refugees seeking a safe haven would soon make the sight commonplace up and down the coast. It was while jotting down information from headstones in the cemetery (almost all the deceased personally known to her) that she experienced a disturbing sense of her own dwindling days. A verse she had written twenty-seven years before came to her mind, a few lines jotted in her diary. It was not death she feared:

> *But since I tasted this ash upon the air*
> *thought turns to stone;*
> *and all the works I plied with patient hand,*
> *my towers of knowledge built from grains of sand;*
> *the lost endeavours that I would redeem,*
> *my proud, enduring faith; my failing dream,*
> *dissolve upon the dark, unbreaking days.*[34]

Witness to the prelude two years earlier, Mary, on travelling to Darwin, was not surprised to learn from Lance Bennett of the irreconcilable discord that had arisen from the fiasco of the Australian presence at the Nigerian festival.[35] Conditions in Lagos had been chaotic. Playing the politics of black power, the urban delegates had decried the inclusion of Lance Bennett and Stefan Haag to coordinate the Aboriginal tribal dancers. In the prevailing melee, the one performance of a genuine corroboree failed, along with the sound and lighting. Eighteen members, disassociating themselves from the messages of discord from their city brothers, pulled out. Unique Australian Aboriginal culture had, in a final mockery, been represented by a sassy urban group dancing Filipino jazz ballet to American soul music. Kath Walker, there to promote black literature, had blamed the whites and the tribal groups for 'being out of their element' and producing a 'flop'. Amid widespread criticism at home, the 203,000 dollar grant that had gone into the project was put down to the folly of the previous government.

On her way south, Mary paid her annual visit to the nuns at the Derby Leprosarium. Viewing the recently completed section to accommodate up to eighty patients, she noted there were only twenty cases remaining. It was apparent that after decades of official indifference to a disease responsible for unimaginable suffering, the up-to-date facilities had arrived too late.[36]

On hearing of the passing of her dear friend Albert Barunga, she had found Albert's widow according to custom camped on the outskirts of the Mowanjum settlement, never again to enter the house they had shared. Nor would the place for Mary ever be the same without the man who had held it together for so long. She would later pay poetic tribute to the Aboriginal elder:

Always he spoke of loving, laughing, giving –
And while we remember his voice, Barunga is living.[37]

Horrie and his eldest daughter within the same abode had meanwhile provoked predictable tension. Fortunately, his son-in-law had been there to listen to verbatim anecdotes from *Early Birds*, and my cooking was accepted with a good appetite. At eighty-four, the legendary airman was still able to climb a ladder and brush a few leaves from the gutter, while creakily descending every few minutes to short circuit the washing-machine cycle 'to save on water', which I was allegedly wantonly wasting. His mechanical skills dwindled with the grey matter, it was also an irritation to me that his fiddling meant the touch of death to anything with a switch or a knob. On her homecoming, Mary was instantly presented with complaints about his having had food 'forced on him' and how the washing machine had been 'thrashed' in her absence. In exasperation, she told him to refrain from his boring vendetta or she would leave him and return to Broome, where the nuns had offered her a convent room as a peaceful writing retreat. Shocked, he turned on her with the anguished cry: 'What am I supposed to do? It's a thousand Duracks against one Miller here!' Was that the way he saw it? An unequal battle against his wife and her family (including shared children)? But Old Man Time, as he had often observed in happy anticipation of a visitation upon others, waited with poised scythe.

Depressed at my departure and once again facing the prospect of trying to work in an atmosphere inimical to concentration, Mary would have been a deal more downhearted had she glimpsed the gathering Fates at that moment conspiring against her – as her diary of 26 September records:

> *This evening to the launching of Bert Vickers latest book. To my surprise Horrie elected to come with me, as he likes Bert whom he meets regularly at cricket matches. He appeared to be enjoying himself and interested in the proceedings when he suddenly slumped in his chair. We got him outside with the help of two doctors there and an ambulance took him to Sir Charles Gairdner hospital. Was told that he had suffered a stroke – the left side affected and speech blurred. Returned home feeling fairly stunned at this bolt from the blue.*

At the patient's side first thing in the morning, she had found him weakly refusing to admit there was anything seriously amiss.

> *His condition is blamed entirely on his having been mistakenly taken to hospital after no more than a slight dizzy spell. He repeatedly declares, 'I just want to get back into my own bed and get on with my normal life.' But a relief that he remembers the occasion last night. Many phone calls as the news spread rapidly owing to the rather public nature of his collapse.*

From this time, Mary's life would become a relentless cycle of hospital attendance. Refusing to eat unless she fed him, Horrie repeatedly insisted that if he came home, he could manage with only her help, 'quite impossible of course as takes two nurses to move him with great difficulty but no amount of reasoning has any effect'.[38] In the mind of the old man, the key to his recovery lay in getting back to the place where he left his independence.

Connie did her best to cancel or defer lesser engagements: a guest of honour appearance at the annual *Overland* dinner, the meeting with Channel 7 executives to negotiate over the *Kings* film rights, a visit to Florence James. But longstanding commitments were harder to put off. A significant talk for WA Institute of Technology students – a revision of her old lecture 'The Aborigine in Australian Literature' – was an obligation fulfilled in the midst of the crisis.[39] Meanwhile, Gran required transportation to and from medical facilities to discuss the possibility of a hip replacement, and Reg was pressing her to write an introduction for, and launch, a book written by a poet friend with whom he had worked on translating a volume of Greek verse. The book was not one, in my opinion, really warranting a Mary Durack endorsement, and she wrote with feeble regret, 'Patsy giving me firm advice which I doubt I can take.'[40] I had begun to perceive a growing lack of consideration in Bet and Reg for their sister's circumstances – one that had the potential for conflict with me.

Worn down by Horrie's unrelenting coercion (as he knew she would be), Mary began investigating homecare services, daily physiotherapy, the house equipped for his incapacities – and the end of a moment's freedom for herself. In the circumstances, the opening of Bet's new gallery ('bright, attractive, family and old friends, many of the latest Broome pictures sold'[41]) got scant attention. Her fortitude was further tested when her long-lost son Andy called to say he was in hospital with injuries sustained as a result of his bull-catching activities. His broken knee encased in plaster, he too would soon require home nursing. Horrie's tactics were meanwhile unremitting:

> *The old man now convinced that the staff, both male and female are trying to kill him. He is the picture of abject misery and despair. He*

asks with my every visit where I have been 'all this time,' and speaks only in a dismal whisper that I feel he reserves for me.[42]

When he asked her to locate his various financial documents, if she thought it an indication of a sense of his mortality she was mistaken. Horrie's actual concern proved to be finding ways to avoid having his private capital, squirrelled away in a number of bank accounts, being used to pay off the large debt to Miller Investments incurred by Debesa. Seeking to recover company funds after depletion at the hands of Harold Dicks, Cyril Gare felt compelled to raise the matter. Mary failed to find his bank books, but among his disordered effects she was dismayed to turn out a distressing letter. Sent from Albury, New South Wales, in 1969, it was from an Annie Kennedy, who revealed herself to be Horrie's never mentioned sister:

Dear Brother Horace, I don't know how to start writing this letter to you.

When you won the East West air race in 1929 I wrote to you and sent a telegram but you never answered. That was forty-eight years ago now. The last time I saw you was when you came back from the war, fifty-nine years ago and it took me many days to find you. Our father died when you were fifteen years and I was seventeen. Do you remember Miss Doyle who adopted me from the Sutherland Home that Dad put us in? She lived at Surrey Hills and you used to come out and stay with us at weekends. Then Dad apprenticed you with Sunshine Harvest Works. You used to think the world of me in those days. We never knew what it was to have a mother's love. You were just six months old when our mother died.

Including a brief account of her marriage and seven children, Annie told of how over the years she had kept a scrapbook of press cuttings on his exploits and followed the career of his wife and – of late – his wonderful daughter Robin. It was after reading *Early Birds* that she had been moved to make an attempt at contact, supposing that the failure to mention her in his memoirs was because he thought she had passed on.

Well brother, I will close, trusting that you will reply to this letter. You used to love me one time. I don't expect we will see one another on this earth but I hope we will meet in the next world. God bless you.

From the unsent stamped and addressed envelope included, Mary presumed Annie had never heard back and, writing at once with diplomatic apologies, she passed on the news of Horrie's indisposition. When confronted, Horrie had refused to explain himself, although he did finally append a shaky 'love H' to the bottom of the page. He might have felt bad about it, but his long neglect had probably placed the situation, to his mind, beyond correction. Or perhaps he had found more mileage in maintaining a sole-survivor image. In any case, Mary embraced her sister-in-law, opening up a long correspondence and future meetings with other members of the Miller family, of whose existence we had known nothing.

In the midst of such domestic preoccupations, the offer on 21 November of her appointment to Dame Commander of the British Empire seemed to Mary no more than incongruous.

> *Wish there was someone who could soundly advise on this without prejudice one way or the other. Heaven knows I don't want the fanfare and letter answering that I suppose would be involved but it is no doubt a singular honour – however puzzling.*

By the next day it was one she was inclined to refuse.

> *Fear it would mean an unwelcome and time-consuming blast of publicity when I so want to get on with the main job in hand which is hard enough as it is.*

For weeks she put off making the decision until telephoned by Government House. When placed on the spot, to decline suggested discourtesy and 'on impulse' she accepted. Within days she would also receive advice of an honorary doctorate of letters to be bestowed by the University of Western Australia.[43]

> *This so soon after the letter from the Governor General was something of a shock to the system. More pleasing than the Dame proposition as I have no hesitation in accepting it as I had in the latter case.*[44]

Andy came home, where he was to remain recuperating for the next seven months. Now aged thirty-three, without a job or prospects, he was dispirited and touchy company, virtually wiped off by other members of the family and regarded as one lost to the battle of life. This was a pity, as there was more to Andy than we gave him credit for, and in later years, he and his sisters salvaged a passable relationship that was all too short. His diaries written from the Bow River diamond mine in the 1980s – an enterprise brought to a close by Aboriginal land claims – give a moving account of his solitary existence as caretaker of the ghostly site, his only companionship the wild creatures of the East Kimberley bush, tamed as in the way of his father.

~

From her letter in early December, I deduced that my mother was stressed to the limit. The only consideration that prevented her from asking the Literature Board to suspend her literary grant was what then to do about Connie, who so relied on the secretarial job. She had also been upset over a misunderstanding on Bet's part when not only was there no sign of the arranged interest on the advance for her new studio, but with a careless wave of her hand, her sister had denied Mary's contribution had been a loan. 'She feels it is her right to be subsidised,' Mary wrote, before the added forgiveness, 'and certainly, her current work is very impressive.'[45]

The last straw arrived with a telegram from Little Jimmy MacLachlan, announcing his intention to visit and, if she was agreeable, move in with the one whose photo he had fallen in love with years ago: 'Feel quite dismayed about this as the old man has been sending me crazed letters for the last two years or so – all I need to send me right round the bend.'[46] When I came to the rescue from Papua New Guinea, it had been a reprieve not without penalties:

> Told Patsy about the free rubbish disposal organised by the Council to be picked up on Monday. The result is that we have now outside the gate the biggest and most hideous pile of rubbish in the neighbourhood. Very embarrassing![47]

Horrie's homecoming for the Christmas break, which he had been so looking forward to, was mercifully short-lived when, after a few hours, he suddenly insisted on being returned to the hospital. Perhaps the failure of the cure he had been so sure of on home ground had been too disheartening. That and the sad sight of his station wagon in the drive as he had left it, packed up and ready to go at a moment's notice.

On Boxing Day the delivery by taxi of a small parcel containing a cufflink wrapped in a food-stained table napkin heralded the arrival in Perth of L.J. MacLachlan:

The poor fellow heavily on my conscience, I asked Patsy to tell him he could visit for one hour only on pretext of urgent appointments. He turned up – old chap, sprucely dressed, vigorous and mad as a March hare, as his letters indicated, his intense monologue shooting off at tangents from the bible to Karl Marx – ancient history, the classics, philosophy, politics and back always to Kings in Grass Castles *and me.*[48]

My mother did not enquire why she was relieved of this problem from the time I drove the gentleman back to his city hotel. Suffice it to say, he was not mad enough to make further personal contact, although the letters only ceased with his (presumed) death.

Mary's final diary entry for 1977 is a well-worn mantra, ending on an upbeat note:

Worried about my inability to even complete a few minor tasks now. Will just have to try to fit more hours into the day by getting up earlier. But a more cheerful aspect the heart-warming and so unexpected gesture of public appreciation and glad cries of so many dear friends. Also the great support of my beloved girls Patsy and Marie Rose and the joy of having the children with me over this season, and please God by this time next year Marie and Mike will have presented me with another grandchild.

CHAPTER 13

GROUNDED (1978–1979)

Arriving at Mildew after a hospital visit to Gran, who was awaiting a hip replacement, Bet was aghast to be met by the ghoulish sight of Horrie being lifted from a vehicle and manoeuvred into a wheelchair. Senescence a subject not in her line of country, her shrinking abhorrence for the infirm and those in their dotage was scarcely concealed. At the age of sixty-two still venturing alone into places beyond the back of anything imaginable, Bet's courage and strength of purpose were never less than extraordinary. All her life, the inner demon driving her on and through, she had overcome the normal prudence restraining most humans from entering the unknown and hazardous, especially when travelling alone. Born thin-skinned, the youthful, rather timid and oversensitive 'Betty' had been thoroughly suppressed, the sheer weight of adversity forcing her to flay her epidermis. Before retreating from the Perth scene on a commission to the company in possession of the former government Aboriginal settlement at Moola Bulla, she made an attempt to deal practically with Gran. Both she and her cohort Reg agreed that a load mostly assumed by their sister would be eased if their mother was moved into care. And there was lobbying from many quarters for Mary to consider doing the same with Horrie, who was now regularly venturing forth, with enormous attendant effort, to spend brief periods at Mildew.

Sniffing the wind, the invalid had fixed his wife with a fearful eye: 'Don't you put me in the Old Man's Home …' This ominous nearby institution, rather bluntly renamed Sunset, would not have been a more sufferable proposition for him if it had been called Sunrise. It had never been other than 'The Old Man's Home', at the end of the road in every sense, and the need to avoid such a pass became his second major preoccupation, the first being his lower intestines. But as long as 'Mum' rose to face another day, he knew he was in no great danger.

~

Somewhat startled to hear her DBE announced from the pulpit during mass on New Year's Day, Mary braced herself for a deluge of publicity and congratulations from all states of Australia and beyond. In case he got a fright to see her photo on the front page of the newspaper, she broke the news in advance to Horrie, whose only comment was, 'But I thought you *were* a dame. What was that other thing you got?' Even Gran did not really register it as once she would have done, her reaction to any event to pronounce with solemn profundity: 'Well, my dear, the longer I live, the more it seems to me that life is just one thing after another.' ('Is this', sighed her daughter, 'the sum total of nine decades of life's rich and varied experience?')

After all, the warm response had revived her spirits: 'Like being present in the flesh at one's own funeral and privy to all the kind things usually only said of the dear departed.'[1] (Less welcome, a marked increase in a variety of causes soliciting financial contributions, as if the conferring of a DBE was akin to a lotto win.) But while in this year the bright flash of her literary plumage was recognised abroad, at home she remained captive and consequently, in terms of creative output, largely featherless. Only by working late into the night had she been able to put together for the Summer School a biographical preview of her father as he would emerge in *Sons in the Saddle*.

Volunteering to hold the yearly FAW party to welcome visiting writers, Mary's cautious foray into life outside hospital visits was rudely checked when Horrie fell and broke his hip. The patient reported at a low ebb, what did the medicos know as they laboured to bring him back to the waking horror of bonded limbs and the prospect of the Old Man's Home? Had they been less assiduous, all concerned might have been spared the next two and a half punishing years. But just as there had been no question other than that Gran, at the age of ninety-five, would receive a spare part and extend into decrepitude a life well lived, so there was no option but to salvage Horrie's wreckage. Regardless of the constant chafing, Mary would never doff her hairshirt.

Very few would know her well enough to discern this aspect of her nature. At a Perth Festival function, she had been beset by people

> *begging me to write more for the theatre* – Leslie Anderson, the Sunday Times *journalist saying, 'Don't make excuses. Just sit down, take up your little pen and get back to it' and Nita chiming in 'Yes, that's what I'm always telling her.' They just haven't a clue.*[2]

With no fresh drama emerging to augment her previous success, Nita would have to be content with revivals and a Queensland production of *Swan River Saga*.

To add to her New Year acclaim, or perhaps because of it, the inconsequential news that one of her books had been banned in the United States became front-page news. *Kookanoo and the Kangaroo*, a collaboration with Bet of twelve years earlier, had been removed from the library of a backwoods primary school in Howard County, Maryland, on the objection from a parent that the word 'piccaninny' had been used in the text. Within hours she became the target of a clamorous press:

> *Most unlooked-for publicity over an obscure and long out of print little book. From 5am continuous calls from every media outlet wanting to know my reaction to the 'banning'. Bet wild about the whole thing but with a new edition of our* Way of the Whirlwind *about to appear, she is going along with it on the grounds that it could in the end only improve sales.*[3]

From her comfortable hospital room overlooking the river, Gran was trying to change the channel of her window view with her nurse call button. 'I've seen this one before,' she said. Sometimes forgetting why she was there, she tended to slip back into the 'unsatisfactory servants' era, telling the staff they were incompetent and that she would not patronise their establishment again. Meaning to pick it up on her return, she had left her diary at home – not realising that after a thirty-year daily record, on 27 January 1978 she had written her final entry, with a reiterated regret over having surrendered her driver's licence:

> *Nothing makes me so sorry than to think that I gave up my car and my independence. Family and friends are all wonderful but I mostly have to go where they are going. I often dream I am driving and it makes me sad to see the wheelbarrow and lawn mower occupying the garage.*

Like the Queen Mother, she stood testimony to the longevous benefits of pampering. While keeping her going 'independently' had become, in terms of the demands on her carers, a right royal luxury, I believed that propping up 'Gran Central' represented a great deal more than the effort involved, and my strong opposition to placing her in an old people's home had earned me no favour with Bet and Reg.

Under my massaging hands, her bones were as frail as a bird's. 'Oh, Pats dear,' she murmured, 'I do feel old age creeping on.'

Through the long, hot summer days, over her once flourishing garden now lay a neglect that stood in potent symbol of her own fading. Mary somehow found time for the daily hand-watering, but Gran's eventual response to her daughter's exertion was disappointing: 'Oh dear, it does look creased. It could do with a good iron.'

Mundane tasks attended to and the rubbish bins put out, Mary was away to a Government House reception for Lady Avon, the widow of Anthony Eden, and another for the governor-general, Sir Zelman Cowen. Going through her wardrobe, she wondered what might be suitable attire for the opening of the Second Session of Western Australia's Twenty-Ninth Parliament. Given her many ready excuses, she may have believed such duties were incurred by her acceptance of the royal award. There was certainly no way she could again put off giving the annual address to the Royal Commonwealth Society or be less than accommodating to requests for nomination from many other worthies. Wearily she saw herself on the 'same old daily circuit':

> *Hardly time to even get to the hundreds of answers required to people who have sent congratulations let alone concentrated work needed on Robin's manuscript and sundry other urgent jobs. Mention to Horrie of pressing reasons to get back only makes him think up more things to delay me. Haven't yet read Donald Stuart's book that I am supposed to launch in three days.*[4]

His hip mended, Horrie had reached a static stage and the hospital wanted him out. As a step towards his gaining a measure of self-reliance, he was placed in a single room, but Mary was not optimistic of success. As she sat with him ready to spring into action at any given moment, she continued with the task of editing Robin's diaries for the sequel, now titled *Sugarbird Lady*, 'a task made much harder than the unscrambling and ordering of events in the dear girl's life by the heartache that accompanies'.[5] Prior to what she described as 'another entirely unnecessary trip to the USA',[6] Harold had been ringing daily to find out how she was progressing, his hectoring tone somehow suggesting she was neglecting the job. His own contribution, as he was at pains to point out, would be to get his surgery receptionist to type out the draft copy 'at no charge to you'. He had also left her with the script for the film cobbled up from *Flying Nurse*, a task Mary would eventually discard with the curt line: 'I really don't want anything more to do with this project.'[7]

As with other detours from her designated path, there had been a cooling of enthusiasm for screenwriting. The four episodes of *Tjakamarra* aired by Channel 9 having attracted small notice, Mary had no further illusions:

Fragmented enough without the commercial breaks. Doubt it will create much of an impression and any chance it may have had anyway seriously strangled by Karl's high-flown stipulations and copyright complications – the Bishop reporting all communication with him becoming very tense and curt. No mention of the booklet.[8]

Published in an optimistic edition of five thousand, the booklet – a compilation of stills from the film and Mary's explanatory text – became another casualty of the cause it was designed to promote. The same could be said for Keith Boombi, the main actor with his wonderful smile, who was killed in a road accident soon afterwards. Karl Stellmach, fallen from grace with his former backers, must have been desperate for a new 'moneybags' or another film script: over the next five years, Mary would become the recipient of 348 letters from the persistent cameraman who (so it transpired), prior to his employment by the bishop, had been working as a window-dresser in Brisbane. The episode in its entirety has been excised from the bishop's memoirs.

Standard commitments and social obligations became major undertakings for Mary, and her appearance at any venue other than the three-times-a-day trek to the hospital required torturous strategy. Deadlines loomed on a history of Broome for the National Trust book *Historic Places of Australia*, a biography of M.P. Durack for the 1979 sesquicentenary, and promised assistance with a WA Institute of Technology pilot program for the print-disabled. She had not even turned her mind to her honorary doctorate speech. Regretfully, she declined the invitation to a DBE investiture in Canberra.[9]

~

The birth of Joseph Megaw was greeted with much joy, but over the ensuing weeks, as the three-weeks-premature babe struggled for survival, this too became a saga of anxiety. Bone-weary, she solicited her doctor for 'energy pills'. Sleepless nights spent on her mother's uncomfortable spare bed when Edith took weekend breaks left her drained and in no fit state to face the day. Rather than bring the matter to the notice of Reg, who handled Gran's finances, Mary, when she discovered that Edith had not liked to ask for essential household items or mention equipment in need of repair, resolved the problem at her own cost.

With Andy still recuperating, Johnson's partner and infant son also in residence and my arrival with children for the university ceremony, every room at Mildew was once again occupied. We made the most of it, knowing that with Horrie's reinstallation the welcome mat would be withdrawn and the house placed off limits until his eventual demise.

For her diary, Mary would confine the big occasion of her doctorate award to a modest two lines: 'So in stately procession down the aisle of Winthrop Hall to the dais. My citation read by the Chancellor before my Occasional Address seemed to go down well.'

From my position, the small figure of Mary Durack was quite hidden amid the throng in colourful faculty gowns and caps. Only as seats were taken did she emerge, composed and dignified in her voluminous scarlet and royal blue array. Near her, equally resplendent in her honorary robes, sat Ida, and seeing the dear ladies, so small in stature and yet so great in the weight of combined erudition, I felt the tears rise on a swell of pride and emotion. Mary was determined not to emulate the stodgy exemplars she had been provided. Her lively discourse made reference to the need for literary self-discipline, the importance of research and the wide-ranging functions expected of an established writer. Using her own experience in illustration, she warned of the pitfalls:

> *It seems often to be thought that writing is an undemanding hobby and that the writer should have the time, inclination and ability to speak at any time, not only on literary subjects but on current political issues such as conservation, uranium mining, electoral disputes, the Constitution and the pros and cons of adding fluoride to the water supply. Why his opinion, unless he has made a special study of the subject, should be of more value than the next man's goodness only knows. Certainly in the process of writing and the inner sifting of ideas and values the writer tends to establish a point of view with which he becomes associated even by those who have read nothing he has written. Rather than being encouraged to go on thinking and developing his thesis, however, he is too often expected to snap out of it, put down his pen, spruce himself up and give the gist of his ideas over the microphone. Another public function expected of the writer is that he act as a source of instant reference as though he were an extension of the telephone service listed in the book under 'Dial an Answer'. One such fairly typical call was from someone wanting information on the introduction and use of camels in the outback. I referred him to a number of sources including the Australian Encyclopaedia, of which publication he had never heard. He did not want to be told where he could find it but what I could find in it for him. Nor does the writer lack offers of collaboration*

from people with no writing experience but with brilliantly original ideas to be divulged only under conditions precluding any crooked dealings with the material. The question of 'copyright' looms large for many unpublished writers. How can one be assured, it is often asked, that the publisher who has rejected the manuscript will not have pinched the plot or central theme? The only answer to this I can ever come up with is 'how indeed?'

In the course of expressing her appreciation of the honour, Mary made mention of her more outlandish mail, some addressed so obscurely as to call for zeal on the part of the postal department:

One correspondent whose envelope I cherish, evidently deciding that 'Mary Durack, author, Australia', looked a bit inadequate had helpfully added the further direction – 'Southern Hemisphere'. One comes to deal with many letters of this sort but not often does one's mailbox contain something so totally unexpected as a letter from the University Senate offering the recipient an honorary doctorate. How to deal with such an unfamiliar situation other than to accept with heartfelt gratitude and hope it will be seen as an acknowledgment of the true function of writers in the community, not as off-the-cuff speakers on current affairs, substitutes for general inquiry bureaus or literary plastic surgeons trained to turn a sow's ear manuscript into a silk purse, but working in their own medium, as the coordinators and interpreters of the world around us.[10]

Could my mother have known her every word strengthened my resolve to stand between her and the worst, she might have chosen a different topic. Alone in that assembly, I stood struck by the irony of how lightly she touched on the sort of imposition that had so compromised her writing life and the penalties awaiting her at the other end of the red carpet.

~

Old associates visiting Horrie had been saddened to see a symbol of Australian aeronautical history at the point of 'chocks away', their kindly recommendations resulting in his being awarded the OBE and the Oswald Watt Aviation Award from the Federation of Aero Clubs of Australia for outstanding service to civil aviation.[11] Having graduated from a fellow in the aviation business to the elevated rating of 'pioneer', Horrie found that, with the added bonus of being certified a 'character', he could get away with almost anything. In company with Hal Porter, of whom he heartily disapproved, he had in effect broken the barrier of accepted behaviour into a stratum of public indulgence for all sorts of antisocial stunting. But he was beyond being cheered by awards, and the investitures became the cause of escalating panic attacks. In the end, he had to be dragged along like a recalcitrant schoolchild.

With the invalid's release from hospital at the end of April, Mary's diary becomes a chronicle of the fatigued carer. It could be no surprise that in a subconscious bid for the maternal love he had never known, Horrie had reverted to helpless infancy. He was the worst of babies, one for whom the exhausting tending had no future.

Arranging an interview with the hospital extended care department, I found the doctor dismissive of the case. Maintaining that my mother had been 'over-protective' with the patient, thus sabotaging the rehabilitation program, the doctor had also understood that it had been she impatient to get him home. My mother was never as forthcoming as was crucial in such circumstances, her dealings with health professionals plagued by mix-ups of this sort. Nor did she act upon my negotiations on her behalf. There would be no good result from placing her problems over my own. Having taken seriously the constant refrain 'if I live to complete the next book' and 'how I long to get down to the job', I felt it incumbent upon me to straighten out the muddle of her life.

My bringing in assessment officers to see the situation backfired: 'Patsy concerned and helpful on all fronts, but the idea of a nursing home obviously a shock to him. I just couldn't do it to the old boy.'[12]

Horrie's reaction, as my record attests, was loud and bitter:

> *If that's what you want, Mum, throw me out of my own home. Throw me on the trash heap. It will be the end of me but now that you are against me you might as well – and after we've been together all these years …*[13]

Conscious that my mother might have some justification for continued meetings with Harold Dicks over the sequel to Robin's book and the impending dedication of the Jandakot memorial, I could see no reason for further association after that. Of late he had been berating her for any mention of Robin in the Miller or Durack context, insisting she be referred to only in connection with himself and the Dicks name. Nothing else left, the theft of Robin's identity was now in progress. At the same time, Harold was assiduous in avoiding public disclosure of his remarriage and now two children. Under no illusions as to the character of the man, my mother could not quite bring herself to shake off the former link to her daughter and his part in her life. My later discovery that she had been accepting his invitations to lunch at the yacht club saw her called to account: 'Well, dear,' she said – facetiously, it seemed to me – 'I do it for Robin's sake.' It was hard to know if she was being deliberately obdurate or, in maintaining civility, simply opting for the more convenient status quo. Ultimatums demanding she make a choice involving conflicting loyalties led Mary into an area she had always been reluctant to negotiate: 'I will miss Patsy when she goes back. She has been *such* a help but fear *too* worried about my situation.'[14]

Before leaving, I privately recruited Ida Mann to keep me regularly informed of happenings on the home front. Full of consternation at the likelihood of no more escapes to Adsett, she would willingly undertake this task, although we were soon spotted: 'Ida cross-examining me, I suspect at Patsy's behest, as to how many times up and down in the night saying, "that's what's going to break you in the end you know".'[15]

~

A crowd of three hundred invited guests attended the unveiling at Jandakot of Robin's memorial, the ceremony officiated by the governor, Sir Wallace Kyle.[16] At the same time, a national appeal was launched for a Flying Nurse Scholarship in her name, a cause made dubious by Harold's having nominated himself to select from the female candidates.[17]

With the bold request that the Miller family cover insurance against damage to the memorial (rusting and a home for bees, one day the alien Mooney bearing the familiar registration would fall off its plinth), Dr Dicks appeared to me to have come to the conclusion that we were such mugs that there need be no end to the extortion. Eventually, even Mary felt he had gone too far:

> *I said I would put my royalties from* Flying Nurse *towards it. Despite saying that he would see to Robin's stated wishes in this regard, he has so far, in three years, not come up with any payments, although the new paperback edition has sold out. He was evasive about it, as before and as in all matters concerning money.*[18]

~

The family in residence at Mildew dispersed prior to the return of the native. Johnson's partner and son had returned to Darwin, their ongoing relationship described by Mary as 'tenuous'. Further to her regret, Andy had taken a job trucking cattle to the Territory meatworks: 'I hate the thought of it myself, a brutalising life if ever.'[19]

Shaping up as a colossal nuisance was the much vaunted sesquicentenary, all ideas somehow requiring a first landing at Dame Mary Durack's door: state history, women's biography, pioneer stories, colonial folk songs, the competition for a live drama on some aspect of state history. An announcement that M.P. Durack would feature on one of the paving stones to commemorate Western Australian notables resulted in numerous calls from citizens seeking her backing to put forward the names of their kin for similar privilege. With not a moment to produce anything fresh, she had begun rehashing old talks to cover the many appeals for a contribution. Seasoned articles, poetry and short stories were also polished up for recycling in anthologies and literary magazines. A 1961 profile of a 'Cinderella' Perth was updated to a 'State of Excitement' for *Vogue*, and the Christmas issue of *The Bulletin* would feature 'Jingle Bells and Didgeridoos', a recollection of the 1930s on an East Kimberley station.

Items from her sentimental back-catalogue illustrated the distance the author had travelled since her rendering of the days when Duracks and their Indigenous employees had ostensibly lived in happy harmony. Long before the stations were sold, she had been alert to an entrenched system of injustice towards the original inhabitants, primarily the unconscionable withholding of citizenship rights. In coming years, while she would follow closely and uphold in principle the long battle over land title and related concerns, she remained wary of being bracketed with those of her associates she deemed well-meaning but deficient in relevant experience. It seemed no issue regarding Aboriginal people was 'safe' or beyond opposition – the proposal for a Yagan memorial being a good example.

Having long lent her voice to the campaign for a fitting marker for the Bibbulmun warrior first restored to public notice through her articles and later book, Mary had urged something other than the white-man concept of a statue – such as a stone or free-form representation in Kings Park. Community feeling going against Premier Court's rejection of the idea, the outcry was settled with an inadequate gesture in the form of a bronze figure sanctioned for placement in an isolated setting inviting to vandals and derided by Mary as 'a crude, un-Aboriginal abomination of a thing'.[20]

Should anyone suppose Mary's days were entirely taken up by a preoccupation with an enfeebled spouse, her diary entry for 7 June, typical of this time, might serve to offset the perception:

Disturbed night haunted by failure on so many fronts. Perhaps today? Not a hope. Discovered the old man had badly blistered his left leg keeping it too close to the radiator. Doctor hardly gone when Hugh Edwards came in wanting me to make a few observations re Aborigines in first contact for his film on coastal wrecks. He was closely followed by a TV team of four. Gave an interview in the garden. Then came artist Brian Card to photograph me for portrait he wants to paint for the Parmelia Prize. Further worries over Mother's missing electric blanket and various other problems. A ring from Laurie Russell wanting me to look over his manuscript on the history of Kwinana Shire. Had a flip through Margaret Hamilton's script on Mollie Skinner. Hopeless as a play – no action – just Mollie relating episodes of her life to her friends and relatives. Wrote Alix Hasluck congratulations on being made first Dame of the Order of Australia. Many letters to HCM re his OBE to deal with! SHOF Budget to look over. Reg Williams wants me to fly to Canberra and persuade Sir Zelman Cowen to become a patron – all expenses paid. Out of the question of course. Couldn't find mother's blanket.

A loud summons to the door in the early hours revealed Hal Porter, complaining that no hotel would take his traveller's cheques:

Obviously too drunk to be trusted. I got him to bed and pulled him round from the jet lag and the hangover but the 'hair of the dog' he treated himself to next morning was actually another dog.[21]

After a holiday in the south of France, his decision to return to Victoria the long way round so that he could see the North West and Northern Territory for the first time would mean a lot of work for those prevailed upon to draw up an itinerary. Mary installed him in her upstairs flat, as far away from Horrie as possible, the separation so successful that she later heard Hal had been spreading the word that she was merely claiming to have a sick husband in residence, an invention to give her more time to write. At this stage any arrangements made or lodgings found for the intemperate writer lasted only until he blotted his copybook – as he inevitably did. With the help of writer Tom Hungerford, acting in his capacity as press secretary for Premier Charles Court, a schedule and tickets were organised, while Mary contacted people to meet and convey the celebrity on tours of the various ports. Meanwhile, the poet and then fellowship president Glen Phillips, whose good offices Mary could call upon in cases requiring more than just kindness, set about organising him for talks to students at the WA Institute of Technology – his involvement, like that of so many others, a narrative of abused effort and hospitality.

Mary's account for Florence of this 'depressing fortnight' tells the sorry tale of her old friend's final visit:

> Over the next few days Hal's fairly steady drinking exposed a different aspect to his normally kind and practical nature. He told me that he found WA writers lacking in any sense of humour and the students dumb. The other side of the story was that the students (and their lecturers) had found Hal quite incoherent. His behaviour over this period was particularly off-putting for Ida Mann who saw no reason why she should tolerate his failing to turn up for dinner and later inviting his taxi driver into her house for a drink. By this time Hal had gone off the idea of the north and was denouncing 'tedious little people' for trying to arrange a trip for him to some place he had no interest in anyway. We'd gone off the idea too when we realised the state he was in so it was cancelled and we poured him onto the plane to Melbourne with sighs of relief. I feel really sad about this as I have a great regard for Hal's writing talent and a genuine affection for him. He has stayed with us many times before here and at Adsett over pleasant interludes, but this time he was quite hopeless. But his account of his sojourn in Perth would no doubt have been amusing and perhaps even perceptive of our local limitations.[22]

An unforeseen event that appealed to Mary's penchant for offbeat plots came with a phone call from Horrie's daughter by his first marriage, the long-lost Auburn, who was anxious to establish contact with her father. 'Horrie has always rebuffed any mention of the girl as none of my business. I'm afraid it *should* have been.'[23] Soon afterwards Auburn McElroy arrived with her husband and children.

> She is a practical, down-to-earth farmer's wife and a nurse, I liked her at once. I had told the old man that she would be coming and brought her to his room to meet him. Predictably unresponsive, as the afternoon progressed he elected to join us for a cup of tea and became quite talkative – seemed to hit it off with Auburn's husband Ron. He retired before long but at least made a gesture towards being civil.[24]

Over the next few months, Auburn made a brave attempt to get to know her 'Dad', whom she resembled more closely than any of his subsequent family did. It was heavy going, but a suggestion that he spend some time at her Kojonup farm and regain his confidence by driving a car around the paddocks hit the right note. He perked up at that!

~

The junket for the purpose of choosing a site for the Stockman's Hall of Fame had been restricted to board members who could be relied upon to understand the requisites. Mary Durack, who had always made plain her preference for regional halls and museums rather than the planned multi-million-dollar edifice of granite and marble, was not included. Alice Springs and Goulburn by now dropped from the shortlist, the shires of Longreach, Rockhampton and Cloncurry turned on lavish mayoral receptions to put their cases. Mary would later protest the final choices for the location being all in Queensland for what was a national concept, and suspecting the decision to have been a 'bulldozing job' by the influential chairman of the Longreach Shire Council, Sir James Walker, she did not submit a vote. Others shared her qualms, and there would be undertones of dissension until the grand opening in 1988. In the interests of a perceived unanimity and after a campaign by Walker to ingratiate himself with her, Mary would eventually back the board's selection of Longreach. For this loyalty she would be rewarded, while others, less diplomatic, were sidelined.

Pining for her presence at Adsett, Ida had reported the place run-down and mouldy and weeds waist-high in the garden. Feeling remiss, Mary could do no more for her companion of the years than head the list of those advocating her for a DBE.

No longer able to travel north or keep up with the FAW, Mary would lament valued friends who were slipping away unfarewelled, not least Broome identities and Aboriginal people from the Kimberley. A downside of her vast catalogue of fond acquaintances was that there would be so many to mourn as they departed, and her diary, the pages marked with crosses, kept the ledger. Grieving the loss of the writer J.K. Ewers, a founding member of the WA fellowship and close associate of long standing, Mary had also been shocked to hear, a full year after the event, that Phyllis Kaberry had died. Having tried in vain for many months to telephone her, she made a call to the London exchange and was advised that Phyllis had been disconnected.

'Disconnected' indeed! Dear friend of my youth dating back to 1934 at Ivanhoe when she arrived as the first woman anthropologist to investigate the Aboriginal woman in her tribal life. So many happy memories of those days and our meeting in London in 1936. She died alone in her bed.[25]

Within weeks, the anthropological world would be further depleted by the sudden death of Ted Strehlow, whose contribution to the understanding of Aboriginal culture Mary declared to have been 'very great'.

Another source of regret was the break-up of familiar partnerships – there they go Charles and Barbara, Rachel and Richard, Donald and Kath, Kira and Jim, Athol and Maureen, Frank and June, Geoff and Nene, John and Barbara – situations often calling for some delicate footwork to maintain impartiality.

But there was compensation for 'Aunty Mary' in a new generation of Duracks, nieces and nephews taking up demanding careers and embarking on their own families, and the abiding delight derived from her grandchildren, Naomi, Yagan, Drew, Marcus and baby Joseph.

~

Bet was enjoying an unusual high. With all pictures on offer at an auction held in Broome sold and examples of her work put on display at the new Derby Shire Cultural Centre, the intrepid traveller was now planning an exhibition in the very hub of the cosmos, the World Trade Centre in New York. Able to move in any direction both physically and artistically, and well established on the art scene, she could only wonder why major gallery recognition had been to a large extent denied her. She chased an elusive phantom. Experience having taught her that talent was never enough, she was convinced that there had to be a 'trick' to success. Did it lie overseas? Was it in a combination of the art and literary worlds? Did the key lie in beauty or bleakness? In the abstract expressionism of Pollock or de Kooning? The writhing Van Gogh mirage? The bold black and white splash effects she would show in New York? She tried them all, and in the 1976 *Two Faces of Elizabeth Durack* covered both bases by exhibiting the graphic beside the same subject matter in stages of disintegration. Any visibly derivative influence was nonetheless so firmly stamped with her singular vision as to often make mincemeat of the source. Leaving no artistic stone unturned, she moved fast through a bewildering variety of styles, and whatever the form of the moment, her work was masterful and, sometimes, sensational.

Steadfastly remaining true to capturing the shapes and elements that pleased her and aloof from any facile analysis, Bet acknowledged that her public face barely hinted at the sometimes savage hunger for success. She had once written to Mary:

> *Outwardly, I conform very prettily. I affect no eccentricities either of manner or dress. I speak quietly, move decorously. I could not stand it if anyone suspected that behind my ribs a tiger pads up and down glowering through the bars.*[26]

Reg, still yearning for the north, had gone against the advice of his sisters and paid a visit to Kildurk. Predictably dismayed by the new reality, he put in an official submission offering his services as an adviser to the traditional landowners running the station. His overture not taken up, Mary made a note of her brother's wry comment:

> *He says the Government attitude seems to be that it's just an experiment anyway so long as they are learning something in the process. He doubts they are acquiring any new knowledge. The lessons will be learned by politicians and department officials.*[27]

The property had been sold as a going concern, but by the 1990s the only profitable 'turn-off' from the renamed Amanbidji would be from the community store.

With each passing day, Gran was perceived to be gently but inexorably fading:

> *Mother as usual gracious and seemingly on the ball but living in a happy fantasy world in which she is quite self-reliant but for a little help from Edith. Horrie thinks she should buy another car with the crazy idea that if she can get behind the wheel again it would be a piece of cake for him.*[28]

To this end, avoiding further consultation with his pessimistic wife, Horrie furtively used the phone to arrange the purchase and delivery of a new vehicle with automatic gears, which practical consideration seemed the answer to his infirmities.

From my perspective, his never-say-die attitude was only marginally less delusional than my mother's belief that she could operate as a full-time carer while keeping up her normal functions. Under the circumstances, anyone else would surely have drawn the line at Jack Saville who, undeterred by the presence of Horrie, arrived on his annual holiday. Laid low by respiratory problems, he too was soon confined to bed and calling for help from his 'mum'.

Sending Connie off early for Christmas, Mary anguished over the renewal of her literary grant. The only book completed during the year had been *Sugarbird Lady*, on which she could expect no return. Despite the line on the title page 'Compiled and edited by Harold Dicks', all the work, except for a few verbal consultations, had been done by Mary, as she later explained to Kath McArthur, who queried it: 'I thought it more appropriate to have Harold's name on it than mine. With his medical practice and RFDS exploits he would never have had the time to do the job.'[29]

To reopen the escape hatch via his car had become Horrie's overriding obsession. That he could no longer come and go as he pleased was to him unendurable, and with the aid of a walking frame he began a grim routine of exercise. His face set in lines of desperation, every day he dragged his limbs round the courtyard, and visitors were coerced into accompanying him on a 'test drive' of his Subaru sedan.

Not given a chance to demonstrate his unfitness to be behind a wheel, the police official failed the applicant at the first post: the eyesight test. The knockback came as a great psychological blow to Horrie, and to add insult, his tame doctor of forty years would not be bullied into signing a declaration that he was in good shape.

Disconsolate and declining to further lift a finger to help himself, he drooped in his wheelchair, the mangy cat by his side allowed an occasional mournful stroke with the ubiquitous shoehorn. Of all the carefully chosen and expensive gifts churlishly rejected over the years, this random lucky dip from an incongruously ho-ho-ho-ing hospital Santa had been an unexpected winner. So partial had he become to the long-handled plastic implement that it could scarcely be prised from his hand, and panic ensued if it was lost sight of for a moment, along with the certainty that it had been stolen. 'It's the very kind of a thing that everybody wants,' he would insist, oblivious to our faintly disguised derision.

On my return to Perth for Christmas, I wondered if it was to augment the thinning family ranks that my mother had invited a number of newly met outsiders to share the festivities. Son Andy many months out of contact, she was also missing Johnson, who had separated from his partner and gone to Sri Lanka. It was a hard thing for their mother to acknowledge, but one son had become a policeman's knock at the door and a solicitor's letter, and the other, his life declared in her diary to be 'all vague, like a disturbed dream', a long-distance cable requesting more money. Above all unconducive to seasonal cheer had been the presence of the Ancient Mariner, repelling guests with the albatross of his predicament. Now, if I so much as dared to speak to my mother in his presence, he would become angry and disruptive, spilling tea, dropping food – lashing out with the shoehorn.

Sidestepping the more doleful picture in a letter to Florence, Mary mentioned only the usual round of literary events:

> *The new year has been ushered in for me with requests to speak at innumerable functions, launch books, write intros and take part in writing and historical gatherings of all kinds. I enjoyed the recent Summer School and meetings with various interstate visitors including Nancy Keesing, James Murdoch and Jean Battersby. The most enlivening episode a public row resulting from playwright David Williamson and his wife Kristin having become emotionally involved with Dorothy Hewett repeating her claim that she had been driven from her home state by a lack of interest or appreciation of her work. Surely a misrepresentation! Now we have Writer's Week upon us and – no getting out of it, I am participating on the theme of dramatisation.*[30]

With her nomination as official historian and researcher for the Stockman's Hall of Fame, it was plain that Mary's notification of her limited availability had been subject to broad interpretation. Faced with reams of documentation and R.M. Williams on the phone at length several times a week, she begged off becoming further embroiled. Brushing aside her excuses, the obstinate magnate refused to believe that she was unable to arrange her affairs to attend meetings or join the fact-finding expedition to the United States. She could barely spare the afternoon to meet Prince Charles (who impressed her by managing to look convincingly as if he had heard of her and the book *Kings in Grass Castles*) or an hour for Rupert Murdoch:

> *To the* Sunday Times *to see Rupert Murdoch. I thought he wanted to speak to me about SHOF, but although interested in this project he really wanted to discuss TV rights for* Kings *– says he would very much like to do it. Told him what I could of the Fairfax option but said best talk to my agent Tim Curnow. With him his right-hand man Ken Cowley who is also on the SHOF Council, keen to cooperate.*[31]

Uncomfortable doses of reality (beyond that she had grown used to fending off from me) did not go down well, and a *Bulletin* article, 'Mary Durack's Literary Race Against Time', was a cause of some affront.[32] Solicitous calls from friends were met with her wiping off as 'silly' the journalist's suggestion that at her age she was going to have to be ruthless and single-minded if there was any hope of producing the self-designated 'history of an era and of the Kimberleys – of men and their times'.

She had already scaled down the initial goal since realising that five decades of vital and complicated family history to bring the saga up to the sale of the properties in 1950 could not be done in one book. Picking up the strands from where she had left them in *Kings*, she had decided to take it only to 1920 and deal with the remaining thirty years in a third volume. The dilemmas of the biographical section could thus be deferred until 'sensitivities' such as the Connor sisters had passed on and they need never know how their despicable mother had for twenty years dragged the Durack firm through the courts to satisfy her rage over their father's come-down.

The task now made manageable, the obstacle to her concentration caused by the distracting undercurrent of moans always within earshot was less easily overcome. Should she leave Horrie for more than an hour or so, she was invariably met on return by accusations of having given herself a holiday and 'leaving me to die'. Remembering that 30 April marked his eighty-sixth birthday, she put all else aside and organised a surprise party for him. Reported in good form on the day, he enjoyed reminiscing with his still surviving colleagues for a recording of aviation memories. The attention and fuss were to some extent calculated to soften the coming blow of a hired housekeeper while Mary went north for the 23 June opening of the Argyle Museum.

It was a big occasion many years in the planning as governments changed and politicians of varied goodwill towards the project came and went. An ABC *Weekend* film team followed the Durack sisters for their reactions and memories as they toured the 170,000 dollar restoration and were reunited with Aboriginal friends. Bet comes across as cool, arch and precise of speech, while the double tragedy and months of broken nights have wrought further damage upon the face of her sister, whose thoughts tend to wander. With a pensive smile, she declares herself 'fatalistic' and pleased that anything at all had been salvaged, especially the legends of the Aboriginal spirit ancestors of the area as captured on her tape recorder. Putting aside her own feelings, she expresses sorrow on behalf of the Miriwoong-Gajerrong people, who had forfeited so much in the name of 'development'. To counteract this negative side to the celebrations, she concedes 'the new beauty and grandeur' created by the lake.

Pragmatic about the CD&D enterprise, Bet recalls her father as never having been closer to the country than required of the manager of a commercial venture. She is critical of his desire to 'die a rich man', a determination she believed behind the sale. Reg, pictured inscrutable among the guests at the opening, was not interviewed. It was a lost opportunity to hear yet another side of the story.

Having put so much into seeing the homestead layout kept as close as possible to the original and gathering historic articles for the display, Mary was genuinely thrilled by the attainment of a goal that had so often threatened to fall by the wayside.

Since the opening, multitudes of tourists have visited the museum overlooking the valley site on the Behn River where Argyle Station stood for eight decades. Walking through the rooms with their photographs and relics, one might get an impression of how it was from the compromised reconstruction, which for want of an authentic kitchen loses a vital part of the less acceptable aspects of homesteads of the era. Under the lake, divers have reported much of the original station and its outbuildings still standing – the laundry taps able to be turned where water is no more needed, saddles on the wooden horses and mule chains hanging from the rafters.

Stimulated by the brief sabbatical, Mary believed the ice had been broken and that with the aid of home nursing help, she would be able to leave Horrie, at least for short periods, while she got back to a semblance of her travelling round. Missing far-flung friends and relations and her many clerical and Aboriginal connections, this restriction had for her always been the hardest to accept. Entertaining guests just required organisation, and she had become quite adept at screening the invalid from those calculated not to appreciate him. For the duration of Barry Humphries's visit, the wheelchair was parked well out of sight, the celebrity's familiarity with 'Norm' she presumed not necessarily having prepared him for an encounter with Horrie.

Ida's summary of the CD&D loose letter files and letter books had brought to light gaps in the otherwise preserved history of the Durack pastoral enterprise, material gone west in the office clear-out. While the loss was regrettable, Mary had also discovered that a surfeit of records tended to complicate rather than clarify the broader picture. In comparison to the relatively straightforward rags-to-riches story of Grandfather Patsy, the complex lives of the Durack sons would not be so easy to deal with.

And what to make of the grandsons? How to explain Reg, having actually made good and left the north behind him, now selling up his retirement properties and talking of going back? More for the pen of a novelist was her contention that his spirit had been, as the Aboriginal people described it, 'sung' by the country. Bet was inclined to dismiss his vacillations as beyond defence. But the eccentricities of family members were of small moment to the artist as she set out once again for New York and an exhibition under the umbrella of the Western Australian sesquicentenary. Fortuitously absent for much family crisis and tragedy, she would miss the next one by a single day.

~

With every plan to renew his driver's licence defeated, Horrie had regressed. After dozing on and off all day, his nights were restless and wakeful. Goaded into a cross word over the constant bell-ringing, Mary was rewarded by his declaring, 'Alright, I'll kill myself,' a threat he attempted to carry out by beating himself (lightly) on the head with his shoehorn.

Doing her best to deflect the unsolicited claims upon her, Mary tried to devise a general letter of refusal, but each one after all required a separate reply. It was only when I was around that cadgers got the message – momentarily, anyway, as most resolved to try again when 'lovely Mary's awful daughter' was out of the way. A matter of stubborn pride in the face of so many warnings that she could not keep it up, she refrained from excusing herself on the grounds of fatigue, but it was obvious that something had to give. Now that I had left Port Moresby and the long-distance to-ing and fro-ing of the past six years to live in Perth, on a daily basis I could see her going to pieces.

Standing at the bedroom door, I observed Horrie as he took his afternoon nap. He looked dead, but even as my hopes rose, he breathed and groaned. Sometimes, as I covertly assessed his condition, he would demonstrate an almost animal sense of danger, stirring and looking round uneasily to find the source of the evil eye. How long, I speculated, could this go on? Well overdue for laudatory eulogies from his old associates and devotees, what a reputation he had for not dying even as he assured us he was on the brink. Would my mother survive the endless ordeal? Ordinary domestic chores got beyond her; the state of the bathroom alone was enough to draw the line. Was there not some way to hasten the process of Horrie's departure? To this end, I conferred with the venerable whodunnit aficionado Ida Mann, who, all too eager to assist, scrabbled round for the least out-of-date barbiturates from her medical sample drawer. There was no doubt in her mind that such a move constituted a mercy killing. Whether I could have steeled myself to the grim task or whether the intervention of fate saved Horrie from patricide remains undetermined.

My mother's diary entry of 20 September was written retrospectively, to the best of her memory:

> Set out after getting the old man to bed to a party for Kay Kinane and her sister. Parked the car and walked in drizzling rain to the median strip on Stirling Highway. Recall watching approaching car lights dim in rain, for a chance to cross – but nothing more. What happened I suppose I will never know. Did I perhaps start to cross and trip? Am told I was hit by a vehicle.

My own diary takes up the story:

> Phone rang about 8pm, an unknown voice: 'We have your mother here in emergency at Sir Charles Gairdner Hospital. She has been in a road accident.' Went at once to the hospital and there met a tearful and shocked Marie Rose. Michael had gone on to Bellevue Avenue to be with Horrie. Mum brought up from X-ray on a trolley and there she was – face relatively OK, still made up for her expected evening with friends. But oh, what a mess! She was on a canvas sheet, her hair matted with blood and gravel, an open cut on the base of her skull, blood oozing from her left ear, leg in an enormous splint. Immediate damage listed as two compound fractures of left leg, shattered kneecap, fractured pelvis and skull with possible neurological complications and some spinal injury seen from leak of lumbar fluid from the ear. She was also badly bruised, blue and purple on all visible areas of skin and lesser cuts and abrasions. With no memory of the accident she was dazed and a little defensive, saying: 'I don't know what happened. I was being careful.' Despite pain and confusion she was frantic about Horrie, needing constant reassurance as to the matter being in hand. There was a long wait as she lay there in blood and debris while the hospital tried to raise a neurosurgeon.

At daybreak I began to phone round the family, only to find the event already in the public domain, triggering calls from across Australia. Michael Megaw rang with an account of his unforgettable night with Horrie, who had been unable to grasp the situation beyond the immediate implications for himself. Mum had put him to bed before she went out for an hour or so and she never came back. All night he had shouted for her, as if his yelling might somehow miraculously produce her and prove the tidings no more than a bad dream.

From her hospital bed, the patient started out of her sick doze: 'Is that his bell?' Constantly looking at the clock, she tried to remember what she was supposed to be doing for 'the old man'. Every few minutes another arrangement of flowers arrived: filling the room, lining the corridor, given to other patients. It was a funeral in advance again. Examining the cards attached to the most extravagant, I registered among many government and vice-regal crests Prime Minister Fraser, R.M. Williams, Lang and Hope Hancock, Sir Charles Court, Barry Humphries and an exotic orchid splash-out from Rupert Murdoch and Ken Cowley. My chronicle continued from a bedside vigil:

> *Mum today looks better thanks to a bit of make-up. She is now feeling a fool for whatever inattention precipitated her into the path of a Kombi-van. Her manner is brisk and business-like as she tries to disguise the fact that she is only half with it, like a drunk doing a passable job of pretending sobriety.*
>
> *Immediate family only allowed to visit at this stage. Round the bed, full-time nurses turning, washing, massaging, shining lights, squeezing hands, wriggling toes, taping drips, changing bottles, taking vital signs, writing notes. Numerous doctors in and out – ward doctors, passing doctors, friend of the family doctors, neuro-surgeons, orthopaedic surgeons ... what a contrast to the long wait on the fatal night now that the super-solicitousness associated with celebrity has kicked in. Reg was sitting by the bed when I arrived today. I could see that his boring old voice droning on with the details of his recent overland journey, soothed her. She drifted in and out of sleep listening – asked a few questions – wanting to hear about something remote from her plight. I bailed him up out in the corridor to put the case for raising Edith's wages from her miserable $50 a week now that Gran is such a cot case. Ran into a blank wall there!*

Her mortal mind hanging together between the perforations like a tattered lace shawl, Gran was perturbed by what she seemed to be hearing about poor Mary. How, she wondered, could such a thing have happened? (She had been similarly perplexed the previous year on receiving news of the death of that favourite of elderly ladies, Sir Robert Menzies.) All she could say was that life was just one thing after another.

Four days after her accident, Mary's diary indicates her worry over letting people down: 'talks I am supposed to give this week – am trying to make notes in hope Nita might act as a stand-in.' From my account, it would seem she had not fully taken in her perilous situation:

The neurosurgeon did not seem bothered about any bedside manner. He told me brusquely that the damage to Mum's head is serious, the fracture still open and fluid loss not decreasing. A CAT scan has been ordered, followed, if no improvement within two days, by a craniotomy to mend the fracture. There is danger of meningitis or other infection. He said it would not have taken a much harder blow to kill her. I think Mum is frightened, but she is brave and fatalistic.

The news is filtering in about Horrie kicking up a terrible fuss at Sunset, shouting at visitors: 'Get me out, get me out – ring Cyril Gare – even if it costs me every penny I've got, get me out of here.' Reg tells me that Horrie's predicament won't happen to him. He says, 'I have a revolver for the purpose.'

The patient's story of the miraculous cure was destined to become a much-repeated anecdote:

Doctor says he will operate on my skull tomorrow. A call from somewhere – Broome? Derby? They said from Aborigines and wheeled me into the corridor where I took the phone to hear the voice of Paddy Roe saying he had organised a ceremonial singing for my return to health – they were all painted up and bearing magical totems. I heard, or at least seemed to hear them chanting. Anyway their message of love got through.[33]

The following day the leakage of fluid from her ear suddenly stopped. No-one was more surprised and impressed by the power of mind over matter than the surgeon. Who knows? It made a good yarn.

Having assessed her charge as a 'nursing-home job', the housekeeper brought in for Horrie had quit after a day. There was nothing else for it. With Horrie booked into Sunset Hospital and Cyril Gare called upon to see him installed, I felt I had to be there to witness the event – like an eclipse of the sun or the passing of Halley's comet. But the moment gave me no satisfaction:

When they came for him, he was sitting half propped on the bed, dressed and gloved, awaiting his fate. In the end, I could hardly bear to look. Puss lay at his feet in a warm patch of sunlight – all coming to an end there too as who wants to deal with an aged incontinent cat that only eats hand-fed prawns? The people from Sunset and Cyril slowly led him out to the car. He dropped his shoehorn and a glove and left his cardigan – all the things he needs around him – even his half-eaten lunch somehow too sad. It was his unprotesting departure, his terrible resignation that tore me – after all, not his fault I suppose that he can't die. At the last he turned and asked, 'No other way Cyril?'

'No other way Horrie.'[34]

What a fool he was to make of me!

It was one of the last good moments I shared with Gran: 'He's not coming out of Sunset?' she asked anxiously.

'Over my dead body, Gran.'

'I feel the same way,' she said. 'Over my dead body.'

'I hope there won't be a lot of dead bodies lying around,' I said, and almost of old, Gran laughed heartily.

Connie had no doubts. Fearfully she predicted: 'He's coming back. I can see it in his eyes!'

~

Set on the path to survival, the cost for Mary would nevertheless be very great. The surgeon who had aligned the bones and pieced together the smashed knee, striving for her cooperation in a strategy of short-term pain for long-term gain, fell into increasing disfavour. And heavier than the thigh-to-ankle plaster weighed the nightmare of Horrie on her mind. Told of the move to Sunset, she had not been fooled by my promise that he was perfectly alright. Every day he had rung the hospital to ensure she hadn't been sneaked back to the house, asking her anxiously how long it would be before she got back to 'normal'. She complained of feeling pressured by too much advice from all sides. 'Of course I don't want him back – it's the *last* thing I want …' It was the proviso that would prevent any hope of a sensible decision: 'If only he would be reconciled!' Another worry for her was 'the poor man who ran into me', and we were urged to contact him and pass on assurances that it had been her fault and he must not blame himself. (He was a decent fellow, and we had not been unsympathetic to his dismay and the bad luck involved in having collided with a National Treasure in a sesquicentennial year.) My mother could wield selflessness like a crusader's sword.

After five weeks she was removed to a private hospital, where the torment of the plaster remained for her bewilderingly unrelieved. A little solace found in the evening glass of brandy from bottles supplied by wellwishers, no-one begrudged her anything that brought her a small separation from the wearing constancy of it.

~

A sinister silence met me as I entered the house. The very walls of Mildew seemed to tremble at the onslaught threatened with my purposeful entrance and armoury of cleaning implements. Launching into a top-to-bottom clearance, I found the place a heart-wrenching time capsule: Robin's cupboards and drawers still containing the clothes and belongings left when she moved in with Harold; hidden corners of Julie's room yet harbouring the poignant residue of her optimistic youth; the writer's upstairs sanctuary forsaken like a sinking ship. A task that had long awaited someone with the mettle to face it, the disposal that followed was tackled with a vision of my mother's renewed spirit to work in a purged environment – the way smoothed for her comeback.

Probing the archaeology of the kitchen cupboards, I dispensed with utensils of forgotten function along with many fondly remembered: a jaffle iron, gem-scone plate, popcorn popper, pressure-cooker, crockpot, fondu set, wok, biscuit shapers, bunny-rabbit jelly mould and an ice-cream maker. No less dispiriting the collections stored in the 'log cabins': birds' eggs, marbles, old glass bottles, geological specimens, remnants of boyhood hobbies to remind me of my mislaid brothers. Christmas cards going back decades – famous senders selectively removed – were donated to kindergartens, yellowing linen assigned to the ragbag, and armloads delivered to the Good Samaritans or set aside for sending to the Kununurra reserve.

Finding occupation for Connie presented a problem. I had for a long time considered her a garrulous dodderer integral to my mother's inefficient daytime routine. Needed when successive drafts of a manuscript were rolling out for typing, in the interim she had lost her purpose, but given taxi chits and firm instruction, she responded surprisingly well and settled into a useful secretarial routine. With her gleeful compliance, I sent severance letters to all those deemed by us both to be lunatics, parasites or pests and binned requests for money.

Re-reading with absorbed interest the completed chapters of *Sons*, I was struck by the quality of the writing and the sheer hard labour expended over nine long years. Mary Durack's style was clear and precise, sentences constructed as to obviate, beyond the occasional dash, the requirement for such contrivances as the colon and semicolon. How familiar to me the pile of A4 pages, stuck over with strips of paper containing corrections, arrows indicating paragraph shifts, pencilled crosses deleting whole sections and margin directives to where further information might be found. Hidden on a window shelf behind a blind, amid the dead flies I found a stack of long Spirax notebooks, the pages crammed with her small handwriting – overwritten and up the sides – beyond even the author's own deciphering. Closer examination found the extraordinarily valuable compendium of firsthand information made in the field over many years. This would have to be rescued and preserved so that future researchers could be amazed, as I was, at how it was done. 'And *transcribed*,' said a firm inner voice.

And as I lost hours going through the boxes and family files in the archives room, what stories to be discovered there! Irresistibly drawn to past dramas, failed enterprises and human relationships, I felt stirring within me the embryo of future addiction. It was a haunted time, and working into the lonely night I turned on all the lights and sang loudly to dispel the shades that emerged to watch their exorcism.

Over the ensuing weeks, with a grinding and groaning of rust and dust, Mildew began to turn once again on smoothly oiled wheels. There came over the place a brightness – a *viability* – that had not been seen in decades. True, there was the ghost of Horrie daily brought home by his hospital visitors, but the need for moment-to-moment assistance meant his stays were perforce brief. And surely worthy of only slight disquiet his insistence on regular transportation to check on the patient and her rate of progress? As matters stood, his tenacious hold on his house and his wife seemed no more than pitiful. Wilfully single-minded, he had let go everything extraneous to this purpose. One day I heard him belligerently challenge my children, as if intruders on the property, and, as they politely repeated their names to him, claim he had never heard of them.

According to my mother (faced with my demands for an explanation), Harold Dicks had taken out a penknife with a file attached and cut a hole in her plaster with nothing but the kindest intent. ('He was the only one to actually do something to help ease the pain.') His signature boldly on the ruined leg cast, it appeared he had performed this act of mercy – which had in fact revealed a raw ulcer – without consulting hospital staff or the doctor concerned. Given my previously having warned her that Harold was on a dangerous collision course with me, I had no compunction in letting the surgeon know that he might like to raise the matter of unethical interference with Dr Dicks. Caught in the middle, the patient, her lofty status cutting no ice here, was told that she should find another physician. The ensuing row, fuelled by feelings of mutual betrayal, was not on any sort of an elevated level, as my diary records:

> *I knew she would be upset but she was more than that. I have never in my life heard Mum so irate with anyone, let alone me – surely the last person who can be accused of acting against her.*[35]

No-one reading Mary's daily jottings over this time would find anything illogical or inconsistent. No sign of irate outbursts, banged fists and rattled rings. My distress at her intransigence and circuitous line of argument is dismissed as 'dear overwrought Patsy'. Her diary resolutely downplaying the discord between us, there is much here she does not want consigned to the record, which is largely confined to her endless stream of visitors. To allow feeling on both sides to subside, I stayed away from the hospital for several days, a strategy that proved a mistake. On the eve of her discharge, I discovered to my apprehension that, shunning the arrangements made by her daughters for suitable short-term carers, she had privately agreed to let her homeless son Johnson, along with his semi-returned partner and little Marcus, move in to look after her 'for bed and board'. Her new and irritating defence was to defiantly agree with me. 'Yes, I suppose I am mad, dear. Yes, I am beyond belief. Yes, no doubt I am a psychiatrist's dream. Yes, I do enjoy my martyr's role.'

Seeing to her homecoming, I left her to a transformed residence and removed myself from the resulting mischief. Presenting the accumulated accounts, I could not prevent the hard-done-by 'No charge for labour and heartburn, Mum'.

For posterity: 'The house in wonderful order when I got back. Patsy has gone through every drawer and cupboard – place repainted and spring cleaned – a genuine lift to the sagging spirits.'[36]

I had cleared the desk, emptied the mail tray, scared off the serial telephoners, looked after Gran – and disposed of Horrie. She had probably never felt so naked and confronted in her life. Despite her endlessly subverted desire to be allowed to get down to her own work and the weariness that had driven her to cry out to me 'Who will rid me of these meddlesome afflictions?', when rid, she was bereft. Her first task was going to be reconnecting with offended parasites and time-wasters, the many complained-of lines that pulled her from 'the main job' and drove her to distraction.

Bet, I noticed, for all her postcard concern from abroad, had slipped back into Perth quietly and was since keeping her distance. Confining herself to 'popping in' on the failing and ailing fronts, she was scarcely able to stay a minute, adroitly skipping off lest there be any possibility of becoming involved. A brief note left under the door also sufficed. And who could blame her?

CHAPTER 14

BENT TO BURDEN (1980–1989)

By New Year 1980, Horrie was being transported to the house every day and returned to Sunset at night. The rationale for this, from Cyril Gare and other well-meaning friends, was that 'it is, after all, his home'. The salient fact that one's 'home' becomes where there is someone able to undertake the nursing care was overlooked. And no-one raised the memory of the many decades when the household had been wholly his wife's responsibility.

My forlorn diary entries testify that I had *finished* with the whole nonsense. Emotionally drained by the many months without a life of my own, I might have been on the verge of a breakdown myself, had I thought of it. From surreptitious and fleeting visits, I had observed Dante's Purgatorio: an exhausted elderly lady in a leg cast struggling at ten-minute intervals to manage a heavy, faltering old man in urgent need of the toilet. This Un-divine Comedy was enhanced by a multilayered sound track combining Johnson's guitar, *Sesame Street* at top volume from the TV, a barking puppy running dangerously underfoot, and Connie's sharp tones directed at the resident mother for her lack of control over her child. But there could be no complaints, and surely this was the unkindest cut of all: the right to a sympathetic ear had been revoked. Only via tearful Connie (restored to uselessness) did I hear of canine and kiddie destruction among the historic papers and photos in the file room, unposted letters torn to shreds, feathers from an exploded cushion blanketing the lounge room and messes in the bathroom.

Acknowledging some justification for her daughter's grievance and determined to restore our relationship, my mother made frequent telephone contact. Skirting round touchy subjects and sticking to bland generalities and discussions on Gran's health, the latter deemed a 'safe' topic of mutual interest, she learned it was unsafe to stray from the sanctioned script:

> *Made the mistake of mentioning to Patsy problems with the old man – merely in passing – she says she fixed that problem for me and that all I am doing is trying to make a ridiculous martyr of myself with which judgment she says 'everyone concurs.' Who 'everyone' is I can't*

think or what else I can do in the circumstances. I married Horrie for better or worse and this patch just happens to be the worst.[1]

Worn to the nub, she was receptive to any and all suggested remedies: 'It's called ginseng, highly recommended as the latest pick-me-up by one of the hairdressers at the salon.' With the blow to her head, the olfactory nerve had been severed, so there was no pleasure in food or drink, the only sensation to be found in something with a kick, spicy hot or alcoholic. The heavy plaster at last replaced with a lighter splint, this too was soon discarded. In consequence her knee, reconstructed from jigsaw puzzle bits, remained unbending and swollen for the rest of her life.

There could be no doubt that the accident caused Mary lasting damage; she was never really the same again. Her memory impaired, long trawls through her diaries for names and dates became a regular occupation. The round, confident Loreto hand became smaller and more untidy, and by the last year of her life only a scratch remained. Alarmed by the effort required for even so ordinary a task as dealing with her correspondence, she knew returning to serious work had never been more important, if only to prove to herself that she could still do it. The family saga, left at chapter twenty, would await the return of her mental discipline and fighting courage.

Other than taking regular phone calls from R.M. Williams, who seemed for a busy man to have a lot of talking time on his hands, Mary was conscious she had been neglectful of her SHOF duties. Still believing her role was to establish a WA branch, she arranged a meeting to discuss the matter with interested parties, taking in representatives from the Department of Tourism, MMA, the Forrest family, historians and the State Library. Reporting to R.M. Williams on the progress being made from her end as he made arrangements for the directors to gather for a Perth seminar in September, Mary found him receptive and apparently keen. But it seemed that having selected a board comprising names of sufficient clout to move mountains, the wily millionaire had perceived the holding of Dame Mary Durack as essential to the public relations aspect of it – the rose in a crown of otherwise thorny men – by whatever means. The lack of direction from headquarters hampering the proper organisation of the WA branch remained for her puzzling and hard to explain to local enthusiasts.

By March the vagabond support team had drifted away, and as Mary became more mobile, she got back to a routine of social commitments that would have daunted one in sound health. Word out that the coast was clear of 'the daughter', the spongers were on the incoming tide. Clergy were the hardest to put off. A persistent priest wanting a biography written of a deceased lay apostle was a fine model of the genre: 'Told him my plate was more than full but he didn't seem to understand.' The only alternative being for her to take on the project, the booklet *Legacy of Love, the Story of Edith Little* was the result.[2]

With the arrival in Perth of her brother Bill and his wife Noni, for the first time in two years Mary made the familiar journey to Adsett. Unprepared for the changes in her absence, she fretted at the untended garden, the visible inroads made by high seas on the fragile seaside haven, and the toll of her many years on Ida, who was in a constant old-lady dither over trivialities. She mourned neighbours of the many years gone and the cherished wilderness overtaken by ugly suburban-style houses. But consoled by the company of her loved Queensland family and with the encouragement of Bill, she began testing her ability to drive again on the quiet country roads. Lack of transport had long been a problem in dealing with Horrie. As soon as he discovered she was able to use the car again, he was certain that they would be back on their old footing in no time.

~

'You know, dears,' said Gran faintly and sweetly as Edith and I tended her bedside, 'I have come to the conclusion it is as hard to die as anything else one is not accustomed to in life.'

My aggravating presence every day in his mother's house meant unavoidable collisions with Reg, who held power of attorney over Gran's assets. From the time of his father's death, as the eldest son of an eldest son, Reg had assigned himself 'Head of the Family', a position he expected other members to take seriously. Apart from looking after his own interests and those of his immediate family, Reg had never earned any kudos for wider duty or generosity. In Aboriginal parlance, he was a 'me-self man'. Now, thumbing her nose at his senior rank, a niece he had never liked was invading his area of authority, carrying with her the taint of goodness knows what views and opinions contrary to his own. His aversion was well founded. I was a regular troublemaker, the self-appointed arbiter of family standards, with a wonderful capacity to bring out the worst in otherwise meritorious people.

Impatient with his mother's prolonged failing, Reg wanted an end to it, just as I resolved to keep her going as long as possible. High-handed demands for such extravagances as air conditioning, a new hot water unit, a vacuum cleaner and even some nonsense about rewiring caused the dutiful son to explode: 'We would be cutting into Gran's capital.'

'Why not? She's hardly going to need it much longer.'

'Who are you to say that? She could live another … ten years.'

'Well, then, she'll get good use out of a few new comforts.'

Reg was incensed. Not in his living memory had he, the Head of the Family, been so brazenly defied. What did I know of hard times or the moral value of frugality, as he did? What was wrong with using the birthday cake candle wired to a stick to light the failing Ascot pilot light? Why buy a new vacuum when Edith was so adept with the straw broom? He felt sure Edith *preferred* to use a straw broom.

'Why doesn't she ask for a vacuum if she wants one?'

'Because she's too scared to, and you know why.'

'She's *not*.'

'She is.'

Hearing the raised voices, Enid came at a run to stand between us, spreading her arms wide to protect her spouse as, broom in hand, I advanced menacingly upon him, thus giving her hero the chance to sprint out the back door and away from the danger zone. It had been a lot safer knocking off the scrub bulls. Unused to being cast as the villain and believing my stance entirely provocative, Reg, like Horrie, found me difficult to adequately condemn. Sotto voce to Edith (fearful lest I be covertly within earshot) he growled: 'Let me tell you something about Patsy.' We waited all agog, Edith and me. 'She could have helped Enid more with the Sunday drives.' He would be extra-receptive to a more substantial indictment against me.

Avoiding any possibility of a run-in with her brother, Mary again picked up the tab and saw to a raise in Edith's wage, taking into account her increased duties and the fact that she did not, as Reg had assured her was the case, receive a pension. The house was rewired without further fuss. Her solution to the vacuum cleaner problem was typical. Remembering that the man who had run her down on the highway was an electrical goods salesman, she rang him to see if he could assist. It was simply not within her powers of comprehension that, with a court case pending, this was inappropriate.[3] I later took it upon myself to send an account of my mother's outlay to Reg, a move that cannot have added to my appeal.

No longer just fading gently, Gran was now in agony. When I looked at her discoloured leg, I was struck by the long-ago memory of Aunt Bird. Called upon for her medical opinion, Ida advised us that gangrene had set in and 'the sooner the better …' Bet felt this an opportune moment to depart for Sydney. She would, of course, return if the news was bad, but she was blithely confident that her mother would go on for at least a year or so.

Her terminal condition confirmed, the patient was given a merciful morphine needle before being transported to hospital. Reg, hostile to any decision not made by himself, raged about what he saw as an 'expediency move'. When he accused me of 'being in league with the doctor', obviously towards the unnecessary prolonging of life, I queried his fitness to make any meaningful judgement.

'Oh Pats, dear,' said Gran from her euphoric state as she was taken aboard the ambulance, 'dreams really do come true ... wonderful we are all going to be together again.'

And so passed the final hours of a long, fruitful and favoured life. Indeed, one of Mary's many unwritten books was a biography of her mother she intended calling 'The Fortunate Child'.

'Oh Pats, this is a new phase in my life.'

'Just temporary, Gran.'

On my last visit, she looked at me as if she would most certainly have recognised me had she been in the business of recognising anyone.

'It's me, Gran.'

'Who's me?' Happily, by this stage she had forgotten about death along with everything else. As I sat by her bed, she all at once roused herself from a semi-coma.

'Tell the staff Mrs M.P. Durack is ready to go home!'

She sounded firm and imperial. I was impressed and moved that she had used her formal title, the one that had always carried weight. Her concluding words spoken, I kissed her and went away with the deathly salt from her brow on my lips.

'With Reg and Enid for a last look at our loved one,' wrote Mary. 'Her wrinkles were smoothed and she looked serene and beautiful.'[4]

Accorded the public deference due the senior member of a renowned family, Gran's passing was radio and television news across the continent, with reporters on the doorstep wanting photographs and biographical details.

Horrie's copious weeping at the tidings seemed not so much on account of his affection for the recently departed but that, to his mind, Gran had stood ahead of him in the queue and with her removal he was the next in line.

'It's the death walk for me now,' he wailed.

Under the officious direction of Reg, the funeral was a divisive affair with separate wakes attended by alienated friends and family, lacking the grace and proper tribute such as would have been seen to by Mary. Offered no place in an official car, Marie Rose, Michael, Edith and I walked with the ranks and stood at the back of the chapel with only a distant view of the proceedings.

Considering that my grandmother had in her final years become the shadow of a shade, I took the loss harder than the situation warranted. The awareness of that particular deficit in my life, the dependable down-to-earth element, has never left me, so I must suppose there lay between us a strong bond. As I had observed since childhood, she was one of the few who *appreciated* me, and indulging her expectations of amusement, I made her laugh and she had always been my best audience.

The aftermath of her death was to have consequences beyond what then seemed no more than a disagreement between legatees. The behaviour of the chief protagonists in this instance goes a long way towards understanding the dispute that was to ravage Mary in her final years and effectively engineer the break-up of the remaining family.

~

Eager to have Gran's will speedily settled, Reg arranged for the more valuable belongings to be removed at once, hustling his brothers Bill and David through the process almost before they had time to adjust to the death. But this was the merest preliminary: 'Inevitable friction arising, which I hope, can be contained. Bill and David have been a great help in negotiating rough corners over the past few days.'[5] Mary's guarded introduction to the unseemly battle unfolding between Reg and Bet might almost be passed over.

Regretful that she had earlier sold her interest in Gran's house, Bet had begun to scheme towards some means of compensation. It was a modest estate: a residence worth about 85,000 dollars and other assets amounting to 30,000 dollars, to be divided between the five surviving children. Bet's reckless proposal that they 'toss' for the assets, 'all or nothing', rejected, she had not felt inclined to contribute to a small settlement on Edith Joshua, who had come to the end of her working life. Since in his opinion Edith had been paid a fair wage for the job, Reg also baulked at the idea. This would be a matter taken care of by Mary and Bill.

After the excitement – and let-down – of the New York exhibition, Bet had found herself in a trough. Her *Black Swan of Trespass on Alien Waters* theme (the catalogue quoting the verse of Ern Malley) had not set the Big Apple alight, and in the process all available finances had been expended.[6] The Perth scene had become depressing, with wheelchairs, walking frames and commodes in bathrooms indicating the presence of the halt and the lame, ailments the prevailing topic of conversation and an absence of fun on all fronts. An invitation to give a lecture for the Art Gallery Society of New South Wales had offered her a temporary escape and the opportunity to visit her daughter Perpetua, who was by now married to Rex Hobcroft, the director of the Sydney Conservatorium of Music. (They would eventually purchase Gran's house.) Returning to Perth for the funeral with nothing much in the pipeline before an exhibition for the Broome Shinju Festival in August, she had been thrown back on herself, with disastrous result. Unless riding on a high or engrossed in a project, Bet could be mercurial.

~

Responding to earnest long-distance entreaties from Aboriginal delegates, Mary returned to Darwin in May with the objective of getting to the bottom of complex and divisive problems arising between the newly named Aboriginal Cultural Foundation and the Aboriginal Arts Board. The project had been reliant on funds from the latter subdivision of the Australia Council which were not forthcoming from the ACF. When the board, under the influence of the urban faction, declared that there was no arts component in Aboriginal ceremony, in effect Nugget Coombs's inspiration would be euthanised. Replaced by a more hard-headed view of 'economic potential' rather than 'preservation', the fragile particularities of dance and culture passed down countless generations would not sit comfortably within the scope of Paul Keating's coming 'Creative Nation'.

After Mary's long absence, it had not been an agreeable reunion. Lance Bennett was in bandages after having been attacked, according to his story, by 'an unspeakable mob of ratbags' who had set him on fire in an atmosphere of rising hostility to the foundation and its hold over their race-related brothers. Now relegated to the role of invited guest, Mary could only promise to make submissions to Canberra on behalf of the tribal delegates who had put so much trust in the original purpose of the venture. She had been saddened to see it falling apart between rival blocs and outside influences, including a group described as 'Marxist orientated'. Her rueful comment as she made her departure was to note that where the Aboriginal people were concerned: 'even our best intentions we have to muck up for them.'[7]

Later putting in order the files and masses of correspondence, she wondered who in future would believe what had gone into the ATF. That there is today virtually no record of this enterprise to be found in any public institution raises conjecture that it has been 'disappeared' as inconvenient to more popular (or less contentious) constructions of Aboriginal contemporary history. Nor would there be any objective account of a seminal period of change, begun with the 1974 Canberra seminar, from which emerged a story of winners and losers among disparate Aboriginal 'mobs'. Information and memories gathered by me in latter days from the surviving main players have been added to the relevant section of Mary Durack's archives, awaiting the interest of some future researcher.

On her way south, it was from the Broome nuns that Mary heard that the bishop was intimating he might sell back to the family the house built by Horrie. This news was also of interest to Johnson, set up in a jewellery-making business in the town and with a new girlfriend, and he urged his mother to take up the option. However, as there was no further mention of selling, we later suspected that his Lordship may have been less than enthusiastic about the prospect of sharing a block with a perceived hippie enclave. Into the 1980s, Mary would investigate other prospects in Broome, all followed through to some point of impossible complication or failure to act, but with Ida beyond participating, it was in reality by then too late.

In the final chapter the tables were turned on the bishop. According to his memoirs, in 1995 he was unceremoniously ordered to hand over the keys to the safe holding the sacred archives and vacate the house forthwith. Notwithstanding his unpopularity in certain quarters, it is hard not to feel affronted on his behalf, given his thirty-six years of service.[8]

During Mary's absence, Horrie had been predictably miserable, and to atone for her brief desertion Mary made plans along the lines of the previous year for his birthday. Friends and MMA associates gathered to pay their respects, and the old man responded to their toasts with heartfelt thanks for their loyal support and hard work of over four decades. Among numerous cards received was an invitation to join commemorative events to mark Amy Johnson's first solo flight from England to Australia – one Mary hoped he would refuse – 'but he was so keen I had to accept for us both as will have to be in constant, and probably embarrassing attendance from go to woe'.[9] On the day, helpers assisted him into a small plane for a spin over the city. It would be his final flight, and although he seemed to enjoy the familiar procedures and sense of being aloft, he was visibly relieved to get down.

Subjected to lengthy long-distance calls from Lance Bennett to discuss arrangements for the August Groote Eylandt Festival, and from R.M. Williams conferring on the design competition for the Hall of Fame, Mary could hardly count a moment without interruption. Both men were a nuisance to her, but with the belief she was contributing to concerns of vital national importance, she continued to allow herself to be earbashed, with no more than weak protest about the brush-off from Williams whenever she mentioned the WA branch.

Years later, when going through an immense pile of paperwork, I could not find much evidence of my mother's latter-day usefulness to the operations of the SHOF, and even in the preliminary stages it was apparent that her drafting to the board had been chiefly on account of her drawcard value. Sensing her initial reluctance, Williams had shrewdly probed until he found a point of entry via her keen interest in local history, and persuaded that the project was by no means a Queensland venture, on a trumped-up ticket she had come aboard a ship steered by Captain R.M.W. towards his predetermined destination. By the time the truth emerged, she was well caught.

My 'withdrawal' by this time having broken down, I was once again on call to sort out my mother's problems, rub the aching leg, give the house a once-over and dispense censure. Why would she not engage a regular cleaner? (No, it was not an *implied* criticism.) How could she seriously allow herself to be worried by the United States' abortive efforts to rescue the hostages from Iran? Why had she agreed to launch and help promote *To Fight the Wild*, a minor book about a young adventurer's survival in the outback?[10]

> *The theme of Patsy's latest diatribe about my wasting time is the reason for my present state of depression – but what to do about it? Get really tough and see the old man once a week? Say 'no' to everything else, as indeed I would like to do?*[11]

~

In an audacious assault on the very notion of family harmony, Bet had decided to challenge Gran's will. Mary's proposal of some allowance for the premature sale of her expectations having been turned down by Reg, Bet's disappointment had prompted a two-pronged offensive.

Recalling Gran's former wish to leave the house to 'the two girls', she proceeded on the grounds that Reg had taken over his mother's mind, causing her to abandon the idea. Making a bid for the silver tea set that had gone to his wife Enid, an item Bet claimed traditionally passed down to a daughter, was also by way of retaliation. Mary noted:

> *She left me a file of correspondence on the subject sent also to Bill and David. As I see it, the resulting publicity of threatened lawsuits would benefit no-one except possibly myself from sale of books. Really! This is the sort of nonsense I dreaded on mother's death but hoped could be avoided by my asking her to be specific in her will.*[12]

My version recalls my aunt's attempts to bring me on side:

> *Bet here in full cry over her claims. I could not recommend further action because she has no case and anyway I have no real sympathy for either party. Reg certainly objected to any suggestion that Gran favour 'the girls' but when I told her at the time that he was 'overseeing' the will, she showed no interest. As for the other issue! She says she does not really care about 'the silly old silver', but that it has become a principle thing – 'a dog that won't lie down'. Apparently the bitterness goes right back to the loss of the stations when Reg 'sold us all down the river' instead of holding the 'united front'. She wants Mum to join her in seeking damages for this long-ago grievance – $100,000 mentioned.*
>
> *When I foolishly pointed out that between the loss of Gran and the retention of Horrie, Mum was in a bad way and not helped by such family quarrels, Bet wondered if I did not think 'a rest home' would be best for her now and urged an advance booking as she had heard places were hard to obtain. As she left she thanked me, in sugary tones, for all I had done for Gran – as if I needed thanking. A most peculiar and subtle insult.*[13]

Faced with a bleak situation as a result of having been left stranded on the comfortless course of the sole parent, I was in no mood for Bet's strident voice in self-interested complaint over a tea set. One day I turned her from the door with the advice: 'I am not loving you right now, Aunty Bet. Best you stay away from me at the moment.' She managed to shrug off what must have given her a reality check. A hardening towards her from the younger generation had not been anticipated. It was an area to be watched and possibly dealt with.

The sordid exchange of letters and imprecations against Reg ended when Bet, in the absence of family support or legal hope, agreed to abandon all other claims for a division of the silver spoils. Still unresolved was the sharing with her sister of Gran's remaining household effects. Fearful of further strife, Mary let herself be taken advantage of in a way that removed any possibility, but Bet's crude manoeuvring in the process reflected little credit on her. Somewhat righteously aggrieved but satisfied at having come out on top, Reg and Enid packed up for a trip around the world, while Bet was diverted by the prospect of a new commission.

At the time, we thought the contretemps just a temporary aberration on Bet's part. None of us saw it as an ongoing trend.

Taking badly the 'concerned criticism' from so many quarters with regard to her wearing herself out over Horrie, Mary believed that had anyone really cared, they might have offered some assistance with the daily run to and from Sunset Hospital. Not only having lost patience with Ida's 'generalities and dogmatic statements, mostly inaccurate'[14] but also believing her to be in cahoots with me – which she was – Mary felt double-crossed. No matter what anyone said to her, she was in the unrelenting grip of a man beyond ordinary reason whose entire existence revolved around being brought home as soon as possible every day and causing havoc for the duration. If she missed a call owing to the prior claims of the invalid, the phone rang and rang again with problems and people and people's problems awaiting her ear. In addition to other claims upon her, she had by now become friendly with other old men at Sunset, for whose modest needs she shopped daily. Obtaining a gun at the request of one desperate fellow had been beyond her remit.

It was as much to save her own sanity as for the longstanding commitments to the Broome Shinju and Groote Eylandt festivals that she headed north with Geraldine Byrne. Meeting up in Darwin with Xavier Herbert, she was amused to learn that while still bitter over his poor treatment in 1964, he was willing to consider giving Perth another chance if invited to return – something he hoped she might facilitate.

Among many distinguished guests invited to the 1980 week-long festival events incorporating five hundred Aboriginal performers had been a choreographer and film team from the Nederlands Dans Theatre. One can only hope the footage has been preserved.

In reviewing accounts of its often fraught and fractious meetings, the many successful events under the auspices of the ATF and ACF tend to be overshadowed. Fulfilling the purpose of their charter, dance groups had attended intertribal gatherings from Cape York to Noonkanbah in West Kimberley, the most impressive of these being the three festivals held at Groote Eylandt facilitated by BHP mining royalties. Moving on from the debacle in Nigeria, a variable company under the title 'Dancers of the Dreaming' would over the next few years tour America, its presentation acclaimed by US critics for its authenticity, which compared favourably to more 'theatricalised' versions of native culture.

In Kununurra Mary found the old people on the reserve looking sick and dispirited. 'Very disturbed at rifts in the community over sacred sites and mining issues – others expressing similar concern and naming the "manipulators".[15] Unable to 'talk good sense' as she had done in the past over less contentious issues, she left them to their new predicaments with perplexed thoughts of the bad old days when the disenfranchised Indigenous people had seemed to her so much happier.

On her return, it came as a shock to find that after decades of declaring himself already there, Horrie did indeed appear to have arrived at death's door. Too weak to walk, he nonetheless insisted on being driven to the house. Unable to leave the car, he shakily drank the cup of tea carried out to him, looking despondently all the while at the great trees he had planted so long ago, down the path to the old brick and tile residence from which he had been exiled. He was like an animal glimpsing freedom through the bars.

It was an inauspicious time for the arrival of notables Sir Rupert and Lady Clarke, Hugh Sawrey, R.M. Williams and his secretary Jane Paul, Gordon Reid, Reynold Chandler, Jill Bowen and Sir James and Lady Walker for the SHOF directors' reception in Perth – a three-day affair that under other circumstances Mary would have enjoyed. A projected book on stockmen to be produced by Lansdowne Press was discussed, R.M. Williams convinced she could get this together in 'her spare time' and have it ready in under six months. On the final day of the conference, Horrie suffered another stroke that paralysed his throat.

As the patient feebly fought to be allowed to lie down, the staff at Sunset, in some well-meaning attempt to keep his chest clear, had propped him up in a chair. He seemed in the lowest of water as my son and I sat with him. His left arm hung useless and icy cold. Massaging some warmth back, I looked at his broad mechanic's hands, scarred veterans of countless hours of labour and know-how, the fingers arthritically bent, palms hard and callused – fit for nothing now. Lifting his head, he stared at me for a moment and I saw the knowledge of death in his eyes. A tray of uneaten food sat on his bedside table, placed there to what purpose I could not imagine. But perhaps he did want something? Slowly he lifted his right hand until it reached a banana and, turning his sorrowful gaze on the grandson he had never acknowledged, he pushed it towards him. He wanted to make some last gesture, I knew that and so did my son, who picked up the fruit with polite thanks. It was a last-ditch concession to the occasion.

Mary's diary shows her in attendance to the end: 'Hardly able to articulate, but he kissed my hand and said, "God bless and thank you darling". Left him feeling very upset.'[16] Once, she had declared, 'There may have been more selfish men than Horrie, but I never met one.' Somehow his final words made up for forty thankless years and cleaned the slate of all but fond and sentimental recollections.

> *He seemed slightly aware of my being there in the morning but unconscious from noon – took turns with him – shared with Marie, Patsy, Perpetua and Geraldine. Call at 10.30pm to say he had just passed away. And so the close of an unusual and remarkable life, the last three years of which have been a misery for us all. He never ceased to fight the inevitable – would not admit the fact that he had suffered a stroke and had lost the use of his left arm and leg. He was waiting to the end to get home again and behind the wheel of his car.*[17]

Accolades and tributes bearing the great names of the nation spoke for the significance of the pioneer's departure. Columns of print were devoted to 'the passing of a chapter in aviation history' and airport flags were flown at half-mast. The coffin passed through a guard of honour formed by MMA pilots and his beloved 'hosties', and mourners in the overflowing chapel wiped their eyes as moving eulogies praised a life of courage and achievement. A Broome service followed (conducted by a genuinely grieved Bishop Jobst), and at the cemetery on the road to Cable Beach there was a final ceremony where the Early Bird was laid to rest beside his two daughters.

It had not been easy for me to connect the conventional observances with the misfit at its centre or to express regret with any conviction. To the end of my days, I will wake from a nightmare where he is still alive and kicking.

~

With the demise of the governing director, the debts owed Miller Investments were extracted from Horrie's assets and Cyril Gare retired. Released from past constraints and the grip of its long-suffering trustee, the company became a tasty fish, inviting to circling predators. It would be a seductive property scheme offered by one of the new entrepreneurial breed emerging in Perth that would, through a punitive process, decimate the remainder of Miller Investments during the 1980s.

Hard put to feel other than relief, it required some adjustment for Mary to lose Horrie's gloomy shadow. In a strange way she missed the encumbrance. Like her father, she had become bent to burden and to a degree the lifting came too late for a proper straightening. Coming to terms with a house to herself, she was further challenged by the removal of the big obstruction to completing the book. For a time she could busy herself with the backlog of mail, the SHOF and fiddling matters, but she acknowledged the subterfuge: 'Oh, my fractured days and the waste of what at least semi-intelligent life remains to me.'[18]

Bet's remedy – movement – was the answer. An invitation to join the directors in Canberra to make a final decision on the winning submission for the SHOF architectural design had the right flavour of a spree about it. Accompanying perks included a billet at the US Embassy, publicity occasions and formal dinners, followed by an overland trip to Queensland with her brother Bill. The ongoing drama of a bizarre tragedy involving a baby taken by a dingo at Ayers Rock provided a talking point during the long haul and on the flight home with fellow passengers. In the process of her uncounted air journeys, Mary invariably found herself sitting beside someone with whom she was able to make a personal connection or from whom she could extract an interesting life story, their names and details preserved in her diaries.

> *Felt the time away has done me a power of good – definitely refreshed and able to cope. The optimism waned somewhat as I got down to opening the mail. Some of the letters formidable – many containing seemingly minor requests – one from a publisher asking me to write a 10,000 word personalised account of Broome. Another to write the intro to a book about Walter Padbury, WA's first millionaire. Bruce Shaw who is documenting the stories of the Aborigines at Kununurra wants more information that will require some tracking down through the files. Usual invitations to functions and two weddings of people I hardly know. Everything can wait as nothing is more important than getting this book finished.*[19]

While not unwelcoming of her gallant visitors in the form of Ian Forbes, a cousin of Nessie Kidson, and the re-encouraged Leslie Rees, Mary fretted at the interruption as they settled in for long yarns and stayed for meals. Admirers from way back, they may have been emboldened by her widowed state, but it was too late for that sort of thing, as far as she was concerned. Looking around her, she observed a once seemingly static social environment now radically altered: the older generation passed and neighbours relocated to self-contained units in preparation for infirmity. Her closest northern friends had gone, among them nuns who had lived to such a great age that it seemed they had been granted dispensation from timely demise. The family was widely dispersed, Reg in Kununurra, Bet travelling, Bill on the other side of Australia and her brother David reported from Melbourne to be terminally ill.[20] She found few sights as reassuring as the unchanging Korwills on their vigorous daily walks, 'looking like two mountain climbers off to pick Edelweiss'.[21]

Circumstances having lessened expectations of family increase, Mary's surviving children had produced between them seven grandchildren, but of these only five would remain to be counted. The doings of my children Naomi and Yagan, the two Megaw sons Joe and Alex and Marcus Miller featured regularly in her diaries, but a child from Johnson's Broome relationship had been taken back to his mother's homeland in Germany, and Andy's ex-wife had remarried and settled in Queensland with Drew. Inasmuch as its full complement is known, the Millers would not burgeon in the way of other Durack lines, Mary's great-grandchildren fewer than her original six – a poor show one might ascribe to the bad karma that came with her inapposite marriage. Her need to be involved in something ongoing extended to the new generation, and nothing brought Mary more joy than the sound of little feet pounding through the house.

~

For the remaining fourteen years of her life, Mary's journals would carefully document the surface detail of her busy days, and there was comfort in the knowledge that to the best of her ability every significant moment was somewhere to be discovered. Even her summarised rendering makes for confounding reading as she presents herself for future scrutiny, and while she would castigate herself for the waste of it, she might well defy anyone to say she squandered or did not make the most of her time.

Crosses in the margin became more frequent, until no more than a handful of those who knew her in her heyday remained. They were all on the last stretch of the conveyor belt, so that by the time she attended the funeral of Nita Pannell in September 1994, it had been open to question who would attend whose. Lines between life and death are apt to become blurred in old age, finally less a great disconnection than a small uncoupling, those falling before calling for little more than a fond wave of farewell. There can be no comparison with the brutal break and terrible scars left by the loss of the young. New names cropped up to be counted among latter-day acquaintances, some no doubt believing they came to know her intimately. But the Mary Durack of the last decade was far removed from the woman who had written *Kings in Grass Castles* and *The Rock and the Sand*.

~

I had advised my mother against her participation in a 'Modern Exploration' project with Geoff Dutton, John Olsen and Vincent Serventy. By May 1982, after months of dedication to the job, *Sons* was in final draft form, and a safari with a coffee table book objective seemed a possibly fatal distraction.

Realising the truth in this but longing to join the party for the Broome to Kununurra section, she had put in a terrific effort that saw the book away to Constable on the very eve of her departure. 'There,' she said, handing me the parcel for posting, 'all I needed was a decent incentive.'

The entrepreneur for this ambitious enterprise was the self-described 'art-lover, dealer and photographer' Alex Bortignon, who had found a major sponsor in Allen Christensen, a philanthropic US mining magnate. According to the promotion, each participant had been selected 'to bring a unique perspective into the mysteries of an ancient land'.[22] From an estimated cost of 700,000 dollars, there would be in the final accounting little change from a million – but what a thrash for all concerned, not least Mary Durack. Her arrival in Broome was captured on video: as she walks across the tarmac, sighting her fellow travellers she breaks into the joyful and relieved smile of one who is home and dry after overcoming great odds. What more could she have asked for than the prospect of an extended picnic with celebrated pals through her beloved country on a not arduous assignment?

For five weeks a convoy equipped with an excess of camping gear traversed over 20,000 kilometres through the Kimberley, while the party, from four-wheel drives, boats and helicopters, exercised their individual talents upon the landscape. Aside from a bout of group food poisoning, the antagonism that developed between Dutton and Bortignon ('so unnecessary', wrote Mary, keen as ever to maintain 'happy families'), and the unfortunate discovery by Ninette Dutton via a letter opened in all innocence that her husband had been bringing his unique perspective to bear on the mysteries of another lady, the tour was an unqualified success. And in due time, Mary having made her stand-out contribution, a 'luxury edition' of *Land Beyond Time* was launched at a very luxurious eight hundred dollars per copy. With intrusions on her time reminiscent of those of John Joseph Jones, Bortignon sought her support for his further 'Artist's Vision' ventures until, like so many 1980s high-flyers, he suddenly vanished from the scene.

Bestowed with the Society of Women Writers' Alice Award for her distinguished contribution to Australian literature, Mary went to Adelaide in October for the presentation. When attending a meeting of the society ten years later, only her name tag would remind her that she was also the federal patron.

At a ceremony attended by a large crowd of family and associates, *Sons in the Saddle* was launched in 1983 by Professor Geoffrey Bolton. Down to the last of its original membership, the FAW was not represented as in days of yore, and listed among absent guests were Hal Porter, who was in a coma after being hit by a car, and Donald Stuart, who had inconsiderately died on the very day.

The sequel was an achievement that over ten years had largely sapped the author's remaining quality writing reserve, so that confident talk of 'the third volume' became ever more fanciful. There was a noticeable letting go. Putting aside the legitimate and lasting, Mary opened her doors and, albeit tacitly, declared herself at home to 'fugitive stuff' and invitations to attend functions across the country.

The July 1984 Sydney launch of the SHOF-funded Lansdowne book *The Stockmen* was typical of the celebrity events to which she added her much-sought presence. One of seven esteemed authorities to contribute to this high-quality compilation of essays and photos, Mary gives a good account in her diary of the lavish function held in the Commonwealth Bank for four hundred select invitees, her many obligatory press and radio interviews serving to also promote *Sons in the Saddle*.

~

My long-held suspicion that despite her emphatic denials, my mother was continuing some form of contact with Harold Dicks was confirmed at this time when I caught him, apparently unaware of her absence, in a surreptitious visit to Mildew. Momentarily taken aback, as was I, he rapidly regained his composure and arranged his face into a smile of pleasure at the prospect of my unexpected company. Suddenly overcome with revulsion and rage, and having the hose in hand, I flushed him off the property – down the garden path, past the 'bear-pit' where with Robin he had so often enjoyed the hospitality of the house, and out the gate. Unfortunately, the weak water pressure made it a symbolic gesture that dampened rather than cannoned him away on the end of a jet.

'How do you live with yourself, Harold Dicks!' I shouted rhetorically, to the wonderment of my watching children.

His shocked reaction indicated this was a fairly novel experience for him, so lest he be left in any doubt I threw in a few specifics before pronouncing him a 'moral bankrupt', my fury also on behalf of many unavenged. Puce-faced and shouting incomprehensibly, he leapt into his car and sped away. Since he had never owned to anything other than conducting himself in the most proper manner while granting us the benefit of his benevolence and scrupulous honesty, I suppose he must have found my aggression perplexing. He did not (to my knowledge) come near my mother again, and I saw him for the last time a year later at the launching of *Speck in the Sky*, the history of MMA by Frank Dunn. Keeping my distance, I gave no sign that I noticed his hurt and pleading eyes fixed on me from across the room.

In 1987 Mary recorded his death in a short line: 'A call from his sister Norah Shepherd to say that Harold had suffered a sudden heart attack and died this morning.'[23] While she did not attend the funeral or place a notice in the paper, she had acquitted herself on that front without offending the ghost of her daughter.

A bright, more youthful social group claimed her: a celebrated littérateur to be produced on all occasions. Bringing a touch of distingué to the merrymaking, she lent her wise counsel to trivial woes, readily composed witty verse to suit and read palms – a *performing* grande dame. One party merged into another; someone brought the curry and everyone brought wine. With the usual overkill, I hoped to provide an exemplar by boringly emphasising my own teetotalism. (How I did bludgeon my poor mother with my dreary rectitude.) Veda Swain and Louise Smith – the ladies who ran Perth's Greenhill Galleries – assumed a prominent place in her life and provided a good deal of the divertissements of the 1980s. Although Marie Rose and I were doubtful about the constant use of her premises, we were glad enough to see our mother amused and feted.

Caught up in this new milieu, attending FAW functions had become for her no more than a sometimes rather melancholy duty of long association and failing faculties. By 1988 and the fiftieth anniversary, Mary Durack was the last surviving member of the founding group, and Tom Collins House itself was under threat of demolishment for a new highway.[24]

In retrospect, writers had perhaps always been relatively heavy going. For her, there was more fun to be had in the company of party people like Barry Humphries and Rolf Harris; artists Clifton Pugh, Pro Hart and John Olsen; the singing bushman Ted Egan; and country music stars Smoky Dawson and Slim Dusty, who somehow became merged into a person referred to as 'Smoky Dusty'. Her old boyfriend Ian Forbes made his yacht available to the swinging crowd, and she could frequently be observed seated uncomfortably on the deck during twilight races and afterwards at yacht club revels in company with such curiosities as Prince Jah, the Nizam of Hyderabad.

After almost a decade of service, following a fall that fractured her knee, Connie Hooker was phased out and replaced by an energetic on-the-ball secretary who brought about a more efficient and up-to-date management of the multilayers that made up Mary's life. While capably dealing in the main with the transitory, Ros Golding was instrumental in salvaging and fostering her employer's residual creative output. She also kept me apprised of matters demanding my intervention, a connivance of which my mother was not unaware.

Bet, while on the face of it maintaining her sociable grace and charm, was vexed by the new crowd in residence, writing to her brother Bill of how 'perfect strangers' seemed to be 'taking over' their sister. Of particular inconvenience had been the advent of a vigilant secretary who kept an account of ingoings and outgoings, and a situation where, as Ros put it to me, 'Your aunt uses up your mother like old scratch'.

~

In November 1981, Mary had unknowingly visited Adsett for the last time. Looking out at the bay as she worked on the final chapters of *Sons in the Saddle*, she had almost forgotten the sense of peace so nourishing to connective thought. But the seaside retreat had come to the end of its term: the long summer days and cosy winter fireside nights, dinners on the terrace under the rising moon, soirees and deep discourse that broke up at dawn – the happy haunt of literary inspiration and a thirty-year close fellowship between two remarkable women.

At the age of ninety, Ida Mann found herself wondering what she should do next. Awarded a DBE in 1980, she had lost count of her honorary doctorates and medals. Deriving little enjoyment or satisfaction from being a celebrity at the wrong end of a phenomenal career, she sat for a while impatiently twiddling her thumbs. Towards the end of 1983, she bowed out in a typically businesslike way:

> *Ida died in her upstairs study this am. I knew she was failing. She repeatedly said she had lived too long and after her busy life was now doing little but reading books about the troubled world. It will be hard none the less to realise that my dearest friend and companion of many years is no longer here.*[25]

Inevitably, Ida's autobiography, in manuscript form, ended up on Mary's plate, but she was now beyond dealing with such a daunting task. Edited by Ros Golding, *The Chase* appeared in 1986, a condensed version of the original, an inspirational story which may someday emerge in a more complete rendering.

The eighties advent of the Hawke Labor Government, Premier Brian Burke in Western Australia, new millionaires and the America's Cup brought a heady, irresponsible atmosphere to Perth. Someone nominated Mary Durack as a suitable candidate for the state's next governor, and the press was happy to run with the diverting idea. It was only slightly less outlandish than speculation in the *Sydney Morning Herald* in 1972 that she – or Germaine Greer – be considered for the position of the first woman governor-general. In her new-found social swim, she had met and liked without reserve most of the profiteers and politicians of the times, so that within a few years there was room for regret when so many of them ended up in prison. Her 'banged up' friends would include Paul Ritter, who had eventually pushed his luck by attempting to fraudulently obtain a Commonwealth grant. His subsequent occupation with a trout farm would bring welcome provision to her door, as would the avocados from the garden of Charles Court.

Scenes of past triumphs were revisited: *Ship of Dreams* was performed again in Broome, *Swan River Saga* toured the North West, and a new edition of *The Rock and the Sand* appeared along with *Kings in Grass Castles* in an illustrated coffee-table volume. More eligible contenders seeking to make a film or television series of the family saga finally narrowed to Paul Barron, manager of a Perth-based film production company, whose entrepreneurial resemblance to Alex Bortignon of the previous venture proved a winning attraction for the author. A script commissioned from David Williamson was followed by reasonable attempts from screenwriters John Goldsmith and Tony Morphett. Passed from the hands of bright sparks to dimwits, with each new mauling a great factual account was further pushed towards pulp fiction and its ultimate destination – a cringe-making two-part television film of dumbed-down trashiness. It still upsets me to think of how seriously my mother took the project and how diligently she laboured to keep the story real. It was as well she did not live to see the result. When in 2003 Barron Films went into receivership, it was a matter of no grief to offended family and fans of *Kings*.

~

Travelling continually on SHOF business, Mary attended fundraising activities as required, her presence gracing bush bash, cowboy night and rodeo until the triumphal opening in July 1988. The successful conclusion of this royally attended occasion was the obvious moment for her retirement, in the way of other notables who had made their contribution, but bending to compliments suggesting her input was vital and unwilling to forgo the gratis travel that kept her in close touch with widespread family, she stayed with it until 1991. At subsequent 'where to from here' meetings, personality differences arising between board members became a cause of embarrassment to her, as was a protracted controversy over Sir James Walker's proposed hotel adjacent to the Hall of Fame site he had so favoured.

Every year an invitation to stand among shire personnel and official guests on the dais drew her to the Shinju Festival in Broome and on to Darwin via the well-worn track. Two free trips a year with Ansett, courtesy of the long MMA association, made her an economical invitee. In transit for four months of 1985, movement and crowds became for her a distraction from the disheartening awareness of her declining faculties. Now and again she opened the transcripts of her father's diaries and took notes from family correspondence files towards the elusive third volume she had tentatively titled 'Full Turn of the Wheel'. The book brought to a halt while in the preparation stage, there is much evidence preserved of Mary's intention.

Her car long taken over by Johnson, she still hoped, when she felt stronger, to get back to driving, a bid firmly discouraged by Ros Golding and me. There was no shortage of willing chauffeurs, though being dependent upon transport meant she was often forced to stay too long and late at events. An Irish acquaintance persuaded her to join PEN International and the W.B. Yeats Society, and the activities of these groups and the 'dear people' met as a result (so many needing her advice on how to get a manuscript or book of verse published) swallowed great swatches of time most satisfactorily. Her blue pencil moving swiftly and surely over alien text, the ability to edit other people's work never left her, and such tasks held in abeyance the moment when she must turn to her own. PEN and W.B. Yeats newsletters joined a multiple of others such, largely unread and left to litter her work room and bedside table, among them a peculiar mix of pamphlets she had not the heart to refuse, along with a donation: Newman Society, *Madonna*, *Watchtower* and the communist *Tribune*.

While Mary was unproductive in terms of serious writing, the years 1987 and 1988 were for her relatively happy and fulfilling. Her lame leg improved with a built-up shoe, and the mysterious back ailment that had so often plagued her kept at bay, she was able to enjoy a privileged circuit of travels, activities and celebrations with her numerous votaries. Her son Johnson was now enrolled in an acting course at the WA Academy of Performing Arts, and she diligently attended plays in which he took part. Closing the book (and her own anguished record) on the past, she stood as his staunchest champion. She would later cut out for her diary newspaper advertisements in which he featured, and she was thrilled to see him appearing in television commercials.[26] Marie's lovely screen prints adorned the walls of Mildew, and her new grandson Alex was adorable. Another source of pride was her high-achieving eldest grandson Yagan, who took off scholastic prizes, sporting trophies and the school captaincy before embarking on a law course.[27]

It was a shame about me – the very embodiment of a Greek chorus, cautioning, disparaging and darkly pessimistic, only serving to emphasise the vagary of fate that had snatched away her lovely golden girls. 'Oh, is that you, dear?' The quick shuffle and slip of papers and letters under cover, and the *brace*.

Fearing loss of control, she obstinately 'supervised' the support team her daughters had set up for her: Flying Domestics, secretary, gardener, handyman, chauffeurs and many friends on call. She refused to consider a telephone answering machine on the grounds that she would have to ring back those who left messages. This explanation she felt watertight in its logic, although in truth she hated the device and the 'ghost voices' encountered on other people's phones, especially mine, on which she left cutting advice that it was 'only your mother' and of no importance to return the call.

During the summer months, we kept up the tradition of evening meals in the garden for family and guests.

Whether at home or abroad, Bet stayed in close touch. Social interchange across the generations was taken for granted as an enduring feature of the Durack clan. But with years and history intervening between the children of M.P. and Bess, the affinity of old had become fragile – a happy legend that could be maintained only so long as no-one rocked the boat or trod on sensitive toes. In a further break with the past, the graceful former Durack home at 263 Adelaide Terrace, where once the six little 'steps and stairs' had lined up for a Christmas photograph against a backdrop of Bess's prize hydrangeas, was demolished for a glass tower. In the process of a film made for the Australia Council archives in 1983, footage taken of Mary on the site of her earliest years did not make it through the cutting process, but having brought her sister into the project, a scene in Bet's house does. The women sitting side by side, rather than their close relationship, it is the distance grown between them that is exposed – a tension on Bet's part as if resenting being involved in something suggestive of their former collaborative era.

For Dame Mary, the accolades continued to roll in: a state ship carrying her name, a Foundation Fellowship of Curtin University in 1987, and the Companion of the Order of Australia in 1989. But conscious that the tributes and recognition were now for past endeavours, she became loath to assume new honours, and agonising over the AC she wired belated acceptance only after someone suggested her inclusion might give needed publicity to the SHOF. Also feeling obliged to prove herself worthy of the Australia Council Emeritus Fellowship awarded in 1983, and increasingly doubtful about her ability to complete any more substantial work, she thought an anthology of her short stories and verse with introductory notes might be an achievable goal, the recycle passed off as something fresh. Files of material were muddled over for a few years, but, sadly, by 1990 it was obvious she was beyond even making a selection.[28]

It had come first as a surprise to her, then as an unacceptable loss, to find that when she tapped the inner sanctum, the writer-in-residence of old was no longer at home. She had been too profligate with her talent, throwing her rare gift in all directions without thought for a bank that might run dry.

~

Her once broad neighbourhood shrunk to those in the immediate vicinity, Mary nonetheless held to her standing as Lady of the Manor and longest resident by inviting the street to a yearly neighbours party. Her aversion to coming home to a dark house saw her happily accommodating for long periods surrogate daughters Geraldine Byrne and Rosy Kerr, the latter another Greenhill Galleries employee, in addition to frequent house guests – prominent among them her steadfast Aboriginal son, Jack Saville. The advent of sculptors Joan Walsh-Smith and husband Charlie Smith, whom she had assisted to migrate to Western Australia from Ireland, provided her with fresh and rewarding company and frequent visits to their country home and studio.[29]

Most of her needs taken care of, could we have averted the never-ending supplicants or changed her nature, all should have been in place for a smooth ride to the end of the road. She saw no reason why there should always be consultation with her secretary or me or another family member before she agreed to give interviews or endorsements or send original material away. Her list of work undertaken in 1990 tells a sorry tale:

> Working on foreword for Bea Darbyshire biography.
> Writing a letter to the editor, with Vin Serventy, in defence of K.S. Prichard.
> Making a list of twenty favourite books for Literacy Year.
> Looking for information on Kimberley identity Tom Pethic for an enquirer.
> Writing lines for Ansett Airlines lunch cards on why Western Australia is a great state to live in.
> Looking up information on pioneer Bob Button for an enquirer.
> Making notes to add to a tribute to Judith Wright from those who knew her.

Looking for information on Tom Quilty for a relative of his. Working on launch speech for Bruce Shaw's latest book of memories from the Aboriginal people of Kununurra.

Weeks of laborious thought went into an appeal from a local school: 'Could you help our young people by explaining what has inspired and motivated you in your life work plus your favourite motto and a photograph.' But she was easy game now, and among her tormentors a small but unshakable clutch of mental cases. One poor soul who regularly evaded her keepers called at frequent intervals to demand the 50,000 dollars belonging to her that she knew Mary Durack was holding in her 'nest of mischief'. A deranged admirer sent weekly screeds and her taped memoirs for 'sponsoring', along with the advice that with the introduction of late-night reduced-rate phone calls: 'When the phone rings after midnight, it will be you-know-who.' And it was!

I could never get over the cheek of people – the 'droppers in' and those who got through by one means or another, so that I would find my mother wasting her days on behalf of distant relatives or vague connections, patiently replying to queries that could have been answered by reading her books. But while she sat at her desk with the phone to hand, as if on duty and open for business, what else could have been expected? Between us, Ros Golding and I dealt with the correspondence, presenting drafts of our replies for her inimitable 'personal touch'. Skulking amid my mother's work-table clutter, awaiting her nervous approval or veto, could usually be discovered copies of letters in my blunt style:

Dear Susan Mitchell,

Re the chapter relating to Dame Mary Durack as taken from a taped interview in your book The Matriarchs. *Dame Mary has never trusted her memory and unlike practised media personalities she is not always clear or accurate in a conversational situation. Her expertise is in the written word where no mistakes of spelling or fact are a matter of pride. Evidently you do not apply the same standards to yourself and it is most surprising that you have no better regard for your own standing than to allow so many erroneous references to pass undetected. It is also obvious that you did not bother to read or familiarise yourself with her works despite the bibliography with which you were supplied ...*

Dear Trish Ainslie and Roger Garwood,

Further to our correspondence concerning the book Til she Dropped her Strides. *Dame Mary Durack has found the continued queries in regard to the fallacious anecdote concerning herself of considerable nuisance and embarrassment ...*

And some drafts handed over, innocent-faced, that she signed a little uncertainly:

Dear Lovejoy,

Thank you for your letters and photo of yourself with goat and the lavender and news of the bees' music and the scarf which is indeed *my colours ...*

Dame Mary Durack was verily famous enough to be a target not only for the demented but for the unprincipled, who shrewdly calculated her unlikely to sue. Considering litigation a horror to be avoided at all costs, she did not react to personal injury and defamation in the normal way. She needed protection, and I was the increasingly impervious shield. Anyone deemed to have offended or misused my mother, even if she forgave them, would find themselves up against the implacable enmity of her daughter. It was into this hardened and defensive atmosphere that Reg and Bet were to recklessly step.

~

With an increasingly high profile and the more profitable marketing of her talents, Bet had become close-mouthed about her financial affairs. There was no mention to her sister of the sale to Alistair McAlpine of her 1947 'big pictures' for 26,000 dollars – a lump sum of the sort Mary's bank account would never see. But the 'tiding-over' loans, often slipping her sister's mind, continued in some form that escaped the account book. Always supposing my aunt was as clueless about money matters as my mother, I was surprised to find later evidence of her shrewdness. Her income such as to make 'tax incentives' attractive, she was as adept at the art of business negotiation as any other.

Appointed in 1982 Companion of the Most Distinguished Order of Saint Michael and Saint George for her lasting contribution to art, at the age of sixty-seven the artist declared herself 'determined to put in an active finish'.[30]

To his wife Enid's dismay, Reg had nostalgically taken up the lease on Bullita, a scenically beautiful but untamed former Durack outpost, the locale of his youthful northern initiation. At an outlay of 300,000 dollars, for two years he would enjoy a semblance of rugged pioneering, until the problems inherent and uncertainty of tenure in the new climate of land rights had placed him in a familiar quandary. When the place was resumed by the government for Gregory National Park at no financial loss to Reg, Bet wrote to Bill that the arrangement had provided him with 'the greatest let out of all time'.[31] His next purchase was Spirit Hill Station, and with other properties in and around the town of Kununurra and frequent trips to Perth, he would avail himself of the best of both worlds and the world beyond. In 1989 he and Enid set out for Paris, the United Kingdom and Ireland, meeting up along the way with Bet, Perpetua, Bill and Noni. (On her return, Bet had amusingly described to me the mortification she had suffered in the company of her elder brother: 'You cannot get a clear picture of Reg until you set him against a great cosmopolitan city like London. He is the quintessential, backwaters Australian – moaning about prices, quibbling over tips, sounding off in public places on a sort of Dad and Dave level.') But nothing would satisfy his unquiet mind and he was ripe for the circumstances to assert his authority as Head of the Family.

CHAPTER 15

RUFFIAN FORCES (1990–1994)

During a New Year visit to Perth, Vin Serventy helped Mary compose a letter to *The West Australian* in defence of Katharine Susannah Prichard after the publication of an article by journalist Hal Colebatch citing the writer's 'darker side' as a reason the Western Australian Government should not subsidise the cost of preserving her Greenmount home as a writers centre.[1] In the process going through material in the archives room, Vin had for the first time taken in the extent of the historic collection. Consequently, Mary notes: 'Vin urging me to consider a sensible disposition of my literary archives I had thought to leave to the Battye Library for want of any other interest. He recommends a consultant be brought in.'[2] She had not considered the possibility of another institution and, until informed by Serventy, was innocent of the concept of payment for documents. From FAW contacts, she had heard stories concerning the State Library of Western Australia's shortage of storage facilities to house donations, material likely to end up in some outer suburban warehouse where it would languish for years untouched and unindexed until beyond the application of a living memory.

The National Library of Australia, on the other hand, distributed glossy brochures extolling their fiduciary credentials. Willing to pay for Australiana, they were selective and acquisitions accordingly accommodated. To avoid resentment from those states losing out, there was some emphasis placed on their readiness to copy and share relevant data.

Gerry Glaskin also gave advice 're the best way of disposing of historical papers. He says I should not will them to the Battye but look for another venue which should pay for same as they have for Vin's.'[3] Gerry had a personal grievance against the State Library, one that, despite lengthy conversations with him, was difficult to grasp. Was the offence that the Battye had refused to give up the manuscript drafts he had deposited with them or that they had returned them (dumped all over his lawn, according to Gerry)?

Since retrieved to write the Durack saga sequel, the archives had been housed in Julie's former room in the backyard. Horrie had once mused on how he had often looked at the old boxes, 'stacked on shelves up to the roof and wondered what you would do with them. What a record of achievement they represent and the sadness which pervades all past and future history.'[4]

Aside from her own literary archives and files, which had seen some ordering, papers taken from the company office forty years before were much as they had been when loaded into Mary's Austin A30. Constant foraging had seen Connie Hooker's system disarranged, and there was no proper inventory of contents. While the general area could be identified, finding a particular piece of information was a task requiring considerable stamina and determination. Between forays, the mouldy documents attesting to enterprises of great pith and moment saw the emergence of frisking silverfish and moths resistant to the curatorial waving about of flyspray.

Notwithstanding the time being right to consider an appropriate public repository, there was no doubt that Mary would greatly miss her archives; it was a situation, as she tried to be practical and sensible, not unlike that faced in 1950 by her father when he came to dispose of his property. The sum total of her assets amounting to the family house and her book royalties, she had not been uninterested in a venue that paid for material over one that did not. Were it not for the Emeritus Fellowship grant, she would have been genuinely hard up. Consulting with her associates, in her modest fashion she took in the general opinion that Mary Durack had transcended the parochial to become an author of national standing. Moreover, the records covered pioneering days in all states of Australia, and her vast correspondence contained letters from the literary and renowned across the continent.

It never occurred to Mary, always so open and up-front in her dealings, that their disposal would be of much concern to her sister and brothers. Her work had made of consequence a mass of papers that would otherwise have been of donation value only. Although Bet had latterly begun to access the correspondence files for claimed 'research purposes', apart from the occasional query neither she nor Reg had ever given them much attention, and Bill, whose interests lay in other spheres, had long been geographically removed.

After discussion with my mother and other family members, I duly wrote and presented for her editing a letter to the National Library, sounding out a possible expression of interest. By the time the draft was retyped, she was in hospital undergoing a replacement of her 'good' knee, so the letter was signed on her behalf.

The proposal was a matter of some personal regret to me, as my hours of fascinated reading had discovered much I had hoped to explore further with no thought other than that there would be ample time to do it. A task begun to sort the material into coded categories would be removed from my hands, but then I thought it might be as well for one of my proclivity for inventories not to have to deal with that mountain of papers. In any case, my mother's decision had absolute priority in the matter.

Some months later, John Thompson, director of collections at the National Library, arrived to investigate and assess the worth of the archives.[5] The reason for his visit was frankly discussed with wider family and no objections were raised. Bet was anyway preoccupied, having shortly before received a worrying health report culminating in an operation for cancer. While the diagnosis following treatment was reassuring, the trauma threw her off balance, and it had required resilience to continue organising a comprehensive retrospective exhibition at the State Library. Opened in February 1991, the showing received a savaging from an art critic, who accused her of 'romantic distortion' of Aboriginal people, celebrating 'second-rate emotions' and, in a particularly mean barb, of being a 'relentless seeker of publicity'.[6] Bet was cut to the quick by the ignorant and unfair review, which raised indignant public protest.

Included in Bet's postoperative and 'active finish' stratagem was the removal from Mildew of her remaining pictures. One by one they vanished, some requested for retrospectives and others without notice or explanation. To avoid any potential objection, she was not above entering the unlocked house when no-one was at home, without thought for her sister's subsequent fright and conviction that she had been the victim of a burglar. A note accompanied the disappearance of the centrally positioned *Paperbark*, purchased at the *Mirage* exhibition in 1963, to the effect that she was allowing space for the obviously more valued art of Marie Rose. Of the uncounted original works bought or exchanged for a loan over the years, only one would remain as a token to her sister's generosity and the days when she had written, 'I'm sunk without you Mary ... tell me you will never fail me although I know full well you never will'.[7] The archives room was regularly ransacked for lurking examples of her early work, such as drawings that had been enclosed in correspondence before the publication of *The Way of the Whirlwind* and *The Magic Trumpet*. But the recent health scare having turned her mind to how she might be seen by posterity, her principal occupation had become the task of censoring her letters. Crudely snipping, liquid-papering and removing entire pages, the decorous matron was set upon excising her imprudent and scandalous youth from hundreds of missives to Mary penned and pencilled in her passionate script over forty years. Alerted to her activities, I was curious as to what Bet was so anxious to hide.

'Well,' said my mother helplessly, 'she says she is just photocopying material that might be of interest to her grandchildren. But I suppose they are her letters and it is her right to look through them for indiscretions.'

I might have accepted this, had a similar courtesy been extended to her sister. Mary's several requests for access to her own letters had met with a vague 'I'm not sure if I kept them', or 'I don't know that I could put my hands on them now'.

Between bursts of focused creative activity, Bet had regularly run off the rails, but she had never failed to get herself back on track. Proficient at smoothly explaining 'misunderstandings' and wheedling a return to favour, she had often pushed the boundaries of family leniency. Over many years, Mary had stood as a barrier against those less forgiving, advising her against, or rescuing her from, ill-advised stunts and impetuous actions. Now her morally stronger sister was growing weaker, no longer able to be relied on to take her side as in the past, and Mary's adult children were beginning to intrude on their sisterly understandings. Given Bet's lifelong claim, the coming battle would ultimately be over who had the right of ownership to Mary.

~

Few people were permitted to know Bet. With a multiplicity of masks, perhaps somewhere along the line she had lost her original face. Anyone wishing to probe deeper than the cosmetically renovated and well-made-up ice-queen countenance that presented for her latter-day appearances will find the authorised version the only one available. But from my earliest years, I had observed her from every perspective – too frank, too open and nakedly unguarded. My eye pierced the armour with an ease that left her in a state of sheer funk.

Now she was facing me across the table in the archives room, the wastepaper basket brimming with the morning's work. Here was a fire-breathing dragon against which she might well need the companionship of Saint Michael and Saint George.

'What do you think you are doing, Aunty Bet?'

Although her reaction at the time had been a glacial calm and an offhand denial of all charges, the 'odium heaped upon her'[8] would reduce Bet, so she subsequently informed her brother Bill, to a wreck unable to rise from her bed for two days.

The files containing her correspondence gathered up and removed to an area of my personal safekeeping, the mystery to me was why she had not simply taken the lot, like her paintings from the walls. If not beyond noticing the loss, Mary was certainly beyond making a fuss. A straight exchange of letter files would also have solved the problem, though perhaps Mary's responses to her less seemly travails and revelations of the extent to which she had been subsidised had been better disappeared. It may have been enough that she perceived the incalculable worth to me of my mother's letters.[9] My mind shies from a scene of Gothic destruction. More likely they had fallen foul of one of her husband Frank's imaginative acts of vengeance – a 'Look what you have driven me to, Elizabeth' moment. Not all the havoc wrought by Frank had she seen fit to pass on to Mary.

Malevolent and dangerous as she mulled over her humiliation, it then came to Bet's somewhat belated attention that a financial consideration, rather than a straight gift, was involved in the proposed disposal of the archival collection. Surely the original plan had been to donate the papers to the Battye? Should she make a push to enforce this? The way was not altogether clear but enough for a start to run interference. Reg was soon apprised of the situation; Bet knew how to pull his strings. Mary's diary entry of 15 August 1991 registers

> *[a] puzzling problem over the family material. It seems to have got around that I have 'settled up' with the National Library for some large figure for a 'treasure' of which I have legally no more than 'custody' for a limited period.*

And the following day:

> *Early ring from brother Reg in Kununurra. He has evidentially been told that I have arranged to sell the papers for some undisclosed sum – all kept 'secret' from family (other than my own) whereas I have no right, only temporary custody of such which belongs to all the immediate family of MPD. I reminded him of the visit from John Thompson and dinner in the garden with family including brother Bill and Bet. John went through the files with the help of Patsy and Ros – said he would keep in touch re a possible purchase of material as a whole rather than gift to Battye as I had intended. I can't find further reference to and certainly no specific offer, let alone payment.*

From Queensland, Bill was drawn into the fray:

> *A ring from Bill as perplexed as I about this sudden explosion of interest in the archival files, previously only of historical value to myself for background of family story of the years. Bill said he remembered interest expressed by John Thompson at the family gathering when he was here. Certainly nothing secret about it. He will ring Reg and try to make sense of it.*[10]

So murky and shifting were to be the motives and demands of the claimants that no-one was ever able to 'make sense of it'. Bet was the driver of this runaway bus and her destination more far-flung than the others were able to grasp. Duplicity her stock in trade, she was a virtuoso when it came to pitting one family member against another and switching sides at will. The alliance she forged with Reg for the duration was a cynical and unholy one. As Mary was wont to recall, her brother had been in many respects an estimable character, and had she got round to a third volume, 'Bids', as he had been affectionately known, would have emerged as integral to the family story. From my own explorations into the family files, I was not unaware of the admirable side to Reg, but that man had been lost somewhere along the years, and now he was a mere vestige, hitting the whisky and complaining of boredom – his sense of humour gone walkabout.

On 4 November, Mary reports her brother's desire to assert his rightful authority:

> *Reg embarked on the issue of family documents. As the eldest he claims he is therefore the head of the family. He insists the documents are his – something that should have been accepted by all from the time of Dad's death, as is any money that they may be worth. Seems he has contacted John Thompson and explained that it was for him to decide where they should be preserved.*

Still unable to take it seriously but getting worried, Mary, in an implicit plea for a 'barleys', wrote for her siblings a wry verse she titled 'Custody':

> *Thank you dears for giving me with such warm geniality*
> *The impetus to carry on with that long-since embarked upon*
> *And rambling documentary now merging into volume three*
> *Should I survive to see it through (or forced to leave the job to you –)*
> *It is my practical suggestion that you make headlines of the question*

> *Of who owns what of source material (good subject for an ongoing*
>   *serial)*
> *Especially should a shrewd relation have cleverly become the*
>   *claimant*
> *Of some considerable payment. But then before we quit it*
> *We might as well admit it – best we encourage family fights*
> *Re ownership and legal rights – thus keeping in the public eye*
> *A story sooner doomed to die.*

Her drollery fell on stony ground.

The National Library in Canberra eventually made an official bid of 61,000 dollars for Dame Mary Durack's personal literary collection, referred to as 'Section One'. Loath to become embroiled in a family disagreement, they recommended she donate the documents from the office of CD&D ('Section Two') to the Battye Library. The impediment for the author was that acceptance of the offer would have meant separating her own papers, with their many connective manuscripts, historical research, field notes and relevant correspondence, from the contested source material. The family sagas had been reliant on the station ledgers belonging to Patrick Durack, the diaries of M.P. and his brother J.W. Durack, a variety of legal documents and the firm's letter books.

An initial objection to the venue set aside, the main focus for Reg and Bet had become a four-way split of the proceeds from 'Section Two' as might be got from a paying concern. Now, given the sum offered by the National Library for 'Section One', their expectations fell far short of the extravagant figures Bet had been bandying about, an amount likely to be further reduced if Mary were persuaded by unscrupulous 'third parties' that her salvage and use of the papers merited a 'value-added' share.

Over the ensuing months and into 1992, the goalposts changed as often as Bet thought up another tactic. Offering, with use of the royal 'we', to end the dispute if her letters were returned, she seemed to be tendering a truce:

> *We require that any material recently removed from your care ... be returned intact. We request that access to all documents be restored to its former rational basis. Provided these reasonable conditions are met we propose to withdraw from any current negotiations regarding the disposal of the family archives.*[11]

Bowing to pressure from both sides to relinquish the confiscated files, I did so, but not before binding them in tape and locking the archives room.

Bill, who had come to Perth to sort things out, returned to Queensland happy that he had seen the matter settled. But Bill's intimate knowledge of his siblings, forged in his youth, had been only intermittently and inadequately updated over the ensuing decades and he had gone with the patently false refrain that there had never previously been any friction in their harmonious family. Unsure of this, Mary had only to look into her own accurate account of thirty years:

> *Found myself looking through 1980 diary – confronted with contention re distribution of mother's possessions after her death. Much of this problem all too similar to the ongoing nonsense of the family papers not 'rightfully' in my possession. The situation getting me down to a deeper level than I can recall ever feeling before.*[12]

My diary provided her with a sharper reminder: 'Patsy's a more forthright record of the years than mine and many more *personal* details.'[13] Perhaps others also needed reminding. As Bet was already well acquainted with the events, copies of relevant sections of my unsparing diaries were sent to Bill and to Perpetua. This transcript was apparently regarded by the chief protagonists as unsportsmanlike. In a field of hit-and-miss tactics, weapons such as journals contravened the Reginald and Elizabeth Durack code of warfare.

Unwilling to make any move that might stir up further dissent, Mary thought it prudent to refuse the offer from the National Library and keep her papers for the remainder of her days – a decision her children unanimously supported. Returning to the fantasy of the third volume, she was only faintly amused at my suggestion that 'Full Turn of the Wheel' should more aptly be titled 'The Wheel Falls Off'.

The feud had taken its toll on her. That her nearest and dearest had turned upon her with intimations of guile and greed! Terribly knocked, she began overdoing the medication for her insistent back pain and the sleeping tablets to relieve her wakeful nights, until one day I found her unconscious and she was taken to hospital. She was cross about this and what she saw as our over-assiduous care, her main fear being that the incident would be made known to Reg and Bet, who would probably interpret her carelessness as a sign of senility. Beside her bed, I found a few scribbled lines that might well have been her last:

> *Well anyway, who grabbed the stuff*
> *That was it seems at least enough*

To somehow document the crap
That put the family on the map ...

Within a few weeks, the embers were relit. On rethinking the ramifications of a return to the status quo, Bet had no compunction about breaching the previous 'agreement'. With her sister nearing the end of the road and the contested papers soon to become an inheritance, it was vital that Mary should be persuaded to sign a letter agreeing to their joint ownership. She could then be forced by a majority vote to give them up, and since she was so anxious to keep her archives together it was likely everything would go. This would serve the objective of having the Elizabeth Durack letter files transferred from what she perceived as hostile hands to a venue compliant with returning them to her for the purpose of 'collation'. Reg was rallied to a renewed offensive.

> *Reg and Bet here with a letter they hoped I would sign at once saying the material belongs jointly to Reg, Bet, Bill and myself who want it assigned to either the Battye or the National Library. Rang Mike Megaw for advice.*[14]

Michael thought the matter had reached a stage where legal opinion should be sought on the matter of ownership. His good reputation and the faith placed in him by his mother-in-law would be an obstruction in the path of the opposition, their only method of dealing with him being to pronounce him 'an outsider' and belittle his much-valued role in the affairs of our family.

As word of the dispute got abroad, Reg and Bet found it something of a loser to work up a case on Mary's infamy. They would have to step around their sister and expose the real villain. Having hoped from the start that selling the material was of more consequence to me than to my mother, they now believed there was a chance that they could convince her it had been my idea in the first place. While maintaining this line, both Reg and Bet knew full well the truth of the circumstances surrounding the approach to the National Library, and Vin Serventy was happy to confirm his role. In his 1990 memoirs, Serventy recalls an occasion when he was confronted by 'a red-faced Reg' who, without preamble, opened with the accusation: 'It's all your fault. You put the idea into her head to sell the papers. They belong to the family.'[15]

Nevertheless, Reg eagerly picked up on the possibility. Going through correspondence obtained from the National Library, the original letter inviting John Thompson to assess the collection was seized upon as all the proof needed.

> *Letter from Reg regretting I have allowed myself to be 'manoeuvred' into claiming 'possession' of Dad's diaries and other old documents – actually a word I can't recall using over the years – but now a claim under dispute. He regrets my having been 'kept in the dark' and letters 'withheld from me' (this referring to a letter I could not find in my complex files while Bet was here but which was soon found by Patsy.) She is naturally indignant at their suggestion that she invited John Thompson here to go through the archives rather than acting on my behalf.*[16]

The plan to convince his sister that she had not given her agreement to an approach from the National Library, and that her daughter had been the snake in the grass behind the whole thing, saw the stern visage of Reg once again on a southbound plane. Raids for the purpose of catching her alone having become hazardous exercises, he often resorted to driving round and round the block until the coast was clear. For both him and Bet, crossing paths with me was an experience worth going to some lengths to avoid.

Bet's most artful designs thus far not having paid off, and being seen as the perpetrator instead of the victim, she complained to Bill of the toll taken on her 'vital psychic energy' and her health, a painful hip and the need for a walking stick attributed to the strain. Lest he be in any doubt over her motives, she continued to emphasise her role in the salvage of family heritage: 'I feel that Mary, the one we all trusted has betrayed not only us, but mother, Dad and Grandfather too.' Unable to work, she could concentrate on nothing else but the 'terrible impasse'.[17] It had also occurred to her that there were reasons why they should return to an insistence that the Battye Library was the only acceptable venue for the collection in its entirety. Unless there was to be a cut for them, then it was only fair that there should be nothing in it for Mary, or her legatees. Bill having indicated that he was unwilling to become further involved in a fight over money, previous talk of a four-way split was now consigned to false memory, along with their former sanction of the National Library as a repository. A 'spoilers' role could be equally damaging, and it was easier to explain the rift as a result of their being at odds with those to whom Mary had given, or not given, authority to act on her behalf.

All that had gone before was dropped for what could be depicted as a parochial and generational issue:

> *Reg, Bet and Bill now contending the papers are more relevant to WA and better all donated (or willed) to the Battye than divided by the NLA. Strange, as I thought their interest aroused by the suggestion of possible payment?*[18]

I could only suppose (her letters aside) that like the fought-over silver tea set, Bet cared nothing for 'the silly old papers' but without the desired victory it had become 'a dog that would not lie down'. Constantly raising the stakes, she recruited Mary's Battye Library friends and associates to personally lean on her. Obsessed by the need to gather allies, sundry supporters were raked up and rallied with her gently aggrieved voice on the phone and elegant script via letters – dupes thrilled to be drawn into the drama and willing to affirm their knowledge of Mary's intentions with regard to her archives. No mention was made to them of pecuniary interest, the concern now entirely confined to the venue. Few would understand that the contested papers amounted to less than a quarter of the whole, an inexpedient fact that had only belatedly come to Bet's attention. To add some bulk to the material under claim, she tried a new tack:

> *Bet asks how I 'came by' boxes of Kim's papers, letters and reports etc, without the consent of the family. She says all this material was 'willed by him to Mother'. Got out my diary of 1968 where I have noted the difficult job putting Kim's effects together – especially as he had no will.*[19]

Bet was beyond scruple. Not herself having kept a daily record, if she wanted something to be so, she simply pronounced it as so and until proved wrong, 'definitely remembered it'.

Not a day passed that I did not lament the diminished strength of the Miller family. The presence of Robin and Julie would have been a powerful deterrent to an unprincipled move on their mother. We were also weakened by the loss of Uncle Kim, whose stance against any scheme attacking the integrity of his sister Mary would have been beyond doubt. And Gran would have had none of it.

~

Ros Golding by now having left for greener and more tranquil fields (a job at the zoo), another secretary was appointed. Elaine Ellis was a lucky find and she grasped the complicated family situation with calm intelligence. Mary took an instant liking to her and was comforted by her gentle and quietly helpful presence. There was little to do now but assist with the daily searches, take phone messages, type letters and provide transport when necessary, but Mary – and we – could not have managed without her.

Anxious to see the family reunited, Professor Geoffrey Bolton came up with a suggestion that perhaps the Battye Library already had a legitimate claim to the papers. For the claimants, the possibility that the state might act as their surrogates was an exciting one. The Library Board was aware that the prospect of a substantial donation had been subverted, but Bolton's notion had not occurred to them, their understanding being that the papers on loan had been returned to the owner in 1971. It was only when Bet notified them that historic documents and others over which she and Reg held 'confidentiality' were being held in – or possibly dispersed from – a shed to which no-one was allowed access and all contact between them and Mary was being obstructed by Patsy, that board members had sat up and taken notice. Mary's old colleagues had likely been deeply affected to hear that her wish to see the archives in their safe hands had been circumvented by an intimidating daughter, and that she no longer had control.[20] In letters to Bill, Bet had begun to refer to me as 'poor Patsy', indicating that I was a mental case deserving of sympathy – a disclosure that had also been useful when putting library personnel in the picture. The Library Board set about raising a case on the strength of little more than a remembered verbal intention.

In February 1993, the Library and Information Services of Western Australia (LISWA), incorporating the Battye Library, wrote to Mary to lay an official claim. Blandly disregarding more than twenty years of silence concerning the material, the letter began: 'We are anxious to update our long-standing agreement with you going back to 1960 when you donated what we have come to speak of as "The Durack Papers".' They offered, in lieu of documents of acquisition, legal agreement or so much as a letter of intent (and the search had been diligent), the loan chit signed by Mary at the time of retrieval, which she had supposed was a standard receipt.

> *Sounds as though [the Library] has been in communication with Bet and Reg re my having 'borrowed' the family papers 'gifted' to the Battye when starting on* Sons *and not since returned – continuation of the issue we all want cleared up.*[21]

With the Library Board demanding an immediate return of their property, now we were fighting on two fronts. While Bet shamelessly declared 'it no longer has anything to do with us', the ceaseless harassment by the original claimants was now on behalf of the Battye Library. The matter seemingly clarified for him, Bill felt better about 'going with the majority' against his sister. This was a hard blow. With few illusions about Bet and Reg, Mary had always relied on Bill's good sense and had valued his counsel in family matters. Was Bill now telling her that she was doing something illegal by not giving up the documents? Nervous of even minor infringements, she had a healthy respect for 'the law', an inherency born perhaps of ancestral oppression. Bewildered and distrait, she complained of sleepless nights, dizzy spells and persistent muscular spasms in her back.

~

As Marie Rose and I sent out invitations across Australia for Mary's eightieth birthday, the shadow of a house divided cast a pall over the intended celebration. Always more comfortable in the giving rather than the taking, our mother had not been overly gratified at the prospect of a lavish party reminding her of the significant milestone. On this occasion, while we went to considerable lengths to contact still-living friends and associates, we were sympathetic to the reason for her lack of enthusiasm.

It was an awkward situation, but civility saw RSVP invitations sent to Reg and Enid, Bet and Perpetua, which went unanswered. Upholding the unmannerly strategy, Reg absented himself, but there under the fairy lights, hobnobbing with the assembled crowd, suddenly appeared a serene and sociable Bet – in her wake, a visibly uncomfortable Perpetua and Enid. Having in the interim advised her sister that her participation would depend upon surrender to demands from the Battye, for Bet, non-attendance had never been an option. Maintaining a perception of unity was vital. Whatever the so-called 'family dispute' was about, it was not between the siblings whose close bond could be observed as unaltered.

The birthday party was the first of a series of tributes. Feted in the press and on television, Mary stoically faced the university lunches and FAW festivities, but given their recent letter of demand, the elaborate homage from the Library Board had seemed an inept gesture and typical of the botch-ups in this special year gone awry. Accepting the story of a great lady unhappily dominated by her children, none of whom were invited to the event, LISWA had reserved front-row seats for Reg and Bet.

~

For the first time in many decades, the previous year had seen an end to Mary's usual travels, and it seemed doubtful that she would ever again go north or visit her Aboriginal friends, who had been anxiously ringing from Kununurra. Among Australian notables interviewed in 1992 by Peter Ross in the ABC TV series *A Life*, she had reminisced about early days on the stations and the many lasting associations made with the Indigenous people, who she loved as well as, and sometimes more than, her own family. Responding to questions with as much accuracy as she was able to muster, elusive matters were passed over with a sad smile and a wave of the hand: 'It's all somewhere in my diaries.'

Apologies were made for SHOF meetings missed, an interview with Ray Martin was declined, and an invitation to attend the elaborate Sydney launch by Rupert Murdoch of R.M. Williams's *Collected Australian Verse* somehow got lost under the table.

~

Operating in the manner of a keen player from a Borgian court, Bet schemed tirelessly, gathering and manipulating a multitude of tenuous threads drawn from a miscellany of spheres. The altercation entirely proactive on their parts, for her and Reg our slowness in responding to each new and groaningly received assault had been infuriating.

With the matter now public knowledge, it was still not easy to explain the nature of the outrage to the many enquirers and Mary Durack fans. The conflict patently lacked an element of wider concern, something that would shock everyone into understanding the claimants' real fears. Bet found it. A letter from Bill dated 20 August 1993 was delivered to Mary's hand with what was, to her, an extraordinary premise:

> We, Reg, Bet and myself, and I am sure you too Mary, do not like to encourage the possibility of the material being fragmented and dispersed and it seems this is likely to occur unless some positive action is taken while we, the senior members of the family, are still about to see that it is properly carried through.

Perhaps Bet had been inspired by rumours that items from the T.G.H. Strehlow collection had been sold overseas for a sum of six million dollars.[22] Even so, it was drawing a long bow to imagine European historians queuing up to bid on documents listing the selling price of Durham Shorthorns in 1912 and the cattle tick infestation of 1902 in a remote corner of the Antipodes. We will never know what exactly was passed to Bill, or how he came to swallow it, but since he did it is no wonder he brought his full force to bear in condemnation. This was information that made everyone pay attention in a most satisfying way. In the absence of tenable wrongdoing on the part of their sister or any member of her family, the opposition could only sustain a case by slanderous and inflammatory bunkum. The downside was Mary's reaction to such a wild assertion. And smelling salts had to be applied to revive me.

To further confuse the issue, the Battye Library undertook to match the National Library's offer for Mary's personal documents, this amount later raised by an unexplained (since they claimed to own the CD&D material) 20,000 dollars. It was an unsolicited tender unlikely to have been approved by the disputants, although to see the papers in the hands of the Battye by whatever means may have represented a win of sorts. Mary could only reiterate that they were no longer for sale. When sought by the press for his reaction, Reg claimed our support for her decision was a ploy to 'hold out for the highest bidder'.[23]

~

As a measure of her low state of health and spirits, Mary had turned down an invitation to a bush bash fundraiser for the RFDS, to be attended by, among many luminaries, her dear pals Barry Humphries and 'Smoky Dusty'. A previous 'Evening at the Homestead' for the SHOF at Carlton Station had been an occasion made most congenial by the royal treatment accorded her by property owners Sue and David Bradley. In her letter of apology, Mary had assured her Kimberley friends that she would see them when 'this sad family contention is at an end'.[24] It did not occur to her that the opportunity might not arise again. But a day before the event, it occurred to me.

All at once, my mother found herself pulled from her vague, muddling routine and swept along in a fury of activity – tickets booked, bag packed, phone calls made – too late for an appointment with the hairdresser. I could see that, although feebly protesting, she rather liked being gathered up willy-nilly by a force beyond her control. Transported from Kununurra to Carlton in the Bradleys' Ultralite helicopter, she found herself as in a dream, skimming the Ord, hovering over House Roof Hill, blowing a myriad of birds from the Ivanhoe Billabong, chasing kangaroos and galloping cattle across the land of her first memories. Beyond the agricultural plots fed by the lake and the place where her brother Kim had first set up his vision of green pastures, she took a turn above the Argyle Museum site where, within a blink of time, would stand her own grave. Later there had been a boat trip on the lake, and with the old 'chisters' for company a picnic at Black Rock, the waterhole of her youthful idyll.

As the moment came for her departure, the Aboriginal women, knowing they would never see her again, began to beat their heads and wail inconsolably. But she was aloft and away to Broome, 'so haunted for me by many ghosts of the past'.[25] It was a 'boom Broome' now and a lifetime's journey from the shabby, white-roofed town where the Miller family had rattled around the dusty roads in Horrie's wartime wagon. And there it goes beneath the wing, the red peninsula jutting into the turquoise sea, the white stretch of Cable Beach, the waves breaking against the jumbled rocks of Gantheaume Point where Horrie had plucked the big fish from the mountainous sea. It goes and goes and goes forever …

And back to purgatory. In the belief that 'constant and sufficient rubbing will finally wear away the stone',[26] never before had the heat been turned up so fiercely as in August and September of 1993. The Battye Library, still hesitant to take off the gloves, hoped the matter could yet be resolved by persuasion from the interested parties. They could not have had stronger champions.

'The papers belong to the Battye Library. Full stop!' was the line Reg favoured for the press. If I had not been so exasperated, I might have wept to see my mother, day after day, sitting at her desk 'working' on the problem. Perhaps if she went back far enough into her diaries – listing dates, transcribing conversations – she could somehow edit this broken text into an intelligible narrative. Sometimes she banged her fists down and rattled her rings in distress: 'I don't want to talk about it *anymore*.' If her life had depended upon it (and it may well have), after four miserable years she could no longer raise an arm against the rogue and ruffian forces calculated to reduce her to a state where, had we allowed it, she would have agreed to anything in order to make it all go away. Mary's siblings had counted on a walkover, and they knew very well that only the intervention of her family, whom they considered not much of a threat, had stood in the way of 'business as usual'.

Unable to contemplate accepting the invitation to open Nutcote, the May Gibbs museum in Sydney, she asked Bet to appear and make a speech on her behalf, knowing that this prestigious all-expenses-paid role was something her sister would be eager to undertake. It was pathetic to see her trying to converse as of old to her sister and brothers, to recover some semblance of normalcy with discussions on other subjects and family matters. But wise to this, Reg and Bet let her know that until she 'did the right thing', they were no longer interested in everyday exchanges, even deputising at the Nutcote event conditional on her capitulation. It was all about punishment now.

By mid-1994 it was clear that further coercion would be of no use. Reg, in his capacity as adviser to the Library Board, thought it timely for the legal guns to be rolled out. Delivered directly to Mary's hand, a requisition order aimed at allowing officers of the library to enter the archives room and forcibly remove the documents unnerved her. While we countered the move, it was not easy to calm her fears of a midnight raid. (How eagerly did her assailants await news of the outcome of each new barrage.) Following this failure, a Supreme Court writ was prepared.

In September Mary was admitted to hospital for tests to get to the root cause of her back pain. Hoping for a rest, the discovery of Reg a few doors down being treated for a prostate problem had set her on edge. Visiting family members from opposing sides (including Bet with a broken arm in this ludicrous geriatric circus) ran into one another, and the temperature of the Riverina Ward at Bethesda Hospital dropped with the frequency of icy encounters.

The doctor's sombre face and manner as he drew me aside signalled what was to be imparted. Barely had the patient been informed before the private tidings were somehow out the door and to the ears of the Library Board. The director, after all a human being, assumed that in the circumstances Reg and Bet would want to put a stop on the delivery of a writ of summons from the Crown Solicitor's Office. However, in a memo of contact dated 29 September, Chris Coggin noted a telephone call from Reg to confirm his sister had cancer, 'seemingly far advanced', and for that reason he urged the pursuance of the papers to be 'expedited as assiduously as possible'. He summed this up in the words 'Go for it!'

Offered a chance of salvation, with those words, Reginald Wyndham Durack lost his own immortal soul. Full stop!

On the defendant's behalf, Michael Megaw received the Command from Elizabeth the Second, by the Grace of God, Queen of Australia, Head of the Commonwealth – the very same who had conferred the honours upon Dame Mary Durack and who had sat beside her at the opening of the Stockman's Hall of Fame – that she should appear in an action at the suit of the plaintiff. Saying she was 'not up to it', Mary turned aside Michael's attempts to inform her of the action. Anticipating that we might try to keep the advice from her, Reg took it upon himself to slide down the corridor for the purpose of passing the bad news to his sister.

A written request from us to Reg and Bet that they show a little compassion (if they wished to visit their sister in her final days) by withdrawing their 'full support' from such savagery went unanswered. Library documents sent to us during the later discovery process confirmed beyond our worst suspicions the degree to which Mary's nearest and dearest had instigated, urged and finally given the green light to the writ. Yet, flatly denying their deep and continued involvement, they had presented innocent public faces, protesting that they should not be held accountable because the Battye Library had made a rightful demand for the return of property.

The threat of the attendant expense of a legal battle (likely to cost more than the papers were worth) beyond our means, we made an appeal for the matter to be settled by mediation or an appointed arbitrator. Despite our conviction that the whole affair had been from the start without merit, we agreed to accept unconditionally the findings. Our proposal was rejected. The library, with access to the public purse, had been made aware of our modest means and it seemed at this point that we had been backed into a corner.

~

Bringing our mother home, with the assistance of Silver Chain carers – the latter always happily embraced with the story of how Frances Cherry, a relative of her mother, had been a founding nurse for the service – Marie Rose and I took shifts so that she was never alone. Disinclined to dwell on the grim prognosis, her diary records only her relief to be once more in familiar surrounds and that 'Patsy and Marie will be with me for a few weeks until I am right again'.[27]

Sitting at her work desk, she diligently applied herself to the mail.

'Who is this from?' she asked. 'Do you recognise the name? They seem to know me well. So many *mysteries*, dear.'

'Don't bother with that, Mum.' From her hand I removed the long yearly photocopied 'catch-up screed'.

'It's some kind of a new idea, I get a lot of these now and I read them for clues to the senders.'

Dictating replies to friends and strangers alike, she added a shaky signature that said it all. Picking up the latest script for the *Kings* TV series, she marked dialogue to be rewritten and noted historical inaccuracies. As the long day faded, she moved to the lounge room to watch the incomprehensible TV news and eat a mouthful of unrelished food.

~

But who is this I perceive lurking in the garden? Why, it's Bet, whose immoderate actions have rendered her, after sixty years of open house, a furtive trespasser. Here is the latest battleline. Forbidden entry, she *will* get into the house by hook or by crook. I hear the back door open, the creak of the kitchen floor and she is standing in the dimly lit hall. I give no indication of it, but she knows I am aware she is there.

'Hello Pat.'

'Hello Bet.'

The television is on. The patient is asleep in her chair.

'I won't wake her.'

She perches on the armrest next to her sister's frail, somnolent form. I sit silent and motionless. She is breathing fast – I can *hear* her heartbeat – she is trying to control her fear. After about ten minutes she rises to leave. Defiance is the name of this apparently thankless exercise.

'Goodbye Pat.'

'Goodbye Bet.'

Suddenly she reaches out and gives my arm a terrible squeeze with her good hand. The other is caught up in a sling. Mary droops between us, unconscious.

'All you have to do is apologise and it's *all over*,' she whispers intensely.

I shake her off, hard and cold. What? Does she think even now she has the power to halt the grinding purpose of the State Library Board, the set-in-motion machinery of the law? Does she think the misery of the last four years of my mother's life, the hounding of her unto her death, can be so easily dismissed? There is no doubt in my mind what she wants the apology for – she has never moved on from our long-ago confrontation in the file room. Now she is begging my complicity in a tactical retreat. She wants to jump this sinking ship.

~

My diary minutes the mind-numbing ritual of the invalid's routine from rise to sink: the blankets, hot pads and pillows, potions, lotions and pills; back rubbing, clock moving, pen finding, foot-stool adjusting, cushion plumping, curtain closing – glasses, lights, cardigans, doors, cool drinks, this and that and that and this. After broken sleep, she rose as ever at seven in the morning and dressed herself before waking me, groggy from the night's disturbance.

'Can you get yourself on deck, dear, in case someone comes? I don't really want to see anyone just yet.' Almost to the last, she – and then we – would make up her face and don the full ensemble, not neglecting petticoat, stockings, beads and earrings. For as long as she was able, she kept to the safety of her beaten track. She did not like people to call in and find her without pen in hand, labouring over some task, and explaining what she was doing also diverted the conversation from paths she preferred to avoid.

With or without advance warning, visitors came in a steady stream. Most were aware that their visit would be in the nature of a farewell and few could resist several encores. Mindful that sick-room attendance may have removed us from immediate earshot, how they did *RINGGG* the doorbell, until we disabled it. If we were distracted, they would find an open door and tiptoe up the passage to her room. As the invalid opened her eyes, there emerged from behind an immense flower arrangement the nightmarish face of Edna Everage, and the next day Barry Humphries with apologies for the intrusion of his inconsiderate alter ego. Then another ordeal was upon us:

> *10 Oct. The West Australian on the phone first thing to say Gerry Glaskin had informed them of the writ, though mentioned to him only in the greatest confidence. He seems to have told them it was about a claim to family diaries. Followed by calls from media in other states, many demanding to talk to MDM personally. Frantic confabs back and forth with Michael who tried to hose things down without much success.*
>
> *11 Oct. Headlines: Author Sued for Diaries. Mike wanting a statement from Mum, Elaine typing for her – dashed it into the city – Naomi tearing down posters all along the Terrace, Dying Dame in Diaries Fight. Johnson fronted the TV cameras on 7.30 Report, Mike doing other news outlets. Yagan took on the Howard Sattler talkback. Gerry seems to have thrust himself forward as MDM's staunchest ally, determined to link our dispute to his own crazy row with the Battye. But as it was he who accompanied Mum to the Library in 1960 when she left the Durack papers for safekeeping, he may be needed as a witness.*
>
> *12 Oct. Headlines: Author Caught in Long Paper Chase. Many calls from supporters. Vin Serventy writing letters to Arts Minister Peter Foss and the Library Board. I am not giving the newspapers to Mum, although she asks every day where they are. I don't want her to see the crude references to her illness, 'stomach cancer' – 'two months to live' and in* The Australian *this am, 'intestinal cancer'. No doubt Reg would call this 'keeping things from her'. Tom Stephens MLC to bring the matter up in Parliament. Gerry Glaskin's protest on our behalf has now taken the form of ripping up his original manuscripts in an act of defiant destruction until the Battye agrees to drop the case.*[28]

From now on, we were under siege. The phone rang nonstop and reporters knocked at the door while photographers, refused entry, scouted round for a through-the-window photo of the dying dame.

Public affront was severely damaging to the plaintiff. Never before in its history had the esteemed State Library been subjected to such censure and vilification, including from potential donors. The very idea of suing a well-loved National Literary Treasure was cause for loud outcry, and had we not been so anxious to close the doors on all but the necessities for a peaceful and dignified passing, the deluge of support would have been heartwarming.

Fearful his surrogates might waver or in some misguided integrity dilute their purpose, Reg divulged certain information to the Library Board. This in turn was passed to the state's newly elected premier, Richard Court. Responding to an attack from the opposition for allowing a government instrumentality to pursue through the courts a woman of Dame Mary Durack's standing, the premier announced in parliament that he had been advised ('through a reliable source') that the Durack papers had been offered for sale overseas.

So quickly and effectively was this statement refuted by our team, now including a law firm, that the Court Government was within a few days forced to concede error, though without an apology. After a damage control meeting with the equally derelict Library Board, the Minister for the Arts let it be known that while the writ remained in force, it would not be executed during Dame Mary's lifetime. The board was ordered to re-enter negotiations with her family. Badly bitten, from this point the library would distance itself from R. Durack and E.D. Clancy.

Reg was now in a frenzy of rage. In his weakening state, for the remaining year until the dispute was settled, according to Bet, its resolution would become the only thing keeping him alive.[29] From this point he took control of the situation so that she was able to begin the process of detaching herself. In a letter to Bill, she professed herself 'bored' with it. One could surmise that she was – the game had lost its zest and the writing was on the wall for the finale. To whatever extent it had emerged as a surreal expression of her innermost commotion, once out of her system it was gone – put aside for the next exploit.

Meanwhile, Mary was dying and she was being kept away. There was some mileage to be extracted from bewailing the cruelty of banishment from the deathbed, but not much. Her last chance came in late October when her sister was readmitted to hospital for a few days. With a nervous eye on the door, wicked Bet could not have been other than impressed at the devastation she had wrought upon the once fair landscape. A lifetime of follies behind her, how to smooth over this one represented a challenge indeed.

Nothing can be said to absolve the actions of Bet and her brothers. In the hands of Mary (or her legatees), the Durack papers were never going elsewhere than to an appropriate venue. But in the light of debts owed, had she wished to sell them abroad or make a grand bonfire of them in the Mildew incinerator, by all that was right under heaven her siblings had no choice but to bow to her will in the matter. So far was Bet in arrears that she could not over several lifetimes have redeemed the overdraft. From the remove of his own good fortune, the tragedies his sister had borne had not given Reg a moment's pause. As for poor bamboozled Bill: for once in his life, his good judgement had failed him.[30] That they had not meant to hurt Mary but her family, and in particular me, is plain enough, but if in the process that was the result, then their relentless pursuit of a barren cause could not then, now or ever be excused.

~

Never in her life idle, Mary felt guilty at her inaction and unsure of her role.

'I don't know what I am supposed to be doing.'

It was not possible that there was nothing outstanding, a 'main job', a meeting to be attended, a plane to catch. She worried about her inability to be at everyone's disposal, as had always been the way of it. I contrived events and cancelled them for her, my subterfuge calming her.

'Well, there is a fellowship do on tonight, Mum, but I thought you wouldn't be up to it, so I sent your apologies.'

'Oh thank goodness, I don't think I could have gone.'

When she became confused by the telephone calls and many voices she knew but could not put a name to, we took over and conveyed messages of thanks and love while filtering out the intrusive demands: the foreword, a glance at a manuscript, a signature on her books, endorsements for sundry honours and awards ...

Once for Bet's amusement, my mother had written an account of a lively night at the mercy of the infant Patsy. As my diary spells out the minutiae of the deathwatch, she is reimbursed:

> *the deadly, long afternoon – the ever-slower haul up the ever-longer passage – step by tiny faltering step. I hold her arm. She stares at her sunken face in the bathroom mirror with bewilderment but without comment – my face behind – reflecting a ghost and a ghost in waiting.*[31]

Her last decipherable diary entry was made on 24 October: 'Sue Bradley rang from Kununurra. She says my Aboriginal relations are singing me better. I hope I can hear them.' The time had come to lay down her pen.

~

We ran a ramp over the front steps for the wheelchair. Enduring a turn around the garden paths worn hollow by her tread, she was embarrassed that the neighbours might see her in such a state of infirmity. There was no relief to be found in any position. As we moved her up and down and from one place to another, anywhere looked better than where she was.

'I want to go home.'

'You are home, Mum.'

She looked at me doubtfully. 'Are you sure?'

'Do you want me to tell Johnson about Bob Hill?'

From her astonishment, I realised that my harbouring of her secret had been unappreciated. She had decided I could not know.

'Well, it's all a very long time ago, so whatever you think you know, you had better keep to yourself.'

'I think Johnson may know anyway.'

'Then it doesn't matter.'

The nights were long and restless, her sick dreams fraught with peril: 'Oh, hold me, don't let me roll into the camp fire.'

The morphine we referred to as 'the respiratory mixture' gave her hallucinations.

'Who are those very nice people over there?' she asked, tremulously pointing to the corner of her room, where there was nothing but an oxygen bottle. 'I am afraid I may have asked them in for a meal, dear. Take them down to the lounge and give them a cup of tea – they seem to be members of the family but I don't know from which branch. You will have to introduce yourselves to one another.' Even in her wanderings, she remained in character.

Her responsible son-in-law Michael, worried that she may not have fully grasped her predicament, believed we had an obligation to make sure she understood in case she wanted to see a priest or relatives, albeit delinquent. We were curious about her apparent state of denial. Had she blinkered herself against the knowledge of her own demise? Or were there perhaps two sides of the story, hers and the doctors', and she was remaining neutral? Tentatively I broached the subject.

'I'm afraid that despite all we are doing, Mum, you might just peg out on us.'

'Oh yes, that's how I feel. Is it too late to call in the Flying Doctor?'

'I don't think … anything much more can be done.'

'But that's mad, dear,' she said faintly.

'The thing is, in the circumstances, do you want to see Reg or Bet?'

'No.' She was quite firm. 'Not right now, at any rate. Later when – and if – I feel better.'

'Do you want a priest to give you the blessing of the church?'

'Oh no, I don't want any of that. Father McMahon comes to see me.'

I knew what she meant. It was mad. Why, the sheer weight of work to be done excluded the indulgence of death. How could all those needy people get on without her? How could such a vast network of connections be broken, that complicated household, rooted and cemented, close down, be lost and brought to dust? We did not raise the subject again, leaving it to her if she felt 'moved to speak'.

On 14 December, when she asked how long until Christmas, I thought we had best bring the celebration forward. The following day, putting away the apparatus of the sick room, we decorated the tree and as she registered the familiar ritual the invalid seemed revived, the mere appearance of normal activity easing her bewilderment at the irregular turn her life had taken. Greeting family, old friends and neighbours affectionately, she rallied to the occasion and, raising a glass of champagne, gave her customary salute, 'Cheers, dears'. With her children and grandchildren present, soothed by the sounds of laughter and life flowing around her, she fell asleep.

Opening her eyes in the morning, she remarked with calm resignation, 'This will be the last day of my life.' Taking off her rings, she placed them in the hand of Marie Rose. She looked sweet and serene, like the good child who had written *Little Poems of Sunshine* to please her parents. Gazing at a creamy magnolia flower picked from the tree outside her window, she made a feeble gesture as if to find the sketchbook and pens once always kept within reach. The phone rang and it was Smoky Dawson with a homely message. She recognised the name.

'Am I in Broome?'

Her surrounds dim and mutable, so had I become a shadowy figure of no defined origin.

'Do you know who I am, Mum?'

After some hesitation, 'I think … I think I call you Patsy.' Then, vaguely accepting me as connected to her in some way: 'I don't know what you are waiting for but I'm waiting for it too.'

Above her bed hung a formal portrait of the proud young mother holding her firstborn child. Looking from the beautiful, vital face to the current reality, I saw it had come to this: the baby seeing her out. But if one contemplated the haphazard nature of mortal existence, then within the great scheme of things this made sense. She had lived a life and a half during her long journey, and bearing in mind the lines from André Malraux she had often quoted:

> *The greatest mystery is not that we have been flung at random between the profusion of the earth and the galaxy of the stars, but that in this prison we can fashion images of ourselves sufficiently powerful to deny our nothingness ...*[32]

Her works would transcend time, and in the process of writing them she had made a lasting mark upon the literary landscape.

~

Taking the night shift, I saw that she had embarked upon the last stretch of the road. Lying beside her, I held her and sang the old songs she used to sing to us as children: 'Daisy, Daisy', 'Row, Row, Row your Boat', 'I Know Where I'm Going' ... For a while she faintly hummed along. Through the long hours, my tearful voice croaked on, 'Waltzing Matilda' with her all the way to the gate through which only she could pass. I sang and talked to her and held her and told her I would not let her roll into the camp fire. I spoke to her of those whose names brought her comfort: Robin, Julie, Horrie, Gran, Kim ... talked and sang and held her. I felt the cold sweat of death, heard her last breath and then the silence. She lay in my arms, the familiar work-worn hands stilled. Only a small uncoupling and yet how strange and wondrous a transition. That great river of life – that force – run its course.

~

There seemed no other place she should go but to her 'spirit country'. After the elaborate Perth funeral, we took her north to the Argyle Museum site and laid her among the family graves rescued from the flood, her grieving 'chisters' and other Aboriginal friends travelling from the reserve and far-flung stations to attend the ceremony. It seemed appropriate that she should have the last word, the silenced voice brought to life on tape speaking the words of 'Lament for the Drowned Country'. Given her gregarious nature, it may have pleased her to know that she would continue to attract visitors, there in the place of her heart and dreams. It was a good idea destined, whether she liked it or not, to be emulated.[33]

EPILOGUE

In March 1995, Marianne Korwill died. During the gathering at the Korwill house after the funeral, Marie Rose and I were suddenly confronted by Bet, whom we had not seen since her well-separated attendance at our mother's requiem mass. Stretching her arms wide, and with a placatory smile, she announced for the benefit of the assembly: 'Now give your old Aunty Bet a kiss and we'll forget all about the silly papers dispute.' Her bid for a public reconciliation openly rebuffed, she would never forgive us for not forgiving her. Fatally freed from Mary's restraining hand, she was soon heading for the next – and ultimate – reckless stunt. Eddie Burrup was just over the horizon.[1]

In the final accounting, Bet would be the engineer of that which she sought most to prevent. Through her letters, I have learned her secrets, followed in her track, walked around in her mind and known her very soul. Reliving her highs and lows, her wild creative urges, I have seen with her eyes and understood the chimera that drove her to an emotional plane beyond the ken of ordinary mortals. Somewhere there is a part of me that will always miss the old 'Aunty Bumbles', whose entrance once picked up the tempo of our lives with her inimitable style and humour. Changing faces and motivations according to requirements, even her pictures subject to caveat emptor, she was a genuine miracle of contrivance – one who would nonetheless produce images powerful enough to eclipse anything that might be revealed by her puny detractors, including this niece.

In a 1995 mediated settlement of their claim, LISWA would take possession of the original diaries of the Durack brothers, M.P. and J.W. – the face-saving outcome, at their behest, kept confidential. Twelve years later, they would acquire the remainder.

The family house having vanished along with the principal actors, still holding the old address, it is a disembodying experience for me to inhabit the same space where once the drama took place, a few trees standing to navigate this or that precise spot.

As I disappeared in a sea of papers, one might have wondered if the conclusive revenge had been wreaked upon me. Lost among the shades of long ago, I worked in my mother's former domain, her sometimes uneasy and reproachful presence at my side. The tedious paper chases of her day are at an end. Although the creative intellect that transformed a mass of disconnected words into memorable prose is gone, where once there was disarray, now there is order. My contribution according to my talents in the area of the practical and prosaic, 150 years of history can now be discovered at the touch of a computer key. Would my mother be pleased, or Horrie grateful for the preservation of his better self? Would Uncle Kim be appreciative of the hours that went into capturing the faint traces on the carbons of his letter books? Or would they tell me I should have got a life?

Through the pages of my mother's diaries, I relive our close and sometimes embattled relationship – the furious love and jealous guardianship of her creative flame that yet demands my vigilance.

CONVERSIONS

acre	0.4 hectare
yard	0.9 metre
mile	1.6 kilometres
foot	30.5 centimetres
square mile	2.6 square kilometres
ton	0.9 tonne

Australian currency changed from pounds, shillings and pence to dollars and cents in 1966. Because of variations in currency values over time, actual conversions are difficult. At the time of the changeover, the following conversions applied:

1 penny	1 cent
1 shilling	10 cents
1 pound	2 dollars

ENDNOTES

LOCATION OF SOURCES
All quotes, unless otherwise noted, are sourced from the Mary Durack Miller papers, held by SLWA (Acc. 7273A). In addition to Mary Durack's literary papers, diaries and correspondence files, the MDM papers include diaries and correspondence of Bess Durack, M.P. Durack, Reg Durack, Elizabeth Durack Clancy, Kim Durack, Bill Durack and Horrie Miller.

Original correspondence between MDM and Florence James is held by the State Library of New South Wales.

Robin Miller's diaries and the Horrie Miller aviation archives are held by the NLA. Personal correspondence between Robin, Horrie and MDM is among MDM papers, SLWA.

ABBREVIATIONS USED IN NOTES
EDC	Elizabeth Durack Clancy
HCM	Horrie Clive Miller
KMD	Kimberley (Kim) Michael Durack
MDM*	Mary Durack Miller
MPD	Michael Patrick Durack
NLA	National Library of Australia
PMM	Patsy Mary Millett
RM	Robin Miller
RMD	Robin Miller Dicks
RWD	Reginald (Reg) Wyndham Durack
SLWA	State Library of Western Australia

*To the end of her days always adding the Miller appendage to her name, Mary Durack Miller was also known by her initials.

PREFACE
1   Brenda Niall wrote a version of the lives of Mary and Elizabeth Durack in 2012. *True North* (Text Publishing) was based on a theme that the sisters' mutual creativity had been founded in an unbroken spiritual link to the East Kimberley region of Western Australia.

1 – MILDEW
1   K.S. Prichard to MDM, 10 October 1939.
2   'The Young Know' remains in manuscript form, unpublished.
3   MDM to EDC, October 1942.
4   The name 'Gertrude' is sometimes included in Mary Durack biographical material;

	this was an informal Catholic confirmation name.
5	The story of how he tampered with the ballot box is in HCM's unpublished memoirs 'Out of the Blue'.
6	HCM (Adelaide) to MDM (Perth), 1941.
7	The prescient views of half a century ago as written by Gordon Colebatch can be found online.
8	The clock was a memorial to WA campaigner for women's rights Edith Dircksey Cowan.

2 – THE WIDER CIRCLE

1	MDM to her brother David Durack, 1943.
2	EDC to MDM, February 1946.
3	ibid., 21 May 1946.
4	MDM to MPD, 7 July 1944.
5	HCM to MDM, 17 March 1946.
6	EDC to MDM, 15 December 1945.
7	HCM to MDM, 17 March 1946.
8	EDC to MDM, 30 August 1944.
9	H. Drake-Brockman, *Australian Writers and their Works: Katharine Susannah Prichard*, Oxford University Press, 1967.
10	E. Hill to MDM, 24 July 1949.
11	ibid., 9 March 1950.
12	B. Humphries, *The Barry Humphries Book of Innocent Austral Verse*, Sun Books, 1968.
13	E. Hill to Anne Tully, a Queensland Durack relative, 4 January 1950, held in MDM papers.
14	EDC to MPD, 8 March 1949. The letter is an impassioned plea from EDC to her father not to sell the stations.
15	Interview with Sandra Simmons, 'Mary Durack's Literary Race Against Time', *The Bulletin*, 17 July 1979.
16	MDM to K. McArthur, 19 October 1950.
17	ibid., 21 June 1953.
18	KMD to MDM, n.d. 1948.
19	ibid., 29 October 1952.
20	MDM to EDC, 29 July 1951.
21	Descriptions of Dampier Downs from MDM to EDC, 29 June 1951.
22	MDM to K. McArthur, 4 July 1951.
23	M.D. Miller and F. Rutter, *Child Artists of the Australian Bush*, George Harrap and Co., 1952.
24	MDM to K. McArthur, 29 October 1952.
25	EDC to MDM, 15 July 1951.
26	Paraphrase of EDC to MDM, 1 August 1951.
27	KMD to RWD, 3 June 1950.
28	F. Clancy, *They Built a Nation*, New Century Press, 1939.
29	EDC to MDM, 26 February 1950.
30	ibid., 12 December 1946.
31	Bess Durack diary, 24 March 1960.
32	MDM to EDC, 1 February 1942.
33	ibid., 25 February 1946.
34	D.C. Congdon, *Casey's Wife*, Artlook Books, 1982.
35	EDC to MDM, 25 July 1951.

3 – BROOME

1. MDM to K. McArthur, 28 April 1952.
2. MMA DC3 crash, 2 July 1949. The aircraft went down nine miles north of Perth.
3. MDM to K. McArthur, 2 December 1952.
4. HCM to MDM, 1959.
5. MDM to EDC, 12 July 1951.
6. EDC to MDM, 9 March 1946.
7. MDM to K. McArthur, 2 December 1952.
8. ibid.
9. M. Durack, 'Lament to Galahan – the Law-Giver', *Winthrop Review*, 1952.
10. 'Ali Bin and the Soldier Crab' and 'Creepy the Crab' remain unpublished.
11. Dr C.E. Cook, CBE, later a director of the Department of Health, Canberra.
12. Incident recorded in diary of Bess Durack, 6 September 1949.
13. EDC to MDM, 18 January 1952.
14. ibid.
15. Pages found among MDM Broome papers, n.d.
16. The Bishop's Palace was a famous landmark. Before it was taken over by the Anglican Church, it had been the residence of a pearl buyer whose ghost was reputed to haunt the place after a series of grim events.
17. MDM diary, 2 August 1981.
18. Japanese attack on Broome, 3 March 1942.
19. MDM to Bess Durack, 18 November 1952.
20. MDM wrote of this phenomenon in 'Wild Geese Calling', an article for *The West Australian*, 19 July 1952.
21. A seafaring superstition, to confer their power the rings were cut from a disc of gold and inserted into the ear by slitting the lobe.
22. Introduction to B. Presser, *Broome Reflected*, B.J. Publications, 1977.
23. H. Miller, 'Out of the Blue', unpublished manuscript.
24. HCM to PMM, 31 December 1967.
25. M. Durack, 'Twentieth Wedding Anniversary', 1950s, unpublished.
26. HCM to K. McArthur, 19 December 1952.

4 – DIVERSIONS AND DEVIATIONS

1. MDM to K. McArthur, 1 July 1957.
2. ibid., 1 April 1957. One of the Aboriginal children thus casually acquired was Boxer, who became a CD&D stockman and a lifelong henchman of M.P. Durack.
3. Paul Haeflinger, 'Amateurish Show by Miss Durack', *Sydney Morning Herald*, 3 January 1947.
4. EDC to MDM, 5 August 1940.
5. ibid., 1 March 1947.
6. ibid., 1 August 1951.
7. ibid., 26 March 1946.
8. Rutter continued to espouse the Carrolup cause from abroad. Her personal collection of drawings found its way back to Western Australia in 2013.
9. Bess Durack diary, 25 November 1953.
10. M.P. Durack co-founded the Okes-Durack Kimberley Oil Company, later Freney Kimberley Oil Company, in 1921.
11. KMD to MDM, 4 January 1950.
12. EDC to MDM, 24 February 1948.
13. The *Cord to Alcheringa* set, purchased by the University of Western Australia in

1953, was part of a series depicting the artist's expression of Aboriginal ritual symbolism, with a claim to ethnological authenticity that would, in 1995, result in the work being banned for public viewing by the Art Gallery of WA.
14   EDC to MDM, 20 September 1944; 25 July 1949.
15   Bess Durack diary, 4 December 1954.
16   Louise Campbell visited Perth in June 1955. She later became Bob Hill's partner.
17   Information from Ernestine Hill's mother, Mrs Margaret Hemmings, as given to Elizabeth Durack. EDC to MDM, 29 December 1944.
18   Author interview with Bob Hill, 20 December 1996.
19   K.S. Prichard to MDM, 11 September 1955.
20   F. James to MDM, 24 October 1955.
21   HCM to MDM, February 1956.
22   RWD to MDM, 16 November 1955.
23   KMD to MDM, 18 September 1955.
24   Author interview with Bob Hill, 20 December 1996.
25   R. Hill to Rene Foster, August 1972, as recorded in MDM diary, 19 October 1972.
26   Author interview with Bob Hill, 20 December 1996.
27   MDM to K. McArthur, 28 September 1955.
28   The aircraft and five aboard were lost while on a mercy flight from Derby, 5 February 1956.
29   Bess Durack diary, 28 March 1956.
30   F. James to MDM, 19 September 1956; 17 November 1959.
31   D. Stuart, *Yandy*, Georgian House, 1959.

5 – BACK ON TRACK
1   K. McArthur to MDM, 16 April 1957.
2   MDM to K. McArthur, 27 April 1957.
3   ibid., 16 June 1957.
4   *Daily News*, 26 July 1957.
5   F. James to MDM, 14 August 1958.
6   MDM to K. McArthur, 9 April 1959.
7   Bess Durack diary, 22 October 1957.
8   KMD to MDM, 20 February 1961.
9   Bess Durack diary, 31 January 1958.
10 ibid., 29 July 1958.
11 MDM to F. James, 22 June 1964. *Wild Cat Falling* was published in 1965.
12 Victoria Laurie, 'Identity Crisis', *The Australian Magazine*, 20 July 1996.
13 Bess Durack diary, 6 January 1959.
14 Australian composer John Anthill created a sensation with his ballet *Corroboree*, first performed in 1950.
15 Reviewed 23 January 1959 by the *West Australian* critic 'Fidelio' as an 'expressive blend ... of moderately modern and quasi-primitive'.
16 MDM to K. McArthur, 23 June 1959.
17 RWD to Bess Durack, 6 July 1959.
18 Bess Durack diary, 12 May 1959.
19 K. McArthur to MDM, 17 December 1959.
20 MDM to K. McArthur, 26 August 1958.
21 MPD diary, 16 November 1938.
22 ibid., 10 August 1950.
23 First MDM diary entry, 1 January 1960.

24 *Flying Nurse*, Rigby, 1971; *Sugarbird Lady*, Rigby, 1979.
25 Bill Harney party 19 February 1960. Ayers Rock is now more commonly referred to as Uluru.
26 MDM diary, 23 November 1960.
27 MDM to K. McArthur, 23 May 1960.
28 Bess Durack diary, 28 December 1960.
29 MDM diary, 27 May 1960.
30 Bishop John Jobst's untitled memoirs, n.d.
31 EDC to MDM, 8 July 1960.
32 HCM to MDM, 1960.
33 MDM diary, 12 July 1961.
34 HCM to RM, 19 November 1960.
35 MDM diary, 27 December 1960.
36 Bess Durack diary, 26 March 1960.

6 – THE ROCK AND THE SAND

1   MDM to K. McArthur, 14 September 1961.
2   O. Ruhen, review of E. Page Smith, *The Beckoning West: The Story of H.S. Trotman and the Canning Stock Route* (Angus & Robertson, 1966), in *The Australian*, August 1966.
3   MDM diary, 13 January 1961.
4   Bess Durack diary, 19 June 1961.
5   MDM diary, 15 May 1961.
6   ibid., extracts June 1961.
7   MDM diary, January 1962. Ida Mann's autobiographies (as Caroline Gye), *The Cockney and the Crocodile* (1962) and *China 13* (1964), were published by Faber & Faber.
8   MDM diary, 21 February 1962.
9   ibid., 22 March 1962.
10 From MDM diary report of the Adelaide Festival, March 1962.
11 Hal Porter comment to MDM recorded in diary, 27 March 1962.
12 MDM diary, 5 May 1962.
13 ibid., 16 July 1962.
14 ibid., 5 December 1962.
15 EDC to MDM, 14 May 1962.
16 *Yagan of the Bibbulmun* and *The Courteous Savage* published by Thomas Nelson (Australia) Ltd, 1964.
17 'Inspiration is for me a sort of bubble that rises quickly to the surface and bursts – bang ...' EDC to MDM, 15 March 1963.
18 M. Durack and E. Durack, *Kookanoo and the Kangaroo*, Rigby, 1963.
19 MDM to F. James, 4 January 1963.
20 MDM diary, 8 November 1963. 'Miracles Are Everywhere' by Brian Collins was featured in *The Catholic Advocate*, 1964.
21 MDM to F. James, 4 December 1963.
22 M. Durack, 'The Friendly Highway', *Walkabout*, 1964.
23 EDC to Bess Durack, March 1963.
24 EDC to MDM, 1 March 1963.
25 MDM to EDC, 8 March 1963.
26 EDC to MDM, 15 March 1963.
27 ibid., 23 April 1963, describing her trip to East Kimberley.

28	KMD to EDC, 11 September 1963.
29	ibid., 6 April 1964.
30	E. Durack, Part 1: 'Enigma of Our North-West', 4 May 1963; Part 2: 'Collapse of an Ideal', 11 May 1963, *Sydney Morning Herald*.
31	MDM to KMD, 25 May 1963.
32	HCM to MDM, 11 September 1963.
33	MDM to PMM, August 1963.
34	MDM diary, 18 April 1964.
35	X. Herbert, *Disturbing Element*, F.W. Cheshire, 1963.
36	*The West Australian*, 30 April 1964.
37	Xavier Herbert party, 29 April 1964.
38	MDM diary, 30 April 1964.
39	R. Stow to PMM, February 1995.
40	MDM diary, 30 April 1964.
41	ibid., 24 November 1966.
42	M. Durack, *An Australian Settler*, Clarendon Press, 1964.

7 – 'A SURFEIT OF THE FULLNESS OF LIFE'

1	MDM diary, 25 December 1964.
2	ibid., 4 February 1965.
3	Elspeth Huxley visit, March 1965; Alan Paton visit, December 1963.
4	Edith Sitwell visit, 28 March 1963.
5	Johnny O'Keefe visit to Perth and country tour, July 1964.
6	MDM to F. James, 12 January 1965.
7	MDM diary, 13 May 1965.
8	ibid., 15 May 1965.
9	MDM to F. James, 22 June 1965.
10	MDM diary, 18 July 1965.
11	ibid., 21 July 1965.
12	MDM to F. James, 8 November 1965.
13	ibid., 30 October 1965.
14	MDM diary, 29 November 1965.
15	HCM to MDM, 2 August 1970.
16	ibid., May 1966.
17	MDM to F. James, 12 August 1966.
18	HCM to C. Gare, 1 March 1966. Following Gare's death, files pertaining to Miller Investments were returned to the Miller family.
19	Bishop J. Jobst to MDM, 1966.
20	MDM diary, 9 August 1966.
21	EDC to MDM, 27 October 1966.
22	MDM diary, 30 January 1966.
23	ibid., 13 February 1967.
24	ibid., 16 January 1967.
25	Published in *The West Australian*, 14 August 1965.
26	MDM diary, 8 February 1967.
27	ibid., 3 November 1966.
28	HCM to MDM, February 1967.
29	MDM to F. James, 16 September 1967.
30	MDM diary, 5 May 1967.
31	ibid., 21 June 1967.

32 HCM to MDM, June 1967.
33 MDM to F. James, 1 September 1967.
34 ibid., 16 September 1967.
35 HCM to C. Gare, 1 August 1968.
36 MDM diary, 20 September 1967.
37 KMD to MDM, 4 December 1967.
38 HCM to C. Gare, 21 September 1967.
39 MDM to F. James, 16 September 1967.
40 ibid., 1 September 1967.
41 MDM diary, 28 September 1967.
42 ibid., 2 October 1967.
43 ibid., 14 November 1967.
44 MDM to F. James, 1 December 1967.

8 – THE COMING OF THE CROWS
1 MDM diary, 17 April 1968.
2 ibid., 29 May 1968.
3 ibid., 30 May 1968.
4 Bess Durack diary, 22 May 1968.
5 *The West Australian*, 31 June 1968.
6 MDM diary, 27 July 1970.
7 HCM to PMM in Canada, 2 November 1968.
8 *Early Birds* (Rigby) was launched 2 August 1968.
9 HCM to MDM, July 1968.
10 MDM to Bess Durack, 6 October 1968.
11 MDM to RM, 13 September 1968.
12 Noted in list of letters sent, MDM diary, 12 September 1968. Dorothy Hewett abandoned her allegiance to the Communist Party soon afterwards. She resigned as FAW president in October 1968.
13 MDM to PMM, 8 October 1968. Premiere of *Ship of Dreams*, 11 October 1968.
14 MDM diary, 14 October 1968.
15 RM to HCM, 14 December 1967.
16 MDM diary, 28 November 1968.
17 ibid., 31 December 1968.
18 ibid., 15 February 1969.
19 HCM to MDM, March 1969.
20 HCM to C. Gare, 21 January 1969.
21 Enclosure, HCM to MDM, 3 July 1969.
22 MDM diary, 10 July 1969.
23 Bess Durack diary, 10 July 1969.
24 Bess Durack diary, 11 July 1969.
25 MDM diary, 12 July 1969.
26 Bess Durack diary, 12 July 1969.
27 Description of Julie's funeral from MDM to PMM, 21 July 1969.
28 A. Miller to C. Gare, 6 July 1969.
29 Australian Land and Cattle Co. Ltd, under managing director J.M. (Jack) Fletcher, purchased two million hectares in West Kimberley.
30 RM to PMM, August 1969.
31 MDM diary, 17 July 1969.
32 MDM to K. McArthur, 1 August 1969.

33 EDC to MDM, 7 August 1969.
34 MDM to C. Gare, 26 August 1969.
35 Barunga's words quoted in MDM's poetic tribute after his death in 1977, 'Barunga Is Dead', later published in M. Durack, *Pilgrimage* (eds P. and N. Millett), Bantam Books, 2000.
36 MDM diary, 8 June 1969.
37 Among those present at the inaugural meeting on 25 November 1969 were Justice R. Blackburn (chair), H. Giese from the Department of Northern Territory Administration (vice president) and Stefan Haag from the Elizabethan Theatre Trust.
38 V. Williams, 'The Undivided Heart', written for Katharine Susannah Prichard, *Harvest Time and Other Poems*, 2008 (self-published).
39 HCM to MDM, 13 November 1969.
40 MDM diary, 25 December 1969.
41 ibid., 18 December 1969.

9 – CROSS THREADS
1 ibid., 14 January 1970.
2 M. Durack and E. Durack, *The Way of the Whirlwind*, first published 1941. The ballet was performed by Perth City Ballet, directed by Diana Waldron.
3 MDM diary, 7 February 1970.
4 Mary Durack wrote 'Johnny Walker-O' in 1972 as a tribute to the blind stockman. The verse was set to music in 1973 for an ABC series on Australian ballads.
5 MDM diary, 30 June 1970.
6 MDM to F. James, 25 July 1970.
7 'Sidelights', written for the US journal *Contemporary Authors*, 1979.
8 MDM diary, 11 July 1970.
9 MDM diary, 11 October 1970.
10 ibid., 27 July 1970.
11 HCM to MDM, January 1970.
12 MDM diary, 20 October 1970.
13 HCM to MDM, September 1970.
14 ibid., January 1970.
15 MDM diary, 1 November 1970.
16 Verse found in pages of MDM diary, November 1970.
17 MDM diary, 15 November 1970.
18 ibid., 25 November 1970.
19 ibid., 12 January 1971.
20 ibid., 27 January 1971.
21 The first performance was on 22 January 1971.
22 MDM report to the Australian Council for the Arts and ATF, February 1971.
23 MDM diary, 27 January 1964.
24 MDM to PMM, 24 July 1973
25 ibid., 17 March 1971.
26 ibid., 26 March 1971.
27 ibid., 14 September 1971.
28 ibid., 8 September 1971.
29 ibid., 6 September 1971.
30 ibid., 18 September 1971.
31 ibid.
32 ibid., 19 October 1971.

33 In November 1975, Mary received her first Public Lending Rights payment: $108 for the only two titles then available in public libraries.
34 *The Fifth Sparrow* was published by Sydney University Press in 1972, shortly before the death of Marjory Rees.
35 MDM diary, 11 October 1971.
36 Extracts from Bess Durack's memoirs of her life prior to her marriage and early days in the Kimberley are included in *Sons in the Saddle*, the sequel to *Kings in Grass Castles*.
37 *Those Were the Days*, the history of Qantas, was televised 26 October 1971.
38 MDM diary, 18 March 1966.

10 – 'EVERYTHING THAT WE BELONG'
1 ibid., 4 February 1972.
2 RM to HCM, 22 May 1971.
3 MDM diary, from the Adelaide Festival, 6–8 March 1972.
4 Report in *Adelaide Advertiser*, 9 March 1972. MDM's comments published 10 March 1973, as noted in her diary.
5 MDM diary, 28 March 1972.
6 ibid., 4 April 1972.
7 ibid., 2 March 1972.
8 KMD to EDC, 18 March 1964.
9 As recorded in an article, 'Argyle Goes Under', by Perth journalist Hal Colebatch, who rowed through the station and surrounds. *The West Australian*, 11 January 1972.
10 A full account of the events of 6 April 1972 can be found in R. Miller, *Sugarbird Lady*, Rigby, 1979.
11 HCM to MDM, 3 July 1972.
12 Bess Durack diary, extracts June–July 1972.
13 HCM to MDM, 29 June 1972.
14 'Consequences of Writing *Kings in Grass Castles*', talk for the Warana Festival, 25 September 1976.
15 The tapes of Aboriginal memories are held by the Battye Library.
16 Ernestine Hill died 23 August 1972. Marj Rees died 4 September 1972.
17 *The West Australian*, 9 November 1972.
18 The restored Wackett aircraft is today on display at the Bull Creek Aviation Museum in Western Australia.
19 MDM diary, 12 January 1973.
20 I. Drysdale and M. Durack, *The End of Dreaming*, Rigby, 1974.
21 MDM diary, 4 January 1973.
22 ibid., 16 January 1973.
23 ibid., 27 April, 5 June, 26 January 1973.
24 ibid., 5 February 1973. Robin and Harold Dicks were married 3 April 1973.
25 ibid., 18 May 1973.
26 The Australia Council, introduced by Whitlam as an interim council in 1973 and made a statutory authority by the *Australia Council Act 1975*, superseded the Australian Council for the Arts (established in 1968) and other arts bodies.
27 MDM diary, extracts from the National Seminar on Aboriginal Arts in Australia, May 1973.
28 Anthony Wallis communication to PMM, 22 November 2011.
29 *Sydney Morning Herald*, 30 July 1973.
30 MDM to F. James, 8 August 1978.
31 MDM diary, 10 June 1973.

32	MDM diary, 4 December 1973. The file of Strehlow correspondence is held by the Battye Library.
33	ibid., 14 November 1973.
34	ibid., 22 November 1973.
35	ibid., 16 August 1973.
36	Durack family reunion at Ithaca, Coolup, 2 December 1973.
37	MDM diary, 4 November 1973.
38	ibid., extracts November 1973.
39	ibid., 7 February 1974.
40	RMD diary, 5 May 1974.
41	RMD diary, 9 May 1974.
42	MDM diary, 9 May 1974.
43	RMD diary, 21 May 1974.
44	MDM diary, election day, 17 May 1974.
45	ibid., 5 June 1974.
46	ibid., 29 May 1974.
47	ibid., 18 June 1974.
48	ibid., 4 May 1977.
49	ibid., 30 June 1974.
50	RMD diary, 20 September 1974.
51	ibid., 30 September 1974; see chapter titled 'Flight to Timor' in *Sugarbird Lady*.
52	MDM diary, 11 September 1974.
53	ibid.; Joe Nangan and Hugh Edwards, *Joe Nangan's Dreaming*, Thomas Nelson, 1976.
54	MDM diary, 2 September 1974.
55	The Furnell Royal Commission into Aboriginal Affairs report was issued August 1974, two months after the Woodward Commission report.
56	N. Keesing to MDM, 5 November 1974.
57	Offers for the television rights to *Kings* were blocked by a contract with Channel 7, which it held for seventeen inactive years.
58	MDM diary, 23 December 1974.

11 – 'CAN THESE BE THE SAME STARS?'

1	RMD diary, 31 March 1975.
2	MDM diary, 11 February 1975.
3	Descriptions of Darwin destruction from MDM diary, 22–23 April 1975.
4	After Ida's death, her eight hundred page autobiography was significantly reduced for publishing purposes: I. Mann, *The Chase* (ed. Ros Golding), Fremantle Arts Centre Press, 1986. The original is held in the Battye Library.
5	MDM diary, 17 June 1975.
6	ibid., 30 May 1975.
7	Sister Ignatius ('Iggy') Murnane of the St John of God order, not to be confused with Dominican Sister Ignatius Prendiville.
8	MDM diary, 2 July 1975.
9	ibid., 24 July 1975.
10	RMD diary, 27 May 1975.
11	A full account of the in-flight birth, 7 May 1975, can be found in *Sugarbird Lady*.
12	Audrey Jordan was killed in 1977 when she accidentally walked into the propeller of an air ambulance.
13	RMD diary, 3 September 1975. Harold Dicks resigned in 1979.

14 ibid., extracts September and October 1975.
15 MDM notes on the meeting, ATF/ATC file, Durack Archives, SLWA.
16 MDM diary, October 1975.
17 The International Aeronautical Association would have no alternative speaker but arranged for Robin's address to be read for her.
18 MDM diary, 6 November 1975.
19 RMD diary, 1 November 1975.
20 ibid., extracts November 1975.
21 ibid.
22 ibid., final diary entry, 19 November 1975.
23 MDM diary, extracts November 1975.
24 ibid., 11 November 1975.
25 HCM to MDM, 30 October 1967.
26 MDM diary, 7 December 1975.
27 ibid., 11 December 1975.
28 EDC to Bill Durack, 20 December 1975.
29 MDM diary, 27 December 1975.
30 ibid., 29 December 1975.
31 ibid., 13 December 1975.
32 ibid., 30 December 1975.

12 – THE MAIN JOB

1   PMM diary, January 1976.
2   MDM diary, 16 January 1976.
3   ibid., 23 January 1976.
4   ibid., extracts January and February 1976.
5   MDM interview with Hazel De Berg, 12 March 1976, held in the Oral History Collection of the NLA.
6   Diamond mining in the Forrest River area of the Kimberley.
7   MDM diary, 5 February 1977.
8   C. Gare to HCM, 30 August 1976.
9   Bishop J. Jobst to MDM, 23 April 1976.
10 MDM diary, 23 May 1976.
11 ibid., 17 May 1976.
12 ibid., 26 May 1976.
13 ibid., 3 June 1976.
14 ibid., 29 June 1976.
15 ibid., 5 July 1976.
16 ibid., 29 June 1976.
17 The eventually heritage-listed Male house was sold in 1997.
18 M. Durack, *To Be Heirs Forever*, Constable & Co, 1976.
19 MDM diary, 3 November 1976.
20 Article by Pamela Brown, *The West Australian*, 30 October 1976.
21 MDM diary, 23 March 1977.
22 Avoiding personal comment, Mary quoted from the diary of M.P. Durack and a newspaper report of the death.
23 MDM diary, 14 February 1977.
24 ibid., 15 February 1977.
25 ibid., 3 February 1977.
26 Attempts to purchase the original aircraft were stalled by the asking price.

Placement at Jandakot had been a stipulation of the fundraising committee.
27   MDM diary, 26 April 1977.
28   ibid., 20 May 1977. Letter from Harold Dicks to MDM sent from the United States.
29   ibid., 21 May 1977.
30   MDM to PMM, 2 June 1977.
31   MDM diary, 25 June 1977.
32   PMM diary, August 1977.
33   MDM diary, 25 August 1977.
34   M. Durack, 'Nemesis', 1949.
35   World Black and African Festival of Arts and Culture, January 1977.
36   The Derby Leprosarium closed in 1986.
37   M. Durack, 'Barunga Is Dead', 1985.
38   MDM diary, 18 February 1977.
39   Later published as *The Aborigines in Australian Literature*, WA Institute of Technology, English Department, 1978.
40   MDM diary, 16 September 1977.
41   ibid., 22 October 1977.
42   ibid., 28 October 1977.
43   Mary, who had left school at the age of sixteen, had no academic degree.
44   MDM diary, extracts November 1977.
45   MDM to PMM, 29 October 1977.
46   MDM diary, 8 December 1977.
47   ibid., 11 December 1977.
48   ibid., 28 December 1977.

13 – GROUNDED
1   ibid., 5 January 1978.
2   ibid., 3 March 1978.
3   ibid., 8 January 1978.
4   ibid., 13 February 1978.
5   ibid., 30 January 1978.
6   ibid., 24 June 1978.
7   ibid., 13 June 1979.
8   ibid., 1 February 1978.
9   The award was bestowed by the governor-general, Sir Zelman Cowen, at the Parmelia Hotel in Perth, June 1978.
10   Extracts from MDM's address at the University of Western Australia on the occasion of her honorary doctorate, 13 April 1978.
11   Awards announced April 1978.
12   MDM diary, 28 April 1978.
13   PMM diary, 27 April 1978.
14   MDM diary, 1 May 1978.
15   ibid., 13 May 1978.
16   Memorial unveiling, 30 May 1978.
17   The first recipient of the Flying Nurse Scholarship was the worthy Helen Reid, in 1986. In 2013, the lapsed award was revived by the Tasmanian RFDS.
18   MDM diary, 26 December 1978.
19   ibid., 16 May 1978.
20   ibid., 12 October 1978.
21   ibid., 22 June 1978.

22 MDM to F. James, 8 August 1978. This account sent in 1983 to Hal's biographer Mary Lord.
23 MDM diary, 16 July 1978.
24 ibid., 27 July 1978.
25 ibid., 7 August 1978.
26 EDC to MDM, 26 January 1947.
27 MDM diary, 8 October 1978.
28 ibid., 31 August 1978.
29 MDM to K. McArthur, 15 December 1979.
30 MDM to F. James, 1 February 1979.
31 MDM diary, 31 August 1979.
32 Interview with Sandra Simmons, *Bulletin*, 17 July 1979; MDM diary, 31 July 1979.
33 MDM diary, 26 September 1979.
34 PMM diary, 2 October 1979.
35 ibid., 6 December 1979.
36 MDM diary, 12 December 1979.

14 – BENT TO BURDEN
1 ibid., 4 April 1980.
2 M. Durack and B. Mulholland, *Legacy of Love, the Story of Edith Little*, Artlook Books, 1981.
3 The case for damages sustained in the accident was settled out of court on a 'shared blame' basis.
4 MDM diary, 10 April 1980.
5 ibid., 15 April 1980.
6 Fifteen paintings on a theme of 'Explorers and Discoverers' were exhibited. In 1993, the Museum and Art Gallery of the Northern Territory would acquire fifteen of this set, valued at $45,000, indicating that none were sold in New York.
7 MDM diary, 26 June 1979.
8 Bishop Jobst oversaw the surrender of mission lands and titles for the establishment of Aboriginal communities. Replaced by Bishop Christopher Saunders, he left Broome in 1996, and in 2000 returned to Austria, where he died in 2014.
9 MDM diary, 23 May 1980.
10 The author, Rod Ansell, dubbed 'the real Crocodile Dundee', went on a rampage in the Northern Territory in 1999, killing a policeman and then himself.
11 MDM diary, 31 May 1980.
12 ibid., 25 May 1980.
13 PMM diary, June 1980.
14 MDM diary, 16 October 1980.
15 ibid., 27 August 1980.
16 ibid., 26 September 1980.
17 ibid., 27 September 1980.
18 ibid., 6 October 1980.
19 ibid., 19 December 1980.
20 David Durack died 19 August 1982.
21 MDM diary, 20 January 1979.
22 Promotional brochure for *Land Beyond Time*, 1982.
23 MDM diary, 11 October 1987.

24 In October 1988 the FAW chair was taken over by Patricia Kotai-Ewers, who during her esteemed stewardship was instrumental in the moving and preservation of Tom Collins House and Mattie Furphy House (the latter named for Joseph Furphy's daughter-in-law, artist Mattie Furphy).
25 MDM diary, 19 November 1983.
26 In later days, John Miller established himself as a successful gold and silver jewellery designer.
27 His promising career cut short, Yagan Millett died of cancer in 1997, at the age of twenty-five.
28 *Pilgrimage: A Journey through the Life and Writings of Mary Durack* (eds P. and N. Millett) was published in 2000 by Bantam Books. The anthology of verse and short stories included a chapter from the unpublished novel 'The Calm Eye'.
29 Among numerous public and commemorative displays, Smith sculptures include one of Mary Durack in the Burswood Park Heritage Trail.
30 Comment made at her birthday celebration, 6 July 1982.
31 EDC to Bill Durack, 10 November 1984.

15 – RUFFIAN FORCES

1 H. Colebatch, 'New Light on Katharine Susannah Prichard', *Antipodes*, vol. 4, no. 2, 1990; M. Durack and V. Serventy, 'In Defence of Katharine Susannah Prichard', *The West Australian*, 3 March 1990.
2 MDM diary, 7 February 1990.
3 ibid., 11 March 1990.
4 HCM to MDM, 17 June 1972.
5 John Thompson visits, October 1990 and February 1991.
6 Review by David Bromfield, *The West Australian*, 28 February 1991.
7 EDC to MDM, 10 November 1942.
8 EDC to Bill Durack, 4 March 1992.
9 The few remaining letters from MDM to EDC are those incorporated into 'The Young Know' and those passed on to and preserved by Bess Durack.
10 MDM diary, 17 August 1991.
11 EDC to MDM, 25 November 1991.
12 MDM diary, 7 November 1992.
13 ibid., 27 January 1992.
14 ibid., 28 May 1992.
15 V. Serventy, *An Australian Life*, Fremantle Arts Centre Press, 1999.
16 MDM diary, 6 June 1992.
17 EDC to Bill Durack, 20 May 1993, 1 August 1993, 9 November 1993.
18 MDM diary, 11 June 1992.
19 ibid., 29 September 1992.
20 Information from draft letter EDC to Wendy Birman, Chairperson, Library Board of Western Australia, 12 August 1993, copy held among the papers of Bill Durack in the Battye Library.
21 MDM diary, 4 February 1993.
22 'Sacred Objects in Sale Row', *The West Australian*, 18 April 1992. The collection is today housed in the Strehlow Research Centre in Alice Springs.
23 Reg Durack, radio interview, 1993.
24 MDM diary, 11 May 1993.
25 ibid., 14 July 1993.
26 Bill Durack to RWD, 5 August 1993.

27 MDM diary, 27 September 1994.
28 PMM diary, extracts October 1994. Torn-up typescripts of G.M. Glaskin books are among his papers held by SLWA.
29 EDC to Bill Durack, 11 June 1995.
30 From 1996, relations were re-established between Bill Durack and PMM. Bill's children were not among those of MDM's nephews and nieces who actively participated in the dispute.
31 PMM diary, November 1994.
32 A. Malraux, *The Walnut Trees of Altenburg* (trans. A.W. Fielding), Lehmann, 1952, © Éditions Gallimard.
33 Reg Durack died in 1998 and Elizabeth Durack in 2000. Their graves were placed in eternal attendance on either side of their sister Mary.

EPILOGUE
1 In 1997 Elizabeth Durack raised a nationwide scandal by revealing that she had assumed the alter ego of a fictitious Aboriginal artist named Eddie Burrup. Under this name she had sold, and continued to sell, work painted in an Aboriginal style.

INDEX

Italics denote titles of books, plays, shows, etc.
Bold type denotes illustrations.
Works of Mary and Elizabeth Durack are indexed under *works of Mary Durack* and *works of Elizabeth Durack*.
Titles beginning with *The* or *A* are filed under the next word, e.g., *A Big Country* is filed under B.
Names starting with Mc and Mac are interfiled as if spelled Mac.

ABC (Australian Broadcasting Commission/ Corporation)
  Big Country, A 252
  Certain Women 295
  Dallying Lama, The (Durack) 131
  English for Aborigines series 251
  Forum 137
  funding cuts 329
  Kookanoo series 104
  Life, A 418
  Mary's talks on Swan River Settlement 94
  Patsy reviews books for 124
  Weekend 368
  Women's Session, The 95, 113, 137
Aboriginal Arts Board 289, 385
Aboriginal Cultural Foundation (ACF) 308, 316, 344, 385, 389
  see also Aboriginal Theatre Foundation (ATF)
Aboriginal culture
  appropriation of 72
  disrespect for 158
  efforts to hold on to 275
  rescue of 245, 250, 303, 313
Aboriginal Land Rights Commission (Woodward) 304
Aboriginal people
  affection for Miller family 65
  AIAS grant for history of 170
  on Argyle Station 244
  Bet's portraits of 91–2
  citizenship rights 360
  displaced by flooding of Argyle Station 244, 389–90
  education 77
  entrenched injustice towards 360
  improvements in health and social services for 264
  Mary records memories from 142, 282–3, 368
  Mary seen as authority on 95
  Mary's Kununurra 'sisters' **217**, 264, 427, 429
  and missionaries 156–7
  pastoral workers' wages 16, 244
  'picked up' 89
  race relations in Broome 81–2
  singing for Mary's return to health 373, 427
  strike at Yandeyarra Station 117
  trachoma 100
  urban 262–3, 289–92, 303, 344, 385
  see also land rights; names of individual groups, e.g. Bibbulmun people; Royal Commissions
Aboriginal Theatre Foundation (ATF)
  1971 conference 271
  aim to rescue Aboriginal culture 245, 288–9, 303
  alcohol problem 275, 301
  Dampier landing re-enactment 260–1, 265, 267
  exploitation of 260, 267–8
  formation of 245
  leadership 271, 294–5
  Mary's involvement with 250–1, 253–4, 263–4, 294–5, 308
  Opera House opening performance 291
  Parkerville Amphitheatre opening performance 259, 262–3
  restructure 294–5, 301
  see also Aboriginal Cultural Foundation (ACF)
ACF *see* Aboriginal Cultural Foundation
Actors, The (Porter) 248
Adam's Rib 304–5, 307
Adelaide Festival Writers' Week 106, 144, 153, 156, 158, 164, 175, 222, 251–2, 275, 328

INDEX

Adsett (Busselton house) **206**
    Mary's love for 128, 148–9, 337, 381, 397
    Porter at 157, 248–9
    purchase of 122–3
    in summer 249, 272, 295
    television banned at 258
    in winter 172, 224–5, 311
Adult Education Board 152, 165
Aherns store account 23
AIAS *see* Australian Institute for Aboriginal Studies
Ainslie, Trish 403
Alice Springs 275
Allawah Grove 93–4
Alphonsus, Sister 327
Amanbidji (formerly Kildurk) 365
America's Cup 397
Anderson, Kathleen 117–18
Anderson, Leslie 352
Angry Penguins journal 154
Ansell, Rod 445
Ansett Airlines 161, 243, 401
Ansett, Reg 243
Antill, John 129
archives
    CD&D 130, 409–15, 419
    Mary's literary 406–7, 411
    see also Battye Library; State Library of Western Australia
Argyle Homestead **197**, 244, 269–70, 277–8, 295, 369
Argyle Homestead Museum 283–4, 286, 368–9, 419, 429
Argyle Station 90, 233, 369
Arrow, Penny **216**
Arthur and Martha (pigs) 133, 136–7
ATF *see* Aboriginal Theatre Foundation
atomic bomb testing 66, 77, 114
Attenborough, David 153
Australian Broadcasting Commission/Corporation *see* ABC
Australia Council 289, 296, 385, 400
Australian Council for Aboriginal Affairs 245
Australian Council for the Arts 245, 251, 259, 289
Australian Institute of Aboriginal Studies (AIAS) 170
Australian Land and Cattle Co. Ltd 239
Australian Society of Authors 173
Aviat 70 air race 256
Avon, Lady 354
Ayers Rock 137

Baard people 142
Bader, Douglas 335
Balgo 141, 309–10, 331
Bali-Hai Caravan Park (Broome) 76
Barron Films 398
Barron, Paul 398
Barunga, Albert **210**, 244–5, 250, 259, 262–3, 275, 299, 323, 344–5
Battersby, Jean 251, 289, 367
Battye Library 130, 265, 287, 405, 411, 415–17, 419–20
Bayley, John 181
BBC TV, visit to Alice Springs 275
Beagle Bay Mission 140–2, 150, 158, 160–1
Beckoning West, The (Smith) 114, 148
Behn River 369
Bell, Mr (Argyle station manager) 244
Belvoir (Shaw property) 273
Bennett, Dorothy 264
Bennett, Lance 263–4, 267, 271, 289, 303, 316, 344, 385–6
Bethesda Hospital 421
Bibbulmun people 51, 278, 313, 360
Big Country, A (television program) 252, 278, 280, 286
Birman, John 180
Birman, Wendy 446
Birrell, Rosemary 239
Bishop's Palace (Broome) 76, 81, 168
Bjelke-Petersen, Joh 179
Black Power movement 275
Black Rock 419
Blair, Harold 290
Blanks, Fred 292
Blumann, Elise 58
Boda, Katerina 'Bodie' 90, 138
Bolton, Geoffrey 94, 179, 287, 335, 394, 416
Bonython, Constance 175
Book of Innocent Austral Verse (Humphries) 42
Boombi, Keith 333, 355
Bortignon, Alex 394, 398
Bousloff, Kira 128, 139, 144, 262, 288
Bow, Mrs (child carer) 55
Bow River diamond mine 349
Boxer (stockman) 278
Brabazon Cup 333
Bradley, David 419
Bradley, Sue 419, 427
Bran Nue Dae (Chi) 188
Brand, David 178
Brand government 269
Brearley, Norman 24, 177
British atomic testing 66
British Empire and Commonwealth Games (Perth, 1962) 139
Broad, Elsie 147

449

Broome
 in 1952 68–87
 as backwater 68
 changes to 76, 176
 Chinatown 68, 76, 81
 Chinese gambling dens 81–2
 in decline 150
 flights to 63–7, 141
 local politics 75–6
 Mary's last trip to 419–20
 Mary's love for 111
 Mary's sketchbooks of 72
 orphanage 141
 pearling industry 67–8, 81
 race relations in 81–2
 royal visit 158, 161
 state school 76–7
 Sun Picture Theatre 81
 surrounds 80–1
 swimming baths 77
 tides 77–9
Broome Cemetery 323, 327, 391
Broome Dramatic Society 230
Broome Historical Society 76, 331
Broome houses (Millers') **196–7**
 in 1952 69–72
 Bet takes up residence in 33–4
 fire 59–61, 70–1
 Horrie takes up residence in 43
 new 69
 purchase of 32
 selling of 257, 260, 266, 268
Broome Jetty 84–5
Broome Road Board 45, 75
Broome Shire Council 76, 260, 267, 286
Bulgroo (property) 175
Bulla (stockman) 264, 278, 283–4
Bulletin, The 360, 368
Bullita (pastoral lease) 404
Bungledoon (stockman) 264
Bunning, Flora 101
Burke, Brian 397–8
Burrup, Eddie 430
Butler, Harry (aviator) 242
Butler, Harry (naturalist) 277, 281–2
Button, Bob 401
Byrne, Geraldine 343, 389, 401

Cable Beach (Broome) 49, 67, 76, 420
Camballin 47, 79, 90–1, 111, 121, 123–5, 160, **203**, 224, 431
 see also Fitzroy River
Campbell, Louise 436
Cape Leveque 146

Capricornia (Herbert) 159
Capuchin Annual 149
Card, Brian 361
Carey, Peter 43
Carlton Hill Station 283, 419
Carroll, Jeff 227
Carrolup School 50–1, 93–4, 313
Carrolup Settlement 50–1
Casey, Dorothy (Congdon) 59–61
Casey, Gavin 60–1
Catholic Weekly 148
Cato, Nancy 153
CD&D (Connor Doherty & Durack)
 documents 46, 94, 130, 311, 369, 406–7, 409–15, 419
 imprudent dealings 128
 poor land management 44
 sale of properties 16, 47, 277
Centenary Cup 335
Certain Women (ABC show) 295
Chamberlain, Bob 335
Chapman, Ernie 264
Charles, Prince 333, 367
Chase, The (Mann) 397
chee fah (gambling game) 81–2
Cherry, Frances 422
Chi, Jimmy, *Bran Nue Dae* 188
Child Artists of the Australian Bush (M.D. Miller & Rutter) 50–1
childcare arrangements 48, 53–5
Christensen, Allen 394
Christesen, Clem 180
'Christmas at Ivanhoe Station' (Durack) 167
Chunuma, Jeff 264
Clancy, Bet *see* Durack, Elizabeth (Bet)
Clancy, Frank 14, 16, 52, 409
Clancy, Michael 33, 114, 276
Clancy, Perpetua 33, 55–6, 92, 114, 173, **202**, 276, 385
Clarke, Kenneth 153
clergy, Mary's affinity with 59, 142–3, 253, 380–1
Clune, Frank 159
Cogan, Helen 144
Coggin, Chris 421
Colebatch, Astrid 29, 58
Colebatch, Gordon 28–9, 54, 104–5
Colebatch, Hal 405
Collected Australian Verse (Williams) 418
Collins, Brian 157
Collins, Tom *see* Furphy, Joseph
Come in Spinner (Cusack & James) 117–18
Commonwealth Games (Perth, 1962) 139
Commonwealth Literary Fund grant 293
communism 39, 57, 125, 229, 247, 329

Congdon, Coralie **207**
Congdon, Sid 61
Connor Doherty & Durack *see* CD&D
Connor, Francis 337
Connor, Kitty 337, 368
Connor, Moira 337, 368
Constable (publisher) 71, 85, 88, 99, 117, 120, 128, 241, 394
Continental Hotel (Broome) 69, 76, 81, 158, 256
Cook, C.E. 'Mick' 73, 99, 236
Cooke, Eric Edgar 137, 162
Coombs, H.C. (Nugget) 130, 245, 250, 253, 289, 385
Coonardoo (Prichard) 107
Cooper, Revel 93-4, 313
coral cups 77-9
Cord to Alcheringa (E. Durack) 100
Country Women's Association 241
The Countryman
  commission on journey to Broome 115-16
  serialises *Keep Him My Country* 107
Court, Charles 131, 178-9, 269, 304, 360-1, 372, 398
Court, Richard 425
Cowen, Zelman 354, 361
Cowley, Ken 367, 372
Crabb, Dawn 118
Crann, David 227
Creative Nation 385
Crick, Don 303
Curnow, Tim 328, 367
Curtin University 400
  see also WA Institute of Technology
Curtis Brown (literary agents) 328
Cusack, Dymphna 118, 252
  Come in Spinner 117-18
Cyclone Tracy 305, 308

Daily News (newspaper)
  article on Horrie 156
  article on Kim 121
Daisy (of Argyle and Kununurra) 15, **217**, 264
Dalgerie (Penberthy & M. Durack) 128-30, 288, 290-2
Dampier Downs (station) 48-50, 53, 59, 62, 68, 73-4, 85-6, 120
Dampier landing re-enactment 260-1, 265, 267
Dampier song cycles 111
Dampier, William 260
Dancers of the Dreaming 389
Darbyshire, Beatrice 12, 41, 401
Darwin 250, 305, 308
Davidson, Doug 281, 297
Davidson, Ken 310, 312

Davidson, Mary (Marie) 17-18
Davis, Beatrice 153, 159, 170
Davison, Frank Dalby 153
Dawson, Smoky 396, 419, 428
Daylight (stockman) 264, 277-8
DCA *see* Department of Civil Aviation
De Berg, Hazel 328
de Havilland, Hereward 184-5
de Pierres, Rosemary 290
Debesa Station
  Andy managing 239, 242, 258
  as bottomless financial pit 98, 166, 234
  disposal of 234, 266
  lease of 120-1, 130
  Rodriguez as partner in 126, 143, 234
Della Marta cafe 112
Dent, Maria 30, 53, 58
Denton, Kit 137
Department of Civil Aviation (DCA) 161
Derby 279
  see also Debesa Station; Mowanjum Presbyterian Mission
Derby Leprosarium 141, 310, 344
Derby Shire Cultural Centre 364
Devonleigh Hospital 235-7
diaries and journals, Mary's 9, 134-5, 168, 393
Dicks, Harold **209**
  character 325, 342
  death of 396
  as family doctor 163, 235-7, 376-7
  final confrontation with Patsy 395-6
  financial dealings by 306-7, 340-1
  Mary's opinion of 145
  overseas junkets 270-1
  propositions Patsy 325, 333-4
  relationship with Mary 358-9
  relationship with Robin 145-6, 161-2, 288, 297-8, 302-3
  remarries after Robin's death 326, 339, 341, 358-9
  as RFDS director 315
  rights to *Flying Nurse* 341
  Robin's diaries for *Sugarbird Lady* 336, 339, 354
  Robin's estate 329-30, 339-40, 342
  Robin's funeral 323
  Robin's memorial at Jandakot 339
  sexual misdemeanours of 186-7, 321
  theft of Robin's identity 358
  on Whitlam 320
'Dispossessed, The' (Johnson) 127
Disturbing Element (Herbert) 164-5
Dixon, Chicka 292, 301
Dodson, Pat 310

Dot (of Kununurra) **217**, 264
Drake-Brockman, Geoffrey 43, 58
Drake-Brockman, Henrietta 39, 101, 165, 222, 229
'Driven, The' (Stuart) 139
droving 131
Drysdale, Ingrid, *The End of Dreaming* 287, 293, 295
Drysdale West Kimberley welfare project 299
Dunn, Frank, *Speck in the Sky* 395
Dunstan, Don 275
Durack, Bess **201**, **208**, **212**
  90th birthday 295
  appearance 35
  appears on *A Big Country* 286
  axioms and survival tips 35
  cars and driving 45, 353
  companions for 163, 328
  on daylight saving 306
  death 382–3
  entertainment 115, 131
  health 132, 156, 163, 252, 352–4
  homes 12–13, 30, 400
  on Jobst 146
  on Julie's death 236
  marriage to M.P. Durack 12
  memoirs 270
  on Menzies' death 372
  on Penberthy 129, 139
  philosophies of 147, 163, 352, 372
  relationship with Aboriginal employees 280
  relationship with Horrie 16–17
  relationship with Kim 139, 224, 281
  relationship with Patsy 30, 35, 296, 341–2, 370, 382–4
  shares 100, 122
  visit to Adsett 269–70
  visit to Kildurk 280
  visit to Kununurra 280–2
  will 310, 384
Durack, Bill
  architect of Mildew 12
  dispute over archive documents 410, 412
  moves to Qld 38
  offered Dampier Downs manager job 62
  relationship with Mary 224, 316, 381, 384
  trek to Thylungra Station 175
  trip to Qld with Mary 392
Durack, Bird (Bridget) 12, 17–18
Durack, David 30, 35, 38, 163, 384, 392
Durack, David (son of Reg) 193
Durack, Dermot 88–9
Durack, Elizabeth (Bet)
  appearance 93, 174, **198–200**, **207**, **212**, **215**, 336, 365
  on Argyle Homestead Museum 369
  articles in *Sydney Morning Herald* on North-West 160–1
  as 'Aunty Bumbles' 33, 430
  and Bess's will 310, 387–8
  in Broome 33–4, 158–60, 364
  censors own letters 407–8
  character 51–2, 101, 160, 312–13, 351, 378, 384, 407–8, 410–15, 418–19
  collaboration with Mary 14, 155–6
  commissions 132, 140, 143, 158, 242
  correspondence with Mary 14, 30
  desert paintings 92, 140
  Eddie Burrup controversy 430
  exhibitions 37, 91–3, 112, 114–15, 123, 150, 155, 290, 336, 364–5, 384, 407
  family papers dispute 409–25
  feud with Reg 384
  financial affairs 93, 338, 349, 403, 426
  goldfields paintings 150
  grants 170, 177
  health 407, 414
  home 92, 155
  home studio opening 114–15
  honours 177, 403
  as illustrator 14, 155–6
  on Jobst 159
  on Kildurk 160
  loan to build new gallery/studio 338, 349
  marriage to Frank Clancy 33
  on motels 143
  murals 91, 112
  new gallery 346
  opening of new gallery 346
  on outback painting 116
  overseas travel 174–5
  paints sets for *Dalgerie* 129
  Papua New Guinea work 251
  Pilbara landscapes 336
  politics 179
  portraits of Aboriginal children 91–2
  poster for Mowanjum dancers 258
  relationship with her children 55–6
  relationship with Horrie 136, 158, 175, 369
  relationship with Mario Giachetti 91, 99
  relationship with Mary 14, 155–6, 349, 388, 397, 400, 407–8, 421–3, 425–6
  relationship with Mick Cook 73, 99
  relationship with Patsy 388, 408–9, 422–3, 430
  relationship with Reg 160, 404

on religion 59
 travels 174–5, 177, 251, 277, 364
 see also works of Elizabeth Durack
Durack, Enid 37, 100, 284, 382, 388, 404
Durack, Eric 95, 105–6, 129, 281
Durack, Jack W. 18, 430
Durack, Jerry Brice 89
Durack, John (son of Reg) 244, 264, 291
Durack, Kim **203**
 Camballin farms project 37–8, 47, 79, 90–1, 100, 111, 121
 character 48, 124–5
 Daily News article on 121
 death 223–4
 ends association with Northern Developments 124–5
 estate 415
 financial support of 35, 48, 139
 health 179
 on *Keep Him My Country* 109
 'Man's Place in Nature' 175–6
 moves to Canberra 132
 offered Dampier Downs manager job 62
 persecution of 125
 philosophical and theosophical studies 160, 175–6
 proposes Northern Water Authority 132
 relationship with Mary 35, 121, 222
 relationship with M.P. Durack 44
 relationship with Patsy 124
 relationship with Reg 132, 163
 on *The Rock and the Sand* 179, 188, 223
 see also Camballin
Durack, Marjory 105–6
Durack, Mary
 40th birthday celebrations 89
 80th birthday 417
 appearance 93, **195–201, 204, 206–8, 210, 212–17**, 270
 awards and honours 174, 348, 351–2, 355–7, 394, 400, 425
 character 19, 21–2, 24, 58, 100–2, 122, 230, 273, 329, 358, 401
 death 428–9
 funeral 429
 health 30, 62, 256, 268–9, 297–300, 371–5, 380
 marriage to Horrie 26, 48, 85, 95, 358
 television appearances 270, 418
 see also works of Mary Durack
Durack, Michael ('Stumpy Michael') 88–9, 120
Durack, M.J. ('Long Michael') 88–9

Durack, M.P. (Michael Patrick)
 death 44–6
 diaries and journals 134, 253–4, 265, 430
 loans to his children 35
 Mary's biography for WA sesquicentenary 355
 Patsy remembers 16
 prevents Bird from marrying 12
 relationship with Horrie 16, 24
 relationship with Mary 11–12, 16, 134
 sale of stations 38, 43–4
 sesquicentenary paver 360
 tributes to 45
Durack, Neal 297
Durack, Noni 38, 316, 381
Durack, Patrick (Patsy) 46, 88
Durack, Peter 179
Durack, Reg **212**
 on Aboriginal employees 265, 284
 at Argyle Homestead Museum opening 369
 Bullita lease 404
 character 404
 family papers dispute 409–25
 as 'Head of the Family' 381–2, 404, 410
 health 421, 425
 Kildurk Station 37, 47, 100, 107–9, 190, 264–5, 312, 365
 objections to Whitlam goverment 312
 opinion of *Keep Him My Country* 109
 relationship with Bet 160, 384, 404
 relationship with Kim 132, 163
 relationship with Mary 190, 264–5, 346, 410, 421
 relationship with Patsy 108–9, 381–2, 413–14
 sees potential for Ord River Dam 244
 South West properties 295
 Spirit Hill Station 404
 travels 388, 404
Dusty, Slim 396, 419
Dutton, Geoffrey 153, 393–4
Dutton, Ninette 394

Early Birds (H. Miller) 161, 176–7, 184, 190, 222, 226–7, 345
Eden House (Porter) 248
Edwards, Hugh 303, 361
Edwards, Robert 289
Egan, Ted 396
Elizabethan Theatre Trust 129, 290
Ellis, Elaine 415–16, 424
Empire Games (Perth, 1962) 139
End of Dreaming, The (Drysdale) 287, 293, 295
European immigrants 90–1

Everage, Edna 424
Ewers, J.K. 144, 242, 363
Farley, Peter 160
Farnsworth Hall, John 129
Farrell, Derm 45, 74, 256
Farrell, James T. 113
FAW (Fellowship of Australian Writers) WA Branch
  Albany branch 152, 166–7
  Corroboree 116, 222
  in disarray 151–2
  formation 38–9
  Hewett as president 151
  Jones as president 151
  Kununurra workshop 289
  loses relevance 242
  male membership 40–1, 60
  Mary as president 137, 143–4, 180, 242
  Mary as vice-president 116–17
  Mary's life membership 232
  memorial for Drake-Brockman 241
  persecution of Greenwood 39
  Serventy as president 116, 151
  Summer School 152
  women members predominate 40
Federation of Aero Clubs of Australia 357
Fellowship of Australian Writers (WA Branch) see FAW
Fifth Sparrow, The (Skinner) 189–90, 233, 257, 269
Fitzgerald, June 222, 229
Fitzroy River 47, 80, 124, 331
  see also Camballin
Flame Trees of Thika (Huxley) 169
Fletcher, Jack 239, 266
Flexmore, Hudson 153
Fluffy (sugar glider) 60
Flying Nurse (R. Miller) 251–2, 257, 271, 335, 341, 354, 359
flying nurse scheme 162, 173
Flying Nurse scholarship 359
Flynn, Frank 155
Foley, Gary 291
Forbes, Ian 392, 396
Ford Foundation 177
Forrest family 149
Foss, Peter 424–5
Foster, Judge 316
Foster, Rene 110
Fraser, Malcolm 326, 329, 372
Freehill, Norman 252
From Patrons to Partners (Zucker) 241
Fryer Memorial Library (Qld) 336
Furphy, Joseph 39

Furphy, Sam 39
Fysh, Hudson 177, 243

Gambleton, Moira 170–2
Gantheaume Point (Broome) 83, 420
Gare, Cyril
  Andy seeks help from 239
  assists former Carrolup artists 93–4
  association with Horrie 64, 138, 187, 233–4, 334, 341–2, 347, 373–4, 379
  as Miller Investments trustee 97–8, 187, 233–4, 240, 266, 334, 341–2, 347
  politics 179
  retires 391
  on Robin's estate 329–30
Gare, Elsie 25
Gare, Nene 117
Garwood, Roger 403
Geraldton Road Board 132
German migrants, internment 53
Giachetti, Mario 91, 99, 101
Gill, Con 81–2, 111
Glaskin, Gerry
  assists depositing CD&D records in State Archives 130
  assists house guest Patsy in Amsterdam 168
  association with Mary 43, 111–12, 114, 117
  breaks confidence on Supreme Court writ 424
  and FAW 151, 184
  grievance against State Library 405, 424
  indecent exposure charge 146
  Literature Board saga 296–7, 304
  phone calls from 293
  welcomes Surkov and Krugerskaya 144
  Windows of the Mind 296
  A World of Our Own 114
Glenn, John 153
Golding, Ros 396–7, 399, 402, 415
Golding, William 312
Goldsmith, John 398
Gorton, John 193
Goulburn (NSW) 175
Governor Broome Hotel (Broome) 73, 76
Graham, Billy 131
gramophones 29, 56, 96, 105, 126
Greenhill Galleries 396, 401
Greenwood, Irene 39–40, 61, 126, **207**, 236, 299, 310, 328
Greer, Germaine 275
Gregory, Ancel 81
Gregory National Park 404
Groote Eylandt Festival 386, 389
Guildford Airport 64

Gulpilil, David 276
Guthrie, Tyrone 255, 257, 265
Gye, Caroline *see* Mann, Ida
Gye, William 90

H-bomb 177–8
Haag, Stefan 129, 153, 290–2, 305, 344
Haebich, Mrs (ironing lady) 225, 327
Haeflinger, Paul 91
Hall, John Farnsworth *see* Farnsworth Hall, John
Hamersley National Park 336
Hamilton, Margaret 361
Hamilton, Roy 171
Hancock, Gina (Georgina) 306
Hancock, Hope 101, 372
Hancock, Lang 101, 266, 299, 372
Hannon, Bob 291
Harney, Bill 117, 137
Harris, Max 153–4, 168, 181
Harris, Rolf 168, 282, 301, 396
Hart, Pro 396
Hasluck, Alix 135, 137, 361
Hasluck, Paul 135, 137
Hasluck, Rollo 137
Hawke government 397
Hawker de Havilland anniversary celebrations 184–5
Hawker, Harry 247, 335
Herbert, Xavier 153, 159, 164–5, 167, 389
  Capricornia 159
  Disturbing Element 164–5
Hewett, Dorothy 151, 181, 229, 247, 367
Hill, Bob (Robert) **200**, **218**
  dodges military service 43
  employment 102
  leaves Perth 109–10
  living with Miller family 42–3, 94, 98–9, 102–3
  parentage 106
  relationship with Mary 43, 102–3, 102–6, 105–6, 109–10, 427
Hill, Ernestine **199**
  attitude towards parenting 43, 94, 102
  Bet's description of 101
  on *Child Artists of the Australian Bush* 51
  death 110, 284
  Mary's friendship with 106
  Patsy remembers 42
  photography 89, 336
  relationship with Mary 106
  on Sorensen 41–2
  travels to Broome 73
  tribute to M.P. Durack 45

Historic Places of Australia (National Trust) 355
Hobcroft, Rex 291, 385
Hole in the Wall Theatre 274
Holt, Harold 179, 193
Hoofs and Horns (magazine) 331
Hooker, Connie 294, 310, 320, 328, 374–5, 379, 396, 406
Horner, Iain 191, 221, 228–9, 234–5, 252, 265–6, 276, 293
Horrie Miller Museum (Broome) 286
House Roof Hill 419
'House that Flew Away, The' (E. Durack) 159
Howard, George 144
Huegel, Father Francis 140, 142, 154, 287, 323
Humphries, Barry 168, **213**, 231, 369, 372, 396, 419, 424
  Book of Innocent Austral Verse 42
Hungerford, Tom 43, 361
Huxley, Elspeth 169

Iddon, Ron 280
Idriess, Ion 159
Ignatius, Sister *see* Prendiville, Sister Ignatius
Ilbarana (Stuart) 268
Ingram, Anne Bower 303
Italian migrants 90–1, 112
Ivanhoe Station 24, 42, 92, 167, 250, 264, 419

Jah, Prince 396
James, Florence 71, 107, 117–18, 121–2, 156–8, 175, **206**, 222
Jandakot airport 314, 325, 327, 339, 358–9
Jobst, Bishop John **209**
  association with Horrie 159, 188–9, 260, 268, 285, 309
  Bess on 146
  Bet on 159
  on Bet's paintings of Aboriginal people 141
  buys Broome house 260, 268, 285, 309, 386
  conducts Horrie's funeral 391
  conducts Robin's requiem mass 323
  Mary on 150
  Petri on 146
  as pilot 188–9, 316, 331–3
  relations with entrenched clergy 151
  and *Rock and the Sand, The* 141–3, 148, 150–1, 154, 188, 192, 241
  and *Tjakamarra – Boy Between Two Worlds* 308–10, 316, 330, 343
  war service 140
Johnson, Babette 225
Johnson, Colin (Mudrooroo) 126–8, 155, 158, 170, 311

Jones, John Joseph (J.J.J.)
 attends Adelaide Festival in Mary's place 164
 as despot 258–9, 262
 as FAW president 151
 Mary dissociates from 263
 Parkerville Amphitheatre 226, 245, 250, 259, 262–3
 Patsy on 151–2
 as singer 144, 154
 Tea Towels and Earrings 146
Jordan, Audrey 315, 320
Joshua, Edith 328, 355, 372, 382, 384
journal keeping 9, 134–5, 393

Kaberry, Phyllis 50, 71, 363–4
Karrakatta Club 113, 152
Katter, Joy 334
Keating, Paul 385
Keesing, Nancy 303–4, 367
Kelly's Knob 250
Keneally, Tom 43, 306
Kennedy, Annie 347–8
Kennedy, J.F. 162
Kerr, Rosy 401
Kidson, Nessie 89–90, 102, 109, 156, 313, 392
Kildurk Station
 Bess visits 280
 Mary visits 170, 190, 264
 Patsy remembers 107–9
 Reg manages 37, 47, 100, 131–2, 160, 190, 264–5
 sale of 284, 286, 312, 365
Kileen, Mick 139, 146, 149, 154, 162
Kilfoyle, Jack 343
Kilfoyle, Tom 167
Kimberley, TV documentaries on 170–2, 180
Kimberley Holdings 160
Kinane, Kay 170, 250–2, 254, 371
King, Catherine 95, 124
Kings Park 31, 181
Kingsford Smith, Rollo 185
Kleinig, Cyril 63–4, 183
Knox, Jean, marriage to Horrie 25
Koolinda (state ship) 73
Korwill, Ferry (Ferdinand) 53–4, 56, 101, 153, 179, 193, **219**, 320, 392
Korwill, Kati 53–4
Korwill, Marianne 53–4, 56–8, 101, 153, 179, 193, **219**, 320, 392, 429
Kotai Ewers, Patricia 446
Krugerskaya, Oksana 143–4
Kuljak theatre group 222, 226, 232, 250

Kununurra Aboriginal reserve 244, 250–1, 264, 280, 375, 389–90, 392, 402
 Dalgerie dancers 290–1
 establishment of 244
 FAW workshop in 289
 irrigation project fades 301
 Mary records Aboriginal memories at 264, 277, 284–5, 316
 Mary's final visit to 419–20
 Mary's 'sisters' in **217**, 264, 300, 417–20, 427
 PWD house at 277, 279, 282–4
 Reg in 404, 409
 TV documentary filmed in 171
Kyle, Wallace 359

La Grange 141, 267
Lake Argyle 369
Lamilarmi, Lazarus 316
land rights 244–5, 283, 304, 349
Laurie, Victoria 436
Lawler, Ray, *Summer of the Seventeenth Doll* 115
leprosy 15, 35, 102, 262, 310
Letters Lunatic file 332
Library Board of Western Australia 416–17, 420–1, 425
Library and Information Services of Western Australia (LISWA) 416, 430
Lindsay, Norman 70
Linklater, William 'Billy Miller' 41
Linley Wilson School of Dance 36
LISWA *see* Library and Information Services of Western Australia
Literacy Year 401
Literature Board 296, 303–4, 349
'Little Black Fingers' *see Child Artists of the Australian Bush*
Liveringa Station 121, 124–5
Lombadina 141, 148
Long Michael Plain 283
Longreach 363
Loreto Convent 21–2, 55, 57–8, 92, **202**
Lorre, Peter (Löwenstein, László) 57
Lucy (leprosy sufferer) 15

McAlpine, Alistair 76, 403
McArthur, Kath
 advance payment for family opus 100, 119
 assistance with *Kings in Grass Castles* 46–7, 88, 119–20
 assistance with *Sons in the Saddle* 312, 334–5
 Horrie propositions 86–7
 on *Kings in Grass Castles* 133

Mary visits 175, 334–5
  unearths historic family feud 88–9
McDaniel, Mrs (shell collector) 77–9
McElroy, Auburn 362–3
  see also Miller, Auburn
McElroy, Ron 362–3
McKenna, Siobhan 275
McKinney, Jack 175
MacLachlan, Jimmy 332, 349–50
McLean family 21
McLeod, Don 117
McMahon, Father Michael 142–3, 227, 260, 323, 343
McMahon, Sonia 281–2
McMahon, William 281–2, 286
MacRobertson Miller Aviation *see* MMA
magpie geese 80
mail 122, 133–4, 357
Male, Kim 260–1
Male, Phyll 75, 260, 333
Male, Sam 74–5, 227, 260, 333
Malraux, André 429
Mann, Ida
  at Adsett 122–3, **206**, 363, 381
  at Kununurra 282
  autobiography *The Chase* 397
  character 89, 122–3, 149, 362
  death 397
  eye clinics 100, 121, 152, 191
  friendship with Mary 89–90, 128, 152, 158, 297, 311, 356, 397
  health 310–11
  honours 397
  retirement 310, 337
  road trips with Mary 158, 175
  summarises CD&D material 311, 313, 337
  travels 89–90, 257, 269
  treats Nessie Kidson 90
  as writer 117, 152
'Man's Place in Nature' (K. Durack) 175–6
Mantova National Nursing Association 223
Marie (of Kununurra) **217**, 264
Marshall, Matron Marjorie 18
Maylands Aerodrome 19
Mayman, Ted 61
Meckering earthquake 230–1
media siege re Durack papers dispute 424
Megaw, Alex **216**, 393, 399
Megaw, Joseph **216**, 355, 364, 393
Megaw, Mary Rose *see* Miller, Marie Rose
Megaw, Michael 271, 371–2, 413, 421, 424, 427
Melitza (companion help) 163
Menzies, Robert 125, 132–3, 160, 174, 372

Michener, James 113
Mildew (12 Bellevue Avenue, Nedlands)
  appearance 12–14, **195–6**, **208**, **219**
  Christmas dinner at 231
  gardens 13
  Horrie suggests selling 279
  Horrie's garage 13, 284
  land purchase and building 12–14
  log cabins 116
  Marie Rose's screen prints 399
  nursery 14
  out of bounds to Patsy and family 300
  parties at 100–2
  Patsy's clean-out of 375
  rooftop balcony 13–14
  self-contained workroom 162
  shows its age 225
  sunken entertainment area ('Bear Pit') 147
  vanished 430
  wildflowers surrounding 20–1
Miller, Andy (Andrew) **195**, **201**, **208**
  at Camballin 79
  birth 30
  bull-catching accident 346
  childhood 31–2, 39, 55–6, 110
  holiday at Kildurk 107–9
  log cabins 116
  managing Debesa 239, 255–6, 258
  marriage to Rosemary Birrell 239, 242, 268
  as member of 'Cnaw' tribe 113
  relationship with Horrie 255–6, 296, 312
  relationship with sisters 349
  returns to Mildew 348–9
  travels 173, 179, 312, 338
  as truck driver 360
Miller, Auburn 25–6, 362–3
Miller, Drew 258, 364, 393
Miller, Horrie (Horace Clive)
  86th birthday 368
  87th birthday 386
  affinity with animals 83
  on air hostesses 256
  appearance 19, **197**, **205**, **207**, **214**
  at Mildew 13, 234–5, 279, 284–5, 288, 311
  attitude towards children 19
  attitude towards grandchildren 286, 376
  attitude towards Mary's writing career 107
  attitude towards money 22, 177, 233–4, 266
  aviation career 14, 19, 24, 27–9, 48, 97, 243, 335
  awards and honours 156, 357
  in Broome 34, 37, 43, 70, 72, 176, 247, 256–7, 286
  cars 18, 112–13

as celebrity 242
character 19–20, 27–9, 59–61, 70, 72, 75, 322–3, 328, 367
childhood 25–6, 29
conversational battlefields 75
Daily News article on 156
Dampier Downs 48–50, 59, 73–4, 85–6
on DC3 flight to Onslow 67
death 390–1
Debesa Station 120–1, 130, 176, 234, 266
despondency 121, 143, 161, 176, 184
on H. Dicks 145–6, 339
Early Birds 161, 176–7, 184, 189–90, 226–7, 234, 345
escapes patricide 370–1
as a father 32, 34
fear of Old Man's Home 351–2
final flight 386
Hawker de Havilland 40th anniversary celebrations 184–5
health 72, 112, 345–6, 352
honours 357
on Horner 234–5
infidelity 26, 30
on *Kings in Grass Castles* 133
loses driver's licence 366
marriage to Jean Knox 25
marriage to Mary 11–12, 24, 26, 48, 85, 358
mechanical expertise 83
and Miller Investments 187–8
moved to Sunset Hospital 373–4
'Out of the Blue' 234
Perth to Sydney air race 335
politics 179
premonition of Julie's death 235
propositions Kath McArthur 86, 87
reaction to Hal Porter 305, 358
recreational pursuits 82–5, 131–2, 305
relationship with Andy 255–6, 296, 312
relationship with Bess 16–17, 112, 374
relationship with Bet 136, 158, 175, 369
relationship with Cyril Gare 64, 138, 187, 233–4, 334, 341–2, 347, 373–4, 379
relationship with daughters 138, 147
relationship with Gordon Colebatch 28–9, 105
relationship with Jobst 159, 188–9, 260, 268, 285, 309
relationship with Johnson 227, 257, 296
relationship with Julie 189, 235, 238
relationship with Marie Rose 189
relationship with M.P. Durack 16, 24
relationship with Patsy 24, 165–6, 189, 227, 285–6, 296, 300, 321, 324, 345, 367

relationship with Robin 17, 138, 187–9, 227, 296, 298
response to *Ship of Dreams* 229–30
sister (Annie Kennedy) 347–8
television appearances 270
Wackett aircraft 49, 80, 161, 185, 247, 286
on women pilots 138, 256
as writer 29, 71, 161, 176–7, 184, 189–90, 226–7, 234, 345
Miller, John (Johnson) **204, 207–8, 216**
at Adsett 221
at Mildew 257, 260, 279, 377
birth 105–6
in Broome 184
character 173
childhood 113, 141
education 183, 228–9, 246, 276
family problems with 231, 246, 278, 282
fronts TV cameras re diaries feud 424
health 123, 141, 162, 191
'hippie' lifestyle 312
jewellery-making in Broome 386
leaves home 278–9, 296
parentage of 105–6, 427
partner Barbara Pedersen 326, 366, 377
relationship with Horrie 227, 257, 296
relationship with Iain Horner 191, 228–9, 265–6
relationship with Mary 231, 234, 399
relationship with Patsy 301–2
relationship with Robin 162, 246
studies fine arts 288
travels to Sri Lanka 366
WAAPA acting course 399
Miller, Julie **195, 197, 201–4, 207–8, 211**
artistic pursuits 138, 146
association with Forrest family 149
birth 15–16, 21
character 19, 65, 134, 141, 147, 192, 224
death 236–41
grave 322, 327
health 73, 235–6
marriage to John Rowney 233–4
as MMA air hostess 161, 173, 232–3
relationship with Horrie 189, 235, 238
relationship with Mary 147, 192, 237, 240–1
relationship with Patsy 237–8
relationship with Robin 237–8
Miller, Marcus **216**, 326, 364, 377, 393
Miller, Marie Rose **197, 201–2, 204, 208, 216**
art 173, 183, 251, 399, 407
birth 43
character 53, 147

marriage to Michael Megaw 271, 284, 328, 330
objection to Ian Horner 228–9
relationship with Horrie 189
screen prints adorning Mildew 399
as stage crew for productions 267, 291–2, 343
Miller, Mary Durack *see* Durack, Mary
Miller, Patsy Mary **195, 201–3, 208, 216, 218, 220**
21st birthday 144
assaults on by H. Dicks 186–7
attitude towards religion 36, 95–6
aversion to Perth Zoo 31, 300
ballet classes 36
birth 11–12
boards with Korwills 53–4
as book reviewer for *Sunday Times* 173
in Canada 194, 246
character 124, 147, 324, 349, 370
childhood 15
diaries 135
as 'drama queen' 61, 77, 84–5
education 21–2, 55, 124
encounter with Hal Porter 261–2
encounter with Johnny O'Keefe 169
friendship with Gordon Colebatch 104–5
health 35–6
leaves home 176
marriage to Robert Millett 191
memorisation compulsion 30–1
as MMA air hostess 165–6, 186
music appreciation 56, 96
in PNG 296, 341–2, 370
proclivity for order 98, 324, 349, 375
propositioned by H. Dicks 325
relationship with Bess (Gran) 30, 35, 296, 341–2, 370, 382–4
relationship with Bet 388, 408–9, 422–3, 430
relationship with Horrie 24, 165–6, 189, 227, 285–6, 296, 300, 321, 324, 345, 367
relationship with Mary 14, 141, 147, 176–7, 191–2, 269, 295–6, 300–1, 349–50, 359, 377–8, 387, 396, 400, 430
relationship with Reg 108–9, 381–2, 409, 413–14, 421
relationship with Robin 301–2
returns to Perth 252, 370
trip to England 153
Miller, Robin **195, 197, 201–2, 204, 207–9**
academic success 124
air races 256, 274, 278, 290
attitude towards religion 36
aviation career 147, 149, 156, 173, 183, 185–6, 223
awards and honours 223, 252, 333
ballet classes 36
birth 15–17
as celebrity 242, 279
character 110, 112, 132, 162, 193, 239–40, 278–9
close call 278–9
contributions to H. Dicks' investments 306–7
death 316–23
diaries 135, 274–5
education 55, 124
Flying Nurse autobiography 251–2
funeral 322–3
grave 322, 327
health 55, 145, 297–8, 301–2, 310, 315–16
marriage to Harold Dicks 145–6, 149, 161–2, 288, 302–3
membership of clubs and associations 141, 252
memorials 327, 333, 339, 359
nursing career 132, 144, 146, 156
objection to Bob Hill 102–3
opinion of television 131
premonition of death 307
relationship with Horrie 17, 138, 187–9, 227, 296, 298
relationship with Johnson 162, 246
relationship with Julie 237–8
relationship with Mary 147
relationship with Patsy 301–2
RFDS career 135, 162, 192, 230, 233, 274–5, 302, 314–15
as Sugarbird Lady 131, 183, 191, 230
Sugarbird Lady 288, 339, 354, 366
tributes to 322
Warrnambool friends 314, 330–1
will 313, 325, 329–30, 334, 339–42
Miller Investments Pty Ltd 97–8, 177, 233–4, 240, 391
Millett, Naomi **216**, 252, 364, 393, 424
Millett, Patsy Mary *see* Miller, Patsy Mary
Millett, Robert 191, 246, 286, 345
Millett, Yagan **216**, 278, 364, 393, 399, 424
Mirima Council 264
Miriwoong-Gajerrong people 250, 277–8, 368–9
mission history project *see Rock and the Sand, The* under works of Mary Durack
Mitchell, Susan 402
MMA (MacRobertson Miller Aviation)
agents 74
air crashes 64–5, 112, 232
Ansett becomes major shareholder 161
during WWII 19–20
establishment 25
flight to Broome with 1952 63–7

Horrie's career with 29, 48, 97, 243
Julie as air hostess 161
logo disappears under Ansett livery 243
new Broome terminal 227
Patsy as air hostess 165–6
Speck in the Sky 395
Sunday Times & MMA North West tour 292, 294
Montebello Islands 66
Moore, Mundae (stockman) 264, 281, 291
Moore, Tom Inglis 153, 181
Morgans Beach (Broome) 78
Morison, Margaret Pitt 101
Morphett, Tony 398
Moss, Father 55
Mowanjum community 250, 275, 299, 303–4, 344
Mowanjum dancers 258–9, 262–3
Mowanjum Presbyterian Mission 244
Moynihan, John Senan 149, 157, 169, 179–81, 192, 231, 241, 252, 255
Mt Tom Price *see* Tom Price
Mudrooroo 127–8, 155
  see also Johnson, Colin
Mulholland, B., *Legacy of Love, the story of Edith Little* 381
Murakami, Yasukichi 81
Murdoch, Iris 180–1
Murdoch, James 367
Murdoch, Rupert 367, 372
Murdoch, Walter 40, 95
Murray, Les 275
Murray-Smith, Stephen 153, 168

Nangan, Joe ('Butcher Joe') 267, 287, 303
National Library of Australia 328–9, 405–7, 411, 413–14
National Literary Treasure 425
National Seminar on Aboriginal Arts in Australia 288–9
Native Welfare Department 258
'Nature Walkabout' (Serventy) 168
Nederlands Dans Theatre 389
Nedlands 'Hot Pool' 54
New Year's Eve 193
Newspaper House 137, 294
Ngigina people 267, 287
Niall, Brenda 9
Nicholas, Anne 101
Nida (of Kununurra) 264
Night Flight (Saint-Exupéry) 323
Nixon, President 295
Njolnjol people 142
Nobel Prize for Literature 144
Noonkanbah Station 304

Noonuccal, Oodgeroo 275
  see also Walker, Kath
Northern Developments 47, 124–5, 160
  see also Camballin
Northern Gateway (Flynn) 155
Nutcote 420

Ockerby, George 67
O'Keefe, Johnny 169
Old Man's Home (Sunset) 351
Olsen, John 393–4, 396
Omodei, Ray 267
Ord River Dam 131, 269, 271, 277
Ord River irrigation scheme 47
  see also Camballin
O'Sullivan, Jack 264
Oswald Watt Aviation Award 357
outdoor dunnies 69
Outhwaite, Ida Rentoul 14
Overland 156
Packer, Kerry 106
Packer, Robert Clyde 106
Padbury, Walter 392
Page, Michael **207**
Page Smith, Eleanor *see* Smith, Eleanor Page
Pallottine priests 142–3
Paltridge, Shane 133
Pannell, Nita 114, **215**, 232, 282, 308, 338, 352, 393
  Adam's Rib 304–5, 307
  Swan River Saga 255, 257–8, 269, 271, 274, 277, 287, 295, 335
Parkerville Amphitheatre 226, 259, 262–3
Parmelia Prize 361
Pash, Frank 270
Pasternak, Boris 144
Patch Theatre 227
Paton, Alan 169
Pearl, Cyril 153
Pearse, Patrick 255
Pedersen, Barbara 326, 355, 359–60, 377
Peggy (of Kununurra) **217**, 264
PEN International 399
Penberthy, James 130, 139, 144, 155, 172, 251, 288
  Dalgerie 128–30, 291–2
Perth
  in the 1980s 397–8
  coffee houses 112
  Herbert's opinion of 164
  isolation of 169
Perth Concert Hall 288
Perth Festival 54, 178, 231, 273–4, 307
Perth Zoo 13, 31, 300
Pethic, Tom 401

Petri, Helmut 146
Phillips, Glen 361-2
Piesse, 'Freddie' 96, 101, 114
Pinkilla (property) 175
Pitt Morison, Margaret *see* Morison, Margaret Pitt
polio 35-6, 183, 191
politics 178-9
Port Keats dancers 290-1
Porter, Hal **213**
   Actors, The 248
   at Adsett 157, 248-9, 307
   at Mildew 259-62, 305, 361
   character 249-50, 261-2, 298-9, 305, 358
   demise of 394-5
   Eden House 248
   Mary's introduction to 153-4
   shenanigans 261-2, 361-2
   Watcher on the Cast-iron Balcony, The 154
Powder Puff Derby 278
Prendiville, Sister Ignatius 181, 252, 261, 312
Prichard, Katharine Susannah 12, 39, 57, 144, 246-7, 401, 405
   Coonardoo 107
Prior, Jack 75
public lending rights 268
public speaking 273
Public Works Department *see* PWD
publishers 241
Pugh, Clifton 313, 396
PWD (Public Works Department) 124, 171, 244, 277, 279, 282

Qantas 143, 226, 270
Quilty, Tom 402

radio serials 30, 56
Ray (property) 175
Reabold Hill 138
Rees, Leslie 285, 392
Rees, Marjorie 120, 138, 190, 269, 283, 294
Reid family 76
Reid, Helen 444
religion, Mary's attitude towards 59
Rennell, Mary 221
RFDS (Royal Flying Doctor Service) 14, 135, 162, 192, 230, 233, 274-5, 302, 314-15
Richardson, Henry Handel 57
Ritter, Paul 181, 398
Roberts, Hew 152, 165-6, 182
Robinson, Roland 153
Rockhole, Biddy 264
Rodriguez, Frank 121, 125-6, 143, 166, 234
Roe, Paddy 267, 373
Ronan, Tom 43, 117

Rose, Canny 99
Rose, Pat and Kim 121
Ross, Peter 418
Rowney, John 232-5, 248, 267
Royal Commission into Aboriginal Affairs (Furnell) 304
Royal Commission into Aboriginal Land Rights (Woodward) 304
Royal Commonwealth Society 351
Royal Flying Doctor Service *see* RFDS
Royal Mail contract 65
Royal Perth Hospital 132, 156, 297-8, 333, 339
Ruby (of Kununurra) 264, 284
Ruhen, Olaf 148, 153
Russell, Bertrand 153, 157
Russell, Laurie 361
Russo, Father 276, 287
Rutter, Florence 93
   Child Artists of the Australian Bush 50-1

Sabin polio vaccine program 183, 191
St Anne's Hospital 149, 323
St John of God sisters 142, 256, 310
Saint-Exupéry, Antoine de, *Night Flight* 323
Sanders, Dorothy Lucie 43
Saunders, Bishop Christopher 445
Saunders, Bob 275
Saville, Jack 171, **216**, 250, 258-9, 274, 307, 366, 401
Sawrey, Hugh 334
Second Vatican Council 181
Selsmark, Mary Lacy **207**, 258, 262
Serventy, Carol **207**
Serventy, Vincent 116-17, 144, 151, 168, **207**, 242, 251, 393-4, 401, 405, 413, 424
Shapcott, Mrs 'Shappy' 114
Shapcott, Tom 153
Shaw, Bruce 392, 402
Shaw, Eliza 255, 269, 273, 294, 335
   see also Swan River Saga and *To Be Heirs Forever* under works of Mary Durack
Sheba (of Kununurra) 264
shell collecting on Broome Reefs 77-9
Shepherd, Norah 187, 325, 339-40, 396
Shinju Matsuri Festival (Broome) 260-1, 265-7, 342, 389, 399
SHOF *see* Stockman's Hall of Fame
Simba Club 169
Sir Charles Gairdner Hospital 132
Sisters of Mercy 149
Sitwell, Edith 169
Skinner, Mollie 164, 184, 361
   The Fifth Sparrow 189-90, 221, 257, 269
Slessor, Kenneth 153

slide shows 89, 100–1
Smith, Charlie 401
Smith, Eleanor Page 157–8, 170, **207**, 276
   The Beckoning West 148, 164
Smith, Louise 396
Smith, Ross and Keith 242
Smith, Shirley 'Mum Shirl' 291–2
Smith's Weekly 106
Society of Women Writers, Alice Award 394
Somerville Auditorium 129
Sorensen, Jack 41–2, 139
Soroptimist movement 50
Soviet Union of Writers 143–4
Speck in the Sky (Dunn) 395
Spirit Hill Station 404
Springfield (property) 175
Stalin Prize 144
State Library of Western Australia 405, 407, 425
   see also Library and Information Services of WA
Stellmach, Karl 309–10, 316, 330, 332–3, 342, 355
Stephens, Tom 424
Stephensen, P. R. 'Inky' 159
Stevens, Nurse 'Snowy' 12, 16
Stewart, Douglas 153
Stirling, Ellen, Mary's play on 94, 113
Stockman's Hall of Fame (SHOF) 270, 331, 334–5, 361, 363, 367, 380, 386–7, 392, 398, 400
stockmen 264
Stockmen, The (book, Lansdowne) 395
Stow, Randolph (Mick) 117, 148, 165, 246
Streeter & Male (store) 74–5
Strehlow, Theodore (Ted) 118, 245, 293, 364, 418
Stuart, Donald R. 43, 117–18, **207**
   death 394–5
   feud with Penberthy 130, 251
   Ilbarana 268
   Patsy on 151
   'The Driven' 139
   welcomes Surkov and Krugerskaya 144
   Yandy 118
Studs Lonigan (Farrell) 113
Such is Life (Furphy) 39
Sugarbird Lady *see* Miller, Robin
Sugarbird Lady (R. Miller) 288, 354, 366
Summer School (UWA) 152, 163–4, 233, 273, 352
Summer of the Seventeenth Doll (Lawler) 115
Sun Picture Theatre 81
Sunday Times 173, 270, 292, 294, 352, 367
Sunset Hospital 351, 389
Surkov, Alexei 143–4
Swain, Veda 396
Swan River Settlement 22, 94, 269
Sydney Morning Herald 107, 133, 138, 160–1
Sydney Opera House 288, 290–2

Tales of the South Pacific (Michener) 113
Taussig, Oska 53, 57
Taylor, David Foulkes **207**
Taylor, P.G. 177
Tea Towels and Earrings (Jones) 146
telegrams 45
television 131–2, 153, 173, 258, 270, 305
Teller, Edward 177–8
Tennant, Kylie 153
Terachy (property) 175
Territorian, Mary article for 167
Thiele, Colin 153
Thomas Nelson (publisher) 313
Thompson, John 407, 409–10, 413–14
Thylungra Station (Qld) 46, 175
Time and Tide exhibition (E. Durack) 37
Tjakamarra – Boy Between Two Worlds 316, 331, 333, 342–3, 354–5
Tobermory (property) 175
Todhunter, Mr (DCA official) 278
Tom Collins House 39, 144, 165, 180, 396
Tom Price (WA) 242
Tommy (stockman) 15
Tonkin government 269
trachoma 100, 152, 191, 337
Trappist monks 157
Tropicana Lodge (Broome) 76
Trotman, H.S. 148

University of Western Australia 100, 367
   see also Summer School

Vickers, Bert 39, 43, 178, 345
Vietnam War 178–9, 310
Vietnamese refugees 343–4
'Virgilia' 294
Vogue magazine 360
von Sturmer, John 271, 291, 316
WA Institute of Technology 346, 355, 361–2
   see also Curtin University
Waldron, Diana 440
Waiting for Godot (Beckett) 131
Walkabout (film) 276
Walkabout (magazine) 94, 158, 167
Walker, James 363, 398
Walker, Johnny 250, 264, 278
Walker, Kath 175, 275, 290, 344
Wallis, Anthony 290
Walsh, Richard 168
Walsh-Smith, Joan 401
Waratah Avenue shops 20
Watcher on the Cast-Iron Balcony, The (Porter) 154
Waten, Judah 303
Watkins man 20

Watty (stockman) 264
W.B. Yeats Society 399
West Australian newspaper
  article re Kim being ousted from Liveringa 124
  letters to editor 131, 405
  Mary's articles and column 22, 94
  Murdoch's 'Life and Letters' column 40
  reporting of papers dispute 424
  reviews of *Dalgerie* 129
  suggests Ord River Dam be named after Kim 224
West Australian Symphony Orchestra 129
Western Australia, sesquicentenary (1979) 355, 360, 370
Western Mail 294
Westralian Secession Movement 299
Wheeldon, John 101, 193
White, Lily 51
White, Noel 51, 313
White, Patrick 43, 117
White Peak Station 294
Whitlam, Gough 289, 298–9, 320, 324, 328
Whitlam government 282, 304, 312, 320, 326
Wild Cat Falling (Johnson) 158, 164, 170
Williams, R.M. 331, 334, 361, 367, 372, 380, 386
  Collected Australian Verse 418
Williams, Vic 246
Williamson, David 367, 398
Wilson, Helen **207**
Winant, Ursula 225
Windows of the Mind (Glaskin) 296
Winship, Mr (American Consul) 114
women pilots 183, 252
Women Pilots' Association (Aus) 162, 183, 252, 256
Women Pilots' Association of Great Britain 333
Women's Session (ABC radio) 95, 113, 137–8
Women's Transcontinental Air Race 290
Women's Weekly, photo of John Miller 106
Woods, Jimmy 20
Woodward Royal Commission 304
works of Elizabeth Durack
  Black Swan Legend 132
  Black Swan of Trespass on Alien Waters exhibition 384
  Cord to Alcheringa set 100
  'House that Flew Away, The' 159
  Kid, The 92
  Magic Trumpet, The 407
  Mirage series exhibition 155
  Paperbark 407
  Rim pictures 299
  Seeing Through series 182, 231, 251, 258, 338
  Two Faces of Elizabeth Durack exhibition 364–5

Way of the Whirlwind, The 250, 252, 353, 407
  'Young Know, The' 14
works of Mary Durack
  'Aborigine in Australian Literature, The' 113, 346
  'Black Swan River' 94
  'Calm Eye, The' 71, 82, 85, 119
  Child Artists of the Australian Bush 50–1
  'Christmas at Ivanhoe Station' 167
  Courteous Savage, The 155
  'Custody' 410–11
  Dallying Lama, The 128–30, 288, 290–1
  'Dilettante' 109–10
  'Friendly Highway, The' 167
  'Grandmother Costello' 338
  'Jingle Bells and Didgeridoos' 360
  Keep Him My Country 71, 99–100, 107, 287
  Kings in Grass Castles 88, 94–5, 119–22, 126, 130, 133–4, 138, 175, **204**, 241, 244, 305, 367, 398
  Kookanoo and the Kangaroo 156, 353
  Kookanoo series 104
  'Lament for the Drowned Country' 284–5, 328, 429
  'Lament to Galalan – the Law-Giver' 72
  Land Beyond Time 394
  Legacy of Love, the story of Edith Little 381
  Little Poems of Sunshine 41
  Magic Trumpet, The 407
  'Missions in a Bypassed Land' 148
  'Postscript to History' 138
  'Really Mr Ritter' 181
  Rock and the Sand, The 141–3, 154, 156–7, 164, 173–4, 179, 184, 192, **206**, 231, 241, 398
  Ship of Dreams 191, **210**, 222, 226–33, 398
  Sons in the Saddle 271, 282, 311, 334–5, 368–70, 376, 393–5, 397
  'State of Excitement' 360
  Swan of the Bibbulmun 139
  Swan River Saga **215**, 271, 273–4, 276, 287, 290, 295, 303, 352, 398
  'They Reached a Land' 22
  To Be Heirs Forever 311, 335
  To Ride a Fine Horse 152, 155
  'Wandering River' 50, 71
  Way of the Whirlwind, The 250, 252, 353, 407
  Yagan of the Bibbulmun 155, 167, 313
  'Young Know, The' 14
World of Our Own, A (Glaskin) 114
World War I veterans 20
World War II 11, 19–20, 23
Worms, Father 71–2, 111, 140
Worora people 244–5
Wright, Judith 175, 222, 275, 401

Writers' Week (Perth) 180, 367
  see also Adelaide Festival Writers' Week
writing
  historical biography 253–4
  life of a writer 356–7
Wyles, Ambrosine 120
Wyndham 280, 316, 343–4

Yagan (Aboriginal warrior) 278, 360
Yampi Sound 158
Yandeyarra Station 117
Yandy (Stuart) 118
Yaoro people 142
Yorkshire House (Perth) 19

Zonta 252
Zucker, Margaret 241

www.ingramcontent.com/pod-product-compliance
Lightning Source LLC
Chambersburg PA
CBHW031323230426
43670CB00006B/218